Energy Security Challenges
for the 21st Century

Energy Security Challenges for the 21st Century

A Reference Handbook

Gal Luft and Anne Korin, Editors

Contemporary Military, Strategic, and Security Issues

PRAEGER SECURITY INTERNATIONAL
An Imprint of ABC-CLIO LLC

A B C • C L I O

Santa Barbara, California • Denver, Colorado • Oxford, England

Library of Congress Cataloging-in-Publication Data

Energy security challenges for the 21st century: a reference handbook / Gal Luft and Anne Korin, Editors.

    p. cm. — (Contemporary military, strategic, and security issues)
  Includes bibliographical references and index.
  ISBN 978-0-275-99997-1 (hardcover: alk. paper) — ISBN 978-0-275-99998-8 (ebook)
  1. Energy policy—United States.   2. National security—United States.
I. Luft, Gal. II. Korin, Anne.
  HD9502.U62E64 2009
  333.790973—dc22   2009016440

13 12   3 4 5

This book is also available on the World Wide Web as an eBook.
Visit www.abc-clio.com for details.

ABC-CLIO, LLC
130 Cremona Drive, P.O. Box 1911
Santa Barbara, California 93116-1911

This book is printed on acid-free paper ∞

Manufactured in the United States of America

To Milton Copulos

Contents

Preface

This book was written and edited in 2008, a year in which oil prices reached a historical record of nearly $150 a barrel, tension grew between the United States and Iran, Russia made power grabs in the energy rich Caucasus and the Arctic and, again, cut its gas supply to Europe, Nigerian rebels intensified their attacks against oil facilities, Somali pirates hijacked a very large Saudi oil tanker, and a global financial crisis of historical proportions induced in part by the rise in energy prices swept world economies. Speaking in Baku, the capital of Azerbaijan, shortly after the Russian invasion of Georgia, U.S. Vice President Richard Cheney concluded that energy security is an "increasingly urgent" issue. This was our conclusion right after the September 11 attacks, when we founded the Institute for the Analysis of Global Security (IAGS) as the world's first independent energy security think tank not funded by corporate and government money. We thought at the time—oil prices were just under $25 a barrel—that the strategic, economic, geological and environmental problems associated with the way the world uses energy require the formation of a new energy paradigm, one that not only focuses on traditional solutions like diversity of geographical sources and energy efficiency but also, taking into consideration the rapid growth of the developing world and the growing tension between oil producers and consumers, aims to reduce the strategic value of oil through competition in the transportation fuel market and international collaboration. We also thought that in order to bring about this new paradigm, there is a need for a dedicated academic discipline that can synthesize the policy and technological issues affecting energy security and provide the tools for researchers and policymakers to devise realistic, balanced and sustainable energy policy. During the years since, we received almost daily reminders of the importance of energy security to global security, and some of those who at first were skeptical of the need for such a discipline became its biggest cheerleaders.

Today energy security is beginning to emerge as a multidisciplinary topic discussed and taught in campuses throughout the world. A growing number of students and policymakers are drawn to the topic and many universities already offer courses specializing in energy security. Policy think tanks around the world are opening energy security programs, and new national and international organizations are being formed to address the growing energy challenge.

But despite the complexity and relevancy of the topic, and while there is a growing body of articles on the topic in academic and popular journals, the energy security discipline still suffers from a dearth of literature for use by students, faculty, and policymakers, and an insufficient effort to document in a balanced manner and in one comprehensive volume the various economic, geopolitical, and technological features that comprise the world's energy security map, describe the strengths and weaknesses of the global energy system, the various approaches nations have toward energy security and the pathways available to them to strengthen their energy security. That is the genesis of this book.

Thanks to the 22 experts who contributed to this volume, all of whom are truly excellent scholars who had to produce articles on extremely dynamic topics that kept on changing as they were being written about, we were able to assemble the main themes of the energy security field into this manuscript. Naturally there is a limit to the number of topics and details that can be included in one volume. There are many components of the problem and even more of the solutions that space did not permit us to include. Our goal was to provide the reader with a bird's eye view of the world's energy system and its vulnerabilities, and then delve into the various approaches that selected producers, consumers and transit states have toward energy security. We then examined the domestic and foreign policy tradeoffs required to ensure safe and affordable energy supplies. We also hoped to explain the various pathways to energy security and the tradeoffs among them and demonstrate how all of these factors can be integrated in a larger foreign and domestic policy framework. If this book has been able to convey the issue's complexity, leaving more questions than answers, then it has achieved its purpose.

We would like to thank the donors, staff and advisors of the IAGS for their friendship and support throughout the years.

We chose to dedicate the book to our friend and colleague Milton Copulos, who died in March 2008 at the age of 60. Milton was one of America's foremost energy security experts. His greatest contribution to the emergence of the discipline was in developing a methodology to assess the hidden cost of oil. Milton taught us that there is much more to the price of energy than what is reflected at the pump or in our utility bill, and that responsible energy decision-making processes must take into account the external cost of energy, which is usually hidden from consumers. A decorated Vietnam War veteran, Milton showed courage also outside of the battlefield. Years before it became widely accepted that oil dependence is a national security and economic problem, and when alternative energy was still solely the a domain of environmentalists, Milton was a unique voice in the conservative movement, calling for a robust effort to rid the country of its toxic and ever-growing dependence on oil and for a massive increase in the use of alternative energy sources as a way to strengthen America's national security. Milton was not only a scholar. He was also a practitioner. Before his premature death he worked with a company specializing in a revolutionary technology which converts wood waste into heating oil. He also led a team which built future House USA, a super energy efficient house which was displayed in the Olympic Games in Beijing, demonstrating the latest advances in energy efficiency, environmental compatibility, and sustainability. Milton called the project "a historical first step towards a sustainable future and a bridge between the U.S. and China." Sadly he never lived to see the house completed. We hope that just like that house, this book will be a tribute to his legacy.

Abbreviations

AFRICOM—U.S. Army African Command
ANWR—Arctic National Wildlife Refuge
APEC—Asia-Pacific Economic Cooperation
AQIM—al-Qaeda in the Islamic Maghreb
Bcm—Billion Cubic Meters
BOTAŞ—Turkish Petroleum Pipeline Corporation
BP—British Petroleum
Bpd—Barrels per day
BTC—Baku-Tbilisi-Ceyhan Pipeline
Btu—British Thermal Unit
CAFTA—Central American Free Trade Agreement
CCGT—Combined Cycle Gas Turbine
CCP—Chinese Communist Party
CCPP—Combined Cycle Power Plant
CDM—Clean Development Mechanisms
CFSP—Common Foreign and Security Policy
CHP—Combined Heat and Power
CIWIN—Critical Infrastructure Warning Information Network
CNG—compressed natural gas
CNOOC—China National Offshore Oil Corporation
CNPC—China National Petroleum Corporation
CO—Carbon monoxide
CTL—Coal to Liquids
DE—Decentralized Energy
DME—Dimethyl ether
DoD—Department of Defense
DoE—Department of Energy
E&P—Exploration & Production
ECI—European Critical Infrastructure
ECOWAS—Economic Community of West African States
EEZ—Exclusive Economic Zone

EFCC—Economic and Financial Crimes Commission
EIA—Energy Information Administration
EPCIP—European Program for Critical Infrastructure Protection
EPDC—Electric Power Development Corporation
ESPO—East Siberia Pacific Ocean
EUCOM—U.S. Army's European Command
EV—Electric Vehicle
FARC—Fuerzas Armadas Revolucionarias de Colombia's
FFV—Flexible Fuel Vehicle
FMF—Foreign Military Sales Financing
FMS—Foreign Military Sales
G8—Group of Eight
GAO—United States Government Accountability Office
GE—Gasoline-ethanol
GECF—Gas Exporting Countries Forum
GEM—Gasoline-ethanol-methanol
GNEP—Global Nuclear Energy Partnership
GNPOC—Greater Nile Petroleum Operating Company
GSPC—Group for Preaching and Combat
GTL—Gas to Liquids
HEU—Highly enriched uranium
IAEA—International Atomic Energy Agency
IAGS—Institute for the Analysis of Global Security
ICSID—International Center for the Settlement of International Disputes
ICT—information and communication technology
IEA—International Energy Agency
IGCC—integrated gasification combined cycle
IMET—International Military Education and Training
IMO—International Maritime Organization
IOC—International Oil Companies
IPCC—Intergovernmental Panel on Climate Change
IPI—Iran-Pakistan-India Pipeline
JODI—Joint Oil Data Initiative
JRC—Joint Revolutionary Council
LAC—Latin America and the Caribbean
LEU—Low enriched uranium
LNG—Liquefied Natural Gas
LPG—Liquid Petroleum Gas
LTTE—The Liberation Tigers of Tamil Eelam
Mbd—million barrels per day
MEND—Movement for the Emancipation of Niger Delta
MITI—Ministry of International Trade and Industry
MOU—Memorandum of Understanding
MTOE—million tonnes of oil equivalent
NAFTA—North America Free Trade Agreement

NDRC—National Development and Reform Commission
NEDO—New Energy Development Organization
NEP—National Energy Policy
NESCO—Network of Energy Security Correspondents
NIMBY—Not in my back yard
NOC—National Oil Companies
NPC—National Petroleum Council
NRDC—Natural Resources Defense Council
OAS—Organization of American States
OCS—Outer Continental Shelf
ODA—Oversees Development Assistance
OECD—Organization of Economic Cooperation and Development
OGP—Organization of European Oil and Gas Producers
OLADE—Organización Latinoamericana de Energía
ONGC—Oil and Natural Gas Corporation
ONLF—Ogaden National Liberation Front
OPEC—Organization of the Petroleum Exporting Countries
PC—pulverized coal
PDVSA—Petroleos de Venezuela
PHEV—Plug in Hybrid Electric Vehicle
PKK—Kurdistan Workers Party
PM—Particulate material
PRC—People's Republic of China
PSA—Production Sharing Agreement
PSC—Private Security Contractors
PV—Photovoltaic
RFS—Renewable Fuels Standard
RPS—Renewable Portfolio Standard
SCADA—Supervisory Control and Data Acquisition systems
SCO—Shanghai Cooperation Organization
SCP—South Caucasus Gas Pipeline
Sinopec—China Petrochemical Corporation
SO_2—Sulfur dioxide
SPR—Strategic Petroleum Reserve
Tcf—Trillion cubic feet
Tcm—Trillion cubic meters
TCP—Trans Caspian Gas Pipeline
TPAO—Turkish Petroleum Corporation
TPES—Total Primary Energy Supply
UNCLOS—United Nations Convention on the Law of the Sea
VLCC—Very Large Crude Carrier
VOC—Volatile Organic Compounds
WADE—World Alliance for Decentralized Energy
WANO—World Association of Nuclear Operators
WTO—World Trade Organization

CHAPTER 1

Energy Security: In the Eyes of the Beholder

Gal Luft and Anne Korin

After nearly a quarter century of relative calm in the world's energy systems, security is again high on the agenda of every nation. There are many good reasons why so many nations are concerned about the future of their energy supply. Perhaps the most important of those is the fact that, despite the current economic slowdown, the world's economy is going through a unique growth period as hundreds of millions of people in the developing world rise from poverty and their need for affordable and abundant energy grows. China and India, together a third of humanity, each has an emerging middle class larger than the entire population of the United States. People for whom ownership of an air conditioner, a microwave, or a family car has always been a fantasy are now edging closer to fulfilling their dream. According to the reference case of the International Energy Agency, China's energy consumption alone is expected to reach 14 quadrillion Btu, which is 11 percent higher than that of the United States, by 2030. Once they pull out of the current recession the other main energy consumers, the United States, OECD Europe, and Japan, together consuming about half of global annual oil output, will also continue to grow, albeit at a slower pace of roughly 2 percent per year.[1] As a result, by 2030 the world's population will need 45 percent more energy than it does today. Unfortunately, it is not at all clear that production of new energy will keep up with the burgeoning demand. The situation is particularly challenging with respect to oil. The projected increase in world oil demand, from 86 million barrels per day (mbd) today to 103 mbd in 2015 and to just over 119 mbd in 2025,[2] would require in the next two decades an increment to world production capability sufficient to supply the additional demand as well as replace the yearly drop in production from known fields due to depletion, which today stands at 5 percent. Predictions about oil depletion have been made since oil was first discovered. Today, too, a growing group of mainstream analysts are positing that the world conventional petroleum production might be closer to peak than expected and that supply of conventional crude will begin to decline, causing chronic shortages.[3] No one knows exactly when this will happen but one thing is certain: key producers already show signs of declining reserves as super giant fields mature, threatening to bring the oil market to a supply crunch.[4] A glimpse into the International Energy Agency (IEA) 2008 World Energy Outlook confirms that the current decline in oil prices is merely a respite and that sooner or later oil prices will rise to much higher levels. The IEA report examined the world's 800 top oilfields and reported an average annual depletion rate of 5.1 percent increasing to 8.6 percent in 2030. The largest declines in oil production between 2000 and 2008 were reported in Mexico, China, Norway, Australia and the United Kingdom. The North Sea's output went down from 6.4 mbd in 2000 to under 2.1 mbd in 2005. Venezuela has been losing output since 2002, and in the United States, production has been sliding for a third consecutive decade. Indonesia recently turned from an exporter into a net importer and as a result decided to leave the Organization of Petroleum Exporting Countries (OPEC). Production decline also plagues the Middle East, home to two-thirds of the world's reserves. In November 2005, Kuwait Oil Company revealed that Kuwait's largest oilfield, Burgan, the second largest oilfield in the world, has reached its peak production at 1.7 mbd.[5] Iran's decline rate stands at 9 percent per year. And in Saudi Arabia, no giant field has been found in 30 years and the probability of making new very large discoveries decreases as a producing area matures. The Saudis have estimated they have 150 billion barrels beyond the 260 billion that are already proven.[6] But various reports question Saudi Arabia's claims that it can significantly expand capacity.[7]

A closer look at some of the major producing countries reveals that geology is not the main party to blame for the declines. Many of the countries where production has dropped have substantial reserves that could enable them to export oil for many decades. What is missing is a political environment conducive to the kind of investment that is needed to meet the energy challenge. The world needs to invest trillions of dollars in the coming decades to meet its growing energy needs. Yet, little investment is made in the places where most of the oil and gas reserves are concentrated. Members of OPEC hold 78 percent of the world's proven oil reserves, but OPEC's production has barely changed in 35 years. Production is hampered by political turmoil, misappropriation of funds, legal constraints on foreign investors, and short-term goals divorced from the long-term investment needs of oil production and exploration. As a result, between 1994 and 2004, 64 percent of the exploration wells drilled around the world were in North America, where only 12 percent of the world's undiscovered oil and gas resources are concentrated. At the same time only 7 percent of the exploration took place in the Middle East, home to 28 percent of the undiscovered reserves.[8] In major oil-producing countries like Iran and Sudan, and until several years ago Libya and Iraq, sanctions have kept international oil companies from investing. A new wave of nationalization in Russia and Latin America has raised the risk of expropriation for foreign companies. Another impediment to investment is lack of political stability in major oil-producing regions. In a *Foreign Affairs* article

Michael Ross points out that despite the general decline in the number of wars fought around the world, oil-producing countries make up the growing part of the world's conflict-ridden countries, and that the number of conflicts associated with oil-producing countries is likely to grow as oil prices rise.[9] This is largely because oil revenues tend to increase corruption, authoritarianism, uneven distribution of wealth, economic stagnation and social discontent. As countries like Algeria, Iraq, Sudan, Nigeria, and Colombia illustrate, those social illnesses increase the risk of civil wars, which further impede foreign investment. Energy supply is also constrained by lack of new pipeline infrastructure and more tankers to transport crude to the world markets and an even more urgent need for increased refining capacity to convert various types of crude oil into various petroleum products. Infrastructure failure can be a result of misuse, natural decay resulting from outdated equipment, and natural disasters. Deliberate interruptions such as sabotage or terrorism are also a major impediment to energy production. As Ali Koknar describes in Chapter 2, throughout the world, terrorists and other rogue elements attack oil, gas and power installations almost on a daily basis with growing impact on the world economy. Striking oil, which *jihadists* call "the provision line and the feeding to the artery of the life of the crusader's nation" is easy and effective.[10] Terrorists can cause enormous economic damage by hitting the world's energy supply at the generating points, where they enjoy strong support on the ground. Outside the Middle East, dissident groups attack energy facilities in order to weaken and humiliate the regimes that they work to undermine. Rebels in Nigeria continuously attack the country's energy facilities and target foreign energy companies operating in the oil-rich Niger Delta. In June 2008, the country's volume of marketable oil held back due to the attacks stood at nearly 1 mbd and its production as a result reached its lowest point in 25 years.[11] No doubt had all the oil lost to malevolent activity been in the market, the price per barrel would have been significantly lower than it is today. Supply disruption risks also exist in the largest part of our globe—the sea—where one-quarter to one-third of the world's oil and gas reserves are believed to lie and on which approximately two-thirds of the world's oil trade is shipped daily. Terrorist groups like al-Qaeda are increasingly focused on the disruption of international maritime trade as a way to hurt Western powers economically. al-Qaeda calls its maritime campaign "a new strategy which permits the mujahedeen" to hijack shipping, since "fighters who aspire to establish the caliphate must control the seas and the waterways."[12] The most important choke points on the transportation water ways where significant energy supply disruption can occur are the Strait of Malacca, the Turkish Straits, Bab-el Mandab, the Suez Canal, the Panama Canal and of course the Strait of Hormuz, through which 17 mbd of oil are transported daily.

Securing those choke points as well as other sea lanes is one of the main challenges for producers and consumers alike. As Donna Nincic concludes in Chapter 3, "the issue of *energy security* is to a large extent one of *maritime security*." But in some cases nations deliberately undermine both maritime security and energy security by using their control over critical supply lines and strategic choke points as a tool of coercion and intimidation. In 2007–2008 Iran threatened numerous times to close the Strait of Hormuz in response to a military attack by the United States and its allies. Such threats, and similar ones by Venezuela's President Hugo Chavez to halt oil supply to the United States, indicate that, contrary to popular belief that the energy weapon died after the 1973 Arab oil embargo, the use of such a weapon is becoming increasingly likely. The combination of heightened geopolitical risk, inhospitable investment climate, terrorism, geological decline and the current credit crunch are causing significant barriers to the expansion of the global petroleum industry at a time the world's needs for energy are more pressing than ever. Considering the long lag time, about 8–10 years, from the beginning of the exploration process until the oil reaches a pipeline from which it can move into the world market, it is almost certain that some significant challenges to supply are already in store.

Power Challenges

When it comes to our electricity supply the situation is not much better than in the oil market. Here too, demand is growing by leaps and bounds while supply is lagging behind due to onerous environmental regulations and insufficient investment in new capacity in many countries. New coal-fired power plants are being blocked by anti-coal groups—in 2007 alone, 59 coal-fired power plants were cancelled in the United States—nuclear power plants still face substantial opposition in many industrialized nations, and transmission systems are highly inefficient.[13] To make things more complicated, environmental concerns are driving many countries to adopt policies aimed at capping or taxing greenhouse gas emissions. Such policies may be good for the environment but they constrain growth in the fossil energy sector which, for now, is, in most cases, more economical than renewable energy. In developed countries such as the United States, where such policies have not yet been adopted, uncertainty about the regulatory future forces energy companies to hold back on their investment until it becomes clear what, if any, additional governmental constraints will be placed on the market. To make things worse, the cost of extracting coal, natural gas and uranium, the main sources of electricity, is rising constantly as reserves are depleted.

Just as in the case of oil, the electricity sector is threatened by terrorists who can cause massive economic disruption by attacking critical nodes of the grid either physically or through cyber-terrorism.[14] In most countries, power grids are extremely fragile and vulnerable to terror attacks, which could cause prolonged dire consequences for nations' security. Electricity infrastructure is increasingly becoming a preferred target of insurgents, rebels and guerrilla fighters around the world. In 2007, it was reported that multimillion dollars' worth of damages were caused to electricity infrastructure in Southwest Pakistan alone, largely as result of pro-Taliban guerillas and Baluchi rebels. Meanwhile, a spree of attacks on Mexican power lines by guerillas has put the economic well being of parts of Mexico in jeopardy. In a sign that sabotage of electrical infrastructure is becoming more of a concern, the Chinese government, in August 2007, announced that any individuals convicted of damaging the electrical infrastructure "causing direct economic losses over $131,500" are subject to the death penalty.[15] The following month, the Nigerian President announced that the government would "deal much more severely" with individuals found guilty of sabotaging electrical infrastructure.[16] Disrupting power infrastructure can also be a means of crippling other sectors of the energy system. For example, power shortages in Iraq have resulted in reduced oil production as much of the infrastructure operating oil wells, pumping stations and refineries relies on electricity.[17] Electricity disruptions are not only due to malicious activity. In August 2003, a fallen tree initiated a mega blackout that cut off large parts of the United States and Canada from electricity, causing economic damage to the tune of billions of dollars.[18] The rolling blackouts in California in 2001 caused $21.8 billion in lost productivity, reducing household income by $4.5 billion and causing 135,000 job losses.[19] Power shortages are prevalent in China and India, costing the Chinese and Indian industries millions of hours of lost productivity every year and in many cases jeopardizing international competitiveness. Developing nations from Afghanistan to Zambia consistently cite power shortages as a major impediment to economic and social development.

What *Is* Energy Security?

The aforementioned energy security challenges are only a sample of the topics this book will describe. The combination of multiple factors affecting supply and demand driven by both state actors and nonstate actors is creating a new energy reality that is no longer transitory but chronic and that begs for the significant reforms described in the second part of this book. Under the above conditions of risk and uncertainty each country is trying to enhance its energy security. But what is energy security anyway? Is there a uniform definition that can encompass the interests of all producers, consumers, exporters, importers and transit states? More than a quarter of the world's population, mostly in Sub-Saharan Africa and South Asia, suffers from acute energy poverty with no access to electricity. In India alone, 600 million people—roughly half the population—are off the electric grid. Hundreds of millions suffer chronic power outages due to an unreliable electricity system. In addition, roughly 40 percent of the world population still relies on traditional wood, crop residues and animal waste as their main cooking and heating fuels. Clearly for this half of humanity the meaning of energy security is different from that of the developed world. It means first and foremost access to energy to supply basic needs like clean water, cooking, lighting and public transportation. In the more developed parts of the world where human needs are more complex, energy security is more about reliability of supply, access to the energy resources in sufficient amounts, affordability, and protection from energy supply interruptions.[20] But, as this book will show, energy security means different things to different countries based on their geographical location, their geological endowment, their international relations, their political system and their economic disposition. While energy importers want security of supply and low prices, energy exporters seek security of demand—the assurance that their production will be purchased at a fair price over a long term, so that national budgets can anticipate a steady and predictable revenue flow. It is also worth remembering that many of the energy-exporting nations also face domestic supply problems of their own driven by economic expansion, high population growth and extremely large subsidies of electricity and transportation fuel prices.

Countries' definition of energy security has much to do with their own particular energy situation and how they view their vulnerabilities to energy supply disruptions. In this, it is important to realize that there are two primary energy usage sectors that pose two different types of energy security challenges. The first sector is electricity. Throughout the world today electricity is generated from coal (41%), natural gas (20.5%), renewables like hydroelectric, biomass, solar, wind and geothermal power (18.5%) and nuclear power (15%). Contrary to popular belief, in most countries electricity is essentially no longer produced from oil. Only 5 percent of world electricity is made from petroleum.[21] According to the 2007 *International Energy Outlook* of the Energy Information Administration, by 2030 oil's share of global power generation will drop to 3.8 percent while coal's share, despite all the concerns about global warming, is projected to climb to 44 percent.[22] This diversity of sources does not exist in the second major sector of energy use—transportation. Transportation energy makes the world go around. It enables the free flow of goods and services onboard cars, trucks, trains, ships and airplanes. Here oil is king, responsible for over 95 percent of the energy used in this sector. In fact, the vast majority of the cars sold around the world today cannot even run on something other than petroleum, in the form of gasoline or diesel.

The distinction between electricity and transportation energy shapes countries' perception of energy security. Some countries, like Russia and Saudi Arabia, are almost fully energy independent, relying on their vast domestic resources for both their power and transportation sectors. Others, like the United States and France—the former thanks to its massive coal reserves and the latter due to an expanded nuclear power industry—are almost self sufficient when it comes to their electricity supply but are heavily dependent on foreign oil imports to power their transportation sector. A few countries represent the opposite situation. Brazil, for example, has reached energy self-sufficiency in its transportation sector by a shift to sugarcane ethanol and expanded domestic drilling but it is dependent for power generation on natural gas primarily imported from Argentina and Bolivia as well as liquefied natural gas from Algeria, Nigeria and the Middle East. (The 2008 discovery of a large natural gas deposit called Jupiter could change all that and make Brazil self-sufficient in natural gas in 5–10 years). Then there are the most vulnerable countries, which are dependent on imports for both electricity sources like coal and natural gas as well as for their transportation needs. In the worst position are those members of the last group that are not only completely dependent on foreign energy but whose energy supply lines are facing constant threat of cutoffs. Russia's December 2005 gas cutoff to the Ukraine, which in turn reduced supply to the EU, as well as repeated threats by Venezuela's President Hugo Chavez and Iran's President Mahmoud Ahmadinejad, all show that the energy weapon is still alive and viable. Even countries rich in energy resources can face severe energy security challenges. One interesting case is Iran, which has the world's third largest oil reserve yet is still energy dependent due to its inadequate refining capacity. Iran's Achilles' heel is its gasoline dependence; more than 40 percent of its gasoline and other refined petroleum products come from abroad. By blocking Iran's imports of gasoline, the West could cripple the Iranian economy and possibly undermine Iran's regime. To reduce its gasoline dependence the Iranian government declared a national project to shift the transportation sector from oil products to natural gas.[23] It also embarked on one of world's most aggressive refinery expansion programs. Additionally, in June 2007, the Iranian government initiated a comprehensive gasoline rationing policy that caused a great deal of anger among Iranians.

Countries facing severe energy security challenges tend to shape their international behavior and national priorities accordingly. China's scramble for African and Middle Eastern oil has drastically increased its interest and presence in those regions. Until the early 1990s, around the same time China turned into a net oil importer, Beijing did not even have diplomatic relations with many African and Middle Eastern countries. But today, as China's dependence on those regions for its energy supply is growing so does its inclination to involve itself in the regions' politics and provide generous foreign aid to energy-rich countries. The downside of its growing dependence on foreign energy is its tendency to turn a blind eye to human rights violations and resist international efforts to impose sanctions on Sudan for mass killing in Darfur and on Iran for its insistence on developing nuclear weapons. China's oil dependence also feeds anxieties about maritime blockades should tension arise between China and potential adversaries like the United States and Japan. This concern has led China to invest a great deal of national resources in the development of a modern blue-water navy and in a strategy dubbed by some as a String of Pearls to extend China's influence along the sea lanes of communication that connect China to vital energy resources in the Middle East and Africa.

Enhancing Energy Security

Countries not only differ in their definition of the energy security challenge but also on how to address it. Chapters 4 and 5 present a debate on the feasibility of the most elementary energy security strategy: the use of force. The militarization of energy security is not a theoretical notion. History is marred with examples of countries that resorted to bullets in order to acquire barrels. Japan's oil dependence in the 1930s brought it to embark on an expansionist and aggressive foreign policy that put it on a collision course initially with China and then with the United States. It ended tragically with two mushroom clouds. Adolf Hitler's decision to attack Russia was, in part, driven by the need to secure oil for the Nazi war machine. His decision to shift his Panzers from Moscow to oil-rich Baku sealed the fate of the Third Reich. Even the 1973 Arab oil embargo brought the United States to the brink of using force. A report delivered to the British Prime Minister in December 1973 warned that the U.S. military would seize oil-producing areas in response to protracted oil sanctions. "The U.S. might consider it could not tolerate a situation in which the U.S. and its allies were at the mercy of a small group of unreasonable countries," the report said.[24] Since then, the United States has used force a number of times to protect its energy supply and deter aggressors from upsetting it. While the role of oil in the current Iraq War is debatable—many believe that access to Iraqi oil was the prime driver for the war, but if oil was what the United States was really after, wouldn't it have been easier to lift the sanctions from Saddam Hussein's regime?—there is no argument about the role energy security played in the 1990–91 Gulf War and the decades of U.S. military presence in Saudi Arabia and, since 2001, in Qatar and Bahrain. An increasing part of the U.S. defense budget and its military deployments is directly related to energy security. U.S. military forces are either deployed in and/ or provide military assistance to energy-rich Azerbaijan, Kazakhstan, Uzbekistan (until 2006) and Kyrgyzstan (until 2008). In Latin America, U.S. Special Forces are deployed in Colombia to help the government protect pipelines that are repeatedly attacked by drug lords and terrorists. And there are the first signs of U.S. military presence along the west coast of Africa. In Chapter 4 Michael Klare holds that with increased global competition over access to energy, the militarization of energy security by the world's superpowers is a harbinger of military conflict and that the tendency of energy consumers to militarize their energy policies increases the risk of resource wars. Christopher Fettweiss offers a diametrically opposed view in Chapter 5, claiming that resource wars are obsolete and that they will not be any more common in the coming century than they were in the 20th century. Whether or not resource wars are more likely is up to each reader to decide. What is clear is that the global struggle for resources is defining the 21st century and that even in the absence of military conflict energy-importing countries align their national strategies in ways that improve their access to energy resources. This is true not only with regards to hydrocarbons and uranium but also to critical minerals which are expected to play an increasing role in the global energy system like lithium, cobalt, platinum, and rare earth elements, as advanced batteries and fuel cells penetrate the transportation sector.

Importers, Exporters and Other Players

From here we move to examine how individual producers, consumers and transit states view energy security and how they address their energy security challenges. We start with the producers. Middle Eastern producers as well as Russia and the Caspian, African and Latin American nations all need to find the right balance between their desire to maximize revenue creation, as many of them rely on oil revenues for their economic well being, and the expectation of the rest of the world that they behave as responsible and fair suppliers. As mentioned before, while importers want security of supply, energy producers seek security of demand—the assurance that their production will be purchased at a fair price over a long term, so that national budgets can anticipate a steady and predictable revenue flow. Guaranteed demand is important at a time when many gas and oil fields have passed their production peaks and development of new fields requires advanced technology and enormous investment over a lengthening time period. One way producers attempt to achieve security of demand is by controlling the supply routes, particularly pipeline corridors. As demand for energy grows, pipelines are getting longer and crossing more than a single country. While they can bring regional stability, modest transit revenues and welfare to the countries that they cross, they can also create instability and competition among exporters over access to markets. In this, Moscow's desire to see a pro-Russia regime in Georgia in the hope of bringing the strategic Baku-Tbilisi-Ceyhan pipeline (BTC) and the Baku-Erzurum (Turkey) gas pipeline under Russian control was one of the main reasons for Russia's attack on Georgia in August 2008. Energy producers also tend to consume large amounts of energy and in most cases are themselves importers of energy products. Saudi Arabia, Russia and Iran are the world's 1st, 2nd and 4th largest oil producers but at the same time they are also the world's 10th, 5th and 15th largest consumers respectively.[25] So despite their ownership of large energy reserves, for those countries energy security also means the ability to provide for their own domestic needs.

Of all the producers, the 13-member OPEC is the most influential. OPEC holds 78 percent of the world proven oil reserves and produces about 40 percent of the world's oil. This allows the cartel a dominant position on the supply side and the ability to dictate the price of oil through its regular meetings in Vienna where members decide on their production quotas. But OPEC's flush-with-petrodollars members seem unconcerned by the pain inflicted on the global economy by oil's meteoric price rise in 2007–8. For them, increasing output is not a matter of capacity, but of will. OPEC members have the geological capability to provide oil for many decades—assuming they are not overstating their reserves—but they have been very sluggish in investing in new capacity. The cartel's production is similar to its 1973 level, while over the same period global demand for oil has nearly doubled. Furthermore, OPEC has repeatedly claimed it holds spare production capacity of more than 3 mbd. This claim is impossible to verify, thanks to OPEC's notorious lack of transparency. If true, it means OPEC can inject a significant amount of oil into the market almost immediately, dropping prices significantly. But this is not what the cartel is after. Since its inception in 1960, OPEC has successfully restricted its member states' petroleum production, artificially distorting the world's oil supply to fill its members' pockets. Production is hampered by political turmoil, misappropriation of funds, and short-term goals divorced from the long-term investment needs of oil production and exploration. Amy Jaffe points out in Chapter 6 that OPEC's focus on short term revenue goals precludes it from forging a policy that would defend security of demand in the long term. Such an approach drives consumers to adopt bolder measures and policies to weaken OPEC's grip over the world economy every time oil prices increase above economically sustainable level.

Another significant producer/exporter and therefore a major player in the world's energy markets, though not a member of OPEC, is Russia, which occupies 13 percent of the world's territory and has less than 3 percent of the world's population but owns 34 percent of global natural gas reserves and some 13 percent of global oil reserves. Russia is today the largest oil exporter after Saudi Arabia and the supplier of 30 percent of the EU's oil and almost a half of its gas. But, as Ariel Cohen describes in Chapter 7, Russia is using its oil and gas exports not only as a powerful economic asset but also as a very efficient foreign policy tool. This creates a growing tension between Russia and Europe, the main market for Russian hydrocarbons, and is a key target of the Kremlin's energy policy and politics. Moscow is pursuing a comprehensive, state-formulated and implemented geo-economic strategy that may exacerbate Europe's political and economic dependence on Russia's energy supply. After the brief gas supply interruption due to the Russian-Ukrainian price dispute and Russia's military attack on Georgia in summer 2008, European countries view Russia as a huge energy security challenge. Cohen's Chapter 8 on central Asia reflects the similar concerns of young energy-producing countries torn between their need for markets and their historical geopolitical and cultural allegiance to Russia.

In Chapter 9 we turn our focus to a fourth energy production region, Latin America. Well-endowed with a large supply of proven oil reserves, natural gas, hydroelectric power and an abundant capacity for biomass energy, Latin America also suffers from the social illnesses prevalent in other energy producing regions—poverty, huge gaps in income, corruption and political instability. Populist regimes in Venezuela, Bolivia and Ecuador have become increasingly anti-American at a time when Chinese interest in the region is developing, turning it into an arena of competition among energy-hungry powers. The biggest energy security challenge in Latin America is Venezuela. In recent years, Venezuela has expressed its intention to part ways from the United States and reduce its dependence on the U.S. market, which now accounts for about two-thirds of the country's oil exports. The acrimonious relations between Caracas and Washington have yielded some stern warnings by Venezuelan officials that Venezuela might use the oil weapon should Washington assume an aggressive posture.[26] Venezuela has already used its natural resources as a tool of foreign policy by providing cheap loans and discounted oil in exchange for political support.

From here we turn to the consumers. They present a whole different universe. While energy-exporting countries wish to ensure reliable demand for their commodities, the importing states commonly strive for diversity of energy supplies to maximize their security. Multiplying a country's supply sources reduces the impact of a disruption of supply from one source or another by providing alternatives. Another principle of energy security adopted by most consumers is the creation of mechanisms to withstand supply disruptions and mitigate their impact. This is most commonly done through strategic petroleum reserves and multinational mechanisms like the IEA, which in the case of disruption oversees the emergency allocation and distribution of oil among consuming countries of the Organization of Economic Cooperation and Development (OECD) But despite the commonality of approaches for dealing with supply disruptions, within the consuming community there are different sets of concerns that are met with different policy responses. For Americans, energy security is about oil and transportation. For Europeans, natural gas poses the most difficult challenges, as the EU becomes increasingly dependent on Russian gas. On both sides of the Atlantic there are efforts under way to formulate an updated energy security strategy, but in both the United States and the EU progress is slow due to political gridlock and lack of consensus on key issues. Kevin Rosner describes in Chapter 11 how within the European sphere countries are in strong disagreement on national energy mixes, the relations with Russia and the degree of effort and resources that should be invested in reducing carbon dioxide emissions. In the United States, despite the general acceptance that energy dependence is a limiting factor behind any notion of American omnipotence, traditional aversion to government intervention in markets coupled with strong political partisanship and conflicting interests among the various states and stakeholders make progress toward energy security extremely slow. In fact, as Gal Luft's chapter describes, the United States seems to be sleepwalking into a growing and dangerous dependence on some of the world's most unstable suppliers.

As major consumers in the transatlantic community are slow to react to the changing energy picture, Asia's future is the biggest wildcard. We chose to dedicate three chapters to Asia as the largest share of growth in demand comes from this continent. In this, Japan, India and China, all heavily dependent on imported energy, present three different approaches to energy security. In Japan, an island devoid of natural resources, with a history of military aggression driven by energy security needs, militarization of energy security is not on the horizon. Instead, efficiency, diversification and the advancement of economic interdependencies are the preferred way to enhance energy security, as discussed by Devin Stewart in Chapter 12. In India, as Jeremy Carl describes, unabated dependence on coal is likely to be the main pillar of the country's energy security, a reality check to those concerned about carbon dioxide emissions. China is perhaps the biggest challenge due to the size of its population and its rapid economic growth. China, discussed by Sabrina Howell in Chapter 13, today accounts for 40 percent of the world's recent increase in demand for oil, consuming twice as much as it did a decade ago, and auto sales in China are expected to exceed those in the United States in about 2015.[27] China's efforts to strengthen its energy security are focused on the physical acquisition of energy assets worldwide, primarily in Africa, Latin America and Central Asia. In this, David Goldwyn compares the United States' and China's scramble for Africa's energy resources in Chapter 15, pointing out the different methods the two countries use to accomplish their goals. China's investment in Africa accelerates infrastructure development but in many cases undermines governance, human rights and environmental quality. The United States, on the other hand, supports international environmental, anticorruption and transparency standards and plays a limited role in promoting infrastructure development and in equity accumulation. While many forecasters worry that China's growing need for imported energy will undermine global security, China's economic boom also provides opportunities to *enhance* global energy security. China's willingness to work in high risk areas and often overpay for energy projects adds product that otherwise would not have been in the market. And Beijing's determination to find alternatives to hydrocarbons and leapfrog oil in favor of the next generation of cars and fuels, along the lines of what happened to telecommunications in the developing world during the past decade (leapfrogging wireline to go straight to wireless) could position China as harbinger of the post-oil economy in the 21st century.

In recent years, a third group of countries is playing a growing role in the energy security discussion—transit states. Those countries are essential bridges connecting exporters with their markets. For energy-starved India, countries like Pakistan and Afghanistan are important bridges to Iran and Turkmenistan where significant natural gas reserves are known to exist. Georgia is an essential land bridge for oil flowing from the Caspian through the Baku-Tbilisi-Ceyhan pipeline. Colombia is contemplating the construction of an oil port on its Pacific coast to enable Venezuelan oil access to Asian markets; and Cameroon provides access to global markets for Chad's oil. By far, the most important transit country is Turkey which, as Necdet Pamir writes in Chapter 16, provides a bridge between energy resources of the Middle East, Russia, and the Caspian Sea and the Western markets. Turkey is becoming increasingly critical to European energy security as the EU seeks ways to become less dependent on Russia. But in the geopolitical chess game Turkey's rise as an energy bridge to Europe is viewed as a challenge to Russia as it undermines its security of demand by providing Europe new alternatives.

A fourth group of actors in the energy security world are international organizations. At this point multinational organizations are struggling to define their role, establish a more proactive role, and enhance their efforts to foster international cooperation on energy issues. Perhaps the most important multinational platform is the IEA, which was formed after the Arab oil embargo and gradually evolved from a system of collective risk sharing to a coordinated system that relies on members to draw down their strategic stocks or reduce demand at the time of a disruption, so that markets can efficiently distribute oil throughout the global system. But the IEA is far from being a perfect platform, as it not only excludes some of the fastest growing consumers like China and India but it also lacks the muscle required to achieve consensus among its members. China for its part is more interested in solidifying its power in a different consortium—the Shanghai Cooperation Organization. The six member countries (China, Russia, Kazakhstan, Kyrgyzstan, Tajikistan, and Uzbekistan) have been cooperating since 2001 to improve regional security and access to energy, not hiding their intention to keep the United States out of their energy club. NATO is another multinational organization that could play a significant role in energy security. In recent years there has been growing pressure within the NATO alliance to define a role and responsibilities in energy security. Robert Bell introduces some of the debates within the Alliance in Chapter 17, showing that even when it comes to a critical issue like energy security member states' priorities do not always coincide.

Enlarging the Energy Pie, Reducing the Risk

While militarization and cooperation are both viable strategies to improve energy security, another approach is an enlargement of the energy pie through a shift to nonconventional hydrocarbons as well as alternative, nonfossil sources of energy. The more energy becomes available, the lower the chance countries would have to compete over it. There are many ways to increase energy production. Some require significant investment in research and development, others can be achieved through changes in national and international regulatory frameworks. The reality is that planet earth still holds enough energy resources for centuries to come, among them hundreds of years worth of coal, trillions of barrels of oil shale and tar sands, a huge endowment of methane hydrates locked under the seabed and substantial reserves of nuclear isotopes like thorium and deuterium and numerous minerals that can make energy storage devices like batteries. Yet, there are economic, security, health, environmental and, in some cases, technological barriers associated with the exploitation of each of the above that take time to surmount. In this book, we chose to focus on two sources of energy that exemplify those tradeoffs: liquefied natural gas (LNG) and nuclear power.

LNG increases energy security through diversification and flexibility by allowing countries to buy natural gas from suppliers with which they have no land bridges, just as with oil. This enables trade relations and political alliances that so far geography has not allowed. As Cindy Hurst points out in Chapter 18, "countries that previously had no energy relations are now growing increasingly dependent on each other thanks to their ability to trade in LNG." But while addressing one energy security challenge, LNG enables relations that are not necessarily conducive to global security. One good example of this is the strengthening ties between China and Iran at a time when the international community tries to pressure Iran to halt its pursuit of nuclear weapons technology and stop its support of terrorist groups. Without LNG there would be no way for Iran to sell its gas to an emerging energy-consuming giant like China. Furthermore, in the context of vulnerability to terrorism, LNG is a dangerous commodity due to its high energy density. LNG tankers or terminals are among the most attractive terrorist targets, a concern that has made the siting of such terminals much more difficult since 9/11. Similar tradeoffs can be found with nuclear power. Concerns about greenhouse gas emissions have given rise to renewed interest in nuclear power, the only nonrenewable form of energy that emits no carbon dioxide. The secure availability of uranium, with Canada, Australia and Kazakhstan being three of the top suppliers, also makes nuclear power a potential energy security enhancer. After years of stagnation the nuclear industry is showing signs of revival. Scores of applications to build new plants are under consideration in the United States and China. In Europe, Finland is building a reactor and even in Australia, which has no reactors, in 2007 then Prime Minister John Howard said nuclear power is "inevitable."[28] Yet, nuclear power still poses significant security challenges with regards to waste disposal and safety of installations. Terrorists could attack plants and steal nuclear fuel, rogue governments can use nuclear technology to develop atomic weapons, and the threat of nuclear accidents like the one in Chernobyl still curbs the public's enthusiasm about this energy source.

No less difficult tradeoffs are found when one tries to reconcile security and the environment. The world's run on energy comes at a time when there is growing awareness of the impact human activities have on the ecosystem. Increased use of fossil fuels is associated with an array of health issues while many tie rising sea levels, desertification and higher than normal extreme weather occurrences to a rise in greenhouse gas emissions. The push to limit greenhouse gas emissions may have merits from an environmental perspective but it often creates new security challenges. Take for example the case of India that, as described in Chapter 14, is heavily dependent on coal for its power generation. The only realistic way for India to cut its carbon dioxide emissions in a meaningful way is by shifting its power sector from coal to less carbon intensive natural gas. Should India decide to make this shift it would become increasingly dependent on nearby Iran, the world's second largest natural gas reserve. India is exploring the possibility of connecting itself with Iran through a natural gas pipeline that would traverse Pakistan and hence create a dependency of one billion Indians on the very same regime in Tehran the international community is seeking to isolate. So while such a shift may benefit the environment, it would surely exacerbate global security. Another demonstration of the tradeoff between security and the environment can be found in Germany, a country that declared that combating climate change is its top priority. Germany has a self-imposed target of reducing greenhouse gas emissions by 20 percent by 2020. The country is in the process of phasing out its coal-mining industrial sector as well as its nuclear power industry (this despite the fact that nuclear power does not emit carbon dioxide). While Germany invests heavily in renewable energy and is now a world leader in solar power in the absence of coal and nuclear, its baseload, 24/7, electric capacity can only come from Russian natural gas. Hence, Germany is now in the process of building an umbilical cord to Russia in the shape of the North Stream pipeline that will make Germany completely dependent on Russia, a country that has shown no compunction using energy as a geopolitical weapon for generations to come. While some are willing to compromise energy security for the sake of planetary concerns, others are pushing in the exact opposite direction, suggesting that urgent security imperatives require that environmental considerations be put on the back burner. Technologies to produce synthetic fuels from coal for use primarily as diesel or jet fuel gain increasing attention as reliance on foreign oil grows, particularly as China invests billions in the technology. The environmental impact of this solution is profound in terms of greenhouse gas emissions. Nonconventional oil from shale and tar sands involves a similar issue as well as a need for large quantities of water. Biofuels that can displace gasoline and diesel for transportation and therefore contribute to energy security also present challenges, as some claim that increased biofuel production may increase deforestation and in some cases put extra pressure on an already strained food market. All these cases and others highlighted by Deron Lovaas in Chapter 22 show that more often than commonly thought, security and the environment do not go hand in hand. If there is an inconvenient truth relating to our energy system it is that while there are some overlapping solutions, we may not be able to address both issues in one strike, and too much emphasis on one could worsen the other. Perhaps one exception is the renewable electricity sector. Solar, wind and geothermal energy are all welcome additions to the global energy mix as they address both security and environmental concerns, but they still play but a small role, about 6 percent, in America's and Europe's energy mix. A different approach to energy security particularly relevant to the electricity sector in which security experts and environmentalists are in full agreement is decentralization, in other words, less dependence on a centralized and highly vulnerable grid. In Chapter 21 David Sweet discusses the role of decentralized energy (DE) as a critical component of any reasonable energy security strategy. As mentioned before, terrorist attacks, simple accidents and overstraining of the grid during peak times of demand can cause parts of the grid to go offline. This can cause a cascading effect that might lead to mega-blackouts. The combination of renewable energy-based decentralized power plus increased deployment of combined heat and power systems can increase the resiliency of our energy system and protect modern economies from price shocks and supply disruptions. All nations have something to gain from decentralized energy. The solar panels on Mongolian yurts, the cell phone chargers in remote Kenyan villages, the fuel cells supplying secure power to research labs in Silicon Valley and the massive heat recovery steam generators in Indian steel mills all fall under the banner of DE. According to Sweet, DE is a cheaper path to global security and peace than efforts to guarantee larger and larger strategic reserves and build expensive, redundant, wasteful central power stations. The efficiency benefits obtainable from increased investment in DE will pay much higher dividends than equal investment in trying to increase supply through conventional means.

This, and many other solutions offered in this book are the foundations for what should be a global energy security strategy. The scale of the solutions is often as large as the scale of the problems. But the nature of the energy security challenges described in the first part of this book is that they do not go away but rather become more taxing and could add unacceptable risks to human life in the 21st century. Luckily, people and governments throughout the world are beginning to understand the gravity of the challenge. It is yet to be seen whether or not the efforts to address the energy challenge will steer us toward a fundamentally changed energy system, one that creates a whole lot more energy for us as well as for those who have not yet had the opportunity to enjoy its benefits as our world becomes more crowded and seemingly more dangerous.

Notes

1. *World Economic Outlook* (Washington DC: International Monetary Fund, April 2008).

2. *International Energy Outlook 2005,* Energy Information Administration, http://tonto.eia.doe.gov/ftproot/forecasting/0484(2005).pdf.

3. Robert L. Hirsch, Roger Bezdek and Robert Wendling, *Peaking of World Oil Production: Impacts, Mitigation and Risk Management,* February 2005, http://www.netl.doe.gov/publications/others/pdf/oil_peaking_netl.pdf.

4. "World Faces Oil 'Supply Crunch' After 2010, IEA Says," *Bloomberg News,* July 9, 2007.

5. "Kuwait Oil Field, World's Second Largest, 'Exhausted,'" *Bloomberg News,* November 9, 2005.

6. "Saudi Arabia: A Whole New Drill," *BusinessWeek,* October 10, 2005, http://www.businessweek.com/magazine/content/05_41/b3954050.htm.

7. Jeff Gerth, "Doubts Raised on Saudi Vow for More Oil," *New York Times,* October 27, 2005, http://www.nytimes.com/2005/10/27/business/worldbusiness/27oil.html.

8. International Energy Agency, *World Energy Outlook 2004,* http://www.iea.org/textbase/nppdf/free/2004/weo2004.pdf.

9. Michael L. Ross, "Blood Barrels: Why Oil Wealth Fuels Conflict," *Foreign Affairs,* May/June 2008.

10. Justin Blum, "Terrorists Have Oil Industry in Cross Hairs," *Washington Post,* September 27, 2004.

11. Spencer Swartz, "Nigeria Oil Output At Lowest in 25 Years," *Dow Jones Newswires,* June 22, 2008.

12. Stephen Brown, "Jihad on the High Seas," *Frontpage Magazine,* September 30, 2008, http://frontpagemag.com/readArticle.aspx?ARTID=32522.

13. Mark Mills, "Brownout," *Forbes,* June 30, 2008, http://www.forbes.com/forbes/2008/0630/038.html.

14. Larry Ness, *Securing Utility and Energy Infrastructures* (Weinheim: Wiley, 2006).

15. "China: Death Penalty for Damage to Grid," *Associated Press,* August 21, 2007, http://archive.newsmax.com/archives/articles/2007/8/21/84043.shtml.

16. "Nigeria to Tackle Power Vandals," *BBC,* September 3, 2007, http://news.bbc.co.uk/2/hi/africa/6975920.stm.

17. "Electric Shortage Forces Iraq to Revise Oil Goal; Year-End Target Is Cut by One-Fifth," *High Beam Research,* http://www.highbeam.com/doc/1P2-274579.html.

18. Final Report on the August 14, 2003 Blackout in the United States and Canada, U.S.-Canada Power System Outage Task Force, April 2004, https://reports.energy.gov/BlackoutFinal-Web.pdf.

19. "Blackouts Will Cost State Billions in Lost Productivity," *Sacramento Business Journal,* May 9, 2001. http://sacramento.bizjournals.com/sacramento/stories/2001/05/07/daily28.html.

20. Leon Fuerth, "Energy, Homeland, and National Security," in *Energy and Security: Toward a New Foreign Policy Strategy,* eds. Jan Kalicki and David Goldwyn (Washington, D.C.: Woodrow Wilson Center Press, 2005), 411, 413.

21. *International Energy Outlook 2008,* Energy Information Administration, http://www. eia.doe.gov/oiaf/ieo/electricity.html.

22. Ibid.

23. Gal Luft and Anne Korin, *Ahmadinejad's Gas Revolution: A Plan to Defeat Economic Sanctions,* IAGS report, December 2006, http://www.iags.org/iran121206.pdf.

24. "UK Feared Americans Would Invade Gulf During 1973 Oil Crisis," *Guardian,* January 1, 2004, http://www.guardian.co.uk/politics/2004/jan/01/uk.past3.

25. Energy Information Administration, http://www.eia.doe.gov/emeu/cabs/topworld tables3_4.html.

26. Anne Korin, "Energy Security in the Western Hemisphere," Testimony before the Committee on Foreign Affairs, Subcommittee on the Western Hemisphere, U.S. House of Representatives, March 2, 2006, http://commdocs.house.gov/committees/intlrel/hfa263 34.000/hfa26334_0f.htm.

27. Arianan Eujung Che, "China's Cars Accelerating a Global Demand for Fuel," *Washington Post,* July 28, 2008.

28. "Nuclear Power's New Age," *The Economist,* September 8, 2007, http://www.econo mist.com/opinion/displayStory.cfm?Story_ID=9767699.

CHAPTER 2

The Epidemic of Energy Terrorism

Ali M. Koknar

Our message to you is crystal clear: Your salvation will only come in your withdrawal from our land, in stopping the robbing of our oil and resources, and in stopping your support for the corrupt and corrupting leaders.
—Ayman al Zawahiri, "Message on Desecration of Holy Koran and the Infidel Democracy"

Over the past 60 years it might seem that the most attractive petroleum reserves are increasingly to be found in parts of the world that are remote and often inhospitable physically, politically, and socially. Petroleum exploration and production companies have gained long and hard experience in coping with these challenging conditions, while often incurring, and being forced to accept, human and financial losses in the process. While the outreach for commercially exploitable reserves has dispersed oilfield operations ever more widely across the globe, the world itself has become a more dangerous, or at least unpredictable, place. Non-state actors, especially multinational companies, have increasingly come to be regarded as legitimate targets by terrorists. Meanwhile, in many regions oil and gas have become strategic resources and hence frequent strategic targets for terrorism.[1] Hundreds of thousands of miles of oil, oil product and natural gas pipelines, many of which are located above ground, crisscross the globe. They are highly visible, largely unprotected targets, as are many of the infrastructure sites servicing them such as the compressor and pumping stations, emergency bypass pipelines and related facilities.[2]

The global jihad and the rising price of oil have contributed to the proliferation of terrorism against energy facilities in countries with Muslim populations. While some of these countries were exposed to energy terrorism in the past, more are expected to face it in the coming years.

The term energy terrorism is not strictly confined to armed attacks against energy generation, storage and transmission facilities. Energy terrorism also includes illegal activity conducted against or in connection with these facilities, such as criminal theft of oil from pipelines or extortion by means of threat of damage to these facilities if such activity is conducted to provide financing and logistic support to a terrorist organization. Terrorist organizations have colluded with criminals who tap oil pipelines, taking advantage of the fact that security forces are preoccupied with fighting terrorist activity. Notwithstanding disagreements about the definition of terrorism, ordinary criminal activity against energy facilities causes significant economic loss.[3] The protection of key infrastructure from terrorist attack is undeniably one of the highest priorities in the safeguarding of a country's security and prosperity. In many countries, the focus is on protection of oil and gas infrastructure such as refineries, tankers, and pipelines. In other countries it is the protection of water pipelines as well as hazardous waste pipelines.[4] With energy costs soaring and finite world oil reserves there is a growing reliance on strategic pipelines to move oil and gas from often challenging drilling environments either to the end user or to safe ports of embarkation.[5] al-Qaeda argues that priority should be given to attacking oil facilities in the Middle East since this would damage the American economy and embarrass the United States as well as apostate regimes al-Qaeda wants to unseat. Such attacks could also embolden other countries seeking to secure their own energy supplies, and force the United States to deploy more troops to the region to stabilize the situation. The terrorists reason that "the United States will reach a stage of madness after the targeting of its oil interests" thus "facilitating the creation of a new front and the drowning of the U.S. in a new quagmire that will be worse than the quagmires of Iraq and Afghanistan." Clearly, the terrorists understand that they can influence oil markets through directed violence, and thus exploit a critical U.S. vulnerability.[6]

Perpetrators of Energy Terrorism

The perpetrators of energy terrorism can be split into two groups:

- Nonstate actors such as politically motivated terrorist organizations, which would include criminals who operate in collusion with the terrorists, and
- Terrorists who act as proxies for state sponsors of terrorism to target energy facilities.

At least four motivating factors drive terrorist groups to target gas and oil sectors:

- The potential to cause catastrophic damage to a nation's economy;
- Retaliation by an extremist group or a disgruntled insider against one of the industry's nodes over a specific demand, issue or general or personal grievance;
- Desire to cause a government to appear inept and incapable of protecting its critical infrastructure and citizens;
- Desire to spread panic throughout society by creating the perception that every critical node in a country's infrastructure is vulnerable to attack.[7]

Terrorists have always been aware of the importance of oil and gas resources for their own political and economical needs and have used attacks on such resources for various goals:

- By attacking oil and gas facilities they can provoke serious economic hardships and endanger the internal stability of the governments they are fighting, thus facilitating their quest for power;
- In many cases, the targeting of these resources is seen as an important step in the fight against foreign powers that have vested strategic or economic interests in these regions and support the legal government, or against international companies involved in the development and exploitation of oil and gas resources;
- Finally, terrorists see the possibility of using their governments' financial wealth from oil revenues as an indirect way to fund their operations. In the Muslim world, where three-quarters of the world's oil is know to exist and where charity is a mandated by Islamic law, the bigger the disposable income of the population the more money trickles down to charity organizations sympathetic to, if not directly supportive of, the terrorists' agenda.[8]

Targets of Energy Terrorism

Electric Utilities

Electric power grids are highly vulnerable and thus have become top targets for terrorist organizations. Terrorists understand that power grids are built-in loops. While this feature allows grids to withstand multiple outages and failures, it is also an advantage to terrorists. Terrorists can identify critical nodes in the power grid and attack designated vulnerable spots to cause wide-scale blackouts over large areas of a country. They can plan attacks in affected regions where response personnel are dealing with blackouts. *Sendero Luminoso,* the Shining Path, launched highly effective terrorist strikes in Peru against Lima's power grid in the 1980s and 1990s.[9] In recent years there have been numerous attacks against power lines in Pakistan's southern province of Baluchistan as well as in numerous locations in Iraq.

Gas and Oil Infrastructure

Oil and gas pipeline systems are also vulnerable networks that are very difficult to secure, a fact that terrorists understand too well. Energy resource extraction and distribution systems are vulnerable both at sea and on land. Once gas or oil reaches land via pipeline networks, it becomes highly susceptible to attack. Established safety precautions require pipeline operators to label and identify their pipes and product every time pipelines cross a road or waterway. These safety precautions enable terrorists to detonate sections of pipelines that carry volatile substances. There are seven principal vulnerable points in any given country's oil infrastructure: production facilities, including oilfields, wells, platforms, and rigs; refineries and other processing plants; transportation facilities, including pipelines, pumping stations, terminals, and tankers; depots; corporate offices; distribution points, both wholesale and retail; and personnel employed at any of these places. A Norwegian study found that the most common disruptions, accounting for nearly two-thirds of attacks on oil infrastructure worldwide, were those relating to pipelines. Since they are relatively easy to repair, it is not particularly cost-effective, generally speaking, to guard long stretches.[10] Oil and gas fields typically pose unusual geographical challenges to security. Their remote locations, and often extensive acreage, make them far more difficult to secure than other industrial facilities. An attack on a pipeline is essentially a soft and effective tactic for the terrorist, as it has an economic, political and environmental impact. Indeed, the mere threat of attack is often sufficient to gain political advantage. This explains why some countries pay local tribes or communities large sums of money to protect pipelines that run through their territory. In most cases these are nothing more than extortion payments made to discourage the tribes or communities from carrying out sabotage attacks.[11]

Zones of Turmoil

Iraq. The future of Iraq is almost wholly dependent on developing its oil reserves. Yet despite its vast reserves the country's oil output since the beginning of the 2003 war has been disappointing—about two and a half million barrels a day. The principal reason for this failure to increase exports has been the disruption caused by terrorism. Through attacks on pipelines, saboteurs have proved themselves adept at maintaining a steady state of disruption.[12] During the war and subsequent occupation of Iraq, forces loyal to the deposed regime of Iraqi dictator Saddam Hussein and other insurgents engaged in a long and steady campaign of disrupting the flow of Iraqi oil to shipping terminals and consumers by conducting sabotage operations on the Iraqi oil pipeline network. Oil and oil products slowed to a trickle through the 5,000 miles of pipelines, and long lines of vehicles queued at filling stations. Despite the presence of tens of thousands of coalition forces in the country, the country's pipeline network could not be protected from acts of sabotage.[13] As of the end of 2007, terrorists continued to attack the Iraqi oil industry infrastructure despite the improved capabilities of the Iraqi security forces. The prime casualty was the Kirkuk-Ceyhan pipeline in Northern Iraq that could, when operational, export 440,000 barrels per day. Since April of 2003 the Iraqi oil industry was subjected to over 500 attacks, nearly 160 attacks by terrorists in 2006 alone, killing and wounding dozens of oil employees and reducing exports by 400,000 barrels a day.[14] A less reported form of sabotage against the Iraqi oil infrastructure is theft via illegal tapping, often by the local tribesmen. The terrorists have realized that stealing oil is not only damaging but is also far more profitable than pure destruction.[15] In 2007 President of the Kurdish Regional Government in Northern Iraq Massoud Barzani estimated the total losses emanating from sabotage and theft at around $12 billion a year.[16] This figure grew considerably with the sharp rise in oil prices. Mr. Barzani offered to deploy 6,000 Kurdish Pashmarga fighters to improve security for the oil infrastructure north of Baghdad from the Baiji refinery to the Kirkuk hub.[17] The local tribesmen hired to protect the pipes are often from the same groups that sabotage them, and tribal bonds are often stronger than national loyalty in Iraq.[18]

Colombia. Marxist terrorists have been carrying out an insurgent campaign against the Colombian government for more than 40 years. While this campaign has mainly been in the form of car bombings, kidnappings and assassinations directed against civilian and military targets, terrorist actions against the Colombian energy infrastructure have caused more financial losses to the government than all other activities combined.[19] The security of the Colombian pipelines is not so much a matter of engineering as one of politics and conflict. The pipelines have frequently been attacked by terrorist groups. The *Ejercito de Liberacion Nacional* (National Liberation Army-ELN) inflicts significant economic damage and gains significant exposure from its regular bombing campaign against the 110,000 barrels per day Cano-Limon-Covenas oil and natural gas pipeline operated by Occidental Petroleum Corporation.[20] The 480-mile pipeline has been hit more than a thousand times, causing close to three million barrels of oil to be spilled, and the pipeline to be nicknamed the flute.[21] A 1998 report by the Colombian Ministry of the Environment stated that spillage from pipeline bombing campaigns had resulted in more oil seeping into the country's water courses than that spilled in the Exxon Valdez incident in Alaska. In October 1998, the ELN blew up British Petroleum's (BP) Oleoducto Central (OCENSA) pipeline at the village of Machuca in the state of Antioquia. The resulting fireball killed at least 70 people. BP and its partner companies predicted even before they had built the pipeline that it would be attacked. Colombia's largest terrorist group, the *Fuerzas Armadas Revolucionarias de Colombia* (Revolutionary Armed Forces of Colombia-FARC) also attacks the pipelines. In 2001, for example, ELN and FARC bombed the Cano-Limon-Covenas pipeline 177 times, crippling it for 266 days.[22] Since the terrorists started attacking the pipelines in 1986, Colombian authorities estimate the damages due to lost pipeline royalty revenue and oil spills to be more than $300 million annually.

Nigeria. Nigeria is of great strategic importance to the United States. It is the largest oil producer in Africa and the 11th largest producer in the world. However, investment in Nigeria's energy sector is threatened by a number of formidable obstacles. The fight over who controls oil revenues in the Niger Delta, where crime and politics are intertwined, underlies many of Nigeria's problems.[23] Since 2004, the Movement for the Emancipation of Niger Delta (MEND) has attacked foreign oil companies, kidnapping and killing foreign oil workers. As a result of dozens of attacks, MEND has succeeded in shutting down 25 percent of Nigeria's oil production, causing 1,000 foreign workers to flee, as well as at least three foreign companies.[24] This caused Nigeria losses estimated at tens of billions of dollars in export revenues since 2005.[25] Following a call by MEND in mid-December 2007 for Niger Delta terrorists to unite,[26] another group called the

Niger Delta Vigilante welcomed 2008 by raiding the center of Nigeria's oil indus-try in the Delta, Port Harcourt, where it killed 16 Nigerians and wounded dozens, as it overwhelmed the Nigerian police.[27] International oil companies operating in Nigeria, most prominently Royal Dutch Shell, are considering scaling back their operations there in light of the risk involved.

Algeria. Algeria has been involved in a long war against domestic terrorism and while there are signs of success in combating these groups, there is the danger of new threats evolving. The Algerian economy is almost entirely dependent on the export of oil and gas, which account for almost all of the country's export reve-nues.[28] *Groupe Islamique Armé* (Armed Islamic Group-GIA) targeted Algerian oil and gas facilities in the 1990s, but more recently a derivative called the Salafist group for Preaching and Combat (*Groupe Salafiste pour la Prédication et le Combat*), has transformed itself into the Algerian al-Qaeda affiliate, the al-Qaeda in the Islamic Maghreb (AQIM), and has started attacking Western and Algerian oil interests. Its ambush, inside a protected military zone, no less, of a bus carrying employees of the American oilfields services contractor Kellogg Brown and Root in December 2006 resulted in the withdrawal of that company's staff from Algeria. In April of 2007, AQIM attacked in the capital city of Algiers, killing 33 people, and later in Septem-ber attempted to assassinate the Algerian president, who had defeated the GIA-led terrorism in the 1990s. Twin suicide car bomb attacks in December 2007 by AQIM in Algiers killed 26 people, including nine UN staff.[29] The November 2007 Nigerian arrest of five suspects trained by AQIM to use high explosives may be interpreted as evidence that the Nigerian MEND may also be loosely affiliated with al-Qaeda in line with the al-Qaeda strategy of attacking the oil industry worldwide. As far as the Algerian authorities are concerned, AQIM is a threat to be reckoned with, as the cancellation of the annual Paris-Dakar rally in January 2008 underscores.

Saudi Arabia. Saudi Arabia, the world's biggest oil exporter with 25 percent of the world's proven oil reserves, also takes al-Qaeda threats against its oil industry seriously. A successful terrorist attack against Saudi Arabia's Abqaiq oil-processing center would easily double the market price of crude oil. al-Qaeda indeed launched an unsuccessful suicide car bomb attack against Abqaiq in February 2006. That attack against the world's largest oil-processing plant immediately sent oil prices up by $2 per barrel and highlighted the sector's vulnerability.[30] Two waves of arrests by Saudi authorities of hundreds of al-Qaeda suspects be-lieved to have planned attacks against Saudi oil facilities in the Eastern Province in April and November of 2007 and seizure of weapons and explosives show that it may be a matter of not if but *when* another attack takes place in the kingdom. Some of the arrested terrorists had undergone flight training with the objective of hijacking planes and crashing them into major oil facilities in the Kingdom. While much of the attention is given to al-Qaeda, the rising bellicosity between Saudi Arabia and Iran raises the threat to Saudi oil infrastructure by radical Shi'a elements, particularly in light of the fact that most of the infrastructure is located in Saudi Arabia's predominantly Shiite Eastern Province.[31]

Yemen and Ethiopia. al-Qaeda attacked the oil industry at sea off the coast of Yemen in 2002, but in the future may choose to do so on land. The Yemeni government derives 70 percent of its revenue from oil production, and in September 2006 Yemeni security forces stopped a group calling itself al-Qaeda in Yemen from detonating vehicle-borne IEDs on oil installations in Hadramawt and Marib Provinces.[32] Just across the Bab al Mandab, in Ethiopia, al-Qaeda affiliated terrorist groups such as the Ogaden National Liberation Front, continue to operate, taking opportunities to target foreign oil workers.[33]

Pakistan. Turbulent Pakistan has also faced energy terrorism in the last decade since the murder of five Union Texas Petroleum workers in 1997. Rocket attacks against gas pipelines in Pakistan's Baluchistan province have taken place since 2001.[34]

Russia and Eurasia. In Russia, the pipeline system consists of 95,000 miles of gas pipeline, 21,000 miles of oil product pipeline, and 10,000 miles of oil pipeline. This huge maze is managed for the state by Transneft, a state-owned company. In crucial locations where energy crosses over national borders from Russia into Ukraine and on to Western Europe, there is a distinct threat not only of sabotage by terrorist groups, but also of tapping by criminals. A disruption of the flow of gas or oil can have a devastating impact upon the economies of a number of European states who are heavily dependent upon oil and gas from Russia and Central Asia.[35] Pipeline sabotage has been of particular concern in Russia's North Caucasus region, where oil, refined products and gas pipelines running through Chechnya, North Ossetia and, increasingly, Dagestan, have become regular targets of attacks. The Mozdok–Gazi-Magomed gas pipeline, running through Dagestan to Azerbaijan, has in recent years been attacked over a dozen times.[36] Like Saudi Arabia, the Russians have also decided to create their own protection force. In July 2007, the Russian Parliament exempted government-owned producer Gazprom and Russia's state oil pipeline operator, Transneft, from a law forbidding companies other than private security firms to arm their employees.[37] In July 2006, Azeri authorities arrested dozens of members of a group called Jamaat al-Muwahiddin that had planned to attack Azeri targets, including the state oil company.[38] In December 2006, a Georgian section of the Baku-Tbilisi-Erzurum gas pipeline from Azerbaijan was blown up by terrorists.[39] In August 2008, the militant arm of the *Partiya Karkaren Kurdistan* (Kurdistan Workers Party-PKK) claimed responsibility for an explosion in an attack on the Turkish sector of the Baku-Tbilisi-Ceyhan (BTC.) In Azerbaijan pipeline security officers serve unarmed, which, in the opinion of the Azeri energy officials, renders them less effective in deterring attackers.[40] In the Caucasus and Near East, the threats against pipelines and other energy facilities are not exclusively by al-Qaeda affiliates. Other terrorist organizations such as the PKK have also declared them as legitimate targets.[41] The PKK has attacked Turkish pipelines, pump stations, refineries and oilfields in eastern and southeastern Turkey at least 20 times since 2004 and has also attacked the Iran-Turkey natural gas pipeline since 2005.[42]

The BTC oil pipeline grew from a vision of an energy corridor that would resurrect the Great Silk Road, articulated at that time by Turkey, Georgia, and Azerbaijan. BTC was commissioned in July 2006. It will reach full capacity of one million barrels of oil per day over the next few years, and connect oil fields in the Caspian Sea with global markets reached from Turkey's Mediterranean Sea port of Ceyhan. A companion natural gas pipeline, the Baku-Tbilisi-Erzurum (BTE), delivers Azeri natural gas from the Shakh Deniz field in the Caspian to Georgia and Turkey.[43] The first year of operation exposed some security vulnerabilities of the BTC pipeline, which was tapped by thieves even before it came online at full capacity.[44] The 1,000-mile-long BTC is most exposed in Turkey, where it stretches for 600 miles. Turkey received more than $100 million in pipeline royalties during the pipeline's first year of operation. It was also tapped more than a dozen times by oil thieves in that period.[45] The PKK, under attack from the Turkish military, has turned to retaliating against softer civilian targets in Turkey. It is conceivable that it may also choose to attack the Turkish sections of these pipelines just as it has attacked the Turkish section of the Kirkuk-Ceyhan pipeline and the domestic Turkish Batman-Dortyol pipeline. A top PKK commander stated in 2006 that they "reserved their option" to attack the BTC pipeline in future.[46] And indeed, on August 5, 2008, just two days before the conflict began over the South Ossetia region, the PKK claimed responsibility for an explosion that forced the closure of the BTC for several weeks.

Mitigation

The economic implications of terrorist attacks on the world's energy infrastructure are potentially enormous. Oil analysts believe that a terror premium of $10-$20 a barrel is now factored into the price of a barrel of oil. There are things that both governments and the energy industry can do to help mitigate these implications and bring a measure of control over drastic increases in the market price of oil by curbing the scale of damage that terrorism can inflict on the industry.

Increased Protection. When operators do the math, Private Security Contractors (PSC) costs often come out as a fraction of the losses suffered as a result of terrorist sabotage and theft. In Colombia for example, in 1997 Occidental Corporation's Cano-Limon-Covenas pipeline was blown up 65 times while BP's OCENSA pipeline was blown up just once. BP's pipeline enjoyed PSC protection while Cano-Limon did not. This means that the terrorist threat to energy facilities is likely to be answered with an ever growing investment in security measures to deter and prevent terrorist attacks and to reduce the likely damage should a successful attack take place. The market for energy security technologies such as sensors, radar and surveillance systems and rapid response capabilities is growing fast and oil states are more inclined than ever to invest in their deployment. More traditional security elements such as specialized protection forces will also be increasingly used. The Saudi government, in collaboration with U.S. defense giant Lockheed Martin, has already begun establishing a 35,000-strong special security force to protect the Kingdom's oil facilities.[47] The new force, called the Facilities Security Force, has already recruited 9,000 members and 8,000 will be added each year until full capacity is reached.[48] This will be highly specialized force and its members will be well vetted to ensure that no religious extremists infiltrate it.[49] Regional states will also increase their efforts to set up mechanisms to enhance maritime security along energy supply routes including growing naval collaboration with NATO militaries.

Creating Alternative Energy Routes. The high rate of demand for oil from the energy-rich regions and the fact that navigation in strategic choke points like the Bosporus and the Strait of Hormuz can no longer be taken for granted are likely to bring oil states to reconsider new energy corridors that could reduce dependence on these chokepoints. For years, Saudi Arabia has maintained capacity to export oil from the Red Sea though the East-West pipeline in the event that Persian Gulf operations are interrupted. But more avenues are needed. The Trans-Arabia oil pipeline project to crisscross the Arabian Peninsula has been in discussion for several years but never materialized due to its high cost. Now, when energy revenues are high and the Gulf economies flourish, oil states are more inclined to take financial risks and commit to multibillion-dollar pipeline projects. Hence the Trans-Arabia pipeline is under serious consideration by Saudi Arabia, Bahrain, the UAE, Oman and Yemen. The UAE has already committed to a major oil project to bypass the Strait: a pipeline between its onshore Habshan oil field, in Abu Dhabi, and Fujayrah. Upon completion in 2009, the pipeline is expected to move 1.5 million barrels a day.[50]

Government-To-Government Aid. Some suggest that oil terrorism is emerging as a major threat to the global economy. Oil markets are tight, with little spare capacity today, and demand is increasing. There is strong evidence that a relatively small disruption to oil production throughout the world could spike world energy prices, severely harming the American economy.[51] There are more than 3 million miles of unprotected oil and gas pipelines worldwide. At an average cost of more than $1.3 million dollars per mile to build, that adds up to $3.6 trillion worth of unprotected pipelines—not to mention the value of the petroleum or gas running through them.[52] Therefore, energy security is a national security issue to which the U.S. government has responded by extending aid to vulnerable governments to help them protect their oil industry infrastructure. One such example of government-to-government aid is Plan Colombia. About 10 percent of this $100 million aid package to help the Colombian government fight terrorism was allocated for the U.S. training of Colombian troops in tactics to defend the Cano-Limon-Covenas pipeline.[53] Following this allocation in April 2002, the ELN declared oil companies a "military target."[54] The U.S. government has also been assisting oil-producing nations in Africa such as Nigeria, Angola and Equatorial Guinea to improve their security capabilities. The creation of a new U.S. Army command dedicated to Africa in 2007 is expected to help this effort. In 2005, the U.S. government unveiled a six-year $135 million initiative called "Caspian Guard" designed to help the governments of Azerbaijan and Kazakhstan improve their defenses against threats aimed at their energy facilities, primarily against the BTC pipeline.[55] The initiative includes the transfer of military technology such as surveillance radars and patrol craft as well as training in small unit tactics, to be provided by the U.S. Army's European Command (EUCOM) and its private military contractors. Similarly the EUCOM ran a $64 million train-and-equip program in Georgia between 2002 and 2004, training and equipping four light infantry battalions and one mechanized/armor company, tasked with protecting the Georgian section of the BTC pipeline. In 2004, BP, the leader of the BTC consortium, contributed $2 million towards the creation of a battalion dubbed the Strategic Pipeline Protection Department, and funds it to the tune of one million dollars annually.[56] Awareness of Georgian shortcomings in properly securing its sections of the critical BTC crude oil pipeline and the Baku-Tbilisi-Erzurum natural gas pipeline has prompted neighboring Turkey, which is the terminus of these pipelines, to extend aid to the Georgian government in order to improve their pipeline security capabilities. The Turkish Gendarmerie, with decades of experience in protecting Turkey's own pipelines, is the lead agency in this effort, in which the Turkish Coast Guard, Special Forces, and Air Force also participate with training and equipment donations.[57] Turkey also conducts annual exercises with Georgians and Azeris, practicing responses to simulated attacks on the BTC pipeline.[58]

Outsourcing. Defense against more concerted attacks by terrorists on a fixed facility such as a production platform or a pipeline is typically the responsibility of the host country's security forces. However, this type of protection may actually be problematic for the company/pipeline operator or its contractor, for a number of reasons. First, the military units or armed police assigned may be inefficient, disorganized and poorly led. This can become a liability for the corporate protectees: conscript soldiers with poor weapons-training may pose a serious safety hazard around production sites. Secondly, in seriously dysfunctional states there may be collusion between individuals in the military and the terrorists threatening the corporate facility. Hence, expatriates are often suspicious, justifiably or not, of the motives and real allegiance of those who are supposed to be there to protect them. Fear of the inside job can lead to distrust of local security resources.[59] PSCs can bridge the gap between the Exploration & Production (E&P) companies/pipeline operators and the host country security forces. Taken together, the changing risk environment, and changing tolerance levels for such risks by companies, is leading E&P companies to revise their old philosophies on security. In the past, smaller E&P players and contractors tended to ignore risks at corporate level, crossing their fingers and leaving it to field management to find the best protection they could in the local market. However, ignoring risks is no longer a good option, for the reasons already discussed. Transferring all risks to insurance is arguably not viable: it is prohibitively expensive to insure against all indirect consequences of a security failure. Since 9/11, in a hardening insurance market, even direct terrorism risks may be uninsurable. A more integrated approach to risk management is therefore being adopted by E&P companies. Although total elimination of risks may be unachievable, it is certainly possible to reduce risks substantially, by becoming a hard target.[60] Thus, oil industry companies are increasingly turning to PSCs to help them become hard targets.[61]

Conclusion

Terrorist sabotage against and terrorist-affiliated theft from oil facilities is almost guaranteed to be a fact of life for the foreseeable future as long as oil prices remain at the current levels.

The E&P sector, and the oilfield services companies and contractor base that support it, has found itself on the front line of energy terrorism, facing physical threats to its people, assets, and operations in many parts of the world. While many old hands in the industry, used to the rigors and risks of expatriate service, might be blasé about this, businesses are finding that individual risk acceptance is no longer a tenable stance. This change in risk tolerance is due to the pressures from stakeholders, who are insisting on ever-higher standards of corporate governance and corporate social responsibility. These stakeholders are not just shareholders and funding institutions; they also include the families of expatriate employees, who these days can be expected to be in regular close contact with their loved ones back at home via email or satellite telephone. Retention of high quality people is becoming problematic for companies that cannot provide a high standard of safety assurance. And, should the worst happen, damage to the company is exacerbated by the likelihood of catastrophic litigation.[62] American, British, French and South African private security companies have provided and continue to provide support to the industry in Iraq, Nigeria, Colombia, Algeria, Angola, Kazakhstan, and other countries with terrorist threats ranging from all-out war to lower threat levels at which they conduct unarmed work under a soft power approach, while the physical protection of their principal's personnel and assets is the foremost concern. But despite the growing investment in security, the booming PSC sector and the tightening intergovernmental cooperation, it will be impossible to eliminate oil terrorism altogether and the cost of energy terrorism to consumers worldwide will be increasingly noticeable.

Notes

1. Jerry Hoffman, "Strategic Security for Oilfields: Countering Terrorism Risks in Unstable Regions," April 10, 2002, ArmorGroup North America, http://www.armorgroup.com.

2. Roman Kupchinsky, "Are Oil Pipelines Sitting Ducks?" February 6, 2004, http://www.rferl.org/reports/corruptionwatch/2004/02/5-060204.asp.

3. Ali Akcoban, "*Hırsızlar petrol boru hattını beş ayda 55 yerden deldi* (Thieves Puncture Oil Pipeline 55 Times in Five Months," *Zaman Turkish daily newspaper,* June 11, 2006.

4. Kupchinsky, Are Oil Pipelines Sitting Ducks?"

5. Erinys International article for the Conference Booklet of the NATO Forum on Energy Security in Prague, November 3–5, 2005.

6. James S. Robbins, "No Blood for Oil," *National Review,* July 12, 2005, http://www.nationalreview.com/robbins/robbins200507120857.asp.

7. Joshua Sinai, "The Terrorist Threats to the Gas and Oil Sectors," *Journal of Counterterrorism and Homeland Security International,* 10, no. 4, 15.

8. Ely Karmon, "The Risk of Terrorism against Oil and Gas Pipelines in Central Asia," January 6, 2002, http://212.150.54.123/articles/articledet.cfm?articleid=426.

9. Christopher Kozlow and John Sullivan, *Jane's Facility Security Handbook* (Alexandria, VA: Jane's Information Group, 2000), 33–34.

10. Ashild Kjok and Brynjar Lia, "Terrorism and Oil: An Explosive Mixture. A Survey of Terrorist and Rebel Attacks on Petroleum Infrastructure 1968–1999," Norwegian Defense Research Establishment, 2001.

11. Erinys International.

12. Ibid.

13. Kupchinsky, "Are Oil Pipelines Sitting Ducks?"

14. "Iraq Oil Industry Hit Hard by Violence, Official Says," *Associated Press,* July 9, 2007.

15. Institute for War and Peace Reporting, "Tribes Sabotage Kirkuk Pipelines," September 7, 2007, http://www.iwpr.net/?p=icr&s=f&o=338515&apc_state=henh.

16. *"Petrol boru hatlarina yapilan saldiri yillik 12 Milyar Dolar zarara neden oluyor* (Attacks Against Oil Pipelines Cause 12 Billion Dollars in Damages Annually)," *Zaman,* July 4, 2007.

17. "6,000 Kurdish Fighters to Guard Iraq Oil Installations," *AFP News Agency,* July 18, 2007.

18. "A Wasted Resource," Institute for War and Peace Reporting, September 12, 2007. http://www.iwpr.net/?p=icr&s=f&o=338633&apc_state=henh.

19. Tom Hunter, "Colombia's Oil Wars," *Journal of Counterterrorism and Security International,* Spring 1998, 4–5.

20. Ibid.

21. Timothy D. Ringgold, "It's On the Pipeline," *Homeland Security Insider,* September 2006.

22. Karl Penhaul, "Along the Pipeline: Tracking Colombia's Revolt," *Boston Globe,* April 21, 2002, 12.

23. Ariel Cohen and Rafal Alasa, "Africa's Oil and Gas Sector: Implications for U.S. Policy," July 13, 2007, http://www.heritage.org/Research/Africa/bg2052.cfm.

24. Spencer Swartz, "Global Oil Firms Confront Fresh Obstacles in Africa," July 13, 2007, http://online.wsj.com/article/SB118426417104364902.html?mod=googlenews_wsj.

25. Ibid.

26. "Nigerian Militants Call for Groups to Unite, Cripple Oil Industry," *Voice of America,* December 17, 2007.

27. George Onah and Jimitota Onoyume, "Nigeria: 16 Killed in P-Harcourt," *Vanguard Lagos,* January 1, 2008.

28. Kupchinsky, "Are Oil Pipelines Sitting Ducks?"

29. Craig Whitlock, "Algiers Attacks Show Maturing of Al-Qaeda Unit," *Washington Post,* December 13, 2007, A25.

30. Roula Khalaf, "Saudis Deploy Special Force to Protect Oil Facilities," *Financial Times,* November 17–18, 2007, 6.

31. Saket Vemprala and Ali al Ahmed, *The Security of the Saudi Energy Infrastructure,* Institute for Gulf Affairs, August 2008.

32. John Solomon, "Expansion of Yemen's Refining Capacity Raises Terrorism Concerns," May 29, 2007. http://jamestown.org/terrorism/news/uploads/tf_004_016.pdf.

33. Anita Powell, "9 Freed After Ethiopian Oil Attack," *Associated Press*, April 29, 2007.

34. Muddassir Rizvi, "Attacks Bode Ill for Mega-pipelines," *Inter Press Service*, January 25, 2003.

35. Kupchinsky, "Are Oil Pipelines Sitting Ducks?"

36. Yuri M. Zhukov, "Addressing Pipeline Security Challenges in Russia," December 7, 2006, http://www.eurasianet.org/departments/insight/articles/eav120706a.shtml.

37. "Gazprom to Form an Armed Security Force," *New York Times*, July 5, 2007.

38. "23 Terrorists Jailed in Baku," *Associated Press*, April 27, 2007.

39. "Terrorist Attack on Gas Pipeline from Azerbaijan to Georgia," *RIA Novosti*, December 23, 2006.

40. Huseyin Sumer, *"BTC boruhattina hirsizlar dadandi* (Thieves Target the BTC Pipeline)," *Zaman*, November 29, 2007.

41. "Kurd Rebels Say May Hit Pipelines if Attacked," *Reuters*, October 19, 2007.

42. Benoit Faucon, "PKK Claims Sabotage Of Iran-Turkey Pipeline-Spokesman," *Dow Jones*, September 10, 2007.

43. Daniel Fried, "U.S.-Turkish Relations and the Challenges Ahead," March 15, 2007 http://www.state.gov/p/eur/rls/rm/81761.htm.

44. Sumer and Ercan Baysal, *"Baku-Ceyhan boruhatti helikopterle korunacak* (Baku-Ceyhan Pipeline to Be Protected with Helicopters)," *Zaman*, March 27, 2007.

45. Ibid.

46. *"Karayilan: Sovenizm derinlesiyor* (Karayilan: Chauvinism Deepens)," *ANF News Agency*, July 15, 2006, http://www.kurdishinfo.com/modules.php?name=News&file=article&sid=8337.

47. Raid Qusti, "Special Units to Protect Oil," *Arab News*, July 2, 2007.

48. "Saudi Force Sent to Guard Oil Facilities," *Financial Times*, November 18, 2007.

49. "US Helps Saudis Train Oil Security Force," *Agence France-Presse*, August 25, 2007.

50. Matt Chambers, "Just in Case," *Wall Street Journal*, August 27, 2007.

51. Statement of Representative Ed Royce, Chairman, Subcommittee on International Terrorism and Nonproliferation, "Terrorist Threats to Energy Security," July 27, 2005 http://www.internationalrelations.house.gov/archives/109/roy072705.pdf.

52. Ringgold, "It's On the Pipeline."

53. Penhaul, "Along the Pipeline."

54. Hoffman, "Security Strategy for Oilfields."

55. "US to Assist Baku in Fleet Building," *AssA-Irada News Agency*, September 22, 2005.

56. Alexandros Petersen, "BTC security questions persist," July 11, 2006, http://www.eurasianet.org.

57. Ali Koknar, "Turkey and the Caucasus-Security and Military Challenges," in Michael Radu, ed. *Dangerous Neighborhood: Aspects of Turkey's Foreign Relations*, (New Brunswick, NJ: Transaction Books, 2002).

58. "Caspian States Practice Pipeline Security," *Interfax News Agency*, August 22, 2005.

59. Hoffman, "Security Strategy for Oilfields."

60. Ibid.

61. Steve Casteel, "Soft Approach Works in Hard Land," May 31, 2007, http://www.eandpnet.com/area/exp/396.htm.

62. Hoffman, "Security Strategy for Oilfields."

CHAPTER 3

Troubled Waters: Energy Security as Maritime Security

Donna J. Nincic

The confluence of the terrorist threat, political instability in key energy producing nations, conflicting claims over access to energy supplies, and new drives of
developing nations for access to oil and natural gas resources has created two
types of threats that impede energy security: the threat of access to oil and natural
gas supplies, and the threat to energy infrastructure, particularly energy transportation infrastructure. Since one-quarter to one-third of the world's oil and gas
reserves are believed to lie offshore, and approximately two-thirds of the world's
oil trade is transported by sea, the issue of energy security is to a large extent one
of maritime security.

The maritime realm is fraught with conflict: piracy, terrorism, conflict over
access to fisheries, and disputes over territorial boundaries and the extent of
Exclusive Economic Zones (EEZs) are common.[1] Since the attacks of 9/11, the
vulnerability of maritime infrastructure has been frequently noted.[2] Concerns
over port security in general, and fears that ships could be turned into floating
bombs or agents of terrorism in particular, have led to the International Ship and
Port Facility Security Code passed by the International Maritime Organization
in 2002, and the U.S. Maritime Transportation Security Act passed by the U.S.
Congress, also in 2002. Meant to address the particular problem of maritime
terrorism, they do not address the more frequent problem of maritime piracy
or other forms of conflict on the world's seas. While all these conflicts combine
to pose threats to merchant shipping, they also threaten the security of access
to maritime energy supplies, and the security of the maritime transportation of
energy resources.

Security of Access: Conflict over Maritime Sources of Oil and Natural Gas

As mentioned, one-quarter to one-third of oil and gas reserves are believed to
lie offshore, mostly on the continental shelf. Some significant reserves lie in areas

of contested EEZs, where in many cases neighboring nations have not yet established mutually-agreed upon maritime boundaries. Disputes are common, and only an estimated 39 percent of maritime boundaries are even partially resolved.[3] Many of these involve disagreements over oil and natural gas exploration, some of which have been settled peacefully, while others remain a source of conflict—even armed conflict.

For example, in August 2002 the Costa Rican government challenged a decision by Nicaragua to grant offshore oil exploration concessions, saying that some of the concessions were located in Costa Rican waters. In the Gulf of Mexico, an area known as the Western Gap had been disputed by the United States and Mexico. Known as a doughnut hole, or an area lying outside of—but surrounded by—the EEZs of both nations, the Gap is believed to contain significant oil reserves. In 2000, the United States and Mexico agreed peacefully on a division of the Gap and its resources.

Some of these disputes have involved military action, or the threat of military action:

- In the 1990s China and Vietnam began oil exploration in two overlapping and disputed tracts of the South China Sea known as Wan An Bet and Tu Chinh. Vietnam leased drilling rights to ConocoPhillips, and China signed an exploration contract with Crestone Corporation. China has on at least one occasion deployed two warships to stop a Vietnamese drilling rig from working in the area.
- In 1994, China claimed Indonesia's Natuanas islands, containing some of the richest natural gas reserves in the world, as part of its historic territorial waters. Indonesia began stepped up naval patrols in the area.
- In 2000 Surinamese military gunboats chased a floating oil exploration rig owned by Canada's CGX Energy from an area disputed with Guyana; the Guyanese government had given the Canadian company a license to explore for oil in the area. After years of bilateral and Caribbean Community proposals for joint exploration and exploitation failed, the International Tribunal for the Law of the Sea was able to settle the boundary dispute, giving each country access to an offshore basin believed to be rich in oil and natural gas.
- While not technically a "sea," the landlocked Caspian contains the world's third largest hydrocarbon reserve with the majority of the offshore energy lying closest to Kazakhstan. While tensions have occurred among all five of the bordering states (Russia, Kazakhstan, Azerbaijan, Iran, and Turkmenistan), the northern countries have largely resolved their disputes. Iran and its neighbors have yet to resolve theirs. In 2001, Iran deployed a warship and fighter planes against two research vessels from Azerbaijan operating on behalf of British Petroleum, and sent troops to its border with Azerbaijan.
- In February 2005, Japanese destroyers chased away Chinese exploration vessels in international waters that were too close to a possible natural gas field (claimed by Japan) in the East China Sea.
- In March 2005 Indonesia sent warships to an island disputed with Malaysia to assert its claims to the oil rich region, and also dispatched F-16 fighters to its border with Malaysia. Malaysia responded by dispatching warships of its own, resulting in several skirmishes.

The Spratlys and the South China Sea

Most, if not all, of the maritime energy disputes to date have taken place in the heavily contested areas of the South China Sea. In 1992, China claimed 95 percent of the South China Sea as its territorial waters. This area extends up to 1,000 miles from the Chinese mainland, and includes the Spratly, Paracel, and Senkaku island chains which China also claimed as sovereign territory and which are contested in varying degrees by six other states: Taiwan, the Philippines, Indonesia, Vietnam, Brunei, and Malaysia. The world's second busiest international sea-lane of communication (after the strait of Malacca) passes through the South China Sea, and over half of the world's supertanker traffic transits the region each year. At stake are the substantial natural resources believed to be in the area. Known as a rich fishing area, many believe the Spratlys also possess significant reserves of oil and natural gas. The energy-poor countries of the region—particularly China—have been awarding oil and natural gas exploration rights to foreign firms in disputed areas. Overlapping claims have resulted in several military incidents since 1974, when China invaded and captured the Paracel islands from Vietnam. Between 1988 and 1998 there have been at least 10 armed conflicts over the islands in the South China Sea. In the early 1990s, China and Vietnam clashed on two occasions. The first was over disputed oil drilling rights, Vietnam accusing China of drilling in Vietnamese waters. China retaliated by seizing some 20 Vietnamese cargo ships between June and September 1992. In 1994, the two sides clashed militarily over two disputed oil exploration blocks, which the international community recognized as belonging to Vietnam.

Much of the maritime conflict in the South China Sea has centered on the Spratly Islands. The Spratlys consist of over 1,000 small islets, reefs and rocks exposed only at low tide, which, along with the Paracels, are believed by the Chinese government to contain up to 105 billion barrels of oil-equivalent hydrocarbons. Western estimates place this figure significantly lower, at approximately ten billion barrels, most of it in the form of natural gas.[4] Despite the wide variation in estimates of *potential* reserves, and the fact that there are currently no *proven* reserves for the Spratlys, the island chain has been the source of armed skirmishes on more than a few occasions. In 1988, ships from Vietnam and China clashed over Johnson Reef in the Spratly chain. The Chinese People's Liberation Army and Navy had dispatched troops to the island to establish an observation station. Vietnam, claiming the reef as its own, deployed forces to the area to thwart this effort. In the resulting skirmish, 6 Chinese and 60 Vietnamese troops were killed and 2 Vietnamese naval vessels were destroyed and sunk. China prevailed and has since retained control over the area. In 1995, China occupied Philippine-claimed Mischief Reef. In the resulting military action, the Chinese were evicted by the Philippine Navy. In 1996, the Chinese engaged in a 90-minute gun battle with the Philippine Navy near Campones Island and in 1997 and 1998, the Philippine Navy drove off various Chinese claimants to Scarborough Shoal. Tensions have abated considerably since the late 1990s as commercial and scientific exploration have repeatedly failed to find commercially viable sources of oil or natural gas beneath the Spratly Island chain or elsewhere in the contested areas of the South China Sea. In September 2003, the disputing countries signed an agreement to promote the mutual development of resources in the disputed islands. And in March 2005, the Chinese, Philippine and Vietnamese national oil companies signed a joint agreement to conduct marine seismic experiments for economic purposes. Confidence-building measures have been discussed, including joint research and economic development of the disputed islands.

The Arctic

As the warming Arctic Ocean is opening up to shipping, tourism, and oil exploration, the eight nations bordering its fringes are increasingly interested in protecting their rights in an area that has so far received very little attention in the world stage. The U.S. Geological Survey estimates that nearly one fourth of global undiscovered oil and natural gas reserves could be found beneath the Arctic Ocean, some of which may be as close as 200 miles from the North Pole.[5] The boundaries are hotly contested: Russia, Denmark, the United States and Canada all have conflicting maritime claims in the region, leading not only to likely legal disputes, but to the possibility of military assertion as well. In summer 2007 Russia made a bold claim to a large swath of the Arctic sea when one of its submarines planted a flag on the sea floor at the North Pole. The expedition's leader, Artur Chilingarov, deputy chairman of the Russian Duma, proclaimed, "The Arctic is ours and we should manifest our presence."[6] Russia declared an underwater mountain known as the Lomonosov Ridge is actually an extension of the Russian landmass and the edge of its continental shelf. If successful (or unstopped) in its claims, Russia could well end up with de facto ownership of approximately half of the Arctic Ocean.[7]

Canada is currently involved in several territorial disputes with its neighbors in the Arctic region:

- Extent of its continental shelf: while Canada has yet to map its continental shelf fully, its boundary claims are widely expected to overlap those of the United States, Russia and Denmark;
- Both Canada and Denmark claim Hans Island, which separates Ellesmere Island from Greenland in the Nares Strait (just north of the Northwest Passage);
- Machias Island in the Gulf of Maine is claimed by both Canada and the United States;
- The United States and Canada dispute the precise location of their border in the productive fishing grounds of the Georges Bank in the Atlantic Ocean;
- Similarly, the delimitations of the Juan de Fuca Strait in Puget Sound, and the Dixon Entrance to the Inside Passage, is contested by Canada and the United States;
- The legal status of the Northwest Passage, which Canada claims as internal sovereign waters, and the United States asserts is an international strait.[8]

Additionally, Canada has issued oil exploration permits for over 6,000 square nautical miles of waters disputed with the United States in the Beaufort Sea.[9]

Despite these disputed territorial claims, oil tanker traffic in the area is rising.[10] Nations littoral to the Arctic are not the only ones involved. China has set up a research station on the Norwegian island of Spitsbergen and deployed its icebreaker *Snow Dragon* twice to the Arctic region. While the voyages were ostensibly to collect climate data, it is entirely possible that energy-poor China is interested in the vast oil and gas fields beneath the Arctic seas. A number of factors have converged to make Arctic oil development and shipping more likely. First, there have been important advances in ship design, specifically in oil tankers, such as double hulling and reinforced bows suitable for passage without icebreaker assistance. Second, as oil prices rise, development of new alternative sources become more economically feasible, even those in harsh and unforgiving climates. Third, as the North Sea oil fields become depleted, there will be an added incentive to develop oil resources in parts of the world more politically stable than the Persian Gulf.[11]

While no one currently believes dispute over the region's vast energy resources is going to lead to armed conflict, there are nonetheless signs of military build-up in the area. In 2006, noting recent reports that U.S. nuclear submarines passed beneath Canadian waters without either notifying or seeking permission from the Canadian government, Canadian Prime Minister Stephen Harper asserted: "The single most important duty of the federal government is to protect and defend our national sovereignty." Canada has been patrolling the Arctic region with a force of 1,500 Eskimo irregulars since the early 2000s, and has launched a satellite system allowing for Arctic surveillance as far as 1,000 miles offshore.[12] While Canada currently lacks the naval capability to stop intrusions into its Arctic waters, Prime Minister Harper has pledged to increase Canadian military presence in the region, including the construction and deployment of three military icebreakers to the Northwest Passage, the development of a new naval base at the deep-water port of Nanisivik, enlarging the port at Iqaluit, and the deployment of an underwater network of listening posts.[13]

Security of Transport: Threats to Oil and Natural Gas Shipping

During some point of their voyages, most ships are forced to transit narrow passages or straits, also known as chokepoints. Ships are often required to slow their speed due to the narrowness, placing them at risk of attack. The small size of their crews, and the proximity to land, also adds to their vulnerability. Nearly all maritime energy trade passes through one or more of three straits: Bab el-Mandeb at the entrance to the Red Sea, the Strait of Hormuz in the Persian Gulf, and the Strait of Malacca between Indonesia and Malaysia. One-quarter of global trade passes through Malacca each year; this includes half of all East Asian seaborne oil trade, half of China's, and two-thirds of global liquefied natural gas shipments. Approximately three mbd of oil flow through Bab el-Mandeb, an area known for increasing pirate and terrorist activity (Somalia and Yemen, respectively). This represents approximately 7 percent of total maritime oil trade.

Concerns about the security of oil transport through the Persian Gulf and Strait of Hormuz has been a global concern since the Tanker War in the early 1980s when over 500 commercial vessels were attacked, killing over 400 civilian mariners. Most of the attacks were carried out by Iran on Kuwaiti oil tankers, resulting in the reregistering of these vessels under the U.S. flag. Some 90 percent of all Gulf oil amounting to nearly 40 percent of the world's maritime oil trade now passes through the Strait of Hormuz each year. The United States depends on Gulf oil for some 22 percent of its imported oil needs; Japan depends on the Gulf for nearly 70 percent. Iran remains a concern, particularly in its occupation of several small islands at the entrance of the Persian Gulf. Tehran has placed anti-ship Silkworm missiles on Abu Musa (also claimed by the United Arab Emirates), and periodically conducts live-fire naval exercises in the area. Nevertheless, despite occasional threats to Gulf shipping by Iran, most of the threats to the world's oil and natural gas transport come from nonstate actors; particularly maritime pirates and terrorists.

Maritime Piracy

While maritime piracy is not a new phenomenon, by the early 1990s the number of pirate attacks had reached a point where the international maritime community decided to take action. In 1996, the International Maritime Organization (IMO) of the United Nations was charged with maintaining details of reported attacks and issuing official reports on a monthly, quarterly and annual basis. The IMO began producing annual reports in 1998, and monthly reports in mid-2000. Since then, as Figure 3.1 shows, it has documented over 3,500 attacks through December 2007. In 2006 there were 240 recorded pirate attacks around the world, translating to one attack roughly every 36 hours; in 2007 with 282 attacks, this increased to one every 31 hours.

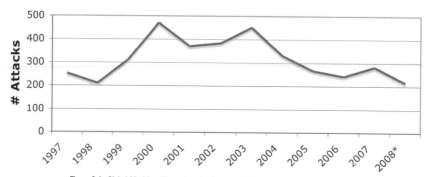

**Global Maritime Pirate Attacks:
Jan 1997–Sept 2008 (N=3566)**

Figure 3.1 Global Maritime Pirate Attacks: January 1997–September 2008 (N = 3566)
Source: International Maritime Bureau

The human costs of maritime piracy can be significant: In 2006, 15 sailors were killed in pirate attacks, 188 were taken hostage, and 77 were kidnapped and held for ransom. From 1995 to 2006, over 350 sailors are reported to have lost their lives in pirate attacks worldwide;[14] this has translated to roughly 30 sailors each year. While the 240 attacks reported in 2006 are the lowest number of attacks reported since 1998, and the 15 deaths in 2006 represent the lowest level of casualties since 2002, 17 sailors lost their lives in pirate attacks in the first two months of 2007.[15] With so many pirate attacks unreported, calculating their financial damage can be difficult. However, the International Maritime Bureau estimates that maritime piracy costs transport vessels between $13 and $15 billion a year in losses in the waters between the Pacific and Indian Ocean alone.[16] Earlier economic estimates had placed the annual global figure at approximately $16 billion.[17] Costs stem not only from stolen cargo and goods (and, in some cases, from the theft of the ship itself) but also from delays in port while the attack is reported and investigated, and from increased insurance rates as well.

As Figure 3.2 shows, energy assets represent an important target of pirate attacks; between 2001 and 2007 attacks on oil tankers and LPG carriers ranged from a low of 12 percent of all pirate attacks to a high of 29.8 percent, with most of the attacks occurring in Indonesia and the Strait of Malacca.

Most pirate attacks—including those on energy vessels—are cases of simple robbery at sea. The pirates board the ship while at anchor, or from small zodiacs while underway, and rob the vessel and crew of whatever can be taken quickly; watches, wallets, jewelry, sometimes the ship's safe, and even coils of rope. Some are more severe, including hijacking and kidnapping for ransom. In August 2003, pirates boarded Malaysian-registered fuel tanker *Penrider* near the Aceh province of Indonesia, and demanded $100,000 in ransom for the release of the ship and the crew. Additionally, there have been cases where the cargo was clearly the main objective of the piracy. In April 1998, pirates seized the *Petro Ranger* three hours

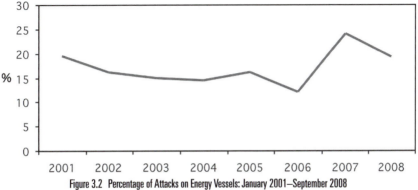

Figure 3.2 Percentage of Attacks on Energy Vessels: January 2001–September 2008
Source: International Maritime Bureau

outside Singapore's territorial waters. The Malaysian-registered vessel was carrying 9,600 tons of diesel petroleum and 1,200 tons of A-1 jet fuel. The pirates repainted the stern with a new name, *Wilby,* and raised the Honduran flag, turning the *Petro Ranger* into a phantom vessel—a stolen ship hidden under a false name, flag and papers. Two other pirate ships rendezvoused with the ship at sea and siphoned off half of the estimated $2.3 million dollar cargo.

In 2007 a number of potentially significant changes have begun to occur. First, as can be seen in Figure 3.2, attacks on energy vessels are rising steeply. In 2007, attacks rose to nearly 30 percent of total pirate attacks worldwide. This is disproportionate to the size of the global tanker fleet: of the approximately 120,000 ocean-going vessels in the world, only about 4,000 (just over 3%) are oil tankers. Second, no longer are most of these attacks confined to Indonesia alone; oil-rich Nigeria emerges as an important locale for pirate attacks on maritime energy assets, accounting for over 29 percent of attacks (Indonesia still remains the largest, with just over 35 percent). The Gulf of Aden has also emerged as a piracy hotbed. On November 15, 2008, Somali pirates audaciously hijacked Saudi VLCC *Sirius Star* carrying 2 million barrels of oil. The ship was released almost two months later with its crew unharmed after a reported $3 million payment by the ship's owners.

Lastly, for the first time since the IMO began keeping records of pirate attacks, no longer are targets confined to oil and LPG carriers. Two liquefied natural gas (LNG) carriers were attacked in 2007; one in Indonesia and the other in the Singapore Strait. Additionally, three offshore drilling platforms were attacked; two in Nigeria (one where a worker was kidnapped for ransom), and one off India.

This suggests that pirates may be acquiring more sophisticated maritime skills. Indonesia has long been the world's prime hot spot for maritime piracy, in large part because boarding vessels is relatively easy in the Strait of Malacca, where ships are required to decrease speed significantly due to navigational challenges. Large ships with small crews are easily boarded by pirates in small vessels who are able to escape into the hundreds of small islands in the area. Significant numbers of attacks on ships in Nigeria (some of which occurred over 30 miles from shore) represent not only a geographical expansion of threats to maritime energy assets, but also perhaps an increasing oceangoing ability on the part of pirates in the region.

Maritime Terrorism

The rise of global terrorism has led to concerns about the security of the maritime domain. Between 85 percent and 95 percent of global trade (depending on measure) moves by ship, with more than 1.2 million seafarers on 120,000 vessels in the global maritime fleet. There are over 2,800 ports in the world, with 361 ports in the United States alone. Attacks on maritime shipping—particularly energy shipping—could have significant implications for the global economy. Additionally, just as cars and trucks are frequently used by suicide bombers, and as airplanes were used in the World Trade Center and Pentagon attacks, so too could hijacked ships be used as weaponized transportation.

Concerns about terrorist attacks on energy shipping also stem, in part, from recent increases in maritime piracy. A January 2004 report by the International Maritime Bureau noted that pirate attacks on tankers in 2003 increased some 22 percent. "That these ships carrying dangerous cargoes may fall temporarily under the control of unauthorized and unqualified individuals is a matter of concern, for both environmental and safety reasons."[18] There are also concerns, particularly in Southeast Asia, that highly skilled pirate groups may join with terrorist organizations to stage larger, more dramatic attacks. A near miss occurred in 1999, when pirates seized the oil tanker *Chaumont* near Singapore. With the crew tied up, the pirates let the ship sail for over an hour with no one at the helm in one of the world's busiest shipping lanes. The pirate attack on the *Chaumont* is widely described as a possible trial run for a terrorist attack. In 2004 it was reported that Jemaah Islamiyah, a terrorist group operating in Indonesia, was planning to seize an oil tanker in the Straits of Malacca for use in a terror attack. Working with an organization calling itself Group 272, Jemaah Islamiyah planned to seize a vessel with the assistance of local pirates. The hijacked ship would then be wired with explosives and directed at other vessels, sailed towards a port, or used to threaten the narrow and congested Straits.

Despite these concerns, there have been very few successful attacks on energy shipping to date. Terrorist organizations have planned several attacks against oil tankers in the Persian Gulf and off the Horn of Africa. According to former FBI director Robert Mueller, "There have been any number of attacks on ships that have been thwarted."[19] In 2002, the Moroccan government arrested al-Qaeda operatives suspected of planning attacks on tankers passing through the Strait of Gibraltar. The few attacks that have been successful have been carried out almost exclusively by al-Qaeda and the Liberation Tigers of Tamil Eelam. al-Qaeda is known to view Western shipping as a key target of future terrorist attacks. Abd al-Rahim al-Nasheri, al-Qaeda's chief maritime strategist and mastermind behind the attacks on the USS *Cole* and the attempted attack on the USS *The Sullivans* detailed al-Qaeda's maritime strategy in an 180-page dossier, which explicitly included attacks on Western merchant shipping and cruise liners, considering them to be both iconic and of significant economic value. The October 2002 capture of al-Nasheri led to the discovery that al-Qaeda had developed a four-part strategy to attack Western shipping interests: (1) ramming vessels in suicide attacks, (2) blowing up medium-sized ships near other vessels or at ports, (3) attacking large vessels such as supertankers from the air by using explosive-laden small aircraft, and (4) attacking vessels with underwater demolition teams using limpet mines or with suicide bombers. al-Qaeda has successfully carried out one attack against a supertanker, the attack on the French-flagged *Limburg* on October 6, 2002. The vessel was carrying crude oil from Iran to Malaysia, when an explosion occurred while it prepared to enter the port of Ash-Shir in the Gulf of Aden off the coast of Yemen. The ship caught fire, which was eventually put out, but not before leaking 90,000 barrels of oil into the sea, and polluting 45 miles of coastline. One crewmember was killed and 17 of the ship's 25 French and Bulgarian crew members were wounded. Although the captain of the *Limburg* reported a small fishing boat approaching the tanker just before the explosion, the explosion was initially reported as an accident. Within days, however, a French investigative team of experts found traces of TNT and parts of a small boat at the blast site inside the tanker, and was able to confirm that the blast was intentional, caused by an explosives-laden boat. Debris consisting of plastic and of a mixed glass-resin material used in Yemeni fishing boat construction was found in the vicinity. The experts also concluded that the explosion bore a strong resemblance to that on the USS *Cole* in 2000. The militant Muslim group Aden-Abyan Islamic Army initially took responsibility for the attack, although Yemeni and U.S. officials believed it did not have the means to carry out such a sophisticated operation. While al-Qaeda never claimed direct responsibility for the *Limburg* attack, it is widely believed to have been responsible. At least 15 Yemenis ultimately were arrested and convicted for their role in attacking the vessel, with two receiving death sentences.

The Liberation Tigers of Tamil Eelam (LTTE) has the most sophisticated maritime capabilities of all known terrorist organizations. The Sea Tigers (the maritime arm of the LTTE) are capable of carrying out attacks well offshore, and have had impressive gains against the Sri Lankan Navy. Most of their targets are Sri Lankan military vessels, or vessels carrying troops and supplies for the Sri Lankan government. On October 2001, the MV *Silk Pride,* an oil tanker hired by the Sri Lankan government to carry oil and other commodities to civilians in the northern part of the country, was attacked by the LTTE. It was carrying 650 tons of diesel and kerosene to the port of Point Pedro off the Jaffna Peninsula when it was attacked. At least five rebel boats took part in the attack, with one finally ramming and detonating an explosive. Seven people were killed: three crewmembers of the *Silk Pride,* and four of the suicide-attackers (two of them women). The Sri Lankan navy rescued the remaining 25 members of the crew. The ship caught fire, which was eventually put out, and the vessel was salvaged from sinking.

Despite the relatively low number of terrorist attacks on energy shipping (for example, maritime targets represented only 1 percent of all terrorist attacks between 1999 and 2003), concerns for the future lie in the inherent vulnerability of the maritime domain, and the potential for catastrophic damage that a successful attack, under certain circumstances, could cause. The nightmare scenario is a successful attack on an LNG carrier, particularly one close to a densely populated urban center or an area of strategic importance. Because of their size, security experts consider LNG tankers to be potential floating bombs. Natural gas is highly pressurized and cooled to a liquid state for transport. In its liquefied state, it can neither burn nor explode. However, if a tanker spill or rupture were to occur, the liquid could return suddenly to its gaseous state, which could then ignite and burn. Sometimes as long as three football fields, a single tanker can hold up to 33 million gallons of liquefied gas (the equivalent of 20 billion gallons of natural gas), and can supply the daily energy needs of over 10 million homes. Concerns about the security of LNG transport stem from two sources—the inherent danger of natural gas in its gaseous state, and the projected increase in LNG trade in the future which, by some estimates, could triple by 2020. As reported in previous works,[20] studies disagree on how catastrophic a deliberate attack on an LNG vessel would be. A report by ABS Consulting to the Federal Energy Regulatory Commission stated that an event powerful enough to rupture an LNG carrier's double hull and cargo tanks "may also provide ignition sources for the spilled LNG."[21] However, a study performed for the Everett LNG facility concluded that the risk of a public catastrophe from a hand-held missile attack on an LNG carrier, or bomb attack from a small boat pulled alongside, would likely be smaller than that of a gasoline or LPG pool fire.[22] Early attempts to detonate LNG vapor clouds failed; explosive triggers have resulted in ignition and burning of the cloud only.[23] A recent report by Sandia National Laboratories concluded that an attack on an LNG carrier could cause "major injuries and significant damage to structures" a third of a mile away,[24] and second-degree burns on people more than a mile away.[25] Despite these differences, the safety and security of LNG transport remains one of vital concern as the world's carrier fleet continues its unprecedented expansion.

Conclusion

The disputes and sources of conflict outlined here are examples of how energy security should be firmly placed within the context of maritime security. With the future of energy exploration lying largely in the world's oceans, and with so many known and potential oil and natural gas reserves lying in areas with disputed maritime boundaries, conflict over access to these resources is bound to continue. The conflicts in the South China Sea and elsewhere, and the potential for conflict in the Arctic, show how willing nations are to take risks over access to energy resources. The resulting conflicts have two effects—to limit access to maritime energy resources while the conflicts are being resolved, and if they turn violent, to threaten the transport of energy when they lie on or near important sea lanes of communication, as they do in the South China Sea. With so much of the world's energy supplies in transit on the world's oceans, safe and secure transit is also a maritime security issue. While many past maritime territorial disputes have eventually been resolved without high levels of violence or casualties, leading to the hope that access to future maritime energy sources will be resolved peacefully as well, threats to energy transportation show only ambiguous signs of abating in the future. While the numbers of pirate attacks have declined in the Strait of Malacca in the past few years (this decline can also be attributed to the tsunami of December 2004, which wiped out most of the bases used by pirates), they are on the rise in other vital energy regions such as Nigeria. And while there has not been a terrorist attack on a maritime energy vessel since the attack on the *Limburg* in 2002, this does not mean the threat of future attack has been reduced to acceptable levels. Until these and other threats and disputes are reduced and resolved, energy security will remain firmly situated in the maritime realm.

Notes

1. According to the United Nations Convention on the Law of the Sea (UNCLOS), nations may claim up to 12 nautical miles of territorial seas, and 200 nautical miles of EEZ. National laws apply in territorial waters; states have the sole right to exploit the economic resources within their EEZ. Where territorial waters or national EEZs would potentially overlap (for example, between Greece and Turkey in the Aegean), nations are enjoined to negotiate separate bilateral agreements. Not all attempts have been successful.

2. Steven E. Flynn, "America the Vulnerable," *Foreign Affairs,* (January/February 2002).

3. Clive Schofield and Ian Storey, "Energy Security and Southeast Asia: The Impact on Maritime Boundary and Territorial Disputes," *Harvard Asia Quarterly,* (Fall 2005), http://www. asiaquarterly.com.

4. Stephen Ruscheinski, *China's Energy Security and the South China Sea,* Ft. Leavenworth: US Army Command and General Staff College, (2002), http://www.stormingmedia. us/26/2607/A260704.html.

5. C. Krauss, S. L. Myers, A. Revkin, and S. Romero, "As Polar Ice Turns to Water, Dreams of Treasure Abound," *New York Times,* October 10, 2005, http://www.nytimes.com. The widely-quoted 25 percent figure comes from an assessment of seven oil and gas basins broadly described as "Arctic" in a USGS report, but which contained substantial tracts of land that were not wholly or even in part strictly within the Arctic Circle. The proper figure for reserves estimated to be wholly within the Arctic Circle is closer to 14 percent of the world's total. "USGS: 25% Arctic Oil, Gas Estimate a Reporter's Mistake," *Petroleum News,* 12, no. 42, October 21, 2007, http://www.petroleumnews.com.

6. Ariel Cohen, "Russia's Race for the Arctic," Heritage Foundation Web Memo #1582, August 6, 2007, http://www.heritage.org/Research/RussiaandEurasia/wm1582.cfm.

7. Scott G. Borgerson, "Arctic Meltdown: The Economic and Security Implications of Global Warming," *Foreign Affairs* (March/April 2008).

8. A designation as "internal waters" would allow Canada to place restrictions on access to, and transit through, the Northwest Passage.

9. Chris Mason, "Is This Our Land?" *Canadian Geographic,* 124, no. 6, (Nov/Dec 2004), 50.

10. Krauss et al., "As Polar Ice Turns to Water."

11. According to some estimates, this could begin to occur as early as 2012. "North Sea Oil Depletion," *Peak Oil News,* (2006), http://www.peak-oil-news.info/north-sea-oil-depletion/.

12. Krauss, et al., "As Polar Ice Turns to Water."

13. Stephen Priestly, "Armed Icebreakers and Arctic Ports for Canada's North?—Costing Out the Plans for a New Deep Water Port at Iqaluit," *Canadian American Strategic Review,* (February 2006), http://www.sfu.ca/casr/id-iqaluitport2.htm; and B. Duff-Brown, "Canada Reasserts Arctic Sovereignty," *Washington Post,* January 26, 2006.

14. Piracy and Armed Robbery Against Ships," *International Maritime Organization,* (various years). http://www.imo.org.

15. Ibid.

16. M. Ryan, "Captain Counts the Cost of Piracy," *BBC News,* February 2, 2006.

17. Dana Robert Dillon, "Piracy in Asia: A Growing Barrier to Maritime Trade," *Heritage Foundation Backgrounder,* no. 1379, (2000).

18. Andrea R. Mihailescu, "Feature: Piracy Still Lurks the High Seas," *Washington Times,* July 16, 2004.

19. "Threats to Oil Transport," *Institute for the Analysis of Global Security* (2004), www.iags.org/oiltransport.

20. Donna Nincic, "The Challenge of Maritime Terrorism: Threat Identification, WMD, and Regime Response," *Journal of Strategic Studies,* 28 no. 4, (August 2005), 619–644. See also Chapter 18, written by Cindy Hurst, in this book.

21. Tom Doggett, "US Lacks 'Real-world' Model to Evaluate LNG Safety," *Forbes,* May 14, 2004.

22. E. Waryas, "Major Disaster Planning: Understanding and Managing Your Risk," *Lloyd's Register America's, Inc.,* Presented to the Fourth National Harbor Safety Committee Conference, Galveston, TX., March 4, 2002.

23. Transportation of liquefied natural gas," *Office of Technology Assessment,* Washington DC: US Congress, (1977), 61.

24. M. Hightower, L. Gritzo, A. Luketa-Hanlin, J. Covan, S. Tieszen, G. Wellman, et al., "Guidance on risk analysis and safety implications of a large liquefied natural gas (LNG) spill over water," *Sandia National Laboratories,* (December 2004), http://www.fossil.energy.gov/programs/oilgas/storage/lng/sandia_lng_1204.pdf.

25. Charlie Savage, "Study Spells Out High Toll on City in LNG Attack," *Boston Globe,* December 21, 2004.

CHAPTER 4

There Will Be Blood: Political Violence, Regional Warfare, and the Risk of Great-Power Conflict over Contested Energy Sources

Michael T. Klare

"Until such time as new technologies, barely on the horizon, can wean us from our dependence on oil and gas, we shall continue to be plagued by energy insecurity," James R. Schlesinger, former secretary of both Defense and Energy, told the Senate Foreign Relations Committee on November 16, 2005. "Instead of energy security, we shall have to acknowledge and live with *various degrees of insecurity*."[1] Although Schlesinger did not spell out what he meant by "varying degrees of insecurity," he indicated they would include assorted types of conflict in the major oil-producing regions. Such instability, he suggested, has become an inescapable feature of the current world energy equation and will not disappear any time soon. With this in mind, it is essential to better understand the link between global reliance on oil and natural gas—together, the source of approximately 61 percent of the world's primary energy supply—and the varieties of violence with which it is associated. As will be shown, these range from localized insurgency and separatist warfare to regional conflict and, potentially, great-power war.

Insurgency and Separatist Warfare

On March 6, 2008, Nigeria's director of Public Prosecution filed charges of treason, terrorism, and gun-running in Abuja's Federal High Court against two detained leaders of the Movement for the Emancipation of the Niger Delta (MEND), Henry Okah and Edward Atatah. Among the charges brought against Okah and Atatah were that they had provided as many as 250,000 assault rifles to armed militias in the Delta region, along with machine guns, rocked-propelled grenade launchers, bazookas, and large stocks of ammunition. These weapons were used, it was claimed, in attacks on oil installations and government facilities throughout the Delta—the source of most of Nigeria's onshore oil and a very large proportion of government revenues. In addition, the two were said to be on a fresh arms-buying mission when captured in Angola in late 2007. If convicted of all these charges, Okah and Atatah could face the death penalty.[2]

For the past few years, MEND and a number of other rebel groups with names like the Coalition for Military Action in the Niger Delta (COMA), the Joint Revolutionary Council (JRC), and the Niger Delta Vigilante, have been kidnapping (and sometimes killing) expatriate oil workers and attacking local offices of the Nigerian federal government in an effort to channel some of the vast oil wealth collected by Abuja to the Delta region, where most of the oil originates. These groups have evolved in a relatively short time from tribal gangs into well-organized militias able to wreak havoc in the swampy morass of the Delta, where roads are few and small boats are often the only viable mode of transport. "From a poorly organized gang fighting with little more than sticks and machetes," the BBC reported in May 2007, "MEND has grown to become a disciplined military machine, using speedboats, machine guns, and rocket-propelled grenades to carry out precise attacks on oil targets."[3]

Although numbering probably no more than a few hundred combatants and equipped with light weapons alone, MEND and its sister organizations have had a devastating impact on oil production in the Delta area. According to the most recent data from the U.S. Department of Energy, as much as 587,000 barrels of oil in daily production has been shut in by Royal Dutch Shell, Chevron, and ENI, the leading producers in the Delta, representing approximately one-fifth of potential daily Nigerian output of approximately 3 million barrels per day.[4] (Some experts say that the shut-in capacity is closer to 700,000 barrels per day, or one-fourth of the country's output.[5]) With violence expected to intensify as a result of the capture and eventual trial of Okah and Atatah, many foreign firms are pulling out of the Delta or confining their operations to far-offshore locations, beyond the reach of MEND's speedboats.[6] MEND may have been weakened by the arrest of two its top leaders, but it is no doubt capable of mounting continuing attacks on vulnerable oil facilities in the months and years ahead. And MEND is by no means the only threat to stability: as noted, it is only one of a number of armed bands that have challenged federal authority in the sprawling Delta region. All of these bands draw on historic grievances against the central government in Abuja— notably, its failure to direct little more than a pittance of its annual oil receipts to the Delta region. According to one report, federal authorities collected more than $400 billion in oil revenues between 1960 and 2000, of which $380 billion was lost to corruption or failed mega-projects in areas far beyond the Delta.[7] Meanwhile, 70 percent of the country's population lives on $1 or less per day—and that percentage is probably higher in the historically disadvantaged Delta region. For many embittered, unemployed young men, enlisting in MEND—or COMA, the JRC, the Vigilantes, or any one of a number of such groups—is thus an attractive option: an opportunity to express hostility toward both the oil companies and the federal government and also, no doubt, to earn some extra cash through kidnapping, looting, and extortion.[8]

It is unlikely, then, that there will be any lessening in the armed violence in the Niger Delta region. Nigeria's president, Umaru Yar'Adua, has pledged to channel more of the country's oil wealth to the Delta and to step up development projects there, but few knowledgeable experts expect anything much to come from these efforts—the level of corruption in federal and state bureaucracies is far too great to allow any of the earmarked funds to reach the people most in need.[9] As a result, MEND and other groups like it will continue to recruit angry young men and conduct raids on the all-too-conspicuous targets offered by the major international oil companies and their government backers. Nor is the Niger Delta region the only area of the world where oil-related political violence is on the increase. In April 2007, for example, rebel forces of the Ogaden National Liberation Front (ONLF) attacked a Chinese-run oil field in eastern Ethiopia, killing 74 people, including 9 Chinese oil workers.[10] A militant group seeking to establish an ethnic homeland in the Ogaden region free of Ethiopian government control, the ONLF immediately claimed responsibility for the attack, sending an e-mail message that read, "We will not allow the mineral resources of our people to be exploited by this regime or any firm with which it enters into an illegal contract."[11] Following the raid, China's Zhoungyan Petroleum Exploration Bureau withdrew its remaining workers from the oil field and refused to resume operations until the Ethiopian government could guarantee their safety—a condition that appears increasingly remote, given an intensified level of fighting between Ethiopian government forces and the ONLF.[12] Chinese oil personnel have also come under attack in the Darfur region of Sudan, another site of recurring combat between rebel armies and central government forces. Although Darfur is most widely known for the bitter conflict between government-backed Janjaweed militias and anti-government rebels, the region also harbors a number of oil fields being developed by Chinese companies and their international partners. In October 2007, forces of the rebel Justice and Equality Movement (JEM) attacked a field in the Kordofan area run by the Greater Nile Petroleum Operating Company (GNPOC), a consortium headed by the China National Petroleum Corporation (CNPC); on December 11 of that year, forces from JEM overran a field in the Rahaw area operated by China's Great Wall Company, killing and wounding several government soldiers posted there; a third attack, on December 18, targeted the Defra oil facility in south Kurdofan.[13] Abdel Aziz Nur al-Ashr, military commander of the JEM, said his forces would continue attacking oil facilities until Chinese companies left the country, claiming they provided funds to the Sudanese government used to buy arms and finance the war against the rebels.[14]

Politically motivated attacks on foreign oil workers are also on the rise in Algeria and Angola. On December 10, 2006, an insurgent group linked to al-Qaeda, the Salafist Group for Preaching and Combat (known by its initials in French, GSPC), attacked a convoy of vehicles transporting employees of Halliburton and the Algerian state-owned oil company, Sonatrach, killing an Algerian driver and wounding four Britons and one American. The GSPC later claimed responsibility for the attack, saying it was determined to drive American companies out of Algeria and impose Islamic law on the country.[15] Although Algeria nationalized its hydrocarbon reserves in 1972 and Sonatrach is bound by law to assume majority ownership of all oil and gas operations in the country, the government is keen to increase foreign participation in new, technically-challenging projects.[16] Since the December 2006 attack, however, some foreign firms have grown skittish about investing in Algeria. These fears were rekindled in December 2007 when al-Qaeda in the Islamic Maghreb—the new name for the GSPC—detonated two bombs in a heavily guarded area of Algiers; 26 people were killed and 176 injured in the attacks, according to Interior Ministry officials. Although foreign energy company offices were not directly targeted in the attacks, officials of the Norwegian oil-and-gas giant StatoilHydro—whose Algerian headquarters are located near the bomb blasts—indicated that al-Qaeda in the Islamic Maghreb had issued specific warnings against Western oil company workers.[17]

In Angola, a low-level insurgency has long been under way in Cabinda province, a tiny sliver of land separated from the rest of the country by the Democratic Republic of the Congo. Although the province itself is desperately poor, Cabinda's offshore waters house some of Angola's richest oil fields—and, as in the Delta region of Nigeria, the local people have seen most of the revenues generated by these fields siphoned off by powerful elites in Luanda, the nation's capital, with very little trickling back home. Not surprisingly, some disgruntled locals have joined the separatist Front for the Liberation of the Cabinda Enclave (FLEC, by its initials in Portuguese) and battled the Angolan army.[18] After being offered some concessions by the central government in 2006, most of the rebels gave up their arms; but one faction continued fighting, and on March 3, 2008 it ambushed an army column, killing three soldiers and severely wounding a Portuguese worker.[19]

The Resource Curse

All of these incidents and upheavals exhibit common features. By and large, they stem from ongoing struggles between minority groups or political factions that dispute the continued legitimacy of the prevailing government or its claim to exercise sovereignty over a particular area of the national territory. Conflicts of these types are not restricted to oil-producing nations, of course; extensive research demonstrates, however, that developing nations that derive a large share of their national income from the extraction of oil or other valuable resources (e.g., copper, gold, or diamonds) are more prone to suffer from internal violence or separatist strife than states that do not.[20] Because the government (rather than private interests) usually exercises ownership over underground resources in these countries, control over the government is tantamount to control over the allocation of resource revenues (or rents). It is not unusual, then, for certain powerful families, tribes, or cliques to acquire and retain control over the government and to use this power to make themselves extraordinarily wealthy while allowing the majority of their subjects to remain immersed in poverty—a surefire recipe for popular resentment, extremist demagogy, and political unrest. This tendency for resource-rich (or rentier) states to generate great wealth amidst unrelieved poverty is widely known as the resource curse.[21]

The mechanisms associated with the resource curse naturally invite political violence, in a number of ways. To begin with, the regime in power—whatever its origins and makeup—has no incentive to hold free and fair elections or to dilute its power in any way; rather, its natural inclination is to cling to power for as long as possible, thereby accumulating more resource wealth and dispensing it among close friends, family members, cronies, and carefully selected members of the national elite. Because governmental income is derived from oil rents rather than taxation, there is no need to placate politically involved taxpayers, as is normally the case in democratic countries. Instead, those in power use a portion of their oil wealth to buy the loyalty of the army and internal security services, and employ these forces as needed to suppress opposition movements. "When governments have an abundance of [resource] revenues they tend to use them to quell dissent—both by dispensing patronage and by building up their domestic security forces," Michael Ross of the University of California at Los Angeles wrote in 2003. "Indeed, oil- and mineral-rich governments generally spend unusually large sums on their military forces."[22] Deprived of an opportunity to redress their grievances through the ballot box or other forms of peaceful protest, opposition forces in these countries perceive no viable option but armed revolt. Oil-producing countries that are governed by entrenched petro-regimes are, therefore, likely to encounter periodic attack from disgruntled military cabals, political factions, or ethnic groups. Typically, these groups seek a larger share of the country's oil revenues, as in the case of the fighting in the Niger Delta, or seek to oust the existing regime and replace it with one more to their liking, as in Algeria. And because the prevailing regime obtains most of its wealth—and the funds needed to retain the loyalty of the security services—from foreign energy firms, these too become targets of the militants' wrath.

The resource curse has also spurred the separatist ambitions of various ethnic groups, especially when valuable oil or mineral reserves are located in their imagined ethnic homeland. In such cases, oil abundance often tends to provoke civil wars "by giving people who live in resource-rich areas an economic incentive to form a separate state," Ross observed. Indeed, the inhabitants of such areas often express "a widespread belief that the central government was unfairly appropriating the wealth that belonged to them and that they would be richer if they were a separate state."[23] It is precisely these views that are often cited by groups like the Ogaden National Liberation Front and the Front for the Liberation of the Cabinda Enclave to justify their ongoing struggles against the national government in their respective territories.

A form of the oil curse can be seen, moreover, in the virulent hatred directed toward the Saudi royal family by followers of Osama bin Laden and other Islamic

extremists in the Middle East. From a purely domestic perspective, the Saudi royals owe their mandate to rule from their guardianship of the Muslim world's two
holiest sites, Mecca and Medina, and through their patronage of one Islam's most
rigid and austere forms of worship, Wahhabism. This religious practice extols
piety and scorns conspicuous expressions of wealth and personal consumption.
Yet the princes of the realm have become known for their luxurious palaces, Mer-
cedes, frequent trips to fleshpots abroad, and other such indulgences—thereby
generating charges of licentious, unIslamic behavior and provoking calls for their
forceful removal.[24] Adding to the sins of the Royals, in the view of bin Laden and
others, is their willingness to allow Western companies to come in and plunder
Saudi Arabia's petroleum wealth. In their quest for lucre, then, the Saudi kings
and princes have facilitated the West's invasion of the Islamic Holy Land and its
subversion of Islam—thus justifying a holy war, or jihad, against both the House
of Saud and its American backers.[25] "You have to realize that our enemy's biggest
incentive in controlling our land is to steal our oil," bin Laden told his sympathiz-
ers in a December 2004 videotaped address. "So do not spare any effort to stop
the greatest robbery in history."[26] Other factors have undoubtedly figured in bin
Laden's thinking, but the link between oil, Western economic interests, and the
corruption of the royal family is a persistent theme in his fatwas and associated
calls for violent attacks on the United States and the House of Saud.[27]

Although bin Laden himself no longer appears capable of playing a direct role
in attacks on U.S. and Saudi interests, shadowy groups that share his extremist
views have continued to attack key elements of the Saudi oil infrastructure with
the goal of frightening expatriate oil workers and causing them to flee, thus undermining the technical proficiency of the Saudi petroleum industry. In response
to these assaults, the Saudis—no doubt in close coordination with American
oil-security and counter-terror officials—have bolstered defenses at their major
oil installations and stepped up their efforts to crush remnants of al-Qaeda in
the kingdom. But while this and other such sweeps may have diminished the
immediate threat to Saudi Arabia's oil infrastructure, it does not eliminate the
fundamental dynamic of the oil curse nor the likelihood that the royal family's
extravagant wealth—and conspicuous ties to the United States—will provoke future resistance of a violent nature.

Regional Conflict

The resource curse and associated discontent over the nature of rentier states
typically leads to internal revolt and separatism, or, as manifested by al-Qaeda,
to international terrorism. But these are only a few of the types of conflict that
are being sparked by the avid pursuit of energy resources and/or resource wealth
in the world today. As doubt increases about the future sufficiency of global
stockpiles of key sources of energy, especially oil and natural gas, states seek to
maximize their control over—or access to—remaining sources of supply, either
to ensure adequate supplies for themselves or to profit from the sale of these

supplies to others. The result is a growing risk of *territorial disputes* over areas harboring valuable reserves of oil and gas and *access conflicts,* involving efforts by outside powers to ensure access to their major sources of supply in conflict-prone resource areas.

This is not the place to comment at length on the current status of expert opinion on the future sufficiency of major sources of energy. Suffice it to say that in place of the optimism that prevailed on this topic up until the start of the 21st century, most energy experts now believe that the international energy industry will be very hard pressed to grow world supplies sufficiently to satisfy the much higher levels of demand that are expected for the decades ahead, largely as a result of continuing high levels of demand from the mature industrial powers along with soaring demand from the economic dynamos of Asia, led by China and India. "Energy developments in China and India are transforming the global energy system by dint of their sheer size and their growing weight in international fossil-fuel trade," the International Energy Agency (IEA) wrote in the 2007 edition of its *World Energy Outlook.* "Although new oil-production capacity additions from greenfield projects [i.e., newly-developed fields] are expected to increase over the next five years, it is very uncertain whether they will be sufficient to compensate for the decline in output at existing fields and keep pace with the projected increase in demand." As a consequence, "a supply-side crunch in the period to 2015, involving an abrupt escalation in oil prices, cannot be ruled out."[28] Two other studies released in 2007 lend further weight to this pessimistic outlook. In its *Medium-Term Oil Market Report* for 2008–2012, the IEA reported that global oil production capacity could rise sufficiently to satisfy anticipated world demand of approximately 96 million barrels per day in 2012, but would not be able to rise much beyond that level because of declining output in existing fields, a disappointing record of new oil field discoveries, and a forbidding investment climate in many producing areas, such as Russia, Central Asia, and Africa. Hence, "oil looks extremely tight in five years' time."[29] A strikingly similar prognosis was offered in *Facing the Hard Truths About Energy,* a report prepared for the U.S. Department of Energy by the National Petroleum Council (NPC), an industry-backed group. Although claiming that the world still possessed ample stocks of oil and natural gas, the NPC report indicated that the actual *extraction* of those supplies could be hampered by political and geopolitical problems and the reluctance of investors to risk their capital in corrupt or conflict-prone areas. "Many of the expected [geopolitical] changes could heighten risks to U.S. energy security in a world where U.S. influence is likely to decline as economic power shifts to other nations," the report noted. "In years to come, security threats to the world's main sources of oil and natural gas may worsen."[30] Under such circumstances, it is hard to imagine that the major oil companies and their major lenders will invest hundreds of billions of dollars to develop new fields in troubled areas, no matter how promising the indications of large reserves.

Despite these pessimistic assessments—and many others like them—the IEA and DoE project that world energy demand will continue to climb as a result of

China's rapid economic growth and other built-in pressures, producing inevitable shortages and accompanying price increases for years to come. This means, of course, that states will have an enormous incentive to hold on to or secure control over contested territories that harbor valuable reserves of oil or natural gas, whether on land or in adjacent offshore areas. It also means that states without adequate hydrocarbon supplies of their own will need to ensure safe and uninterrupted access to overseas sources of supply, including sources in chronically troubled areas like the Middle East and Africa. This can—and has—led to a policy of relying on military force to ensure such access, as exemplified by the Carter Doctrine of January 23, 1980.[31]

In the past, most resource-related territorial disputes occurred on land, in contested border regions or ethnic enclaves coveted by two adjoining states. For example, some analysts believe that Saddam Hussein initiated the Iran-Iraq War of 1980–88 with the intent (among other things) of gaining control over Iran's key oil province of Khuzistan, on the Iran-Iraq border, near the northwest corner of the Persian Gulf. An area that once claimed a majority Arab population and then housed four-fifths of Iran's oil installations, Khuzistan was an attractive prize for Hussein; but despite vigorous Iraqi efforts to win their support, Khuzistan's Arabs did not rally to the Iraqi side and the Iranians eventually drove Hussein's troops out of the territory.[32] Control over oil resources again figured in Hussein's decision to invade Kuwait in August 1990. In this case, the center of controversy was a major oil reservoir, Rumaila, that straddled the border between Iraq and Kuwait. According to Baghdad, the Kuwaitis had installed oil wells on their side of the border and sucked up an estimated $2.4 billion worth of oil from the Iraqi side; when all Iraqi requests for compensation were denied, Hussein ordered an invasion. Here again, other factors undoubtedly entered into Hussein's decision, but with his country impoverished by eight years of war with Iran, he evidently concluded that the theft (as he saw it) of Iraqi oil by Kuwait could not be allowed to continue.[33]

Territorial disputes like this over contested border regions may well break out again in the future, but it is far more likely that they will occur at sea, where boundaries are harder to define and the international strictures against aggression are less easily applied.

With the coming into force of the United Nations Convention on the Law of the Sea (UNCLOS) in 1994, maritime states became eligible to claim an exclusive economic zone (EEZ) extending 200 nautical miles from their coastlines in which they enjoyed the right to exploit all undersea resources, including oil and natural gas reserves. However, UNCLOS does not provide formal mechanisms for resolving disputes arising from claims to overlapping EEZs in contained bodies of water, such as the Persian Gulf, the East China Sea, and the South China Sea. One provision of UNCLOS calls for dividing such areas along a line equidistant from the shorelines of the contending states; another provision of international law gives coastal states control over undersea resources all the way to the edge of their continental shelf, even if it extends beyond 200 nautical miles. Further complications are posed by the question of whether islands should be factored into any decision regarding the drawing of an "equidistant" line between the coastlines of contending states seeking to define their overlapping EEZs—and, if so, which ones. All of this, needless to say, provides ample fuel for offshore boundary disputes—especially when ownership of valuable oil and gas reserves is at stake.[34]

One extremely worrisome example of such a dispute is the contest between China and Japan over ownership of the Chunxiao natural gas field in the East China Sea. Citing conflicting provisions of UNCLOS, Beijing and Tokyo have proclaimed different offshore boundaries in this area. Japan insists that the common offshore border falls along the median line between the two countries; China opts for its outer continental shelf (which lies much closer to Japan than to China). Between the two competing lines, of course, lies an area claimed by both. The Chunxiao field (called Shirakaba by the Japanese) lies partly in this contested area and partly in uncontested Chinese territory. Beijing has, for the time being, pledged to refrain from extracting gas in the disputed zone pending resolution of the issue; it has, however, insisted on its right to drill on the Chinese side of the Japanese-claimed median line, even though Tokyo responds that this will inevitably suck up gas from the disputed region. For its part, Tokyo claims the right to drill for gas in the contested zone, even though Beijing insists that the area is part of its own sovereign territory.[35] In 2004, with Chinese firms already probing for gas deposits in places adjacent to the median line, Japan commenced a survey of the disputed zone, insisting it was operating in its own national territory. Needless to say, this produced an angry reaction from Beijing and a demand from Vice Foreign Minister Wang Yi to the Japanese ambassador to cease and desist. He specifically characterized the Japanese survey of the disputed zone as an infringement of China's sovereignty[36]—a powerful signal indeed in the Asian historical context. When Tokyo refused to halt the survey, Beijing acted forcefully. In early November, it dispatched a submerged submarine into waters claimed by Japan, prompting the Japanese navy to go on full alert for the first time in five years.[37] The Chinese later apologized for the move, saying it was an accident, but the message was clear: Beijing was prepared to employ force if necessary to defend its claim to the contested area.[38] Although several rounds of negotiations were then held in an effort to resolve the boundary dispute, no substantive progress was achieved; and, in early 2005, the China National Offshore Oil Corporation (CNOOC) began drilling in the Chunxiao field from a position just a mile or so beyond the median line claimed by Japan. At about this time, protests broke out in Beijing and other Chinese cities against the publication in Japan of new history textbooks that downplayed Japanese atrocities in China during World War II. Soon thereafter, Tokyo announced that it would allow Japanese firms to apply for drilling rights in the contested zone, melding ancient grievances and recent ones.[39] In July of 2005, Tokyo raised the ante once again, by actually awarding drilling rights in the contested zone to Teikoku Oil Company. This prompted another sharp protest from Beijing and ominous warnings in the Chinese press. "Giving Teikoku the go-ahead to test drill is a move that makes conflict between the two nations inevitable, though what form this clash will take is hard to tell," declared the government-backed newspaper *China Daily*.[40] Both sides quickly removed any uncertainty as to what form their immediate responses would take. By early September 2005, patrol planes of the Maritime Self-Defense Force—Japan's navy—had commenced regular flights over Chinese drilling rigs along the disputed median line. Not long after, there was an unprecedented sight in these waters: the arrival of a Chinese naval squadron of five missile-armed destroyers and frigates.[41] Within days of their arrival, a gun turret on one of the Chinese ships was aimed at a circling Japanese patrol plane. No shots were actually fired, but an ominous precedent for a future confrontation over disputed energy resources in the East China Sea had been set.[42] Possibly chastened by this incident, Beijing and Tokyo did agree to undertake a new round of negotiations over the disputed boundary. These commenced in January 2006 and proceeded on an irregular basis even as the Chinese continued to pump gas from rigs along the median line under the watchful eyes of Chinese and Japanese air and naval forces. Hopes for an early settlement were raised in October 2006, when Shinzo Abe replaced Junichiro Koizumi as prime minister and, in a state visit to China, pledged to invigorate the negotiations.[43] But Abe resigned in disgrace in September 2007 before any progress had been made.[44] Although his successor, Yasuo Fukuda, is thought to be more conciliatory on matters involving China, the dispute remains unresolved and, with both sides building up their naval capabilities, there is every prospect that additional instances of mutual gunboat diplomacy can be expected in the East China Sea.

Gunboat diplomacy of this sort has also occurred in disputed waters of the Caspian Sea claimed by both Azerbaijan and Iran. Although three of the Caspian states—Russia, Azerbaijan, and Kazakhstan—have now delineated their maritime boundaries in the Sea's northern section, Iran and Turkmenistan have as yet failed to agree on a legal regime that would determine their offshore boundaries in the Caspian's southern reaches, with each asserting a claim to ownership of undersea oil and gas fields also claimed by Azerbaijan. The Azerbaijanis, for their part, have awarded production-sharing agreements (PSAs) to foreign energy firms to explore for and produce hydrocarbons in the disputed areas—prompting predictable protests from the other two. In July 2001, Iran took its wrath one step further when one of its warships approached an oil-exploration vessel in a field being developed by BP under a PSA granted by Azerbaijan and ordered it out of the area at the risk of being fired upon. The survey ship complied, but Azerbaijan reportedly responded by sending in a patrol boat of its own that chased off the Iranian vessel; warplanes from the two countries may also have been involved.[45] (The Azerbaijanis and Iranians provided conflicting accounts of what occurred.)

Conflicts like this over contested maritime resource zones are certain to grow even more heated in the years ahead as onshore energy reserves are depleted and more attention is paid to untapped offshore reserves. The fact that offshore boundaries have proved so difficult to delineate also makes such areas likely sites of future contestation. In fact, even the Arctic Ocean—whose maritime boundaries remain undefined—has been identified as a possible arena of geopolitical friction as a warmer climate makes the area more accessible and its undersea energy reserves become more valuable.[46]

Military Aid and Access Wars: The Carter Doctrine

Yet another type of conflict over energy arises from the perceived need of oil- and gas-importing states to ensure their continued access to foreign sources of supply—especially when said sources of supply are located in areas that are prone to conflict or political disorder. In such cases, the major importing states may feel inclined to provide military assistance to regimes in the affected areas that can be relied upon to safeguard the export of oil, or provide protection to these regimes with their own forces when such action is deemed necessary. In extreme cases, they may also engage in direct military action to overcome a threat to the continued flow of oil or natural gas from a major foreign supply zone to markets at home.

The United States has long considered it essential to engage in both forms of military activity in order to ensure continued access to overseas sources of energy, especially oil supplies from the Middle East. This link between military action and access to foreign oil was initially established in February 1945, when President Franklin D. Roosevelt met with King Abdul Aziz ibn Saud of Saudi Arabia aboard the USS *Quincy* at the entrance to the Suez Canal and forged a de facto alliance between the two countries, under which the United States agreed to protect Saudi Arabia and the House of Saud in return for privileged American access to Saudi oil. As part of this agreement, the United States subsequently established an air base at Dhahran and provided substantial arms and technical support to the Saudi Army and the National Guard (which has responsibility for protecting the royal family). This arrangement remains intact today, providing the foundation for U.S. ties with Saudi Arabia's current rulers and the cornerstone of American strategic policy in the greater Gulf area.[47] Despite the growing importance of Saudi Arabia and other Gulf producers in supplying the world's energy needs, however, American policymakers of the early postwar era were largely content to allow Great Britain to shoulder primary responsibility for maintaining regional stability and propping up local regimes. And when London announced that it would withdraw its forces from "East of Suez" by the end of 1971, Washington again looked for someone else to carry the burden of regional security—on this occasion, selecting the Shah of Iran, Reza Mohammed Pahlavi, whom the Americans and British had helped install in a CIA-orchestrated coup in 1953.[48] From 1971 to 1978, the Shah was the leading foreign recipient of U.S. arms aid and technical support, investing his forces with a wide array of advanced military equipment.[49] But all these arms and advisory services did not enable the Shah to overcome a domestic upheaval led by rebellious Shiite clergy, and in January 1979 he was forced to abdicate— once again forcing Washington to ponder the safety of America's access to vital Persian Gulf oil supplies. And, just a few months later, the security equation in the region received a further jolt when the Soviet Union commenced its invasion and occupation of Afghanistan.

In reviewing the strategic equation in the Gulf, President Jimmy Carter and his top associates concluded that given the magnitude of U.S. interests and the nature of the threats arrayed against them, it was no longer possible to rely on surrogates to guarantee regional security—henceforth, this task would have to be assumed by American forces. "The region which is now threatened by Soviet troops in Afghanistan is of great strategic importance: It contains more than two-thirds of the world's exportable oil," Carter told Congress in his State of the Union address of January 23, 1980. "The Soviet effort to dominate Afghanistan has brought Soviet forces to within 300 miles of the Indian Ocean and close to the Straits of Hormuz, a waterway through which most of the world's oil must flow. The Soviet Union is now attempting to consolidate a strategic position, therefore, that poses a grave threat to the free movement of Middle East oil." America's response to this threat, he avowed, cannot be equivocal. "Let our position be absolutely clear: An attempt by any outside force to gain control of the Persian Gulf region will be regarded as an assault on the vital interests of the United States of America, and such an assault will be repelled by any means necessary, including military force."[50]

Again and again, American officials have reaffirmed this basic principle, known ever since as the Carter Doctrine. When Iranian naval forces began attacking Kuwaiti and Saudi oil tankers in the Gulf itself during the Iran-Iraq War of 1980–88—thus jeopardizing the flow of crude to American refineries—the administration of President Ronald Reagan threatened to employ military force to keep the oil flowing. "We would regard as especially serious any threat by either party to interfere with free navigation or act in any way that would restrict oil exports from the Gulf," Deputy Assistant Secretary of State Robert H. Pelletreau asserted in 1983.[51] When the Iranians failed to heed this and subsequent warnings, President Reagan authorized the reflagging of Kuwaiti tankers with the American ensign and ordered U.S. warships to escort them while traversing the Gulf.[52]

American determination to ensure the safety of Persian Gulf oil supplies in accordance with the Carter Doctrine was next affirmed in 1990, when Iraqi forces invaded Kuwait and appeared to pose a threat to Saudi Arabia, the world's leading producer. In a nationally televised address on August 8 announcing his decision to employ military force in the Gulf, President George H. W. Bush cited America's energy needs as his primary impetus for intervention in the region. "Our country now imports nearly half the oil it consumes and could face a major threat to its economic independence," he declared. Hence, "the sovereign independence of Saudi Arabia is of vital interest to the United States."[53] Only later, when American troops were girding for combat with the Iraqis, did administration officials come up with other justifications for war—the need to liberate Kuwait, to destroy Iraqi weapons of mass destruction (WMD), to bolster international sanctions against aggression, and so forth. The record makes it clear, however, that the President and his senior associates initially viewed the invasion of Kuwait through the lens of the Carter Doctrine: as a threat to Saudi Arabia and the free flow of oil from the Gulf.[54] Following the expulsion of Iraqi forces from Kuwait, the first President Bush considered—but eventually rejected—plans to invade Iraq and eliminate the threat posed by Saddam Hussein once and for all. Instead, he chose to weaken the regime and hopefully spark a military coup d'etat through a punishing system of economic sanctions—a policy subsequently embraced by his successor, President Bill Clinton. Despite ruinous consequences for ordinary Iraqis, however, the sanctions failed to achieve their intended goal of regime change in Baghdad, making U.S. policy look increasingly ineffectual. It was on this basis (among others) that President George W. Bush eventually concluded that direct military action was needed to complete the task left unfinished at the conclusion of the first Gulf War in February 1991.[55] Today, with American forces still occupying Iraq and the task of creating a stable, self-sustaining regime there far from finished, the United States continues to adhere to the basic premise of the Carter Doctrine—that the application of military force is required to ensure the uninterrupted flow of Persian Gulf oil. "If we were to be driven out of Iraq," President Bush told a national television audience on September 13, 2007, "extremists of all strains would be emboldened. [. . .] Iran would benefit from the chaos and be encouraged in its efforts to gain nuclear weapons and dominate the region. Extremists could control a key part of the global energy supply."[56] Of all the arguments wielded by Bush to elicit support for his invasion and occupation of Iraq—the presence of WMD, links to al-Qaeda, the promotion of democracy, and so on—this is the only one that appears to have gained any traction with his critics. As suggested by the president's September 2007 address, this same principle has been extended by the Bush administration to Iran—another perceived threat to the free flow of Persian Gulf oil. Although Washington's chief argument with Tehran has been its suspected pursuit of nuclear weapons, U.S. officials are also worried that the Iranians are prepared to mine the Strait of Hormuz, fire anti-ship missiles at tankers in the Gulf, and otherwise seek to impede oil shipping in the area in the event of a future confrontation with the United States.[57] To deter such action, the Bush administration has conducted highly conspicuous naval maneuvers in the Gulf and issued stern warnings of likely U.S. countermeasures. "With two carrier strike groups in the Gulf, we're sending clear messages to friends and adversaries alike," Vice President Cheney declared during one such exercise, in May 2007. "We'll keep the sea lanes open. We'll stand with our friends in opposing extremism and strategic threats. . . . [And] we'll stand with others to prevent Iran from gaining nuclear weapons and dominating this region."[58] And while the risk of an armed encounter with Iran appeared to drop after the release in December 2007 of a National Intelligence Estimate claiming that Iran had suspended its efforts to develop nuclear weapons in 2003, Washington's commitment to the use of military force in the event of any perceived threat to the free flow of Persian Gulf oil remains very much in force.

The Globalized Carter Doctrine

At present, U.S. efforts to defend key foreign providers of energy and to ensure access to overseas sources of supply remain centered on the Persian Gulf, where they have been focused for the past six decades. In recent years, however, this policy has been extended to other regions, including the Caspian Sea basin and West Africa, as U.S. energy policy has come to emphasize the diversification of oil supplies. The first chief executive to stress this approach was President Clinton, who crafted what might be termed a globalized Carter Doctrine and applied it to the Caspian Sea region in the late 1990s.[59] Carter viewed this region as a promising new source of oil and as an attractive alternative to the ever-turbulent Middle East. At that time the newly independent states of Azerbaijan and Kazakhstan were eager to sell their petroleum riches to the West, but lacked an autonomous conduit for exports—all existing pipelines from the land-locked Caspian passed through Russia—and also faced serious challenges from ethnic minorities and internal opposition movements. Clinton agreed to assist in the construction of the Baku-Tbilisi-Ceyhan pipeline and to help these states enhance their military capacity.[60] U.S. military aid began flowing to the Caspian Sea states in 1997, at which time U.S. troops also began a series of joint military exercises with forces from the region. Although never formally invoking the Carter Doctrine when announcing these actions, Clinton applied the same national security umbrella to Caspian Sea oil as had Carter to Persian Gulf oil.

The regional security ties President Clinton built were later utilized by President George W. Bush to facilitate the U.S. intervention in Afghanistan following 9/11 and to support the ongoing campaign against remnants of al-Qaeda and the Taliban. This, in turn, has led to a substantial increase in U.S. military aid to these countries. Although the Global War on Terror is usually cited as the principal justification for these allocations, a close reading of State and Defense Department documents suggests that the protection of oil remains a paramount concern in the Caspian. In requesting $51.2 million in assistance to Azerbaijan for fiscal year 2005, for example, the State Department affirmed that "U.S. national interests in Azerbaijan center on the strong bilateral security and counter-terrorism cooperation [and] the advancement of U.S. energy security."[61] Meanwhile, in Kazakhstan, the United States is helping to refurbish the old Soviet air base at Atyrau, near the giant offshore Kashagan oil field. This base will be used to house a Kazakh "rapid reaction brigade" whose task, according to the Department of State, will be to "enhance Kazakhstan's capability to respond to major terrorist threats to oil platforms or borders."[62]

If President Clinton was largely responsible for extending the Carter Doctrine to the Caspian region, it is President George W. Bush who has extended it to Africa. Although American military involvement in Africa is at a less advanced stage than it is in the Caspian, growing U.S. reliance on African oil has given the continent increased strategic significance from Washington's point of view.[63] The growing importance of Africa in satisfying America's energy needs was first highlighted in the National Energy Policy of May 2001: "Sub-Saharan Africa holds 7 percent of world oil reserves and comprises 11 percent of world oil production. Along with Latin America, West Africa is expected to be one of the fastest growing sources of oil and gas for the American market."[64] This obviously gives Africa a strategic dimension it did not possess before. "African oil is of national strategic interest to us," Assistant Secretary of State Walter Kansteiner observed in 2002, "and it will increase and become more important as we go forward."[65] On this basis, African oil is being exposed to the same sort of Carter Doctrine military initiatives, the opening wedge of which is military assistance and training—an approach that facilitates the establishment of close ties with the region's (often dominant) military elites. Military aid to the African oil producers is supplied both in the form of bilateral assistance to individual nations as well as through multilateral security initiatives. Angola and Nigeria have been the principal recipients of bilateral aid, jointly receiving approximately $180 million in Fiscal Years 2004–2006. This has included transfers of arms and military equipment via the Foreign Military Sales (FMS) and Foreign Military Sales Financing (FMF) programs, along with specialized training given to Angolan and Nigerian military personnel under the International Military Education and Training (IMET) program. Other West African recipients of IMET assistance have included such oil-producing states as Chad, Congo-Brazzaville, Equatorial Guinea, and Gabon.[66]

In providing such aid, American officials are well aware of the vicious logic of the resource curse and the discontent this has aroused in the Delta region of Nigeria, America's leading African energy provider. Not surprisingly, then, a major objective of U.S. aid is to enhance the Nigerian government's capacity to address the Delta insurgency. "Nigeria is the fifth largest source of U.S. oil imports, and disruption of supply from Nigeria would represent a major blow to U.S. oil security strategy," the State Department noted in its Fiscal Year 2006 request for economic and military assistance to Nigeria. It is for this reason, the document asserts, that the United States should help bolster Nigeria's internal security forces and protect its vital oil installations—especially "in the vulnerable oil-producing Niger Delta region."[67] For fiscal years 2005 through 2007, this translated into a proposed allocation of $30 million in direct U.S. support to Nigerian security forces along with $50 million in "development aid" pegged to improving the security situation in the Delta and other troubled areas.[68] In addition, Nigeria is a participant in several Pentagon-sponsored multinational programs that serve, under the rubric of the Global War on Terror, as additional conduits for American military aid, including the African Contingency Operations Training and Assistance Program and the Trans-Saharan Counter-Terrorism Initiative.[69]

To better coordinate all of these aid programs and facilitate any future involvement of American forces in African conflicts, in February 2007 the Bush administration announced the establishment of the U.S. African Command, or AFRICOM. Although oil is rarely mentioned when Pentagon officials seek to justify the formation of AFRICOM—insisting instead that its focus will be on the conduct of humanitarian operations and counter-terrorism—there is no doubt that senior officers are well aware of the violence in the Niger Delta and the priority placed by Washington on restoring stability to this vital oil-producing area.[70] Thus, in a Power Point presentation given at the National Defense University on February 19, 2008, Vice Admiral Robert Moeller, AFRICOM's Deputy Commander, noted that among the major challenges facing the new command in West Africa were "illegal arms and drugs; oil disruption; corruption; political instability; and frozen conflicts."[71]

Few American analysts are prepared to acknowledge that the United States is likely become *directly* involved in addressing these dangers, though—as part of the programs described above—U.S. military advisers, instructors, technicians, and intelligence officers are *indirectly* assisting the Nigerian military in efforts to enhance their counterinsurgency capabilities.[72] It is entirely possible, however, that internal conflicts of this sort could escalate to a higher level of hostilities and prompt some future president to conclude—as Carter did in 1980 with respect to the Persian Gulf area—that vital U.S. interests demanded direct American military involvement. In fact, a senior Pentagon official predicted as much when commenting on his efforts to secure basing rights on the African mainland in 2003. "A key mission for U.S. forces would be to ensure that Nigeria's oil fields, which in the future could account for as much as 25 percent of U.S. oil imports, are secure," he said.[73] A similar comment, one might surmise, could likewise be made about the safety of the now-operational BTC pipeline in the Caspian Sea region.

The Risk of Great-Power Competition and Conflict

It is the United States that, until now, has devoted most effort to the protection of foreign oil-producing regimes and that has most vigorously employed military force to ensure safe access to overseas sources of energy. As we have seen, moreover, this remains a major aspect of U.S. foreign policy and has been extended from its initial focus on the Persian Gulf area to the Caspian Sea basin and West Africa. But the United States is no longer the only nation that is pursuing such policies: Increasingly, the People's Republic of China is providing military aid to its major foreign energy providers and, though it is not yet capable of engaging in access operations of the sort long conducted by the United States, appears to be acquiring a capacity to do so. There is a growing risk, therefore, that U.S. and Chinese efforts to militarize their foreign energy endeavors will produce a competitive stance between them and someday spark a dangerous confrontation.[74] The militarization of China's foreign energy ties is most evident in Africa and Central Asia. China first became involved in the delivery of arms and military services to African oil providers in 1996, when it acquired a majority stake in the Greater Nile Petroleum Operation Company, Sudan's leading producer. At that time, Sudan faced a severe challenge from rebel forces in the south (where most of the country's oil fields were located) and desperately needed a fresh infusion of weapons for its army; when rebuffed by Western powers, the Khartoum regime turned to Beijing, which proved far more accommodating. Eager to ensure the safety of its recently acquired oil assets in southern Sudan, China provided a wide array of modern arms, which were then used to drive the rebels out of the oil-producing region in what many observers termed a scorched-earth campaign.[75] The Sudanese government has since reached a cease-fire agreement with the southern rebels, but has stepped up its efforts to suppress insurgents in the Darfur region—again reportedly using weapons supplied by China.[76]

As China has increased its reliance on other African suppliers, it has increased its military ties with them as well. Thus, when Chinese firms made their first significant bids for oil assets in Nigeria in 2005, Beijing promised to provide— probably at reduced prices and concessional lending rates—twelve F-8IIM multi-purpose combat jets to the Nigerian air force, along with numerous light patrol boats for guarding the labyrinthine waterways of the Niger Delta.[77] At the same time, a Chinese munitions firm, China North Industries Corporation, agreed to help reinvigorate Nigeria's state-owned arms company, the Defense Industries Corporation of Nigeria.[78] The Chinese are also supplying arms and ammunition to a number of other African oil suppliers and, like the United States, is supplementing these deliveries with training programs, joint combat exercises, and intelligence-sharing activities.[79] There is a danger, then, that China and the United States will spark an arms-supply contest on Africa, with each side trying to outbid the other in their competitive efforts to establish ties with the continent's major energy suppliers.

In the Caspian region and Central Asia, China has been reluctant to play an overly conspicuous role as an arms supplier in its own right, fearful of giving the impression that it has imperial designs on the region, but has instead worked through the Shanghai Cooperation Organization (SCO), the regional body (whose members also include Kazakhstan, Kyrgyzstan, Russia, Tajikistan, and Uzbekistan) it helped launch in 1996. Originally created to enhance counter-terrorism operations and bolster border security in Central Asia, the SCO has evolved into a robust regional security organization with a decidedly anti-American cast.[80] (At a 2005 summit meeting, for example, SCO member states called on the United States to vacate its military bases in the region.[81]) As China has become more reliant on the Central Asian countries for supplies of oil and natural gas, it has increased the importance given to the SCO in its foreign policy and the resources devoted to the organization's growth. This has led to an accelerated tempo of joint military exercises and the delivery—under SCO auspices—of Chinese arms to the Central Asian republics.[82]

Until now, China's efforts to protect its access to overseas sources of energy have been limited to the delivery of arms and military-support services. The U.S. Department of Defense (DoD) has indicated, however, that the Chinese are beginning to build up a capacity to engage in access operations of the sort long conducted by the United States. "China's reliance on foreign energy imports has affected its strategy and policy in significant ways," the DoD reported in the 2008 edition of its annual report on the *Military Power of the People's Republic of China.* Although Chinese officials have considered the need to better protect access to foreign sources of supply, the report notes, they still lack adequate capabilities to accomplish this. However, "China's leaders may seek to close this gap" by acquiring a broad spectrum of "extended-range power projection" capabilities, including aircraft carriers and associated support vessels, long-range missiles, expeditionary (i.e., interventionist) forces, and overseas bases.[83]

Should Chinese leaders proceed down this path, one could imagine a situation where efforts by China to secure access to overseas sources of energy would collide with similar efforts by the United States, producing a direct confrontation between the two. This would not be due to a deliberate effort on the part of either country to provoke a conflict, but rather the result of unintended escalation arising out of a regional dispute that imperils the vital interests of both great powers, prompting them to deploy their forces in what quickly—and unexpectedly—erupts into a larger conflagration. As we have seen, there are many conceivable sparks for such a regional conflict, and more are likely to emerge in the years ahead. Add to this the growing resource requirements of the great powers along with their growing inclination to rely on force to secure access to oil in inherently unstable areas, and the potential for unintended clashes of this sort is certain to grow.

Returning, then, to former secretary Schlesinger's comments about the "various degrees of insecurity" we can expect from the world's continuing dependence on oil and natural gas, it is evident that these encompass a wide spectrum of conflict types, ranging from internal strife, ethnic separatism, and terrorism to regional warfare and the prospect of all-out war between the major powers. Many of these conflict types are being practiced today or have been witnessed in the recent past. As the gap between energy demand and supply widens, moreover, the risk of further outbreaks of conflict—all across the spectrum of violence—is bound to increase. The only way to reduce this risk, as Schlesinger made quite clear, is to accelerate the development of alternative sources of energy and reduce the inclination to rely on military means to ensure access to contested sources of supply.

Notes

1. Statement of James Schlesinger before the Committee on Foreign Relations, U.S. Senate, November 16, 2005, http://www.planetforlife.com/oilcrisis/oilschlesinger.html.

2. Funso Muraina, "MEND Chief Charged with Treason," *This Day* (Lagos), March 6, 2008, allafrica.com.

3. Senan Murray, "The Shadowy Militants in Nigeria's Delta," *BBC News*, May 10, 2007, http://www.news.bbc.co.

4. U.S. Department of Defense, Energy Information Administration (DoE/EIA), "Nigeria," Country Analysis Brief, April 2007, www.eia.doe.gov.

5. Spencer Schwartz, "Nigeria's Strife Forces Shell to Cut Outlay," *Wall Street Journal*, June 15, 2007.

6. Jad Mouawad, "Growing Unrest Posing a Threat to Nigerian Oil," *New York Times*, April 21, 2007.

7. Ibid.

8. Murray, "Shadowy Militants in Nigeria's Delta." See also Thomas Catan, Dino Mahtani, and Jimmy Burns, "The Warriors of Warri: How Oil in Nigeria Is Under Siege," *Financial Times,* April 7, 2006; Lydia Polgreen, "Blood Flows With Oil in Poor Nigerian Villages," *New York Times,* January 1, 2006; Polgreen, "Armed Group Shuts Down Part of Nigeria's Oil Output," *New York Times,* February 25, 2006.

9. Senan Murray, "Tackling Nigeria's Violent Oil Swamps," BBC News, May 30, 2007, news.bbc.co.uk. For background, see Human Rights Watch (HRW), *Criminal Politics: Violence, "Godfathers," and Corruption in Nigeria* (New York and Washington, D.C.: HRW, October 2007).

10. Jeffrey Gettleman, "Rebels Storm a Chinese-Run Oil Field in Ethiopia, Killing 70," *New York Times,* April 25, 2007.

11. Cited in Gettleman, "Rebels Storm a Chinese-run Oil Field."

12. Eric Watkins, "China Calls for Oil Worker Safety in Sudan, Ethiopia," *Oil & Gas Journal Online,* December 13, 2007, www.ogjonline.com; Tsegaye Tadesse, "Ethiopia Rebels Say Killed 43 Soldiers in 2 Weeks," *Reuters Africa,* February 27, 2008, africa.reuters.com.

13. Watkins, "China Calls for Oil Worker Safety in Sudan, Ethiopia"; Eric Watkins, "Darfur Rebels Halt 50,000 b/d Defra Oil Production," *Oil & Gas Journal Online,* December 18, 2007, www.ogjonline.com.

14. Cited in Watkins, "China Calls for Oil Worker Safety in Sudan, Ethiopia."

15. Craig S. Smith, "Qaeda-Linked Group Claims Algerian Attack," *New York Times,* December 13, 2006.

16. DoE/EIA, "Algeria," Country Analysis Brief, March 2007, www.eia.doe.gov.

17. Mariam Fam and Guy Chazan, "Algeria Blasts Reverberate Abroad," *Wall Street Journal,* December 12, 2007.

18. For background, see Philippe Le Billon, "Drilling in Deep Water: Oil, Business, and War in Angola," in Mary Kaldor, Terry Lynn Karl, and Yahia Said, eds., *Oil Wars* (London: Pluto Press, 2007), 100–129.

19. "'Deadly Attack' in Angola Enclave," *BBC News,* March 7, 2008, news.bbc.co.uk.

20. See, for example, Paul Collier and Anke Hoeffler, "On Economic Causes of Civil Wars," *Oxford Economic Paper,* 50 (1998), 563–573; Collier and Hoeffler, "Greed and Grievance in Civil War," (World Bank, October 21, 2001).

21. For background and discussion, see Michael Ross, "The Natural Resource Curse: How Wealth Can Make You Poor," in Ian Bannon and Paul Collier, eds., *Natural Resources and Violent Conflict* (Washington, D.C.: World Bank, 2003), 17–42. See also the essays in Kaldor, et al., *Oil Wars.*

22. Ibid., 25.

23. Ibid, 27–28.

24. For background and discussion, see Gwenn Okruhlik, "Networks of Dissent: Islamism and Reform in Saudi Arabia," *Current History* (January 2002): 22–25.

25. The author first made this argument in Klare, "Fueling the Fires: The Oil Factor in Middle Eastern Terrorism," in James J. F. Forest, ed., *The Making of a Terrorist, 3, Root Causes* (Westport, CT: Praeger Security International, 2006), 140–159.

26. From an audiotape address released on Islamic websites on December 16, 2004, as transcribed by and posted at www.jiadunspun.com on December 24, 2004.

27. Klare, "Fueling the Fires," 151–155.

28. International Energy Agency (IEA), *World Energy Outlook 2007* (Paris: IEA, 2007), 41, 43.

29. As quoted in Javier Blas, "World Will Face Oil Crunch 'in Five Years,'" *Financial Times*, July 10, 2007. See also James Kanter, "Rise in World Oil Use and a Possible Shortage of Supplies Are Seen in Next 5 Years," *New York Times*, July 10, 2007.

30. National Petroleum Council (NPC), *Facing the Hard Truths About Energy*, draft report (Washington. D.C.: NPC, July 18, 2007), 26.

31. For background and discussion, see Michael T. Klare, *Blood and Oil: The Dangers and Consequences of America's Growing Dependence on Imported Petroleum* (New York: Metropolitan Books, 2004), esp. 26–55, 74–144.

32. See Anthony H. Cordesman and Abraham R. Wagner, *The Lessons of Modern War*, vol. 2, *The Iran-Iraq War* (Boulder: Westview Press, 1990): 12–13, 31–32, 33, 95.

33. See Lawrence Freedman and Efraim Karsh, *The Gulf Conflict 1990–1991* (Princeton, N.J.: Princeton University Press, 1993), 48, 57, 59.

34. For discussion of how this plays out in the South China Sea, see Michael T. Klare, *Resource Wars* (New York: Metropolitan Books, 2001), 109–137.

35. For background on this dispute, see James Brooke, "Drawing the Line on Energy," *New York Times*, March 29, 2005; Norimitsu Onishi and Howard W. French, "Japan's Rivalry with China is Stirring a Crowded Sea," *New York Times*, September 11, 2005.

36. As cited in "China Condemns Japanese Survey," BBC News, July 8, 2004, news.bbc.co.uk.

37. The assertion that Beijing deliberately sent the submarine into Japanese waters to signal Tokyo over the territorial dispute is the author's alone; Japanese authorities did not formally take this position, although they protested the action vigorously. See "Japan Protests to China over Sub," BBC News, November 12, 2004, news.bbc.co.uk.

38. Mure Dickie and David Pilling, "Tensions Ease as China Admits Its Submarine Entered Japanese Waters, *Financial Times*, November 17, 2004.

39. "Japan Risks China Anger over Gas," BBC News, April 13, 2005, news.bbc.co.uk.

40. "Japan's Dangerous Move in E. China Sea," *China Daily*, July 18, 2005, www.china.org.cn.

41. Onishi and French, "Japan's Rivalry with China is Stirring a Crowded Sea."

42. "Oil and Gas in Troubled Waters," *The Economist*, October 2005, 52–53.

43. Joseph Kahn, "China and Japan Take Steps to Mend Fences," *New York Times*, October 9, 2006.

44. Eric Watkins, "China, Japan Postpone Dispute Resolution Talks," *Oil & Gas Journal*, October 1, 2007, 26.

45. "Iran is Accused of Threatening Research Vessel in Caspian Sea," *New York Times*, July 25, 2001.

46. For background and discussion, see Clifford Kraus, et al., "As Polar Ice Turns to Water, Dreams of Treasure Abound," *New York Times*, October 10, 2005.

47. For background and discussion, see Klare, *Blood and Oil*, 26–55, 84–94. On the Roosevelt-Ibn Saud meeting, see Aaron Dean Miller, *Search for Security* (Chapel Hill: University of North Carolina Press, 1980), 128–131. For background on U.S. military aid to Saudi Arabia, see David E. Long, *The United States and Saudi Arabia* (Boulder, Colo.: Westview Press, 1985).

48. For background on these events, see Stephen Kinzer, *All the Shah's Men* (Hoboken, N.J.: John Wiley, 2003).

49. For background and discussion, see Michael T. Klare, *American Arms Supermarket* (Austin: University of Texas Press, 1984), 108–126.

50. Jimmy Carter, State of the Union Address, January 23, 1980, www.jimmycarterli brary.org. For background, see Michael A. Palmer, *Guardians of the Gulf* (New York: Free Press, 1992), 101–111.

51. Statement before the Subcommittee on Near Eastern and South Asian Affairs of the House Foreign Affairs Committee, Washington, D.C., September 26, 1983, as cited in Palmer, *Guardians of the Gulf,* 118.

52. For background on these events, see Palmer, *Guardians of the Gulf,* 118–127.

53. As quoted in *The New York Times,* August 9, 1990.

54. For background, see Bob Woodward, *The Commanders* (New York: Simon and Schuster, 1991), 225–226, 230, 236–237.

55. Klare, *Blood and Oil,* 94–101. See also Bob Woodward, *Plan of Attack* (New York: Simon and Schuster, 2004).

56. Address by the President to the Nation on the Way Forward in Iraq," the White House, September 13, 2007, www.whitehouse.gov.

57. For an assessment of U.S. security concerns regarding Iran, see Kenneth Katzman, *Iran: U.S. Concerns and Policy Responses,* CRS Brief for Congress (Washington, D.C.: Library of Congress, Congressional Research Service, September 25, 2007).

58. As quoted in David E. Sanger, "Cheney on Carrier, Warns Iran to Keep Sea Lanes Open," *New York Times,* May 12, 2007.

59. The author first discussed this concept in Klare, *Blood and Oil,* 132.

60. The author first discussed these efforts in Klare, *Resource Wars,* 81–108

61. U.S. Department of State, *Congressional Budget Justification: Foreign Operations, Fiscal Year 2004,* February 2003, www.fas.org.

62. As paraphrased by Jim Nichol in *Central Asia's New States* (Washington, D.C.: U.S. Library of Congress, Congressional Research Service, December 11, 2002), 3.

63. The author first advanced this argument in Klare, *Blood and Oil,* 143–145.

64. National Energy Policy Development Group, *National Energy Policy* (Washington, D.C.: White House, May 17, 2001), chaps. 8, 11.

65. Quoted in Mike Crawley, "With Mideast Uncertainty, U.S. Turns to Africa for Oil," *Christian Science Monitor,* May 23, 2002.

66. U.S. Department of State (DoS), *Congressional Budget Justification, Fiscal Year 2006* (Washington. D.C.: DoS, 2005), 191–198, 287–289, 443, 587–590.

67. U.S. Department of State (DoS), *Congressional Budget Justification for Foreign Operations,* Fiscal Year 2007 (Washington, D.C.: DoS, 2006), 307.

68. Ibid., 307–309, 589, 628. The $30 million includes Foreign Military Sales Financing (FMF), International Military Education and Training (IMET) grants, narcotics and law enforcement assistance, Emergency Support Funds (ESF) assistance, and commercial and Pentagon-managed arms transfers. Due to a Congressional impasse on foreign aid funding for Fiscal Year (FY) 2007, the *Congressional Budget Justification* for FY 2008 did not include updated information for FY 2007, but included a $5 million request for security aid in FY 2008.

69. On indirect sources of military aid to Nigeria, see Michael Klare and Daniel Volman, "The African 'Oil Rush' and U.S. National Security," *Third World Quarterly,* 27, no. 4 (2006), 609–628. For background on these multilateral programs, see Lauren Ploch, *Africa Command: U.S. Strategic Interests and the Role of the U.S. Military in Africa,* CRS Report for Congress (Washington, D.C.: Congressional Research Service, U.S. Library of Congress, July 6, 2007), 18–21.

70. For background on AFRICOM, see Ploch, *Africa Command.*

71. "United States Africa Command," Power Point Presentation, February 19, 2008, electronic document, www.ndu.edu/ctnsp/NCW_course/Moeller_08%2002%2014%20 DCMO%20Brf%20v2.pdf.

72. For background and discussion, see Klare and Volman, "The African 'Oil Rush' and U.S. National Security"; Ploch, *Africa Command,* 18–21.

73. Quoted in Greg Jaffe, "In Massive Shift, U.S. is Planning to Cut Size of Military in Germany," *Wall Street Journal,* June 10, 2003.

74. The author first wrote of this danger in Klare, *Blood and Oil,* 146–179.

75. For background and discussion, see Human Rights Watch (HRW), *Sudan, Oil, and Human Rights* (New York and Washington, D.C.: HRW, 2003).

76. See Eric Reeves, Prepared Statement, in U.S.-China Economic and Security Review Commission (USCC), *China's Role in the World: Is China a Responsible Stakeholder?* Hearing, 109th Cong., 2nd Sess., August 3, 2006, www.uscc.gov.

77. Dino Mahtani, "Nigeria Shifts to China Arms," *Financial Times,* February 28, 2006.

78. See Ruby Rabiu, "China Donates $3m Military Equipment to Nigeria," *Daily Trust* (Abuja), October 20, 2005, www.dailytrust.com/archives. See also "Nigeria to Mass-Produce Nigerian Version of AK-47 Rifles, Xinhua News Service, October 2, 2006, english.people. com.

79. For background on Chinese arms transfers to Africa, see Amnesty International, "People's Republic of China: *Sustaining Conflict and Human Rights Abuses,* The Flow of Arms Accelerates," June 11, 2006, www.amnesty.org. See also David H. Shinn, "Africa and China's Activism," paper presented at National Defense University Pacific Symposium, China's Global Activism, Washington, D.C., June 20, 2006. On Chinese training and advisory programs, see Susan Puska, "Resources, Security, and Influence: The Role of the Military in China's Africa Strategy," *China Brief,* Jamestown Foundation, May 30, 2007, 2–6.

80. For background on the SCO, see Bates Gill and Matthew Oresman, *China's New Journey to the West* (Washington, D.C.: Center for Strategic and International Studies, 2003), 5–8.

81. See C. J. Chivers, "Central Asians Call on U.S. to Set a Timetable for Closing Bases," *New York Times,* July 6, 2005.

82. Gill and Oresman, 20.

83. U.S. Department of Defense (DoD), *Military Power of the People's Republic of China 2008* (Washington, D.C.: DoD, 2008), 10, 13.

CHAPTER 5

No Blood for Oil: Why Resource Wars Are Obsolete

Christopher J. Fettweis

Is oil worth fighting for? For most observers, the answer might seem obvious. After all, there is no commodity more crucial to industrial age societies, and no national interest more vital, then access to oil at a stable price. Over the course of the coming decades, as supply shrinks while demand steadily grows, heightened competition over fading resources may lead to a whole new species of conflicts: resource wars, in which consumer countries fight each other to assure steady supplies of oil and other natural resources. Oil is like oxygen to industrial age societies, some of which may prove susceptible to desperate action in order to assure a steady supply. As Michael Klare has argued on behalf of the conventional wisdom, "that conflict over oil will erupt in the years ahead is almost a foregone conclusion."[1]

Fortunately, there is good reason to believe that resource wars will not be any more common in the coming century than they were in the last. There has never actually been a war over fossil fuels—the closest call was in 1973, when the Arab members of OPEC stopped selling oil to the United States and the Netherlands. Washington drew up plans to break the embargo by force and seize Arab oil. Secretary of State Henry Kissinger told *Business Week* that it was "one thing" to use oil as a weapon in the case of dispute over price, but it was quite "another where there is some actual strangulation of the industrialized world."[2] U.S. Secretary of Defense James Schlesinger apparently wrote to his British counterpart that the United States would not tolerate threats from "under-developed, under-populated" countries and that it was "no longer obvious" that the United States could not use force to resolve the stand-off.[3]

That is as dangerous as the situation was to get, however. Despite the contingency planning, using force never appears to have been a serious option to resolve the crisis. Kissinger repeatedly stated afterward that he determined military solutions to be "totally inappropriate" to the problem; the prospect of using military force to end the oil embargo died without serious debate.[4] In 1975 Congress commissioned a feasibility study to explore the potential for a military seizure of the oil fields of the Gulf, in case the crisis should ever be repeated. The report concluded that such an action would be both practically and strategically unwise, for the fields would likely be damaged in any such operation, and assuring their long-term viability would probably prove costlier than any benefit that could be gained from their possession.[5]

Political scientist Robert Tucker was hardly alone when he noted with some amazement that the crisis was resolved in the absence of any meaningful threat of force. "Suddenly," he wrote, "we find ourselves in a strange universe," where 20th century Melians could withhold a vital product from the Athenians of the day.[6] The United States was not the only inhabitant of this bizarre world—Tucker noted in 1981 that the Soviets too had proven to be oddly cautious and tentative in their actions in the Gulf.[7] As it turns out, Moscow had come to the same conclusions as Washington about the feasibility of seizing Arab oil. Even though the Soviets had the obvious advantage of proximity and a massive imbalance in available forces in the region, they did not seem to ever have seriously considered making such a move.[8]

Military power played no role in the resolution of the 1973 crisis, nor did it factor into oil politics in any serious way during the Cold War. In fact, as a general rule force has not proved to be useful in oil politics. There has never been a war to control territory that contains fossil fuels, and there are good reasons to believe it is likely that there never will be. The conventional wisdom concerning the inevitability of energy wars is probably wrong.

War for Oil?

At some point in the 21st century, the world will begin to run low on oil. Demand around the world is skyrocketing for the nonrenewable resource, far outpacing the growth of supply, and all projections suggest the pace will continue. While oil will not likely ever run out in the literal sense, geologists warn that in the not-so-distant future oil may well be a relatively scarce commodity.[9] Per capita energy use may hold steady or even decline across much of the industrialized world, but projected growth in population will more than compensate. In the U.S. Energy Information Agency's mid-range projection, even with higher prices world oil use will grow from 86 mbd in 2007 to 103 mbd in 2015 and 119 mbd by 2025.[10] Such growth would obviously require a major increase in the current production capacity of the industry. Few think that supply is likely to be able to keep pace. War need not result from such shortages, however. There are at least three good reasons to believe that war to control the territory that contains fossil fuels will continue to be a very rare phenomenon as the new century unfolds: First, fighting to control oil is likely to be a self-defeating proposition. It will always be cheaper to buy oil than to seize it. Second, the interests of consumers and producers do not conflict—all parties involved in oil production have serious interests in stability, without which no one can benefit. Finally, and perhaps counter-intuitively, all kinds of warfare are becoming more and more rare. The 21st century is likely to be a great deal more stable than the 20th century, and oil politics should prove to be no exception.

The Utility of Seizing Oil

A common refrain arising from the anti-war left is that the war in Iraq is being fought for oil. Perceptions across the region certainly back this up—large majorities of Arab publics are convinced that the United States is in Iraq merely to control the flow of its oil, and that it has no intention of leaving.[11] To these groups, one needs look no further to find the kind of resource war that so many scholars and analysts have long anticipated. Iraq provides the only proof they need. But if the oil was the main goal of the invasion, the United States certainly has acted rather strangely. Iraqi oil production has not met pre-war expectations, and it is hardly bringing riches to U.S. coffers. While Iraqi oil fields under-produce, U.S. troops participate in otherwise peripheral activities like pacifying Baghdad, battling al-Qaeda in Anbar province and building relationships between feuding Shi'ite clans. If the war was truly fought for oil, it has been an unqualified disaster. Indeed, if the United States had been primarily interested in Iraqi oil, it would have been far cheaper to simply buy it rather than go to war to seize it. Saddam Hussein would have been quite happy to sell as much of his oil as the world would have purchased, if only the United Nations sanctions were lifted. The cost incurred by the war—approaching one trillion dollars with no signs of slowing— far outweighs any possible benefit that could come from dominating the distribution of Iraqi oil. Oil companies stood to benefit from Saddam selling his oil just as much as they would if the United States had liberated it—after all, democracy is hardly a sine qua non for energy resource development. If the descendents of the Seven Sisters were indeed driving U.S. policy, the sanctions would be lifted and Saddam would now be selling his oil on the world market. The Iraqi experience demonstrates vividly what security analysts have known for a long time: War for control over oil reserves is usually a self-defeating proposition, since the cost involved in replacing the inevitable damage, and protecting the seized territory, outweighs the benefits that could be gained by conquest.[12] The infrastructure involved with oil exportation—from rigs to pipelines to tankers—is very fragile and costly to replace. Maintaining the flow from seized fields would present an additional problem, since that infrastructure is more easily sabotaged than protected. This seems to be especially true for offshore infrastructure, which is simultaneously more expensive and more vulnerable to attack. The fragility of petroleum infrastructure, therefore, provides powerful incentives for cooperative behavior. Oil rigs make easy targets.

There is good reason to believe that most states realize the limited utility of seizing oil fields. Even in those few areas where oil has been discovered under weakly held or disputed territory, the disputes have been resolved without even the realistic threat of force. If conflict breaks out, then no oil can get to market, and no one benefits. As the old saying goes, money is a coward—investment dollars flee away from the slightest hint of instability, providing powerful incentives for cooperation over resource development issues. It is in the interest of all sides to continue to seek solutions to their disagreements at the bargaining table rather than on the field of battle.

The Caspian Sea provides a great example of low utility of military force in oil disputes. Early on, all states surrounding the sea (Russia, Azerbaijan, Iran, Turkmenistan and Kazakhstan) realized that two major issues had the potential to pit regional states against one another, and bring in outside states on behalf of their allies. First and foremost, pipelines had to be constructed to bring the oil to market. Because the Caspian has no outlet to the oceans, there is no easy way to get its resources to international buyers. In order for the Caspian to realize its potential, massive investment was needed to create or improve extraction equipment, such as rigs and platforms, and transportation equipment, such as pipelines and tankers. The question of who would provide that investment has sometimes pitted national against corporate interests. Analyses of potential pipeline routes tended to emphasize either their significance as instruments of external control over the destiny of the region, regarding profits as incidental, or their economic viability, treating politics only as a variable of risk.[13]

The second potentially explosive issue was the undefined legal status of the Caspian Sea.[14] The heart of the dispute is whether the Caspian, which is an entirely land-locked, salty body of water, is a sea or a lake. The distinction is important not only for geography buffs—if the Caspian is a sea, then according to international law, each riparian state can claim ownership of the seabed adjacent to its coast; if it is a lake, then its riches must be shared equally by all surrounding states. Unsurprisingly, the states with large oil and gas deposits close to their shores (Azerbaijan and Kazakhstan) believe that the Caspian is a sea. The states whose coastlines hold fewer deposits (Russia, Turkmenistan and Iran) have argued that the Caspian is a lake and therefore its resources should be shared equally among the five states. Each side constructed an argument based on various precedents in international law, some of which date back to agreements signed by the Soviets and the Iranians in 1921.

Little would be gained by repeating the intricacies of these issues, both of which have been addressed at length elsewhere. The important point for the purposes of this discussion is that, despite the fears of pessimists, neither of these issues has come close to sparking conflict. The states of the region, in conjunction with the energy companies, have reached a series of agreements on export routes, including the well-known pipeline from Baku to Ceyhan (BTC), which started carrying Caspian oil in mid-2006.[15] The littoral countries have also held a series of meetings on the legal status issue, the most recent of which was in Tehran in October 2007, and may well be close to reaching a lasting agreement. Russia has dropped its objections to considering the Caspian to be a sea, and Iran may well be close to doing the same. All sides seem to realize that the absence of a well-defined legal status of the Caspian Sea prevents maximum exploitation of resources of the region. Many major agreements for exploration and production, which faced seemingly insurmountable problems only a decade ago, have been reached.[16]

The most important and obvious fact about Caspian geopolitics is this: no side has ever used force, or even threatened to use force, in order to bring about its preferred outcome in either the pipeline or legal status dispute. Despite the pessimistic predictions to the contrary, great power politics in the Caspian have evolved without a significant military component. The relative power of the actors has not mattered in any of the outcomes, perhaps because the utility of force is clearly minimal. The language that the players are using may resemble traditional realpolitik, but the issues over which they are arguing—and, much more importantly, the tools that they are using to pursue them—are entirely diplomatic and economic.[17]

The danger of conflict over either pipelines or the legal status issue is likely to shrink further as time goes on. Each year that goes by without the threat of war sets precedents for peaceful resolution of disagreements. Over the course of the coming decade, other agreements will likely emerge on how to bring oil to market, and construction may begin on new routes. Conflict over pipelines is highly unlikely now that BTC has set a cooperative precedent, and as time goes on it will become even less plausible. The risk of conflict is surely highest before the cement of agreement on the steel umbilical cords dries. Martha Brill Olcott, arguably the leading American expert on the region, wrote that:

> It certainly seems predictable that the level of Western interest in the region will diminish once the Caspian export routes are firmed up and the construction of pipelines begun . . . . Once pipelines are built and production begins, the focus on the region is likely to shift to potential new areas of energy exploration. There will of course be interest in maintaining the flow of oil, but relations will move to a 'maintenance' phase.[18]

This "maintenance phase" is unlikely to be as contentious as the initial negotiations, which, though sometimes spirited, are by no means explosive. In oil politics, these phases rarely are.

Common Interest

Today oil is traded on a global market—supply disruptions anywhere affect the price everywhere. It is of course the price of oil is that is most clearly correlated with economic performance in consumer and producer states alike. Although their interests diverge on precisely what that price should be—producers want it to be relatively high, and consumers relatively low—they both want to see it remain fairly stable. Any war in a resource-rich area that would disrupt the supply and raise the price would prove to be counterproductive. A certain amount of predictability is necessary to assure that disruptions in price, the kind that have far-reaching implications for an entire economy, do not occur. In order for any energy company to be interested in developing the resources of this region, ju-risdictional issues must be settled. As long as higher risks mean higher costs, the perception of instability will remain an important factor driving potential inves-tors away from energy resource development.[19] No state is able to benefit from oil and gas fields until ownership issues are settled.

Oil does no one any good in the ground. In order for any country to profit from owning large stocks, it must sell. Control over the territory that contains oil is therefore hardly necessary to assure access to its resources. Whoever controls the territory where oil is extracted will face the same incentives to sell it on the world market. States of the 21st century may well reach the conclusion that it does not much matter who controls oil, as long as those who do seem willing to sell it.

No matter who is in charge of Saudi Arabia, or Kuwait, or the UAE, for ex-ample, there is every reason to believe that they will have strong incentives to sell their oil to the industrialized consumer states. In one of the very few studies of the issue, political scientist Shibley Telhami found that "a change in regime from moderate to radical in one state does not appear to alter the pattern of that state's foreign trade."[20] Throughout the Cold War, the nature of Gulf regimes had little or no impact on who they traded with, or how much. In other words, market forces have a greater impact than national policy in determining the flow of oil. Even the 1980–88 Iran-Iraq war failed to have much of an impact on oil production, despite the fact that much of the fighting occurred within artillery range of major oil terminals and facilities.[21]

Even if profoundly unfriendly regimes were to come to power in the Persian Gulf or in any other oil-producing region, they would still need to sell their oil. Any government determined to act with profound economic irrationality would be quickly displaced by those eager to maximize the amount of oil revenue com-ing into their country. Also, unlike in 1973 when boycotts could target individual countries, today the oil companies control distribution and will make adjust-ments to keep their customers satisfied and protect their profits. The market will bring stability, perhaps better than that currently provided by the over-strapped U.S. taxpayer.[22]

Oil-producing countries have an interest in keeping the price high; consumer states wish to see it low. Both, however, want it to keep flowing. Instability in oil-producing regions prevents that from happening. The fact that there no one on either side has an interest in seeing the spigot turned off provides powerful, stabilizing incentives encouraging the peaceful development of these resources.

War Is Rare, and Getting Rarer

International precedents for oil exploitation certainly suggest that future re-source competition issues could be settled peacefully. In fact, war has never broken out over the ownership of oil deposits, even when that ownership was hotly contested. There are a few rather significant, disputed fields that have been discovered in the past few decades, from the North Sea to the Gulf of Mexico to the Caspian Sea.[23] In all cases, agreements have been reached to develop the oil and gas fields without conflict. Of course peaceful precedents do not guarantee peaceful futures—Norway and the United Kingdom are obviously quite different from China and Taiwan—but still it is worth noting that when vast offshore hydrocarbon fields have been discovered before, despite the energy autarky and billions of dollars at stake, lasting agreements have emerged that benefit all parties. Despite the fact that the strategic and economic importance of oil grew steadily throughout the past century, there has never been a time when states have determined that assuring access to petroleum was worth the risk of war.

The final and perhaps most important reason to not expect a rise in resource wars in the next century is due to what may be the most under-reported—and perhaps counter-intuitive—phenomenon in international politics: War is disappearing from the planet. A number of both academics and practitioners, from Richard Nixon to John Mueller, have argued for years that due to a combination of nuclear weapons, economic interdependence, institutions and the evolution in ideas, major war has become all but obsolete.[24] "Apart from an occasional Cod War," argued Samuel Huntington, wars in the industrialized north are "virtually unthinkable."[25] If it is true that war is obsolete for the strongest of powers—and a growing number of experts believe that it is—then the weakest can reasonably hope that it will soon be for them too, as their societies and economies develop, and as they adopt the institutions, technology and ideas of the industrialized world.[26] As a result of something akin to a trickle-down effect for peace, conflict may well wane everywhere as the post-Cold War era unfolds. This utopian future seems to be unfolding, if the data on global warfare can be believed. Figure 5.1 outlines what may turn out to be one of the more astonishing developments in human history: the decline of war as an instrument of policy.

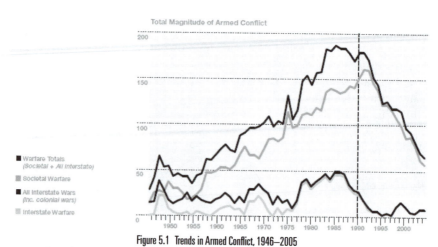

Figure 5.1 Trends in Armed Conflict, 1946–2005
Source: Center for International Development and Conflict Management, University of Maryland, College Park

Major wars tend to be quite memorable, so there is little need to demonstrate that there has been no such conflict since the end of the Cold War. But the data seem to support the trickle-down theory of stability as well. Every extant empirical analysis of warfare has found that the frequency and intensity of *all types* of wars—interstate, civil, ethnic, revolutionary, etc—declined throughout the 1990s and into the new century, after a brief surge of postcolonial conflicts in the first few years after the collapse of the Soviet Union.[27] The magnitude and intensity of warfare is steadily declining. At the end of 2007, Africa is more peaceful than it has ever been (despite its other problems); Europe, South America, and most of Asia are the same. Although no one seems to have noticed, warfare—whether over resources or anything else—is disappearing from the Earth.

For resource wars to become a reality, not only would substantial economic incentives for peace and the common interest of consumers and producers have to be overcome, but also international trends of peaceful conflict resolution would have to be reversed. If indeed conflict is becoming a rare event, then the risk of war over oil in the coming century is even lower than it would have been otherwise. And that risk was probably never particularly high.

The China Wildcard

One of the truly significant moments in the history of international politics took place in late 1993. The exact date it occurred is unclear, since at the time no one seemed to take much notice. There were no headlines, no news coverage, no analysis from CNN pundits, not even hyperbolic warnings from Congress. Looking back, it seems remarkable that no one in 1993 took note of the moment that the People's Republic of China (PRC) became a net importer of oil.[28] Few events were to have as much lasting importance for economics, politics, and national security affairs, for the transition to oil importer status was an early symptom of the rapid growth that the Chinese economy was to experience over the next decade (and counting).[29] The effects on the price at the pump are clear, the implications for international politics significantly less so.

Traditional realist analysis would suggest that the growing economic power of China will inevitably be turned into military power which, when coupled with its new thirst for oil, will lead to expansion, and perhaps even to conflict with the United States. According to this litany of pessimistic projections, China will seek to maximize its power and influence throughout the next century, and will do so by military means whenever necessary.[30] The rise of China may be accompanied by balancing, suspicion, security dilemmas and instability. The oil supplies of the region just add to its problems, inspiring self-interested littoral states to vie for their control.

Will China's growing thirst for oil bring it into conflict with the United States as the century unfolds? All projections suggest that both India and China will need more and more oil to fuel their booming economies. Nightmare scenarios have the Chinese presence in the Persian Gulf and other resource-rich areas growing, igniting competition and perhaps even conflict with the other consumer states. However, as is the case everywhere in petroleum politics, consumer states' interests align far more than they conflict. During the mercantilist era, states would commonly attempt to control territory and keep vital resources out of the hands of their potential enemies; today, they trade with one another to get what they want. All consumer states want to see oil be cheap. In any disagreement over oil, it is more likely that the United States and China would find themselves on the same side rather than opposing one another. A Chinese challenge to the status quo in the Pacific would entail an enormous risk for a questionable reward, which is a calculation that Beijing seems to have made.[31] In the East China Sea, China and Japan have taken active steps to begin developing what has been called a conflict avoidance regime to address their many overlapping claims, from fishing rights, scientific research notifications, and ultimately for military and intelligence activities.[32] Since 9/11, the Chinese relationships with both the United States and ASEAN have improved dramatically, leading to the signing of a code of conduct for parties in the various South China Sea disputes.[33] Regional trends suggest that risk of war seems to be decreasing as time goes by. Alistair Iain Johnston, one of the most important living China scholars, is not alone in believing that fears of a rising dragon are misplaced, and that China exhibits all the signs of being a status quo power.[34] The idea that oil is not worth fighting for may have taken hold in the Pacific Rim.

The first decade-and-a-half of post-Cold War international relations in the Pacific have not unfolded as early pessimist forecasts predicted. In fact, the states of the region have acted almost as if they were unaware of the inevitability of rivalry. No alarms seem to have been rung in response to the growth of China. The post-Cold War period has been marked by a notable (and, to realists, puzzling) lack of balancing behavior in East Asia.[35] Today both the evidence and theoretical logic support the belief that major war to assert control over the potentially vast petroleum deposits in the South and East China Seas, despite lingering disputes over their ownership and rapidly increasing regional demand, is not very likely in the indefinite future. If indeed the use of force to assure access to oil is not a realistic option even between China and the other East Asian states over the potential riches of the East and South China Seas, then can it be an option anywhere?

Conclusion

Overall, there seems to be little reason to believe that the world is on the verge of a series of resource wars that will define the new era. Although the demand for oil will be growing steadily, market forces are likely to determine how it is distributed; the interests of consumers and producers are likely to align far more than they conflict; and the overall trends in warfare will also likely affect decisions regarding oil politics. In other words, there is much room for optimism. Despite common perceptions to the contrary, the world is a far safer place than it was in the 20th century. We are living in a golden age of international security, where war is rare and major war is non-existent. While international rivalries and disagreements will never go away, the odds are good that their solutions will be peaceful. If states prove unwilling to fight over control of the most vital of national resources, will they ever again come to blows?

Notes

1. Michael T. Klare, *Resource Wars: The New Landscape of Global Conflict* (New York: Metropolitan Books, 2001), 29. See also John Orme, "The Utility of Force in a World of Scarcity," *International Security*, 22, no. 3 (Winter 1997/98): 138–167; Thomas F. Homer-Dixon, *Environment, Scarcity and Conflict* (Princeton, NJ: Princeton University Press, 1999); and C. J. Campbell, *The Coming Oil Crisis* (New York: Multi-Science Publishing, 2004).

2. Quoted in James M. Collins and Clyde R. Mark, *Oil Fields as Military Objectives: A Feasibility Study* (Washington, DC: Government Printing Office, August 12, 1975), 79. Kissinger mentions in his memoirs that he requested a variety of contingency plans to be drawn up to address the crisis. *Years of Upheaval* (Boston: Little Brown, 1982), 871.

3. Glenn Frankel, "U.S. Mulled Seizing Oil Fields in '73: British Memo Cites Notion of Sending Airborne to Mideast," *Washington Post*, January 1, 2004, A1.

4. Kissinger discusses his reasoning in *Years of Upheaval*, 871. For a review of the non-debate over the use of force, see Collins and Mark, *Oil Fields as Military Objectives*, 77–82.

5. Collins and Mark, *Oil Fields as Military Objectives*.

6. Robert W. Tucker, "Oil: The Issue of American Intervention," *Commentary*, 59, no. 1 (January 1975): 22.

7. Robert W. Tucker, "The Purposes of American Power," *Foreign Affairs*, 59, no. 2 (Winter 1980/81): 247.

8. Joshua M. Epstein, "Soviet Vulnerabilities in Iran and the RDF Deterrent," *International Security*, 6, no. 2 (Fall 1981): 126–158; Robert H. Johnson, "The Persian Gulf in U.S. Strategy: A Skeptical View," *International Security*, 14, no. 1 (Summer 1989): 135.

9. Kenneth S. Deffeyes, *Hubbert's Peak: The Impending World Oil Shortage* (Princeton: Princeton University Press, 2003); Richard Heinberg, *The Party's Over: Oil, War and the Fate of Industrial Societies* (British Columbia: New Society Publishers, 2003); Mamdouh G. Salameh, "A Third Oil Crisis?" *Survival*, 43, no. 3 (Autumn 2001): 129–144; Collin J. Campbell, *The Coming Oil Crisis* (New York: Multi-Science Publishing, 2004); and Paul Roberts, *The End of Oil: On the Edge of a Perilous New World* (New York: Houghton Mifflin, 2004).

10. *International Energy Outlook 2005* (Washington, DC: Energy Information Administration, June 2005), http://tonto.eia.doe.gov/ftproot/forecasting/0484(2005).pdf.

11. Shibley Telhami, "What Arab Public Opinion Thinks of U.S. Policy," Brookings Institution Forum, December 2005, http://www.brook.edu/fp/saban/events/20051212.pdf.

12. Amy Meyers Jaffe and Robert A. Manning, "The Myth of the Caspian 'Great Game': The Real Geopolitics of Energy," *Survival*, 40, no. 4 (Winter 1998–99): 112–129.

13. For an example of the former, see Svante Cornell, "Geopolitics and Strategic Alignments in the Caucasus and Central Asia," *Journal of International Affairs*, 4, no. 2 (June-August 1999): 100–125. For the latter, Robert Ebel and Rajan Menon, eds., *Energy and Conflict in Central Asia and the Caucasus* (New York: Rowman and Littlefield Publishers, 2000).

14. Bernard H. Oxman, "Caspian Sea or Lake: What Difference Does it Make?" *Caspian Crossroads*, 1, no. 4 (Winter 1996); Mehdi Parvizi Amineh, *Towards the Control of Oil*

Resources in the Caspian Region (New York: St. Martin's Press, 1999); and R. Hrair Dekmejian and Hovann H. Simonian, *Troubled Waters: The Geopolitics of the Caspian Region* (New York: I.B. Tauris, 2001).

15. Brenda Shaffer, "From Pipedream to Pipeline: A Caspian Success Story," *Current History*, 104, no. 684 (October 2005): 343–346.

16. Philip D. Rabinowitz, Mehdi Z. Yusifov, Jessica Arnoldi and Eyal Hakim, "Geology, Oil and Gas Potential, Pipelines, and the Geopolitics of the Caspian Sea Region," *Ocean Development and International Law*, 35, no. 1 (January-March 2004): 19–40.

17. Edward Luttwak, "From Geopolitics to Geo-Economics: Logic of Conflict, Grammar of Commerce," *The National Interest*, no. 20 (Summer 1990): 17–23.

18. Martha Brill Olcott, *Revisiting the Twelve Myths of Central Asia* (Washington, DC: Carnegie Endowment for International Peace), Working Paper No. 23 (September 2001), 9.

19. Daniel Yergin, Dennis Elkof and Jefferson Edwards, "Fueling Asia's Recovery," *Foreign Affairs*, 77, no. 2 (March/April 1998): 47–48.

20. Shibley Telhami, *Power and Leadership in International Bargaining: The Path to the Camp David Accords* (New York: Columbia University Press, 1990), 72–73.

21. See C.J. Campbell, "Running Out of Gas: The Time of the Wolf is Coming," *The National Interest*, no. 51 (Spring 1998): 48.

22. For a good, if a bit dated, discussion of the power of market forces in the oil industry, see Philip K. Verleger, Jr., *Adjusting to Volatile Energy Prices* (Washington, DC: Institute for International Economics, 1993).

23. For a discussion of the connection between oil hot spots and war, see Christopher J. Fettweis, *Angell Triumphant: The International Politics of Great Power Peace* (New York: Oxford University Press, forthcoming), Chapter 3.

24. Richard M. Nixon, *No More Vietnams* (New York: Arbor House, 1985), 225; John Mueller, *Retreat From Doomsday: The Obsolescence of Major War* (New York: Basic Books, 1989); Michael Mandelbaum, *Ideas that Conquered the World: Peace, Democracy, and Free Markets in the Twenty-First Century* (New York: Public Affairs, 2002); Robert Jervis, "Theories of War in an Era of Leading Power Peace," *American Political Science Review*, 96, no. 1 (March 2002): 1–14; and Raimo Väyrynen, *The Waning of Major War: Theories and Debates* (New York: Routledge, 2006).

25. Samuel Huntington, *The Clash of Civilizations and the Remaking of World Order* (New York: Touchstone, 1996), 302.

26. Mueller elaborates upon and supports this point in *The Remnants of War* (Ithaca, NY: Cornell University Press, 2004).

27. See Ted Robert Gurr and Monty G. Marshall, *Peace and Conflict 2005: A Global Survey of Armed Conflicts, Self-Determination Movements, and Democracy* (College Park, MD: Center for International Development and Conflict Management, 2005); Human Security Centre, *Human Security Report 2005* (New York: Oxford University Press, 2005); Peter Wallensteen, and Margareta Sollenberg, "Armed Conflict, 1989–99," *Journal of Peace Research*, 37, no. 5 (2000): 625–649; and Ted Robert Gurr, "Ethnic Warfare on the Wane," *Foreign Affairs*, 79, no. 3 (May/June 2000): 52–64.

28. Mamdouh G. Salameh describes this quiet transition as one of the "true watershed moments of international politics," in "China, Oil and the Risk of Regional Conflict," *Survival*, 37, no. 4 (Winter 1995/96): 141.

29. For other early, pessimistic forecasts, see Kent E. Calder, "Asia's Empty Gas Tank," *Foreign Affairs*, 75, no. 2 (March/April 1996): 55–69; and Robert A. Manning, "The Asian Energy Predicament," *Survival*, 42. no. 3 (Spring 2000): 73–88.

30. Thomas J. Christensen, "China, the U.S.-Japan Alliance, and the Security Dilemma in East Asia," *International Security,* 23, no. 4 (Spring 1999): 49–80, and "Posing Problems without Catching Up: China's Rise and Challenges for U.S. Security Policy," *International Security,* 25, no. 4 (Spring 2001): 5–40; Richard K. Betts, "Wealth, Power, and Instability," *International Security,* 18, no. 3 (Winter 1993/94): 34–77; John W. Garver, *Face Off: China, the U.S. and Taiwan's Democratization* (Seattle: University of Washington Press, 1997); Arthur Waldron, "How Not to Deal with China," *Commentary,* 103, no. 3 (March 1997): 44–49; Richard Bernstein and Ross H. Munro, *The Coming Conflict with China* (New York: Knopf, 1997); Bill Gertz, *The China Threat: How the People's Republic Targets America* (New York: Regnery, 2000); and Ted Galen Carpenter, *America's Coming War with China: Collision Course over Taiwan* (New York: Palgrave-Macmillan, 2006). Gertz, a journalist for the *Washington Times,* is perhaps the most consistently, unrelentingly pessimistic.

31. Hongyi Harry Lai, "China's Oil Diplomacy: Is It a Global Security Threat?" *Third World Quarterly,* 28, no. 3 (October 2007): 519–537.

32. Mark J. Valencia and Yoshihisa Amae, "Regime Building in the East China Sea," *Ocean Development and International Law,* 34, no. 2 (April-June 2003): 189–208.

33. See Yann-Huei Song, "The Overall Situation in the South China Sea in the New Millennium: Before and After the September 11 Terrorist Attacks," *Ocean Development and International Law,* 34, nos. 1–2 (July-December 2003): 229–277; and Nguyen Hong Thao, "The 2002 Declaration on the Conduct of Parties in the South China Sea: A Note," *Ocean Development and International Law,* 34, nos. 1–2 (July-December 2003): 279–285.

34. Alastair Iain Johnston, "Is China a Status Quo Power?" *International Security,* 27, no. 4 (Spring 2003): 5–56.

35. Daniel Kang makes this point very convincingly in "Getting Asia Wrong: The Need for New Analytical Frameworks," *International Security,* 27, no. 4 (Spring 2003): 57–85.

CHAPTER 6

OPEC: An Anatomy of a Cartel

Amy Myers Jaffe

The history of the Organization of Petroleum Exporting Countries (OPEC) has been a successful one, and it remains one of the most important multinational energy institutions outside the Western industrial world. Founded in 1960, OPEC's original aim was to wrest higher fixed crude oil prices and royalty tax payments for oil-producing host governments from the international oil companies that owned and operated Middle East and South American oil fields under concessionary terms in the post-World War II period. As the 1960s progressed, OPEC ultimately got the upper hand in negotiations with the international oil companies and took control of their own national oil resources through massive nationalization of in-country oil field and infrastructure assets. OPEC's actions to "assert its member countries legitimate rights" and gain "a major say in the pricing of crude oil on world markets" made history in 1973, when the organization initiated its famous oil embargo that rocked the international community and quadrupled the price of oil.[1] OPEC's membership originally included only five countries (Venezuela, Saudi Arabia, Iraq, Iran, and Kuwait) but today 13 countries are members, including Saudi Arabia, Venezuela, Kuwait, Iraq, Iran, the UAE, Qatar, Libya, Nigeria, Algeria, Indonesia, Ecuador and Angola. Throughout the years, OPEC has stuck with a very basic objective: it defends and supports the income and revenue aims of its members and forces any burden of that economic adjustment of higher oil prices on to other countries, namely large oil consuming nations such as the United States, the EU, Japan, and China. OPEC's ability to achieve its revenue aims has varied over the years, rising and falling on the fate of global economic growth and the increasing ability of the world's citizenry to attain a high enough standard of living to own an automobile.[2] Starting with the end of the Asian financial crisis in the late 1990s and the dramatic boom in world economic growth into the turn of the century, OPEC's ability to influence oil prices grew dramatically between 1999 and 2007 and with this greater market power also grew its oil price ambitions. Oil prices hit $147 in July 2008, highlighting the cartel's critical role in the energy security debate worldwide. But OPEC's fortune reversed four months later when a global economic crisis brought to the collapse of oil prices to under $40, forcing the perplexed and economically damaged cartel to cut its daily production by more than 4 mbd.

Torn between Greed and Heed

Western nations often reference the risks associated with producer cartelization like OPEC as a reason to adopt new energy security measures. OPEC's very existence, against the backdrop of the 1973 oil embargo, raises the risks that a grouping of oil producers could use oil supply as a political weapon or economic lever to force some political end on vulnerable oil-consuming economies. OPEC is equally cognizant of the risks to its members of unified responses by large consuming nations to limit oil demand through a variety of policy tools including alternative energy, austerity measures and energy taxes. Japan and the European Union imposed huge taxes on oil consumption of 400 percent or more, virtually halting the growth in oil demand and promoting energy-efficient technologies, including automobiles that allow drivers to travel more each year using less fuel. Nuclear power was also utilized in the industrialized West to almost eliminate oil use in the electricity sector. OPEC became acutely aware that these kinds of diversification and demand-constraining policies of consuming countries had bearing on its goals and aims when oil prices began to slip dramatically in the 1980s. The producer group initiated a price war in 1984–1985 that failed to achieve its goal of reducing competition and market volatility continued into the 1990s. As a result, OPEC was forced to reconsider its approaches. The cartel responded by calling for a consumer-producer dialogue to find a middle ground to protect demand for its oil while at the same time achieving reasonable prices. OPEC became increasingly concerned about security of demand for its oil and the international oil industry began to debate openly the topic of reintegration. Vertical integration of the international industry in the 1950s when the owners of the oil production had also controlled the downstream petroleum refining and marketing outlets had provided for market stability. As Edward Krapels noted in 1993, the large degree of vertical integration in the 1950s had provided a high degree of "common interest" in stable prices where oil companies would "routinely take losses selling oil products in order to maximize the profits of crude oil production."[3]

Key OPEC members redoubled their efforts to acquire downstream assets. Then Saudi oil minister Hisham Nazer noted in several policy addresses in the late 1980s and early 1990s that the acquisition of oil refineries and marketing networks by oil exporters would enhance both supply security and price stability.[4] In 1981, he made an important policy statement during a speech at Harvard University where he called for a system of "reciprocal energy security" and implied that in return for demonstration of security of demand on the part of the West, the United States and other consumer nations could gain guaranteed access to a "fairly priced ocean of oil."[5] Nazer and his generation of OPEC ministers focused their attention on reintegration of the oil industry—a strategy that included OPEC countries like Saudi Arabia, Venezuela and Kuwait buying large or controlling interests in downstream refining and marketing assets in key consumer countries such as the United States, Japan, South Korea, and the EU. Since oversupplied oil markets and falling prices were perceived to be a key risk to OPEC's market control, producing countries recognized energy security "required unfettered access to the downstream petroleum sectors of the United States and other major industrial countries."[6] But increased ownership of downstream assets failed to provide OPEC with the market stability it sought and oil prices came under fire again in the late 1990s when oil demand took a sudden downturn during a major recession and financial crisis in Asia.

The impact of the crisis on OPEC's export revenues was dramatic. Oil prices reached their highest level of the decade in 1996–1997 of around $26 a barrel, and total export earnings for the OPEC countries, as shown in Table 6.1, hovered around $170 billion (in nominal dollars of the day). By 1997–1998, the circumstances in Asia, the return of Iraqi oil exports to the market, and the market share struggle between Venezuela and Saudi Arabia, led oil prices to collapse below $10. The collapse ushered a plunge in export earnings, in some cases by almost 50 percent. The internal economic pain inside OPEC, as well as in other oil exporting countries, including Mexico and Oman, was intense. Unable to provide basic services, governments lost authority and changes occurred, sometimes peacefully and sometimes not, in Indonesia, Iran, Nigeria, Russia, and Venezuela. The changes came on the heels of subtle shifts in the dynamic of Saudi internal politics, which was facing a transition in the aftermath of King Fahd's debilitating stroke in 1995. The price collapse of 1998 not only drove home the need for collective action. It also prompted new politics inside the producer organization. OPEC's commitment to protect revenues and increase oil prices gained momentum after the 1998 oil price collapse. With the survival of regimes at stake from falling revenues, intensive diplomacy began, with Venezuela and Mexico actively working to pave the way for a major agreement among oil producers to trim output and propel oil prices back above $22 a barrel.[7]

The 1998 agreement stands as a recent turning point for OPEC. Since its 1998 agreement, which quickly lifted oil prices off their floor and back to a $22 a barrel target price, OPEC has successfully orchestrated and jointly implemented production cuts to defend dramatically higher prices, first in the $30 level, and then subsequently to $50 and then to record levels of $100 a barrel and beyond. OPEC's turnaround March 1998 agreement mandated 1.485 mbd in cuts, with pledged contributions also from non-OPEC producers Mexico, Russia and Oman. The 1998 plan was designed to create a floor under world oil prices.[8] Following the implementation of the March 1998 plan, OPEC continued to work together to address any rise in global oil inventories that might threaten the rebound in prices. The cuts implemented over the summer of 1998 brought global supply to levels well below global demand, forcing market players to draw down bulging inventories that had been overhanging the market and pressuring prices.

Table 6.1 OPEC Export Revenues, 1998–2007 (in billions of US$, nominal)

	1998	1999	2000	2001	2002	2003	2004	2005	2006	2007
Saudi Arabia	28.6	40.2	74	60.1	58	80.8	103.6	156.9	182.8	194.3
Iran	10.5	14.6	22.6	19.8	19	23.9	32.3	48	54.2	57.1
Kuwait	8.1	10.8	18.7	15.3	11.6	18.7	26.3	40.4	50.6	54.9
Iraq	6.9	12.9	20.2	15.9	12.4	9.6	18.4	23.8	31.8	37.5
UAE	12.2	15.7	25.5	21.2	18.7	23.7	29.7	44.2	57.5	63
Venezuela	11.5	14.9	25	20.6	19.7	20.6	25.5	37.1	41.9	44.2
Others	26.7	36.1	60.1	51.1	49.5	62.9	99.6	157.7	192.3	219.6
Total OPEC	104.4	145.3	246	204.1	188.9	240.2	335.4	508.1	611.1	670.6

Source: U.S. DOE, independent estimates

By September, OPEC could boast 81 percent compliance with production quota allocations, uncharacteristically high for the producer organization.[9] The success reinvigorated OPEC and by March 1999, the producer group adopted another set of agreements that triggered continued price rallies. By the spring of 2000, ambitious OPEC members such as Venezuela and Iran began pressing for a framework to adjust output regularly to ensure that the OPEC basket price remained between $22 to $28 a barrel. Behind the scenes, U.S. Secretary of Energy Bill Richardson pressed U.S.-friendly OPEC members to raise output to keep oil prices closer to the $20 to $25 end of the spectrum. Over time, OPEC came to endorse the $25 target. Unexpected circumstances, including an oil workers' strike in Venezuela that drastically cut its exports, and attacks on American oil personnel in Saudi Arabia, unnerved markets, creating a war premium. With globalization proceeding, OPEC became more concerned about its own economic performance that lagged in the 1990s relative to other nations. By the end of the last decade, OPEC rejected the notion that low oil prices were good for everyone. Key nations inside OPEC whose oil revenues were critical to fuel government budgets perceived the domestic impact of falling oil prices as far greater than the impact of higher prices on most oil-importing countries, whose oil import bill is only a fraction of their total trade. Oil-importing countries gained this advantage partly because of policies taken in the 1970s and 1980s to diversify to other fuels or to tax oil use to hold down demand growth for oil. Key OPEC members began to resent the suffering they experienced during the low oil prices in 1997–1998, which also appeared to be providing a sort of subsidy for growth for other countries. OPEC therefore decided to shift the burden of price adjustment back on to the oil importing community.

As OPEC entered 2003, news of an impending U.S. military action in Iraq sent oil prices to close to $40 despite a quiet prewar production increase by Saudi Arabia in March to more than 9 mbd. By early 2004, OPEC, including Saudi Arabia, was endorsing production cuts even though prices were above $35 a barrel. By October 2004, U.S. oil prices had hit a record at $55 a barrel as hurricanes pummeled oil production platforms in the U.S. Gulf of Mexico and OPEC was left producing flat out with little dampening effect on markets. By year end, OPEC's shifting attitudes towards its old price targets became apparent, as the organization agreed to institute new counter-seasonal production cuts during the high winter demand period, effectively defending prices above $40. The decision came against the backdrop of a terrorist attack on U.S. targets inside Saudi Arabia and rising revenue needs against a weakening dollar. In explaining its decisions to defend prices well above its $22 to $28 price band, OPEC explained that, after adjustments for inflation and the accelerated depreciation of the dollar, the OPEC basket price of oil reflected its $22 to $28 target price in purchasing power parity terms.[10]

OPEC politics have continued to favor an appreciating nominal price path, with $55 becoming a price floor instead of a price target by 2006, and OPEC countries have been slow to respond to rising oil prices with high output or major new oil production investment programs in recent years. Underlying OPEC's apathetic response to a tightening market and projections of continued rises in demand is the view that the future is putting OPEC squarely in the driver's seat, with enhanced market power and ever improving revenue streams. With over 78 percent of the world's oil reserves under their control, OPEC countries have banked their future on a combination of growth in oil demand and a presumed natural limit to the growth of non-OPEC production. OPEC governments, responding to pressing social and economic pressures of rising populations and aging infrastructure, favor the realization of greater short term revenue, which will be best achieved not by bringing on line new oil production capacity, but rather by curtailing output.[11]

Enjoying increased market power and organizational success in implementing higher prices, and thereby higher revenues, OPEC members have similarly and conscientiously been careful not to over-invest in new productive capacity. As Table 6.2 shows, OPEC's total sustainable production capacity has not increased between 1998 and 2005, despite a rising call for OPEC crude oil supply and the rapid growth of developing Asia. Capacity gains made through added investments in Iran, Saudi Arabia, Kuwait, Algeria, Qatar and Libya and the accession of two new members, Angola and Ecuador, in 2007, have barely managed to offset the losses in Iraq, Venezuela, Nigeria and Indonesia.[12]

Table 6.2 OPEC Average Daily Production (in mbd)

Member country	1999	2001	2003	2005	2007
Saudi Arabia	7.6	7.9	8.4	9.35	8.8
Iran	3.4	3.5	3.7	4	4
Iraq	2.8	2.5	1.3	1.8	2.1
Kuwait	1.8	1.9	2.1	2.5	2.5
UAE	2.1	2.2	2.3	2.4	2.5
Qatar	0.72	0.75	0.75	0.82	0.84
Venezuela	2.8	2.7	2.6	3	2.9
Nigeria	1.8	2	2.2	2.3	2
Indonesia	1.35	1.2	1.15	1	0.83
Libya	1.2	1.3	1.45	1.6	1.6
Algeria	0.7	0.7	0.9	1.35	1.37
Ecuador	NA	NA	NA	NA	0.51
Angola	NA	NA	NA	NA	1.7
Total	26.27	26.65	26.85	30.12	30.12
Spare capacity	5	3.5	1.25	0.7	2.5

Source: OPEC Annual Statistical Bulletin 2007

In some cases, notably Nigeria and Iran, capacity gains have been delayed or derailed by civil unrest, bureaucratic infighting, corruption and sector mismanagement. In other cases, such as Qatar and Algeria, geological constraints limit the potential for expansion, while in Kuwait decision-makers have been conservative about committing broad resources to capacity expansion, with some parliament politicians arguing that Kuwait's oil will become more valuable over time. Only Saudi Arabia has invested heavily in recent years to bring on new fields to revive its 2 mbd cushion of spare capacity in the face of declining output capacity at some of its mature fields. In June 2005, Saudi Aramco's leadership stated that Saudi Arabia would raise production capacity to more than 12 mbd by 2009, and then possibly to 15 mbd "if the market situation justifies it." Official statements added that by 2006, Saudi Arabia would have 90 drilling rigs in the kingdom, more than double the number of rigs operating in 2004.[13] In December 2006, as prices continued to rise, Saudi Aramco's board approved an aggressive 2007 operating plan, which according to press reports is "the largest spending program in the company's history."[14]

OPEC rhetoric has matched its new focus, and the producer group has noted that its aim was to attain a "fair" price for its oil. The debate highlighted the true nature of the geo-economic issues underlying OPEC's relations with the rest of the world; at issue was an economic struggle for rents between oil producers who demand high revenues and major consumers whose economies can grow faster with low oil prices. In its policy pronouncements, OPEC targets OECD consumer governments, who have been capturing rents via high national Western energy taxes. "People always talk about the revenues of OPEC," said OPEC president Chakib Khelil to the press following the March 2001 OPEC meeting held in Vienna. "Before they point a finger at OPEC, they should probably reduce taxes in their own country."[15] While the anti-tax rhetoric is not new to OPEC, its political weight has a different, more radicalized character today and serves as a clearer justification and impetus to production restraints that do not accommodate Western interests. OPEC's anti-tax, anti-Western rhetoric comes against the backdrop of popular domestic sentiment inside OPEC countries that their governments are not doing enough to deliver economic benefits to a substantial portion of the population. Leaders in OPEC countries cannot be seen as delivering benefits to Western consumers at the expense of their own citizens because such perceptions would leave regimes more vulnerable to public attack and more susceptible to the efforts of opposition groups.[16]

Producers Are Also Consumers

Beyond the larger energy security of demand issue facing OPEC countries, many of the producer group's member nations also face domestic internal energy security of supply problems of their own. OPEC consumption of refined products has been growing rapidly in recent years, from 5.4 mbd in 2002, to 6.43 mbd in 2006.[17] Fueled by large consumer subsidies, the Middle East Gulf has become the second largest region of growth in oil demand after Asia, with consumption rising by more than 5 percent a year since 2003—similar to growth rates seen in recent years in China. The Middle East Gulf's demand for oil now represents over 7 percent of total world oil demand and increases are being driven by economic expansion, high population growth and extremely large subsidies to electricity and gasoline prices. Subsidies for gasoline in the region keep domestic prices as low as 9 to 10 cents a liter. The resulting boom in energy demand has meant that some countries, notably Iran, have experienced fuel shortages and others, like Saudi Arabia and Kuwait, are struggling to meet rising electricity demand and have resorted to burning increasing amounts of crude oil for power generation despite negative environmental consequences and the loss to the federal treasury of potential export revenues. A recent report of CIBC World Markets calculated that "soaring rates of consumption in Russia, in Mexico and in member states of the Organization of Petroleum Exporting Counties would reduce crude oil exports by as much as 2.5 mbd by the end of the decade."[18] The issue of cheap and available fuel is a political hot potato inside OPEC countries. Many OPEC countries view their oil industry as a vehicle to achieve wider socio-economic objectives including income redistribution and industrial development. Among the noncommercial objectives imposed on national oil companies inside OPEC by political interests, subsidizing domestic fuel in an effort to redistribute oil proceeds to the general public and to promote economic development has been among the most debilitating policies to OPEC countries' long term economic future. On a macroeconomic level, low petroleum product prices can stimulate growth in energy intensive sectors and limit incentives for energy efficiency, which in high population societies only exacerbates the budgetary problems faced by the national oil company and the government. This problem creates a treadmill effect where the subsidies serve as a drain on the budget of the government and the national oil companies, leaving fewer and fewer funds to reinvest in expanding oil production over time as internal oil demand grows. At the extreme, the combination of rising oil demand and flagging domestic production following investment constraints can reap political and economic crises. OPEC member Indonesia flipped from a net oil exporting country to an oil-imported country in the last four years because of flagging oil production in aging oil fields combined with soaring demand driven by fuel subsidies. Those fuel subsidies, which by the late 1990s had reached almost one quarter of the Indonesian government's entire federal budget, caused such massive economic dislocation for the Indonesian government that the long time rule of President Suharto was ended as a result. As a result of these new conditions, Indonesia, OPEC's sole member from Southeast Asia, has announced that it would leave OPEC by the end of 2008.[19] Other major OPEC countries such as Iran and Algeria face a similar prospect: they could potentially become net oil importers in the years ahead, with dire economic consequences. Iran is particularly exposed, with Iranian domestic demand for fuel skyrocketing so high that the country has had to import expensive petroleum products from the international market. This has forced Iran's state oil company NIOC to sell hard currency in order to import gasoline back into the country to meet growing demand that is driven by large subsidies. The country's product import bill now runs in the billions of dollars, with NIOC predicting that the gasoline subsidies will be costing the industry $15 billion to $20 billion annually by the next decade. The subsidies, while extremely helpful to average Iranians, are becoming increasingly damaging to the Iranian treasury and have created a mounting deficit that even high oil prices have not been able to countermand. Ironically, OPEC's own struggle to provide energy security for its own citizens at subsidized prices is perhaps one of the greatest risks to its ability to offer secure export supplies to the industrialized West and the entire dynamic becomes a self-propelling chicken-egg problem that is driving global insecurity today.

Threats to Security of Demand

OPEC's perspective was summarized clearly by current Saudi Oil Minister Ali Naimi in an address given to the OPEC International Seminar on Petroleum in an Interdependent World in September 2004. Naimi noted that national oil companies engage in the efficient extraction, production and marketing of oil to "provide the needed revenues and foreign exchange for the non-oil sector to grow and the economy to be more diversified." But beyond revenue needs and feedstock for national industries, Naimi noted that national oil industries must work to "enhance the role of oil in global energy mix." He warned that "environmental and energy security concerns have been channeling technologies and research towards alternate fuels . . . the research and investment in those technologies pose long-term challenges to the oil industry in general and to the NOCs including our own."[20] OPEC's joint desires to garner maximum revenues for its oil and its long term aim to attain energy security of demand are at odds with each other. After its 1998 agreement, which quickly lifted oil prices off the floor and back to a $22 a barrel target price, OPEC successfully orchestrated jointly implemented production cuts to defend dramatically higher prices, first in the $30 level, and then subsequently to $50 and then to record levels of over $100 a barrel. But the exceedingly high oil prices stimulated consumer country responses and encouraged oil conservation and investment in alternative energy. High prices did not convince consuming countries to remove energy taxes; and high oil prices contributed to a global economic slowdown that negatively impacted oil demand and oil prices. Moreover, high prices played into the cycle by rendering many promising new energy technologies more commercial and adding to the possible alternative fuels that will compete with oil in the coming years, leaving the oil producer group with possible shrinking markets over time. This new economic reality is already affecting consumers' energy policies in a significant way. For example, in a historic shift, in December 2007 the U.S. Congress passed the most aggressive energy legislation it has adopted in over two decades, including a renewable fuel standard and an increase in fuel efficiency standards which could, between now and 2030, push oil use about 2.5 mbd of oil lower than previous projections. U.S. President

Barack Obama has initiated even more strict fuel efficiency standards and other new programs to encourage conservation and expansion of renewable energy. For its part, the EU has even tighter mileage standards and is targeting mandates for both renewable energy and biofuels. The EU is targeting biofuels to make up 5.75 percent of transportation fuels (measured by energy content) by 2010. Aggressive consumer country conservation and alternative energy policies will likely undo some of OPEC's 1998–2007 gains as an organization in defending security of demand while still garnering high prices. Oil demand rose steadily between 2003 and 2007, accompanying rapid growth in the global economy and straining existing global oil supply infrastructure. However, due to persistent high oil prices and changing national policies in large consumer countries, it is estimated that oil demand in the industrialized West fell by 0.4 percent in 2007. As a result, the estimated increase in total global oil demand was only 1 percent in 2007, which is slower than the historical average of 2 percent a year. By April 2009, global oil demand had fallen 3.5 percent versus levels the year before, and analysts are now projecting that oil demand growth may fail to return to previous growth paths in the coming decades. OPEC has reacted to these new Western policies and slowing growth in oil demand by warning that a shift to alternative energy will discourage its own investment in future oil supplies, potentially forcing oil prices through the roof. Speaking the day before a meeting of the G-8 group of industrialized nations meeting in June 2007, OPEC Secretary General Abdalla el-Badri said OPEC was considering cutting its investment in new oil production: "If we (OPEC) are unable to see security of demand . . . we may revisit investment in the long term." He warned that the U.S. and European biofuels strategy would backfire because "You don't get the incremental oil and you don't get the ethanol," alluding to the fact that a biofuels strategy might not prove successful.[21] OPEC President Chakib Khelil, for his part, blamed "the intrusion of bioethanol on the market" for being responsible for 40 percent of the rise in oil prices.[22]

Yet, overall, OPEC does not believe that the West has created a viable competitor to its key product, oil. OPEC countries still believe that world demand for energy will grow so astronomically in the coming decades through economic expansion in developing Asia, among other regions, that biofuels and competing fuels for power generation such as solar energy, wind power, clean coal and nuclear power will barely make a dent in the rise in demand for their oil. The International Energy Agency forecasts do not agree with OPEC's optimism. As security of supply becomes a critical geopolitical issue, and partly in response to OPEC actions and rising oil prices, consumer governments and citizens are searching for new solutions. This is leading to increasingly strict regulation and public outcry for new technologies and policies. In its 2006 World Energy Outlook Alternative Policy scenario analysis the IEA suggests that alternative policies would mean that oil use climbs to 103 mbd in 2030, 13 mbd less than the business as usual case. The IEA predicts that about 60 percent of that oil savings or about 7.6 mbd will come in the transportation sector, mainly from lower oil demand in the United States, China and Europe.[23] According to Baker Institute calculations, the schedule for the phase in of the new fuel-efficient cars could reduce oil demand in the transportation sector in the United States by about 9.5 percent, putting U.S. motor fuel demand in 2017 at 12.0 mbd instead of the 13.3 mbd previously projected for 2017. In total, between now and 2030, the new fuel efficiency regulations could push oil use about 2.5 mbd of oil lower than previous projections, assuming the average rate of vehicle purchases experienced in recent years. This savings could be even higher under the stricter efficiency regulations that were adopted in 2009.[24] In addition, ethanol production is targeted to reach 15.2 billion gallons a year by 2012 and billions of gallons of other alcohols and alternative fuels are likely to penetrate the market. Further improvements in vehicle efficiency beyond those imposed by the new fuel efficiency standards could also be potentially very important down the road. Efficiency in the transportation sector is being viewed by some as a virtual source of supply, as evidenced by new legislation in the United States and elsewhere. If, for example, a major breakthrough in car technology and innovation were to occur such that new vehicle fuel efficiency accelerated after 2015 to an average of 50 mpg by 2020, the implications for oil use in the United States would be substantial, even if no other regulatory policies are enacted. A technological breakthrough in vehicle technology, such as in plug-in hybrid vehicles technology, could push oil demand even lower. OPEC will have to consider the impact of alternative energy policies on the long-term future path of oil prices. Some politicians and government leaders inside the oil-producing countries believe that oil left under the ground will be worth more in the coming years than it is now. However, hawkish oil pricing strategies could threaten OPEC's long term security of demand as both industrial and major developing nations accelerate energy diversification and conservation policies. Adoption of alternative energy technologies, particularly in the transportation sector, by the OECD and developing Asia could have a large impact on oil exporting countries. Once these technological alternatives are adopted, the market will be altered forever. As Saudi oil minister Ali Naimi told his colleagues in 2004, the role of national oil companies and OPEC itself is to enhance the role of oil in global energy mix. He warned that environmental and energy security concerns have been channeling technologies and research towards alternate energy, including fuel cells and hybrid vehicle design, and added that the research and investment in such technologies pose long-term challenges to OPEC's national oil companies. Prior to the collapse in oil prices in 2008, his warning seemed to have fallen on deaf ears as OPEC has focused on short term revenue goals instead of forging a policy that would defend security of demand in the long term. However, by early 2009, as the outline of new U.S. energy policies were emerging, OPEC members appeared to be in agreement that a more moderate, $45 oil price, would be more in the producer group's immediate interests. Members hoped this lower price would be enough to discourage oil conservation policies in the West. The question remains whether this price will be low enough to be effective in convincing consumers to put aside security of supply concerns and whether oil exporters can sustain strategies that will protect the long term growth in oil use. Should OPEC return to price maximizing behaviors after the global economy recovers, OPEC may face a new supply-demand cycle that may conclude with the end of the oil era as OPEC's policies, combined with global climate concerns, usher in a new age of emerging energy technologies.

Notes

1. "A Brief History of OPEC," www.opec.org/aboutus/history/history.htm.

2. See Kenneth Medlock and Ronald Soligo, "Economic Development and End-Use Energy Demand," *The Energy Journal,* 22, no. 2 (2001); Kenneth Medlock and Ronald Soligo, "Automobile Ownership and Economic Development—Forecasting Motor Vehicle Stocks to 2015," *The Journal of Transport Economics and Policy,* (Spring 2002).

3. Edward N. Krapels, "The Commanding Heights: International Oil in a Changed World," *International Affairs,* 69, no. 1 (January 1993): 71–88.

4. "The Need for Stability and Predictability in the Oil Market" *Middle East Economic Survey,* 30, no. 20 (February 20, 1989).

5. Edward L. Morse, "When It Comes to Dialogue, Small is Better" *Petroleum Intelligence Weekly,* May 27, 1991, 7.

6. Ibid.

7. Edward L. Morse and Amy Myers Jaffe, "OPEC in Confrontation with Globalization," in *Energy and Security: Toward a New Foreign Policy Strategy,* ed. Jan H. Kalicki and David Goldwyn (Baltimore: John Hopkins University Press, 2005).

8. *Petroleum Intelligence Weekly,* 37, no. 13 (March 30, 1998): 1.

9. *Petroleum Intelligence Weekly,* 37, no. 37 (September 14, 1998): 1.

10. "OPEC Talks Dollar, Market Ahead of Meeting," *Oil Daily,* November 30, 2004.

11. There is a rich literature on the subject of the trade-offs between volume and price with respect to OPEC revenue. The most recent contributions to these debates are found in Dermot Gately's recent pieces in the *Energy Journal.* See, H.G. Huntington and Dermot Gately, "Crude Oil Prices and US Economic Performance: Where Does the Asymmetry Reside? *Energy Journal,* 19, no. 4 (2002): 19–55; "How Plausible is the Current Consensus Projection of Oil Below $25 and Persian Gulf Oil Capacity and Output Doubling by 2020?" *Energy Journal,* 22, no. 4 (2002): 1–27; and "OPEC's Incentives for Faster Output Growth," *Energy Journal,* 24, no. 2 (2003).

12. Morse and Jaffe, "OPEC in Confrontation."

13. Saudi Arabia Country Analysis Brief, August 2005, Energy Intelligence Agency, U.S. Department of Energy.

14. Ian Talley, "Saudis Adjust Long-Term Oil Strategy," *Dow Jones News Wires,* January 10, 2007, http://www.rigzone.com/news/article.asp?a_id=39941.

15. For an even fuller statement, see his opening statement to that OPEC meeting, www.opec.org, press release no. 3/2001.

16. For a discussion of the impact of this trend on U.S. policy, see *Strategic Energy Policy: Challenges for the 21st Century,* Report of an Independent Task Force Co-sponsored by the James A. Baker III Institute for Public Policy and the Council On Foreign Relations, April 2001, http://www.rice.edu/energy/publications/PolicyReports/study_15.pdf.

17. OPEC Statistical Bulletin, 2006, www.OPEC.org.

18. Clifford Krause, "Oil-Rich Nations Use More Energy, Cutting Exports," *The New York Times,* December 9, 2007.

19. "Indonesia to Withdraw from OPEC," *BBC,* May 28, 2008, http://news.bbc.co.uk/2/hi/business/7423008.stm.

20. Amy Myers Jaffe and Jareer Elass, "Saudi Aramco: National Flagship with Global Responsibilities," www.rice.edu/energy/publications/nocs.html.

21. Javier Blas and Ed Crooks, "Drive on Biofuels Risks Oil Price Surge," *Financial Times,* June 5, 2007.

22. "OPEC President Blames Ethanol for Crude Price Rise," *MarketWatch,* July 6, 2008, http://www.marketwatch.com/story/opec-president-blames-oil-prices-on-ethanol-weak-dollar-reports.

23. *World Energy Outlook, 2006* (Paris: International Energy Agency, 2006), http://www.iea.org/weo/2006.asp.

24. Amy Myers Jaffe, Kenneth B. Medlock, and Lauren A. Smulcer, U.S. Energy Policy FAQ: The U.S. Energy Mix, National Security and the Myths of Energy Independence, www.bakerinstitute.org.

CHAPTER 7

Russia: The Flawed Energy Superpower

Ariel Cohen

As a giant energy producer and a major energy transit country, Russia is an important player in the field of global energy security. The country has the largest proven gas reserves (1,688 trillion cubic feet) and the eighth largest proven oil reserves (60 billion barrels) in the world.[1] It is the number one natural gas producer and exporter in the world and is producing about as much energy as Saudi Arabia. According to BP 2007 Statistical Review of World Energy, in 2006 Russia accounted for 21.3 percent of total world natural gas production with its output of 612.1 bcm of gas. In oil production, Russia accounted for 12.3 percent of world output, with its 9.7 mbd second only to Saudi Arabia's.[2] Total Russian net oil exports reached 7 mbd in 2006.[3] In addition to that, large areas of eastern Siberia and the Arctic are still unexplored and, according to experts, are expected to yield up to a quarter of the world's energy supply.

Despite its vast resource base and its formal assurances of reliable partnership, Moscow has already proved that it is willing to hike up oil and gas prices, engage in anti-free market practices and use energy as a foreign policy tool. Control of energy corridors from the Caspian Sea to the Black Sea and beyond was the target of the Russian military operation against Georgia in August 2008. This is clearly confirmed by other incidents involving delays in energy supply to Ukraine, Azerbaijan, Belarus, Georgia and the Baltic states. Many argue that Moscow's international energy behavior leaves its partners insecure and makes observers doubt that Russia is rising as a responsible player. Russia's policy is also facilitated by the Soviet-era oil and gas infrastructure that ties Central Asian producers to Russia for their access to external markets. As part of its strategy, Russia pushes to maintain control over energy transportation routes and opposes any projects that could provide Europe with alternative energy supplies. European demand is very high and is projected to grow further. In 2006, the EU consumed a total of 14.9 mbd of oil and a total of 476.4 bcm of natural gas.[4] Oil exports from Russia and Central Asia to Europe reached 5.9 mbd[5] in the same year, and Russia supplied European countries with some 132 bcm of natural gas by pipelines.[6] Eastern Europe consumes even higher percentages of Russian energy, with several countries being entirely dependent on Russian gas.

Russia's Revisionism

To Europeans energy dependence on Russia is unsettling. The Kremlin through its two state monopolies, Gazprom (for natural gas production and gas pipelines) and Transneft (for oil pipeline transit), has demonstrated its readiness to use hydrocarbon muscle and newfound wealth as a political tool in its relations with neighboring states, while reaching out to bolster anti-status quo energy exporters, such as Venezuela and Iran, endangering international security.[7] These concerns became even stronger with Russia's invasion into Georgia in summer 2008. On August 8 that year, as the Beijing Olympics started, Russia decided to rewrite the rules of post–World War II European security. It effectively repudiated the Helsinki Pact of 1975, which recognized sanctity of borders in Europe, and violated the sovereignty and territorial integrity of the NATO aspirant Georgia, whose troops had attacked South Ossetia, an integral part of Georgia, the day before. In the process, Russia also tore up its own peacekeeping mandate in South Ossetia and Abkhazia, and soon thereafter recognized declarations of independence by the secessionist, pro-Moscow regimes of South Ossetia and Abkhazia. The Georgian war brought Russia back to the Southern Caucasus in force, outflanking oil-rich Azerbaijan, and effecting control over the principal energy and rail arteries bringing natural resources from the Caspian Sea and Central Asia to the West, and consumer and industrial goods to the East. The Russian military practically destroyed the Georgian military, which protected the energy pipelines, and the Georgian port of Poti, the important Black Sea terminal of the East-West corridor. Russia proclaims that it wants to shift the global balance of power away from the United States, "Finlandize" Europe, revise global economic institutions, and return to highly competitive and often confrontational great power politics reminiscent of the 19th century. Such anti-status quo revisionism is the stuff of which world wars are made. Think of the Balkan wars that preceded World War I or Adolf Hitler's invasion of the Sudetenland in Czechoslovakia in 1938—with Europe's acquiescence.

Western analysts and officials accuse Moscow of hindering energy security through its politically motivated decision-making in the energy sphere and excessive emphasis on control of the energy markets and resources. However, as a major energy producer whose economy is heavily dependent on energy exports and who is vulnerable to fluctuations in global commodity prices, Russia views energy security in a very different way.

A View from the Kremlin

Russia has criticized Europe's approach to international energy security as limited to the energy importers' interests.[8] Under Russia's presidency in the Group of

Eight (G8), then President Vladimir Putin made energy security a central theme at his 2006 summit in St. Petersburg, presenting his own vision for global energy security. While talking of interdependence and dialogue, Russia insisted on providing demand guarantees for the producers, and sharing responsibilities and risks among energy suppliers, consumers, and transit states. Putin spoke of joint commitments on the energy arena with coordination and distribution of profits and risks to prevent energy conflicts.[9] This would not be a problem if Russia allowed minimally restricted access to its energy resources for international oil companies (IOCs). Unfortunately, since 2003 this hardly has been the case, as the state has not budged from monopolizing gas production or oil and gas pipeline transportation, and has tightened its grip over the quickly growing oil production sector by effectively expropriating YUKOS and buying Sibneft and Russneft oil companies. Russia's Energy Strategy, adopted in 2003, sets the framework for the county's energy policy. Thus, Russian energy security builds upon "protection of the country, its citizens, and economy from [external and domestic] threats to reliable energy supply," including geopolitical and energy market risk factors.[10] Moscow is set to promote a nondiscriminative regime for the Russian companies to access foreign energy markets and advance their participation in large international oil and gas projects. Energy factors are put in the center of Russian diplomacy. As President Putin noted in one of his speeches, "the place Russia takes in global energy cooperation directly impacts its current and future wellbeing."[11] With ample energy resources and an increasingly dominant position in the European market, Russia's hydrocarbon power is on the rise. Beyond that, Russian decision makers sense that consumer governments and companies, anxious to get coveted barrels and cubic meters, do not want to challenge the supplier's assertive foreign policy.

Russian strategy in the energy sector seeks to maximize its economic and geostrategic advantages as a major energy producer with vast hydrocarbon reserves. The Kremlin has advanced Russia's energy strategy through an array of security and economic policies, which aim at a common strategic goal. These policies create customer country dependency by locking in demand with energy importers and consolidating oil and gas supplies by signing long-term contracts with Russian and Central Asian state-owned or state-controlled energy producers and Russian state-owned pipeline monopolists.

Moscow prefers to deal with the EU member states separately rather than as a group. This way it can price-discriminate among its customers, charging each country as close to its full paying potential as possible.[12] The second prong of Russia's strategy is to lock in supply by consolidating control over strategic energy infrastructure throughout Europe and Eurasia. Russian state-owned or dominated companies use outright equity ownership or joint ventures to control supply, sale and distribution of natural gas. Moscow is steadily and inexorably buying up major national energy infrastructure companies, such as pipelines, refineries, electric grids, and ports. For example, in 2002, Russian state-owned Transneft attempted to gain control of the Mazeikiu Nafta refinery in Lithuania as well as the Ventspils oil export terminal in Latvia. When the two governments refused to sell their stakes to Transneft, Moscow sharply cut oil deliveries, forcing Ventspils to obtain oil by rail at a greater cost.[13] In Lithuania, Russian pursuit of the Mazeikiu refinery was cut short when the Polish company PKN Orlen bought the asset in 2006.[14] In May 2007, a top executive at Ventspils said, "the company was prepared to take on a strategic Russian investor."[15]

Gazprom, fully supported by the Kremlin, is pushing to gain greater access to European gas distribution networks. In 1998, Gazprom took over shares of Topenergy, a Bulgarian company dealing with commercial distribution of gas.[16] As of 2004, Gazprom had $2.6 billion invested in 23 big joint ventures, including Slovrusgaz in Slovakia (50% stake), Europol Gaz in Poland (48%), and Eesti Gaas in Estonia (30.6%).[17] In 2007–2008, Moscow has completed acquisitions of companies, pipelines, and storage facilities in Bulgaria, Serbia, Hungary, and Austria, in preparation for the roll-out of its South Stream project, which is aimed at derailing the competing Nabucco EU-backed gas supply project. Gazprom's acquisitions of strategic infrastructure companies in Georgia, Hungary, Ukraine, and Belarus, are followed by Rosneft, LUKoil and other actors. Russia aggressively tries to consolidate control over major European oil and gas transportation routes through multibillion-dollar transnational pipeline projects from the Baltic to the Black Sea, including Blue Stream and South Stream. The existing Soviet era pipeline system gives Russia strategic control over oil and gas flows throughout the former Soviet Union. The Putin era expansion of this system would add redundancy and bypass problematic transit countries, such as Ukraine and Georgia, while consolidating Russia's control over Europe's supply. The EU and the United States have supported several large projects to diversify energy supply routes to Europe. The Kremlin, however, is assertively opposing the Western-controlled pipeline projects directly linking Eurasian energy-producing countries to European markets. Moscow fulminated against the Baku-Tbilisi-Ceyhan (BTC) oil pipeline and the Baku-Erzurum gas pipeline, but despite the fact that a fully functional BTC could reduce Russia's current Caspian oil transit by one-third, it did not take action on the ground to prevent those projects from materializing.[18] With lessons learned from BTC, Gazprom and Transneft are consistently working to undermine the European Nabucco project, which aims to bring Caspian gas from Turkey via Bulgaria, Romania and Hungary to Austria and the heart of Europe, by diversifying their European network. Moscow is signing multibillion-dollar deals with individual European states to construct the following pipelines, as shown in Figure 7.1, under Russian control.

Nord Stream Pipeline

In 2003, German Chancellor Gerhard Schroeder and President Putin agreed to build the North Transgas (Nord Stream Pipeline) to supply Germany with Russian natural gas. This $16 billion pipeline will cross the Baltic Sea from Russian port Vyborg to German Greifswald, bypassing Ukraine, Belarus and Poland. Nord Stream is expected to become operational by 2010 with the initial annual capacity of 27.5 bcm of gas.[19] Russia's Gazprom owns 51 percent of the Nord Stream AG

Figure 7.1 Russia's Major Oil and Gas Pipelines in Europe and Eurasia
Source: Energy Information Administration

(formerly North European Gas Pipeline Company), created to build the pipeline's submarine section.[20] Constructing a seabed pipeline is, by some estimates, three times as expensive as an overland pipeline of comparable capacity, but the overland options have been rejected by the Kremlin and its German partners.[21] The Nord Stream Pipeline would further tie European energy security to the Kremlin and Russian gas deliveries, extend Gazprom's reach in Europe, and cultivate nontransparent practices in the EU markets.[22] Opposition to this pipeline among the Northern and Central European states is growing, however. First Estonia, and now Finland and Sweden have expressed concerns about the environmental safety of the pipeline and have pressured Gazprom to make a costly re-routing decision.[23] Sweden has opposed the construction of a compressor station near its Gotland Island out of security considerations.[24] Poland and the Baltic states have been outspoken about political motivation for the pipeline.[25] In addition, the German consumer associations are beginning to raise concerns about pricing arrangements of the Nord Stream project and their effect on energy prices for the end consumers.[26] Yet chances for its derailment remain slim.

Burgas-Alexandroupolis Pipeline

In March 2007, Russia signed an agreement with the EU members Bulgaria and Greece to construct an oil pipeline with the initial capacity of 35 million metric tons of oil a year, bypassing the Turkish-controlled and congested Bosporus Straits. The Burgas-Alexandroupolis oil pipeline will be the first Russian-controlled pipeline on EU territory.[27] Russian companies Transneft, Gazpromneft and Rosneft will control 51 percent of the pipeline. Bulgaria and Greece will control the rest.[28] Russia is also developing plans to build a second Bosporus oil bypass from a Turkish port on the Black Sea (such as Samsun or Trabzon) to the Mediterranean, possibly the oil port of Ceyhan.

Prikaspiisky Pipeline

At a May 2007 summit in the Turkmen port city of Turkmenbashi, Russia, Turkmenistan and Kazakhstan reached a preliminary agreement to upgrade the Prikaspiisky gas pipeline to carry gas from Turkmenistan, through Kazakhstan, to Russia.[29] According to the Russian estimates, the expansion would allow the pipeline to carry 10 bcm per year by 2009, and up to 30 bcm per year by 2015, up from 0.4 bcm of gas in 2006, thus further tying the Caspian gas producers to Russia for their access to the Western markets. In November 2007, Russia agreed to pay a higher price for the Turkmen gas supplies—removing a price disagreement that analysts believed was a major obstacle to the deal.[30] On December 20, 2007, a trilateral agreement was signed in the Kremlin between Russia, Kazakhstan and Turkmenistan on the construction of the Caspian Coastal gas pipeline (from Turkmenistan through Kazakhstan to Russia), which is expected to increase annual exports of Turkmen gas to Russia to 20 bcm.[31] The Prikaspiisky expansion thwarts the plans for the U.S.-and EU-backed Trans-Caspian gas pipeline (TCP) that would have delivered Turkmen and possibly Kazakhstani gas across the Caspian Sea via Nabucco and would have enabled Central Asian exporters to circumvent Russian-controlled routes.[32]

Blue Stream and South Stream Pipelines

The Blue Stream gas pipeline from Russia's North Caucasus coast across the Black Sea to Turkey's Durusu terminal, near the port-city of Samsun, also competes with the TCP project. By 2010, Blue Stream is expected to be operating at full capacity, delivering 16 bcm of Russian gas per year. The total length of the pipeline is 758 miles. Russia's land section is 233 miles long; the offshore section is 247 miles long; Turkey's land section is 277 miles up to Ankara. In an attempt to enter the Italian energy market, in June 2007, Russia's Gazprom and Italy's ENI signed a memorandum of understanding to build the South Stream gas pipeline from Russia to Italy. This pipeline, with planned capacity of 30 bcm a year, would run across the Black Sea from Russia to Bulgaria, bypassing both Ukraine and Turkey. From Bulgaria, the pipeline may either run southwest via Greece and the Adriatic to southern Italy, or northwest via Serbia, Hungary (or Austria), and Slovenia to northern Italy. The South Stream pipeline will increase the EU's dependence on Russian energy supplies. It rivals the proposed extension of the EU-backed Baku-Erzurum gas pipeline via Turkey either to connect to Nabucco pipeline or continue to Greece and Italy. Most critically, South Stream competes directly with the EU and U.S.-backed Nabucco project. Nabucco's chances are shrinking as Gazprom is building up its influence in Europe and reaching agreements on alternative routes.

Controlling Eurasia's Energy

Another tenet of Russia's energy security strategy is the consolidation of control over oil and gas supplies throughout Eurasia. Though possessing the world's largest gas reserves, Russia seeks to acquire a significant share of exported natural gas from Central Asia and elsewhere, in order to be able to dictate prices—especially in Europe. The Kremlin also says that it is interested in the long-term availability of Central Asian energy so that it can "preserve Russia's northern gas fields for next generations, avoid boosting investment in their development, and decrease the pressure on the markets presenting strategic interests for Russia itself."[33] Since 2002, Moscow has reached long-term exploration and supply deals with Kazakhstan and Uzbekistan to preempt them from reaching independent exporting arrangements with the West.[34]

Turkmenistan is an ace in Russia's Eurasian gas supply deck of cards and a good example of such policy. Today, Turkmenistan supplies the bulk of Russia's Central Asian gas, including most of the gas sold to Ukraine. Russia buys up to 30 bcm of Turkmen gas a year compared to Russia's total 2006 exports to Europe of some 132 bcm. Access to Turkmen gas is strategically important for Russia to be able to meet its international commitments. Out of similar considerations, in May 2006 Gazprom agreed to pay a higher price ($140/tcm) for gas supplies from Kazakhstan. A Russian energy analyst commented that "fair distribution" of incomes from Central Asian gas exports is vital for preserving the post-Soviet gas transportation system, which opens the way to creating a new "gas OPEC."[35]

In July 2006, when Russia was hosting the G8 summit, Vladimir Putin and Kazakh president Nursultan Nazarbayev, his personal guest, created a joint venture to process and export natural gas from the Karachaganak oil field in Kazakhstan. This took cooperation between the two regional heavyweights to a new level. At the August 2007 summit of the Shanghai Cooperation Organization (SCO), the presidents of Kazakhstan and Russia called for establishing an "Asian energy club" to extend energy ties between the member-states, including the creation of unified energy infrastructure to serve as a basis for a common SCO energy market.[36] If successfully launched, such a body would further increase Russia's geopolitical role as the linchpin of energy supply in Europe and Eurasia.

Uzbekistan remains an important source of gas for Russia, supplying up to 10 bcm of gas a year.[37] In January 2007, a Gazprom subsidiary started exploration and development on several gas deposits in northwestern Uzbekistan. An agreement entails a five-year exploration license for the Russian company and its exclusive right to export the gas.[38] A year earlier, Putin and Uzbek President Islam Karimov signed a deal awarding exploration and development rights to Gazprom for 35 years.[39] These developments cement Russian hegemony over Central Asia's energy ties with the outside world, overturn Western companies' leadership in the Caspian energy developments that characterized the 1990s, and defeat the EU's major goal to diversify its oil and gas imports.

Internal Consolidation

The Russian oil and gas sector is notorious for easing domestic and foreign corporations out of majority equity stakes in Russian mega-projects and for consolidating domestic ownership by the government-controlled entities. The two Russian energy national champions—vertically integrated state-owned or controlled global companies capable of competing with foreign corporations—are headed by senior officials close to Vladimir Putin. Putin's successor as president, Dmitry Medvedev, is the ex-officio chairman of Gazprom. President Putin confidante and Deputy Chief of Staff Igor Sechin chairs the board of Rosneft, Russia's largest state-run oil company, which took over the bulk of YUKOS assets. This management scheme ensures that Gazprom and Rosneft are reliable foreign policy arms for the Kremlin. Moscow is pushing major international energy corporations out of Russia or at least forcing them to give up their majority stakes in lucrative projects. The new investment law draft limits foreign participation in energy exploration projects to minority stakes—25 percent in strategic oil and gas fields, and 49 percent in other energy projects. Limited in their rights to own exploration licenses, the transnational corporations are reduced in many cases to operator or technical service provider roles. In June 2007, First Deputy Prime Minister Sergey Ivanov said that foreign companies "will never operate" Russia's major fields again.[40]

Although leading officials, including Mr. Medvedev, have explicitly rejected state capitalism as a model for Russia, the Kremlin is consolidating its ownership in the energy sector. Putin envisages the state not as the great re-nationalizer, but the biggest shareholder in a newly privatized society.[41] Return of strategic assets under state control is often presented to the public as restoration of national property illicitly acquired in the mid-1990s by corrupt and politically manipulative oligarchs at deeply discounted prices. This, however, certainly was the case with the state-owned Rosneft's 2004 murky acquisition of Yuganskneftegaz, the key production unit of forcibly bankrupted YUKOS. The Kremlin dismantled and amalgamated the YUKOS oil-producing company into its state-owned flagship after bankrupting the company through dubious and grossly inflated tax bills in 2003 after the company got a clean bill of health by tax authorities. Since then, the YUKOS affair has become a byword for Russia's judicial arbitrariness and politically motivated justice. The Kremlin's push for asset consolidation has touched the major energy companies working in Russia. Royal Dutch Shell has been pushed out of a major Russian energy project. Under pressure from the Kremlin for alleged environmental breaches, Shell announced in 2006 the sale of its majority stake in Sakhalin-2 oil and gas fields, off Sakhalin Island in Russia's Far East, to Gazprom.[42] While announcing the entry of Gazprom into the project, Putin said that the threats by the government's environmental agency to take legal action over the alleged ecological breaches are likely to be resolved, demonstrating once again that Russia's state environmental regulator can be used by the Kremlin as a tool of exerting pressure on the international energy companies working in Russia.[43] Later, British Petroleum was evicted from the lucrative Kovykta gas field in eastern Siberia after the sale of its 62.9 percent stake to Gazprom in June 2007. TNK-BP joint venture was unable to meet the production quotas prescribed by the Kremlin since Gazprom had refused to develop any export pipelines. After officials threatened to cancel the license, and the courts refused to intervene, BP-TNK agreed to sell its Kovykta stake to Gazprom at a fraction of its market value.[44] Later on, in 2007–2008, TNK-BP joint venture, with its unique 50–50 control between the Russian and British partners almost fell apart. This was due to pressure by the Russian partners, known as Alfa Access Renova (AAR) to oust the BP-appointed CEO and gain more control of the company. Many experts suspected that the ultimate goal was to force the British to sell to AAR or to a Russian state-owned oil company; however, falling oil prices and the precipitous Russian stock market slide of 40 percent from May to August 2008 may have put pressure on the Russian partners to settle. A compromise, rare in the Russian oil sector, was achieved in early September 2008, and for now, the joint venture is continuing.

The Kremlin-affiliated structures are squeezing independent energy companies to get hold of their assets. In a ground-breaking interview to *Kommersant,* Oleg Shvartsman, head of the Finansgroup financial-industrial group close to the *siloviki* (security services leaders) faction, revealed a scheme of pressuring private companies that the Kremlin finds insufficiently accountable to the state.[45] Among the group's key assets is the Russian Oil Group that appeared as a joint activity with Rosneft, TNK, and Lukoil. After an initial push for trading alliances, Finansgroup began to acquire small and medium-sized oil-refineries, using illicit activities to bring down corporate values prior to the acquisition.[46] Finansgroup is also managing the so-called Social Investments Corporation to exercise what Shvartsman called the "velvet re-privatization" of strategic assets based on various voluntary and coercive market instruments of asset absorption. Shvartsman said the group enjoys the full support of the Russian power ministries.[47]

Domestic consolidation of Russian oil and gas industry under the Kremlin's direct ownership or control increases Moscow's options in the continued use of energy as its foreign policy tool. These major takeovers and evictions further limit the opportunities for foreign investment and technology transfer to the Russian energy sector and beyond it. They signal the return of statist economic policies, widespread corruption, and a major departure from market liberalization.

A Gas OPEC?

Russia is stealthily and steadily developing an international cartel to control the price and output of gas. A new gas OPEC is emerging based on the Gas Exporting Countries' Forum (GECF), created in 2001. In addition to Russia, this cartel is supposed to include the world's major gas producers in Latin America and the Middle East. The group members plan to "reach strategic understandings" on export volumes, production and delivery schedules, and pipeline construction. They also speak of joint exploration and development of gas fields. To continue their work, the participating states plan to create a permanent secretariat. Despite protestations to the contrary, this looks like a cartel in the making.

Russia is steadfastly putting the components of a gas cartel into place without making any official proclamations. Russia's Energy Strategy document briefly mentioned Moscow's aim to negotiate "just prices for energy resources" with other producing states.[48] During his February 2007 visit to Qatar, President Putin called the gas OPEC "an interesting idea."[49] In Doha, Russia initiated the creation of a High Level Group to "research" gas pricing models, and an unnamed "high ranking member of the Russian delegation" told *RIA Novosti* that "as the gas market undergoes globalization, such an organization, a gas cartel, will appear and is necessary."[50]

The GECF members agreed to discuss dividing up the consumer markets between them, particularly in Europe, where Russia and Algeria are major players. The EU's dependence on such a cartel will diminish its ability to deal bilaterally with gas exporting countries bypassing Russia, challenge its energy liberalization and gas deregulation policy, and perhaps have dire foreign policy consequences. The Kremlin will gain more leverage in Europe where Russia's direct national interests range from preventing NATO expansion and deployment of ABM defenses in Poland and the Czech Republic, to fostering division between the EU and the United States, and regaining more comprehensive control over the post-Soviet space.

Arctic Energy Rush

If the development of a gas cartel has been stealthy, Russia's August 2007 flag-planting on the Arctic seabed under the North Pole has been overt and audacious. Moscow is claiming a sector of the energy-rich Arctic continental shelf the size of France, Germany and Italy combined. Vladimir Putin weighed in during a speech on a Russian nuclear-powered icebreaker in early 2007, urging greater efforts to secure Russia's "strategic, economic, scientific and defense interests" in the Arctic.[51] Moscow's moves are dictated by energy-driven geopolitics and geo-economics. Geologists believe the Arctic Ocean's seabed may contain nearly 25 percent of the world's hydrocarbon deposits. It is also rich in diamonds, and precious ferrous and non-ferrous metals.[52] As the ice cap melts and shrinks, these resources will become more accessible and a new sea passage along the northern coast of Eurasia may provide a cheaper transportation route. From a geopolitical perspective, the exploration of polar petroleum reserves may be the kind of opportunity that allows Russia to become what then President Putin termed "an energy superpower." Russia seeks to expand its continental shelf beyond the 200-mile economic zone through the mechanism provided by the UN Commission on the Limits of the Continental Shelf under the 1982 U.N. Law of the Sea Convention (UNCLOS), to which Russia is a party. Moscow claims that two underwater mountain ridges jutting into the Arctic Ocean from the Russian continental shelf—the Lomonosov Ridge and the Mendeleev Ridge—are extensions of the Eurasian landmass.[53] Russia's first claim with the UN, submitted in 2001, has failed due to insufficient evidence. After a recent scientific expedition to the Arctic, Russia is preparing to resubmit its claim with new arguments. The Russian media has applauded the "Arctic heroes" and talked of "the start of a new distribution of the world."[54] International experts, however, doubt that the ridges extend far enough to justify Moscow's claims. Russia's flag-planting has alarmed other Nordic states with territories inside the Arctic Circle—Canada, Denmark, Norway and the United States—who also have their eye on the vast hydrocarbon deposits under the Arctic seabed and have potential territorial claims in the region.[55] Thus, the Kremlin has triggered a strategic race for the Arctic and one more subject of geopolitical and energy security contention between Russia and the West. The energy-rich Arctic is too valuable of an asset to be surrendered to Russia at a time when global energy demand is growing and supply remains limited and unreliable.

Conclusion

Russia is pursuing a comprehensive energy strategy, which masterfully integrates geopolitics and geo-economics. Its assertive Cold War-style posture is a growing concern for Brussels as well as for Washington. For Europeans, the concerns stem not only from Russia's monopolistic behavior but also because of the opaqueness regarding its supply capabilities. European demand for Russian energy is projected to grow by leaps and bounds. According to the 2006 European Energy and Transport Report, in 2030 the EU will consume 15 percent more energy than it did in 2000.[56] Natural gas demand is projected to grow considerably through 2030 (by some 140 mtoe compared to the 2000 level.)[57] At the same time, Europe is experiencing a steep decline in its indigenous energy production. Consequently, by 2030 Europe will rely on imports for two-thirds of its overall energy needs. Gas import dependency is projected to rise from some 50 percent today to 84 percent in 2030.[58] This begs the question whether Russia will be able to satisfy this growing energy demand and meet its international commitments. In its public pronunciations, Russia says it expects its natural gas exports to increase from 185 bcm in 2002 to 275–280 bcm by 2020.[59] However, many experts doubt Russia's capability to ensure the needed energy supply. Leonid Fedun, the vice-president of LUKoil, Russia's largest independent oil company, said he believed that Russia's oil production in 2007 was the highest he would see "in his lifetime."[60] When it comes to gas the uncertainty is even greater. The output of Gazprom's three giant fields in West Siberia, which account for three-quarters of its production, is declining at a rate of 6 to 7 percent a year, and the output from a gas field brought online in 2001 has already peaked.[61] Gazprom's latest decision to develop a field in the Arctic (Yamal peninsula) will take years. Exploration of new deposits has been underinvested since the 1990s, causing steep decline in oil and gas reproduction rates. Russia's official statistics indicate that the extraction of mineral resources in 2006 has grown by as little as 2.3 percent in comparison to 2005, when the World Bank reported a mere 1.3 percent increase (compare this to 6.8 growth in 2004, and 8.7 percent in 2003.)[62] Availability of Central Asian gas, which makes up a lion's share of total gas exports from Russia, is critical for Gazprom's ability to maintain its international commitments. Gazprom is also behind when it comes to investment in new fields. Many hopes are connected with the exploration of Shtokman gas field, located over 300 miles offshore in the Barents Sea with local sea depths exceeding 300 meters.[63] After many delays, Gazprom reconsidered its earlier decision to go it alone and in July 2007 signed an agreement with France's Total and in October 2007 with Norway's Statoil Hydro on the first phase of Shtokman development.[64] However, the agreement gives Total and Statoil Hyrdro no ownership rights to the gas. Gazprom, through its 100 percent-owned subsidiary Sevmorneftegaz, remains the full owner of the Shtokman development license and will be the full owner and sole exporter of products.[65] Gazprom's choice of partners was politically motivated. First, U.S. companies were kept out despite earlier promises to include Chevron and possibly Conoco Phillips. Second, Europe is a principal part of Russia's geopolitical energy game. While Norway's Statoil Hyrdro has vast experience drilling off shore in the northern longitude, Total is cash-rich but has no experience working in Arctic conditions.[66]

Russia's obsolete energy infrastructure raises additional concerns. Deterioration of Soviet-era major export pipelines is close to critical levels. According to Gazprom's own data, almost 14 percent of the pipelines have served for over 33 years and must be fully renovated, with an additional 20 percent of the pipes being over 20 years old.[67] EU's high representative for common foreign and security policy Javier Solana said in 2006 that "due to Russia's outdated oil and gas pipelines, the equivalent of a quarter of Russia's total gas exports to Europe was being lost in transport."[68] Russia will need tens of billions of dollars to bring the gas transit infrastructure up to speed. Meanwhile, its own energy consumption is growing. Fueled by cheap subsidized domestic gas the Russian economy is extremely energy intensive, with sectors such as aluminum and pet-rochemicals enjoying an undue advantage. The ratio of domestic energy consumption to GDP in Russia is 2.3 times above the world average, and 3.1 times higher than the EU average.[69] Thus, Russia is subsidizing its exports through cheap energy, which may partially explain its reluctance to join WTO and sign the Energy Charter. In addition, seasonal fuel consumption hikes may cause supply interruptions. The 2006 long and intense cold wave increased Russian domestic gas demand and strained Gazprom's delivery capability.

European energy supply may also suffer from Russia's growing commitment to Asian markets. By 2020, Russia expects to sell 30 percent of its oil and 15 percent of its natural gas to Asia. To achieve this ambitious target, Russia needs to invest in exploration of East Siberian energy deposits and build an export pipeline to Asia. Currently, Russia has built less than a half of the projected oil pipeline to Nakhodka on the Pacific Coast, and has not started building a long-promised gas pipeline to China. Both projects will be long and costly. Wary of the threats to its energy supply, the EU has been working to engage Russia in a more reliable energy cooperation framework based on the Energy Charter, designed to promote energy security through greater openness and competitiveness of the energy markets, while respecting the principles of sovereignty over energy resources. Compliance with the Charter would increase Moscow's predictability and transparency in energy markets and attract foreign investments. In particular, Russia would have to offer foreign investors fair access to its oil and gas deposits and export pipelines.[70] Unfortunately, despite its assurances of being a responsible and reliable partner in energy matters, Russia refuses to ratify the Energy Charter. For Russia, the Charter's key negative aspect is its provision allowing open access of third parties to Russian deposits and energy transit facilities. Russian critics say this would imply a loss of sovereignty in Russia's strategic energy industry. The Kremlin could consider granting European companies broader access to Russia's energy assets in exchange for Russian companies getting access to equally valuable assets in European gas transportation and distribution networks.

However, Moscow's ambitions may suffer a blow as Europe forges ahead with its energy liberalization policy. The regulations introduced in July 2007 keep energy-producing companies from controlling distribution networks in Europe. Gazprom, now banned from acquiring European gas-delivery networks, has harshly criticized this proposal as "the most absurd idea in the history of the world economy."[71] Further, the European Commission included a "reciprocity clause" informally dubbed as a "Gazprom clause" in its September 2007 energy liberalization proposals. This provision would prevent foreign companies from acquiring energy assets in Europe unless their home countries reciprocate.[72] In October 2007, the EU and Russia agreed to set up a joint panel to assess the implications of the new energy policy that drew harsh criticism from Moscow.[73] In spite of the arguments, the two sides remain interdependent, as Russia will need European technological and financial support to fully exploit its vast resources.

From an American perspective, growing dependence of European energy supply and infrastructure on monopolistic Russia is a negative long-term geopolitical trend. But there are other issues. Despite being the world's largest energy consumer, the United States has limited energy relations with Russia. In 2002–2003 Russia refused to construct projects dedicated to oil exports to the United States, such as the Murmansk pipeline, suggested by the then-privately held YUKOS, LUKoil and Sibneft oil companies. Moscow has also derailed attempts by U.S. oil majors to buy a significant noncontrolling stake in a large private Russian company such as YUKOS. While both countries can afford not to collaborate on the energy front, they cannot afford not to collaborate on major foreign policy matters. In this, Russia's behavior has been a source of frustration in Washington. Russia is becoming an assertive anti-status quo power that challenges the U.S. and its allies on many fronts, especially in territory of the former Soviet Union, the Balkans and the Middle East. This is both because of ample funding available to finance a more ambitious foreign policy due to energy revenue and general economic prosperity, and because of its use of energy as a foreign policy tool. Washington understands that Russian strategic goals are to prevent countries around its borders from becoming pro-American and to increase control over the transportation of Russia hydrocarbons through the territory of its neighbors, as well as to control export of the neighbors' oil and gas by directing their flow via the Russian pipeline system. By locating pipelines and gas storage facilities in Austria, Hungary, Bulgaria, Greece and Turkey, Russia connects them to Moscow by the ties that bind. Russia is also active in pushing the United States out of Central Asia and excluding it from the SCO's energy club. The United States, for its part, supports diversification of energy transportation routes in Eurasia. From the Russian perspective, the U.S. and EU-backed pursuit of diversified energy sources and transportation routes is unfriendly towards Russia, politically motivated, economically unfeasible and environmentally damaging. The Kremlin is likely to use Europe's dependence to insert wedges in transatlantic relations and use its influence to promote an anti-American foreign policy agenda. In this situation, the maneuvering space for America's allies in Europe will be significantly limited as they face tough choices between cost and stability of energy supply, on one hand, and siding with the United States on some key issues, on the other hand.

In sum, the world economies will benefit from greater stability, security, and the rule of law in energy-exporting states to ensure that oil and gas remain readily available, ample, affordable, and safe. The Kremlin, on the other hand, views energy as a tool of assertive foreign policy and uses it broadly, often without much concern for diplomatic niceties. If current trends prevail, the Kremlin might translate energy monopoly into untenable foreign and security policy influence in Europe. In particular, Russia is seeking recognition of its predominant role in the post-Soviet space and Eastern Europe. This will affect the geopolitical issues important for the West, such as NATO expansion, ballistic missile defense, the status of Kosovo, and influence in the post-Soviet space. Furthermore, Moscow is seeking to re-engage in a centuries-old balance-of-power game in the Middle

East, from Algeria, where it attempted a gas condominium, to Syria, where it is rebuilding naval bases in Tartus and Ladakiye, to Iran and India.[74] During diplomatic crises over the Iranian nuclear enrichment program, Moscow provided Tehran ample diplomatic cover in the United Nations and elsewhere, as well as expanded arms supplies.

To increase their energy diversification, major consumers of Russian oil and gas should work to support alternative transit lines throughout Europe and Eurasia to diversify their supply routes. It is vital for EU members to come up with a joint position on energy security despite the splits on policy toward Russia in the EU apparatus and among national chanceries and foreign ministries. It is also necessary to insist that Russia lives up to its commitments to uphold and implement the rule of law, without which its economic development and civil liberties will remain in limbo. Finally, it is essential that energy importers join their effort in finding and implementing innovative ways to discourage Russia from using politically-motivated pricing schemes and monopolistic practices. Otherwise, Russia will apply the ancient Roman principle—*divide et impera*—to 21st century energy geopolitics.

Notes

1. BP, "BP Statistical Review of World Energy 2007," June 2007, 6, 20, 22, at www. bp.com/productlanding.do?categoryId=6848&contentId=7033471; estimates from *BP Statistical Review* and *Oil & Gas Journal*, reported in U.S. Department of Energy, Energy Information Administration, "World Proved Reserves of Oil and Natural Gas, Most Recent Estimates," January 9, 2007, www.eia.doe.gov/emeu/international/reserves.html.

2. Ibid.

3. U.S. Department of Energy, Energy Information Administration, "Russia," *Country Analysis Brief,* April 4,2007, www.eia.doe.gov/emeu/cabs/Russia/pdf.pdf.

4. Ibid., 11–12, 27–28, 41.

5. Ibid., 20.

6. Ibid., 30.

7. Ariel Cohen, "How to Confront Russia's Anti-American Foreign Policy," Heritage Foundation *Backgrounder* #2048, June 27, 2007, http://www.heritage.org/Research/Russia andEurasia/upload/bg_2048.pdf.

8. The World Bank estimated that in 2005 energy sales generated 61 percent of Russia's export revenues. The World Bank, "Data and Statistics for the Russian Federation: Latest Macroeconomic Indicators," http://siteresources.worldbank.org/INTRUSSIANFEDE RATION/Resources/macromay2006.pdf.

9. Nina Kulikova, "Voprosy energeticheskoy bezopasnosti—pozitsiya Rossii [The Issues of Energy Security—Russia's Position]," *RIA Novosti,* September 1, 2006, http://www. rian.ru/analytics/20060901/53406077.html.

10. "Energy Strategy of the Russian Federation for the Period till 2020," http://www. minprom.gov.ru/docs/strateg/1.

11. V. Salygin, "Globalnaya energeticheskaya bezopasnost' i vneshnyaya energeticheskaya politika Rossii [Global Energy Security and Russia's Foreign Energy Policy]," *Neftegaz,* June 28, 2007, http://www.neftegaz.ru/analit/reviews.php?id=548.

12. Ariel Cohen, "The North European Gas Pipeline Threatens Europe's Energy Security," Heritage Foundation *Backgrounder* #1980, October 26, 2006, http://www.heritage.org/Research/Europe/upload/bg_1980.pdf; Judy Dempsey, "Gazprom plans to re-route controversial European pipeline," *International Herald Tribune*, August 23, 2007.

13. Judy Dempsey, "Poland supports purchase of refinery," *International Herald Tribune*, October 31, 2006.

14. "PKN Orlen, Mazeikiu Nafta to complete deal in Nov.," *RIA Novosti*, September 27, 2006, http://en.rian.ru/world/20060927/54311008.html.

15. "Ventspils Nafta ready to cooperate with Russia," *The Baltic Times*, May 2, 2007, http://www.baltictimes.com/news/articles/17809.

16. Judy Dempsey, "Russia casts energy web over East Europe," *International Herald Tribune*, October 1, 2004, http://www.iht.com/articles/2004/10/01/energy_ed3_.php.

17. Ibid.

18. Yuriy Solozobov, "Energeticheskaya bezopasnost': ponyatie po interesam [Energy Security: Interests Based Concept]," *Promyshlennye Vedomosti*, no. 7–8, August 2006, http://www.promved.ru/articles/article.phtml?id=882&nomer=32.

19. Nord Stream AG, "Nord Stream: The new gas supply route to Europe," Press-Release, July 20, 2007, http://www.nord-stream.com/uploads/media/Nord_Stream_Press_Release_Background_info_eng.pdf; "Company Structure," http://www.nord-stream.com/company.html?&L=0.

20. Ibid.

21. "Baltic Pipeline Poses Environmental Threat—Estonian Premier," *RIA Novosti*, March 11, 2005; Vladimir Socor, "Questions Multiply on the Baltic Seabed Pipeline Project Viability," Jamestown Foundation, *Eurasia Daily Monitor*, April 23, 2007, www.jamestown.org/edm/article.php?article_id=2372117.

22. Ibid., and Cohen, "The North European Gas Pipeline."

23. Dempsey, "Gazprom Plans to Re-Route Controversial European Pipeline," and "Finland Wants Environmental Study of Nord Stream Gas Pipeline," *RIA Novosti*, November 12, 2007.

24. "Poland Bent North the Gas Pipeline of Russia," *Kommersant*, August 22, 2007.

25. "We Are Very Vigilant When it Comes to the Polish–German Relationship: Spiegel's Interview with Poland's Kaczynski," *Der Spiegel*, March 8, 2006.

26. Socor, "Questions Multiply on the Baltic Seabed Pipeline Project Viability."

27. "A Bear at the Throat; Europe's Risky Dependence on Russian Gas," *Economist*, April 12, 2007.

28. "Russia, Bulgaria, Greece Sign Balkan Pipeline Deal," *RIA Novosti*, March 15, 2007, http://en.rian.ru/russia/20070315/62048590.html.

29. "Russia Clinches Gas Pipeline Deal," *BBC News*, May 12, 2007, http://news.bbc.co.uk/2/hi/asia-pacific/6649169.stm.

30. Sergei Blagov, "Russia Renews Interest in CIS, Agrees to New Price Deal for Turkmen Gas," *Eurasia Insight*, November 27, 2007, http://www.eurasianet.org/departments/insight/articles/eav112707.shtml.

31. Lucian Kim, "Putin Secures New Gas Pipeline, Undermining U.S. Plan, http://www.bloomberg.com/apps/news?pid=20601087&sid=aZAoqlSorbFA&refer=home.

32. Sergei Blagov, "Russia Celebrates its Central Asian Energy Coup," *Eurasianet*, May 16, 2007.

33. "Energy Strategy of the Russian Federation for the Period till 2020," 53.

34. "Turkmenistan Raises Gas Prices by 50 Percent, Russia Pays," *Asia News,* August 2006, http://www.asianews.it/index.php?l=en&art=7152.

35. Solozobov, "Energeticheskaya bezopasnost': ponyatie po interesam."

36. Peter Fedynsky, "Shanghai Cooperation Organization Seeks to Expand Energy and Security Influence," *Voice of America,* August 16, 2007.

37. "Turkmenistan Raises Gas Prices by 50 Percent, Russia Pays."

38. Vladimir Socor, "Uzbek Gas Output, Export Set to Grow under Russian Monopoly Control," Jamestown Foundation *Eurasia Daily Monitor,* February 22, 2007.

39. Socor, "Caspian Gas and European Energy Security."

40. Torrey Clark and Lucian Kim, "Gazprom Gains BP Gas Field as Putin Tightens Control," *Bloomberg,* June 22, 2007.

41. Nick Paton Walsh, "Meet the Chief Exec of Kremlin Inc.," *The Guardian,* July 6, 2005.

42. Andrew Kramer, "Shell Cedes Control of Sakhalin-2 to Gazprom," *International Herald Tribune,* December 21, 2006.

43. "Gazprom Grabs Sakhalin Gas Stake," *BBC News,* December 21, 2006.

44. "Russian Arm Twisting: Another Energy Firm Backs Down," *The Economist,* June 22, 2007.

45. "Partiyu dlya nas olitsetvoryaet silovoy blok, kotoryy vozglavlyaet Igor Ivanovich Sechin [The Party is embodied for us in the power bloc led by Igor I. Sechin]," *Kommersant,* November 30, 2007, http://www.kommersant.ru/daily.aspx?date=20071130http://www.kommersant.ru/doc.aspx?DocsID=831089.

46. Jonas Bernstein, "Finansgroup: How Russia's Siloviki Do Business," Jamestown Foundation *Eurasia Daily Monitor,* November 30, 2007, www.jamestown.org.

47. "Partiyu dlya nas olitsetvoryaet silovoy blok, kotoryy vozglavlyaet Igor Ivanovich Sechin," http://www.kommersant.ru/daily.aspx?date=20071130.

48. "Energy Strategy of the Russian Federation for the Period till 2020."

49. Ariel Cohen, "Gas OPEC: A stealthy cartel emerges," *The European Journal* (print edition), 14, no. 5, May/June 2007, 15.

50. Ibid.

51. Ariel Cohen, "Russia's Race for the Arctic," Heritage Foundation *WebMemo* No. 1582, August 6, 2007, http://www.heritage.org/Research/RussiaandEurasia/upload/wm_1582.pdf.

52. Alexander Gabuev, "*Print* | Cold War Goes North: Russia and the West begin the race for the Arctic Region," *Kommersant,* August 4, 2007.

53. "Russia: Polar Expedition Means 'Very Little' For Territorial Claims," RFE/RL, August 3, 2007.

54. "Russia Greets Flag Team 'Heroes' as the World Condemns Arctic Stunt," *The Times,* August 4, 2007.

55. "The Hunt for Red Gas: Putin Triggers Arctic Energy Rush to the North Pole," *The European Weekly,* no. 741, August 4, 2007.

56. European Commission, Directorate-General for Energy and Transport, "European Energy and Transport: Trends to 2030—update 2005," 2006.

57. Ibid.

58. Ibid.

59. "Energy Strategy of the Russian Federation for the Period till 2020."

60. "Fears Emerge over Russia's Oil Output," *Financial Times,* April 14, 2008.

61. "A Bear at the Throat."

62. The World Bank, "Data and statistics for the Russian Federation: latest macroeconomic indicators," June 2006, http://siteresources.worldbank.org/INTRUSSIANFEDERA-TION/Resources/macromay2006.pdf; Federal Statistics Committee, "Production indicators by the types of economic activity," http://www.gks.ru/free_doc/2007/b07_11/14-03.htm.

63. Gazprom JSC, "Shtokman Project," http://www.gazprom.com/eng/articles/article 21712.shtml.

64. "Statoil Hydro to Develop Shtokman field," *New Europe,* Issue 753, October 25, 2007, http://www.neurope.eu/articles/79155.php.

65. Vladimir Socor, "The Shtokman Gas Deal: an Initial Assessment of Its Implications," Jamestown Foundation, *Eurasia Daily Monitor,* July 17, 2007, http://jamestown.org/edm/article.php?article_id=2372294.

66. Marina Pustilnik, "LNG Politics," *Moscow News,* July 19, 2007, http://mnweekly.ru/business/20070719/55262808.html.

67. Solozobov, "Energeticheskaya bezopasnost': ponyatie po interesam."

68. "Energy Disputes Set Stage for Difficult EU-Russia Summit in Helsinki," *International Herald Tribune,* November 22, 2006.

69. "Energy Strategy of the Russian Federation for the Period till 2020."

70. Associated Press, "Energy Disputes."

71. "A Bear at the Throat."

72. "EU, Russia to Explore 'Reciprocity' in Energy Trade," *Euractiv,* October 17, 2007.

73. Ahto Lobjakas, "Russia Weighs in on EU's Tough New Energy Policy," *RFE/RL,* October 17, 2007.

74. Ariel Cohen, "Putin's Middle East Visit: Russia is Back," The Heritage Foundation *Web Memo,* March 5, 2007, http://www.heritage.org/Research/RussiaandEurasia/wm1382.cfm.

CHAPTER 8

Energy Security in the Caspian Basin

Ariel Cohen

After the collapse of the Soviet Union in 1991, Caspian gas and oil became an attractive option as instability in the Middle East underscored the importance of supply diversification and overall energy security as a key portion of strategic national security.

The Caspian littoral states are landlocked and surrounded by two great powers and one aspiring regional power: Russia, China and Iran. They are also in relative proximity to the European Union and NATO borders. The Caspian region is surrounded by four nations (Russia, China, India, and Pakistan) with nuclear capabilities. A fifth neighbor, Iran, may be well on its way to achieving its nuclear ambitions as well. Afghanistan remains a regional source of instability, divided by its ongoing conflict and threatening overall regional stability with the spread of Islamic extremism and an influx of refugees into poor, fragile states such as Tajikistan, which already struggles to enable a minimal living standard for its current population. The desire to counter-balance Moscow's growing influence, the global war on terror, and exploitative energy contracts with Russia has led to increased Western interest and presence in the region, thus causing additional foreign interests to influence the agendas of the Caspian governments. This presence is not welcomed by Beijing and Moscow, who, like the United States and EU, have a vested interest in the region's energy resources. The unique and precarious location demands that the Caspian states balance their foreign and security priorities, including energy security, with the strategic agendas of Beijing, Moscow, Brussels and Washington. The four external players all have somewhat conflicting agendas and are competing for regional influence, access to energy and control of its transit, with various forms of carrots and sticks. Thus, the Caspian states must carefully weigh their ties with each of the four external competitors, as well as the extensive consequences of their new energy policies in the ongoing geostrategic tug-of-war.[1]

In many ways, the international competition centered around the Caspian Basin has proven harmful to regional growth, development and stability. It is true that the Caspian littoral states share the common threat of radical Islamic terrorism with China, Russia and the United States. However, competing geopolitical and geoeconomic objectives have debilitated potential international cooperation and prevented formulation of consistent regional policies working towards growth and stability in the Caspian basin. In terms of economic benefits resulting from influence in the Caspian, Washington, Brussels, Moscow and Beijing tend to view the regional situation as a zero-sum game; all four players are seeking to gain the largest piece of the resource pie possible. While this competition has brought investment, economic and institutional development to some countries, others have experienced cool diplomatic relations with regional powers, particularly Russia, thus slowing their development.

Relying on Russia for approximately 40 percent of gas imports and the Middle East for 45 percent of oil imports, the EU has increasingly looked to the energy-rich Caspian Basin as a key component of future energy security.[2] Given the proximity of the Caspian Basin to the EU's ever-expanding borders, the region offers a variety of overland transit options, avoiding costly and time-consuming shipping methods required to obtain hydrocarbon resources from more distant and remote locations. As Kazakhstan seeks to become one of the 50 most competitive countries in the world, and Turkmenistan opens up to foreign investment after years of isolation after the death of former President Saparmurad Niyazov, nicknamed Turkmenbashi (the leader of all Turkmen), the Caspian states represent an investment environment of unparalleled opportunity for Western energy companies willing to venture into a still volatile business sector. As demand for Caspian energy exports increases, Western technology and investment will be necessary for Caspian producers to increase production, develop new fields and build long pipelines to markets. Economic growth and mutual dependence make the future partnerships between Europe and the Caspian ones of enormous potential, both in terms of economic opportunity and security. This potential partnership, however, will not come without its obstacles. The energy resources of the Caspian states also represent a significant source of revenue for Russia, as well as a diversification strategy for China. As the world's hydrocarbon deposits shrink, the largely untapped resources of the Caspian Basin, as outlined in Table 8.1, will be the focus of intense competition, the scale of which will reflect the broad economic and strategic implications of securing access to such resources.

Table 8.1   Proved Oil and Gas Reserves at the end of 2006

	Azerbaijan	Iran	Kazakhstan	Russia	Turkmenistan	Uzbekistan
Oil (Billion barrels)	7	137.5	39.8	79.5	0.5	0.6
Gas (TCM)	1.35	28.14	3	47.65	2.68	1.87

Source: 2007 BP Statistical Review of World Energy

Reviewing the Players

Kazakhstan

Kazakhstan has formulated its "multi-vector" policy that took into account and carefully balanced regional geopolitical and energy interests. Though Kazakhstan's relations with Russia have generally remained strong, since the 1990s Kazakhstan has been pursuing an independent policy as it continued to amass its considerable economic might. With the ascendancy of President Vladimir Putin and strengthening of the Russian state, Kazakhstan adjusted its course, prioritizing Moscow's concerns. Nevertheless, in 2006, Kazakhstan raised the price of its gas, though still selling it to Russia below market price for $145 per 1000 cubic meters (Russia resells the gas to Europe for an average of $250 per 1000 cubic meters)[3] and cutting Russia's sizeable profits from selling Russian natural gas mixed with cheaper Central Asian gas. Kazakhstan remains heavily dependent on Russia as a transit country for its primary export routes: its cheapest oil export routes include the Atyrau-Samara pipeline, Caspian Pipeline Consortium (CPC) that exports oil from Karachaganak and Tengiz field to the Russian Black Sea port of Novorossiisk, and cross-Caspian shipping routes that take Kazakh oil to Baku and then to Georgia's port of Batumi on the Black Sea by rail.[4] However, although Kazakhstan remains highly reliant on Russian transportation networks, it is increasingly diversifying its export routes, looking to China and the West as key investors. Kazakhstan's state-run energy giant KazMunayGaz has recently acquired Romania's Rompetrol, giving Kazakhstan access to EU markets through its ownership of several oil refineries in Romania, as well as Rompetrol's former distribution networks throughout the region.[5]

The West has played a key role in Kazakhstan's energy sector, especially in the 1990s. Kazakhstan has also exported oil directly to the West by delivering it to Novorossiisk via the CPC pipeline, to the Georgian port of Supsa, and to the Baku-Tbilisi-Ceyhan (BTC) pipeline. Kazakhstan also sought to export oil to the Odessa-Brody pipeline in Ukraine, undercutting Kazakh dependence on Russian pipelines and Ukrainian/EU dependence on Russian oil. Moscow eventually blocked the Odessa-Brody project through its influence in Kyiv, but Astana remains interested in the potential pipeline, which recently received support from European states at the 2007 Vilnius Energy Summit. In addition, Kazakhstan has continually expressed interest in plans for a trans-Caspian gas pipeline.[6] It also has advanced proposals on the Caspian Sea's legal status, which would curtail Russian and Iranian influence by allowing each of the five littoral states to build underwater cables or lay pipelines across its own seabed sector without approval of the other states. Russia and Iran seek veto power over pipeline proposals that are contrary to their own energy interests.[7] In addition to Russia's intimidating opposition, the trans-Caspian pipeline faces other impediments, including the lack of feasibility studies, financing, and allegations of questionable cost effectiveness and limited volumes of gas available for the next few years.[8] However, recent developments in the Nabucco negotiations (see Chapter 7) may assist in creating the initiative and commitment needed to transform the trans-Caspian pipeline from a dream to a reality.

Kazakhstan begun to open its oil and gas fields to Western companies in the early 1990s but the country's commitment to opening its energy sector to outside operators is still under scrutiny. The 2007 conflict between the Kazakh government and Italian ENI concerning the Kashagan consortium's work in that oil field has led some Western companies to raise questions regarding the Kazakhstani investment environment. After receiving notification of "massive cost overruns, technical difficulties, environmental challenges, and a continually growing delay to the start of production," the Kazakh government suspended the consortium's work for a three-month period citing environmental concerns and contractual violations.[9] However, Kazakhstan's minister of Energy and Mineral Resources stated that the government saw "no reason to suspend the project over environmental issues."[10] The Kazakh government has listed conditions that the consortium must meet if it is to continue working in Kashagan, including: (1) compensation for the state's lost revenue due to the three-year delay in production, (2) a commitment from the consortium to capture and deliver the gas coming from the oil field, (3) a higher equity stake for state company KazMunayGaz, as well as granting it the role of joint operator, and (4) increased purchase and usage of Kazakh materials and labor.[11] The consortium will likely suffer considerable losses due to its own miscalculations and cost overruns. The dispute with ENI typifies the regional trend of maintaining and at times expanding sovereign control of energy resources.

As relations with the West became somewhat complicated, China emerged as a major customer for Kazakhstani energy. A formidable rising energy consumer, whose oil imports have more than doubled since 2000, China has looked to neighboring Central Asia as an alternative to Russia's somewhat unreliable and expensive Siberian railway exports. Kazakhstan and China have recently completed a direct oil pipeline from Atasu in Central Kazakhstan to China's Xinjiang province. The pipeline has been in service since May 2006 and future extensions, linking to other pipelines in Kazakhstan, are planned.[12] Discussions are already underway between China and Kazakhstan regarding potential contributions of the two sides to the Sino-Turkmen gas pipeline currently under construction, which will cross Uzbekistan and Kazakhstan and contribute gas from the two countries.

Turkmenistan

The sudden death of Turkmenistan's President Saparmurat Niyazov in December 2006 has led to considerable uncertainty regarding Turkmenistan's position vis-à-vis Russia, China and the West. It seems that Niyazov's successor, Gourbangouli Berdimoukhamedov, will manage to fill the considerable political vacuum left by Turkmenbashi. Though it is still difficult to predict Turkmenistan's new foreign policy, Berdimoukhamedov's commitment to continue supplying countries other than Russia, such as China and Ukraine, and his intensive contacts with the EU and the United States indicate that he may be seeking to remove Turkmenistan from the Kremlin's chokehold by decreasing Ashgabat's dependence on Russian pipelines. The state's strict control of the energy sector, as well as the underdeveloped banking system, makes foreign direct investment difficult at best and impedes the country's economic development and geopolitical position. Turkmenistan has made considerable strides in courting both China and the West. Although Ashgabat remains hesitant to allow foreign companies to develop its inland energy fields, it is increasingly receptive to foreign operations in its offshore fields. Dragon Oil (the UAE-Irish firm) is currently operating in Turkmenistan successfully, LUKoil is close to securing deals for two offshore blocks, and TNK-BP and Chevron have both visited the country to discuss possible ventures.[13] Likewise, Berdimoukhamedov used his visit to the UN General Assembly in New York to court Western investors and "to present Turkmenistan as a safe and lucrative opportunity for foreign investment."[14] Berdimoukhamedov hopes his recent economic liberalization policies, particularly the country's new law "On Foreign Investment" (which allows foreigners to acquire more assets and incorporate enterprises in Turkmenistan) will lead to the investment needed to increase Turkmenistan's gas output and modernize the country.[15] He is capitalizing on Turkmenistan's strategic location and abundance of energy resources to play competing powers (namely Russia, China, Iran, and the West) against each other in order to enhance the country's geopolitical position. In that, one may see continuity with Turkmenbashi's "positive neutrality" stance. The Turkmenistan leader's recent moves include a non-binding memorandum of understanding with Vladimir Putin to export all existing gas output to Russia, but also plans to pursue future pipeline projects based on new discoveries bypassing Russia. This may be an important step in the country's post-Niyazov foreign policy and may indicate the reconsideration of Ashgabat's long-standing declared neutrality. Turkmenistan's isolation, it would seem, is coming to an end and the country has become the most recent addition to the multi-actor geopolitical competition, which has been dubbed The New Great Game.

Turkmenistan is currently a key player in four proposed pipeline projects. The most significant for Turkmenistan is the scheduled construction of a direct pipeline that will link the country to China, thus eliminating Moscow's control over gas deals between Ashgabat and Beijing. Pipeline construction will be funded by China. In preparation for construction, China has actively championed the pipeline by negotiating separate gas deals with Kazkahstan and Uzbekistan, in order to ensure smooth transit of Turkmen gas through its Central Asian neighbors.[16] The 1,800-mile pipeline is scheduled to be in operation in 2011 and will carry 30 bcm of Turkmen gas per year.[17] Berdimoukhamedov has also expressed considerable interest in the realization of the proposed trans-Caspian gas pipeline. Turkmenistan thus may also contribute to the proposed Nabucco pipeline, which would also bypass Russia and carry the Central Asian state's gas to Europe via the South Caucasus (Azerbaijan and Georgia), and Turkey. However, to participate in the Nabucco project, whose pipeline extension routes have yet to be planned, Turkmenistan and Azerbaijan need to agree on the route for the trans-Caspian pipeline. These plans remain tentative at best as Russia and Iran vehemently oppose them. The two interconnected projects remain in the stage of political negotiations for now. The same Russian and Iranian intransigence prevents an oil pipeline from being built across the Caspian from Kazakhstan to Azerbaijan, to connect to BTC.

In order to construct a pipeline on the bottom of the Caspian Sea, the littoral states must first agree on the demarcation of their respective national sectors of the seabed. Under Turkmenbashi, Turkmenistan was opposed to the national sector regime of Caspian Sea claims, hoping to get a better deal demarcating its border with Azerbaijan and retaining control over more hydrocarbon reserves. Iran, Turkmenistan's neighbor and one of the littoral states laying claims to a relatively large part of the southern Caspian Sea and its resources, has made negotiations nearly impossible and used force against Azerbaijan to prevent hydrocarbon exploration. On July 23, 2001, an Iranian warship and two jets forced research vessels working on behalf of British Petroleum-Amoco in the Araz-Alov-Sharg field out of that sector. That field lies 60 miles north of Iranian waters. Due to that pressure, BP-Amoco immediately announced that it would cease exploring that field, which it did by withdrawing the research vessels.[18] Like Iran, Russia is also blocking negotiations needed to demarcate the Caspian Sea and provide the necessary legal framework to begin construction of the trans-Caspian pipelines.

As the trans-Caspian pipelines would bypass Russia, Moscow has no incentive to cooperate and may take steps to sabotage the project. Russia's recent gas deals with Turkmenistan and Kazakhstan have limited availability of gas supplies Western consumers had hoped would eventually go to the proposed trans-Caspian pipeline. The Tehran Caspian Summit in October 2007 saw Putin and Ahmadinejad further their position that each littoral state must approve pipeline construction in the Caspian Sea; this proposal would give Iran and Russia de facto veto power over the trans-Caspian pipeline and similar projects inconsistent with their strategic regional interests.[19] Ashgabat also has aspirations of constructing a pipeline through northern Afghanistan, Pakistan and across India, the so called TAPI (Turkmenistan-Afghanistan-Pakistan-India) pipeline. However, the cost of such a project through inhospitable mountainous terrain and Taliban- and drug warlord-controlled territories, coupled with Afghanistan's and Pakistan's instability, make the project risky and costly, as the gas shipments' security would be jeopardized.

Russia is more likely to secure Turkmenistan's participation in a new Caspian gas pipeline known as Prikaspiiskaya, which would carry gas from Kazakhstan and Turkmenistan along the Caspian coast to Russia. This is a Moscow-sponsored alternative to the proposed trans-Caspian pipeline. Ashgabat has already agreed to upgrade the existing CAC gas pipeline system, in order to increase future capacity. It seemed that Moscow's vision of a new Caspian pipeline via Russia may soon materialize, but the September 1, 2007, cutoff date to sign the relevant agreements has come and gone and President Berdimoukhamedov has been unavailable in Ashgabat due to his extensive visits to the United States and Europe.[20]

EU Energy Commissioner Andris Piebalgs' November 2007 trip to Ashgabat to discuss the trans-Caspian pipeline highlights the political jockeying between East and West over Turkmen's rich endowments of gas and oil. Turkmenistan, it seems, has quickly mastered the New Great Game.[21]

Azerbaijan

Azerbaijan, together with Kazakhstan, has been the major energy player in the Caspian region. The discovery of oil in Azerbaijan in the late 19th century established Baku as an important economic force of the Russian Empire and Soviet Union. As a province, Azerbaijan was divided between the Persian and Russian empires by the Treaty of Turkmanchay in 1828, 20 years before the world's first industrial oil well was discovered south of Baku.[22] British support of Azerbaijani independence in 1918–1920 can be partially explained by the country's oil riches. After the collapse of the Soviet Union, Azerbaijan began to pursue an independent energy policy, greatly reducing Moscow's control of its gas and oil exports. In 1994, a consortium of Western companies signed the deal of the century with the Azerbaijani government to export the country's oil to the West, thus decreasing Baku's (and Europe's) dependence on Russia's pipelines.[23] At the time of the signing, a route had not yet been established, yet the desire for greater energy security on the part of Europe, and independent energy policies in the Caucasus, lead to the establishment of the BTC pipeline. Azerbaijan's participation in the Nabucco and BTC pipeline projects, both of which bypass Russia to serve as alternative energy supply routes, represents a clear split between Baku and Moscow. As Azerbaijan asserts its independence, it has become a strategic partner for the West. Both Russia and Iran have placed considerable pressure on Azerbaijan, blocking Caspian delineation, challenging Azerbaijan's claims to Caspian off-shore oil fields and pursuing closer relations with regional rival Armenia. Azerbaijan has become the ally of the West out of necessity, both in terms of energy and of being militarily sandwiched between two volatile, increasingly anti-Western powers.

Azerbaijan may also become a transit country for the future trans-Caspian oil pipeline, bringing Kazakh oil to the markets if the export capacity via Russia through tanker shipping across the Caspian, and through China will be insufficient (the current pipeline between Kazakhstan and China is unlikely to have excess capacity). Recently, Azerbaijan and Turkmenistan have made considerable strides in improving their bilateral relations, which had been complicated by the erratic rule of Turkmenbashi that emphasized territorial disputes between the two in the Caspian for some time. Azerbaijan is the principal supplier of the Shakh Deniz-Baku-Tbilisi-Erzurum gas pipeline to eastern Turkey, which mostly runs parallel to BTC.

In March 2007, Azerbaijan's Minister of Foreign Affairs Elmar Mammadyarov signed a memorandum of understanding on energy security cooperation with Secretary of State Condoleezza Rice. The memorandum codifies the important role

Baku has played in promoting Caspian energy security and regional development.[24] The two countries agreed to enter a high-level dialogue on energy security, focused on Azerbaijan's expanding gas and oil exports, and particularly the realization of the Turkey-Greece-Italy and Nabucco pipelines.[25] Also in March 2007, Azerbaijan's veteran Deputy Minister of Foreign Affairs Araz Azimov adamantly stated Azerbaijan's commitment to the Nabucco project during a joint hearing of the European Parliament's Committees on International Affairs and Energy and Transport in Brussels. Azimov's emphasis on supply diversification refuted Hungarian Prime Minister Ferenc Gyurcsany's dismissal of the Nabucco project as a "dream" and his clear preference at the time for Gazprom's Blue Stream project, which would continue the EU's dependence on Russia's energy exports.[26] Baku's ties with Europe and the United States and its continued commitment to serving as an alternative supplier/transit route indicate its attempts to avoid dependence on Russian energy transit and on Moscow in general. This is in line with the Azerbaijani elite's historic preference of a secular Western path of development demonstrated as early as the emergence of the multi-party government in Baku in 1918–1920 and introduction of universal suffrage, the first in any Muslim country.

In reference to Russia's active opposition to the construction of trans-Caspian pipelines, Great Britain's energy minister, Malcolm Wicks, stated, "The right to decide on this matter is Turkmenistan's and Azerbaijan's and nobody else's. Oil and gas issues are not just energy issues; they are national security issues for many countries. The EU's cooperation with countries in the [Caspian] region should be seen through the prism of the energy security and national security of all states involved in these projects."[27]

Azerbaijan's energy security is a complex issue that is linked to Baku's key domestic and foreign policies. In his 2007 New Year's address to the country, President Ilham Aliyev discussed the importance of Azerbaijan's energy-related developments in 2006, most notably the operation of the BTC pipeline and the first gas extractions in the Shakh Deniz deposit. "These two historical events will determine Azerbaijan's long-term development strategy, will strengthen Azerbaijan economically and certainly contribute its worldwide positions."[28] Azerbaijan's oil wealth has contributed to the country's exceptional economic growth and its regional development projects. Azerbaijan's rapprochement with the West is due, in part, to tensions and problems with Russia. Aliyev's refusal to pay the higher gas prices demanded by Gazprom for gas supplied to Azerbaijan, which the Azerbaijani president described as "commercial blackmail,"[29] marked the underlying tensions between the two countries. In order to meet its energy shortage, Azerbaijan was required to use internally produced gas, as well as fuel oil. The increased domestic fuel oil consumption did not reduce volume from the BTC pipeline, but rather from the pipeline that runs to Russia's Novorossiysk Black Sea port.[30]

Significant tensions between Azerbaijan and Iran force President Aliyev to carefully balance his country's regional interests with Western energy needs and tense relations with Russia. Namely, Baku must exercise caution when pursuing ties with Washington and Brussels. Iran expressed its discontent with Azerbaijan's rapprochement with the West in February 2007, when Iranian helicopters violated Azerbaijan's air space, flying over administration buildings in the southern town of Astara for over 20 minutes.[31] "The incident with the helicopters, as well as the sudden termination of the duties of the Iranian ambassador to Azerbaijan, Afshar Suleymani, has led the local pundits to believe that something has gone off track in Azbaijani-Iranian relations due to the growing insecurity on Tehran's part."[32] Tehran has reason to be concerned. In addition to Baku's Western orientation, Iran fears calls for autonomy, if not outright succession in Iranian Azerbaijan in the country's north, which is populated by more than 25 million (Azeri) Turkic-speaking ethnic Azeris.[33] Representing over one-third of Iran's entire population, Azeris' sympathy towards Baku could be problematic for Tehran in the event that tensions escalate further.

In an attempt to further the country's economic growth, Aliyev is actively promoting foreign investment in nonenergy sectors of the economy, such as tourism. It is hoped that the country's economic growth will extend beyond Baku and create jobs and develop industries throughout Azerbaijan, thus stemming the influx of rural inhabitants to Baku in search of economic opportunities.[34] Aliyev has continually emphasized Azerbaijan's underlying policy priority—the resolution of the Nagorno-Karabakh conflict. Baku hopes that growing economic capacity, geopolitical importance and regional development projects will entice Yerevan to cooperate and withdraw its troops from occupied territories. In his 2007 address to the nation, Aliyev acknowledged the economic and political significance of his country's strategic cooperation with the EU's energy sector. Aliyev stated that, "Our international activities are worthwhile and all efforts of Azerbaijan in international organizations are directed at a resolution of a single issue," the Nagorno-Karabakh conflict. "Our position remains unchanged. Azerbaijan's territorial integrity must be restored."[35] But Aliyev's failure to meet with Armenian President Robert Kocharian has also raised questions as to his true commitment to resolving the territorial dispute.[36] The extent to which Azerbaijan remains preoccupied with Nagorno-Karabakh is exemplified by the country's 2005 commitment to create a military budget equal to Armenia's entire national budget; this goal was realized in 2007.[37] Thus, while Azerbaijan is currently making overtures to the West through its cooperation in the War on Terror and commitment to Caspian energy projects and Western energy security needs, its underlying objective remains gaining support for its claim to Nagorno-Karabakh. This goal may largely determine its international position within organizations such as the OSCE Minsk group, as well as regarding future pipeline projects.

Uzbekistan

For all of the Caspian states, rich endowments of oil and natural gas are a source of increased geopolitical power. In these countries, the benefits of these energy resources are distributed unequally, with the ruling elite receiving most of the profit; and investment in national development varying considerably among the countries. Even in the company of its fellow Caspian states, however, Uzbekistan seems to suffer the most from resource curse, despite being least endowed in oil and gas. Uzbekistan may be a case where energy exports generate more insecurity for the regime and the society, as will be demonstrated below. One may determine that the growth of the Uzbek energy sector has been detrimental for the country at large, with the profits going to the narrow elite, and most of it remaining outside the country. As the International Crisis Group states, "domestic gas supplies are often cut in winter so the gas can be sold abroad raising half a billion dollars; entire cities sit unheated in freezing weather, often provoking protests."[38] Rising poverty and urban overcrowding only exasperate the Uzbek population's plight. More importantly, energy profits have allowed the Uzbek government to continue its hard-line policies; energy profits are used to finance extensive security measures and authoritarian controls such as the regime's systematic violation of human rights, free speech, democratic activity and civil society.

Uzbekistan's relations with the United States has gone through ups and downs, and at the time of this writing are in deep freeze. In the 1990s, Tashkent rejected U.S. calls for greater regional cooperation, which would have made attempts by Russia to return to the region more difficult and would have created a basis for economic development. At the time, President Islam Karimov entertained ambitions for regional leadership, if not hegemony. As the Taliban and al-Qaeda grew stronger in neighboring Afghanistan and Islamic radicalism spilled over to Uzbekistan through a terrorist Islamic Movement of Uzbekistan (IMU), Hizb ut-Tahrir, and Akramiyah extremists, Tashkent's calls for anti-terrorist cooperation fell on deaf ears in Washington. The September 11 attack changed all that. The United States needed Uzbekistan for resupplying its troops in Afghanistan. Many IMU fighters and some of its leaders were killed fighting alongside al-Qaeda and Taliban. 2002–2004 was the honeymoon of U.S.-Uzbek relations, but Tashkent did not pursue the liberalization or economic reform Washington called for. The U.S. air force base in Karshi-Khanabad was shut down under President Islam Karimov's orders in 2005, less than six months after the Islamist revolt in Andijan in which several hundred protestors were gunned down by Uzbek interior troops. U.S. protests notwithstanding, Tashkent's increased human rights abuses, combined with the government-mandated closing of almost all NGO offices and subsequent imprisonment of activists and NGO members, made Uzbekistan the least desirable Central Asian partner in Washington. Thus, while investment and political engagement with Uzbekistan sustains a hard-line authoritarian regime and is contrary to the democratic principles proclaimed by the Bush administration, a lack of foreign investment and engagement could prove even more detrimental to an increasingly frustrated Uzbek population. Russia, however, could not care less about democracy and human rights, either in Uzbekistan or elsewhere in the post-Soviet space. In November 2007, LUKoil inaugurated a major gas field in Uzbekistan.[39] The Khauzak field is part of the wider Kandym-Khauzak-Shady-Kungrad project, developed jointly by LU-Koil, with a 90 percent stake, and Uzbek state energy company UzbekNefteGaz, which controls the rest.[40] Gazprom's continued willingness to buy the relatively moderate amount of gas Uzbekistan exports to Russia—approximately 13 bcm/year, up from 9 bcm/year in 2006—at the expense of its population, does provide the country with considerable external revenue; where gas sale profits go is entirely another matter.[41]

Nevertheless, there are signs that Uzbekistan is not yet prepared to sever ties with Washington. The appointment of an allegedly pro-Western foreign minister,[42] cultural diplomacy with the United States and Uzbekistan's sole automobile plant's recent partnership with General Motors may signify an important window of opportunity for Western engagement in this important and unstable state.[43]

Russia

Russia has dominated Central Asia, then known as Turkestan, since the second half of the 19th century. Many in Moscow still view the vast region as Russia's past and future sphere of influence, although the recognition of Central Asia's Islamic roots, Chinese aspirations, and Western influence is clearly understood by experts and policy makers. Yet Russia is committed to playing a key role in the region without plans to formally absorb any country, with the possible exception of Kazakhstan. Russia continues to rely heavily on Central Asian gas to meet its contracts with Western consumers. As domestic demand rises and production slows down, Russia will apply increased pressure on Caspian energy providers to protect its strategic interests and continue its stranglehold on much of the energy sector. In short, Russia's pipeline politics will pose a considerable barrier to the region's integration into the global economy and will remain a formidable factor for Caspian states' and Western energy security for decades to come. Moscow's relations with Tehran may shed additional light on Russia's future energy strategy. A bilateral joint statement between Putin and Ahmadinejad laid the groundwork for future bilateral cooperation in the energy sector, including what appears to be the intent to work toward coordination of a gas cartel.[44]

Iran

Tehran has pursued strategic rapprochement with Moscow in recent years, largely due to both countries' distaste for perceived American superpower status, aspirations to dominate the Persian Gulf, and also because they have similar views on the issue of the Caspian Sea demarcation. During his 2007 visit to Tehran for the Caspian summit, Putin demonstrated the convergence of Russian and Iranian views on the Caspian, as he eagerly promoted overall strengthening of bilateral ties, including in the military, diplomatic and economic areas.[45] Russia's assistance in constructing Iran's Bushehr nuclear power plant is the fruit of the countries' rapprochement and a source of increased tension between Iran and the United States and its allies.

The issue of demarcation of the Caspian Sea, which is the largest salt lake on the planet, may have escaped headlines, but is vitally important for the future of hydrocarbon development and energy security in the region. While both Russia and Iran have stalled the demarcation of the Caspian, largely over the rights of each littoral state to veto proposed undersea pipelines, the two countries are at odds with each other as to how exactly the Caspian should be split. Iran, which possesses only 13 percent of the coastline, has advocated a condominium, with all countries sharing equally in mineral wealth of the sea. If that is not acceptable, Iran advocates an even split, awarding each Caspian state 20 percent of the seabed.[46] The Iranian position contradicts those of Azerbaijan, Kazakhstan and Russia. These three littoral states have implemented a "modified median line" approach, well recognized in international law, to the demarcation of sovereignty over resources under the bed of the Caspian Sea. This offers a precedent for the resolution of the territorial conflict between Azerbaijan and Turkmenistan over the Kyapaz/Serdar field, which lies in the middle of the southern Caspian Sea, divided by a median line between the Azerbaijani and Turkmenistani coasts if such a line were to be drawn. For this, it would not be necessary to resolve boundary questions between Azerbaijan and Iran, between Turkmenistan and Iran, or even between Turkmenistan and Kazakhstan. It would only require Turkmenistan to agree on such a "modified median line" principle to demarcate its boundary with Azerbaijan over use of undersea resources.[47]

Turkmenistan has occasionally backed Iran's position; primarily because its principal oil fields would be split with Azerbaijan under the modified median line approach. Ownership of these fields is still contested. Russia's position, adhering to the modified median line, is strongly backed by Kazakhstan, who, having 28 percent of the coastline, stands to lose the most under Iran's terms.[48] Azerbaijan also backs Russia's model, under which it would be awarded 21 percent of the Caspian, largely at Iran's expense.[49] Under Russia's model, Iran would be the biggest loser (Turkmenistan would receive around 17 percent and Russia around 20.)[50] Iran has several distinct advantages under its model, in addition to an increased share of the Caspian seabed. Iran's demarcation model of the Caspian is not limited to the seabed; thus, it would limit the free travel of Russian (and other Caspian states') naval forces and stop Russia's industrialized fishing fleet from operating in other national sections.[51] Iran's section of the Caspian under the Russian model is very deep and would require advanced technology in order to extract oil from the seabed; given Iran's increased international isolation, it is unlikely that Western companies will invest in Iran's oil fields and provide it with the necessary technology and equipment.[52] However, strategic cooperation between Moscow and Tehran is unlikely to allow disagreements over the Caspian to derail Russian-Iranian relations, while Iran is unlikely to rush to settle the legal claims to the Caspian Sea.

China

In the larger picture of energy diversification and Euro-Atlantic security, China should be viewed as a competing consumer with vast economic clout, who, when successfully securing direct pipelines and supply contracts from its Central Asian neighbors, sends valuable non-Russian energy resources East instead of West. As China is attempting to maximally diversify geographic sources of energy imports and Russia proves to be a somewhat unpredictable supplier, China looks increasingly to Central Asia to meet its rapidly growing energy needs. China also views ex-Soviet Central Asia as a target of economic expansion and eventual integration into the Chinese sphere of influence.[53]

China views the Shanghai Cooperation Organization (SCO) as a framework that allows it to gain influence in Central Asia at the expense of the United States and Russia.[54] Indeed, China's growing energy demands have led to significant Chinese regional investment, particularly in the energy sector; these growing investments rival Russia's own regional investments and influence.[55] Energy export routes from the Caspian to China and Europe prove to be costly and risky. In the case of Europe, deep sea routes, deployment of advanced technology and possibly LNG infrastructure will be required. Direct pipeline construction between Central Asia and China is less geographically challenging, though also extremely expensive due to the length of the routes. However, China's energy security calculus is dictated by the ruling Politburo and Communist Party Central Committee and thus is less market-driven than Europe's and the United States. Beijing wants to secure reserves in the ground and supply contracts for a long term, not to buy oil and gas in unpredictable spot markets. It does not want to depend on energy imports via sea routes, which China lacks naval power to secure. Thus, given supply, geographic, and financial restraints, the Western governments and companies must carefully plan its Caspian energy projects in order to ensure viable proposals that can compete with bids from China.

Regional Projects and Agreements

Significant competition, primarily between Russia and the West for access to Caspian energy resources has led to a number of developments and agreements regarding international pipeline construction. Perhaps the most significant development was the 1990s division of Azeri oil exports from the Caspian between Russia, which controls the Baku-Novorossiisk pipeline, and a consortium of Western oil companies led by BP, which controls the BTC pipeline. A desire for greater regional independence from Russia, combined with growing Western interest in supply diversification, helped to make the BTC pipeline a reality. The pipeline was a key step in establishing an alternative, non-Russian controlled export route for Caspian gas and oil. As the primary supplier to the BTC pipeline, Azerbaijan has assumed a prominent regional position directly challenging Russia's influence in the former Soviet Union. A source of great cohesion between Azerbaijan and neighboring Georgia, the BTC has also led to increased interest from Kazakhstan, thus further weakening Russia's control of key energy resources in the Caspian Basin. But Russia's attack on Georgia in August 2008 has shed a new light on the balance of power in the region and cast doubts about Georgia's ability to continue to serve as a reliable transit state.

In recent years, the main factor defining energy security in the Caspian basin is the competition between Europe and the United States on the one hand and Russia on the other. The EU's push for Nabucco, which would bypass Russia, as well as a trans-Caspian gas pipeline from Turkmenistan to Azerbaijan to supply Nabucco, have raised strong Russian opposition. Russia insists on control of Turkmen gas exports, proposing instead the South Stream pipeline that will go through the bottom of the Black Sea to Bulgaria and then via Romania to Hungary and Austria, with a possible spur via Serbia to Italy.

As can be seen in Figure 8.1, several Central Asian states have shown an increased interest in further exploring the possibility of constructing a trans-Caspian pipeline, which would run through Central Asia, under the Caspian Sea, and onward to Europe (via the new Shakh Deniz-Baku-Tbilisi-Erzurum and Nabucco pipeline systems). The proposal is still in the very early stages and faces considerable political and environmental challenges. Nevertheless, the regional countries' newfound cooperation, especially Turkmenistan, emphasized by a variety of state visits and bilateral agreements, has added a new vitality to Caspian energy security cooperation.

The Energy Security Conference held in Vilnius, Lithuania, October 10–11, 2007, also yielded promising results for the future of EU and Eurasian energy security.[56] During the summit, Azerbaijan, Ukraine, Lithuania, Georgia and Poland signed agreements backing the proposed and much delayed Odessa-Brody-Plotsk oil pipeline, which had been put on hold due to the Ukrainian leadership's ambiguity, lack of commitment, as well as Russian pressure and possible corruption, and Azerbaijan's inability to commit the necessary oil. The proposed pipeline, which would carry Caspian crude from the Black Sea to Poland's Baltic Sea refinery of Gdansk, creates additional incentives for Western investment and support of infrastructure to carry Caspian oil to the EU without going through Russia. Also discussed was the White Stream project, which would carry Caspian gas to the EU via Georgia and the bed of the Black Sea, then either through Ukraine or to Romania's Black Sea coast. The difficult deep-sea construction will rely on the experience and technology used in Russia's North Stream project, which also travels along the Black Sea's seabed. It is estimated that the project will initially deliver gas from Azerbaijan and eventually from the eastern Caspian basin, presumably Turkmenistan and Kazakhstan.[57]

Russia, along with Kazakhstan and Turkmenistan, will upgrade and extend the existing Soviet-era Central Asia-Center (CAC) pipeline system, which is already operating at capacity. The agreement would allow Russia to supply Central Asian gas at below-market prices to its quickly developing economy, while the Russian gas will be sold to Europe. The modernization and expansion of the CAC system, as well as the proposed construction of a similar pipeline extending up the Caspian coast from Turkmenistan through Kazakhstan to Russia, will increase

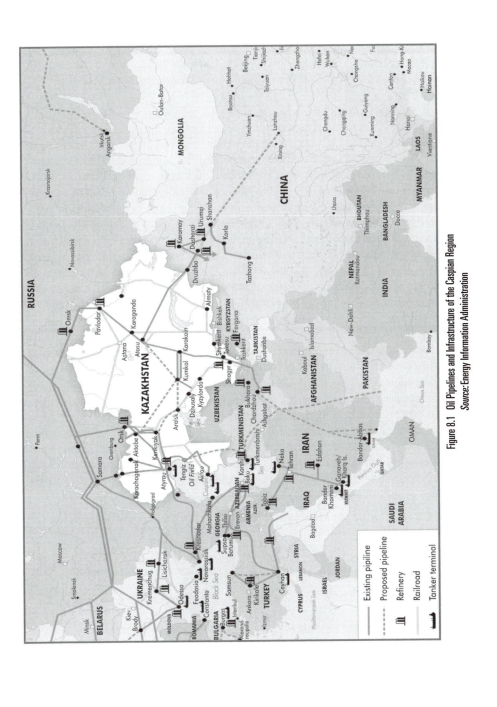

Figure 8.1 Oil Pipelines and Infrastructure of the Caspian Region
Source: Energy Information Administration

exports of Central Asian gas to Russia from 60 bcm/year to 90 bcm/year.[58] It is estimated that the initial expansion of 10 bcm/year will occur by 2009 and full capacity may be reached as early as 2010.[59] The agreement between Russia and two former Soviet Central Asian republics was a decisive victory for Moscow and has enhanced the increasingly pivotal role Russia's pipeline system plays in the global energy sector.

Conclusion

The Caspian Basin represents an important source of energy in light of growing global demand and increased instability in the Middle East. This region is strategically extremely important, straddling Eurasia borders and key countries of interest to the West, namely China, Russia, Iran, and Afghanistan. The region's relative stability, strategic geographic location and increased openness make it an attractive alternative for Western companies and consumers. While each Caspian state has a unique national security position regarding its energy exports, the general regional trends include increasing investment opportunities for Western influence and investment in Azerbaijan and Turkmenistan, unclear prospects in Kazakhstan, and nonexistent ones in Russia and Iran. Once firmly fixed in the Russian sphere of influence, the former Soviet Republics around the Caspian Sea are looking west to the United States and Europe, and east to China, for economic and political gains. Each country must be viewed independently in its own unique domestic and foreign context. Although the region generally lacks transparency, good governance and the rule of law at the level of developed Western economies, and remains subject to strong Russian influence, the strategic geographic location and increased openness of the Caspian states make them obvious targets in the 21st century energy investment projects that some view through the geopolitical prism of the New Great Game. This openness, combined with unsurpassed global energy demand, make the region a new, profitable investment environment for Western gas and oil companies. While the rules of engagement remain uncertain and conditions risky, the political and economic payout of increased Western presence in the region compels decision-makers and investors to take risks.

Notes

1. Gawdat Bahgat, "Central Asia and Energy Security," *Asian Affairs,* 37, no. 1 (March 2006): 1–16, http://www.informaworld.com/smpp/content~db=all?content=10.1080/030 68370500456819

2. Geopolitics of EU energy supply, September 24, 2007, http://www.euractiv.com/en/industry/geopolitics-eu-energy-supply/article-142665.

3. Vladimir Socor, "Kazakhstan's Growing Gas Exports to Go Russia's Way," *Eurasia Daily Monitor,* 4, no. 97 (May 17, 2007), http://www.jamestown.org/single/?no_cache=1& tx_ttnews%5Btt_news%5D=32749.

4. Ariel Cohen, *Kazakhstan's Energy Cooperation With Russia* (London: GMB Publishing Limited, 2005), 15.

5. Vladimir Socor, "Bridgehead in Europe: Kazakhstan Acquires Romania's Rompetrol," *Eurasia Daily Monitor,* 4, no. 165 (September 7, 2007), http://www.jamestown.org/single/?no_cache=1&tx_ttnews%5Btt_news%5D=32976.

6. Sergei Blagov, "Russia Tries to Scuttle Proposed Trans-Caspian Pipeline," *Eurasianet. org,* March 28, 2006, http://www.eurasianet.org/departments/insight/articles/eav032806. shtml.

7. Vladimir Socor, "Discussions Intensify with Kazakhstan on Trans-Caspian Gas Pipeline," *Eurasia Daily Monitor,* 1, no. 29 (June 11, 2004), http://www.jamestown.org/single/?no_cache=1&tx_ttnews%5Btt_news%5D=32549; "Caspian Summit Balances Interests and Differences," *Eurasia Daily Monitor,* 4, no. 192 (October 17, 2007), http://www.jamestown.org/single/?no_cache=1&tx_ttnews%5Btt_news%5D=33084.

8. Ibid.

9. Vladimir Socor, "Kazakhstan Confronts Oil Consortium Over Setbacks at Kashagan," *Eurasia Daily Monitor,* 4, no. 166 (September 10, 2007), http://www.jamestown.org/single/?no_cache=1&tx_ttnews%5Btt_news%5D=32982.

10. Farkhad Sharip, "Kazakhstan Seeks Full Control Over Kashagan Oil Tap," *Eurasia Daily Monitor,* 4, no. 169 (September 13, 2007), http://www.jamestown.org/single/?no_cache=1&tx_ttnews%5Btt_news%5D=32993.

11. Vladimir Socor, "Kazakhstan Confronts Oil Consortium."

12. Jim Nichol, "Central Asia: Regional Developments and Implications for U.S. Interests" *CRS Report for Congress* (July 5, 2007): 28, http://www.au.af.mil/au/awc/awcgate/crs/ib93108.pdf.

13. "A New Broom," *Petroleum Economist,* August 3, 2007, http://www.petroleum-economist.com/default.asp?page=14&PubID=46&ISS=24016&SID=690553

14. Roger McDermott, "Turkmenistan Ponders Partnership with Washington," *Eurasia Daily Monitor,* 4, no. 183 (October 3, 2007), http://www.jamestown.org/single/?no_cache=1&tx_ttnews%5Btt_news%5D=33050.

15. Kommersant.com, "Turkmenistan Passes New Foreign Investment Law," October 15, 2007, http://www.kommersant.com/p814971/economic_legislation/.

16. Stuart Elliot with Winnie Lee, "Turkmenistan, China Agree to Speed up Gas Pipeline," *Platts Oilgram News,* 85, no. 141 (July 19, 2007), http://construction.ecnext.com/coms2/summary_0249-250151_ITM_platts.

17. Ibid.

18. Ariel Cohen, "Iran's Claim Over Caspian Resources Threaten Energy Security," *Heritage Backgrounder,* September 5, 2002, http://www.heritage.org/Research/Iraq/bg1582.cfm.

19. Vladimir Socor, "Caspian Summit Balances Interests and Differences," *Eurasia Daily Monitor,* 4, no. 192 (October 17, 2007), http://www.jamestown.org/single/?no_cache=1&tx_ttnews%5Btt_news%5D=33084.

20. M.K. Bhadrakumar, "A Massive Wrench Thrown in Putin's Works," *Asia Times,* September 29, 2007, http://www.atimes.com/atimes/Central_Asia/II29Ag01.html.

21. "EU's Piebalgs Says Turkmenistan Could Sell Gas Directly to Europe," *Forbes,* November 15, 2007, http://www.forbes.com/markets/feeds/afx/2007/11/15/afx4342271.html.

22. "Timeline: Azerbaijan," *BBC,* September 26, 2007, http://news.bbc.co.uk/1/hi/world/europe/country_profiles/1235740.stm.

23. Liz Fuller, "Caucasus: The BTC—Settling On A Route," *Radio Free Europe/Radio Liberty,* July 12, 2006, http://www.rferl.org/featuresarticle/2006/07/2008aefc-45a2-44d6-badd-8733098b37a5.html.

24. Vladimir Socor, "Azerbaijan at the Forefront of Caspian Basin Energy Initiatives," *Eurasia Daily Monitor,* 4, no. 57, (March 22, 2007) http://www.jamestown.org/single/?no_cache=1&tx_ttnews%5Btt_news%5D=32615.

25. U.S. Department of State Media Note, "U.S.-Azerbaijan Sign Memorandum of Understanding on Energy Security Cooperation," March 22, 2007, http://www.state.gov/r/pa/prs/ps/2007/mar/82072.htm.

26. Ibid.

27. Vladimir Socor, "Gas Discussions in Turkmenistan, Azerbaijan after the Budapest Nabucco Conference," *Eurasia Daily Monitor,* 4, no. 176 (September 24, 2007), http://www.jamestown.org/single/?no_cache=1&tx_ttnews%5Btt_news%5D=33020.

28. Ilham Aliyev, "Azeri Leader Sets Key Priorities for 2007," *BBC Monitoring Trans Caucasus Unit,* January 1, 2007, http://www.armeniandiaspora.com/forum/showthread.php?t=75310.

29. Vladimir Socor, "Azerbaijan's President Turns Down Gazprom's 'Blackmail' Prices," *Eurasia Daily Monitor,* 4, no. 4 (January 5, 2007), http://www.jamestown.org/single/?no_cache=1&tx_ttnews%5Btt_news%5D=32360

30. Ibid.

31. Fariz Ismailzade, "Tehran Reminds Azerbaijan to Keep Distance from Washington," *Eurasia Daily Monitor,* 4, no. 43 (March 22, 2007), http://www.jamestown.org/single/?no_cache=1&tx_ttnews%5Btt_news%5D=32550.

32. Ibid.

33. Ibid.

34. Fariz Ismailzade, "Regional Development on Top of Aliyev's Agenda," *Eurasia Daily Monitor,* 4, no. 34 (February 16, 2007), http://www.jamestown.org/single/?no_cache=1&tx_ttnews%5Btt_news%5D=32504.

35. Ilham Aliyev, "Azeri Leader Sets Key Priorities for 2007," (January 1, 2007), http://www.armeniandiaspora.com/forum/showthread.php?t=75310.

36. Ibid.

37. Ibid.

38. International Crisis Group, "Central Asia's Energy Risks," *Asia Report,* no. 133 (May 24, 2007), http://www.crisisgroup.org/home/index.cfm?id=4866&l=1.

39. Sergey Karpoukhin, "Russia, Uzbekistan Light Flame at Major Gas Field," Reuters, November 29, 2007, http://uk.reuters.com/article/oilRpt/idUKL2987617820071129.

40. Ibid.

41. Vladimir Socor, "Uzbek Gas Output, Export Set to Grow Under Russian Monopoly Control," *Eurasia Daily Monitor,* 4, no. 37 (February 22, 2007), http://jamestown.nvm-server.com/124/?no_cache=1&tx_ttnews%5Btt_news%5D=32516.

42. Ruslan Nagaev and Ulhom Ahmedov, "Uzbekistan Considers Rapprochement with the West," *Eurasia Daily Monitor,* 3, no. 229 (December 12, 2006), http://forum.arbuz.com/archive/index.php/t-34327.html.

43. Ibid.

44. Vladimir Socor, "Caspian Summit Balances Interests and Differences," *Eurasia Daily Monitor,* 4, no. 192 (October 17, 2007), http://www.jamestown.org/single/?no_cache=1&tx_ttnews%5Btt_news%5D=33084.

45. "Lecturers in Iranian Province Comment on Caspian Sea Summit in Tehran," *BBC Monitoring International Reports,* October 27, 2007, on Lexis-Nexis.

46. John C.K. Daly, "Analysis: The Caspian's division," *UPI Energy,* October 11, 2007, http://www.upi.com/Energy_Resources/2007/10/11/Analysis-The-Caspians-division/UPI-46341192135315/.

47. Ibid.

48. Mark N. Katz, "Russian-Iranian Relations in the Putin Era," *Demokratizatisya,* (Winter 2002): 3, http://mars.gmu.edu:8080/dspace/bitstream/1920/3046/4/Russian-Iranian%20Relations%20in%20the%20Putin%20Era.pdf.

49. Alex Vatanka, "Azerbaijan-Iran Tensions Create Obstacle to Caspian Resolution," *Eurasianet.org,* January 29, 2003, http://eurasianet.org/departments/business/articles/eav012903.shtml.

50. Bahman Aghai Diba, "Iran's National Interests in the Caspian Sea," *Times of Central Asia,* March 19, 2006, http://www.iranian.ws/cgi-bin/iran_news/exec/view.cgi/7/14204.

51. Ibid.

52. Ibid.

53. Author's personal interviews with Chinese researchers, Beijing and Shanghai, September 2006. Interviewees requested anonymity.

54. Andrei Piontkovsky, "China's Strategic Threat to Russia," *The Korea Herald,* August 27, 2007, http://www.turkishweekly.net/news/47949/china-s-threat-to-russia-by-andrei-piontkovsky-.html.

55. Andrew Neff, "China Competing with Russia for Central Asian Investments," *Oil and Gas Journal,* March 6, 2006, http://www.ogj.com/display_article/249454/7/ARCHI/none/none/1/CENTRAL-ASIAN-OIL-AND-GAS-1—China-competing-with-Russia-for-Central-Asian-investments/.

56. Vladimir Socor, "Vilnius Energy Summit Institutionalizing a Process," *Eurasia Daily Monitor,* 4, no. 189 (October 12, 2007), http://www.jamestown.org/single/?no_cache=1&tx_ttnews%5Btt_news%5D=33072.

57. Vladimir Socor, "White Stream: Additional Outlet Proposed for Caspian Gas to Europe," *Eurasia Daily Monitor,* 4, no. 189 (October 12, 2007), http://www.jamestown.org/single/?no_cache=1&tx_ttnews%5Btt_news%5D=33073.

58. Nadia Rodova, "Russia Wins Backing for Caspian Gas Line; Turkmenistan, Kazakhstan Agree to Support New Export Line via Russia," *Platts Oilgram News,* May 15, 2007, http://www.platts.com/search_premium.jsp.

59. M. K. Bhadrakumar, "A Massive Wrench Thrown in Putin's Work," *Asia Times Online,* September 29, 2007, http://www.atimes.com/atimes/Central_Asia/II29Ag01.html.

CHAPTER 9

Latin America: America's Forgotten Energy Barn

Johanna Mendelson Forman and Susana Moreira

Latin America is well-endowed with natural resources. It owns the world's second largest supplies of proven oil reserves, natural gas, hydroelectric power, and abundant capacity for biomass energy (40 percent of the world's biodiversity is in this hemisphere). It is therefore ironic the United States has paid so little attention to working with the region in a coherent and systematic way. U.S. energy security is tied closely to the resources in the Western hemisphere. According to the Energy Information Administration, in 2007 the United States imported 28.3 percent of its oil from Latin America and the Caribbean—outweighing the 16.6 percent imported from the Middle East. From reliance on Canadian oil, to the use of LNG from Trinidad and Tobago, to the recent efforts to develop a relationship with Brazil about biofuels there is ample reason for the United States to focus even greater resources on strong relations with its neighbors. Until 2007, when the United States and Brazil signed a memorandum of understanding to jointly develop renewable energy in the Western hemisphere, scant attention was paid to the issues of energy security, save for the way energy has been linked to the diplomacy focused on the new populist regimes in Venezuela, Bolivia, and Ecuador. Recent new discoveries of large deep-sea petroleum reserves off the coast of Brazil also indicate that the long-term potential for Latin America continuing to play a major role in the U.S. supply of hydrocarbons is assured.

In June 2007, at the General Assembly of the Organization of American States (OAS), Secretary of State Condoleezza Rice explained the U.S. approach to energy security in the Americas. She said "we seek to promote the democratization of energy in the Americas, increasing the number of energy suppliers, expanding the market and reducing supply disruption. We are starting this work now with El Salvador, the Dominican Republic, Haiti and St. Kitts. And we are eager to expand our cooperation on energy with more countries and especially with the OAS. Our goal should be nothing less than to usher in a new era of inter-American security in energy."[1] This statement plus the Bush administration's focus on renewable energy as memorialized in the U.S.-Brazil biofuels agreement, are among the clearest statements we have on what a Western hemisphere energy security strategy might entail.[2] But how does the United States "democratize" energy when its key suppliers are themselves having problems meeting their own energy commitments? And how does the United States help ensure its own energy future if many of those countries with large reserves are not yet able to export sufficient amounts of energy to make a real difference in filling the gap in our own country's increasing energy consumption?

There is a general consensus among leading energy information sources that energy consumption will surge as much as 30 percent by 2020. A growing world population and strong economic growth in developing countries will propel energy consumption, and the twin forces of urbanization and industrialization will accelerate this trend. Latin America, which has experienced a healthy increase in energy consumption, is expected to face a doubling of demand for all forms of energy in this time period.[3] The impact of this demand spike will be felt differently across the region. The rates of energy intensity and the annual per capita energy consumption levels of the Caribbean are quite distinct from those of the Andean countries, for example.[4] In addition to distinct consumption patterns, resources are distributed unequally throughout the region. Even the areas that have ready access to gas and oil, like the Southern Cone, also have their own specific energy issues related to lack of integration and asymmetric distribution of natural resources. There are thus a host of compelling reasons for the United States to work with countries of the hemisphere to develop strategies that will address the growing energy demand and its environmental impact.

Overview of Latin America's Energy Potential

Hydrocarbons

At the end of 2006, Latin America and the Caribbean (LAC) had 9.7 percent of world proven oil reserves and only 4 percent of the world's proven natural gas reserves. In terms of production, Latin America ranked third for oil and natural gas globally after the Middle East and Eurasia. According to the Energy Information Administration, in 2007 the United States' top sources of crude were Mexico, Venezuela, Ecuador, Colombia and Brazil. Mexico and Trinidad & Tobago are the only Latin American exporters of natural gas to the United States but they have a significant share of U.S. imports: 11 percent in 2007. In 2007 the Western hemisphere, including, of course, Canada, supplied 93 percent of America's natural gas.

Mexico is the most significant supplier of both oil and natural gas to the United States but its relative position within the region is being increasingly challenged by the depletion of its reserves, the decline of its production, and by recent developments that have favored both Venezuela and Brazil's relative position in oil while dramatically increasing Latin America's level of proven reserves: The

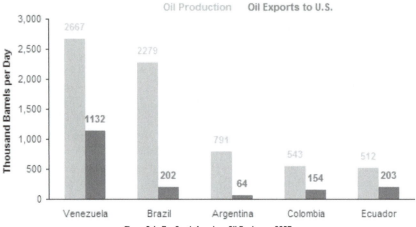

Figure 9.1 Top South American Oil Producers, 2007
Source: EIA Short Term Energy Outlook

2007/2008 Tupi, Carioca and Bem-te-vi discoveries point to the existence of oil (sweet crude) in a very large pre-salt area, on the southern Atlantic coast of Brazil, and the January 2008 Jupiter discovery is a large natural gas deposit estimated to contain approximately 5 billion to 8 billion barrels of oil equivalent, which could make Brazil self-sufficient in natural gas 5–10 years out, impacting Bolivia and others in the region.[5] The Brazilian government estimates the new reserves to be between 40 billion and 50 billion barrels. Added to the 2007 proven reserves of 14.4 billion barrels of oil and natural gas equivalent, they would potentially make Brazil the eighth biggest oil nation in the world, overtaking Russia.[6] In May 2008 Venezuela's government declared that the proven crude oil reserves had increased by 30 percent to reach 130 billion barrels, the largest reserves outside the Middle East.[7] In addition to conventional hydrocarbons, Latin America is rich in nonconventional crude. About 1.2 trillion barrels of extra heavy oil are in place in Venezuela. At current technology and prices, only 2–3 percent of this endowment is economically recoverable but it is likely that 100–270 billion barrels will eventually be economically recoverable.

Venezuela

Venezuela, once a major supplier of oil, has seen its production decline since 2002. This drop in production follows the government's growing intervention in the hydrocarbons sector, starting in November 2001 with President Hugo Chavez's enactment by decree of the new Hydrocarbons Law, which raised the royalties that oil companies had to pay to the Venezuelan state from 16.6 percent to 30 percent for heavy and for light crude, and from 1 percent to 16.6 percent for extra-heavy crude.[8] In February 2003, Chavez solidified his control over the hydrocarbons sector by firing the Petroleos de Venezuela (PDVSA) upper-echelon management along with another 18,000 PDVSA employees, following a two-month long strike that sought to force Chavez out of office by completely removing his access to the all-important government oil revenue. By then, the price of a barrel of crude had started to rise from the average price of under $25/barrel that had been in place since the mid-1980s. In 2004, the price of oil reached $50, giving Chavez access to billions of dollars, which he rapidly used to establish Venezuela's status as an energy powerhouse in Latin America and to counter U.S. influence in the region. As part of this strategy, in 2005 alone, Chavez inked preferential oil deals, barters and loans with Argentina, Brazil, Cuba, Uruguay, and Paraguay and with 13 Caribbean nations, which resulted in the establishment of PetroCaribe.[9] Chavez has also looked to other markets like China to reduce Venezuela's dependence on the U.S. oil market, signing several agreements and rapidly increasing exports: between 2001 and 2007, Venezuelan oil exports to the PRC rose 74 times, albeit starting from a small base.[10]

The enormous costs of these undertakings draw away from productive investments in energy, which combined with inefficient management of PDVSA and an aging oil infrastructure, explain Venezuela's inability to reach 2002 levels of production. At the same time, as Genaro Arriagada points out, Venezuela's demand is increasing, as is smuggling to Colombia, (100,000 bpd in 2006),[11] which has made it very difficult to predict whether Venezuela will be able to meet its own needs and simultaneously those of its preferential regional and extra-regional partners. Although the United States remains the main destination of Venezuelan crude production, PDVSA's shipments to the United States have been declining, particularly since 2004, resulting in a drop of 3 percent in Venezuela's share of U.S total oil imports to 10 percent between 2001 and 2007. Faced with declining oil production, Venezuela has turned to its vast natural gas reserves—the largest in the region and equivalent to 2.4 percent of the world's reserves in 2006. It is actively looking for partnerships to rapidly expand its production, which has been significantly below Venezuela's reserve potential. As part of this effort, Venezuela has launched the Delta Caribe Oriental LNG project. In contrast to previous natural gas projects, this one grants Caracas the freedom to choose between premium markets, namely the United States, Europe and Asia.[12]

Ecuador

Ecuador has the third largest reserves of oil and it is the fifth largest South American producer. In 2007 Ecuador sent 42 percent of its oil exports to the United States and was the second-largest source of U.S. crude oil imports from South America, after Venezuela. Like Caracas, Quito is highly dependent on oil as the main source of export earnings and tax revenues. After a sizable increase in production following the 2003 opening of the Oleducto de Crudos Pesados that doubled Ecuador's oil pipeline capacity, production has fallen in recent years. This drop has been attributed to aging equipment, natural decline, the lack of investment, and some operating difficulties at existing fields. One of the consequences of this decline has been Ecuador's failure to meet the production quota it received after rejoining OPEC in 2007. Future increases in Ecuador's crude oil production will likely come from development of the Ishpingo-Tapococha-Tiputini (ITT) block located in Ecuador's Amazon region, with potential recoverable reserves of heavy crude oil as high as 1.3 billion barrels, according to EIA.

Brazil

Brazil has the second-largest crude oil reserves in South America and is one of the fastest growing producers. In 2007, Brazil produced 2.2 mbd, only 14 percent less than South America's largest producer, Venezuela. This increase in production allowed Brazil to meet its rapidly expanding demand for oil. Brazil also exported 8.8 percent of its production to the U.S., making it the region's third largest supplier by providing 1.5 percent of U.S. oil imports in 2007. Brazil's role as a global hydrocarbons producer is set to expand in the next 5 to 10 years, thanks to the recent discoveries on its South Atlantic Coast. These colossal finds that prompted President Lula da Silva to exclaim that "God is Brazilian" pose significant engineering hurdles that will drive up costs in tapping the field.[13] Experts are confident that Brazil has the expertise to overcome these challenges, especially since Petroleo Brasileiro SA (Petrobras) is a global leader in deep water oil exploration. Brazil has become the region's success story in terms of transforming itself from a net importer of oil into a major crude producer, which will allow it to project its power globally. Key to this success was Brasilia's decision to strip Petrobras, the nation's oil company, of its regulatory role and open the way for energy competition in 1997. This fostered Petrobras' evolution into a competitive, efficient, and accountable company, attracting private investment and energy partnerships with foreign companies along the way.[14]

Colombia

Colombia has small natural gas reserves and the fifth-largest reserves of crude oil in South America. Much of Colombia's crude oil is lighter and sweeter than that of other major Latin American oil producers. About half of Colombia's oil production is exported, 28 percent of which went to the United States in 2007, making it the fourth largest regional source of U.S. oil imports with a 1.2 percent market share. Since 1999, Colombia's oil production has declined steadily, from its peak of 830,000 bpd to the current average of 540,000 bpd in the past three years. This production decline is a product of mature oil fields and a lack of sizable new reserve discoveries. The Colombian government has tried to reverse the current trend by introducing a series of measures to make the investment climate more attractive to foreign oil companies: partially privatizing the national oil company, Ecopetrol, allowing foreign oil companies to own 100 percent stakes in oil ventures; and the establishment of a lower, sliding-scale royalty rate on oil projects. These favorable measures combined with the improvement in

Colombia's security situation, to which the United States has contributed, have led to renewed interest by international oil companies. As a result there has been a significant increase in exploratory and development drilling and investment, $5.4 billion in 2006 and 2007, according to Proexport Colombia. There is hope that these investments will result in significant finds, particularly in the vast unexplored and potentially hydrocarbon-rich territories, which until recently were under Fuerzas Armadas Revolucionarias de Colombia's (FARC) control. Colombia's offshore Caribbean basins have also received more attention in recent years and new technology is expected to produce better results than in the past.

Renewable and Biomass

In terms of energy, Latin America is distinctive for its large renewable resources: hydropower, solar, wind, geothermal and biomass. As of 2005, Latin America had 19.2 percent of the world's technically exploitable hydropower capacity. The three countries with the largest potential in the region are Brazil (with almost 50 percent of Latin America's total capacity), followed by Peru and Venezuela. Most of this potential has remained unexplored due to engineering difficulties, environmental concerns and lack of investment. Brazil, for example, which has the highest installed hydropower capacity, was only exploiting 27 percent of its potential by the end of 2006. At present, there are talks of constructing six bilateral hydroelectric stations involving Brazil with Argentina, Bolivia and Peru. The region has had previous success in bilateral cooperation with Itaipu, which is one of the largest dams in the world and was still providing 8 percent of Brazil's energy needs in 2007.[15]

The exploration of solar and wind energy in Latin America is still in its infancy, despite the reduced costs in generation and maintenance of these energy sources. They are now reasonably priced renewable energy sources. Large areas of Latin American countries do not have access to grid electricity, thus making renewable sources like solar and wind energy an attractive alternative. The region's potential for solar power use is significant, particularly in Mexico, the Andean countries, the Caribbean and Southeast Brazil. Solar energy technologies themselves are expected to continue to improve, promising higher efficiencies and lower costs.[16] Wind power is one of the most promising renewable resources in Latin America. Government incentives and programs are evidently the main wind market drivers in the region, coupled with the need for enhanced energy security, rural electrification and energy diversification. Overall, the Latin American wind power installed capacity was expected to grow by 50 to 55 percent in 2007 and burgeon in 2008, as governments across the region begin implementing new wind power projects.[17] By mid-2008 several new projects had been launched in the region, including a joint venture between an American and Caribbean companies to develop 600MW of wind power in the region,[18] and the temporary concession for the construction of Las Lomas Wind Farm in Peru that will have a 240 MW capacity.[19]

According to the World Energy Council, 17 percent of the world's annual geothermal electricity generation occurred in Latin America in 2005. The top three Latin American producers were Mexico, the world's third largest geothermal producer, followed by Costa Rica and El Salvador. About 12 percent of the total electricity generation of Costa Rica, El Salvador, Guatemala and Nicaragua was provided by geothermal power stations. In terms of direct use of geothermal power, Brazil was the top producer, then Mexico and Argentina. There are still large untapped geothermal resources, and Mexico and Central America have significant experience in the technology.[20] This has attracted the interest of international companies like Enel (Italy), Ormat Technologies (U.S.) and Polaris Geothermal (U.S.).[21] Geothermal energy can play an important role in Chile, Peru, and the Caribbean area[22] but it is still in the early stages of development (except for Guadeloupe) due to insufficient government support, weak or nonexistent legislation, limited financing and economic incentives.

Energy from biomass has become a central focus of the U.S.-Latin American energy security relationship. First, it has been the source of an important bilateral diplomatic effort between the United States and Brazil to expand to other nations of the hemisphere the benefits of Brazilian and American experience in the production of ethanol. The U.S.-Brazil Biofuels Pact of March 2007 may be one of the most important legacies of the Bush administration in this hemisphere. Second, the debate over the use of different feedstock for the production of ethanol for transport has been subsumed by a larger global conversation about the use of food sources for fuel. Corn, the primary feedstock used in the U.S. biofuels industry, has been incorrectly targeted as the main source of increased commodity prices. Sugar, the source of Brazil's ethanol, is also being discussed as a culprit, despite the advanced technology and hybrids of sugarcane that Brazil has developed to produce ethanol most efficiently. The debate has also assumed a political dimension in the hemisphere as Chavez in Venezuela and Castro in Cuba have both condemned the use of biofuels made from food as a driver of increased poverty and hunger in Latin America. No matter where one stands on the food versus fuel debate, one thing is clear. Brazil, whose ethanol industry started thirty years ago, has greatly helped alleviate its dependence on fossil fuels for transportation. Brazil is the world's leading producer of ethanol. It is also the most efficient, using sugar cane that yields ethanol, and also using the cane waste or bagasse to generate electricity that runs the production facilities and the communities where the ethanol is produced. Brazil's success story has generated considerable interest in biofuels across Latin America, but no other industry in the region has yet approached the size or sophistication of Brazil's.[23] Brazil is now actively conducting ethanol diplomacy with neighbor countries, signing technology exchange agreements with Peru, Colombia, Argentina, Venezuela, Panama and Cuba. Not only has Brazil reduced the cost of ethanol production, but it has transformed its transport industry through the use of advanced flex-fuel engines that allow the consumer to drive on blend gasoline, pure ethanol, or any combination of the two.[24] Compared to U.S. corn ethanol, which costs $65 per oil equivalent barrel, Brazil's ethanol is far less expensive to make. As long as oil prices remain over $40 dollars a barrel Brazil's ethanol will remain competitive.[25] This investment in ethanol has allowed Brazil to leverage its experience, investments and technology to advance its own geopolitical role around the hemisphere and globally. Now the only remaining obstacle in the U.S.-Brazil relationship, the imposition of a 54 cent per gallon tariff on Brazilian ethanol imported to the United States, must be lifted so that the United States is able to get enough biofuels to meet the targets for the blending of renewable resources with fossil fuels mandated by recent U.S. energy legislation. One beneficiary of the food versus fuel debate may very well be Brazil, as the U.S. corn lobby faces greater public criticism of its use of a food crop for production of fuel. The biofuel debate has also opened up an international conversation in the United States and Europe about commodity subsidies that may once and for all end these practices.[26]

Opportunities in biofuels are not limited to Brazil, however, and include Colombia's promising biodiesel program, Chile's potential for cellulosic ethanol production, and the sugar export centers of Central America and the Caribbean. Many countries in Latin America have fitting climate and ample farmland available for cultivation of energy crops. The Caribbean and Central America, but especially the Dominican Republic, Cuba, Guatemala, Costa Rica, and El Salvador, which once relied on sugar exports to support their economies, are now ripe for conversion of that commodity to ethanol.[27] Given the absence of fossil fuels in this part of the hemisphere the advent of biofuels offers these countries a new commodity for internal use but also for export. Under regional trading agreements like the Central American Free Trade Agreement (CAFTA), which also includes the Dominican Republic, ethanol production from these countries is easily exported to the United States without a tariff, creating yet another incentive for investment and future growth.[28]

Development of biofuels also offers an important social dimension. It is a source of increased jobs not only in the agricultural sector, but also in the other industries that have grown up around the emergence of bioenergy production. In a region where the gap between rich and poor is most pronounced (30–50 percent of the region still lives in poverty, in spite of improved growth rates) renewable energy development offers an industry that will positively impact the region's most vulnerable populations. It is appropriate technology that can be used for large-scale production, but also lends itself to small farmer solutions as well. There is also growing evidence that rural development could be sustained by the creation of segmented biofuels markets to provide communities with fuel for cooking, transport and electricity generation. In some poor countries like Haiti, it is clear that using biomass to produce energy may well offer an exit from the extreme poverty that has paralyzed economic growth. In Haiti's case the use of a nonfood crop, jatropha, which can be made into biodiesel, promises a new beginning for rural farmers.[29]

Soybeans, African palm, castor, and jatropha are the main feedstocks for biodiesel production in the hemisphere. Brazil, Argentina, Paraguay, Colombia, and Guatemala have been the main centers of biodiesel production. But other countries in Central America and the Caribbean are also picking up production, though the volumes are quite small. In the case of Brazil, soybeans are also major export crops to China, hence the competition between production of oil for transport and for food. The other crops are not edible, though in the case of African Palm early results in Colombia are proving it less effective because the crop consumes great amounts of water. Jatropha, an indigenous crop in the Caribbean and Central America, offers the most promise as a nonfood feedstock for biodiesel.[30] In this context, biofuels have emerged as a strong transport fuel alternative. The Kyoto Protocol has provided an additional impetus to biofuels development as industrialized countries seek to meet their emissions reduction targets. The advantages offered by biofuels, such as lower carbon dioxide emissions and competitive production techniques, rely on existing technology. Latin America is second only to Asia as a location for Clean Development Mechanisms (CDM) projects, with 47 percent of the projects in 2006. There is interest in investing in these types of projects in the region, and there are parties already experienced in the CDM process.[31]

Looking forward, Colombia and Peru, which have negotiated free trade agreements with the United States (though Colombia's is still pending Congressional approval), have a potential advantage because of that access to the U.S. market. Indeed, Colombia is planning a major expansion of its palm oil production as a biodiesel feedstock, with an eye to the export market. Similarly, Mexico, with its proximity to the United States and open access to the U.S. market under the North America Free Trade Agreement (NAFTA), has strong external incentives to produce biofuels, including reducing air pollution, promoting rural development, and potentially supplementing its declining oil reserves through biofuels production and use. In Central America, Guatemala holds great potential for ethanol production as the largest sugar producer in Central America. The country harvests 197,000 hectares of sugarcane, using 15 sugar mills for processing. Its sugar industry earned the country nearly $500 million in 2005, and Guatemala ranks fifth in terms of global sugar exporters, exporting 72 percent of its production. In the Caribbean, Jamaica also has great potential for expanded ethanol production and exportation with roughly 347 million liters of ethanol production capacity and expansion plans for up to an additional 220 million liters in the short- to medium-term. In addition, sugar lobbies in El Salvador and the Dominican Republic that still receive subsidized sugar prices on their crop from the U.S. sugar quotas are reluctant to transform their sugar industries into biofuels operations until that benefit ends.[32] Even if there were an immediate decision to undertake a massive conversion of sugar plants to ethanol installations in the Caribbean, there would still be a delay as the sugar industry infrastructure is outdated and in need of large investments for modernization. There is also the uncertainty of the relationship of oil prices to ethanol development, though it is highly unlikely that we will ever see cheap oil again.

Challenges

Today Latin America's energy sector is facing multiple challenges, product of an oil price hike, declining production in several major hydrocarbons producers, energy disintegration, a growing concern with climate change and its disproportionate impact on the poor, and finally, the persistent energy inequality that affects nearly 45 million Latin Americans that live without electricity, half of them in Bolivia, Haiti, Honduras, Nicaragua, and Peru.[33] Probably the most significant challenge is whether Latin America will be able to meet its own growing demand. In recent years, energy insufficiency in South America has appeared as an important political, economic and social issue. The main reasons behind it are the lack of availability and instability in the supply of natural gas resulting from regional disintegration and underinvestment in the sector.

According to EIA's World Energy Outlook of 2007, Latin America needs to invest approximately $1.3 trillion in overall investment in the energy sector until 2030: 50 percent for power projects, 28 percent for oil, 19 percent for gas and less than 1 percent for coal.[34] Specifically in the case of biofuels, insufficient infrastructure translates to a lack of production facilities that take advantage of cogeneration for electricity, and inadequate storage and pipelines for transporting biofuels. Given limited local capacity, attracting private know-how and funds is essential to further fossil fuel production. According to the World Bank's Private Participation in Infrastructure Database, Latin America had the second largest number of privately funded projects in natural gas and electricity between 2000 and 2006.[35] In terms of investment, Latin America received 41 percent of all private funds coming into electricity and natural gas between 1992 and 2006. Unsurprisingly, the years of highest investment coincided with the liberalization of the Latin American energy sector. Between 2001 and 2004 investment declined but recovered again in 2005 and 2006. At the same time, Latin America has the highest incidence of projects being cancelled or considered under distress. 50 projects were valued at $20 billion, which is 67 percent of the total value of private investment at risk in the world. Recent estimates of current and planned investment in energy supply infrastructure investments in Latin America are lower than in all other developing regions (including Africa).[36] The "Doing Business Report 2008" by the International Finance Corporation provides an insight into this lack of enthusiasm by investors. Key Latin American energy producers perform significantly below average according to main business indicators: notoriously bad red tape, difficulties of doing business, complex and rigid labor rules, high and complex taxation, costly and time-consuming enforcement of contracts, and, most importantly, weak protection of investments. This weak general performance bodes ill for the prospects of the region's energy sector, especially when combined with resource nationalism that has gained momentum following the sustained rise in world prices since 2002. The price hikes have shifted the bargaining power away from foreign oil companies and toward oil-producing countries. The upsurge of leftist governments in Latin America in countries like Venezuela, Bolivia and Ecuador, major energy producers, has also favored resource nationalism. This recurring phenomenon in Latin America is characterized by tightening state control on energy assets, increasing royalties for private energy investors, and redistribution of proceeds, be it directly or through publicly-funded social programs.[37]

Bolivia, for example, nationalized its hydrocarbons industry in May 2006. On October 27, 2006, Petrobras, Bolivia's largest investor in the energy sector, accepted the increase of taxation on hydrocarbons, from 50 percent to 82 percent, to ensure supplies to Brazil. A year later, Venezuela's President, Chavez, as part of his renationalization campaign, tightened control over joint oil ventures in the Orinoco Belt, where he in essence confiscated approximately $6 billion in foreign assets.[38] These and other similar developments have led international oil companies to shift their operations elsewhere and have produced a growing number of requests for arbitration at the International Center for the Settlement of International Disputes (ICSID), making Latin America the region of the world with the largest share of claims (56%) since 2000.[39] Although foreign national oil companies (NOC) like Sinopec have also sought international arbitration, Chinese NOCs as well as NOCs from other countries like Malaysia, India, Iran and Russia have decided to stay in Latin America, taking over some of the concessions previously owned by international oil companies. Most of these NOCs are starting from a low base, however, which means that they will still play a relatively small role in the region's energy sector.

Latin America suffers simultaneously from too much and too little legislation. Regulations often delay the approval of projects in Latin America. They are complex, intricate and, at times, contradictory. A good example is the Angra III nuclear project in Brazil, which has been pushed for by the minister of Mines and Energy, but has seen its licensing process impeded by a court order.[40] At the same time, there are areas, particularly alternative energies, that are not covered by legislation or are under very rudimentary regulatory systems. While half of the countries in Latin America and the Caribbean have regional plans to develop biofuels industries there are still great gaps in the legal-regulatory frameworks necessary to actually implement changes in blending of fuels, and conversion to flex-fuel vehicles that allows for transitions to happen very quickly.[41] As mentioned earlier, regional disintegration may also jeopardize Latin America's ability to ensure its own energy supply. Despite the establishment of several institutions like Organización Latinoamericana de Energía (OLADE) in 1973 and, more recently, PetroCaribe (2007) and the Energy Council of South America (2007), de facto energy integration is almost nonexistent. OLADE, for example, focuses on peripheral issues, perhaps a result of the difficulty of generating consensus among its members on how to proceed with regional integration.[42] PetroCaribe is clearly not a long-term solution for the sub-region's high dependency on oil imports, but instead a political instrument used by Chavez to secure the influence of Caribbean states in Inter-American systems.[43] The lack of coordination among countries for their energy needs and the absence of overarching regional policies about energy defy common wisdom and economic logic—a profit of $90 billion by 2018 for natural gas alone[44]—that joining together to complement resources and capacity should be in the interests of all Latin American states.

Conclusions

The energy security relationship between Latin America and the United States is complex. The respective potential of different countries and regions demonstrates that the United States must craft a policy that takes into consideration our own national needs for resources, but also recognizes the hemisphere's requirements for sustainable economic growth.[45] The United States and Latin America are highly dependent on each other. The United States needs the fossil fuels, but Latin America needs U.S. trade, investment, and technology. The energy dynamic in the region is changing. Although U.S. dependency on Venezuelan oil is expected to continue in the near term, the production limitations at PDVSA will force it to seek a more diversified source of fuel. On the other hand, Brazil is poised to increase its importance as a supplier of fossil fuels to the United States, thanks to recent pre-salt discoveries of oil. The benefits of these discoveries will not be realized for at least a decade. As Brazil assesses its place in the world of major oil players there are signs of energy nationalism that may conflict with U.S. private sector interests. This situation makes it even more important for the United States to continue its positive relationship with Brazil.

Because there is no one specific solution to the diversity of problems from poor infrastructure, to lack of integrated energy systems, to poor legal-regulatory schemes, the United States will need a multidimensional approach to its energy relationships in the Americas. Such a policy framework will require sensitivity to environmental needs, energy inequality, and the impact that high costs of energy have on socioeconomic development. In the future, the U.S. can build on relationships that have started to grow around different types of energy solutions. For example, the continuation of the U.S.-Brazil biofuels pact to include additional countries and technical support would be welcome in other Central American and Caribbean nations. Alternative energy options should also form a basis for advancing a new energy framework for the hemisphere given the potential of wind, solar, and geothermal sources. And advanced biofuels will also play an important role in any future collaboration with the region as the biodiversity of the Americas offers ample opportunity for expansion of this type of fuel source.

Energy diplomacy is a tricky subject. Even if Chavez's regional petro-diplomacy is a source of friction with the United States, it is also pushing the United States to find closer alliances with countries like Brazil, Colombia, and the Caribbean. Washington will also need to pay closer attention to Cuba as a crossroads of two competing types of regional energy developments, particularly in light of foreseeable political changes in Havana as the Castro era comes to an end. Brazil is counting on new agreements with Raul Castro on cooperation to develop renewable energy sources, thus paving the way for Cuba's potential as an ethanol production and refining center just 90 miles from the U.S. market. On the other hand, Venezuela continues its petro-diplomacy in Cuba, which has helped sustain the Castro government since the signing of the bilateral "Convenio Integral de Cooperación" (2000) and Venezuela's decision to increase discounted oil shipments in 2005.[46]

It is likely that energy security will continue to dominate the geopolitical conversation in the years ahead. But it will remain only one element of a complex set of shared interests that will require cooperation and dialogue. For example, transnational crime, drug-trafficking, immigration, illicit arms transfers, free trade agreements and response to global warming and environmental degradation will also demand attention. For the U.S. to successfully pursue its geopolitical interests in Latin America it will need to address all these issues in a comprehensive way that once again puts Latin America on the top of the foreign policy agenda in Washington.

Notes

1. "Remarks at Organization of American States General Assembly Plenary Session," Secretary Condoleezza Rice, Panama City, Panama, June 4, 2007, http://www.state.gov/secretary/rm/2007/06/85968.htm.

2. "Memorandum of Understanding Between the United States and Brazil to Advance Cooperation on Biofuels," Office of the Spokesman, U.S. Department of State, Washington, D.C., March 9, 2007, http://www.state.gov/r/pa/prs/ps/2007/mar/81607.htm.

3. According to BP Statistical Review of 2007, Latin America's energy consumption grew 15.3 percent between 2000 and 2006, http://www.bp.com/sectiongenericarticle.do?categoryId=9023753&contentId=7044109.

4. "Energy Policy Scenarios 2050," World Energy Council, 2008, http://www.worldenergy.org/documents/scenarios_study_online_1.pdf.

5. Brian Fonseca, "Energy Outlook: Brazil," Pensar Internacional, March 14, 2008, http://pensar-internacional1.blogspot.com/2008/03/energy-outlook-brazil.html.

6. "Petrobras halla crudo ligero en cuenca Santos," *Reuters,* May 29, 2008, http://ve.invertia.com/noticias/noticia.aspx?idNoticia=200805292323_RTI_1212103406nN29461986&idtel=; Jonathan Wheatley and Richard Lapper, "Brazil Oil Field Poised to Transform Economy," *Financial Times,* June 9, 2008, http://www.ft.com/cms/s/0/31ba6024-35bc-11dd-998d-0000779fd2ac.html.

7. "Venezuela's Oil Reserves Swell to 130 Billion Barrels," *AFP News Agency,* May 8, 2008, http://www.breitbart.com/article.php?id=080508195126.9cnubmcr&show_article=1.

8. Gregory Wilpert, "Chavez Announces that Venezuela will Raise Oil Production Royalties," Venezuelanalysis.com, October 11, 2004, http://www.venezuelanalysis.com/news/730.

9. Danna Harman, "Chavez Seeks Influence with Oil Diplomacy," *Christian Science Monitor,* August 25, 2005, www.csmonitor.com/2005/0825/p01s04-woam.html.

10. Wenran Jiang, "China-Latin America Energy Relations," presentation at the School of Advanced International Studies (SAIS), April 8, 2008.

11. "Petropolitics in Latin America," Wilson Center Event Summary, February 15, 2007, http://www.wilsoncenter.org/index.cfm?topic_id=1425&categoryid=34EDAB85-AA6E-B2C4-4F2AD620BFBE0F2A&fuseaction=topics.events_item_topics&event_id=224298.

12. "Venezuela LNG Development—Delta Caribe Oriental LNG Project," 17th Latin American Energy Conference, Institute of the Americas, May 2008.

13. "'God is Brazilian,' Lula Says After oOil Find," *AFP,* November 20, 2007, http://afp.google.com/article/ALeqM5gYFLi2U6rrZ2YFmKvpLaO5rAGHfg.

14. "Petropolitics in Latin America."

15. "Brazil to Construct Hydroelectric Stations with Peru, Argentina and Bolivia," *Xinhua*, March 29, 2008, http://english.people.com.cn/90001/90778/90858/90864/6383288. html; Nielmar Oliveira, "Lobão diz que Brasil, Argentina e Bolívia deverão construir hidrelétricas em área de fronteiras," *Agência Brasil*, March 10, 2008, http://ultimosegundo.ig.com. br/economia/2008/03/10/lobao_diz_que_brasil_argentina_e_bolivia_deverao_construir_ hidreletricas_em_area_de_fronteiras__1223426.html; Paulo Maciel, "Celso Amorim Defends Venezuelan Entry Into Mercosur," *Agência Estado,* March 25, 2008, http://www.mre. gov.br/portugues/noticiario/nacional/selecao_detalhe3.asp?ID_RESENHA=436488;Milena Fiori, "Brasil não pretende rever acordo de Itaipu com o Paraguai, diz Marco Aurélio," *Agência Brasil*, April 2, 2008, www.agenciabrasil.gov.br/noticias/2008/04/02/materia.2008-04-02.9516202486/view.

16. "2007 Survey of Energy Resources," *World Energy Council 2007,* http://cesenet.org/ documents/ser2007_final_online_version_1.pdf.

17. "Latin American Wind Power Installed Capacity is Expected to Burgeon in 2008," *Business Wire,* September 27, 2007, http://www.allbusiness.com/energy-utilities/utilities-industry-electric-powerity/5258396-1.html.

18. "Latin America Jt. Wind Power Venture Formed," WindEnergyNews.com, May 21, 2008, http://www.windenergynews.com/content/view/1284/45/.

19. "Wind Farm For Energy Studies to be Built in Peru," *Living in Peru,* February 5, 2008, www.windenergynews.com/content/view/1165/45/.

20. "2007 Survey of Energy Resources," *World Energy Council, 2007,* http://cesenet.org/ documents/ser2007_final_online_version_1.pdf.

21. Ian Simpson, "Enel Eyes Volcanic Latin America for Geothermal Growth," *Reuters,* April 18, 2008, http://uk.reuters.com/article/oilRpt/idUKL1876417820080418; Wendell A. Duffield and John H. Sass, "Geothermal Energy as a Natural Resource," *USGS Circular 1249,* 2004, http://pubs.usgs.gov/circ/2004/c1249/c1249.pdf.

22. Lúdvík S. Georgsson, "Geothermal Training Program and Capacity Building in the East Caribbean Region," United Nations University, 03/25–27/2008, http://www. un.org/esa/sustdev/sids/2008_roundtable/presentation/energy_georgsson.pdf; Erouscilla P. Joseph, "Geothermal Energy Potential in the Caribbean," University of the West Indies, March 2008, www.sustainabilityforum.com/forum/sustainable-energy/3408-geothermal-energy-potential-caribbean-region.html.

23. Sergio C. Trindade, "Beyond Petroleum and Towards a Biomass-based Sustainable Energy Future: Opportunities for Financing Sustainable Development and Carbon Trade," presented at Biomass Energy Workshop, World Bank, Washington, D.C., February 2003.

24. World Bank, "Potential for Biofuels for Transport in Developing Countries," Chapter 2, *International Experience,* (Washington, D.C., 2005).

25. Energy Future Coalition, *Biofuels Facts: A Primer* (Washington, D.C., 2006), 9, 28.

26. Sawar Anil, "Brazil Rejects Biofuel Criticism," *The Guardian,* April 17, 2008, http:// www.guardian.co.uk/environment/2008/apr/17/biofuels.food.print.

27. Marcos J. Jank, Geraldine Kutas, Luiz Fernando do Amaral, and Andre M. Nassar, *U.S. and EU Policies on Biofuels: Potential Impacts on Developing Countries* The German Marshall Fund of the United States, Washington, D.C., April 2007, http://gmfus.org//doc/ GMF_US-EU_Final.pdf.

28. Ariel Cohen, "Two Cheers for the President's Brazilian Ethanol Initiative," Web-Memo #1401, March 20, 2007. The Heritage Foundation, 2.

29. Eric Kroh, "Can Biodiesel Power Haiti?" *Biodiesel Magazine,* May 2008, http://www.biodieselmagazine.com/article-printe.jsp?article_=2296.

30. Johanna Mendelson Forman, "Jatropha and Peacebuilding," Testimony before the House of Representatives, Western Hemisphere Sub-Committee, March 13, 2007.

31. "A Blueprint for Green Energy in the Americas—Strategic Analysis of Opportunities for Brazil and the Hemisphere, Featuring: The Global Biofuels Outlook 2007," Garten Rothkopf for the IADB, 2007.

32. Daniel de la Torre Ugarte, Johanna Mendelson Forman, and Charlotte McDowell, *Dominican Republic's Biofuel Potential: A Report Prepared for UNCTAD and the UN Foundation,* unpublished, November 2005.

33. Ibid.

34. Veronica Prado, "Energy Infrastructure in the Western Hemisphere," in *Energy Cooperation in the Western Hemisphere: Benefits and Impediments,* ed. Sidney Weintraub et al. (Washington, D.C.: Center of Strategic International Studies, 2007), 406.

35. Private Participation in Infrastructure Projects Database, *The World Bank Group,* 2007.

36. Georg Caspary, "The Energy Sector in Latin America," Deutsche Bank Research, September 7, 2007, http://www.dbresearch.com/PROD/DBR_INTERNET_EN-PROD/PROD 0000000000215273.PDF.

37. Ibid.

38. Ray Walser, "Meeting Energy Challenges in the Western Hemisphere," *Heritage Lecture #1079,* November 3, 2008.

39. Christopher J. Gonçalves, "Energy Disputes in the Americas: Bringing Method to Madness," presented to XVII Annual Latin American Energy Conference, *Navigant Consulting,* May 2008.

40. Alana Gandra, "Eletronuclear recorre de decisão judicial sobre novas audiências públicas para Angra 3," *Agência Brasil,* January 25, 2008, http://www.agenciabrasil.gov.br/noticias/2008/01/25/materia.2008-01-25.0222121499/view.

41. "Sistema de Informacion Energetica Legal," *OLADE,* June 9, 2008, http://www.olade.org/siel.html.

42. OLADE's official Web site, News and Organization sections, June 9, 2008, http://www.olade.org.ec.

43. "Petropolitics in Latin America."

44. Mauricio B. Garron, "OLADE: Thematic Planning Meeting on Comprehensive Energy Planning," *International Atomic Energy Agency,* October 30, 2006, http://tc.iaea.org/tcweb/abouttc/strategy/Thematic/pdf/presentations/energysystemplanning/LA_Energy_Perspective-OLADE_Workplan.pdf.

45. Brazil Institute, "The Global Dynamics of Biofuels: Potential Supply and Demand for Ethanol, and Biodiesel in the Coming Decade," *Brazil Institute Report,* April 3, 2007, 3. This report noted that "alternative energy policies that protect against hydrocarbon price volatility, promote technological research, and stimulate investment can lead in the direction of less reliance on hydrocarbons and greenhouse gases." The problem now is that we lack such a policy today.

46. "Venezuela/Cuba: Accord Seeks Regional Integration," *Oxford Analytica,* January 6, 2005.

CHAPTER 10

United States: A Shackled Superpower

Gal Luft

When Americans think about energy security they think petroleum and transportation. Unlike Europeans or Japanese, whose electricity generation is dependent on imported natural gas or coal, the United States is almost self-reliant for its power generation. It owns a quarter of the world's proven coal reserves; it operates more than 100 nuclear reactors; it has untapped natural gas reserves, and its system of rivers and dams produces hydroelectric power that meets nearly 5 percent of its electricity needs. Only 2 percent of U.S. electricity is generated from petroleum. When it comes to the transportation sector, the situation is completely different. Energy consumption in the transportation sector relies almost exclusively (97%) on petroleum-based fuels. Nearly 85 percent of the energy consumed in this sector is for vehicle travel, followed by air (9%) and rail and water (6% combined).[1] The United States consumes a quarter of the world's oil supply, a gigantic amount of 21 million barrels per day (mbd), an amount of oil that can daily fill a container the size of the Twin Towers. Yet, it is the locus of a mere 3 percent of global conventional oil reserves. Putting aside the current economic recession, U.S. gross domestic product is projected to grow at an average annual rate of roughly 3 percent from 2005 to 2030 and, barring a change of course, its oil consumption is projected to jump from 21 mbd to 25.5 mbd over the same period. Domestic oil production, at 5 mbd, is expected to stay almost flat.[2] Consequently, the United States is heavily—and increasingly—dependent on foreign oil. In fact, as can be seen in Figure 10.1, U.S. dependence on imported oil has increased from 30 percent in 1973, when Arab countries imposed their oil embargo, to over 60 percent today. By 2030, the United States is expected to import close to 70 percent of its oil and a growing portion of it will come from the Persian Gulf, Nigeria and other politically unstable regions.[3]

Historically, when it comes to oil American energy policy has been focused on a narrow definition of energy security that strived to ensure sufficient supply at affordable prices. This has translated primarily into policies promoting increased

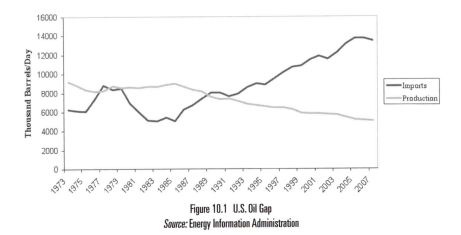

Figure 10.1   U.S. Oil Gap
Source: Energy Information Administration

and diversified production of energy from a range of foreign suppliers, effective measures to respond to physical oil supply disruptions through the use of strategic stocks, and a dialogue with major oil producing countries aimed to maintain responsible production policies. Conservation was also historically part of this, less so since the 1980s, when oil prices collapsed. While these policies have been successful in providing decades of relative stability in the energy market they now seem to be failing in the face of what Senator Richard Lugar calls "the new energy realism" in the global energy market, one that gives inordinate power to a small club of nondemocratic, largely anti-American oil-producing countries that otherwise would have little influence on the world scene.[4]

Because the American way of life is one of the most energy-intensive in the world, U.S. oil dependence is a source of great national security threats—"the albatross of U.S. national security" in Lugar's words—and an economically destabilizing factor. The rise of Islamic fundamentalism, the instability in the Middle East and Africa, and the natural disasters in energy producing areas are constant reminders to Americans that their oil supply, and, by extension, their way of life, is increasingly vulnerable.

Perhaps the biggest concern associated with oil dependence is that it undermines U.S. foreign policy objectives. "I can tell you that nothing has really taken me aback more as secretary of state than the way that the politics of energy [is] 'warping' diplomacy around the world," said then Secretary of State Condoleezza Rice in a 2006 testimony before the Senate Foreign Relations Committee.[5] The impact on foreign policy expresses itself in various ways. First, the United States finds itself in an odd situation in which it funds both sides of the war on terror. On the one hand it carries most of the financial burden associated with fighting the war on radical Islam and defending the Persian Gulf from aggressors, and at the same time through its oil imports it funds the very same regimes of Iran and Saudi Arabia that are most responsible for the spread of this ideology.[6] Second, the excessive power wielded by other oil and gas producing countries like

Venezuela and Russia enables those countries to use their wealth to undermine U.S. interests in Latin American and Eurasia. Third, China is today the world's second largest petroleum user after the U.S. and its dependence on Iran and Sudan prevents Beijing from siding with the Washington on vital issues like Iran's nuclear program and the genocide in Darfur. In the future, China's pursuit of oil could create increasingly tense Sino-American competition over access to oil.

Oil dependence has considerable economic implications. Disruptions of foreign oil supplies sparked the two most serious recessions of the post World War II period. The massive rise in gasoline price in 2007–2008 has taken a considerable economic toll on working families, and petroleum purchases are responsible for roughly one-third of the U.S. trade deficit and a slew of economic dislocations from declining currency to inflation. For the two decades between 1988 and 2007, U.S. expenditures on petroleum imports averaged $78.5 billion annually. In 2008, the United States paid nearly half a trillion dollars for foreign oil, an amount that far surpasses its defense budget. This loss of national wealth is believed to be one of the causes of the economic crisis that hit the United States in full force in September 2008.

In a Hole, Yet Keeps Digging

The danger of America's growing dependence on oil from unstable regimes has been on the mind of every American president since Richard Nixon. On January 30, 1974, several months after the Arab oil embargo, President Richard Nixon addressed the nation, saying: "Let this be our national goal: At the end of this decade, in the year 1980, the United States will not be dependent on any other country for the energy we need to provide our jobs, to heat our homes and to keep our transportation moving." On July 15, 1979, President Jimmy Carter made a similar pledge: "I am tonight setting a clear goal for the energy of the United States. Beginning this moment, this nation will never use more foreign oil than we did in 1977—never."[7] Carter requested of Congress "the most massive peacetime commitment of funds and resources in our nation's history" to develop efficiency measures and alternative energy sources. In the next several years, conservation proved to be America's fastest growing energy sector. Fuel efficiency of the average American car nearly doubled. Fuel switching brought down the share of homes using oil for heating from 31 percent to 10 percent. Electricity generation from oil dropped from 17 percent of the nation's total power output to its current 2 percent (a fact that seems to have eluded many in the public sphere who incorrectly persist in calls for increased solar, wind, or nuclear power generation as ways to reduce oil consumption.) The oil shocks of the 1970s also launched a wave of technological innovation in alternative energy and gasoline substitutes. Energy saving patents were registered by the thousands, and several government bureaucracies to enforce and encourage conservation were established. As a result of all these measures, between 1979 and 1985 oil consumption in the U.S. decreased by 15 percent, oil imports fell by 42 percent and imports from the Persian Gulf by 87 percent.[8] But America's progress toward energy independence was stopped by the collapse of oil prices in the mid-1980s. Many investors in alternative energy lost their shirts and the improvement in fuel economy of American cars stalled; in the two decades following 1987 it remained essentially unchanged. In recent years, the aforementioned impact on the U.S. economy and foreign policy brought oil dependence to the top of America's national priority list. Then President George W. Bush, a president who emerged from the petroleum industry, acknowledged in his 2006 State of the Union Address that: "We have a serious problem: America is addicted to oil," while his successor, President Barack Obama said in January 2009: "At a time of such great challenge for America, no single issue is as fundamental to our future as energy."[9]

Despite the broad agreement on the urgent need to reduce petroleum dependence, America's energy policy still suffers from institutional paralysis. Fuel economy standards in the United States are lower than any other industrial country and alternatives to oil face significant barriers to market penetration. This is caused partly due to partisan bickering but mostly due to a poor definition of the energy problem. After a century of a transportation sector dominated by petroleum—almost all of the world's cars, trucks, ships and planes can run on nothing but petroleum—Americans accept oil's strategic status as a fait accompli. As a result, instead of addressing oil's virtual monopoly in the transportation sector—the reason for oil's status as a strategic commodity—as a problem to be solved, the focus has been on policies that increase either the availability of petroleum or the efficiency of its use. This led to a public discourse that is focused too much on solutions that are politically contentious (like domestic drilling and increasing mandatory fuel efficiency standards) and by and large tactical rather than strategic or, in the case of solar, wind and nuclear power, irrelevant to the problem, as almost no electricity is generated from oil. The reality is that neither efforts to expand petroleum supply nor those to crimp petroleum demand will be enough to reduce America's strategic vulnerability. The reason for this is that such solutions do not address oil's monopoly over transportation fuel and the stronghold of OPEC over the consuming nations' economies. Yet, while there is a near consensus about the danger of continuous reliance on oil, and while it is clear that the transportation sector is, and will continue to be, the main petroleum consuming sector, every year the United States continues to put on its 10–15 million new gasoline only cars, each with a street life of 16 years, hence locking its future to petroleum-exporting nations for many years to come. Cars that can run only on petroleum are perhaps the biggest obstacle to U.S. energy security as they essentially guarantee the perpetuation of the petroleum standard and the oil cartel's continuous domination over the global transportation sector.

A new energy security paradigm is therefore urgently needed, one that requires deployment of diplomatic, military, scientific, and economic resources toward solving the energy problem, and, most important, one that enables the United States to shift the economic and geopolitical balance of power to its advantage by shifting from a petroleum-dominated transportation system to one in which petroleum alternatives can play a significant role, and doing this while providing for the petroleum needs of the 220 million cars and trucks that will be running on America's roads during the transition period.

Militarization of Energy Security

An American columnist who was asked after 9/11 what U.S. energy policy is replied with two words: "aircraft carriers."[10] Behind the sarcasm lies a plain truth: the use of military power to ensure free flow of oil from the Persian Gulf has been the main tenet of U.S. national energy security policy since the 1980s. According to the Carter doctrine coined by President Jimmy Carter after the oil crises of the 1970s, any effort by a hostile power to block the flow of oil from the Persian Gulf to the United States will be viewed as an attack on America's vital interests and will be repelled by any means necessary including military force. Since 1980, the United States has exercised the Carter doctrine several times. When, during the Iran-Iraq War, Iranian forces attacked Kuwaiti tankers, President Ronald Reagan authorized reflagging and provided them with U.S. Navy protection. Then, following Iraq's invasion of Kuwait in 1990 President George H.W. Bush authorized military action to defend Saudi Arabia's oil fields and restore Kuwait sovereignty. In the decade between the Gulf War and the 2003 Operation Iraqi Freedom the United States strengthened its military presence in the region, building bases in Qatar, Bahrain, and Kuwait. At a cost of $50-$60 billion per year (in a non-war year) it patrolled the waters of the Gulf, imposed a no-fly zone in Iraq and provided training and equipment to the region's militaries. During the Second Iraq War, coalition forces invested a great deal of resources in critical energy infrastructure protection. Since the last several years of the 20th century, with increased geographical diversification of America's oil supplies, the Carter Doctrine has gone global, and military protection is now granted to new, albeit smaller, oil-producing regions.[11] Both the Clinton and the second Bush administrations made significant efforts to strengthen U.S. ties with emerging oil producing nations in Central Asia, West Africa and Latin America. U.S. military forces are deployed in and/or provide military assistance to Azerbaijan, Kazakhstan, Afghanistan (not an energy producer but one that could become an important transit state for Caspian energy), until 2006, Uzbekistan and until 2008 Kyrgyzstan. In Latin America, U.S. Special Forces are deployed in Colombia to help the government protect pipelines that are repeatedly attacked by drug lords and terrorists. With increased interest in African oil, U.S. military presence along the west coast of Africa, where some of the most promising offshore oil fields are known to exist, has grown considerably. In 2007, the U.S. military created the Africa Command, AFRICOM, to address security challenges in the African continent.

The problem with militarization as a way to achieve energy security is that often it delivers the opposite result. U.S. military presence in energy domains feeds a perception that the United States is an imperialist power that intends to take over oil fields. This, in turn, invites antagonism, anti-Americanism and terrorism. U.S.

military presence in Saudi Arabia was a rallying cry for Islamic fundamentalists and a prime motivator of al-Qaeda's 9/11 attacks. Iraq provides an example of the limitation of military power in providing energy security. More than 150,000 U.S. troops were deployed for several years in the country that holds the second largest conventional crude reserve. Yet, during the U.S. occupation Iraq has exported less oil than it did prior to the first Gulf War. The U.S. presence has not enabled the country to fulfill its potential to emerge as a major oil producing country, and may have caused the exact opposite. Terrorists who believe the United States is out to rob the Muslims of their oil have identified the country's energy infrastructure as a prime target. Between 2003 and 2007 Iraq's pipeline system has been attacked more than 500 times.[12] This has hindered investment in Iraq's energy sector and scared away multinational oil companies, denying the global oil market millions of barrels per day that otherwise could have been available for export.

Diversification

Contrary to common belief, the United States is *not* heavily dependent on Middle East oil. As Figure 10.2 shows, about a third of total U.S. imports come from Canada, Mexico, and Venezuela, whereas the Middle East (primarily Saudi Arabia) accounts for a little more than 18 percent of total imports. U.S. relations with its neighbors are therefore critical to its future energy security. Of the three Western hemispheric neighbors, Canada, America's top trading partner overall and also its number one source of foreign oil, offers the most promise. U.S.-Canada relations are stable and the Canadian resource base holds great potential for America's future. Apart from large reserves of conventional oil and natural gas, Canada's oil sands in Alberta, 174 billion barrels in total, are second only to Saudi Arabia in terms of proven oil resources, albeit significantly more difficult and costly to extract. Output of marketable oil sands production increased to over 1 mbd in 2007. With anticipated growth, this level of production could reach 3 mbd by 2020 and possibly even 5 mbd by 2030. But due to Canada's growing demand and the rise of China, only a fraction of this oil will be directed to the U.S. market. The situation in Mexico is different. Though it is the fifth-largest producer of oil in the world, the country's production and proven reserves are in acute decline. Mexico produced an average of 3.74 mbd during 2006, a 1.2 percent decline from 2005 and a 2.5 percent decline from 2004. Its reserves/production ratio fell from 20 years in 2002 to 10 years in 2006.[13] Mexico's largest producing field, the Cantarell offshore field in the Gulf of Mexico, is facing a steep annual decline of roughly 14 percent from the current 2 mbd to anywhere between 1.5 mbd and 0.5 mbd.[14] Apart from natural geological depletion the Mexican oil sector suffers from excessive government control, insufficient investment, corruption and mismanagement. Be it due to geology or mismanagement Mexico's oil decline could cost the United States more than 1 mbd.

An even more complicated challenge for U.S. energy security is Venezuela. The United States and Venezuela are interdependent. Venezuela supplies about 11 per-

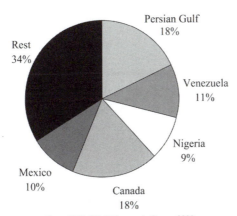

Figure 10.2 U.S. Oil Imports by Source, 2008
Source: Energy Information Administration

cent of U.S. oil imports and the United States purchases roughly 60 percent of Venezuela's oil output. Yet, relations between the two countries are acrimonious. In recent years, Venezuela's populist leader Hugo Chavez has tightened his grip over the country's state owned oil company, Petroleos de Venezuela (Pdvsa) and his heavy-handed policies have caused a rapid decline in Venezuela's production. His tense relations with the Bush administration brought him in September 2008 to expel the U.S. ambassador from Venezuela and recall his envoy to Washington. He also threatened more than once that "oil is a geopolitical weapon" and that he would not hesitate to use it should the bilateral relations continue to deteriorate. Chavez has also stated his intent to drive oil to $200 a barrel and to divert an increasing portion of Venezuela's oil exports from the United States to China.[15] In the near term, these threats are hollow, as the United States is the only country with significant infrastructure to refine Venezuela's specific type of crude, but as China and Venezuela develop such refining capacity more and more oil will be diverted into the Asian market at the expense of the U.S. market.

The decline of Western hemispheric producers will force the United States increasingly to turn to alternative suppliers. The National Energy Policy (NEP) report released by the White House in May 2001 (also known as the Cheney report) put strong emphasis on obtaining access to petroleum sources abroad by removing political, economic, legal, and logistical obstacles in Caspian and African nations "to provide a strong, transparent, and stable business climate for energy and related infrastructure projects."[16] At first glance, diversification of sources may seem to be a sound approach. But this solution is no more than a Band-Aid, and, in the long run, it could breed stronger reliance on the club of countries on which the United States would like to be less dependent. There are two downsides to this approach. First, oil is a globally traded, fungible, commodity, so stifling

U.S. purchases from the Persian Gulf and buying from other regions like Africa would just mean that somebody else would buy more from the Persian Gulf with no impact on price and availability. Second, reserves outside of the Middle East are being depleted almost twice as fast as those in the Middle East. The overall reserves-to-production ratio—an indicator of how long proven reserves would last at current production rates—in non-OPEC countries is about 15 years comparing to roughly 80 years in OPEC. With current growth in global demand, many of today's large non-Middle East producers such as Russia, Mexico, Norway and China are running a marathon at the pace of a sprint, and, if production continues at today's rate, many of today's largest producers will cease to be relevant players in the oil market in less than two decades. At that point, the Middle East will be the remaining major reservoir of abundant, cheap crude oil and the world's dependence on it will grow rather than diminish. This could allow Middle Eastern producers even more leeway than they have today to manipulate prices and increase their political leverage on U.S. foreign policy.

Second, deepening alliances with various African and Central Asian energy exporters may be beneficial to energy security, but by relying on additional non-democratic countries the United States runs the risk of undermining its own foreign policy priorities such as human rights and democracy promotion. Supplying nondemocratic oil producers with advice and state-of-the-art weapons enables these regimes to stay in power and oppress their people. Such relations have proven in the past to be extremely problematic and in conflict with America's prime foreign policy goal of spreading freedom and democracy in countries where they are lacking. In the 1970s, energy security considerations dictated forgiving treatment of the Shah of Iran despite his corruption and abysmal human rights record. When the Shah fell, the Iranian people responded with an outpouring of anti-Americanism that reverberates to this date. America's support for the House of Saud and reluctance to criticize Saudi Arabia's dreadful human rights record openly, its mistreatment of women and its lack of religious freedom and contempt for Shiites, Sufis and other non-Wahhabi Muslims is already producing similar sentiment. Like the Middle East, both Central Asia and West Africa suffer from territorial disputes, authoritarian regimes, bad governance, corruption, ethnic and religious strife and terrible human rights records. Nigeria, expected to supply a quarter of U.S. oil imports by 2030, is one of the most corrupt countries in the world and despite its oil riches most of its people live on less than $2 a day. The situation in Angola and Equatorial Guinea is not much better. Central Asia's most important producers, Azerbaijan and Kazakhstan, both have human rights records that would normally deny them U.S. support. Yet, by becoming increasingly dependent on new energy producing regions the United States is forced to turn a blind eye to these social illnesses and in doing so it undermines the prospects for the kind of reforms that are the keystone of its own diplomatic efforts.[17] It is therefore not clear whether the rush to the new oil domains will improve America's energy security or replay in other arenas the problems the United States currently faces in the Middle East.

Schizophrenia Regarding China

As President John Kennedy once noted, in the Chinese language the word crisis is composed of two characters. One represents danger, and the other represents opportunity. In the same vein, the rise of China creates both dangers and opportunities for U.S. energy security. To date the United States is undecided as to whether China is a friend or foe in this respect. With 1.4 billion people and an economy growing at a phenomenal rate, China is today the world's second largest oil consumer and is becoming heavily dependent on imported oil. By 2030 China is expected to import as much oil as America does today. To fuel its growing economy China is following in America's footsteps, subjugating its foreign policy to its energy needs as Chinese oil companies buy stakes in foreign oil fields in Africa, Central Asia and the Western hemisphere. In a lecture at Beijing University in March 2004, China's deputy foreign minister, Wang Yi, admitted that Chinese foreign polices are "at the service of China's economic development."[18] China's pursuit of energy could present an opportunity to enhance cooperation, integration and interdependence with the United States. Its willingness to invest in high-risk energy-producing countries adds to the tight energy market product that otherwise would have been available. At the same time, there are ample signs that China's pursuit of energy runs counter to key strategic goals of the United States. China's attempts to gain a foothold in the Middle East and build up long-term strategic links with key energy producers is likely to challenge the Pax Americana that has prevailed in the Middle East since the end of the Cold War. In the past several years, U.S.-China competition has extended far beyond the Middle East, including Africa and the Western hemisphere, where half of U.S. petroleum imports come from. Unlike the United States, which bars companies from doing business with some unsavory regimes, China's state-owned companies turn a blind eye to the way petrodollars are used by countries like Burma, Sudan and Uzbekistan. In the global contest for oil the United States loses ground as a result of its pressure for government reform. Dictators who view democracy with suspicion much prefer to sign E&P deals with the Chinese, who pay top dollars and do not lecture them on democracy and human rights. Furthermore, if Chinese companies increase their ownership of energy assets in these countries, this may increase China's propensity to intervene in order to protect its investments. This will force the United States to invest increasing diplomatic and economic efforts to court energy-producing nations in an attempt to prevail in the global competition over access to energy. While U.S. official statements call for increased energy collaboration, the two countries are highly suspicious of each other's motives. The U.S. Congress has been exceedingly critical of China's activities and has worked to undermine Chinese acquisition of an American energy company. American technology firms are reluctant to share technology with the Chinese due to their abysmal property rights record. The Chinese, for their part, do not hide their concern about U.S. domination of the high seas and America's ability to block energy shipments to China should a crisis develop.

The Piggybank Dilemma

According to the U.S. Department of Interior there are 21 billion barrels of conventional crude oil and 187 trillion cubic feet of natural gas below federally controlled lands, mostly in the western part of the United States and in Alaska. (To put these figures in proportion U.S. annual oil consumption in 2007 stood at 7.5 billion barrels and its natural gas consumption stood at 23 trillion cubic feet.) An additional 85 billion barrels are believed to lie offshore, in the outer continental shelf. The United States also accounts for 60 percent of the world's endowment of oil shale. This alone constitutes a potential of 1.5–2.6 trillion barrels, primarily concentrated in the Green River formation in Colorado, Utah, and Wyoming, if technology is developed to extract it economically, a task made easier by high oil prices but uneconomic when prices are lower. A U.S. government-commissioned Task Force on Strategic Unconventional Fuels Resources concluded: "Depending on technology and economics, as much as 800 billion barrels of oil equivalent could be recoverable from oil shale resources yielding roughly 25 gallons per ton. Production of fuels from domestic oil shale, under various growth assumptions, could potentially exceed 2.5 mbd within 30 years."[19] A significant amount of shale gas, porous sedimentary rocks, and sandstone that stores natural gas, is located primarily in deposits in Texas, Oklahoma, Alabama, Colorado, and Arkansas. Despite America's wealth of energy resources and the plethora of political speeches calling for energy independence, over the years both Republican- and Democratic-controlled congresses have refused to increase access to oil and gas resources in federal lands, and 51 percent of America's oil and 27 percent of natural gas reserves are off limits.

The debate over the utilization of domestic reserves is complex. Environmental activists oppose drilling in Alaska on the grounds that it would hurt sensitive terrain and wildlife. Coastal states relying on tourism like Florida and California are worried about the risk of oil spills associated with offshore drilling. Despite the prominence of the debate it is not clear that increased use of domestic reserves would do much to bring down oil prices. A recent study by the Energy Information Administration estimated that under the best-case scenario opening up the Alaskan National Wildlife Reserve (ANWR) would reduce prices by $0.41-$1.44 per barrel by 2027.[20] Drilling off the continental United States would hardly affect prices until 2030. There is also a moral question: Alaskan and offshore oil are probably America's last remaining conventional reserves. Breaking this piggy bank to power SUVs would mean consigning future generations to reliance on foreign sources of oil for applications in which oil is likely to remain essential, like drugs, chemicals, paints and plastics. There is also another concern raised by the EIA: "Assuming that world oil markets continue to work as they do today, the OPEC could neutralize any potential price impact of ANWR oil production by reducing its oil exports by an equal amount."[21] Experience of the past three decades clearly shows that whenever non-OPEC producers increase their production, OPEC decreases supply accordingly, keeping the overall amount of oil in the market essentially the same.

A Blueprint for Energy Security

The popular debate on energy security in the United States leans toward the pursuit of energy independence, a concept that has been ridiculed by many policymakers. A 2007 report of the National Petroleum Council refers to energy independence as "unrealistic in the foreseeable future and incompatible with broader foreign policy objectives and treaty obligations. Policies espousing energy independence may create considerable uncertainty among international trading partners and hinder investment in international energy supply development."[22] A Council on Foreign Relations report went as far as accusing those working for such independence of "doing the nation a disservice."[23] Such voices interpret energy independence simplistically as autarky—that is, complete self-sufficiency, or not importing energy from any foreign source. But self-sufficiency is not what energy independence means. Energy independence means reduction of the role of oil in international politics by turning it from a strategic commodity to just another commodity. Independence would not necessarily lower the price of energy or reduce price volatility but it would break oil's monopoly over transportation fuels, a monopoly that gives intolerable power to a small group of oil producers. Independence could, over the long run, rid the United States of many of its foreign policy constraints.[24]

How can the United States achieve such a goal? Surely, much more can be done to squeeze more domestic oil and gas and increase the use of America's huge endowment of non-conventional petroleum sources. New technologies, such as deep water drilling and enhanced oil recovery, are reducing the environmental effects and the economic costs of accessing technically challenging oil and gas reserves. But tapping into conventional domestic reserves that, all included, amount to less than 3 percent of the world's reserves, will never be more than a stopgap solution. Increased production from nonconventional petroleum sources like tar sands and oil shale would certainly add product to the market but they are not likely to be competitive with OPEC's production costs. As long as the petroleum standard dominates the global transportation sector, the oil cartel will be in the driver's seat of the world economy. Long-term security and prosperity require the development of sufficient, affordable, reliable, and sustainable petroleum alternatives that can compete against oil-derived transportation fuels at the pump. Getting to a point where alternative fuels comprise a significant portion of America's energy supply will take many years, substantial investment and strong political will. The latter is particularly necessary in light of the political clout of some of the industry groups that prefer to defend the status quo. For nearly three decades the auto industry effectively blocked efforts to increase fuel efficiency standards. This opposition was broken with the signing of the Energy Independence and Security Act of 2007, which required automakers to boost fleet-wide gas mileage to 35 miles per gallon by 2020, and in May 2009 the Obama administration introduced an even more stringent requirement of 35.5 miles per gallon by 2016. The oil industry enjoys billions of dollars worth of tax credits and is collecting a

45 cents-per-gallon federal subsidy for each gallon of ethanol it mixes with gas but its control over the fuel distribution system allows it to block any significant market penetration of petroleum alternatives.[25] The corn ethanol lobby also supports policies that undermine energy security. In the United States corn-derived alcohol is blended with gasoline and is on track to supply about 10 percent of America's fuel supply. The United States has 100 ethanol refineries that, in 2008, produced roughly 7 billion gallons a year from corn. Additionally, there are 76 plants under construction.[26] Yet, corn is not the best crop for ethanol production. Sugarcane is a far better. It has higher energy content and it is cheaper to grow. But the ethanol industry, through its champions in Congress, restricts imported sugar ethanol from entering the U.S. market through a 54-cent per gallon tariff. No such tariff is imposed on imported oil. Such protectionism is inconsistent with the intention to reduce oil dependence as billions of gallons of ethanol are kept away from the U.S. market this way.

The first thing the United States must do to bring choice and competition to its petroleum-dominated transportation sector is to ensure that the cars rolling on to its roads are platforms on which fuels can compete. For a cost of roughly $100 extra as compared to a gasoline-only vehicle, automakers can make virtually any car a flex-fuel vehicle, capable of running on any combination of gasoline and a variety of alcohols such as ethanol and methanol, made from a variety of feedstocks, including agricultural material, waste, coal, natural gas, and even carbon dioxide. Flex-fuel vehicles let consumers and the market choose the winning fuels and feedstocks based on economics. In Brazil, where ethanol is widely used, the share of flex-fuel vehicles in new car sales rose from 4 percent to 80 percent in under five years. These cars entail no size, power, or safety compromise by consumers, and ironically, they are manufactured by the same automakers that sell to the U.S. market. The U.S. alternative fuels market is dominated today by corn ethanol. But potential cellulosic biomass resources, from wood waste, food crop waste and dedicated crops, are as large in the United States as coal, and both would be an effective way to ramp up alcohol production. The U.S. Departments of Agriculture and Energy estimate that the United States could generate sufficient biomass to produce up to 4 mbd of oil-equivalent liquids.[27]

Despite the environmental issues associated with coal, it has a major role in energy security. The United States is home to a quarter of the world's coal reserves, and 50 percent of its electricity supply is already coal-based. Today coal plays almost no role in the transportation sector and hence is not perceived as a substitute for oil. This could change if coal-to-liquid (CTL) technologies become more competitive, allowing the production of diesel, gasoline and jet fuel via Fischer-Tropsch processes. No less promising are the technologies to produce the alcohol fuel methanol from coal. Coal-to-methanol technology is mature and economic and most of the alcohol supplying the Chinese market is produced this way. Technologies to convert carbon dioxide to methanol are currently in the development stage and could become an elegant solution for greenhouse gas emissions.[28]

Despite the potential of alcohol fuels as replacement to gasoline, there are still significant challenges to the nationwide deployment of alcohol fuels, including the need for rail, waterway, and pipeline transport capacity, the need for distribution systems—less than 1 percent of U.S. gas stations have the ability to sell alcohol—and balancing food uses and water requirements. Opening the U.S. transportation fuel market to competition would require imports from developing countries where such fuels can be made cheaply and in large scale. Sugar, from which ethanol can be cheaply and efficiently produced, is now grown in 100 countries, many of which are poor and on the receiving end of U.S. development aid. Encouraging these countries to increase their output and become fuel suppliers, opening the U.S. fuel market to them by removing the protectionist 54 cent a gallon ethanol tariff, could have far-reaching implications for their economic development. By creating economic interdependence with biomass-producing countries in Africa, Asia, and the Western hemisphere, the United States can strengthen its position in the developing world and provide significant help in reducing poverty.

Electricity is another game changer. Since so little of U.S. electricity is generated from oil, using electricity as a transportation fuel enables the full spectrum of electricity sources to compete with petroleum. Plug-in hybrid electric vehicles (PHEVs) can reach oil economy levels of 100–150 miles per gallon of gasoline without compromising the size, safety, or power of a vehicle. If a PHEV is also a flexible-fuel vehicle powered by 85 percent alcohol and 15 percent gasoline, oil economy could reach over *500 miles per gallon* of gasoline (each gallon of gasoline is stretched with alcohol and electricity.) In addition, the United States is the world's biggest potential market for pure electric cars that can be sold as second or third family car. 38 percent of America's households own two cars and an additional 20 percent own three or more vehicles. That makes over 64 million households in the U.S. that own more than one vehicle and that can potentially replace one or more gasoline-only cars with a car powered with made-in-America electricity.[29]

Grid Concerns

Ideally, electric cars and plug-in hybrids would be charged at night in home or apartment garages, when electric utilities have significant reserve capacity. The Department of Energy estimates that over 80 percent of the U.S. vehicle market could shift to plug-in hybrids without needing to install additional base load electricity-generating capacity, assuming off-peak charging.[30] But to electrify America's transportation system the electric grid will have to be greatly bolstered, creating sufficient redundancies and storage capacity. This is true even without electric transportation, as domestic electricity needs are growing. At the moment, the physical and human elements that make a strong grid—generation and transmission capacity, distribution lines or control equipment and service personnel—are being stretched to the limit. Perhaps the most troubling is the shrinkage of generating capacity reserve margins, found in virtually every section of the country. Strict environmental regulations and not-in-my-back-yard (NIMBY) considerations currently limit the growth of electricity infrastructure, making siting of new facilities such as nuclear power stations, coal-fired power plants, LNG terminals, and even windmills a regulatory nightmare. Environmental activists like former

Vice President Al Gore, who in September 2008 called for civil disobedience to stop coal plants, take pride in the fact that 59 coal-fired plants were cancelled in 2007 alone and that nearly 50 more in 29 states are being contested.[31] For a nation of plasma screens, iPhones and computers, such resistance to expand the power sector means that sooner or later millions will be left in the dark. Back in 1982 a book by the Rocky Mountain Institute, *Brittle Power: Energy Strategy for National Security*, warned of the weakness of the grid, describing it as a disaster waiting to happen. "The United States has for decades been undermining the foundations of its own strength," it said. "It has gradually built up an energy system prone to sudden massive failures with catastrophic consequences."[32] To strengthen energy security the United States would need to increase its power-generating capacity significantly, in addition to investing a great deal to ensure sufficient redundancies and overall reliability. Notwithstanding concerns about safety, security, radioactive waste, and weapons proliferation, there is also likely to be an increased role for nuclear power. It is estimated that up to 17 new nuclear plants may be online by 2020, predominantly in the Southeast.[33] Wind, solar and geothermal power will also have an increased role. In the first ten months of 2008, wind power experienced a 38 percent growth from the year before. Solar and geothermal are poised to greatly expand their market share in the near future.[34] However, coal-fired power plants are projected to continue to be the dominant source of electricity generation through 2030. Coal's share in total electric generation is projected to increase from 49 percent to 54 percent.[35]

Other Energy Security Mechanisms

In addition to reducing the importance of oil to the transportation sector, and improving the domestic electricity system, America's energy supply will depend on the security and reliability of a wide network of critical energy infrastructure. In the United States itself oil flows through roughly 200,000 miles of pipelines and 130 refineries. 18 million tank-truck journeys a year move gasoline from refineries to gas stations. In addition, there are 1,300 natural gas drilling rigs, 300,000 miles of natural gas pipelines, and 10,000 power plants, including 104 nuclear reactors.[36] This vast network is vulnerable to disruption by either man or nature. The 2003 Northeast blackout was a reminder that an attack on America's electricity grid could cripple the U.S. economy. It also demonstrated the main problem of America's grid: the interdependency of the system's components and the dependency of the entire system on the weakest link in the chain. One failed transformer on a hot summer day (or cold winter day for that matter) becomes the epicenter of a catastrophic failure and the entire system collapses like a house of cards. This means that if a terrorist attack disables one or more elements in the generation or transmission system the ripple effect is certain. Such an attack could take place either physically or virtually. As former CIA Director James Woolsey warned, terrorists are smart enough to identify weaknesses in every system, including our electricity grid, "where the equivalent of flimsy cockpit doors might be found."[37]

Even if U.S. energy infrastructure were perfectly secure the United States would not be immune to supply disruptions caused by terrorists abroad. Energy security therefore depends also on the ability to protect critical facilities abroad. The United States, as the largest participant in the global energy system, has a stake in strengthening global energy security. This requires the United States to create multilateral, regional, and bilateral security arrangements and to provide oil-producing nations with counter-terrorism training and technology so they can better protect petroleum supplies. To increase supply and encourage competitiveness and investment the United States should also promote more favorable conditions for global energy trade and investment through multilateral and international institutions—including the World Trade Organization, G-8, Asia-Pacific Economic Cooperation (APEC), IEA, and the Joint Oil Data Initiative (JODI). Finally, if all fails and supply disruptions do occur the United States will need to fall back on its Strategic Petroleum Reserve (SPR). The energy security program designed to safeguard the U.S. economy from supply disruptions began collecting oil in 1977 and has the capacity to hold approximately 700 million barrels. This oil stockpile enables the federal government to release oil to the local market in time of emergency. According to the DOE, oil could be drawn from the SPR at a rate of 4 mbd for the first three months, falling progressively after for the next seven months until reaching zero. Alternatively, it could be drawn down at a rate of 1 mbd for a year and a half. At its current capacity, the SPR barely suffices to tide the U.S. economy over in case of a severe disruption of oil supplies, which is why, in his 2007 State of the Union address, President Bush announced his intention to almost double the SPR from its current capacity, 700 million barrels, to 1.5 billion barrels. But when oil prices soared in summer 2008 Congress decided to stall the expansion program.

Conclusion

There is no silver bullet solution to America's energy security predicament. If there is any realistic way to strengthen America's energy security it is in devising an energy policy that has a healthy balance among a variety of policies and technologies. Unfortunately few nations have the discipline and common foresight to address a collective problem a moment before they must do so. As President Barack Obama said in his first address on the issue: "Year after year, decade after decade, we've chosen delay over decisive action. Rigid ideology has overruled sound science. Special interests have overshadowed common sense. Rhetoric has not led to the hard work needed to achieve results. Our leaders raise their voices each time there's a spike in gas prices, only to grow quiet when the price falls at the pump."[38] Paradoxically enough, energy security can only be achieved through a common sense of insecurity. Without constant reminders of the vulnerability of the American way of life to energy supply disruptions and the heavy price in blood and treasury Americans pay each day to fuel their economy it is unlikely that the country will master the necessary political will and the huge investment necessary to embark on a major energy reform. Therefore, the terrorists who blow up facilities in the Persian Gulf and the hurricanes crashing against U.S. shores are likely to be the most important drivers of America's energy policy in the years to come.

Notes

1. Energy Information Administration, *Annual Energy Outlook 2007 with Projections to 2030,* http://tonto.eia.doe.gov/ftproot/forecasting/0383(2007).pdf.

2. Ibid.

3. Ibid.

4. "Energy is the Albatross of U.S. National Security, Lugar Says," Press Release, Senator Richard Lugar, March 13, 2006, http://www.brookings.edu/comm/events/20060313lugar.pdf.

5. Condoleezza Rice, Testimony before the Senate Foreign Relations Committee, April 5, 2006, quoted in Steven Mufson, "As China, U.S. Vie for More Oil, Diplomatic Friction May Follow," *Washington Post,* April 15, 2006, http://www.washingtonpost.com/wp-dyn/content/article/2006/04/14/AR2006041401682.html.

6. While the United States does not import oil from Iran it is affected geopolitically by Iran's strong standing in the global oil market. Oil is a fungible commodity so even if the United States imported all of its oil from friendly and stable sources it would still be beholden to the growing power of those who control the lion's share of the world's reserves.

7. Jimmy Carter, televised speech on July 15, 1979, http://www.pbs.org/wgbh/amex/carter/filmmore/ps_crisis.html.

8. Amory Lovins and Hunter Lovins, "Mobilizing Energy Solutions," *The American Prospect,* January 28, 2002.

9. George W. Bush, "State of the Union Address by the President," January 31, 2006, www.whitehouse.gov/stateoftheunion/2006; Remarks by President Obama on Jobs, Energy Independence, and Climate Change East Room of the White House, January 26, 2009, http://www.whitehouse.gov/blog_post/Fromperiltoprogress/.

10. Irwin M. Stelzer, "Can We do Without Saudi Oil?" *The Weekly Standard,* November 19, 2001.

11. Michael Klare, "The Futile Pursuit of 'Energy Security' by Military Force," *The Brown Journal of World Affairs* (Spring/Summer 2007).

12. Institute for the Analysis of Global Security, Iraq Pipeline Watch, http://www.iags.org/iraqpipelinewatch.htm.

13. Energy Information Administration, Mexico Country Brief, http://www.eia.doe.gov/cabs/Mexico/Background.html.

14. "Mexico: Pemex Oil Field Declining," *New York Times,* February 8, 2007.

15. "Chavez starts OPEC Summit with 200-dollar Oil Warning," *AFP News Agency,* November 17, 2007.

16. *Report of the National Energy Policy Development Group,* The White House, http://www.whitehouse.gov/energy/2001/index.html.

17. Glenn Kessler, "Oil Wealth Colors the U.S. Push for Democracy," *Washington Post,* May 14, 2006.

18. Maurizio d'Orlando, "Need for Oil Draws China Close to Saudis and Iranians," *Asia News,* April 13, 2004, http://www.asianews.it/index.php?l=en&art=615.

19. *Development of America's Strategic Unconventional Fuels Resources,* Task Force on Strategic Unconventional Fuels, Report to Congress, September 2006, http://www.fossil.energy.gov/programs/reserves/npr/publications/sec369h_report_epact.pdf.

20. "Analysis of Crude Oil Production in the Arctic National Wildlife Refuge," EIA Report #: SR-OIAF/2008-03, May 2008, http://www.eia.doe.gov/oiaf/servicerpt/anwr/results.html.

21. Ibid.

22. National Petroleum Council (NPC), *Facing the Hard Truths About Energy*, (Washington. D.C.: NPC, July 18, 2007), http://www.npchardtruthsreport.org.

23. *National Security Consequences of U.S. Oil Dependency*, Council on Foreign Relations Task Force Report, 4, http://www.cfr.org/content/publications/attachments/EnergyTFR.pdf.

24. James Woolsey and Anne Korin, Turning Oil into Salt, *National Review*, September 25, 2007, http://article.nationalreview.com/?q=OTlmMjFjYWRjOWI3ZGI0MzUxZD JjYTBlMmUzOTc2Mzc=.

25. David Kiley, "Big Oil's Stall on Ethanol," *BusinessWeek*, October 1, 2007.

26. Renewable Fuel Association, Industry Statistics, http://www.ethanolrfa.org/industry/statistics/.

27. The "Billion Ton Study"—*Biomass as a Feedstock for a Bioenergy and Bioproducts Industry: The Technical Feasibility of a Billion-Ton Annual Supply*, USDA and USDOE, April 2005, http://www.osti.gov/bridge.

28. George Olah, Alain Goeppert, and G. K. Surya Prakash, *Beyond Oil and Gas: The Methanol Economy* (Weinheim, Germany: Wiley, 2006); See also Robert Zubrin, *Energy Victory: Winning the War on Terror by Breaking Free of Oil* (Amherst, NY: Prometheus, 2007).

29. *Pocket Guide to Transportation 2008*, Bureau of Transportation Statistics, U.S. Department of Transportation, http://www.bts.gov/publications/pocket_guide_to_transportation/2008/.

30. According to the DOE's Pacific Northwest Lab report there is sufficient off-peak reserve capacity in the electricity grid to power up to 84 percent of today's vehicles before new power plants of any kind need to be built. See: Jennifer Kho and Brian Caulfield, "US Could Plug in Most Cars," *Red Hering*, December 10, 2006, http://www.redherring.com/Home/20179.

31. Mark Mills, "Brownout," *Forbes*, June 30, 2008, http://www.forbes.com/forbes/2008/0630/038.html.

32. Amory Lovins and Hunter Lovins, *Brittle Power: Energy Strategy for National Security* (Andover, MA: Brick House: 1982).

33. Goldman Sachs Power Survey: Outlook for Nuclear Development, August 2007.

34. Energy Information Administration, Renewable Energy Production and Consumption by Source, http://www.eia.doe.gov/emeu/mer/pdf/pages/sec10_3.pdf.

35. *Annual Energy Outlook 2008 with Projections to 2030*, Energy Information Administration, http://www.eia.doe.gov/oiaf/aeo/pdf/0383(2008).pdf.

36. *Siting Critical Energy Infrastructure: An Overview of Needs and Challenges*, National Commission on Energy Policy, June 2006, http://energycommission.org/files/contentFiles/Siting%20Critical%20Energy%20Infrastructure_448851db5fa7d.pdf.

37. R. James Woolsey, "The War on Terrorism," The Pitcairn Trust Lecture on World Affairs, Foreign Policy Research Institute, http://www.fpri.org/enotes/20021010.woolsey.waronterrorism.html.

38. Remarks by President Barack Obama on Jobs, Energy Independence, and Climate Change East Room of the White House January 26, 2009, http://www.whitehouse.gov/blog_post/Fromperiltoprogress/.

CHAPTER 11

The European Union: On Energy, Disunity

Kevin Rosner

When a North American travels to India, China or Africa he or she readily assumes that the local culture, customs, practices and perspectives will differ from his or her own. This is not the case when the same North American visits Paris, London, Rome or Vienna. Behavioral and attitudinal differences between Euro-Atlantic partners are swiftly pigeon-holed as 'European' by the North American or uniquely 'American' by the European partner. The differences between these two groups however are largely marginalized, based on the assumption of a fundamental unity in how problems are defined and how they are solved. The fact is that on the issue of energy security Europeans, or more precisely the European Commission as the executive branch of the European Union, has developed a unique set of practices driven by a specific set of assumptions on what energy security is and what should be done about it. Just like the United States, Europe is heavily dependent on imported energy. Today, oil, natural gas, and coal account for 80 percent of the energy consumed in the EU and collectively, EU member states import half of their energy needs. This figure is expected to rise to 65 percent by 2030. But despite the similarity in the level of dependence the practices and assumptions of the European concept of energy security fundamentally differ from the North American concept and solutions to these problems as practiced by the U.S. government. What follows is not a comparative analysis of differing attitudes to the challenges posed by energy insecurity, nor an exercise in deconstructing the social, historical, or cultural determinants of policies put in place to solve energy related problems. What follows is an interpretation of what energy security means in the European context and how the institutions of the European Union are attempting to deal with it.

European Approach to Energy Security

The European Union's approach towards the broad and complex issue of energy security follows three separate but interrelated policy paths:

- internal mechanisms to ensure sustainable energy supply
- external steps to integrate energy into a European common foreign and security policy
- internal and external steps to deal specifically with critical infrastructure protection

Together this mosaic of policies links problems facing the 27 member states of the European Union to those in the global environment. As a report to the Trilateral Commission states, "The energy issue has been more broadly addressed by the EC in the security of supply-competitiveness-climate change triangle."[1] These policies are outlined in a series of three papers and detail the steps the Commission and, by consequence, member states will take in tackling these three facets of energy security simultaneously.[2]

Internal Mechanisms

EU heads of states and governments broadly endorsed the Commission's proposals at their annual spring summit on March 24, 2006, on a European strategy for a secure energy future. The strategy embraces all three priorities. The summit agreed on the following main points on enhancing internal measures for improving the energy security of European Union member states:

- diversification of energy sources—including a re-examination of 'indigenous' sources of energy and power such as nuclear
- a common approach to address crisis situations "in a spirit of solidarity"
- development of regional gas and electricity energy markets within the EU
- developing electricity interconnections to reach the target of "at least 10 percent of member states' installed production capacity" (financing borne "mainly by the enterprises involved")
- "considering raising by 2015 the share of renewable energies" to 15 percent; increasing the share of biofuels to 8 percent by the same date; implementing the biomass action plan[3]

In seeking to diversify primary energy utilization particularly for power generation the Commission has had to avoid the highly contentious issue of presuming to dictate Europe's energy mix. No state was or is willing to have Brussels dictate the form and type of energy consumed and power generated on a national level. National governments largely retain the right of determining their own energy future, based on national access to resources, nationally determined and developed power grids and generating facilities, access to legacy systems and grids (particularly in Central and Eastern Europe), and differing and competing national decisions taken on the desirability of one type of power generation over another (e.g., nuclear-coal-natural gas in large part).[4] In short, Europe seeks to secure a diversified yet clean and environmentally sound energy mix that can adequately meet the EU's future energy demand. The goal of diversification is prompting EU members to reevaluate the contribution that nuclear energy can make to the European energy mix. Already 60 percent of Europe's power is generated from either nuclear or coal. In 2005, nuclear provided 31 percent of EU electricity while 30 percent comes from coal resources. According to the IAEA, nuclear energy's prominence as a major energy source will continue globally over the next decades while Europe remains undecided on the technology. Altogether, Europe has 166 reactors in operation and 6 under construction. However, the distribution of electricity generation from nuclear varies widely between EU member states. In France, over 80 percent of power generation comes from nuclear power plants, followed by Germany (31%) and the UK (roughly 15%). Some countries such as Germany, Belgium and Spain have committed to phasing out their reactors, despite the fact that together nuclear power accounts for a significant part of their power generation. Other states such as the UK, Finland, and Lithuania are working to introduce a new generation of reactors. The resurgence of nuclear power in these countries reflects the political acceptability of nuclear power generation, the existence of national energy champions traditionally active in the nuclear field, economic realities, and the growing acknowledgement that nuclear energy contributes to all three facets of the EC's supply strategy triangle: security of supply, competitiveness and climate change. Proponents of nuclear energy in Europe point out that the rising costs for primary input gas and coal energy resources for electricity generation relative to the rising cost of uranium makes nuclear energy cost competitive, if it is not already. This is excluding the external costs of carbon dioxide emissions, which are important for European compliance with its commitment to capping greenhouse gas emissions under the terms of the Kyoto Protocol. Under the 1997 Protocol, the EU, by 2012, is obligated to reduce its gas emissions by 8 percent from its 1990 levels. To the extent Europe intends to meet its obligations, decisions by the member states regarding the energy mix will be important. Proponents of nuclear power also argue that it can provide Europe with base-load electricity without increasing imports of fossil fuels, which is an obviously important external dimension of EU energy policy. But these views are not shared throughout the EU. In 2000 Germany became the first major economic power to announce its intention to phase out the use of nuclear energy by 2021. This decision was taken in spite of the fact that 31 percent of the country's power is nuclear generated (a noncarbon dioxide-emitting fuel). It also runs contrary to public opinion in Germany—in 2007 polling indicated that 61 percent of the German population was against this decision.[5] Another trend that complicates diversification of German power generation is that the anti-nuclear lobby has become an anti-coal lobby. While admittedly many of Germany's electricity-generating plants based on coal should be upgraded, promoting the wholesale closure of the coal-fired electricity industry borders on the irresponsible. Austria took a similar anti-nuclear position in 1978 and has blocked the development of any nuclear facility since despite the fact that it is becoming increasingly dependent on hydrocarbon imports from the Russian Federation.

Power generation from coal has also been opposed by the European Union as dirty and contrary to Europe's commitment to fulfilling the terms of the Kyoto Protocol in limiting greenhouse gas emissions. Again the EU's criticism is a nuanced one, which avoids an anti-coal argument by insisting on the introduction of clean coal burning technologies. As a U.S. Congressional Research Service report states, "coal burning is a major source of carbon dioxide and so for environmental purposes a European Commission Directive was put into force years ago that could force many coal fired plants to be shut down unless they install clean burning technology. That technology, although expensive, does exist and in theory can capture 80–90 percent of the carbon (CO_2) by-products of burning coal. While several electricity producers in a few countries that currently rely on coal for power generation, such as Spain 22 percent, Germany 52 percent, UK 35 percent and the Czech Republic 62 percent, have indicated an interest in upgrading their generation facilities with new clean coal technology, none of the European countries has adopted this technology on a broad commercial basis."[6] Renewable energy presents much less controversy. The EU views itself as the world's leading promoter of renewable energy.[7] In terms of internal *supply* diversification, this is by far the most politically correct solution to meeting its goal of secure energy supply. As of 2004, the leading sources of renewable energy in the EU-27 energy mix in terms of contribution levels were biomass, hydro, solar, wind and geothermal (in this order). But, as Figure 11.1 shows, renewable energy still plays a relatively minor role in Europe's energy basket, providing roughly 7 percent of the total energy mix.

In March 2007, European heads of state and government concluded a "firm independent commitment," which in effect is a legally binding agreement to meet 20 percent of each member state's energy needs by renewable energy by 2020. Included in this is a minimum target of 10 percent for biofuels subject to supply availability and second generation technology by 2020.[8] The EU also agreed to cut greenhouse gas emissions by 20 percent by 2020 compared to 1990 levels and to reduce energy demand by 20 percent. It is difficult to imagine how Europe is going to meet these binding targets without revisiting the nuclear question,

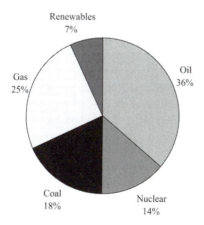

Figure 11.1 EU-27 Energy Mix
Source: European Commission

paying a significant economic toll and compromising the supply needs of European consumers. In short the 20–20–20 Program by 2020 is much more of an environmental program than an energy security strategy and one that clearly demonstrates that for Europe environmental stewardship trumps energy security considerations. The plan runs the risk that as the EU 27 develops as a global strategic player it concurrently marginalizes itself as master of its own energy destiny. North Sea oil production peaked in 1999. European coal production has declined significantly over the last 25 years, in part due to political decisions, while demand for coal exceeds supply, prompting major European nations to import coal from newer mines as far away as Columbia, Indonesia and Australia. Between 1990 and 2004, EU-15 greenhouse gas emissions decreased in most sectors. However emissions from the transport sector increased by nearly 26 percent and are projected to increase to 35 percent above 1990 levels by 2010.

Internal Market Bundling and Un-Bundling

At the heart of EU energy policy is the successful completion of a common internal market for energy and power among the EU 27. The reasons for this are well documented and understood: difficulties faced by new entrants into the market, highly concentrated, vertically integrated energy markets, and the concentration of market power among incumbent players have all led to a noncompetitive environment within Europe for energy and power resources. The lack of interconnections between national transmission systems is but one example that creates energy vulnerabilities, particularly for the newer members of the EU across Central and Eastern Europe. Building additional European resiliency through network and power interconnections would help to bridge these island regions to the larger European network, contribute to the development of an interconnected European internal market for energy and power supply and provide a much needed layer of security, particularly to the newer EU members whose network and grid connections are much stronger in an eastward direction than to the south and west.

The Baltic states for one consider themselves an energy island largely dependent on Russia for their energy needs. Strengthening of the EU's internal market for energy and power is a key step towards reducing energy-related vulnerabilities for all 27 member states. In the power sector, a main strategy is to interconnect national transmission grids by building a series of interconnections among and between states and their national electricity grids. These grids were initially constructed to be independent and stand-alone. Enhancing power connections among and between states is a viable diversification strategy that may provide power in the event of national power failure or emergency and concurrently may contribute to effective growth of the economies of scale in the European internal market for power. While interconnections between national grids ostensibly can be pursued without reference to the other major barrier, as perceived by EU regulators, which is the un-bundling of ownership in generation and transmission of power, the entire process is in fact bundled together. The insistence on the un-bundling of ownership and control over the entire supply chain is nuanced between established and mature large European national energy markets that exercise national monopoly control over power and in those in smaller and less extensively developed markets. Even then, however, the international trend in power markets is one of vertical consolidation. This creates on the one hand important economies of scale that should enhance cost efficiencies but may on the other hand create insecurities by giving priority to profit maximization over safeguarding the long term security interests of consumers through maintenance of resiliency in redundant lines and grid connections.

External Dimensions

Europe is becoming increasingly dependent on imported hydrocarbons. It imports over 80 percent of its oil, close to 55 percent of its natural gas and an increasing percentage of its coal. Within the current business as usual scenario the EU's import dependence will jump from 50 percent of total EU energy consumption today to 65 percent in 2030, with reliance on imports of natural gas expected to increase to 84 percent and of oil to 93 percent.[9] Forty-five percent of all EU oil imports originate in the Middle East and roughly 30 percent from Russia. This oil dependency is not equally distributed, as the new EU 10 of former Central and Eastern European nations are far more dependent on Russian hydrocarbons than the old Europe of 15.

Thirty percent of the EU's natural gas imports come from Russia, followed by Algeria and Norway. But there are several EU member states, like Finland and Estonia, that are totally dependent on Russian natural gas (see Table 11.1).

By 2030, European gas imports are expected to reach slightly over 80 percent with 85 percent of all imports coming from Russia. There are several issues at work here that must be addressed concerning the security of energy supply. In terms

Table 11.1 Dependence on Imported Gas, 2006

Country	Dependence on Imported Gas	Dependence on Russian Gas
Austria	88%	74%
Czech Republic	98%	70%
Estonia	100%	100%
France	98%	26%
Finland	100%	100%
Germany	81%	39%
Italy	85%	30%
Poland	70%	50%

Source: International Energy Agency

of oil, given its location and availability there is a global supply shift underway back to the Middle East. To paraphrase the words of American President George W. Bush, while America may be addicted to oil, Europe is decidedly addicted to Middle East oil. The implications of growing dependence on the volatile Middle East are clear. Another source of concern is that Russian oil output is set to plateau in 2010, according to the International Energy Agency (IEA). The IEA warned that Russia's 20 biggest development projects scheduled to come on-stream in the next five years could face delays due to uncertainty over Russia's investment climate and tight drilling capacity.[10] Energy security in a European context is linked to natural gas as much as American security is linked to oil. Natural gas is the fuel of choice for power generation—though there is a good reason to question the logic of this choice—as its carbon dioxide emissions are lower than coal, and until 2000 it was historically moderately priced. Forecasters predict that natural gas consumption in the EU will double over the next 25 years.

Already in July 2007, Russia's Gazprom's natural gas output fell by 3.5 percent or some 1.131 bcm over June's output, and as of July overall Russian gas production was down 1.5 percent year-on-year.[11] Gazprom, the world's largest supplier of natural gas, is increasingly crippled by a lack of investment in technology and infrastructure, a lack of available capital for extremely expensive but necessary upstream development, and by a lack of political willingness to engage non-Russian entities in new upstream exploration and development on equitable terms. This is particularly worrisome for European states that are physically coupled to the Soviet legacy natural gas pipeline system. Even if Russia's capacity to supply Europe's needs were undisputed there are significant concerns about its reliability as an energy partner. The Russia-Ukraine and Russia-Belarus natural gas and oil crises that demonstrated Moscow's willingness to use its energy power as a political weapon were early wake up calls that exposed Europe's energy security vulnerability to both intended and unintended supply disruptions. Russia's August 2008 invasion of Georgia is only the most recent crisis that puts European supply security in question. Georgia is a key transit state for both Caspian oil and gas and provides the only land-bridge for hydrocarbons tying Central Asia to downstream European markets that obviates Russian territory. If Russia succeeds in casting a shadow over the future of the Caucasus energy corridor then other flagship projects such as Nabucco for further diversifying energy supply and related infrastructure away from Russia are in peril. All of these crises highlight the urgent need to present a unified front to Russia and to craft policies to secure and diversify energy supply. In terms of European oil and gas country-of-supply diversification there are alternatives, such as Azerbaijan, a large exporter of oil (1 mbd through the Baku-Tbilisi-Ceyhan pipeline), which will become an increasingly important supplier of gas to Western markets when the South Caucasus (gas) Pipeline (SCP) comes on line. In the East Caspian there is Kazakhstan, which has had the third largest growth in proven oil reserves over the last decade, and Turkmenistan, which has large gas reserves, though they are largely underdeveloped with no direct pipeline access to Western markets other than through Russia. Unless the EU can begin to use its leverage and influence as Russia's largest downstream market for both Russian oil and gas exports to achieve Russian political acquiescence in allowing Kazakh oil and Turkmen gas to reach Western markets in the most economically expedient fashion, EU energy supply diversification from Central Asia will largely fail over the short-to-medium term. Without pipeline diversification in the gas industry there can be no gas supply diversification in the European theatre.[12] Europe is clearly looking elsewhere for alternative oil and gas supply. Turkey's investment in Iran's South Pars gas field and the possibility of construction of the Nabucco pipeline, connecting Turkey and Central Europe, could eventually position Iran, which sits on the world's second largest natural gas reserve, as a major gas supplier to Europe, despite current efforts to isolate Iran due to its pursuit of nuclear power. However, for the EU to enhance its own energy security requires a unity of voice and purpose in negotiating with Russia. Thus far this has failed to materialize. Russia's policy in forging ahead on establishing bilateral energy ties with individual EU member states has thus far succeeded in rendering the EU effectively mute and moreover impotent in confronting Russian aggression, within or outside an energy specific policy framework, on issues of fundamental importance and principle to the democratic nations of the EU. Should this continue, the EU's grasp on controlling its own energy security future is sure to slip even further vis-à-vis a fossil-fueled Russian Federation.

Africa is another destination of interest for Europe. With countries such as Angola and Nigeria now in the league of major global oil suppliers, other countries in the Gulf of Guinea are seeking to emulate their success. EU relations with the region have centered on development cooperation with the Economic Community of West African States (ECOWAS), in particular on issues such as peace, security and good governance with a strong emphasis on economic and trade integration. Since January 2007, representatives from both sides have been engaged in more intensive discussion on the possibility of creating an Africa-Europe Energy Partnership.[13] In November 2007, key energy players from the EU, Africa and the Middle East came together for the first time to debate common challenges and policies in the field of energy security. European Neighbourhood Policy Commissioner Benita Ferrero-Waldner stated at this event that "When the EU thinks of energy security it looks not only East but also South," she said. "We are determined to expand our network of energy partners by building on bilateral partnerships and regional initiatives."[14] Taken together, North Africa and West Africa already supply Europe with 136.1 million tons of combined crude and product imports annually and this is set to expand, with Libyan oil and gas output coming back on line in increased volume over the next several years. In sum, energy security can be achieved through a bouquet of measures that focus on diversification in country of supply, diversification in transport route, and diversification in energy sources themselves. In the EU all of these challenges must be pursued concurrently through a clear and coherent common energy policy. This is something that the EU has thus far been unsuccessful in constructing.

Collective energy security requires the willingness to speak with the collective strength of European nations. This is relevant not only to the supply side of the equation but to the protection of critical energy infrastructure.

Critical Energy Infrastructure Protection

European *security* policy on critical infrastructure protection and pipeline security is led by the European Union's Directorate General for Justice, Liberty and Security. *Energy* issues on a European level remain the area of responsibility of the Directorate General for Transport and Energy (DGTREN). Together these two bodies have driven forward energy and security policy in creating a European Program for Critical Infrastructure Protection (EPCIP). The EPCIP finds its origin in the issuance of a Green Paper in November 2005. This Green Paper itself was generated in response to the March 11, 2004, terrorist attacks in Madrid. The initiative was directed by the Council of the European Union in June 2004 and expanded on an earlier piece of EU legislation that focused on the adoption of an appropriate response to the 9/11 attack in the United States. Since the issuance of the Green Paper in November 2005, The European Union and its institutions have adopted a package of measures to protect Europe's critical infrastructure.

The package consists of:

- A proposal for a Directive on the identification and designation of European Critical Infrastructure and the assessment of the need to improve their protection, which proposes the main foundations for an EPCIP.
- A [nonbinding] Communication on a European Programme for Critical Infrastructure Protection, which contains nonbinding measures designed to facilitate the implementation of EPCIP, including an EPCIP Action Plan.

These steps resulted in a Council Directive (2008/114/EC) adopted on December 8, 2008 on the identification and designation of European critical infrastructures and the assessment of the need to improve their protection. This directive is significant for a number of reasons: It constitutes "a first step in a step-by-step approach to identify and designate European Critical Infrastructures (ECIs) and assess the need to improve their protection."[15] Its initial focus is on the energy and transport sectors and it points out that "[it] should be reviewed with a view to assessing its impact and the need to include other sectors within its scope, inter alia, the information and communication technology (ICT) sector."[16] The step of issuing a directive is particularly significant. A directive in Brussels requires member states to adopt compliant legislation on a national basis thereby superseding national authority in rejecting its individual articles. In short, the directive requires member states to adopt its tenets (articles) into national law. The directive importantly defines critical infrastructure in common form as "an asset, system or part thereof located in Member States which is essential for the maintenance of vital societal functions, health, safety, security, economic or social well-being of people, and the disruption or destruction of which would have a significant impact in a Member State as a result of the failure to maintain those functions."[17] In Article 2 (b) it goes on further to define European critical infrastructure (ECI) as meaning "infrastructure located in Member States, the disruption or destruction of which would have a significant impact on at least two Member States. The significance of the impact shall be assessed in terms of cross-cutting criteria. This includes effects resulting from cross-sector dependencies on other types of infrastructure." European critical infrastructures fundamentally include the electricity, oil, and gas sectors as well as virtually all transport sectors, (e.g. road, rail, air, and marine transport and ports). The assessment of whether a national critical infrastructure meets the definition of ECI is dependent on a host of other requisite analysis including risks assessment, criticality, transnationality and other criteria beyond the scope of this initial discussion.

The legal ramifications on a member state for ignoring or implementing—in part but not in whole—the articles of the directive notwithstanding have broad implications for European energy security. The adage that "a chain is as strong as its weakest link" is most appropriate here. Should one or more member states linked contiguously by energy networks fail to, or refuse to, adequately take national measures to protect their own national energy infrastructure, it would have cross-cutting implications for energy security within the EU as a whole. Further, ECIP is based on an all hazards approach, taking into account man-made (accident), technological (failure), natural disaster, or asymmetric (terrorist) causes of critical energy infrastructure disruption or debilitation. Given the history of European policy development regarding critical infrastructure protection, the true focus on this directive is on the terrorist consequences and response management of attacks carried out against ECI. Having said that, many of the transnational disruptions in European energy flow (such as the one in Switzerland in 2003 caused by a fallen tree that cascaded into the worst power outages in Austria and Italy since WWII) or the more recent cut offs of natural gas from Russia through Ukraine (which had impact across Southeastern Europe) were caused by casual factors rather than terrorism. What the directive does accomplish should also be acknowledged. The crux of the directive is to define critical infrastructure and help determine common standards for ECIP across the European community. This is vitally important for European energy security, particularly from a resiliency standpoint given all of its supporting measures (the development of interconnections and enhanced and necessary information-sharing among them). Yet lingering questions remain regarding which body has enforcement authority over the institutionalization of the directive's measures and what to do in the event of noncompliance. The security components of energy states and companies are reluctant to share vital information over what systems are in place and what measures have already been taken to protect their own critical assets, and, should this information be shared, the European Union does not have an institutional legacy of protecting such information nor does it have at present the necessary mechanisms for accomplishing this task.

When it comes to critical infrastructure and pipeline security, a distinction needs to be drawn between national critical infrastructure and European critical infrastructure as Directive 2008/114/EC. The 2004 Communication on a European Program for critical infrastructure protection states that the responsibility for protecting National Critical Infrastructures located in member states belongs to the state or the owners/operators and on the member states. The Commission acknowledges that it will support the member states in these efforts where requested to do so without defining from whence this assistance will emanate. It should be pointed out that risk assessment and analysis of pipeline vulnerabilities is left up to individual member states to be executed under the aegis of a National Critical Infrastructure Protection program. While the Commission has set out specific framework criteria for the organization of these programs their composition and functionality will remain nationally determined. In contrast, pipelines in a European context are often transnational in nature. Countries are often relatively small compared to U.S. states or Canadian provinces and pipelines often traverse contiguous borders over very short distances, subject to multiple jurisdictions, ownership, security, and regulatory policy regimes. This is the real value of the directive's definition of European critical infrastructure as distinct from national critical infrastructure.

Pipelines

Pipelines are the white elephants of critical infrastructure. They are large, long, and for the most part difficult to protect unless buried. Holding the risks and vulnerabilities of pipelines, ceteris paribus, critical energy infrastructure must overcome the legal challenge of subsidiarity, which was set out in the 1992 Maastricht Treaty and amended in the Treaty of Amsterdam in 1997 as set forth by a Protocol on Subsidiarity and Proportionality. In essence, subsidiarity first and foremost seeks to regulate the relationship between the EU and its member states. It is the fundamental principle of European law, which states that the EU can only enact laws when member states agree that the action of individual countries is insufficient. The EPCIP and, in particular, the protection of pipelines and particularly sensitive technical nodes (as indicated above) are identified as ECIs. On this issue however, industry federations such as the Organization of European Oil and Gas Producers (OGP) have stridently fought to prevent the EU from regulating pipeline and infrastructure protection and have sought support from their respective member states, using the concept of subsidiarity as the legal mechanism to argue (unsuccessfully) against the directive's passage. OGP member companies, as already indicated, are also reluctant to provide detailed information on their hard assets to the Commission, seeing it as a sieve for the release of sensitive information versus a more trusted repository for proprietary knowledge.

A key component of European pipeline protection in parallel with the proposed EPCIP is the development of a Critical Infrastructure Warning Information Network (CIWIN). The need for such an early warning network has been voiced for years by industry confederations such as the European Gas Confederation (Eurogas). The CIWIN would set up a community framework for critical infrastructure protection leading to increased capabilities and the identification of vulnerabilities to ECI. Complementing this proposal was the establishment in May 2007 of the Network of Energy Security Correspondents (NESCO), comprising representatives of the Commission, member states, and the Council Secretariat. The NESCO's tasks include the monitoring and exchange of information. Its purpose is to serve as a new instrument to step up the Union's capacity to collect information and provide early warning of potential threats to the security of energy supply in complementing the focus on distinct threats against European infrastructure. In 2006 the European Union's Joint Research Center in Ispra, Italy, launched a program to track, on a global basis, attacks against critical infrastructure. Hence, human, technical, and intellectual resources are being mounted jointly for European pipeline protection, but until there is implementation agreement on a common EPCIP these steps remain nascent in their development. The development of the NESCO is an expression of the EU external policy on energy security and as such goes hand in hand with the EU's Neighborhood Policy, in working with European energy transit countries such as Ukraine and Turkey. There is another complementary effort at shoring up European energy supply security through the creation of a European Energy Community, bridging EU member states and nonmember states in Southeast Europe. The energy community aims to create compatibility in energy legislation and market development in nonmember states, thereby facilitating foreign investment, and the construction of transborder interconnections for electricity transmission and cross-border energy trade. Turkey holds a key role here for the entire EU in terms of energy trade and maintains the status of observer within the Community framework. A major challenge to the protection of Europe's pipeline network is that all of the legislation that has been mentioned has been, and continues to be, couched within the broader concept of creating a common European Security and Defense Policy. Because security and defense policies are driven by national priorities, domestic considerations, and the perception of threats in the global security environment from a national perspective, there are large and broad divisions among EU member states for giving the EU the authority for enacting and pursuing a common foreign policy. While pipeline integrity can be construed fundamentally as a technical issue, it takes place in a complex and varied security and defense framework.

Energy security, principally supply security as differentiated from pipeline or infrastructure security, is the responsibility of the EU High Representative for Common Foreign and Security Policy (CFSP) and the EU Commissioner for External Affairs. Under the terms of the EU Reform Treaty agreed to in Lisbon, a new post of EU foreign policy chief will be created. The formal title is High Representative of the European Union for Foreign Affairs and Security Policy, instead of Foreign Minister of the EU as envisaged in the constitutional treaty, due to Britain's opposition. The new foreign policy chief will take over the jobs from present foreign policy chief Javier Solana and EU External Relations Commissioner Benita Ferrero-Waldner. Historic disagreement on the creation of a common European Foreign Policy has in part retarded the development of a common European energy policy to which it is linked. Further impeding progress on the development of far reaching measures that would allow for enhanced pipeline security from Belfast to Vladivostok has been the European penchant for insisting that external energy policy must await the completion of the common internal market for energy. While this may be preferable it certainly is not necessary, as both internal and external energy policies can be developed concurrently. The new EU foreign policy chief (theoretically), who is at the same time a vice president of the European Commission, will chair meetings of the 27 EU foreign ministers and head a combined foreign service with both national and EU diplomats. He or she must address the acute reality that overall EU pipeline integrity rests on the entire supply chain with the vast majority of product as well as the pipeline network itself originating outside the EU, and much of this network is beyond its engineering lifespan. In short, a main threat to the integrity of European gas supply rests outside the control of the EU and its member states from the standpoint of hard asset ownership and control.

Common External Policy

The discussion of development of a common European external policy on energy has been eclipsed by the Commission's focus on the creation of a common and competitively driven internal energy market. At the same time the European public's focus has been on the external dimensions of EU energy security, particularly as it relates to the Russian-EU energy dialogue. The common misconception that completion of the internal market must occur before consolidation of a common external policy has provided foreign firms with a window of opportunity to invest in and gain access to strategic European downstream energy markets. In fact, consolidation of the EU's external policy could assist in regulating access to internal European energy assets and thereby bolster overall EU energy security. The issue of reciprocity in asset ownership has already been mentioned as one way of reining in the interests of foreign (non-European) companies in these assets. Another step towards consolidating an external policy on energy security would be to deem certain energy assets as strategic. If certain energy assets were indeed deemed strategic, control over these assets could be either outright forbidden or at least limited by imposing certain legal restrictions, in the form of a licensing regime on prospective foreign ownership. In this case foreign owners would be subject to EU rules on owning and operating any energy asset inside the EU. These rules might be extended to conduct, obligations and financial security of foreign firms operating in the EU.[18] In practice the absence of any common EU energy policy has allowed the Russian Federation in particular to divide EU members from one another and in some cases has allowed it to succeed in gaining access to strategic assets that would fall under an external policy control regime.

There is at least at present no evidence for optimism that there will be a substantial change in this absence of policy.

Conclusion

The European approach to energy security, with its focus on security of supply, competitiveness, and climate change, is under increased scrutiny and uncertainty about its ability to deliver on all three simultaneously. Efforts to secure alternative oil and gas resources from Central Asia have been successfully thwarted by Russian interests, to the detriment of country of supply diversification for EU members. Competitiveness is hampered by the lack of a comprehensive mechanism of tying together European energy networks and markets through a robust system of interconnections and there is no single comprehensive European electricity grid even on the horizon. Climate change, and the European commitment to providing leadership on lessening the environmental effects of greenhouse gas emissions, is laudable, but the sun is setting on Kyoto and any follow-up blueprint to advance global progress on the issue has yet to be determined. Concurrently European imports of liquid hydrocarbons are increasing with no realistic evidence of abating. Energy has simultaneously become a tool in the foreign policy toolbox of nations outside of the EU from Russia to Venezuela and across the Middle East with no comprehensive policy response to fight its effects. A comprehensive and ongoing reassessment of EU energy policy must be expected if this group is to successfully face and combat its own internal challenges to the energy question let alone address the external dimensions of energy from a traditional national-international security perspective.

Notes

1. Anne Lauvergeon, "Energy Security and Climate Change: A European View," in *Energy Security and Climate Change, Task Force Report #61*, ed. John Deutch, Anne Lauvergeon, and Widhyawan Prawiraatmadja (Washington D.C.: Brookings Institution Press, 2007), 52.

2. See official European Union documentation for further detail: "A European Strategy for Sustainable, Competitive, and Secure Energy," European Commission, COM (2006) 105 Final, Brussels, August 3, 2006; "An External Policy to Serve Europe's Energy Interests," European Commission/Secretary General-High Representative, a paper adopted into a Communication to the European Council, "External Energy Relations-From Principles to Action," European Commission, COM (2006)590 Final, Brussels, October 12, 2006; and the Green Paper "On a European Programme for Critical Infrastructure Protection," European Commission, COM (2005) 576 Final, Brussels, November 17, 2005.

3. European Commission, *Green Paper: Toward a European Strategy for the Security of Energy Supply*, http://ec.europa.eu/energy/green-paper-energy-supply/doc/green_paper_energy_supply_en.pdf.

4. Notable exceptions to this exist in the form of the dismantling of Lithuania's Ignalina nuclear facility by 2009; within the framework of the accession negotiations, the institutions of the European Union made the Slovak Republic consent to the early closure of two

units of the Jaslovské Bohunice nuclear power plant, despite the fact that the International Atomic Energy Agency has confirmed that the plant meets the criteria for long-term safe operation. Dismantlement was also a precondition set by the European Commission for Lithuania's accession to the EU as a full member. The Ignalina plant is often characterized as a Chernobyl type reactor (utilizing a Russian built RBMK-1500 type reactor). Ostensibly the objection of the Commission to the Lithuanian reactor was based not on an objection to nuclear energy per se but on safety concerns on the channel type reactor installed at this facility.

5. Specifically, the agreement worked out limits of the operational lifetime of a nuclear plant to 32 years. "Nuclear Power in Germany," World Nuclear Association, December, 2008, http://www.world-nuclear.org/info/inf43.html.

6. Vince Morelli, *The European Union's Energy Security Challenges,* Congressional Research Service Report RL 33636, September 11, 2006, http://www.fas.org/sgp/crs/row/RL33636.pdf.

7. This claim, if it is to be justified, has to be narrowly defined. It could feasibly be argued that the EU as a source of public funding is *one* of the world's major proponents.

8. As of January 2008 the EU's biofuels program was under increasing criticism that it would drive food prices upwards and contribute to deforestation and a loss of biodiversity, just as the OECD had criticized in September 2007. In response to this criticism, Stravos Dimas, the EU's environmental chief, stated, "We have seen that the environmental problems caused by biofuels and also the social problems are bigger than we thought they were. So we have to move very carefully." "EU Rethinks Biofuels as Criticism Mounts," *Deutsche Welle,* January 14, 2008.

9. *Communication from the Commission to the Council and European Parliament: An Energy Policy for Europe,* Brussels, January 10, 2007, COM 2007(1) Final. Additional information can be found in *Presidency Conclusions: Council of the European Union,* 7224/1/07 paragraphs 36–39, http://register.consilium.europa.eu/pdf/en/07/st07/st07224-re01.en07.pdf. For a full discussion of the European Union's policy orientation on energy and growing import dependence see the statement by His Excellency John Bruton, Ambassador, Head of Delegation of the European Commission to the United States to the Committee on Finance, United States Senate, 29 March 2007, http://www.eurunion.org/eu/index.php?option=com_content&task=view&id=2539&Itemid=152.

10. Russian oil output actually began to fall in 2008 and since then has continued its downward slide. This decline is expected to accelerate given downward pressure on new oil and gas investment in Russia by the global economic recession. This comes at a time when Russia needs more, not less, investment for new oil and gas greenfield development. See for example, Kevin Rosner, "Russia's Financial Market Meltdown: Energy Security Implications," *Journal of Energy Security,* December 2008, http://www.ensec.org/index.php?option=com_content&view=article&id=168:russias-financial-market-meltdown-energy-security-implications&catid=90:energysecuritydecember08&Itemid=334.

11. "Russia's Gazprom Gas Output Falls in July," *Reuters,* August 2, 2007, http://uk.reuters.com/article/oilRpt/idUKL0285155720070802.

12. Critics will be quick to point out that the growing market for LNG has not been addressed. In 2005 LNG satisfied approximately 7 percent of world gas demand and it is expected to expand over and above this figure by 10 percent per annum over the next decade. Certainly this will help diversify the global gas market and ease pressure on regional pipeline networks, but the vast majority of future gas will continue to be shipped by pipe.

See for example the comments by Linda Cook, Shell Executive Director of Gas and Power to the Oil and Money Conference in London on September 21, 2005. "The Role of LNG in a Global Gas Market," http://www-static.shell.com/static/media/downloads/speeches/lcook_speech_oilandmoneyconf.pdf.

13. EurActiv: Geopolitics of EU Energy Supply, July 18, 2005: Euroactiv, http://euractiv.com/en/industry/geopolitics-eu-energy-supply/article-142665.

14. "EU Deepens Energy Relations with Africa and the Middle East," November 2, 2007, http://euractiv.com/en/energy/eu-deepens-energy-relations-africa-middle-east/article-168097.

15. Council Directive 2008/114/EC of December 8, 2008, on the identification and designation of European critical infrastructures and the assessment of the need to improve their protection, paragraph 5, http://eur-lex.europa.eu/LexUriServ/LexUriServ.do?uri=OJ:L:2008:345:0075:0082:EN:PDF.

16. Ibid.

17. Ibid Article 2(a).

18. Dieter Helm, "The Russia Dimension and Europe's External Energy Policy," Oxford University, September 2007, http://www.dieterhelm.co.uk/publications/Russian_dimension.pdf.

CHAPTER 12

Japan: The Power of Efficiency

Devin Stewart

Energy security concerns are nothing new in Japan. The oil embargo during World War II and the 1970s oil shocks shaped much of Japan's recent history. The island of Japan is unique among industrialized nations in that it is virtually devoid of natural resources. Foreign suppliers must be found for all components of its energy portfolio except hydro and renewables: oil (47% of total energy supply), coal (21%), liquefied natural gas (13%), and nuclear (15%).[1] Long the technology leader in Asia, Japan finds itself preparing for a future in which its energy policy must weigh increased global energy demand, emerging resource nationalism, and stagnating upstream development. Japanese energy policy is built upon an understanding that resources are finite and that it has maxed out its domestic resources. This is the main factor behind Japan's relentless drive for efficiency and diversification. By putting efficiency at the center of its policies, since 1973 Japan's energy intensity has improved by 37 percent, and its oil dependency has dropped by 30 points, making it one of the largest, most energy-efficient economies in the world.

A History of Energy Insecurity

Japan's current energy approach, emphasizing efficiency, diversification, and international cooperation, evolved out of its wartime experience. Oil supply security played an important role in the imperial policies leading to World War II and in the period that followed, when energy policy was directed at reconstruction of the country.

Soon after the eruption of hostilities with China, many Western powers curtailed oil shipments to Japan out of fear that British and Dutch colonial possessions in South Asia could be threatened. While the United States used its position as Tokyo's main oil supplier to restrain the Japanese, President Franklin D. Roosevelt resisted sanctions proposed by members of his cabinet. Roosevelt suspected that cutting the Japanese off from their only reliable supply of oil was likely to drive their military south toward the East Indies. He sustained the flow of petroleum products to Japan even as its war against China continued. FDR overruled Petroleum Coordinator Harold Ickes's proposed halt to petroleum exports out of east coast ports, which was intended to maximize availability of petroleum to support Britain in its war against Germany. Nevertheless, a restriction in 1940 on the types of petroleum products available for export to Japan was implemented to ensure enough fuel was available for U.S. aircraft.[2] Embargoes on Japan grew tighter, and by August of 1941, oil exports to Japan had effectively dried up, causing great anxiety in Tokyo.[3] Just as Roosevelt predicted, Admiral Yamamoto's fleet steamed for the East Indies, simultaneously attacking Hong Kong, Singapore, the Philippines, and Borneo. The attack on Pearl Harbor was aimed at securing the advancing Imperial navy's rear flank, ensuring that that the United States could not interfere in Japan's efforts to gain the oil it needed.[4]

After the war, with the collapse of the Japanese industrial base, a general decimation of its infrastructure, and policymaking decisions in the hands of the Supreme Commander of the Allied Powers, General Douglas MacArthur (SCAP), the development of a coherent energy policy receded as a priority.[5] Instead, growing industries such as iron and steel took precedence, boosting demand for the only energy source available domestically—coal. Power demand began to rise, and by the early 1950s electricity shortages and outages became a reality of daily life.[6] In response, the Japanese government put together its first energy policy, the Matsunaga Plan. Despite objections from inside and outside the government, the Matsunaga Plan was forced through the Diet on General MacArthur's instructions.[7] By May 1951, the national electricity monopoly had been dismantled and nine vertically integrated private utilities were formed.[8] Just over a year later, with rates up 30 percent and public opinion turning against the reorganization, the government created the Electric Power Development Corporation (EPDC), which was tasked with using government resources to develop hydropower plants to supply the nine regional monopolies.[9]

Because of oil's key role in the Japanese war machine and the dearth of domestic sources, SCAP's initial stance was to dismantle the petroleum industry in Japan. By the early 1950s, however, oil was seen as an increasingly attractive alternative to dirty, though abundant, coal. Worsening pollution combined with union unrest among coal miners and escalating costs to reduce Japanese international competitiveness.[10] The shift to oil gathered momentum with the outbreak of the Korean War, as U.S. forces began to require ever greater amounts of petroleum products, and the oil infrastructure began to improve.[11] This pattern of development set the tone for the next 20 years, particularly as labor unrest and cartelism persisted in the coal sector. The introduction of the First Coal Program in 1962, nationalizing the mining industry and capping prices, was not enough to preserve coal's role in the economy, and by 1964 its share of the total primary energy supply (TPES) dropped below oil's.[12]

The absence of a Japanese company from the roster of the oil majors did not go unnoticed by the government, which established the Japan Petroleum Development Corporation in 1967. Modeled on the French and Italian oil firms (ELF and ENI, respectively), JPDC (later the Japan National Oil Company, or JNOC) was initially tasked with providing capital for projects using revenues collected from oil consumption taxes.[13] This arrangement was meant to ensure a stable flow of energy through the development of oil and gas resources by Japex and Inpex, two major oil companies established through government initiatives. The nascent nuclear power industry, a source of pride for some, remained a marginal player in Japan's energy mix during this period. The public's ambivalence toward nuclear technology, along with the need to import much of the hardware, restricted initial investment to the government-sponsored Japan Atomic Power Company (JAPC).[14] Established in 1957, JAPC took nine years to put into service its first nuclear reactor, the 166 MW gas-cooled Tokai Power Station, and it was another four years before the first Boiling Water Reactor produced electricity commercially at Tsuruga.[15] Both power plants were based on imported designs, the first from Britain and the second from America's General Electric.[16]

This energy-intensive stage of Japanese development, with heavy industry and manufacturing serving as engines for the reconstruction of the country, required coordination of industrial and energy policy. By focusing investment on exporting industries, Japan sought to generate foreign exchange with which to satisfy its energy needs.[17] Few countries were as affected as Japan was by the Arab oil embargo of 1973. The resulting changes in the industrial landscape, the economic slowdown that followed, and dramatic increases in energy prices helped to mobilize the Japanese population in support of energy efficient policies. By the second oil shock six years later, Japan was in a position not only to weather the storm better than most developed countries, but also to capitalize on the world's newfound desire for energy conservation by exporting fuel-efficient cars and other technology.[18]

The Path to Diversification and Efficiency

The mid-1970s saw a wave of energy-related legislation in Japan. Enacted in December 1973, the Emergency Law for the Stabilization of National Life gave the government the ability to set prices for everyday products during times of severe inflation. The Petroleum Supply and Demand Optimization Law of the same year set oil supply targets and restricted oil use.[19] To insulate the economy from turbulent market effects, the Petroleum Stockpiling Law of 1975 provided financial assistance to private companies for the maintenance of a 70-day supply of petroleum products.[20] The Law Concerning the Rational Use of Energy, enacted in June of 1979, encouraged efficiency on the part of Japanese consumers.[21] Setting out specific efficiency goals for factories, buildings, and machinery, this law demonstrated recognition that while some industries had responded early to the call for efficiencies, government-mandated goals had to be tailored to specific sectors. Japan succeeded in reducing its dependence on oil through a rapid improvement in energy intensity, while maintaining healthy rates of economic growth. The beginnings of antinuclear sentiment in Japan may have been established in World War II, but it had been truly ignited by the exposure of Japanese fishermen to radioactive ash from an American nuclear test in 1954, and the public failure of the *Mutsu* nuclear-fueled cargo ship. While general pacifism remains, this opposition became easier to overcome in the aftermath of the first oil shock, and three laws passed in June of 1974 gave the nuclear industry the support it needed to dramatically accelerate development.[22]

In 1970, Kansai Electric Power Company put into service its first reactor. Along with the JAPC's two commercial nuclear reactors, this accounted for just 0.5 percent of all electricity in the country.[23] By 1974 the number of reactors increased to eight and to 46 by 1993.[24] Nuclear energy's share in electricity production climbed up from 2 percent in 1975, to 17 percent by 1980, to 30 percent today.[25] Domestically, however, nuclear power has not been received without trepidation. A spate of problems after 1991, averaging one incident per reactor per year, undermined public confidence in the technology.[26] Starting with the 1991 accident at the Mihama nuclear plant and gradually escalating in severity to a level-3 fire and explosion at a fuel-reprocessing plant, the Japanese nuclear industry and bureaucracy have faced growing skepticism from the public. An October 1999 Japan Public Opinion Company survey found 52 percent of people were "uneasy" about nuclear power. A March 2000 Asahi Shinbun poll found that 75 percent of Japanese did not trust the bureaucracy.[27] These polls took place before the 2002–2003 shutdown of TEPCO's 17 reactors in reaction to public outcry following falsified safety reports. The Kashiwazaki-kariwa plant, which suffered a major earthquake in mid-2007, revealed some weaknesses in the reporting procedures that eclipsed the otherwise excellent performance of the emergency shut-off system and a follow-up clean bill of health by the International Atomic Energy Agency (IAEA). Thus, despite Japan's need for nuclear power and increasing public understanding, it is no surprise that a not in my back yard mentality still persists.

While Japan is undecided about the future of its nuclear industry, coal is enjoying resurgence. Because of its relatively low cost and long-term viability, it now accounts for approximately 20 percent of the energy mix.[28] Coal is also attractive because of its wide geographic distribution in stable countries, with over half of Japan's coal imports coming from Australia, and the remainder from China, Indonesia, the United States, Canada, and other countries. Like many other nations, Japan has increased its use of natural gas since the oil shocks. Imported liquefied natural gas (LNG) currently provides 14 percent of total energy supply, primarily for electricity generation.[29] Though Japan was a pioneer in the LNG trade, it now finds itself in an increasingly competitive international market, accounting for only half of global demand.[30] Hydro-generation accounted for 9.5 percent of electricity production in 2004.[31] By the 1960s virtually all hydroelectric potential in Japan had been exhausted (all major Japanese rivers have been dammed—many more than once) leaving this sector with little additional capacity.[32] Finally, alternative sources make up only 2 percent of Japan's total primary energy supply. Given the country's relatively high energy use for electricity, however, this sector has great potential for growth. The country has embraced solar power as a growing part of its energy mix and has continued to build large-scale wind farms in many areas.[33] Alternatives and renewables have expanded by 50 percent per year for the past decade.[34]

The Ministry of International Trade and Industry (MITI) also created a subsidiary agency tasked with developing alternative energies not related to nuclear power. The New Energy Development Organization (NEDO) was created to support projects focused on reducing Japan's oil dependency through technology development.[35] NEDO concentrates its efforts on three core technologies—coal-to-liquids, geothermal, and solar—while also providing domestic support to the promotion and dissemination of these technologies, and participating in overseas mining and geological surveys.[36] The government encouraged a switch in electricity generation away from oil through the imposition of tariffs on petroleum imports, with the revenue directed toward implementing the Stockpiling Law and non-oil energy-related research and development. One of the effects of this policy shift was an increased use of LNG. Prior to the oil shocks, LNG comprised 2 percent TPES.[37] Though the Tokyo Electric Power Company (TEPCO) had begun the development of transportation, regasification, and distribution networks for Alaskan LNG in 1969, it was not until 1979 that a significant increase in the use of LNG for power generation occurred.[38] This policy environment made TEPCO an early adopter of gas combined-cycle (GCC) technology, the most thermally efficient form of electricity generation from fossil fuels. Motivated by a wider distribution of natural gas throughout the world, and its low emissions, the Japanese government exempted LNG from taxes on energy imports imposed in 1980.[39] Gas's share of Japan's TPES rose to 7 percent in 1982, and 11 percent in 1990—a six-fold increase in less than 20 years.[40]

Economic Adjustments

Instability in world energy markets led the Japanese government to a conscious decision not to shield domestic consumers from rising global energy prices.[41] The result was a rapid market-driven increase in the price of petroleum products, and consequently of electricity for Japanese consumers and industry. With energy becoming a significant drag on their budgets, and the general impression of scarcity in the oil market, Japanese industry began an adjustment that allowed for the decoupling of economic growth and energy consumption.[42] The government worked to ensure energy supplies as the private sector responded by improving energy efficiency and conservation. Concurrent with the shift toward more efficient equipment and manufacturing processes was the development of the high technology and microelectronics industries, which by their nature were much less energy intensive and became the cornerstones of the new Japanese economy.[43] By the 1980s, Japan also became an importer of processed materials and commodities requiring great amounts of energy input in the refining process, effectively exporting some of its energy consumption to less developed countries.[44] Japan came out of the 1980s with a high degree of energy security for a country so poorly endowed with domestic resources.

The economic slowdown of the 1990s in Japan had far-reaching consequences. During this period unemployment rose and homeless appeared in major cities, with some labeling this the nation's lost decade. For the outside world, this period marked the end of the Japan, Inc. economic juggernaut. For the Japanese, it was a time when *shoganai*, the sense that little can be done, replaced a steely national confidence. During this period energy consumption in Japan's industrial sector remained flat and conservation efforts plateaued as Japanese manufacturers reached the upper limit of efficiency gains through the turnover of capital stock to more efficient machinery. An economic downturn and historically-low energy prices weakened the pressure to conserve, refocusing government efforts on other concerns. The internationalists at MITI (now METI—Ministry of Economy, Trade, and Industry) felt partly vindicated, having advocated reliance on the global market and an end to large-scale oil-substitution research and development. Some blamed spending on grandiose schemes of the 1980s for the economic malaise of the 1990s.[45] After a decade of economic drift, Japan began to rebound in 2002. Unlike previous periods, during which economic growth and low energy prices coincided, growth accelerated from 0.13 percent in 2002 to 2.63 percent in 2005, even as oil prices in the wake of the Iraq War rose from $24.96 per barrel in 2002, to $51.57 in 2005. Unlike other OECD economies, Japan did not experience inflationary pressures brought on by rising energy prices. At the time, however, Tokyo viewed this as a disappointment because the economy had suffered a decade of deflation, which acted as a drag on consumption.

This most recent period has coincided with an inverse energy-income relationship: tightening conservation measures may indeed have little impact on growth.[46] Toyota's surpassing GM as the world's largest car company on the strength of its sales of hybrids and fuel-efficient compacts, and the expansion of production capacity by Honda to satisfy higher-than-expected demand for its most fuel efficient models provide further proof that energy conservation and high fuel prices do not always translate into job losses and industrial decline.[47] The growth in Japan's automobile industry has received much attention, but growth in sales of energy-efficient technology is also visible across a range of other industries. The solar sector received support from NEDO from 1994 until 2002 and has reduced prices of photovoltaics by 60 percent, making them a good buy for many households.[48] Japan provides nearly 40 percent of the world market and leadership in thin-film technology.[49] Steelmaking, shipbuilding, glassmaking, transportation, and home heating are just a few other fields in which Japanese companies have taken a leadership position through gains in efficiency and pollution reduction. The 1980s era investment in technologies meant to prepare Japan for the next oil shock, such as hybrid-engine automobiles or waste-heat recovery, have begun to pay off.[50]

Current Energy Security Challenges

While oil remains the primary source of energy in Japan, its share in the total energy mix has fallen dramatically from a high of 77 percent in the 1970s to below 50 percent today. Prior to the oil shocks, more than half of all electricity in Japan came from oil-fired thermal power plants. Currently, oil accounts for only 8 percent of electricity production.[51] Despite that, Japan still remains the world's third largest oil importer, with its transportation sector 98 percent reliant on petroleum.[52] Unlike most OECD member states, it depends on the Middle East for most of its oil, particularly Saudi Arabia, the UAE, and Iran.[53] An additional vulnerability is the near-total dependence on the Malacca Strait as the transit route for this oil.

An important tenet of Japan's energy security is its relations with Russia. Capitalizing on Japanese weakness at the end of World War II, Russia claimed sovereignty over part of Japanese-controlled Sakhalin Island, as well as some of the Kuril Islands. These islands, known as the Northern Territories, had previously been part of the Japanese archipelago. Japan's refusal to accept these acquisitions continues to complicate energy relations with Russia.[54] The East Siberia Pacific Ocean (ESPO) pipeline, first proposed by YUKOS in 1998, has generated both cooperation and contention among Russia, Japan, and China.[55] The pipeline is to carry oil pumped from fields in East Siberia to Asia, with the terminus located at either Nakhodka, a short ferry trip from the tip of Japan, or Skovorodino, in Eastern Siberia.[56] Though the project initially suffered delays due to funding and environmental concerns, record-high oil prices have rekindled progress. Beijing's growing interest in the project may persuade Transneft, the Russian pipeline monopoly, to designate Skovorodino, near the Chinese border, as the terminus for not only the first stage of construction, but for the entire project. Beijing already has plans to build a trunk line to Daqing, while the remainder of the oil would be shipped by rail to Nakhodka or Vladivostok.

Second to Russia, China has long exerted influence on Japanese energy security. Energy has been an important part of the economic relationship between Asia's two biggest trading powers.[57] Disagreements over claims to East China Sea gas resources persist, with periods of heightened tension, but overall the two countries have maintained a dialogue on the issue and produced a steady stream of positive pronouncements.[58] Six working groups relating to energy have been established between China and Japan: oil and natural gas, electricity, power generation (including nuclear), coal, renewables, and perhaps most importantly, conservation. With eight times the energy intensity of Japan's economy, improving efficiency is an important part of Chinese attempts to meet growing energy demands.[59] Helping China would have strategic, economic, and environmental benefits for Japan. Japanese consumers ultimately pay for inferior Chinese environmental standards through pollution that wafts across the East China Sea and high levels of toxins captured in fisheries common to the two nations. While the Chinese are eager to access superior Japanese technology and know-how, the pitfalls associated with an aggressive approach to energy security are plainly obvious in the Japanese historical example. By helping China manage the environmental effects of its rapid growth, Japan strengthens its claim to regional and international leadership.

Iran poses a specific challenge for Japan, one that demonstrates the delicate balance that Japan must pursue between fulfilling its energy needs and living up to its responsibilities as a member of the international community. After years of negotiations over a contract to explore and develop the vast Azadegan oil field in southwest Iran, Inpex was forced to reduce its stake in the project to 10 percent from an original 75 percent after negotiations faltered, purportedly over responsibility for cleaning up landmines.[60] The field was to produce 260,000 bpd and form a central component of Japan's strategy to pursue independent upstream development of overseas oilfields. The debate over Azadegan reflected the struggle within the Japanese bureaucracy between METI and the Foreign Affairs Office, and within METI between internationalists and autonomists.[61] Whereas the internationalists look to downplay the severity of Japan's supposed vulnerability to the disruptions from Persian Gulf countries, seeing the market as the great equalizer, the more hawkish faction is reluctant to do business with the regime in Tehran at a time when the Bush administration is looking for ways to isolate it internationally. But by supporting the United States and Europe in their efforts to prevent Iran from developing nuclear weapons, Japan proved that its global responsibilities trump narrower interests of energy security and economic growth. In the case of Iran, Japan's choice to side with the United States was almost natural—after all, Japan's military dependence on the United States is no less important for its energy security than Iran's oilfields. Despite the fact that the Japanese Maritime Self-Defense Force (MSDF) is the most capable blue-water navy in East Asia, Japan still relies on the U.S. Navy for trade route security. But there are increasing pressures within Japan to assume more responsibility for its military needs and amend Article IX of the constitution, which commits Japan to a pacifist foreign policy. This issue has been at the center of a wider debate that has gone on for years over attempts to project an image more befitting a "normal country." As part of Japan's assistance to the United States in the war on terrorism, Tokyo assumed responsibility for refueling in the Arabian Sea operations against the Taliban. This requires, among other things, MSDF to traverse the route over which 90 percent of Japanese oil travels. This oil-carrying umbilical cord, traditionally prone to piracy, has experienced a significant reduction in attacks since the MSDF began its operations in 2001.[62] The MSDF's participation in the annual Cobra Gold military exercises as well as the recent Malabar Exercise, involving American, Australian, Singaporean, and Indian naval forces, suggest the possibility that aspects of Japanese energy security have in fact already been partially militarized.

Policies for the Future: International Leadership, Regional Cooperation

When world leaders gathered in Kyoto in 1997 to discuss global warming, they came to an agreement that required a collective reduction in greenhouse gas emissions to at least 5 percent below 1990 levels by 2008–2012.[63] For Japan, this translated into a 6 percent cut in its emissions.[64] In the years that followed, the Kyoto Protocol experienced complications. Citing economic burdens not borne by developing nations such as China and India, the United States withdrew its signature. Other countries have failed to meet their commitments. Aside from excluding developing countries, the agreement failed to account for energy intensity. Given that Japan had the most energy efficient baseline in the world for 1990, it was said that achieving a 6 percent reduction would be like wringing water out of a dry towel.

The development of Asian economies over the past quarter century has complicated energy security for Japan. By harnessing its experience in technology and efficiency efforts, Japan aspires to regional leadership in energy, security, and environmental efforts. The increased commitment to helping other Asian nations in their energy concerns was expressed explicitly in the New National Energy Strategy of 2006.[65] Through regional organizations such as the Asia Energy Conservation Collaboration Center, Japan has promoted the adoption of "widely conceived emergency response options" aimed at encouraging stockpiling strategies that will forestall panic purchasing in the event of supply disruptions.

Nobuo Tanaka, Executive Director of the International Energy Agency, is a cosmopolitan thinker who has emerged as one of Japan's voices for a fairer approach to energy, admonishing rich countries for not following a sustainable energy path.[66] Unlike his predecessors at the IEA, the former METI official has become a global advocate for more responsible energy policies. Tanaka's leadership at the IEA is a source of pride for Japanese bureaucrats and symbolizes Japan's conception of its role in regional and international energy security. Japan hopes its leadership role will ensure stable resource markets for developed and developing countries and facilitate the establishment of a post-Kyoto framework to control the effects of greenhouse gases.

Technology Development

As one Japanese official remarked, energy security is seen as sacrosanct in Japan—it is not questioned. In the short term, the Japanese focus is on highly feasible, immediately effective projects that promote energy conservation. These include power storage, superconductors, and other products that improve conservation at the commercial and residential levels.[67] NEDO also works to develop more forward looking, long-term technology projects that include solar and highly efficient coal technology.[68] In keeping with its commitment to international cooperation in the development and dissemination of energy-related technologies,

Tokyo has taken the lead in the effort to advance the study of coal liquefaction. This technology allows countries to use an abundant resource for development purposes while mitigating its harmful environmental impact.[69] After sponsoring a pilot project in Australia, Japan donated equipment to a coal plant in Indonesia that will use Japanese liquefaction technology when it comes online in 2013.[70]

In line with Japan's diversification-centered policy, LNG continues to play an important role as a non-oil fuel alternative. But what was once a duopoly of LNG consumers, with France in the Atlantic basin and Japan in the Pacific, is now a varied and vibrant market. As this market continues to grow, Japanese power companies have begun to question the viability of take-or-pay contracts.[71] Though the Japanese government continues to promote take-or-pay, there may only be so much support for this policy before buyers move to a market-based system, something that has already taken place in Europe and North America.[72]

The Japanese auto industry has played an important supporting role in the country's energy security strategy. After nearly 30 years of conservation measures in industry, the doubling of energy consumed by Japan's fleet of cars, trucks, and trains has made the transportation sector a prime target for efficiency efforts.[73] Transportation accounts for nearly half of oil consumption, making it an important arena for diversification away from petroleum.[74] Japanese companies were the first to commercialize hybrid automobiles and the government expected diesel-powered automobiles to displace gasoline-powered ones, lowering fuel consumption in the transportation sector while helping to diversify fuel sources. Diesel can be obtained through traditional refining processes as well as through gas-to-liquids (GTL), coal-to-liquids (CTL), and biomass conversion. Despite efforts on the part of the public and private sector, however, METI expects the transportation sector's dependence on oil to decline only 20 percent by 2030.

Finally, Japan has long recognized the need to enlist ordinary Japanese in conservation efforts.[75] One Japanese official explained that the Shinto tradition embraces conservation since it posits spirits in all things. This tradition manifests itself in the Japanese mindset of "*mottainai*" or "don't waste."[76] The wartime effort to encourage civilians to collect pine roots for processing into synthetic fuel has evolved into measures that affect the way Japanese people dress, drive, and consume.[77] Japan aims to achieve a 30 percent improvement in conservation and a 40 percent reduction in oil dependence by 2030. Shifting policies may nevertheless prove challenging. As IEA's Tanaka said in an interview, it is difficult to change policies when previous ones were successful.

The ability to tailor energy policy to fit each stage of development and to acknowledge the transition from one stage to another may depend on values inherent in the Japanese experience, but the government's willingness to frame consumption choices in terms of energy security can serve as a model to many nations. As one Japanese official put it, increasing energy efficiency is like finding new energy resources.

Overall, Japanese officials interviewed for this chapter mentioned several approaches suitable for duplication: the mixture of global market prices and domestic regulation; emphasis on energy efficiency; use of cross-sector consultations to set standards; and promotion of new technologies. But if they had to put Japan's strategy in one word, it was efficiency. Indeed, at the 2008 World Economic Forum, it was suggested that Japan's energy efficiency achievements could be of "great aid" to the world as it attempts to deal with energy and environmental problems.[78]

Resource demands have long been among the strongest forces shaping a country's foreign policy. From the development of trade relationships to the acquisition of colonies, countries have looked for ways to gain materials from beyond their borders to fuel their development. In a globalized economy, in which the demands of development and the environment constrain many actors, nations must take every measure within their power to ensure that their people and economies remain competitive and well supplied.

Increased interdependence has given states more leverage over one another, creating superpowers in various fields. If Japan can continue to lead in its use of technology to overcome the restraints of an ever-changing energy environment, it may stake a claim as an "efficiency superpower" in the 21st century's struggle for energy security.

Notes

1. International Energy Agency, *Share of Total Primary Energy Supply in 2004: Japan,* http://www.iea.org/Textbase/stats/balancetable.asp?COUNTRY_CODE=JP.

2. Jonathan Utley, *Going to War with Japan, 1937–1941* (New York: Fordham Univ. Press, 2005), 100.

3. Daniel Yergin, *The Prize: The Epic Quest of Oil, Money and Power* (New York: Free Press, 1993), 316–318.

4. Ibid., 326.

5. Richard J. Samuels, *The Business of the Japanese State* (Ithaca, NY: Cornell University Press, 1987), 186–187.

6. Julian Kinsley, "The Kansai Electric Power Company," *Enotes.com Business: Company Histories,* http://www.enotes.com/company-histories/kansai-electric-power-company-inc.

7. Samuels, *The Business of the Japanese State,* 156–158.

8. Kansai Electric power company Web site, www.kepco.co.jp/english/.

9. Samuels, *The Business of the Japanese State,* 160.

10. Yagi Kiichiro, *Japanese Theory of Modernization/Industrialization Between Liberalism and Developmentalism,* (Kyoto, Japan: Kyoto University, 2004), 8.

11. Yasumasa Kuroda, Fereidun Fesharaki, and Wendy Schultz, "Historical Perspectives on Japanese Energy Policies" *Energy Systems and Policy,* 11, 121–141.

12. Kiichiro Yagi, *Japanese Theory of Modernization/Industrialization Between Liberalism and Developmentalism,* http://www.siue.edu/EASTASIA/Yagi_110800.htm; Samuels, *The Business of the Japanese State,* 117.

13. Samuels, *The Business of the Japanese State,* 208–209; Peter C. Evans, "Japan," in *The Brookings Foreign Policy Studies: Energy Security Series,* (Washington, D.C.: The Brookings Institution, 2006), 20, http://www.brookings.edu/reports/2006/12japan.aspx.

14. Mindy L. Kotler and Ian T. Hillman, "Japanese Nuclear Energy Policy and Public Opinion," in *Japanese Energy Security and Changing Global Energy Markets: An Analysis of Northeast Asian Energy Cooperation and Japan's Evolving Leadership Role in the Region* (Houston, TX: James A. Baker III Institute for Public Policy of Rice University, 2000), 2.

15. "Corporate Overview: History," Web site of The Japan Atomic Power Company (JAPC), http://www.japc.co.jp/english/company/history.htm, Accessed September 21, 2007.

16. Samuels, *The Business of the Japanese State,* 240.

17. Bai Gao, "The Search for National Identity and Japanese Industrial Policy, 1950–1969," *Nations and Nationalism,* 2, no. 2 (1998): 227–247.

18. Steven W. Lewis and Amy Myers Jaffe, et al., *Japanese Energy Security and Changing Global Energy Markets: An Analysis of Northeast Asian Energy Cooperation and Japan's Evolving Leadership Role in the Region* (Houston, TX: James A. Baker III Institute for Public Policy of Rice University, 2000), 1.

19. Mikio Sumiya, *A History of Japanese Trade and Industry Policy* (Oxford University Press, 2000), 554

20. The composition of the stockpile will differ, depending on the type of product the private entity imports, produces, or distributes.

21. United Nations- Selected National and State Laws and Regulations for the Promotion of Energy Conservation and Efficiency in Countries of Asia and the Pacific Region, http://www.unescap.org/esd/energy/publications/compend/ceccpart4chapter5.htm.

22. The Law on the Development of Areas Around Power Plants, the Law on Taxation to Promote Power Generation, and the Law on the Special Account on Measures to Promote Power Generation, Tatsuo Masuda, *The Japanese Energy Model- Lessons from 60 Years Policy Making* PowerPoint Presentation given on March 21, 2007 at Centre de Géopolitique de l'Energie et des Métiers Premières, Université Paris Dauphine, 21.

23. Mika Goto and Masayuki Yajima, "A New Stage of Electricity Liberalization in Japan: Issues and Expectations," in *Electricity Market Reform,* eds. Fereidoon P. Sioshansi, Wolfgang Pfaffenberger (New York: Elsevier, 2006), 621.

24. *Current Status of Nuclear Power Facilities in Japan—2006 Edition* (Tokyo: Japan Nuclear Energy Safety Organization, March 2006), 2, http://www.jnes.go.jp/english/database/unkanhp2006-e.html.

25. Kenneth B. Medlock and Peter Hartley, "The Role of Nuclear Power in Enhancing Japan's Energy Security," Baker Institute working paper, www.rice.edu/energy/publications/docs/TEPCOweb_FinalPaper.pdf.

26. Mindy L. Kotler and Ian T. Hillman, *Japanese Nuclear Energy Policy and Public Opinion,* 6.

27. Ibid, 10.

28. *Energy in Japan 2006: Status and Policies* (Tokyo: Agency for Natural Resources and Energy, Ministry of Economy, Trade and Industry, March 2006), 20.

29. *New National Energy Strategy (Digest)* (Tokyo: Ministry of Economy Trade and Industry, May 2006), 5, http://www.enecho.meti.go.jp/english/report/newnationalenergystrategy2006.pdf.

30. *New National Energy Strategy (Digest),* 7, http://www.enecho.meti.go.jp/english/report/newnationalenergystrategy2006.pdf.

31. IEA Web site, "Electricity/Heat in Japan in 2004," http://www.iea.org/Textbase/stats/electricitydata.asp?COUNTRY_CODE=JP.

32. Julian Kinsley, "The Kansai Electric Power Company."

33. *Energy in Japan 2006,* 13.

34. *Electricity Review Japan 2007,* 13.

35. Takashi Honda, "NEDO's Solar Energy Program," *Renewable Energy,* (September-December 1998), 115.

36. Richard J. Samuels, *The Politics of Alternative Energy Research and Development in Japan,* 157.

37. *Energy in Japan 2006,* 5.

38. Roger W. Gale, "Tokyo Electric Power Company: Its Role in Shaping Japan's Coal and LNG Policy," in *The Politics of Japan's Energy Strategy: Resources-Diplomacy-Security,* ed., Ronald A. Morse (Berkeley, CA: Institute of East Asian Studies, 1981), 98–99.

39. Yasumasa Kuroda et al., *Historical Perspectives,* 132.

40. Ibid., 131.

41. Chikashi Moriguchi, "Japan's Energy Policy During the 1970s" in *Government Policy towards industry in the United States and Japan,* ed., John B. Shoven, (Cambridge, UK: Cambridge University Press, 1988), 307.

42. Takao Tomitate, "Japan-U.S. Energy Interests and Relations: An Overview from the Japanese Perspective" in *U.S.-Japan Energy Policy Considerations for The 1900s,* eds., John E. Gray and Yoshihiro Nakayama (Lanham, MD: University Press of America, 1988), 4.

43. Ibid., 6.

44. Chikashi Moriguchi, "Japan's Energy Policy," 306.

45. Peter C. Evans, "Japan," 6–7.

46. Chien-Chiang Lee, "The Causality Relationship between Energy Consumption and GDP in G-11 Countries Revisited," *Energy Policy,* 34, no. 4 (UK: Elsevier, 2006): 4.

47. "Toyota Is Poised to Supplant G.M. as World's Largest Carmaker," *The New York Times,* December 23, 2006; "Honda to Expand Production in U.S.; Demand for Fuel Efficient Civics Soars on Record Gas Prices," *The International Herald Tribune,* November 7, 2006.

48. Makoto Tanaka, General Manager, Advanced Energy Research Center, SANYO Electric Co., Ltd., "Recent Status and Future Prospects of Photovoltaic Solar Cells," presentation given at the Japan/China Joint Seminar on Energy Conservation and New Energy in Cooperation, at Shanghai Jiao Tong University on October 27, 2006, http://www.nedo.go.jp/kokusai/kouhou/181027/3222.pdf.

49. "Japan Cements Position as Solar Cell Leader," *Financial Times,* November 30, 2007.

50. Peter A. Petri, "High-Cost Energy and Japan's International Economic Strateg," in *The Politics of Japan's Energy Strategy: Resources, Diplomacy, Security,* ed., Ronald A. Morse (Berkeley: University of California Press, 1981), 28–29.

51. *Energy in Japan 2006: Status and Policies,* Agency for Natural Resources and Energy, Ministry of Economy, Trade, and Industry, March 2006, 6.

52. The New National Energy Strategy Digest, Ministry of Economy Trade and Industry, May 2006, 19.

53. 90 percent from Mideast OPEC members: Saudi Arabia at 25.9 percent, the United Arab Emirates, at 25.3 percent, Iran at 15 percent, Qatar, at 9.3 percent, Kuwait, at 8.6 percent, Oman, at 2.4 percent, Iraq, at 2.2 percent, and Yemen, at 0.1 percent, round out the list of Middle Eastern suppliers, while Indonesia, at 3.5 percent, and Nigeria, at 2.2 percent, complete the OPEC list. Only 5.5 percent of Japanese oil comes from non-OPEC sources (MITI).

54. Shoichi Itoh, "Can Russia Become a 'Regional Power' in Northeast Asia? Implications for Contemporary Energy Relations with China and Japan," in *Security Challenges in the Post-Soviet Space: European and Asian Perspectives,* eds. Adam Eberhardt and Akihiro

Iwashita (Sapporo, Japan: Polish Institute of International Affairs Research Center, Hokkaido University, 2007), 93.

55. Shoichi Itoh, "Sino-Russian Energy Relations: The Dilemma of Strategic Partnership and Mutual Distrust," in ERINA Report, 77 (Niigata, Japan: The Economic Research Institute for Northeast Asia, September 2007), 67.

56. Olga Minina, "Pipelines of Eastern Siberia: From Local Supplies To Large-Scale Exports," *Pipeline and Gas Journal,* August 2007, 66.

57. See Kent Calder, "Sino-Japanese Energy Relations: Prospects for Deepening Strategic Competition," presented at the Conference on Japan's Contemporary Challenges, Yale University, New Haven, Connecticut, March 9–10, 2007.

58. For example, Prime Minister Fukuda and Premier Wen Jiabao made a joint statement on December 28 that said "We both hope for joint development, to turn the East China Sea into a sea of peace and cooperation. Let's work for more progress on common points. We hope for settlement as early as possible."

59. Sebastian Moffett, *Wall Street Journal,* April 9, 2007.

60. Peter C. Evans, "Japan," 15.

61. Ibid., 6–7.

62. International Maritime Bureau reports a decline in pirate attacks in Indonesian waters from 121 in 2002 to 43 in 2007; Marcus Hand, "African Hot Spots Worst Hit as Piracy Surges 10 Percent," *Lloyds List,* January 10, 2008, 4.

63. Kyoto Protocol to the United Nations Framework Convention on Climate Change, http://unfccc.int/resource/docs/convkp/kpeng.html.

64. Energy in Japan, 2006, 9.

65. Tatsuo Masuda, "The Japanese Energy Model: Lessons from 60 Years Policy Making," PowerPoint Presentation given on February, 14 2008 at Centre de Géopolitique de l'Energie et des Métiers Premières, Université Paris Dauphine, 3, http://www.dauphine.fr/cgemp/masterindustrie/cours%20geopolitics/geopolitics%202008/Presentation%20Masuda%207feb/pdf/Japan%20EnergyPolicy%2014Feb2008.pdf.

66. The author was Nobuo Tanaka's assistant at the Research Institute of Economy, Trade and Industry in Tokyo. Judy Dempsey, "New Energy Agency Chief Sees Household Energy Use Rising in Industrial Countries," *International Herald Tribune,* September 10, 2007.

67. "Outline of NEDO," New Energy and Industrial Technology Development Organization, 2008–2009 (Tokyo, Japan: October 2008), 97–99, http://www.nedo.go.jp/kankobutsu/pamphlets/kouhou/2008gaiyo_e/all.pdf.

68. Ibid., 102, 106.

69. The New National Energy Strategy Digest, Ministry of Economy Trade and Industry, May 2006.

70. Monika Boyle, "JBIC Seeks Guarantee for Coal Liquefaction Plant in Indonesia," *Platt's International Coal Report,* October 8, 2007.

71. Ryoichi Namikawa, "Take-or-Pay under Japanese Energy Policy," *Energy Policy,* 31, 1329.

72. Ibid., 1330.

73. "Breakdown of Sectorial Final Consumption by Source in 1973 and 2004," *IEA Energy Statistics,* IEA Web site, http://www.iea.org/index.asp.

74. *Energy in Japan 2006,* METI, March 2006.

75. Joseph Kahn, "Cheney Promotes Increasing Supply as Energy Policy," *New York Times,* May 1, 2001.

76. For more on this topic see David Kestenbaum's "Mottainai Grandma Reminds Japan, Don't Waste" on *National Public Radio* (October 8, 2007), http://www.npr.org/templates/story/story.php?storyId=14054262.

77. But to argue that conservation is unique to Japan may be an overstatement. According to TEPCO's Aug. 2007 report "Recent Challenges and Solutions of the Energy and Electric Utility Industry in Japan" (85); studies show that Japanese are as inclined to pay for green energy as others.

78. World Economic Forum Web site, http://www.weforum.org/en/knowledge/KN_SESS_SUMM_23969?url=/en/knowledge/KN_SESS_SUMM_23969.

CHAPTER 13

Jia You! (Add Oil!)*: Chinese Energy Security Strategy

Sabrina Howell

Like other major energy consumers, the Chinese are concerned about maintaining affordable, secure and reliable access to increasing amounts of energy. China exported oil and coal until the early 1990s, when the booming economy inspired by Deng Xiaoping's reforms transformed China into an energy importer. Mao-era emphasis on self-sufficiency, however, remains deeply rooted in the Chinese psyche. Current oil import dependency, now at over 50 percent, causes alarm in Beijing. And yet, just like many other major energy-importing countries, China has no overarching energy security strategy. Centralized policy sometimes gives way to competing interest groups, exaggerated rhetoric and province-level initiatives. Lacking a powerful Energy Ministry, China's energy policy is in fact more disaggregated than that of many other countries. Though the Chinese government may be secretive, particularly on energy and military issues, it is not a monolith and is rapidly evolving.

Five vulnerabilities drive Chinese energy policy. First, China is located far from its petroleum suppliers. In 2007, 30 percent of U.S. oil imports came from Canada and Mexico, both countries that border the United States and lie securely within its sphere of influence. Meanwhile, China relies on long-haul tankers maneuvering through dangerous straits for 90 percent of its imported oil. Second, China suffers from a poor geologic endowment, with only 1.3 percent of known world oil reserves.[1] Third, demand is increasing faster than supply can keep pace. China is already the world's second-largest energy consumer and its increase in total delivered energy consumption between 2005 and 2010 is projected to be 40 percent of the global increase.[2] Fourth, China believes that it has little sway in

---

* "Jia You" literally means "Add Oil." It is a Chinese cheer roughly equivalent to "Let's Go!" At the Olympics it became a ubiquitous motto supporting the country's larger economic and political rise as well as the effort of individual athletes.

the global arena. Chinese leaders often point out that China, despite its permanent Security Council seat, is a developing country not yet admitted to the G8 great-power club.[3] Finally, the Chinese Communist Party (CCP) is committed to continued improvements in the Chinese standard of living, believing that fulfillment of this commitment is vital to the regime's survival. Prosperity brings energy demand, and for 1.4 billion people, this is a tall order.

Policy Formation and the National Oil Companies

Today, China's top political leaders proactively shape energy policy and respond in times of crisis.[4] They guide the National Development and Reform Commission (NDRC), established in 2003, which produces high-level regulations and handles daily oversight of the energy sector. Increasingly, think tanks like the China Institute for International Studies and academic institutions like the Shanghai Academy of Social Sciences are influencing policymakers, creating a more pluralistic environment. While the oil companies and ministries are certainly powerful stakeholders, they tend to exercise their power through selective implementation of directives, rather than shaping policy.

From the 1950s, the Ministry of the Petroleum Industry (MIPI) planned and oversaw all activities relating to oil and gas exploration, production, refining and distribution. Mao prioritized petroleum production, leading to the 1959 discovery of the supergiant Daqing fields, which in 2005 were still responsible for 25 percent of Chinese output.[5] In the initial reform push of the mid-1980s, MIPI delegated upstream (exploration and production) to the China National Petroleum Company (CNPC) and downstream (refining and distribution) to the China Petrochemical Corporation (Sinopec).[6] This semi-corporatization of ministry-level organizations fed into a broader round of state-owned enterprise restructuring in the 1990s.[7] In 1997, the Fifteenth Congress of the CCP approved the reform program known as "Grasp the big, enliven the small."[8] The energy industry transformed into an economic free-for-all at lower levels but consolidated power at high levels. The State Council maintained tight control over the high levels of policy decision-making, but deregulated lower levels to stimulate competition. This arrangement continues to produce narrow-minded state management struggling with thinly veiled chaos on the ground.

Concerned by the decline of the Chinese oil industry, policymakers decided in 1998 to transform CNPC and Sinopec into integrated, more fully corporatized oil companies with both upstream and downstream operations. This, it was argued, would put them on the same playing field as the international oil companies (IOCs).[9] However, CNPC was assigned to dominate the north of China and Sinopec the south to limit competition.[10] Corporatization continued after 1999 when CNPC, Sinopec and the China National Offshore Oil Company (CNOOC) floated listed holding companies. The government maintains majority ownership of all three. Not only are the managers of these companies governmental viceministers, but the CCP appoints and evaluates all top oil and gas executives.[11] Yet no institutional structure has been built to govern their activities. One critic described the effort to create internationally competitive oil enterprises as "Welding sampans together to form an aircraft carrier."[12]

The flagship element of the 10th Five Year Plan (2001–2005) was the 2003 "Twenty-First Century Oil Strategy." The document was China's first public energy policy, and used the term "energy security" (*nengyuan anquan*) for the first time. It fed into a State Council report in 2004 entitled "National Energy Strategy and Policy."[13] High level policy is now supposed to be planned and implemented by the new Energy Bureau and State Energy Office (SEO), respectively. Both are under the purview of the NDRC.[14] Yet these new agencies, with few employees and little power, are largely viewed as a cosmetic maneuver.[15] Indeed, a number of analysts have argued that the "decentralized privatization" of the petroleum sector prevents the design of a national energy security policy.[16]

We see this failure in the recent effort to build a Strategic Petroleum Reserve (SPR). Increased import dependence created fear of a temporary reduction in crude oil supply, leading to an internal debate over whether to build an SPR, with some parties in favor and others arguing that a reserve would be an expensive waste and unhelpful in the event of a real crisis.[17] CNPC and Sinopec are already required to maintain stockpiles, some of which were employed in the aftermath of the 2008 Sichuan earthquake.[18] Nonetheless, the 10th Five Year Plan (2001–2005) called for 35 days of import storage by 2008.[19] In 2006, China began to fill the first of four initial stockpiles. The Energy Leading Group, a high-level energy strategy committee established in 2005 and led by Premier Wen Jiabao under the aegis of the NDRC, has revised targets upward in the hope of meeting the International Energy Agency (IEA) recommendation of 90 days of net imports. The United States has around 60 days of imports in its SPR and another 60 days in private company import protection.[20] At current high prices, China's SPR will be extremely costly and may affect the global oil market. Dr. Kang Wu suggests that China would be better off following South Korea's example and pursuing a more flexible stockpiling system that exploits market mechanisms by committing the government-controlled NOCs to maintain more long term storage.[21] Yet, even as China tries to build a traditional SPR, it avoids joining the IEA, which coordinates global storage facilities, because it does not want to relinquish control. Here, the need for self-reliance prevents cooperation that would be vital in a crisis. China's reserves will therefore be limited to a flexible buffer system in case of short term supply shocks.

Venturing Overseas

Beijing's push to acquire diverse foreign equity oil and gas holdings is considered in China to be a means to a sort of overseas Strategic Petroleum Reserve. There is much controversy over Chinese energy security strategy abroad, however, both in China and among Western analysts. While some point to oil policy as an arm of a military grand strategy, others argue that energy policy emerges from economic forces. For example, in a 2004 article in Beijing's Foreign Affairs University Journal, Tang Weibin concludes that "The competition among oil importing countries revolving around the source of oil must follow an increasing trend, and our country should more intensively build our own energy security strategy."[22] Though this represents one aspect of Chinese thinking, Phillip Saunders at the National Defense University points out that "When strategic concerns threaten to interfere with economic growth, Chinese leaders have repeatedly compromised or pursued policies that allow growth to continue."[23] Examples include extensive trade with Taiwan and Japan, both of which are seen in China as politically hostile neighbors, and participation in international institutions with whose values China may not agree.

Chinese energy policy and business ventures abroad exist at the nexus of political, economic and military agendas. It is important to remember that the NOCs have prioritized domestic exploration and development. The three companies' spending on domestic upstream rose from $12.6 billion in 2004 to $21.5 billion in 2006. The two-year increase in domestic investment was greater than their total international expenditure, including acquisitions, in the same period.[24] Despite great investment in advanced recovery, China's large domestic fields like Daqing are in decline. China also worries about its dependence on Middle Eastern imports, and hopes to achieve security of supply through diverse holdings abroad. The Chinese pursue a Sun Tzu-like strategy: "Go into emptiness, strike voids, bypass what he defends."[25] This method was articulated in a 2004 article from the Beijing Foreign Affairs University's journal. "Russia, Asia, Africa and other oil producers that have not yet been controlled by America have become the focus of competition among those desiring oil."[26] An expert at the government-affiliated China Contemporary International Relations Institute, Chen Fengying, has written: "Chinese companies must go places for oil where American [and] European companies are not present."[27] In general, when discussing their ventures abroad CNPC's executives consider themselves underdogs against stacked odds.[28] And indeed, as Figure 13.1 shows, China's sources of imported oil are not exactly paragons of stability.

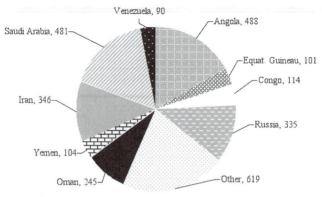

Figure 13.1 China's Oil Imports by Source, 2006 (in thousand barrels/day)

At the top of China's national security concerns are the Malacca Straits, through which 80 percent of China's oil imports must pass on their way from the Persian Gulf and Africa. Oil tankers in the Straits, only 1.7 miles wide at one point, risk collisions, oil spills, hijacking, piracy, and terrorism.[29] China is also worried that the U.S. Navy, which acts as a policing force in the Straits, might blockade China's oil in the event of war with Taiwan. Hu Jintao was quoted by the official Chinese news agency as saying that "certain major powers" might seek to control oil transit in the Strait.[30] Beijing's multi-pronged strategy to deal with these threats include overland oil sources from central Asia, oil pipelines in Malaysia and Myanmar, and increased naval capacity in the region.

China first proposed a pipeline through Kazakhstan in 1996. Western analysts deemed the pipeline unfeasible in the long term because of its extreme length, the engineering challenge of its construction, and the difficult politics of the region.[31] Both Russia and the United States opposed the project. Russia pushed the Kazakh government to rely solely on Russian export pipelines, and the United States argued that the excess oil from the rich Tengiz field ought to be shipped across the Caspian towards Europe by barge.[32] Yet, the Chinese pushed ahead with construction in 2004. As Figure 13.2 shows, the pipeline originates in Atasu in central Kazakhstan, and runs 750 miles, to Alashankou in Xinjiang. By 2006, the pipeline carried about 200,000 barrels per day to China's Dushanzi refinery.[33] PetroKazakhstan's new Chinese Vice President, Zhou Jiping, exclaimed, "This is the new Silk Road."[34] However, the Chinese have found themselves foiled by Kazakh resource nationalism and a strong IOC presence. The Chinese have not been able to enter any of the three major projects in Kazakhstan (Tengiz, Kashagan, and Karachaganak). These large fields are controlled by the Kazakh government and the IOCs that operate them, such as Chevron and Italy's ENI.[35] Thus, despite a doubling of Kazakhstan's oil output since the late 1990s, when the pipeline was originally negotiated, the Kazakhstan-China pipeline operates far below capacity.[36]

A second nearby source of oil is Russia's rich Eastern Siberian fields. As early as 1993, China and Japan faced their own diplomatic and engineering challenges as they worked with Russia to build a pipeline eastward. Though they had a shared interest in the pipeline, the two consumer nations clashed over where it would terminate—the northern Chinese city Daqing or the Russian port of Nakhodka, where oil can be shipped to Japan and other markets. In 2003 negotiations about the $2.5 billion pipeline ground to a halt. By way of explanation, Russian Prime Minister Mikhail Kasyanov said that the plans endangered Lake Baikal's "UNESCO-protected" environment.[37] The Russian delay was perceived in China as a major diplomatic failure, but it seemed that China had foregone the project because it could not have control. CNPC later re-engaged with Russian oil company Rosneft to build a branch off the main route from Skovorodino to Daqing. The pipeline, operated by Russia's Transneft and called the East Siberia Pacific Ocean (ESPO) pipeline, will carry 1.6 mbd and cost China $11 billion.[38] By June 2008, the pipeline was 75 percent complete, according to Transneft.[39] The pipeline helps Russia diversify away from its traditional European market.

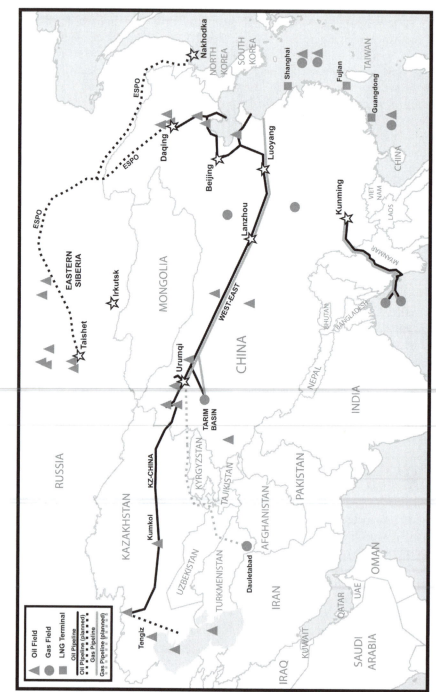

Figure 13.2 Key Chinese Oil and Gas Infrastructure

The ESPO will connect to pipelines in the West, so Russia will have the leverage to divert supplies potentially withheld from Europe to energy-hungry China and Japan.

Despite the obstacles, Chinese academics continue to regard transport from Central Asia as the "first choice for solving the energy transport security and bottleneck issues."[40] Referring to a continuation of the Great Game, Fang Yixian of the Xinjiang University School of Politics and Public Management argues that U.S. efforts to break Russia's stranglehold on Central Asian exports through the BTC pipeline and to promote democracy in the region create an opening for China to seek its own influence in this complicated but increasingly vital region.[41]

More directly, China hopes to solve what Hu Jintao has called the "Malacca dilemma" by building a pipeline across Myanmar.[42] Gas is now produced in the reclusive Southeast Asian nation by a consortium of South Korean and Indian companies. Originally Myanmar planned to send a gas pipeline to India, but Bangladesh's transit conditions prevented the project.[43] Negotiations over a pipeline to China began shortly thereafter. Meanwhile, China defended Myanmar's interests in the United Nations Security Council, vetoing sanctions on the Burmese junta in 2007.[44] In exchange, the Burmese regime pressed the foreign consortium in mid-2008 to commit to selling their gas to PetroChina, CNPC's listed subsidiary. Though PetroChina will pay market prices, the deal was still a major disappointment to India.[45] Furthermore, in bidding for as-yet-untouched offshore blocks worth as much as $50 billion, Chinese companies later beat out Korean Daewoo, which had offered the junta an arms factory, and India's ONGC, whose government had offered loans.[46] The gas deals paved the way for China's ultimate goal, an oil tanker port at Kyaukphy. With the port now under construction, CNPC is building an oil pipeline parallel to the gas pipeline to bring crude to a new refinery in Yunnan province. This will reduce tanker transport from the Middle East by as much as seven days while avoiding the Malacca Straits. Beijing hopes to use Myanmar's port for naval operations and has built listening-posts in the Bay of Bengal. These moves form part of China's "string of pearls" strategy to increase control over the sea lanes from the Persian Gulf.

Another pearl is the new port at Gwadar in Pakistan. In 1999, a program on Radio Pakistan said that "Pakistan is China's window to the Islamic world."[47] Building on a long history of strong ties, China built the Gwadar port both to receive oil supplies from the Gulf and to extend the presence of the People's Liberation Army Navy. China has also renewed its interest in participating in the Iran-Pakistan-India (IPI) gas pipeline to bring gas overland from Iran's rich Yadavaran field. Though discussed for many years, Indian concerns have long stonewalled the project. To entice Beijing to join the project Pakistan has proposed to extend the pipeline to China.[48] Additionally, China's presence in Pakistan threatens to diminish U.S. influence. In 2006, then-president Pervez Musharraf said "If Pakistan suffers pressure from certain major powers, I believe China will come forward to help us apply pressure on the other side."[49] In turn, China values Pakistan's support of its Tibet and Taiwan policies.[50]

The IPI (or IPC) pipeline highlights China's global energy rivalry with India. The two countries competed in Turkmenistan, where China eventually won the rights to explore and produce in the Amudarya region. Though some analysts doubt Turkmenistan's capability to produce all the gas that it has contracted to Russia and China, construction on a Turkmenistan-China pipeline began in 2007 and, despite enormous financial and engineering challenges, is expected to be operational by 2011.[51] China has also competed with India, as well as Japan, in Iran. Though China supports the Treaty on the Non-Proliferation of Nuclear Weapons, as one of Iran's largest foreign investors its official policy is that actions against Iran should not affect economic cooperation, and therefore it refuses to join Western powers in imposing punitive measures against Tehran for its insistence on developing nuclear capabilities.[52] In 2004, Iran agreed to supply China with a stake in the Yadavaran oil field and 25 years of LNG supply for $100 billion.[53] Shortly thereafter Chinese delegates began to oppose UN Security Council sanctions on Iran.[54] After three years of negotiating and an initial $2 billion contract, China was rewarded with 51 percent of the 30 billion barrel Yadavaran field. Sinopec is developing this field in a joint venture with India's ONGC, which has 29 percent.[55] Overcoming more than 50 years of rivalry, Yadavaran joins assets in Sudan, Syria and Columbia, where China and India also have joint ventures. Here similar economic and strategic goals overcome the traditional antagonism.

Farther afield, China has established energy interests in Latin America, provoking worry in the United States of losing ground in its own backyard. Chinese companies have won the rights to explore and produce oil off Cuba's coast. A recent discovery indicates that there could be as many as 10 billion barrels of oil in Cuba's waters, prompting American oil executives to seek an end to the long-time U.S. trade embargo against Castro's regime.[56] Were the embargo ended and open bidding established, no Chinese company could compete with the IOCs for offshore exploration capability. A similar situation exists in Venezuela, where Hugo Chavez has recently nationalized U.S. assets. In May 2008, the Chinese government contributed $4 billion to a $6 billion joint Chinese-Venezuelan fund to finance development projects in Venezuela and enable increased oil exports to China.[57] Caracas has also given Chinese companies preferential access to new field development.[58] Venezuela will sell increasing amounts of crude to China, with contracts requiring 1 mbd by 2012, up from 350,000 bpd in 2008.[59] Shipping heavy fuel oil such a long distance to a country without refineries capable of processing it makes little economic sense. It is not insignificant, then, that according to China's government-run newspaper, Venezuelan officials "will support China's reunification and territorial integrity at any international forum or organization."[60] Energy affairs bleed into purely political goals, which, in this case trump strict economic goals. Establishing firm supporters is vital to China's peaceful rise strategy.

With about 8 percent of the world's known oil resources, along with extreme poverty and instability, Africa presents major consumers with opportunities to establish influence and to extract cheap resources. Ideological differences about development and governance, combined with the continent's resource potential, make Africa a focus of Sino-U.S. competition.[61] In addition to widespread investments in African minerals, China has oil interests in Algeria, Angola, Chad, Sudan, Equatorial Guinea, Gabon, and Nigeria. Sudan sends 80 percent of its oil to China. The rest goes to Japan, Malaysia, and India, who also have investments in Sudan's upstream oil industry.[62] As CNPC's largest and most successful overseas enterprise, Sudan is the most important example of the Chinese go into emptiness strategy. In 1996, the exodus of Western oil companies allowed CNPC to buy 40 percent of the Greater Nile Petroleum Operating Company (GNPOC).[63] In 1999, Chinese and northern Sudanese laborers completed the Greater Nile Oil Pipeline from the south to the Red Sea.[64] Sudan's oil production has expanded dramatically, and in 2006 CNPC completed a major addition to the Khartoum Refinery.[65]

Yet, for nearly 20 years Sudan has caused China diplomatic problems and forced the government to recognize the global power of interest groups and human rights organizations. China has consistently blocked UN action on the atrocities in Sudan's western province of Darfur, rejecting calls for sanctions and peacekeepers. Matthew Chen has written that "China's drive for energy resources risks gravely weakening international human rights and obstructing global energy security objectives."[66] Sudanese oil revenues, according to Human Rights Watch, are largely used to buy weapons, and the GNPOC has been accused of horrific work conditions for its more than 10,000 Chinese laborers.[67] China first faced the consequences of its actions in 1999, when CNPC sought an initial public offering (IPO) on the New York Stock Exchange, hoping to raise $10 billion in the first stock offering of a state-owned Chinese firm. Instead, public opposition to the IPO led to an embarrassing showing that raised only $2.9 billion.[68] Under pressure surrounding the 2008 Beijing Olympics, China has conceded that it must explain its position in Sudan, and even helped convince the Sudanese government to accept a hybrid AU/UN peacekeeping force in 2007.[69] China's official representative to Darfur, Liu Guijin, has pointed out in the Chinese press that "The oil cooperation between China and Sudan is helping Sudan develop its economy and is helping to solve the war in Darfur." Liu further argues that it is "unfair" for other countries doing business in Sudan not to be subject to the same criticism as China.[70] Many Sudanese resent the Chinese, whose projects must now operate under heavy guard. One southern rebel group that has repeatedly attacked Chinese infrastructure has also threatened to expel the Chinese if they gain power.[71] This only provides Beijing with a larger incentive to support the existing government. CNPC's Sudanese assets are a source of pride and energy security for China, and are unlikely to be relinquished in the near future.

With production success in Sudan as a stepping stone, CNPC is advancing into the traditional African territory of the IOCs: Nigeria and Angola. Two of the world's most tragic examples of the resource curse, these impoverished countries remain highly dependent on oil revenues. In 2007, Angola was China's second-largest source of oil after Saudi Arabia. China hopes to own and operate some of these resources, and has successfully used no-strings-attached aid and loans to access producing blocks.[72] These deals, which involved acquiring assets from Shell and Total, required strong muscling on the part of the Angolan national oil company Sonangol. Since 2004, Angola received between $8 and $12 billion in loans from China.[73] The contracts stipulate that the loans will be used for infrastructure, and Chinese companies will receive preferential treatment in the contracting process.[74] This benefits China because improved roads and railways make oil development less expensive. Second, the contracts to Chinese companies ensure that the money will circle back home in the form of low-skill jobs. This strategy is mimicked from Vietnam to Venezuela. Government intervention allows Chinese construction and railway companies to piggyback on the national oil companies. Angola has simultaneously decided to dismiss IMF recommendations, a policy consistent with its failure to reduce endemic corruption.[75] However, it has yet to be seen whether China will be able to enforce Angola's promise of future oil delivery. Angola may renege on its contract, calling China's loan strategy into question.

In Chapter 15 of this book David Goldwyn faults the policy of acquisition directly from producers. He correctly argues that this will not stabilize prices and, if exercised by other consumers, might disturb global oil markets. He writes, "Imagine a world where China had to buy oil from the United States. or the UK, and not from private companies. China's access might well be conditioned on changes in internal or foreign policy." However, today over 90 percent of the world's oil reserves are in the hands of national governments. Saudi Arabia and Venezuela *do* control the sale of their oil and have conditioned that sale on foreign policy prerogatives in the past. The United States and the UK are no longer net exporters of oil. From China's point of view, particularly since it has only engaged in the global oil market since the early 1970s, it makes sense to engage directly with those who control supply.

The United States should not perceive China's efforts to acquire overseas oil fields and lock-in long term purchase agreements as a threat. When China invests billions to find and produce oil in countries unappealing to developed nations and their companies, they do the global oil market a favor. The locked-up oil satisfies a certain amount of world demand that would otherwise have to be supplied by existing sources. If China does so inefficiently, transporting oil from far-away Chinese fields in Africa and South America, it is equivalent to them paying a higher price than other consumers. Chinese import sources do not have much in common with CNPC's upstream investment. The global liquid oil market pushes CNPC to sell around 90 percent of its overseas production to foreign countries.[76] Eugene Gholz and Daryl Press argue that "Chinese efforts to lock up supplies with long-term contracts will at worst be economically neutral for the U.S. and may even be advantageous."[77] While many experts agree that Chinese demand has contributed to oil price increases since 2000, China's overseas acquisitions and contracts, though sometimes politically motivated, have not.

Military Buildup and Diplomacy

Overseas acquisition of oil and gas fields is just one element in a larger effort to remedy what China perceives as energy-related diplomatic and military vulnerabilities. China hopes to establish increasing influence among developing countries worldwide, as was clear from President Hu Jintao's 2004 trip to Latin America and his 2007 tour of Africa. Upon receiving Chinese investment, governments often make a public statement supporting the PRC's claims to Taiwan.[78] It is important to keep in mind, however, that the current Chinese leadership is most concerned with domestic stability and continued growth. To this end, leaders have maintained a highly defensive posture and emphasized that China's rise will be peaceful.[79] Yet China does seek to gradually and peacefully replace the America's influence in Asia with its own. China also hopes to woo important energy producers worldwide with diplomacy, arms sales, and aid, usually filling a gap left by the. United States and its allies. Lastly, China seeks to build a military capable of securing energy infrastructure and trade routes.

A new institution that may impact China's energy security is the Shanghai Cooperation Organization, a group of six nations (China, Russia, Kazakhstan, Uzbekistan, Tajikistan and Kyrgyzstan). Formed in 2001, the SCO suffers from an unclear mandate. Some people, like U.S. Senator Sam Brownback and the late General William E. Odom, have described the SCO as an aggressive Eastern counterbalance to NATO.[80] Most observers agree, however, that the SCO does not pose a credible joint military threat in the near term. Martha Brill Olcott has even called it no more than an ineffective discussion forum.[81] Though many SCO meetings have failed to produce real group action, the SCO has implemented measures combating terrorism, nuclear proliferation, and the trafficking of drugs and weapons. Pan Guang, the Director of the SCO Studies Center in Shanghai, praised the SCO's August 2007 Bishkek summit but stated that "economic and energy cooperation remain substantial weaknesses" in the organization.[82]

Iranian President Mahmoud Ahmadinejad recently watched SCO joint military exercises in Siberia from the sidelines.[83] As one of four SCO observer nations (the others are Pakistan, India, and Mongolia) Iran publicly seeks full membership.[84] Were these countries to join the SCO, increased mutual trust and cooperation might make an overland pipeline from Iran, terminating in India or China, more feasible. On the other hand, Russia and China distrust each other and have competing energy interests.[85] Russia resents China's expanding influence in the former Soviet Union's hydrocarbon infrastructure and was not pleased with the completion of the Kazakhstan-China pipeline, the first Central Asian pipeline to bypass Russia and Georgia. With no compensation, Moscow canceled substantial agreements between Chinese companies and YUKOS, the former Russian oil company. More recently, Russia and China disagreed over Russian handling of the breakaway Georgian provinces of Abkhazia and South Ossetia. The future of the SCO and indeed stability in the region depend on the resolution of regional pipeline and resource controversies. If the SCO can accomplish its mission of creating greater economic interdependence and interconnectivity, the result is likely to be a more stable and peaceful Eurasia, which is arguably in NATO's interest.[86]

Chinese leaders believe an essential part of "great power" status is a military that can credibly project power across Asia. Despite past Uyghur terrorism in energy-rich Xinjiang, Chinese officials and companies do not believe that domestic energy infrastructure is at high risk. Instead, as pertains to energy security, the focus is on threats to China outside its borders. China is investing in a blue-water navy with state-of-the-art submarines and technological equipment.[87] Though most analysts agree that China's most immediate concern is Taiwan, many argue that more far-reaching energy security issues are also driving China's military modernization.[88] China wants to protect tankers traveling through the tight Malacca Straits and exert control over contested areas of the East and South China seas.

As the shortest route from the North Pacific to the Indian Ocean, the South China Sea is a vital shipping lane. Though estimates vary widely, significant oil and natural gas deposits have long been known to lie beneath the South China Sea floor. When the World War II victors divested Japan of its empire in 1951, they left a power vacuum that has never been resolved. Today 6 of the 10 countries that border the South China Sea vigorously claim overlapping pieces. In 1947, Beijing issued a map with nine undefined dotted lines claiming sovereignty over most of the South China Sea.[89] Yet under Communist rule China was largely closed off from the world and the ASEAN countries were able to stake claim to much of the Sea, leading China in the early 1980s to begin an effort to reclaim its "lost territories." Today, China, Vietnam and Taiwan claim the whole Sea and its islands, while Brunei, Malaysia, Indonesia and the Philippines claim certain parts.[90]

It was hoped that skirmishes in the 1970s would end with the 1982 UN Convention Law of the Sea (UNCLOS). However, UNCLOS further complicated the situation by allowing bordering nations to set up military posts on the islands and use the region's complex marine geography to claim "Exclusive Economic Zones." In the 1990s heightened tension with Taiwan led China to become more assertive in the South China Sea.[91] China and Vietnam began drilling for oil in contested waters, and on a number of occasions Chinese military vessels expelled foreign oil company ships working for another country. The United States entered the equation by putting two aircraft carriers in the area and stationing forces in the Philippines.[92] Though ASEAN nations sought to negotiate with China, hardline military factions in Beijing seemed to prevail over the economic and foreign ministries, preventing the exploitation of much of the South China Sea. Some analysts argue that China's refusal to relinquish its claim to the entire South China Sea, established in a 1992 declaration, made resolution impossible.[93] After 2000, however, China's increasing sense of energy insecurity and its desire to establish influence among ASEAN nations, preventing their alliance with either Japan or the United States, led Beijing to switch tacks and pursue cooperation. An official statement in 2000 announced that "China is ready to shelve the disputes for the time being" and by 2005 Vice President Zeng Qinghong said it was time to "actively push forward the joint exploration of the disputed areas in the South China Sea."[94] Since then, China and ASEAN countries have discussed joint ventures between their national oil companies and the terms under which foreign oil companies, who possess the technology necessary for the deep water of the South China Sea, could be involved to all parties' mutual benefit. After conducting seismic surveys with PetroVietnam and the Philippine National Oil Company, CNOOC began drilling exploratory wells around the Spratly Islands in 2008.[95] China's intransigence on sovereignty and insistence on self-reliance here gave way to the needs for regional stability and immediate access to new energy supplies.

A similar story surrounds the East China Sea, where China and Japan both claim the Diaoyu Islands (commonly called by their Japanese name, Senkaku) and the Xihu basin (which Japan calls the Okinawa Basin). There are significant oil and gas reserves in the basin, and the problem with dividing the basin by its median line, as Japan has historically proposed, is that the oil and gas on one side can be extracted from wells drilled on the other side.[96] China refuses to accept the "median line" principle and instead draws a line substantially east of the Diaoyu Islands, which also gives its navy an outlet to the high seas other than the Taiwan Strait.[97] With the help of foreign companies Royal Dutch Shell and Unocal Corporation, China began to successfully produce moderate amounts of oil and gas from the contested Chunxiao field area in 2003. Japan protested that the area was in dispute, forcing the foreign companies to exit. In 2005, Japan authorized one of its oil companies to begin exploring but left upon the arrival of Chinese warships.[98] Though negotiations began in 2004 to resolve the issue, they floundered for three years amidst heightened political tension. Finally, in June 2008 the two countries produced a plan to jointly develop a specifically delineated block surrounding the Chunxiao field area while putting the competing territorial claims on hold.[99]

Though increasing energy demand yields incentives for cooperation and stability, it also produces the need for a navy capable of protecting maritime claims. In 1996 Kent Calder wrote "A naval arms race among China, Japan, and possibly South Korea sparked by the changing oil equation is the greatest long-term security danger the region faces."[100] Today, the growth of China's navy is a source of worry not just for regional governments but also for the incumbent naval power in the Pacific, the United States. The U.S. Department of Defense has become increasingly vocal about the lack of transparency in Chinese military spending, and in March 2008 released a report that criticized China's military development, citing secretive spending and advances in space and cyberspace.[101] Media attention linked this report to China's aggressive energy policy, and did not mention the report's conclusion that China "is neither capable of using military power to secure its foreign energy investments nor of defending critical sea lanes against disruption."[102] The Chinese Ministry of Foreign Affairs called the Pentagon report a "distortion of facts," and proposed that the United States "drop its Cold War mentality."[103] Indeed, Chinese defense spending, even in this growth stage, is only a fraction of that spent by the U.S. According to the Center for Arms Control and Non-Proliferation, the United States spent $711 billion on the military in 2008 while China spent $122 billion.[104] According to Lt. Col. Dennis Blasko, a former U.S. defense attaché to Beijing, Chinese sources indicate that Chinese military leaders believe they are seriously under-funded.[105] The PLA seeks more funding for its modernization effort, which aims to win technology-intensive conflicts by the mid 21st century.[106]

Besides straightforward military build-up, China exploits its comparative advantage in missile capabilities to enhance its energy security. In the mid-1980s, China sold Riyadh ballistic missiles and sent Chinese military personnel to maintain them.[107] More recently, this cooperation has increased, and includes intercontinental missiles with ranges of up to 3,500 miles. Such deals helped lead Chinese President Jiang Zemin, on the first trip ever of a top Chinese leader to the Saudi kingdom in 1999, to announce a "strategic oil partnership" between China and Saudi Arabia.[108] China interprets international arms agreements to which it is party with strict legalism, arguing in almost every case that its policy of "non-interference" permits arms trade. As China's footprint grows, however, this position is becoming difficult to maintain. In 2008, China faced global outrage when one of its cargo ships attempted to deliver secret weapons to Zimbabwe's Robert Mugabe.

The Home Front

It is clear to Chinese policymakers that while establishing a sphere of influence and acquiring resources abroad are important, relying on regimes like Mugabe's is no match for the self-sufficiency of energy produced on the mainland. The stated goal of alternative fuel and power generation initiatives is to increase energy security through decreased dependence on oil imports. China hopes to replace declining output from domestic oil fields by exploiting its huge coal reserves (the world's third-largest) in large-scale projects that convert coal into methanol, the simplest alcohol fuel, and other liquid fuels. Even as high coal prices led to electricity blackouts, coal-to-methanol plants produced 20.6 million metric tons of fuel in 2007 (about half the global figure).[109] Large new plants, aiming to produce as much as 6 million tons annually, are under construction by Shenhua Group Co, the nation's largest coal producer.[110] In coal-rich northern China, a number of cities already have taxi and bus fleets running on methanol, and domestic automobile companies like Chery are manufacturing methanol flexible-fuel vehicles.[111] In 2006 it was expected that coal-to-liquids would supply 10 percent of China's liquid fuel needs by 2011.[112] A study last year by the Chinese Academy of Sciences said: "Production of liquid fuels from coal is, practically, the most feasible route to cope with the dilemma in oil supply."[113]

A strong push in the early 2000s for biofuels to make up 15 percent of China's automotive fuel by 2020 led to an entirely state-owned corn ethanol production program that in 2007 produced 486 million gallons of fuel ethanol, the third largest after the United States and Brazil (both of which produced more than 5 billion gallons).[114] PetroChina responded to the national goals by investing in a 40,000 hectare jatropha plantation in China's southwest to produce biodiesel from the oily seed.[115] There are also projects, many involving foreign companies like GE Energy, producing fuel from cellulose, cassava, and cooking oil. China's decreasing availability of arable land and projected water constraints may serve as bottlenecks for non-cellulosic biofuel expansion. After growing demand for grain for food, animal feed and biofuel production drove large grain price hikes in early 2008, Song Yanqin, a codrafter of China's national energy strategies, asserted that "Food security comes first in China, more important than fuel."[116] The NDRC has in fact discouraged biofuel projects since 2006, and banned the use of corn for ethanol in June 2007.[117] The focus is now on non-grain feed stocks and gasified waste biomass, but recent projects in Guangxi Province that make ethanol from sweet potatoes and cassava have failed because their output cannot compete with subsidized oil.[118] Before China can seriously exploit its biofuel potential, it must first bring domestic petroleum product prices nearer to international levels by reducing subsidies.

China faces a fundamental conflict between on the one hand rapidly expanding coal-fired base load electric capacity to meet the needs of a vast number of Chinese who do not yet have access to electric power, and on the other hand addressing the environmental impacts of burning fossil fuels, and global pressure to reduce greenhouse gas emissions. Inefficiency and shortages plague China's electric power generation sector. Despite ample coal reserves, the discrepancy between coal and capped electricity prices forces many power plants to shut down or operate at a loss, which they are loathe to do in their newly privatized condition.[119] According to the IEA, China must *add* at least 1,300 GW of electricity supply just to meet demand in 2030. This could cost around $2.5 trillion in 2006 dollars and does not include urgently needed repairs to existing infrastructure, much of which is outdated.[120] In 2008 coal generated 78 percent of China's electricity, and the People's Republic accounted for over 70 percent of the increase in global coal demand.[121] It was to no one's surprise, therefore, when in 2006 China became the largest global carbon dioxide emitter.[122]

In a state known for meeting its policy goals, it is notable that China has not met 10 of 13 critical environmental targets laid out in the 10th Five Year Plan (2001–2005).[123] Prioritizing social harmony through steady improvements in the standard of living, often at the expense of economic efficiency and environmental protection, is the root cause of this failure. For example, the NDRC is intent on creating "national champions" in the automobile industry. Chinese are encouraged to buy domestically-manufactured private vehicles. In 2007, 9 out of every 1000 Chinese people had a private car, compared to 450 per 1000 people in the United States.[124] As China's middle and upper classes expand, this gap represents massive growth potential. Indeed, automobiles are the strongest driver of China's increasing oil demand, with car sales in China expected to exceed those in the United States by 2015.[125] Yet, air pollution and fuel consumption constraints mean that China cannot follow the Western pattern of development.[126] According to Worldwatch Institute, half of the 800,000 yearly deaths attributed to urban air pollution are in China.[127] Recently the vice minister of construction, Qiu Baoxing, has said that the growth in China's vehicles "is posing grave challenges to energy security."[128]

Qiu's comment is symptomatic of a new freedom among Chinese academics and policymakers to point out the downsides of the economic growth incentive system.[129] In order to maintain "social harmony," Beijing ensures very low fuel and electricity prices. Oil subsidies alone were expected to reach $40 billion in 2008.[130] Despite the subsidies, the gap between international market prices for crude oil and China's low domestic product prices mean NOCs still cannot break even. In 2007, Sinopec shut down a number of refineries that broke even at $60 a barrel, causing shortages and riots at the pump.[131] The new leader of the Energy Bureau, Zhang Guobao, was prompted to remark, "The oil shortage is in fact a problem of price."[132] Electricity prices are also subject to strict ceilings and by June of 2008 over 80 percent of China's power plants reported operating losses. Beijing's initial response was to set an artificially low price for coal, creating an incentive for miners to export illegally.[133] Yet brownouts continue to plague China's urban centers, decreasing productivity. Besides shortages, the long-term drawback of China's strategy of economic growth through artificially low energy prices is tremendous waste. China requires seven times the energy to produce the same value of GDP as the United States, and three times that of India.[134] Given China's energy security and environment vulnerabilities, this is an unsustainable situation.

In an article in Shanghai Jiaotong University's journal in March 2008, former President Jiang Zemin advocated a drastic move to market-based pricing systems for all types of energy.[135] In a shift from traditional state policy, he proposed an energy policy of diversification, advanced electricity generation and energy conservation.[136] Jiang argued for the use of market mechanisms and private companies to effectively allocate energy resources *and* to prevent environmental damage.[137] Partially in response, the government increased fuel prices by 17 percent in June 2008 (the most recent price increase had been 10 percent in November 2007), and in the same month raised electricity prices by a more meager 4 percent.[138] After the Olympics in August 2008, the State Electricity Regulatory Commission considered further hikes for retail electricity prices.[139] There has been, in fact, a gradual shift toward more efficient private and foreign ownership in the electricity sector. In 2005, Hong Kong-based China Light & Power (CLP) was permitted to be the first non-mainland company to control a power plant, with 70 percent ownership of a new super-critical, energy efficient power plant in southern Guangxi province.[140]

China also continues to increase its natural gas-fired power generation capacity, a program that began in the 1990s with aggressive moves to ship gas across the country through the West-East pipeline and build liquefied natural gas (LNG) terminals to import natural gas from overseas. The Guangdong terminal received its first LNG shipment in 2006. The imported natural gas is impacting oil use, as one of Guangdong's biggest cities, Shenzhen, has put 10,000 compressed natural gas (CNG) vehicles on the roads and is building CNG stations throughout the city. Shenzhen also has three gas-fired thermal power plants (TPP).[141] However, LNG prices have risen dramatically since 2004, causing CNOOC to balk at recent deals to buy natural gas for the Fujian and Shanghai terminals and the government to halt construction at planned terminals.[142] Yet the failure to raise electricity prices has meant that pipelined natural gas from the West is too expensive for most consumers. It is clear that Chinese policymakers are not ready to force people to pay a premium for clean energy. Indeed, China has rejected binding targets for cutting carbon dioxide emissions, indicating its first priority is lifting its population out of poverty, an effort facilitated by cheap and plentiful energy.[143]

China has, however, demonstrated a commitment to scaling up nuclear power. In a period of relatively little global construction, China has commissioned eight new nuclear power plants. Many more will be required for nuclear energy to meet China's target of 4 percent of its overall electricity supply by 2020.[144] Currently, China's 11 nuclear power plants are all in coastal provinces, and only produce about 1 percent of China's total power. New plants will be in interior provinces and will be built by foreign companies, like France's Areva and the United States's Westinghouse. However, high prices for uranium have generated a black market in production and trade, prompting worry from Israel to Australia that Chinese uranium might pass to terrorists in the Middle East.[145] China also has inadequate safety standards for nuclear technology, and its lack of transparency may worsen the impacts of an accident.[146] Chinese-American joint nuclear power authentication and inspection mechanisms are one of many areas where China hopes to use cooperation and technology transfer with countries such as the United States and Japan to improve its energy system.[147] In 2007, the State Commission of Science and Technology for National Defense Industry announced that foreign companies could hold a non-controlling stake in nuclear power plants, which paved the way for the Areva and Westinghouse deals.[148] Safety and business cooperation is very much to the benefit of the developed powers as it helps to build a cleaner, safer China and a degree of security interdependence that may help prevent future conflict.

Recent Chinese development plans present some of the world's most aggressive targets for renewable energy development. Beijing's long term development plan calls for renewable energy in primary energy consumption (including coal and oil) to reach 15 percent by 2020, up from 8.5 percent in 2007.[149] Hydropower is the only renewable arena where China has already invested substantial sums, with around half the world's number of dams and 500 GW of annual power generation.[150] At full operating capacity, the Three Gorges Dam will be the largest producer of hydroelectricity in the world, though at a significant environmental and human cost. There are also concerns that the massive dam could be a potential terrorist target. Yet hydropower's attraction as a clean and relatively cheap source of energy means that investment in this sector will continue.

The newest frontier of renewable energy in China is in the country's massive wind and solar power resources. Li Junfeng, former leader of the NDRC's Energy Research Institute and the present Secretary General of the China Renewable Energy Industrial Association, claims China is in a "golden age" of wind power development and goes further, saying, "It is widely believed that wind power will be able to compete with coal generation by as early as 2015."[151] Indeed, China leads the world in potential wind power.[152] Though the Chinese wind turbine market was traditionally dominated by European companies, by the end of 2007, 55 percent of newly added turbines in China were produced domestically.[153] This was made possible through government encouragement and company-level efforts to access technology.[154] New wind farms, particularly in the northwest, are of globally unprecedented magnitude. A Beijing-based consultancy, Azure International, estimates that China has 130 GW of planned wind generation.[155] Similarly, China's solar industry is burgeoning and the country is now the world leader in the manufacture and use of solar thermal systems.[156] The Chinese press has begun to promote domestic solar companies and research as evidence of China's rising technical and economic prowess. Central policy encourages this sort of development by mandating that the electrical grid buy all the electricity produced by renewable energy projects at state-determined prices.[157] Chris Flavin, president of Worldwatch Institute, said in 2008 that "I think China will be number one in less than three years in every renewable energy market in the world."[158]

Some critics suggest that renewable energy companies, particularly in wind and solar, are more politically than economically motivated, and fear that the sector may crash after the 2008 Olympic games and 2010 Shanghai World Expo.[159] However, Chinese policymakers seem genuinely dedicated to renewable energy, and the regime has a history of accomplishing staggering feats of infrastructure in short periods of time. In a sense, where market incentives and military strategy leave off, the Scientific Development Concept picks up as a very real third aspect of Chinese energy policy.

As China develops, Beijing is hoping to turn from a purely supply-side oriented energy policy to one in which demand is managed more effectively. Increasingly, conservation is a matter of energy security. In the *Report on National Energy Security* of 2005, three out of the five policy directives focus on saving energy.[160] Indeed, by 2004 China had stricter fuel economy standards than the United States.[161] Ma Fucai, the former president of CNPC and now the vice chairman of the Energy Leading Group, has said, "Our country must prioritize saving energy, diversification, environmental protection and global cooperation in order to have harmonious economic, social and energy development."[162] In addition to emphasizing the "green Olympics," the 11th Five-Year Plan (2006–2010) calls for reducing the energy intensity of GDP by 20 percent.[163] The Plan's first year saw a $610 million investment and the incorporation of energy efficiency in evaluating managers at state-owned firms.[164] President Hu Jintao does his part, appearing with other leaders in short sleeved, open-necked shirts and mandating that no government office should be cooler than 26° Celsius.[165]

Conclusion

To achieve its energy security goals, China will continue to act in sync with the OECD and the IEA regime, but it will not place its full trust in the global energy market. Some in the West hold that the laws of supply and demand ensure that energy is secure in its diversity. Mark Qiu, chief financial officer of CNOOC, echoed this sentiment when he said, "China has to look at supply security and the name of the game in energy security is diversification."[166] Yet the Chinese approach to supply security is more complex. Their emphasis on diversification is couched within the need for control and self-reliance rather than a belief in the power of markets.[167] Though China has recently employed capitalism to great success, its leaders have consciously avoided unfettered capitalist orthodoxy in matters of energy policy. Beijing seeks to make the 21st century the age of Chinese economic and military dominance. To fuel their rise, they turn to an old paradigm of energy security and will continue to employ a mixture of state and market forces.

However, in ways often neglected by Western China-watchers, this traditional psychology can feed into dramatic policy shifts. China has proven that it can develop quickly, adapting to new exigencies with remarkable flexibility. Within a generation, urban Chinese transitioned from a nutrition-poor subsistence diet to ample McDonalds and finally pricy weight-loss programs. Their energy policy matches this pattern. Under Hu Jintao and Wen Jiabao, the world has witnessed an aggressive foreign acquisition strategy complemented with conservation and serious investment in alternative energy. Self-reliance and control are easily applied to this new paradigm of alternative energy, conservation and efficiency. In his 2008 article Jiang Zemin urged the Chinese people to take an "open-minded and long term view to devising and prioritizing energy security policy."[168] A real push to improve efficiency and save energy can be expected over the next decade. The most credible threat faced by the United States is that it will fail, or already has failed, to keep up.

Notes

1. BP Web site, *BP Statistical Review of World Energy,* June 2007, www.bp.com.

2. Calculated from: Energy Information Administration Web site, "International Energy Outlook 2008" (Tables F1 and F13), June, 2008, http://www.eia.doe.gov/oiaf/ieo/ieoenduse.html.

3. Yong Deng and Thomas G. Moore, "China Views Globalization: Toward a New Great-Power Politics?" *The Washington Quarterly,* 27, no. 3 (2004): 129.

4. Christian Constantin, "Understanding China's Energy Security," *World Political Science Review* 3 (2007), http://www.bepress.com/wpsr/vol3/iss3/art2/.

5. Tatsu Kambara and Christopher Howe, *China and the Global Energy Crisis* (Cheltenham, UK: Edward Elgar Publishing, 2007), 18–19.

6. Fereidun Fesharaki and David Fridley, eds., *China's Petroleum Industry in the International Context* (Boulder: Westview Press, 1986), 2–3.

7. John Hassard et al., *China's State Enterprise Reform: From Marx to Market* (New York: Routledge, 2007), 42.

8. Russell Smyth, "Should China be Promoting Large-Scale Enterprises and Enterprise Groups?" *World Development,* 28, no. 4 (2000): 722.

9. Kambara, *China and the Global Energy Crisis,* 7–36.

10. Robert E. Ebel, "China's Energy Future," *Center for Strategic and International Studies Significant Issues Series,* 27, no. 6 (2005): 10.

11. Erica Downs, "China," *The Brookings Institution Energy Security Series* (December 2006), http://www.brookings.edu/reports/2006/12china.aspx.

12. Hassard et al., *China's State Enterprise Reform,* 46.

13. Leland R. Miller, "In Search of China's Energy Authority," *Far Eastern Economic Review* (January 2006), http://feer.com/essays/2006/january/in-search-of-chinas-energy-authority.

14. Xin Qiu, "China Overhauls Energy Bureaucracy," *Asia Times,* June 3, 2005, http://www.atimes.com/atimes/China/GF03Ad01.html.

15. "China's Crisis-Hit Energy Bureau Lacks Tools For Job," *Radio Free Asia,* December 16, 2004, http://www.rfa.org/english/features/lelyveld/2004/12/16/china_energy/.

16. See Stephen W. Lewis, "Privatization and Decentralization in China's Oil Industry," (presented at the Workshop on Energy and Environmental Awareness in China, James A Baker III Institute for Public Policy, Rice University, June 30, 2004), www.rice.edu/energy/research/asiaenergy/docs/BIPP_UFJ_SWLEWIS_063004.pdf; Erica Downs, "China," *The Brookings Institution Energy Security Series* (December 2006), http://www.brookings.edu/reports/2006/12china.aspx.

17. Premier Zhu Rongji led this anti-SPR group until 2003, when the leadership changed. Song Guoqing, an economist at Beijing University, has argued that China has more pressing economic concerns. See Downs, "China."

18. Lee Geng and Michael Economides, "China's SPR Pumping Up Prices," *Energy Tribune,* July 21, 2008, http://www.energytribune.com/articles.cfm?aid=953.

19. Jeffrey Logan, "China Scrambles for Energy Security" (International Energy Agency presentation at the Center for Strategic and International Studies, Washington, D.C., March 23, 2005), www.iea.org/textbase/speech/2005/jl_csis.pdf.

20. U.S. Department of Energy, "Strategic Petroleum Reserve: Quick Facts and Frequently Asked Questions," http://www.fossil.energy.gov/programs/reserves/spr/spr-facts.html.

21. Kang Wu, "China's SPR: Massive Buildup, Policy Imperatives," *FACTS Global Energy* via *Reuters News,* April 2, 2007.

22. Translated from Chinese: Tang Wei-Bin, "China's Petroleum Security and Energy Diplomacy," *Journal of China's Foreign Affairs University,* 76 (June 2004).

23. Phillip C. Saunders, "China's Global Activism: Strategy, Drivers and Tools," (Occasional Paper 4), Institute for National Strategic Studies, National Defense University Press (October 2006), www.ndu.edu/inss/Occasional_Papers/OCP4.pdf.

24. Wood Mackenzie Web site, "Chinese NOCs Double Domestic Upstream Spend," (Press Release), July 26, 2007, http://www.woodmacresearch.com/cgi-bin/corp/portal/corp/corpPressDetail.jsp?searchStr=return&oid=834995&origSessionID=@@@@102840 8771.1228493173@@@@&origEngineID=cccdadefkmkeiflcflgcegjdffjdgih.0.

25. Sun Tzu, *The Art of War,* trans. by Samuel B. Griffith (Oxford: Oxford University Press, 1971), 96.

26. Translated from Chinese, Tang Wei-Bin, "China's Petroleum Security."

27. Peter S. Goodman, "China Invests Heavily in Sudan's Oil Industry," *Washington Post,* Foreign Service, December 23, 2004.

28. Author's interview with CNPC Western Bureau Deputy Vice President Wang in Jiuquan (Gansu Province), July 2007.

29. Energy Information Administration (U.S. Department of Energy), "World Oil Transit Checkpoints: Malacca," January 2008, http://www.eia.doe.gov/cabs/World_Oil_Transit_Chokepoints/Malacca.html.

30. Ioannis Gatsiounis, "Delay Adds to Doubts about Trans-Malaysian Pipeline Project," *International Herald Tribune,* February 17, 2008.

31. Energy Information Administration (U.S. Department of Energy), "Kazakhstan—Oil," (Country Analysis Briefs), October 2006, http://www.eia.doe.gov/emeu/cabs/Kazakhstan/Oil.html.

32. Lutz Kleveman, *The New Great Game: Blood and Oil in Central Asia* (New York: Grove Press, 2003), 90.

33. Petrochina, "Crude Oil Imports Reach PetroChina Dushanzi Refinery Via China-Kazakhstan Pipeline," (Press Release), July 29, 2006, http://www.petrochina.com.cn/english/xwhgg/englishnews/200608010011.htm.

34. Christopher Pala, "China Pays Dearly for Kazakhstan Oil," *The New York Times,* March 17, 2006.

35. PFC Energy, "China's Share of Kazakh Production," (Memo), National Oil Company Strategies Service, June 27, 2007.

36. "Kazakhstan Oil Piped into China," *Xinhua,* May 25, 2006, http://www.chinadaily.com.cn/china/2006-05/25/content_600060.htm.

37. "Russia: Prime Minister Tells China Oil-Pipeline Deal Postponed," *RFE/RL,* September 24, 2003, http://www.globalsecurity.org/military/library/news/2003/09/mil-030924-rferl-094623.htm.

38. "Russia, China Close to Deal on ESPO Oil Pipeline Branch," *Russian News and Information Agency (RIA Novosti),* May 22, 2008, http://en.rian.ru/russia/20080522/108111646.html.

39. Tanya Mosolova, "Russia Pipeline to China 75 pct Built," *Reuters News,* June 4, 2008.

40. Translated from Chinese: Fang Yixian, "Contention between the US and Russia in Central Asia and the Effects on China's Energy Security—the Geo-political Perspective," *Guizhou Normal University Journal Social Science Journal,* (February, 2008), 1.

41. Ibid., 2.

42. Graeme Jenkins, "Burmese Junta Profits from Chinese Pipeline," *The Daily Telegraph,* January 16, 2008.

43. Mriganka Jaipuriyar, "Myanmar Offers China New Energy Corridor," *Platts Oilgram News,* 85, no. 165 (August 22, 2007).

44. Jenkins, "Burmese Junta."

45. Jaipuriyar, "Myanmar offers China New Energy Corridor."

46. Jenkins, "Burmese Junta."

47. "Radio Comments on Scope for Enhanced Military Cooperation with China." (program on Radio Pakistan, Islamabad, February 18, 1999).

48. "China Shows Interest in Iran-Pakistan-India Gas Pipeline," *Associated Press of Pakistan,* April 25, 2008.

49. David Montero, "China, Pakistan Team Up on Energy," *Christian Science Monitor,* April 13, 2007.

50. "Joint Statement Issued by the People's Republic of China and the Islamic Republic of Pakistan," (document distributed by Xinhua), November 25, 2006, http://pk.china-embassy.org/eng/svhjt/t282202.htm.

51. Daniel Kimmage, "Central Asia: Turkmenistan-China Pipeline Has Far Reaching Implications," *RFE/RL,* April 10, 2006, http://www.rferl.org/content/article/1067535. html; "Turkmenistan-China Gas Pipeline: A Gas Processing Plant to Be Constructed," *State News Agency of Turkmenistan,* July 2, 2008, http://turkmenistan.gov.tm/_eng/2008/07/02/turkmenistanchina_gas_pipeline_a_gas_processing_plant_to_be_constructed.html; "CNPC Starts Building Turkmenistan-China Gas Pipeline," *News Central Asia,* August 30, 2007, http://www.newscentralasia.net/Regional-News/160.html.

52. Sun Zifa, "Liu Jianchao: Iranian Nuclear Issue Should Not Affect Relevant Countries' Normal Economic and Energy Moves With Iran," *China News Bureau,* February 28, 2008; and American Enterprise Institute Web site, "Global Business in Iran," (Interactive Country Listing), http://www.aei.org/iraninteractive/.

53. Wang Ying and Dinakar Sethuraman, "China, Iran Sign $2 Billion Oil Production Agreement," *Bloomberg,* December 10, 2007.

54. Joseph Cirincione, Jon B. Wolfsthal and Miriam Rajkumar, *Deadly Arsenals: Nuclear, Biological and Chemical Threats* (Washington, D.C: Carnegie Endowment for International Peace, 2005) 165–166, 172.

55. Siddharth Srivastava, "China, India Firms in Energy Alliances," *Business Times Singapore,* September 25, 2006.

56. Tim Padgett, "A New Cold War in the Caribbean?" *Time Magazine,* July 24, 2008.

57. "Venezuela-China Fund Likely to Double in Size," *The International Herald Tribune,* August 29, 2008; Simon Romero, "Chavez Steps Up Government Takeovers." *The International Herald Tribune,* May 19, 2008.

58. Vandana Hari, "China, Venezuela Agree Two New Oil Deals," *Platts Oilgram News,* May 13, 2008.

59. "China Teams up with Venezuela to Produce, Refine Heavy Oil," *Xinhua,* May 13, 2008, http://english.peopledaily.com.cn/90001/90776/90883/6409840.html.

60. "Venezuela Eyes Better Relations," *China Daily,* November 16, 2007.

61. Chietigi Bajpaee, "Sino-U.S. Energy Competition in Africa," *Power and Interest News Report,* October 7, 2005, http://www.pinr.com/report.php?ac=view_report&report_id=378&language_id=1.

62. "China Rising: China's Influence in Africa," (Five part series), NPR Morning Edition, July 28, 2008 and July 29, 2008, http://www.npr.org/templates/story/story.php?storyId=92990229.

63. Goodman, "China Invests Heavily."

64. Greater Nile Petroleum Operation Company Web site, "Brief History," http://www.gnpoc.com/history.asp?glink=GL001&plink=PL005.

65. Khartoum Refinery Company, Ltd Web site, "Introduction," http://www.krcsd.com/e-krc/e-index.htm.

66. Matthew E. Chen, "Chinese National Oil Companies and Human Rights," *Orbis* (Foreign Policy Research Institute) 51, no. 1 (2007), linkinghub.elsevier.com/retrieve/pii/S0030438706001086.

67. Human Rights Watch Web site, "China's Involvement in Sudan: Arms and Oil," (Publications), November 2003, http://www.hrw.org/reports/2003/sudan1103/26.htm.

68. Human Rights Watch Web site, "Sudan: Events of 2007," (World Report 2008), January 31, 2008, http://www.hrw.org/englishwr2k8/docs/2008/01/31/sudan17759.htm.

69. Jim Yardley, "China Defends Sudan Policy and Criticizes Olympics Tie-In," *New York Times,* March 8, 2008; Human Rights Watch Web site, "Sudan: Events of 2007."

70. Translated from Chinese: Qian Ming, "The politicization and Special Treatment of China-Sudan Oil Cooperation is Unfair," *Xinhua,* May 31, 2007.

71. Danna Harman, "How China's Support of Sudan Shields a Regime Called 'Genocidal'," *Christian Science Monitor,* June 26, 2007.

72. Jad Mouawad, "Angola: Oil-Rich but Dirt-Poor," *International Herald Tribune,* March 20, 2007.

73. Lucy Ash, "China in Africa: Developing Ties," *BBC World News,* December 4, 2007, http://news.bbc.co.uk/2/hi/africa/7047127.stm.

74. The recent $2 billion loan requires that 70% of public works contracts go to Chinese firms. In Adam Wolfe, "The Increasing Importance of African Oil," *Power and Interest News Reports,* March 20, 2006, http://www.pinr.com/report.php?ac=view_report&report_id=460&language_id=1.

75. "Special Reports: A Ravenous Dragon," *The Economist,* March 13, 2008.

76. Gary Dirks, "Energy Security: China and the World," (speech delivered at the International Symposium on Energy Security: China and the World, Beijing, May 24 2006), Transcript available at www.bp.com.

77. Eugene Gholz and Daryl G. Press, "Energy Alarmism: The Myths That Make Americans Worry About Oil," *Policy Analysis* no. 589, CATO Institute, April 5, 2007, http://www.cato.org/pub_display.php?pub_id=8161.

78. Amy Meyers Jaffe and Kenneth B. Medlock III, "China and Northeast Asia," in *Energy and Security: Toward a New Foreign Policy Strategy,* eds. Jan H. Kalicki and David L. Goldwyn (Washington, D.C.: Woodrow Wilson Center Press, 2005).

79. According to "China's National Defense Policy" on the Ministry of Foreign Affairs Web site, "China has been and will remain firm in safeguarding international and regional peace, security and stability. China hopes the international community will view China's national defense construction in an objective and fair manner," (February 29, 2008), http://www.mfa.gov.cn/eng/wjb/zzjg/jks/kjlc/gjjk/t410720.htm.

80. See U.S. Senator Sam Brownback's remarks at the United States Commission on Security and Cooperation in Europe (Helsinki Commission) Hearing: "The Shanghai Cooperation Organization: Is it Undermining U.S. Interests in Central Asia?" Washington D.C., September 26, 2006, http://www.csce.gov/index.cfm?Fuseaction=ContentRecords.ViewTranscript&ContentRecord_id=381&ContentType=H,B&ContentRecordType=H&CFTOKEN=79136338; "Q&A: U.S. Military Bases in Central Asia." *New York Times,* July 26, 2005.

81. Nicklas Norling and Niklas Swanstrom, "The Shanghai Cooperation Organization, Trade, and the Role of Iran, India and Pakistan," *Central Asian Survey* 26, no. 3 (2007); and Lionel Beehner and Preeti Bhattacharji, "The Shanghai Cooperation Organization," (Backgrounder), Council on Foreign Relations, http://www.cfr.org/publication/10883/; Martha Brill Olcott's remarks at the Unites States Commission on Security and Cooperation in Europe.

82. "New Developments in the Shanghai Cooperation Organization," (CACI Forum), Central Asia-Caucasus Institute, Johns Hopkins University, May 22, 2008, Audio available at http://www.sais-jhu.edu/media/caci/may08/NewDevelopmentsInSCO5-22-08.mp3.

83. Christian Caryl, "Asia's Dangerous Divide," *Newsweek,* September 10, 2007.

84. "Iran Keen on Joining Shanghai Cooperation Organization—Minister," *Islamic Republic News Agency,* March 24, 2008.

85. Dennis J. D. Sandole, "Central Asia: Managing the delicate balance between the 'discourse of danger,' the 'Great Game,' and regional problem solving," *Communist and Post-Communist Studies* 40, no. 2 (2007).

86. Johannes Linn and David Tiomkin, "The New Impetus Towards Economic Integration Between Europe and Asia," *Asia Europe Journal* 4, no. 1 (2006); see remarks by Richard Boucher, Assistant Secretary of State for South and Central Asian Affairs, at the United States Commission on Security and Cooperation in Europe.

87. Thomas M. Kane and Lawrence W. Serewicz, "China's Hunger: The Consequences of a Rising Demand for Food and Energy," *Parameters* (US Army War College) 31, no. 3 (2001).

88. Toshi Yoshihara and James R. Holmes, "China's Energy-Driven 'Soft Power,'" *Orbis* (Foreign Policy Research Institute) 52, no. 1 (2007), linkinghub.elsevier.com/retrieve/pii/S0030438707001196.

89. J. Peter Burgess, "The Politics of the South China Sea: Territoriality and International Law," (Special Section: The Politics of the South China Sea) *Security Dialogue* 34, no. 1 (2003): 8.

90. Energy Information Administration (U.S. Department of Energy), "South China Sea Territorial Issues," (Country Analysis Briefs), March 2008, http://www.eia.doe.gov/cabs/South_China_Sea/SouthChinaSeaTerritorialIssues.html.

91. Leszek Buszynski and Iskandar Sazlan, "Maritime Claims and Energy Cooperation in the South China Sea," *Contemporary Southeast Asia* 29, no. 1 (2007),152–154.

92. Nilanthi Samaranayake, "Oil and Politics in East Asia," *Online Journal of Peace and Conflict Resolution* 1, no. 2 (1998): http://www.trinstitute.org/ojpcr/toc1_2.htm.

93. Leszek Buszynski, "Maritime Claims," 144.

94. Ministry of Foreign Affairs of the People's Republic of China, "Basic Stance and Policy of the Chinese Government in Solving the South China Sea Issue," November 17, 2000, http://www.fmprc.gov.cn/eng/topics/3754/t19230.htm; "China, Vietnam Likely to Complete Border Demarcation Work Before 2008: Chinese Vice President," *People's Daily,* October 19, 2005.

95. Energy Information Administration (U.S. Department of Energy), "South China Sea Regional Conflict and Resolution," (Country Analysis Briefs), March 2008, http://www.eia.doe.gov/cabs/South_China_Sea/RegionalConflictandResolution.html.

96. Energy Information Administration (U.S. Department of Energy), "East China Sea Territorial Issues," (Country Analysis Briefs), March 2008, http://www.eia.doe.gov/emeu/cabs/East_China_Sea/Territorial_Issues.html.

97. James C. Hsiung, "Sea Power, the Law of the Sea, and the Sino-Japanese East China Sea 'Resource War,'" *American Foreign Policy Interests* 27 (2005): 515.

98. Janet Xuanli Liao, "Sino-Japanese Energy Security and Regional Stability: The Case of the East China Sea Gas Exploration," *East Asia* 25 (2008): 61–66.

99. "China, Japan Reach Principled Consensus on East China Sea Issue," *Xinhua,* June 18, 2008.

100. Kent Calder, "Asia's Empty Tank," *Foreign Affairs* 75, no. 2 (1996): 58.

101. "Military Power of the People's Republic of China 2008, Annual Report to Congress." Office of the Secretary of Defense, March, 2008, available at http://www.defenselink.mil/pubs/china.html.

102. Cindy Saine, "Pentagon Says China Continues Military Build-up," *Voice of America News,* March 3, 2008, http://www.voanews.com/english/archive/2008-03/2008-03-03-voa63.cfm?moddate=2008-03-03; Daniel Griffiths, "Fears over China Military Build-Up," *BBC News,* February 15, 2007, http://news.bbc.co.uk/2/hi/asia-pacific/6365167.stm; "Military Power of the People's Republic of China 2008, Annual Report to Congress."

103. "China to Raise Military Spending," *BBC News,* March 4, 2008.

104. Christopher Hellman and Travis Sharp, "The FY 2009 Pentagon Spending Request—Global Military Spending U.S. Military Spending vs. the World," (Policy and Research Release), Center for Arms Control and Non-Proliferation, February 22, 2008, http://www.armscontrolcenter.org/policy/securityspending/articles/fy09_dod_request_global/.

105. Dennis J. Blasko, "The Pentagon-PLA Disconnect: China's Self-Assessments of its Military Capabilities," *China Brief* (The Jamestown Foundation) 8, no. 14 (2008), http://www.jamestown.org/programs/chinabrief/single/?tx_ttnews[tt_news]=5034&tx_ttnews[backPid]=168&no_cache=1.

106. Translated from Chinese: "Central Government and State Council Issue '2006–2020 State Informatization Development Strategy'," Chinese Government Internet Portal, May 8, 2006, http://www.gov.cn/jrzg/2006-05/08/content_275560.htm.

107. Gal Luft and Anne Korin, "The Sino-Saudi Connection," *Commentary Magazine,* March 2004.

108. Robert A. Manning, "The Perils of Being Number 1: East Asian Trends and US Policies to 2025," in *East Asia and the United States: Current Status and Five-Year Outlook,* (Conference Report), National Intelligence Council, September 2000, http://www.dni.gov/nic/confreports_asiaUSoutlook.html.

109. Gregory Dolan, "China Takes Gold in Methanol Fuel Blending," *Journal of Energy Security,* October 2008, http://www.ensec.org/index.php?option=com_content&view=article&id=148:chinatakesgoldinmethanolfuel&catid=82:asia&Itemid=324.

110. "China's Coal-to-Liquid Plant Eyes 2010 Expansion," *Reuters,* January 28, 2007; and "China to Produce Liquid Fuel from Coal," *Xinhua,* March 30, 2007.

111. "Methanol-blended Fuel Standard to be Approved," *Xinhua,* December 9, 2007.

112. Richard McGregorin, "Beijing Sets National Standard for Methanol as Automotive Fuel," *Financial Times,* November 24, 2006.

113. David Adam, "Fuel Made from Coal Ignite Green Row," *Guardian,* April 8, 2008.

114. Antoaneta Bezlova, Biofuels Eat into China's Food Stocks," *Asia Times Online,* China Business, December 21, 2006, http://www.atimes.com/atimes/China_Business/HL21Cb03.html; Renewable Fuels Association Website, "2007 World Fuel Ethanol Production," (Industry Statistics, Table 6), http://www.ethanolrfa.org/industry/statistics/#E.

115. Yingling Liu, "Chinese Biofuels Expansion Threatens Environmental Disaster," Worldwatch Institute Energy & Climate Analysis, March 13, 2007, http://www.worldwatch.org/node/4959.

116. "China not to Sacrifice Food for Fuel: Energy Expers," *Xinhua,* June 6, 2008.

117. Kevin Latner et al., "Strict Government Control Characterizes Biofuel Development," (United States Department of Agriculture, Foreign Agricultural Service, Market and Trade Data, September 2006), http://www.fas.usda.gov/info/fasworldwide/2006/09-2006/ChinaBiofuels.pdf; Dennis Avery, "China Releases Biotech Rice, Bars Biofuel to Protect Food Supply," *Canada Free Press,* July 29, 2008, http://www.canadafreepress.com/index.php/article/4174; Le Tian, "Ban on Use of Corn for Ethanol Lauded," *China Daily,* June 22, 2007.

118. Lou Schwartz, "China Fuels Ethanol Industry with Yams, Sweet Potatoes and Cassava," RenewableEnergyWorld.com, May 16, 2008, http://www.renewableenergyworld.com/rea/news/story?id=52450.

119. Daniel Ikenson, "China's Energy Woes," *Far Eastern Economic Review,* June 30, 2008, http://www.feer.com/economics/2008/june/Chinas-Energy-Woes.

120. International Energy Agency, "World Energy Outlook 2007: Fact Sheet—China," http://www.iea.org/textbase/papers/2007/fs_china.pdf.

121. Energy Information Administration (U.S. Department of Energy), "International Energy Outlook 2008," June, 2008, http://www.eia.doe.gov/oiaf/ieo/highlights.html; World Coal Institute, "Coal Facts 2007," October, 2007, http://www.worldcoal.org/pages/content/index.asp?PageID=188.

122. Netherlands Environmental Assessment Agency, "China Now no. 1 in CO2 Emissions; USA in Second Position," http://www.mnp.nl/en/dossiers/Climatechange/moreinfo/Chinanowno1inCO2emissionsUSAinsecondposition.html.

123. The World Bank Web site, "Cost of Pollution in China: Economic Estimates of Physical Damages," (Joint Report with the State Environmental Protection Administration of the PRC), February, 2007, www.worldbank.org/eapenvironment.

124. Jackson Dykman, "China Counts . . . And Counts," *Time Magazine,* March 8, 2007.

125. Ariana Eunjung Cha, "China's Cars, Accelerating A Global Demand for Fuel," *Washington Post,* Foreign Service, July 28, 2008.

126. Juli S. Kim and Jennifer L. Turner, "Urban Transport Development in China—Trends and Challenges," (China Environment Forum, Woodrow Wilson International Center for Scholars, Princeton University, November 30, 2006), http://www.wilsoncenter.org/index.cfm?topic_id=1421&fuseaction=topics.event_summary&event_id=207527.

127. Worldwatch Institute Web site, "State of the World 2007: Notable Trends," January 10, 2007, http://www.worldwatch.org/node/4840.

128. "China Construction Minister Laments Cars, Praises the Bicycle," *Platts Commodity News,* June 15, 2006.

129. Wang Mingyuan, "Efforts in Moving Towards a Low Carbon Future: China's Energy Conservation and Renewable Energy Laws," (presentation at the China Environment Forum, Woodrow Wilson International Center for Scholars, Princeton University, February 13, 2008), http://www.wilsoncenter.org/index.cfm?topic_id=1421&fuseaction=topics.event_summary&event_id=370725.

130. "The Cost of Oil Subsidies" (Editorial), *New York Times,* August 1, 2008.

131. Oster, Shai, "Oil Prices Prod Beijing to Try to Ease Strain," *Wall Street Journal,* November 8, 2007, A4.

132. Ma Wenluo, "Sinopec a Victim of China's Price Distorting Energy Policy," China Stakes.com. April 9, 2008. http://www.chinastakes.com/story.aspx?id=302.

133. Daniel Ikenson, "China's Energy Woes," *Far Eastern Economic Review,* June 30, 2008.; and Yang Yue and Li Qiyan, "China Hikes Prices for Refined Oil, Power," *Caijing Magazine,* June 20, 2008.

134. Economy, Elizabeth C. "The Great Leap Backward?" *Foreign Affairs,* September/October 2007.

135. Jiang Zemin, "Reflections on Energy Issues in China," *Shanghai Jiaotong University Journal* 42, no. 3, April 3, 2008 (translated from Chinese).

136. Earlier state policy is articulated in a 2006 comment from the Chairman of the State Assets Supervision and Administration Commission. He said that in oil, petrochemi-

cals and coal, "State capital must play a leading role in these sectors, which are the vital arteries of the national economy and essential to national security." In "Oil One of China's Key Sectors," *China Oil & Gas Monitor* 124, Week 50 (2006).

137. Jiang Zemin, "Reflections on Energy Issues in China."

138. Yang Yue and Li Qiyan, "China Hikes Prices for Refined Oil, Power," *Caijing Magazine,* June 20, 2008.; Shai Oster, "Oil Prices Prod Beijing to Try to Ease Strain," *Wall Street Journal,* November 8, 2007, A4; Patrick Barta, "Oil demand in Asia shows signs of easing," *Wall Street Journal,* July 9, 2008.

139. Du Xiaodan, China Mulls Hikes in Retail Electricity Prices," CCTV.com, BizChina Program, September 14, 2008, http://www.cctv.com/program/bizchina/20080914/101871.shtml.

140. Rowan Callick, "Coal-fired Power Heats up in China," *The Australian,* March 17, 2008, http://www.theaustralian.news.com.au/story/0,25197,23386057-643,00.html.

141. "Shenzhen to Boost CNG, LCNG Vehicles," *China Oil & Gas Monitor* 94, Week 20 (2006).

142. "Muted Celebrations as First LNG Cargo Heads for China," *China Oil & Gas Monitor* 94, Week 20 (2006).

143. David Adam, "China Rejects Binding Target to Cut Greenhouse Gas Emissions," *The Guardian,* July 6, 2007.

144. "China's nuclear power capacity expected to be 60m kW by 2020," *Xinhua,* March 8, 2008.

145. John Garnaut, "Bright Glow is Black Market Uranium Trade," *Sydney Morning Herald,* April 7, 2008.

146. Toru Miyazawa, "China to Build 30 Nuke Plants," *The Nikkei Weekly,* September 3, 2007.

147. "Chinese Vice Premier Hopes US Strength Cooperation With China in Nuclear Power Field," *Xinhua,* September 20, 2007.

148. "China Opens Nuclear Power Industry to Private, Foreign Investors," *Xinhua,* May 31, 2007.

149. "Long Term Renewable Energy Development Plan," National Development and Reform Commission, September 28, 2007, http://www.ndrc.gov.cn/fzgh/ghwb/115zhgh/P020070930491914730 2047.pdf; Wang Xu, "Energy: Nation to Get Key Oil Bases by Year End," *China Daily (BizChina),* August 19, 2008.

150. Yang Jianxiang, "Hydropower: A Viable Solution for China's Energy Future?" (Energy and Climate Analysis), Wordwatch Institute, February 13, 2007, http://www.world watch.org/node/4908.

151. Jonathan Watts, "Energy in China: 'We Call It the Three Gorges of the Sky. The Dam There Taps Water, We Tap Wind,'" *Guardian,* July 25, 2008.

152. "Nation Pins High Hopes on Green Alternatives," *China Daily,* April 27, 2006.

153. 2nd China (Shanghai) International Wind Energy Exhibition & Conference (CWEE2008) Website. Accessed August 10, 2008, http://www.cwee.com.cn/en/.

154. Liu Yingling, "Made in China, or Made by China? Chinese Wind Turbine Manufacturers Struggle to Enter Own Market," Worldwatch Institute, May 19, 2006, http://www.worldwatch.org/node/3931.

155. Watts, "Energy in China."

156. "State of the World 2007: Notable Trends," Worldwatch Institute, January 10, 2007, http://www.worldwatch.org/node/4840.

157. Wang Mingyuan, "Efforts in Moving towards a Low Carbon Future: China's Energy Conservation and Renewable Energy Laws," (presentation at the China Environment

Forum, Woodrow Wilson International Center for Scholars, Princeton University, February 13, 2008), http://www.wilsoncenter.org/index.cfm?topic_id=1421&fuseaction=topics.event_summary&event_id=370725.

158. Ken Silverstein, "China's Real Challenge," *Energybiz Insider,* July 16, 2008, http://www.energycentral.com/site/newsletters/ebi.cfm?id=536.

159. Zhang Pinghui, "Wind Power Could be Booming for Wrong Reasons, Expert Warns," *South China Morning Post,* November 3, 2007.

160. Translated from Chinese. *Report on National Energy Security,* (Beijing: People's Publishing, 2005).

161. Amanda Sauer and Fred Wellington, "Taking the High (Fuel Economy) Road: What Do the new Chinese Fuel Economy Standards Mean for Foreign Automakers?" (Capital Markets Research Report), World Resources Institute, November 2004, http://archive.wri.org/publication_detail.cfm?pubid=4003.

162. Translated from Chinese. Li Bin, "How Can China's Energy Be Sustainable? Ma Fucai's Four Points," *XinhuaNet,* March 6, 2008, http://www.gov.cn/2008lh/content_911792.htm.

163. National Development and Reform Commission Web site, "The Outline of the 11th Five Year Plan," http://en.ndrc.gov.cn/hot/W020060531535874229725.jpg.

164. Ding Yimin, "Combating Climate Change: China Goes on Offensive," *ChinaView.net (Xinhua).* October 4, 2007, http://news.xinhuanet.com/english/2007-10/04/content_6829889.htm.

165. Ibid.

166. Brian Bremner, "Asia's Oil Hunt," *BusinessWeek,* November 15, 2004.

167. Erica Downs, a China specialist at the Brookings Institution, argues that Chinese policymakers continue to stress self-sufficiency through supply-side oil access. See Erica S. Downs, "The Chinese Energy Security Debate," *China Quarterly* 177 (2004).

168. Jiang Zemin, "Reflections on Energy Issues in China."

CHAPTER 14

India: Addicted to Coal

Jeremy Carl

In many respects, India's energy security challenges are among the world's most difficult. Surrounded by unfriendly and unstable neighbors, possessed of a rapidly-growing population of more than one billion people, and owner of relatively modest domestic energy resources (with the exception of its substantial coal reserves), India faces many roadblocks in its quest for energy security. In 1991, India imported just 17.8 percent of its commercial energy—today it imports more than 30 percent and the percentage of imports is steadily growing.[1] In addition to the disadvantages of its resource endowment and geopolitical position, India's quest for energy security is also hampered by strategic uncertainty in the Indian policy community. As Montek Singh Ahluwalia, the influential deputy chairman of India's Planning Commission, said bluntly: "it was never clear in anybody's mind what energy security [is]."[2] Given the uncertainties, both definitional and strategic, within the Indian policy community, it is scarcely surprising that India's energy security strategy is less than fully formed. However, India does have certain advantages with respect to energy security. Compared to China and the United States, India is far less dependent on obtaining expensive forms of energy such as oil and natural gas in order to continue its existing growth trajectory. And while India has grown rapidly, it still consumes only about 4 percent of the world's energy, far less than one quarter that of China and one fifth that of the United States[3] Unfortunately for India, the reverse is also true. Even with its substantial coal reserves, India has just 4 percent of the world's primary energy to supply 17 percent of the world's population.[4] Despite its resource deficiencies, India is already the world's fifth largest energy consumer and its appetite for new energy sources is growing rapidly and reshaping its military, political, and diplomatic strategies.[5] An official planning document from the Indian government projects that India's energy demand could more than quadruple by 2031.[6]

Indian Policymakers' View of Energy Security

Energy security has become an increasing concern of Indian policymakers. India has a tradition of self-reliance that stems from the colonial experience and the views of Gandhi and Nehru, India's most important founding fathers. As one recent commentator noted: "India has often been hampered by an overly extensive emphasis by defining Energy Security purely in terms of self-sufficiency. . . . It flows from the desire of Indian nationalists to break away from the shackles of empire; the mindset and the term continue to have resonance even today." For a few observers and decision makers, the solution, at least rhetorically, lies in developing "a strong, self-reliant hydrocarbon sector," which they aver "must be a national imperative."[7] But India is also saddled with the Nehruvian legacy of political nonalignment, a strategy that was low on realpolitik. Thus India has been slower to develop the relationships in power politics that are often necessary for success in today's competitive global energy marketplace. Despite this mixed legacy, energy security has had a high profile in India in recent years. India's then-president, A.P.J. Abdul Kalam, a scientist who gained fame as a father of India's nuclear program, used it as the theme of his 2005 Independence Day speech. According to Kalam, demand for energy would be "a defining characteristic of our people's life in the 21st century."[8] He defined energy security as "ensuring that our country can supply lifeline energy to all its citizens, at affordable costs at all times."[9]

For Indian policymakers, energy affordability is at the heart of their notions of energy security. The influential recent Expert Committee on Energy Policy formed by the Indian government defined energy security as a condition in which "we can supply lifeline energy to all our citizens as well as meet their effective demand for safe and convenient energy [. . .] at affordable cost."[10] India's per capita GDP is around $1,000, about 1/44th of the United States, which means the Indian consumer is much more price sensitive than the American one. Furthermore, 40 percent of Indians do not have electricity in their homes, and only 14 percent of Indian families own vehicles of any kind (including motorcycles). Just 1 percent own automobiles. Affordability is a profoundly important aspect of India's energy security calculus.[11]

A more expansive view of energy security was offered by Indian Prime Minister Manmohan Singh in an August 2007 address. Singh's conception of energy security, endorsed by the ruling coalition (the United Progressive Alliance), implicitly lays out a coal-based vision for India's energy, one which has profound implications in a post-Kyoto world. Singh explicitly stressed pricing in his conception of energy security, noting that "By energy security, we refer not merely to the assurance of the supply of energy. Real energy security implies assured supply of good quality energy at a reasonable price."[12] Singh also stated that such security could not depend on oil and gas and that even the relatively modest existing oil and gas import bill was a crushing burden to India's economy. Singh's speech also stressed the importance of developing nuclear energy in India, which may help explain his strong advocacy of the U.S.-India nuclear deal, a key, though extremely controversial, element of India's proposed energy security strategy, which will be discussed more later in this chapter. Also, befitting his personal history as an economist, Singh called for market-rate pricing of energy in hopes of discouraging profligate use. In this sense, India's internal restructuring of its domestic energy markets can be seen as a key element of its energy security strategy.

Increasingly, India's diplomatic corps has also become involved in India's quest for energy security. In 2007, the foreign ministry announced the formation of an energy security unit in an effort to make better deals abroad for resource acquisition in the oil, gas, and coal markets, markets where India has frequently played second fiddle to a more aggressive China. Yet, such "going out" in the past has been fraught with difficulty. Japan wasted billions on such an energy strategy in the 1980s and while China has lucked out with a similar strategy in recent years, benefiting from global oil and gas price rises, only a small percentage of the oil and gas delivered from these projects goes back to China.

Despite the unified push from both domestic and foreign governmental actors to develop energy security, the often-dysfunctional Indian political environment makes it a challenging goal to achieve. For example, India spends $4 billion per year to use expensive natural gas for the low-value task of making fertilizer in the name of having "security" in this globally traded and widely-available commodity. This represents an enormous expenditure in the context of India's overall economy, which is roughly 1/13 the size of the U.S. economy. In reality, this subsidy has merely served to prop up India's woefully inefficient but politically connected fertilizer production sector.

Another current and significant problem is current energy supply shortfalls. Energy supplies, especially in the electricity sector, remain notably insecure. Not only do 40 percent of Indians still lack access to electricity,[13] peak deficits are officially as much as 15 percent of the power total, with an implied peak deficits are closer to 30 or 40 percent if unmet potential demand is considered.[14] Meanwhile, India's annual additions to its power grid are consistently below government plans, with the government achieving a fairly typical 55 percent (21 GW) of the stated goal in the last five year plan. While India looks to have finally turned the corner in power plant construction and figures to add approximately 42 GW—during the current plan period, that will still be well short of the 70 GW in the plan.[15] The specter of narrowly-averted rolling blackouts in 2006 in the financial capital of Mumbai further underscored the precariousness of India's energy infrastructure, and these deficits contribute significantly to energy insecurity in India.

India's coal, oil, gas, and utility sectors have traditionally been state run. Historically, this policy decision has created a barrier that is arguably one of the country's most profound energy security challenges. While all sectors have opened up to varying degrees of private competition in the wake of India's 1991 economic reforms, each is still dominated by state production. State ownership contributes to India's energy insecurity in several ways. First, poor management and low technology availability means that existing domestic resources are not utilized efficiently and, in fact, are often permanently destroyed. (This has been particularly epidemic in the coal sector, where poor mining techniques have rendered millions of tons of coal unextractable). The recent Integrated Energy Policy Committee of the Indian government echoed this concern.[16]

Second, public ownership has kept these sectors from expanding sufficiently through the introduction of private sector capital and know-how. Finally, by having the public sector effectively control prices for these resources (in conjunction with their respective ministries) prices invariably come under political influence and are often kept artificially low, depressing resource supply. For example, programs to give free power to farmers, a constituency that includes approximately 60 percent of all Indians, have been tried in several states, resulting in poor quality power for farmers and bankruptcy for utilities.

While the state-owned companies' grip over India's fuel industries is loosening, Coal India Limited (CIL) and other state-owned companies still produce over 90 percent of India's coal, NPCIL (The Nuclear Power Corporation of India Limited) owns and operates all Indian nuclear reactors, GAIL (Gas Authority of India Limited) dominates natural gas sales with an almost 80 percent market share, and state owned oil companies produce 87 percent of India's domestic oil.[17] In the power sector, National Thermal Power Corporation (NTPC) and various power companies operated by various Indian states own the vast majority of current power generation assets. Cross-subsidization and transfer of bureaucrats from one inefficiently run ministry to another is a hallmark of the existing Indian system, along with constant political interference by India's omnipresent politicians.

With such relatively limited scope for market activity, India loses billions of dollars per year through government-set pricing as the left-wing parties make it almost impossible to raise energy prices, even when global energy costs are soaring. As a result, state-owned oil and gas companies are only partially reimbursed, representing a drain on the finances of these companies and preventing them from further expansion and resource exploration. With state-owned companies controlling an estimated 75 percent of India's energy assets, this debilitates substantial portions of India's domestic energy wealth.[18] Finally, excessively low prices encourage wastage and overconsumption of fuels, leading to poor allocation decisions.

The state-owned companies are well entrenched and myths of pro-poor pricing are enthusiastically propagated by much of the Indian elite. For example, between September 2005 and June 2006, despite soaring global oil prices, there was no increase in state controlled oil prices.[19] During a period between 2002–2005 when gas prices rose 124 percent in the United States they rose only 49 percent in India.[20] As long as India's energy prices are set by the state rather than the market, true energy security is likely to remain elusive. While pricing and state ownership are not always considered under the rubric of energy security, in the Indian scenario, they clearly are at the heart of the country's most profound energy security challenges.

King Coal

While other fuels have more prominence in international markets, coal has been and will continue to be the bulwark of any Indian energy security strategy for the foreseeable future. India has more than 10 percent of global reserves, coal makes up 54 percent of India's total primary energy supply,[21] and as Figure 14.1 shows, there is enough coal at current rates of consumption to last more than 200 years.[22]

Coal reserves represent between 85 percent and 98 percent of India's total fossil fuel reserves by total energy content. This coal is used largely in the electricity sector, where it is by far the predominant fuel, but coal also plays a key role in India's industrial sector.

From an energy security perspective, coal is appealing partially because the alternatives are so unappealing. Domestic natural gas reserves are very modest (representing less than 1% of global reserves), and while natural gas might be seen as tempting to bring by pipeline or through expanded LNG terminals, the reality remains that the risk of upstream shut-off of supply (as Russia has recently threatened in Europe)or a terrorist attack on the pipeline makes imported gas unappealing as a backbone of India's energy security. Given that the most likely current pipeline to India would go through Pakistan, this is hardly a merely theoretical consideration.

Similarly, while nuclear energy has its advantages, there are problems with obtaining uranium fuel (India has only 0.8% of the world's uranium reserves).[23] Perhaps more important, with India's poor industrial safety record, often corrupt business practices, and proneness to industrial accidents as exemplified in the Bhopal disaster of the 1980s, which killed thousands, it is questionable whether building an extensive nuclear power network in India is in either Indian or global interests. It would take only one meltdown or dirty bomb either in India or elsewhere to put this strategy for energy security at fundamental risk.

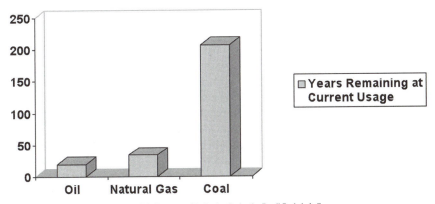

Figure 14.1 Reserve to Production Ratios for Fossil Fuels in India

However, taking a coal-based path towards energy security presents many problems for India—state-run behemoth Coal India Limited, which controls 85 percent of India's coal mining market, is extremely inefficient, employing 50 times the manpower of U.S. private sector leader Peabody Coal while producing only 33 percent more coal. The company is rife with corruption and inefficiency and its failure to increase mining production sufficiently has put India's economic growth at risk. While capacity projections have been boosted substantially in the current 5 year plan, it seems unlikely that India will be able to make this plan, a fact that has essentially been acknowledged by Coal India's current chairman.[24] Given Coal India's failures to meet domestic demand, India has increasingly had to expand its import capacity (where it is heavily reliant on Indonesian and Australian suppliers) and it is also looking to take equity stakes in mining operations outside of the country to supply domestic needs. India has made initial moves to introduce more private participation in the coal sector through loosening restrictions on so-called captive mining and generally increasing the pace of reform in the sector. These reforms have begun to take hold in the past couple of years, but they are also very incomplete. India also suffers from a critical shortage of coking coal for use in steel production. Domestic supplies are almost nonexistent and India's imports only figure to increase over time in this critical sector. India is also crippled by a dilapidated port infrastructure (often run by public-sector unions) that stymies import capacity growth—and its rail system, which is the backbone of coal transport, is notoriously inefficient and accident prone. This sharply limits Coal India's ability to get coal from its sources largely in East-Central India to its primary consumption centers, which are often located far from the mining districts.

However, despite all of the challenges mentioned above, coal's abundance and low cost in India makes it clear that it will continue to be the key fuel source powering India's future. Though environmental constraints in a post-Kyoto world may cause India to rely somewhat less on coal, given India's fundamental interests it is difficult to imagine that the growth of coal use will be significantly reduced.

Oil

When global policymakers consider energy security, oil is usually the first thing that comes to mind. It has been the proximate cause of the world's major energy security crises in recent years and stands at the center of much of the volatile politics in the Middle East. Yet, while India's oil security is of growing importance, its relatively modest current imports suggest it has a less critical role here than in many other countries. However, even with its modest oil needs, India imports about 70 percent of its oil vs. 50 percent in the case of China.[25] India's imports are expected to be as much as 85 percent of demand by 2012.[26] This rapid increase in import percentage will occur because India's oil demand seems likely to grow dramatically and, despite significant new domestic exploration efforts, domestic supply seems unlikely to increase significantly.

India's oil exploration began in the 1860s, but did not really hit stride until the 1974 offshore discovery at Bombay High. But with modest domestic oil resources, India's oil security has often been intertwined with international politics. Just before the discovery at Bombay High, India's nonaligned approach to international affairs was undermined in the 1973–1974 Arab Oil Embargo, when India's suppliers, lacking a special relationship with India, deserted the country for other markets. India's imports were further disrupted when foreign oil companies suspended oil sales during India's war with Pakistan.[27]

Another foreign adventure not of India's making proved equally disastrous in the short term for India in 1991, when the first Persian Gulf War sent prices soaring. These high oil prices were in a significant part responsible for the ensuing depletion of India's currency reserves, which ironically ended up being a long-term boon, as it forced India to engage in long-term financial restructuring to put its economy on its current growth path.[28]

To some extent, the growth in oil demand is being driven by the growth of automobile sales in India. From a baseline of just 5.7 million privately-owned cars in 2003–2004, automobiles are expected to grow to as much as 200 million cars by 2030 (although estimates of this range widely and the true number could be as little as 40 million.)[29]

India's automobile market, while dynamic, sold approximately 1.3 million vehicles in the 2007 fiscal year (along with a world-leading 8 million motorcycles).[30] While this growth is impressive and promises to increase at a greater rate as India's per capita income rises and lower-cost cars (including an automobile projected to cost just $3000) become available, these numbers are dwarfed by the estimated 5 million autos that will be sold in China in 2008 and the 16 million autos sold annually in the United States. The total number of autos currently on the roads in India represents less than one year's output for the U.S. auto industry. India is still less 2.4 percent of the global auto market for all types of vehicles, though this is expected to rise rapidly. The amount of this rise, and the pressure it may put on India's energy security, is inherently uncertain. But India may become the world's third biggest auto market by 2030.

One possible domestic substitute for oil to power India's transportation sector is coal. This can be done by either converting coal to the alcohol fuel methanol—as China is doing—for use in flexible fuel vehicles, by producing synthetic petroleum and refined products from coal, or by using coal-fired electricity to power plug-in electric vehicles. The Indian government has also focused on biofuels, and in 2006 directed oil companies to blend ethanol into gasoline at a level of 5 percent for a large part of the country, with an increase to 10 percent by October 2008.[31] In September 2008 the government announced a target blend ratio of 20 percent by 2017 for both ethanol and biodiesel, with a focus on fuels produced from nonfood crops on degraded land.[32] From an Indian perspective there are urgent reasons to reduce oil demand as soon as possible. Due to both increased demand and prices, India spent $38.8 billion to import crude oil in 2005–2006, up from just 25.9 billion the previous year, a number that represents a substantial portion of

India's imports and trade deficit.[33] One potential way to curb dramatic price rises is to institute a strategic petroleum reserve, which, though expensive for a country such as India, is being looked at increasingly by policymakers. Meanwhile the production of state-owned Oil and Natural Gas Corporation (ONGC) has been consistently short of targets, reflecting both India's increasingly depleted reserves and ONGC's poor extraction strategy.

As Figure 14.2 shows, like many countries, India is seeking diverse sources of oil supply, and like many countries it is finding that such diversification is difficult in a world with globally concentrated oil reserves. Currently India imports most of its oil from Saudi Arabia, Nigeria, Kuwait, Iran, and Iraq, which together provide more than 71 percent of India's imports.[34]

In an attempt to stimulate domestic exploration, India instituted the New Exploration and Licensing Policy (NELP) in 1998, which made it easier for foreign oil firms to do business in India. Private foreign bids for Indian oil blocks have since increased significantly, but this has been a slower process than anticipated initially. Corruption, India's stultifying bureaucracy, and other failings have made sure that major foreign players have stayed out despite extensive recruiting by the Indian government (save for BP which had a pre-existing business in India focused on lubricants). Corruption in the bidding process has often forced foreign firms to work in concert with a politically-connected local partner.[35] It is possible that further domestic exploration in India will yield at least somewhat improved exploration results. Nonetheless, it seems very unlikely that India will be able to supply a major portion of its oil demand domestically going forward.

By virtue of its prime location near major Middle Eastern and African producers, India is well positioned to increase its oil imports. India's state-owned companies have been exploring the foreign blocks extensively, attempting to lock up foreign exploration licenses. Indian oil companies have made substantial investments in the Sudan, Vietnam, Iran, Iraq, Russia and even the United States.

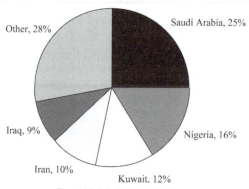

Figure 14.2 India's Oil Imports by Country

However, the government has often been criticized for its amateurish approach and packaging of these deals, particularly in comparison to the Chinese. As one Indian oil executive noted: "Dealing with foreigners is always a cakewalk compared to dealing with our own ministries."[36] Generally speaking, the Ministry of Petroleum and the Ministry of Foreign Affairs have had regular battles over the role of petroleum diplomacy in India, with oil ministry "diplomats" often stepping on toes in the foreign ministry in their quest to get deals done, particularly under the recent oil minister Mani Shankar Aiyar, a former diplomat. It is arguably partly in response to this that the foreign ministry has created its own energy security department. Some observers, such as the head of Shell India, applauded this move, while others worried that the creation of competing authorities will simply lead to more policy confusion. One major improvement in India's recent oil diplomacy was joint understandings reached with China in 2006 to attempt to bid together for more equity oil projects in order to avoid driving up prices. While the agreement was an informal one with no binding constraints, it may be significant to the extent it reduces competition between the two Asian giants.

India has also stepped up its relationship with key suppliers such as Saudi Arabia, Iran, Kuwait, and Nigeria. In general, India probably has less to fear than countries like the United States in its relationship with these countries. As a traditionally nonaligned country and home to the world's second largest Muslim population (after Indonesia), it is relatively unlikely that India's foreign policy would cause it to run dramatically afoul of Arab states such that it would be subject to an oil boycott though, conceivably, antagonism toward India's Muslim minority by a Hindu Nationalist government could cause friction.

India has recently warmed its relationship with Saudi Arabia—Saudi King Abdullah was the chief guest at India's Republic Day celebrations in 2006, the first time a Saudi monarch had visited India in 51 years, and an indication of the increased importance that India put on the Saudi relationship. Given that this followed chief guest visits for Republic Day from Nigeria's president Obasanjo in 2000, Algeria's President in 2001, Iran's President Khatami in 2004, it is clear that India places a high priority on bolstering relationships with key energy providers.[37]

Natural Gas

The Indian gas market is in the midst of a radical transformation. Historically, India has been a relatively sleepy market with the vast majority of all gas production controlled by state owned ONGC. India has two primary LNG terminals at Hazira and Dahej, both in the state of Gujarat, with the latter set up by state-owned company Petronet.[38] India began importing LNG from Qatar in 2004, and has plans to further enhance imports. Historically, natural gas has been misallocated in India, with the bulk going to the fertilizer sector and power sectors. Recently, there has been increasing use of natural gas in urban transport (such as the universal conversion of taxis and buses in Delhi and Mumbai to natural gas power), which if more broadly adopted could lead to changes in India's demand dynamics. Likely future sources of natural gas supply will come through pipelines either from Iran or from Southeast Asian suppliers.[39] Natural gas demand could easily triple by 2025 in an aggressive scenario. In a high demand scenario based on existing known Indian reserves, 25 percent of the gas could be supplied by an international pipeline and 20 percent from LNG tankers.[40] However, due to the massive infrastructural investments required to deliver natural gas and the high costs of gas relative to coal, its primary competitor, gas seems likely to be a relatively small part of India's energy supply, representing less than 10 percent of India's energy by 2030 according to the IEA.

India's relationship with Iran also promises to be critical to its future natural gas (and oil) development. Iran is a critical global energy supplier and particularly critical for India, because Iran is ideally positioned geographically to supply India with oil and gas. Iran's oil resources are the world's third largest and its gas reserves the second largest. India's most critical current energy project with Iran is in the gas sector and involves a much-debated natural gas pipeline from Iran to India. While the economics of such a pipeline remain questionable, and its route through Pakistan highly problematic, it is still viewed as a critical component of India's energy strategy by some Indian policymakers. In many ways, this pipeline is a potential key to India's expanding its gas supply, especially as India is geographically constrained from obtaining large quantities of Russian gas, a problem not faced by other potential Asian gas customers such as China. While gas is exceedingly unlikely to replace coal as India's staple fuel, India seeks to increase imports of Iranian gas to improve its diversity of supply and, by extension, its energy security.

India has generally had good relations with Iran, including substantial military and intelligence cooperation, and their friendship threatens to complicate Western efforts to isolate the Iranian regime. Iran's assistance is seen as central to furthering India's ambitions in central Asia, and India's foreign minister visited Iran in 2007. While India has taken sides against Iran on the nuclear issue, it is clear that as much as possible, Indian officials are attempting to have it both ways. India does not want another nuclear power in its home region—at the same time, it has steadfastly opposed sanctions against Iran in favor of a diplomatic track, and in the past its scientists have aided Iran's nuclear program. Such coziness with Iran complicates U.S efforts to isolate the Iranian regime. However, to some extent India's relationship with Iran will be balanced by its need to maintain its strong relationship with both the United States and Israel, India's largest arms suppliers. These interests are still competing actively to nudge the Indians away from or toward the pipeline project. If completed, the proposed pipeline would import 30 million cubic meters of natural gas between Iran and India per day.

Nuclear

India has always pursued an independent nuclear policy, and this pursuit appears to have paid dividends with its recent signing of a strategic nuclear agreement with the United States that secures nuclear fuel supplies and technical assistance for India in exchange for limited inspections and safeguards to ensure such nuclear technology and materials are not repurposed for military use. While this agreement had been much discussed and debated in both countries, it was eventually ratified by India's government, but only after a firestorm of domestic political protest that nearly brought the government down. Many deal opponents professed worry that India would sacrifice its sovereignty by agreeing to the monitoring of some of its nuclear facilities under the terms of the deal. Also, Communist party partners of the then-ruling coalition, who made up a key base for its political support, were disturbed by the prospect of an Indian alliance with the United States, which has always been a bete noire of the Indian political left. After the agreement, which technically did not require approval of the Indian legislature, passed the U.S. Congress, it became clear that the deal threatened the entire ruling coalition. India eventually shelved the implementation of the agreement for an extended period of time at the cost of considerable domestic and international embarrassment, before finally passing it after a vote of no-confidence against the government (based solely on the nuclear deal) failed. In the wake of final Indian approval, the deal was passed in its final form by the U.S. Congress before being signed in October 2008 by Indian Foreign Minister Pranab Mukherjee and then-U.S. Secretary of State Condoleezza Rice.

In the wake of the deal's approval, India is currently constructing reactors of over 3GW and has cleared more than 6GW more.[41] Caution is in order though, as Indian nuclear plans have consistently fallen behind schedule and it can fully be expected that India's plants, even those currently under construction, may not be completed. India also continues to have issues with disposing of nuclear waste (similar to those in the United States and many other countries) and its lack of a significant domestic uranium supply also constitutes an impediment to growth. When the initial nuclear deal with the United States was announced by George Bush and Manmohan Singh, many predicted a renaissance for Indian nuclear providers as India would now be able to get reliable access to uranium fuel to power future reactors. However, the great difficulty in implementing the deal, despite the fact that independent analysts saw it as highly favorable to India, indicates that domestic politics continue to interfere with India's quest for energy security.

Renewable Electricity

Energy sources such as wind power, hydroelectricity and solar power have generated a great deal of publicity, though somewhat less energy, in recent years. Large scale hydroelectricity is currently a substantial contributor to India's current power production; however, expanding this substantially beyond its present capacity could prove difficult. Domestic hydropower has only limited possibilities for expansion. There is some scope for increased imports of hydropower from Bhutan and Nepal, but such projects face substantial political and environmental hurdles, and relying on foreign hydropower would not greatly increase India's domestic energy security. Nonetheless, hydropower is they key

commercial source of renewable energy in India today. While the remainder
of India's renewable energy growth is notable for a developing country (it has
one of the world's largest installed power wind capacities and a entire government ministry dedicated to renewable energy), the fact remains that, as in many
other places in the world, it is very unlikely that wind, solar, or other renewable sources of energy will be a meaningful part of the country's energy strategy
in the next two decades. India produces less than 1 percent of its energy from
non-hydro commercial renewables. India's wind power potential is relatively
low, and its capacity factor for wind turbines currently installed is a very low
17 percent, with private estimates being even lower.[42] While theoretical solar
potential is high and India has a fairly extensive rural solar program, the overall
contribution of both wind and solar is miniscule. While both of these figures
can increase significantly in the coming decades, India's wind potential has been
described as "marginal" even by government sources. Wind currently comprises
0.2 percent of India's total primary energy and solar is far below that. Even if
these renewable power sources grow by more than an order of magnitude in the
next two decades, they cannot provide a significant measure of near-term energy
security to India. Other, more speculative forms of renewable energy are even
less likely to be important in the near future.

Conclusion

India faces very substantial, but not insurmountable, energy security challenges in the years ahead. As it becomes wealthier and more globalized, its concerns have moved from mere subsistence and survival to taking its place on the
stage of global powers. In part, India's ascent will give it added leverage in the
international energy markets, but it also presents a host of challenges. At the same
time, Indian policymakers have been clear both in speeches and in writing that
their conception of energy security extends not just to the realms of international
geopolitics, but is very much related to the affordability of energy for the average Indian family. India's dependence on foreign oil and natural gas seem sure to
increase. Its domestic coal, the bedrock of its energy security, is primarily mined
by a highly inefficient state-owned industry, and its extraction and combustion
presents a host of environmental problems. Nuclear energy has some potential,
but Indian nuclear development has disappointed time and again in recent decades. While the potential for a deal with the United States could open up the
nuclear window for India, the future of that deal is very much in doubt at present. Meanwhile, while non-hydro renewable power will continue to get extensive
press, especially internationally, they are likely to do little to address India's near-
term energy security needs. State interference in energy markets and governance
continues to be a substantial detriment to Indian consumers.

But there are hopeful signs as well. India's unleashed private sector is increasingly able to provide various energy services in ever-larger quantities to Indian
consumers. A much stronger macroeconomic outlook ensures that a situation

such as the one during the first Persian Gulf War, in which an increase in India's oil import budget drained virtually all of foreign currency reserves, seems very unlikely today. Similarly, India's increased international profile means that it has more leverage in negotiating global deals than it could have dreamed of just 15 or 20 years ago. While energy security challenges remain, India has overcome far greater obstacles in its turbulent, 60-year history.

Notes

1. *Integrated Energy Policy, Report of the Expert Committee*, Planning Commission, Government of India, April 2006, http://planningcommission.nic.in/reports/genrep/rep_intengy.pdf.

2. Tanvi Madan, *Energy Security Series: India,* The Brookings Institution, Washington, D.C. November 2006, 14, http://www.brookings.edu/fp/research/energy/2006india.pdf.

3. *BP Statistical Review of World Energy, 2007,* 40, http://www.bp.com/liveassets/bp_internet/globalbp/globalbp_uk_english/reports_and_publications/statistical_energy_review_2008/STAGING/local_assets/downloads/pdf/statistical_review_of_world_energy_full_review_2008.pdf.

4. Rangan Banarjee, *Overview of Renewable Energy Scenario in India,* Lecture delivered in Bombay, September 21, 2006, http://www.ese.iitb.ac.in/events/other/renet_files/21-9/Session%201/Sceneario%20of%20renewable%20energy%20in%20india(R.B.).pdf.

5. S. Sengupta, "India's Quest for Energy Security is Reshaping its Diplomacy," *International Herald Tribune,* June 6, 2005.

6. *Integrated Energy Policy.*

7. Madan, *Energy Security,* 63.

8. A.P.J. Abdul Kalam, Address to the Nation on the Eve of the 59th Independence Day, http://www.education.nic.in/Elementary/Policyel/presidentspeech-14082005.asp.

9. Ibid.

10. *Integrated Energy Policy,* 57.

11. World Bank Policy Document, http://web.worldbank.org/WBSITE/EXTERNAL/COUNTRIES/SOUTHASIAEXT/EXTSARREGTOPTRANSPORT/0,,contentMDK:20694248~pagePK:34004173~piPK:34003707~theSitePK:579598,00.html.

12. Manmohan Singh, Speech delivered in New Delhi, India, August 19, 2007, http://pmindia.nic.in/speech/content.asp?id=572.

13. "World Bank Approves Loan to Rampur Hydropower Project," http://web.worldbank.org/WBSITE/EXTERNAL/NEWS/0,,contentMDK:21471216~pagePK:34370~piPK:34424~theSitePK:4607,00.html.

14. Jeremy Carl, *The Indian Coal Sector, An Overview,* manuscript in review for publication, 2007.

15. Author estimates from interviews with government and private sector sources.

16. *Integrated Energy Policy.*

17. Madan, *Energy Security,* 28–30.

18. Ibid., 28.

19. Ibid., 20.

20. Ibid., 22.

21. Carl, "The Indian Coal Sector."

22. *BP Statistical Review of World Energy, 2007.*

23. "Towards an Energy Independent India." Nuclear Power Corporation of India, ltd. Accessed at http://www.npcil.nic.in/nupower_vol11_1-3/chidambaram.htm.

24. Bhattacharyya Partha, Presentation at McCloskey's Coal Markets India Conference, August 2007.

25. "Oil and Energy Trends," http://www.oilandenergytrends.com/ger/ger_india.asp.

26. Doordarshan News, August 8, 2007.

27. Madan, *Energy Security,* 34.

28. Ibid., 35.

29. Madan and author estimates.

30. "Indian Auto Industry," http://knowindia.net/auto.html.

31. "Use of Alternate Fuel," Government of India Ministry of Petroleum & Natural Gas March 11, 2008 press release, http://pib.nic.in/release/release.asp?relid=42733.

32. "Cabinet approves the National Policy on Biofuel," Government of India Ministry of New and Renewable Energy September 12, 2008 press release, http://pib.nic.in/release/release.asp?relid=42733.

33. Madan, *Energy Security,* 23.

34. Ibid., 11.

35. Mike Jackson, Personal Communication, June 2007.

36. Madan, *Energy Security,* 42–44.

37. "Meet India's Republic Day Chief Guest," *Rediff,* January 4, 2006. http://www.rediff.com/news/2006/jan/04look.htm.

38. "Gujarat—Energizing the Nation with Power and Natural Gas," *The Hindu Business Line,* October 9, 2007.

39. Mike Jackson, *The Future of Natural Gas in India: A Case Study of Major Domestic Consuming Industries,* Working Paper, Program on Energy and Sustainable Development, Stanford University, http://pesd.stanford.edu/publications/india_gas_synth/.

40. Author calculations based on data from "The Future of Natural Gas in India: A Case Study of Major Domestic Consuming Industries."

41. Madan, *Energy Security.*

42. *Integrated Energy Policy,* 40.

CHAPTER 15

Squaring the U.S.-Africa-China Energy Triangle: The Path from Competition to Cooperation

David L. Goldwyn

The United States and China, more than any other two countries in the world, share an interest in global energy security and the steady and stable development of Africa's energy resources. Both nations seek stability of energy supply, stable prices, access to exploration acreage and a secure operating environment. Both have strong political and economic interests in the stability and prosperity of the host countries. Africa has parallel interests in security of demand, stable prices, and maximization of revenues from their resources, social peace and economic development. Despite their common interests, the United States and China engage African energy producers in very different ways and hold the companies who carry their nation's flag to different standards. The impact of these competing approaches on African development is mixed; Chinese investment accelerates infrastructure development but in many cases undermines governance, domestic job growth and environmental quality. U.S. investment drives energy development, and the U.S. government supports international environmental, anticorruption and transparency standards; but plays a limited role in promoting infrastructure development. There is great potential for a more compatible and more harmonious U.S.-China approach to Africa's energy development, one which promotes energy security, energy development and better governance. Whether this approach will come to pass will depend on whether China comes to view advancement of anticorruption norms and improved governance as part of its responsibilities as a global player, and more critically, on whether resource-rich African governments are truly committed to reducing poverty by improving governance. If African governments insist on high standards of conduct by the companies that develop their resources, and take responsibility for managing their own wealth in a transparent and effective manner, then healthy U.S. and Chinese economic competition can help drive African prosperity and global energy security. If African governments shift responsibility solely to the business sector to police itself, then economic competition is likely to erode governance, increase corruption and foster instability, and Africa's future will look much like its past.

Common Energy Security Interests

The United States and China are the world's two largest consumers of oil, and, respectively, the first and third largest importers. This will remain the case for the foreseeable future. While the rate of growth of U.S. demand for oil is expected to be modest, the quantity of oil the United States will consume will grow from 20.7 mbd in 2007 to between 23.7 and 29.7 mbd by 2030, representing an average annual growth of between 0.5 percent and 1.4 percent. China's economy is growing faster, as it is at the stage of industrialization where it is building the power and transportation infrastructure needed to move from a largely agrarian economy to an industrialized one. China is expected to consume between 13.6 and 18.1 mbd by 2030, up from 7.7 mbd in 2007 at an average annual growth of between 2.9 percent and 4.1 percent.[1] With these needs to acquire enormous quantities of oil by import, both nations have five major interests in common.

The first is *security of supply*. Consuming nations need to be confident that energy producers will produce enough to meet demand, and that they will have the right to buy the oil (or natural gas) they need without political or military interference.

The second interest is *stable prices*. Consumers, whether individuals, companies, or governments, need to be able to anticipate the price of energy in order to plan their budgets. Price shocks, from interruptions of oil supply as a result of war, internal unrest, weather or embargo, cause economic pain because consumers cannot rapidly adjust to them. While consumers bear the pain of this dislocation in a market economy, governments (like China's and India's) that subsidize the price of fuel or gasoline must also either reduce subsidies or pay the cost of the price shock from government funds.

The third interest the United States and China share is the desire to gain *access to exploration acreage*. Both nations seek to influence the supply of oil they consume by enabling their companies to explore for oil and produce it to meet market (or national) demand. Fourth, both nations seek to have a *safe and secure operating environment* for their citizens who work in exploration and production overseas and the assets of their companies. The United States and China both saw their citizens kidnapped in Nigeria in 2007. Four U.S. oil workers were kidnapped and released in May, and one in June. China saw at least two of its workers kidnapped that year.[2] Nine Chinese citizens were killed in Ethiopia in April 2007 as well. In addition to protecting their citizens, both nations want to see the substantial economic investment of their countries protected from destruction, strikes or expropriation. Finally, both the United States and China have an interest in *promoting economic development* in the nations that host their energy companies. Both have an interest in promoting development for political reasons (to earn the good will of the host country), for moral reasons (to ensure that the benefits they gain in energy security do not come at the cost of the well-being of the citizens of the host country) and for security goals (internal stability to provide a safe investment climate).

Complementary African Interests

Africa's energy producers have interests that are compatible with those of the United States and China. While importers want security of supply, energy producers seek *security of demand*. Security of demand is the assurance that their production will be purchased at a fair price over a long term, so that national budgets can anticipate a steady and predictable revenue flow. Energy producers also seek *stable prices*. While windfall profits are welcome, producers value a steady income stream. Income shocks, like the oil price crash of 1998 to $10, wreak havoc on national budgets. The rock bottom oil prices of 1998 exacerbated domestic political tensions and enacted strong pressure on the ruling regimes of the OPEC member states.[3] With government budgets pegged to at least $40 or $50 oil, a price crash would devastate the operating budgets of most energy-producing governments. Energy producers should also seek to *maximize the revenue* they earn from national resources, and to minimize the risk to their own capital. In theory, they have an interest in maximizing the return from every barrel and to expanding the life of the resource. Fiscal systems that maximize return are in the national interest. Many African producers utilize international tenders for production-sharing contracts to shift the cost of exploration and production to private companies, taking their share of profits when costs have been repaid. Countries also have an interest in ensuring that the highest bidder is qualified to do the job. They want to ensure that the acreage they put out for development is actually explored and produced and that the costs of doing so are reasonable and held to the minimum necessary. Where oil is in deep offshore reservoirs, or even geologically complex locations, producers therefore have an incentive to try to get the best technology and the most efficient producer to develop their oil or natural gas acreage. Producing countries should also be motivated to ensure a *safe and secure environment* where companies extract oil, natural gas, or minerals safely. Countries should have multiple reasons for this. From a moral point of view, they should take care that the companies use safe practices so their own citizens are not harmed, that company practices do not harm local fisheries or farms, and that local communities are compensated for the disruptions they may suffer. From an economic point of view, local security is indispensable to sustained operations of oil companies and therefore for government revenue. From a security point of view, countries can avoid internal unrest by addressing the needs of local communities before exploration begins. Finally, African governments should have an interest in using oil and gas production to *promote economic development* in their own nations. This is an interest that has not been pursued effectively by most African (or other resource-rich) governments. Governments should leverage oil and gas wealth to promote overall development, such as by investing in infrastructure, education, health and private sector development. Governments should respect the impact of energy development on local communities and strategize to target investment locally to maintain social peace. While energy development is a specialized, capital-intensive business, it has proven to be a successful platform to create jobs, such as plumbing, electrical services, construction and in later stages, and part fabrication. Despite prior oil price booms, African governments have failed to advance this interest because their leaders have taken public monies for personal gain, and because weak governments have squandered national income. In the absence of strong political reformers, African countries like Nigeria have had to deal with problems inherent to an untamed oil industry: Dutch disease, volatility and asymmetry in the oil market, expansion of the public sector, inefficient investment, excessive credit expansion, weak institutional capacity, diminished accountability, political sensitivities, revenue sharing issues, and corruption.[4] Indeed, between 1960 and 1999, Nigeria's Economic and Financial Crimes Commission (EFCC) estimated that the government stole or wasted $380 billion in public funds.[5] With the government as part of the problem instead of the solution, Nigeria has been unable to use its estimated $300 billion in oil revenue over the past 25 years to raise its GDP per capita above $400, and 60 percent of the population still lives on less than $2 per day.[6]

Africa's Importance

One factor which impacts the different ways in which the United States and China compete for influence in Africa is Africa's relative importance as an energy supplier to each country. African oil is indisputably important to global energy security. According to Cambridge Energy Research Associates, one out every five new barrels of oil delivered to global markets between 2004 and 2010 will come from West and Central Africa.[7] While the United States imports far more oil from Africa than China, and from more countries, Africa is a much more strategic supplier to China than it is to the United States. For the United States, which imports nearly 60 percent of the oil it consumes, Africa is a very important supplier.

African countries supply roughly 2 mbd, representing 10 percent of U.S. total consumption and 18 percent of U.S. imports. Nigeria and Angola are the two largest suppliers, providing 11 percent and 5 percent of U.S. imports respectively. Africa is key to fulfilling the U.S. government's goal of reducing dependence on imports from the Middle East, but Latin America and Canada provide greater sources of alternative supply.

For China, Africa is a critical strategic supplier. China imported nearly 44 percent of the oil it consumed in 2005. Africa provided 775,000 bpd, or 31 percent of China's imports. Four of China's top ten oil suppliers are from Africa: Angola (14%), Sudan (5%), Congo/Brazzaville (4%) and Equatorial Guinea (3%). Other African countries provided another 5 percent in aggregate. For China's goal of reducing its dependence on Middle East imports (45% in 2005), Africa is indispensable.

Africa is also important to both the United States and China as a destination for oil investment. U.S. companies have billions of dollars invested in Nigeria, Angola, Equatorial Guinea, Chad and Gabon. China has acquired major shares of production in Sudan and Angola and has signed deals for equity shares of existing producing assets in Algeria, Chad, Cote d'Ivoire, Gabon, Equatorial Guinea, Kenya, Libya, Mauritania, Niger, and Nigeria, Sao Tome, and Principe, and Somalia. China is also pursuing exploration in Cote d'Ivoire, the Democratic Republic of Congo, Ethiopia, Equatorial Guinea, Gabon, Kenya, Liberia, Madagascar, Mali, Mauritania, Morocco, Namibia, Niger, and Somalia.[8]

Taken in perspective, at this time, the United States is more important to Africa as an investor and as a consumer than China. Nigeria and Angola are the most important suppliers and those countries plus Equatorial Guinea and Chad the most important investment destinations for U.S. investment. For China, Africa is a critical supplier, with Angola and Sudan the most important sources of supply and Sudan the most important investment destination.

Different Approaches

While the United States and China have common energy security interests, they have different governmental approaches to pursuing their interests. In addition, they take different approaches to the manner and degree to which they support or constrain the operations of the oil companies they have legal power over. These differing approaches produce unhelpful geopolitical competition between the United States and China, and adversely impact African development.

The U.S. Approach to Energy Security

For the United States, energy security, particularly *security of supply,* comes from a diverse set of supplies, drawn from open and efficient global markets.[9] U.S. consumers, and the private companies that buy the energy and deliver the products they demand, count on the existence of crude oil and product markets to make supplies available on demand regardless of who produces them. When Hurricane Katrina disabled large amounts of crude oil production in the Gulf of Mexico in August 2005, efficient markets enabled U.S. companies to bid for crude oil supplies from other regions, and for gasoline and other products to meet U.S. demand. Markets enable this to happen nearly instantly, at reasonable prices and at no geopolitical cost or risk. The United States pursues *stable prices* by encouraging transparency in the supply of data to the oil markets, in the belief that accurate, timely information about market supply and demand will provide producers with incentives to invest and produce oil in quantities desired by the markets. The United States hedges against supply disruptions by holding strategic stocks of oil, primarily the Strategic Petroleum Reserves, so that oil can quickly be brought to the market to supply liquidity in the event of a disruption. The United States subscribes to the International Energy Agency, a collective energy security mechanism, to share the burden and benefits of a collective response to oil emergencies. The United States also pursues stability in prices by resisting the monopolization of oil markets, by OPEC or other countries. Monopolies (or cartels in the case of OPEC) tend to be poor predictors of market demand and inhibit the flow of capital to countries to produce oil when it is needed. The United States promotes a free market in *access to exploration acreage* by U.S. government support for free markets in general. While the U.S. government may advocate for its companies to win competitions for an oil block, it primarily supports the use of transparent mechanisms, based on merit and price. U.S. policy seeks a level playing field for U.S. companies, bolstered by the belief that whoever wins, if the oil is produced, the global market benefits. The U.S. government promotes a *safe operating environment* overseas in multiple ways. First, it encourages host governments to exercise their sovereign duty to protect people and assets in their country. Second, recognizing the limited capacity of some governments to do so, it offers security assistance or training where host governments are willing and able to respect human rights norms. Third, the United States both mandates and encourages its companies to respect certain standards of integrity and transparency when operating overseas. The U.S. government influences the actions of its private companies overseas in extreme cases, by economic sanctions prohibiting them from investing. The United States does this where its national security or moral interests supersede its economic interests. Today, it limits its companies from investing in Iran, Sudan, Syria, Burma, North Korea, and in the past has sanctioned investment in Libya, and Iraq, among other oil producing states. It enforces anti-corruption practices through the Foreign Corrupt Practices Act.[10] In an effort to create a level playing field for its companies, the U.S. government supports international voluntary standards, which it encourages its companies to subscribe to. In the area of transparency, these standards include the Extractive Industries Transparency Initiative (EITI) and the Voluntary Principles on Security and Human Rights. In the environmental sector, the United States subscribes to the Equator Principles, by which it (and any private financial institution that subscribes to the principles) conditions any support for infrastructure projects through the international financial institutions to prevention of environmental harm.[11] Even in lending, the United States subscribes to the OECD Export Credit Arrangement, which discourages OECD members from using subsidized loans to countries in order to avoid destructive competition.[12] The U.S. government promotes *economic development* in a manner independent of U.S. companies. It promotes development bilaterally through diplomacy, through incentive-based foreign aid, such as agreements with the Millennium Challenge Agency, through trade-based incentives such as the African Growth and Opportunity Act and through foreign assistance from the Agency for International Development. In places like Nigeria and Angola, U.S. support may be directed at governance, health, and education. The United States tends to support infrastructure development multilaterally, through its shareholding in the World Bank or regional development banks. These agencies, in turn, apply standards to their own work, such as requiring environmental impact statements and adherence to poverty reduction strategy programs before they provide financing. The U.S. government also supports other forms of conditionality by the World Bank and International Monetary Fund, such as a recipient country's agreement to a staff monitoring program of its finances, or disclosure of its finances to the IMF as a precondition to any assistance program. U.S. companies engage in social investment programs on their own, often providing local support (such as schools, local roads, and heath care support or vocational education). In some cases, U.S. companies may partner with U.S. development agencies to provide a program, such as USAID's Global Development Alliance, which "mobilizes the ideas, efforts and resources of governments, businesses and civil society by forging public-private alliances to stimulate economic growth, develop businesses and workforces, address health and environmental issues, and expand access to education and technology."[13] U.S. companies tend not to provide funding directly to governments for their voluntary community investment programs both to maintain control of the development projects and to avoid any appearance of impropriety that might violate the U.S. Foreign Corrupt Practices Act. U.S. companies increasingly demonstrate their social responsibility to the places they invest by subscribing to international voluntary standards, such as the Extractive Industries Transparency Initiative and the Voluntary Principles on Security and Human Rights. These commitments hold a company to a higher standard than its competitors may practice, but companies increasingly believe it is good business to do so, and institutional shareholders, such as pension funds and investment funds, increasingly restrict or threaten to restrict their holdings to socially responsible companies.

China's Approach to Energy Security

China's approach to energy security is different from the U.S. approach (and that of most OECD countries), although it is reminiscent of the strategies these countries applied in the 1960s and early 1970s. The key components of China's strategy are (1) secure direct access to oil supplies through equity interests or long term contracts, (2) leverage government to government support packaged with commercial bids by Chinese oil companies to secure that access, (3) attach no strings to the government or commercial bids, and (4) pursue unilateral rather than collective approaches to energy security.

On close examination, China's strategy seems to serve neither China's own long term energy security interests nor Africa's development interests. China will not provide itself with *security of supply* by long term contracts with particular suppliers, or by the kind of package deals it uses to procure the right to purchase equity shares of existing production. First, China cannot possibly buy enough existing production to meet its demand. Indeed, if it bought every barrel of oil now produced by ExxonMobil, it would only secure 2.68 mbd (China's 2007 demand is nearly 7.7 mbd). Second, China is unlikely to be able to buy shares of production in the kind of oil it needs from producers close to its markets. Indeed, China already trades a good deal of the oil it has an equity interests in and imports the oil it consumes from Western producers of African oil. Third, China's vaunted package deals, whereby it provides debt relief, low interest loans or infrastructure support, only amount to a likely overpayment for assets. Indeed China is as reliant on the spot market for oil as any other consumer and it has no problem accessing the supplies it needs by simply paying the market price. If other countries were to follow China's example—seeking agreement of producers to provide purchasers to the exclusive right to purchase oil at a market price—then the oil market might become highly politicized and China's ability to access oil could be greatly constrained. Imagine a world where China had to buy oil from the United States or the UK, and not from private companies. China's access might well be conditioned on changes in internal or foreign policy. China's strategy also seems to do little to provide China with *stable prices* or a hedge against price volatility. Securing access to oil at a market price does not provide insurance against a spike in prices in another part of the world. China is as likely to be harmed by a market disruption due to internal unrest, armed conflict, or weather as any other country. Furthermore, buying existing assets does not add to global oil supply. Actions which impede the spot market, like long term supply contracts, are more likely to increase price volatility since the closest supplies might not move to Chinese markets in the event of a disruption. China also does not yet contribute positively to the efficient functioning of oil markets either by supplying data about its own demand (which would help producers anticipate demand) or by allying itself with other consumers to take measures to respond to oil emergencies. China is taking steps to build strategic oil reserves, and may have enough oil in storage to replace 30 days of its own supply by 2010.[14] But it has sought advice on the management of these reserves from Saudi Arabia and not sought to ally itself with the International Energy Agency or other consumers.

China does take steps to obtain access to acreage. As noted earlier it does so by using its political leverage as a great power, grants of development assistance and debt relief to countries, and by offering subsidized state financial support to its companies. China has offered multi-billion dollar low interest loans to Angola for the purchase of equity rights, offered nearly $50 billion in aid to the continent overall, offered billions of dollars in infrastructure for a stake in the Kaduna refinery in Nigeria, and offered to finance two dams in Uganda in exchange for exploration rights for CNOOC.[15] China also produces oil where many Western countries refuse to because of the actions of the host governments. The most obvious case of this strategy is China's pursuit of Sudan, where it not only owns a number of producing blocks, but where China has also built the 930 mile export pipeline, a refinery near Khartoum and an export terminal at Port Sudan.

China has as much right as any country to use its diplomatic power to advocate for its companies. Its efforts to lock up supply have not in fact resulted in commitments for significant amounts of oil.[16] The most serious critique of the Chinese government's actions is its use of predatory lending, a form of government lending and subsidization that can distort market-based competition, hamper African development, and undermine energy security. China's ability to use government bonds to finance private transactions and to sweeten the deals with large aid packages is seen as unfair competition, as they are, in effect, subsidizations of Chinese companies that undermine free-market competition. Private companies cannot compete with the extremely low-interest loans that China offers its companies, such as the 3.5 percent interest rate on a $4.5 billion loan it offered to CNOOC for its controversial bid for UNOCAL in 2005.[17]

China's acquisition strategy is inefficient from an economic point of view—it probably overpays for the assets it acquires. But providing direct support to governments surely pays political benefits in earning the loyalty of the host governments. "China sees its partnerships with African nations, in particular, as being essential to its rise as a global power. It specifically sees its official government-to-government relations as being indispensable, and beyond its investments, it has spent millions in debt reductions, public works projects and cultural and educational exchanges in an effort to obtain a preferential standing with African governments."[18] As China competes with Taiwan for recognition, it can swap cash for both recognition and assets.[19]

China's strategy is, however, proving to be politically costly. China is paying a heavy price for its support for Sudan, despite significant recent efforts to use quiet diplomacy to address the conflict. China is also learning that support for a government does not earn you the welcome of its people. Indeed in oil-producing countries where governments are perceived as not addressing the needs of the people of the producing regions, China's failure to address development and governance makes it no different from Western producers. In Nigeria, the insurgent guerilla group MEND, responsible for attacks on Western assets land and kidnapping of western oil workers, issued a plain warning to China when it entered the Nigerian market.[20]

China at this point is taking no discernible steps to address the environmental protection of the *operating environment* where it operates. The Chinese government and the major Chinese extractive industry companies are not members of most international voluntary initiatives, particularly the Equator Principles which are directed at project finance. By focusing on bilateral rather than multilateral aid, China competes with development agencies that loan to infrastructure projects. Indeed, some analysts have labeled China's no strings approach as rogue aid because it crowds out World Bank projects which require both adherence to environmental and safety standards and progress on basic governance issues. For example, when the World Bank went into Nigeria to clean up widespread corruption in the railroad industry with a conditioned $5 billion project for private companies, China countered with a $9 billion offer to rebuild the railroad with no conditions attached, pushing the World Bank out.

China does not yet engage on the issue of how it will protect its workers overseas. Given the high number of workers it relocates to build projects, China will need to be cautious is in its interactions with host government security officials. Western companies have learned the dangers posed by host governments that may seek to use a company's own security personnel or equipment to aid the government's enforcement efforts, as well as the dangers of using paid personnel who have not undergone careful vetting for human rights violations. As China operates in Sudan and Burma, two countries where host governments already stand accused of human rights abuses, the risk are high. China's approach to *promoting development* is impressive in its scale. It has used bilateral aid, debt relief, and infrastructure support to gain access to oil and mineral rights. The November 2006 China-Africa summit (FOCAC) was the largest diplomatic gathering China has ever hosted. The development impact cannot be denied. China has built roads, hospitals, power plants, pipelines, railroads and soccer stadiums. Many African governments have not mustered the administrative or financial capital to do these things for themselves. The volume of China's assistance itself is staggering. China has fully or partially cancelled debt in 31 African countries, writing off a full $1.2 billion in 2000, and $750 million in 2003. The World Bank estimates that, as of mid-2006, China's Export-Import Bank had loaned over $12.5 billion in total for infrastructure projects. As a rough means of comparison, Oversees Development Assistance (ODA) from the OECD was just over $4 billion in 2004, and total USAID loans and grants to sub-Saharan Africa were just over $4.9 billion in 2005.[21]

The criticism of China's economic development approach to Africa is that it undermines governance and that it is not sustainable. China's no strings approach enables governments to reject World Bank or IMF good governance conditions on their development assistance. Governments are excused from using their own funds to develop their own countries, efforts to get those government to be transparent about what they are being paid for exploration rights or for equity shares are defeated, and the citizens of these countries remain uninformed and uninvolved. The two most widely cited cases are that of Angola and Sudan—which unsurprisingly are two of China's most important oil suppliers. Angola ended talks with the IMF in February 2006 over an arrangement that would have provided IMF loans for reconstruction in exchange for Angola's transparency about its oil revenues. Angola believed that the IMF was being too critical of its governance, transparency, macroeconomic structure, and structural reform throughout the entire loan negotiation process. Angola was able to withdraw from the IMF deal financially because China was waiting on the sidelines with multi-billion dollar loans, a rehabilitation project for the Benguela railroad, and a new airport, all with fewer strings attached and fewer tough questions asked of the Angolan government.[22] No one knows what the loans can be used for, how much oil is pledged to repay it. Despite Angola's oil wealth, reconstruction efforts are slow, job creation is modest, and national elections are repeatedly postponed. China's no strings approach with Sudan is cited as the primary reason the government of Sudan can resist international efforts to end the genocide there.

China's turnkey approach to infrastructure development, where it brings in workers and creates self sufficient Chinese enclaves to perform the work, is also criticized for not being sustainable. China creates few local jobs and even monopolizes support industries by providing food and other support from Chinese workers as well. Some critics say the Chinese have "simply come to take the place of the West as the new colonizers of Africa" for extracting resources and building infrastructure that governments cannot maintain on their own.[23]

China's strategy, taken as a whole, is sadly familiar. Western oil companies also developed their access to acreage in earlier decades by dealing with governments, paying little heed to investment in local communities, and with little regard for the environmental impact of their actions.[24] Later on, they too tried to build roads, hospitals and other forms of infrastructure without insisting on complementary host government investment. Enormous enmity emerged from the lack of environmental sensitivity. Millions of dollars in investment were wasted. The U.S. government, as well as other governments, paid little heed to the way governments treated their own citizens as long as they agreed to address our energy security needs. The results were not good for energy security or for African development. Indeed, the Niger Delta crisis highlights how misguided governmental and commercial strategies produced human tragedy, corruption and in the end enormous insecurity and volatility because of the failure to properly address the rights and development needs of the citizens of oil producing regions. While oil pumped from the Niger Delta region helps to make Nigeria the seventh largest exporter of crude in the world, its residents remain among the poorest in the country. Indeed it is the monumental mistakes of the past which have produced collective energy security, environmental standards, and modern development strategies.

China will need to decide for itself whether it believes that the no strings approach serves its own interests. It is widely accepted in Western circles that the resource curse or negative impact of high resource revenues on governance is a primary reason why energy-rich nations have failed to develop, and continue to suffer instability despite enormous wealth.[25] China will also need to decide whether it has a duty as a global player, or responsible stakeholder, to try to help the nations it aids to improve governance for China's own sake as well as the host country's. So far China does not seem to accept the resource curse as a problem it needs to address. Chinese companies, still heavily influenced by their government, will also need to address whether corporate social responsibility or even sustainable development practices, are in their self-interest. So far they have not. The concept of corporate social responsibility is still quite new in the West, and so it is no surprise that Chinese companies, who have come late to the global market, are even slower to reach this agenda. Similarly China will need to consider how its own arms sales to African nations, and the interactions of its companies with host country security forces, impact its own interests. It appears that for now, Chinese companies are on track to repeat some of the most costly errors of their western predecessors.

Africa's Choice

China and the United States, and the companies that operate under their sovereignty, have different strategies for achieving their own energy security. As competitors for global influence as well as energy resources, neither country is likely to convince the other of the rightness of its approach. The key determinant of the conduct of these nations in Africa will be what rules African governments choose to impose on them. In the resource sector, the host government sets the rules. If a government chooses to have an open tender to market its resources, all competitors must bid to win. If a government mandates that producers disclose what they pay in taxes, royalties or bonuses, they must publish it. If a government has building standards or demands environmental assessments, the competing companies must produce them. Four key strategic choices for African governments will be their approach to maximizing revenue, to promoting development, to improving extractive industry governance, and to providing security.

Maximizing Revenue. If African producers seek to maximize revenue, will they put exploration blocks out for international competition through a tender, or will they pursue deals with individual companies, where the price of acquisition may be muddled by barter of rights or pledges of investment? From an economic point of view it is in a country's self-interest to require transparent bidding for its assets. Certainly there are cases where technological capacity and managerial capacity matter more than price alone, but even a tender can be structured with technical requirements that weed out unqualified companies. If African governments choose to sell the right to develop their resources through competition, all companies will have an equal chance to compete and open competition can maximize income and deter corruption. If governments choose to deal privately, there will be no independent way to for them or for their citizens to determine if they are receiving value for money from bidders, and the terms of a transaction may never be known.

Promoting Sustainable Development. If African governments seek to promote development will they do so by accelerating investment regardless of the consequences or will they support environmental or safety standards for that investment? All governments face challenges in mustering the capital and managerial capacity to build major infrastructure projects such as roads, bridges, and railroads. These projects are enormous capital expenditures, with complex procurement and safety requirements. It is easy to understand why African governments are tempted to welcome China's turnkey approach whereby it will deliver these critical infrastructures in exchange for preferential rights and save a government with thin administrative capacity the burden of managing and financing construction. The problems with this approach is that without a competitive tender for infrastructure project (or the mineral or hydrocarbon rights) the government does not know whether it is overpaying or underpaying for either asset. In addition, the host government often cedes the benefits of job creation and support which a domestic procurement project could bring. In addition, host governments often fail to impose safety or environmental standards on these projects. As China itself has learned, at great human cost, the failure to impose these standards can lead to death and disaster. In Chambishi, Zambia, in 2005, an explosion at a Chinese mine killed 46 people, making it one of the worst industrial disasters in the country's history.[26] Once one of the world's largest sources of fish, more than 80 percent of the East China Sea is now rated unacceptable for fishing.[27] Today, some African governments will forgo infrastructure support from international financial institutions, or even loans, choosing to welcome China's no strings approach. The question for these governments is, what will truly provide stability and growth in the long run?

Promoting Governance. The rhetorical commitment of African governments to improved governance, transparency and integrity in procurement is strong and inspiring. Both the New Partnership for Africa's Development (NEPAD) and the accord which produced the Africa Union are unequivocal on these goals. NEPAD lists "good governance as a basic requirement for peace, security and sustainable political and socio-economic development" as its first Principle, and the African Union's fifth Mission out of seven in its Strategic Plan is to "play a leadership role for promotion of peace, human security, and good governance in the Continent." But the actions of governments lag far behind the rhetoric. Even Nigeria, which has made enormous strides in demanding due process in procurement and has led the world in the implementation of EITI, exchanged construction of railroad and low interest loans from China for the right to preferential right to bid on oil blocs. African governments will need to choose whether they will outlaw corruption, and put in place the legal framework to fairly investigate and prosecute it. They will need to decide whether to enforce transparency norms on themselves as well as companies that operate in their country. As nations they can publish what income they receive, they can require public officials to disclose their assets, they can require public tenders for oil or infrastructure, they can allow public expenditure reviews to be conducted by the World Bank, and they can require investors to adhere to international codes such as the Equator principles or EITI. If African governments decline to take these actions, and to require higher standards for their own sake, no amalgam of international pressure and voluntary actions will change the behavior of companies. Either the nascent consensus for socially responsible behavior in Africa will erode under Africa's own lack of interest, or Western companies will increasingly leave the field to competitors who do not operate under the constraints they impose on themselves.

Providing Security. Finally, African governments will need to address how they will provide security for the investments in their country and what rules of engagement will apply in conflict areas. The first step for government should be to build institutions for law enforcement and security which are professional, honest and effective. Security should be a sovereign responsibility. Governments such as the United States and China can play a role in providing help with this training, but companies should not. African governments will have to decide whether to make improved capacity in this area a priority. In the interim, it is clear that most resource-rich African governments lack the capacity to protect the billions in infrastructure that provide the primary source of revenue for their countries. In these cases, there should be clear rules about what companies can do to protect their people and their assets. It should be equally clear that governments will not expect companies to serve as proxies for government when governments lack the personnel to conduct enforcement actions. The United States and UK led Voluntary Principles on Human Rights and Security is one such set of rules. What is needed is a common understanding.

The Path Forward—A Trilateral Agenda

The United States and China are now leading competitors for Africa's resources and political support. If all parties see their long term interests clearly, there is a chance for a more harmonious approach which can enhance the prosperity and security of all parties. An official trilateral dialogue, on the model of some promising private U.S.-Africa-China dialogues now under way, could provide a useful platform for discussion.[28] Any such dialogue should have a private sector counterpart, where U.S., Chinese and African companies can meet face to face and address issues from their perspective. The four corners of a trilateral agenda are:

Agreement on Common Objectives. This should be the starting point. The three parties might discuss whether they can agree on issues like security of energy supply, price stability, efficient allocation of acreage and sustainable development. From there the parties can move to discussion of what policies might help to achieve those objectives.

Agreed Standards for Fair, Sustainable and Transparent Investment. Based on probable common interests in a level playing field for investors and revenue maximization for host countries, a trilateral dialogue could address standards for fair, sustainable and transparent investment. At minimum it would be useful for China to understand the practices of the past which African governments do not want to see repeated and the ways in which the U.S. government, and industry itself, has tried to create new standards to correct these errors. The utility of the Equator Principles and the OECD Guidelines on Export financing would be ripe topics for this dialogue. The parties should at least discuss the utility of mandatory U.S. and Chinese, as well as African, standards for government procurement or transparent bidding.

Support for Improved Governance. In various contexts (NEPAD, AU and the Evian, Sea Isle and Gleneagles G-8 meetings), African leaders seem to have approved adoption of higher standards for transparency and governance. A trilateral dialogue could discuss how African leaders believe these aspirations should be translated into practice. The agenda for this dialogue could include current international standards, such as EITI and the OECD Anti-bribery Convention, national standards (like the U.S. Foreign Corrupt Practices Act), or perhaps more tailored ones, and whether it is useful for African governments to require these standards in order to advance their own interests.

Cooperation on Conflict Prevention and Resolution. As dominant investors (along with Europe) the actions or inaction of the United States and China can have enormous impact on areas in conflict or in preventing conflict in areas where they operate. Many of Africa's resource rich countries nations are enduring conflict today (Nigeria, Chad, DRC, Sudan), or have been threatened by coups (Equatorial Guinea, Sao Tome and Principe), or are recovering from conflicts (Angola). Without imposing their will on these nations, the United States and China can discuss rules of the road for governments and companies for avoiding aggravation of conflicts in Africa, as well as positive actions they might take from limiting arms sales to providing training assistance for the professionalization of coast guard and police forces.

Conclusion

The confluence of factors we see today—China's rising demand for energy and rising global influence, Africa's great resource potential and attention to governance issues, and the U.S. and European focus on corporate social responsibility—can rapidly foster either a three way partnership that will promote Africa's development or a destructive scramble for African resources. There are compelling common interests among the parties to create both healthy competition and responsible investment. The United States will have to seriously engage China on energy security in way that it has not done for almost a decade. China will need to decide if it—and its companies—will be responsible stakeholders in Africa and balance their short term energy needs against their long-term national and energy security interests. Resource-rich African governments will need to sustain their nascent commitment to transparency and improved governance, by resisting the historical temptations to maximize short term (and sometimes personal) gains in the face of huge short term profit. The challenge is steep. But the first step, simply to discuss these issues in a sustained manner and at a high level, is possible, practical and overdue.

Notes

1. The EIA range of 2030 projections are based on four cases: high economic growth, low economic growth, high oil prices, and low oil prices. In all cases, the EIA projects that the United States and China will remain the first and second largest consumers of oil respectively in the year 2030, with China barely surpassing the aggregate European OECD

countries' consumption by 2030 in the high economic growth case and almost equaling it in the other three. http://www.eia.doe.gov/oiaf/ieo/pdf/0484(2007)pdf.

2. "Nigeria: Gunmen Seize 4 U.S. Oil Workers," *New York Times,* May 10, 2007.

3. Edward L. Morse and Amy Myers Jaffe, "OPEC in Confrontation with Globalization," in *Energy and Security: Toward a New Foreign Policy Strategy,* eds. Jan Kalicki and David Goldwyn (Washington, D.C.: Woodrow Wilson Center Press, 2005), 70.

4. Charles McPherson, "Governance, Transparency, and Sustainable Development," in *Energy and Security: Toward a New Foreign Policy Strategy,* eds. Jan Kalicki and David Goldwyn (Washington, D.C.: Woodrow Wilson Center Press, 2005), 464–467.

5. "Chop Fine: The Human Rights Impact of Local Government Corruption and Mismanagement in Rivers State, Nigeria," *Human Rights Watch* 19, no. 2(A), (January 2007): 16.

6. McPherson, "Governance, Transparency,"464.

7. "Promoting Transparency in the African Oil Sector: A Report of the CSIS Task Force on Rising U.S. Energy Stakes in Africa," (Washington D.C.: Center for Strategic and International Studies, March 2004).

8. Erica Downs, "The Fact and Fiction of Sino-African Energy Relations," *China Security,* 3, no. 3 (Summer 2007): 43.

9. "July 2007 International Petroleum Monthly," Energy Information Administration, August 7, 2007.

10. "The anti-bribery provisions of the FCPA make it unlawful for a U.S. person, and certain foreign issuers of securities, to make a corrupt payment to a foreign official for the purpose of obtaining or retaining business for or with, or directing business to, any person. Since 1998, they also apply to foreign firms and persons who take any act in furtherance of such a corrupt payment while in the United States." http://www.usdoj.gov/criminal/fraud/fcpa/.

11. The Equator Principles were launched by a group of banks in 2003 and updated in 2006 through collaboration with the World Bank and the IMF. The Principles address and assess social and environmental risks of a project during the financing stage, and require a plan to mitigate them, in an effort to promote investments that are socially and environmentally responsible, http://www.equator-principles.com/index.html.

12. Specifically, the OECD Export Credit Arrangement regulates the terms of official export credits and foreign aid, with the objective of controlling predatory lending and unintentional financial transfers from supplier countries to buyer countries (China is not a member). Peter C. Evans and Erica S. Downs, "Untangling China's Quest for Oil through State-backed Financial Deals." Policy Brief #154, The Brookings Institute, May 2006.

13. USAID's Global Development Alliance Web site, http://www.usaid.gov/our_work/global_partnerships/gda/.

14. Ying Lou, "Oil May Reach $70 as China Imports Rise on Stockpile, CLSA Says," *Bloomberg,* April 24, 2007, http://www.bloomberg.com/apps/news?pid=newsarchive&sid=aWerPLvknIHw.

15. Peter C. Evans and Erica S. Downs, "Untangling China's Quest."

16 "In 2006, the total African output of the Chinese NOCs was about 267,000 barrels of oil equivalent per day (boe/d). This is only one-third of that produced by the largest foreign producer in Africa, ExxonMobil—which pumped 780,000 boe/d—and a mere 7 percent of that of the continent's largest producer, Sonatrach, which pumped 4.1 million boe/d." [Erica Downs, "The Fact and Fiction of Sino-African Energy Relations," *China Security,* 3, no. 3 (Summer 2007): 44–45.]

17. Evans and Downs, "Untangling China's Quest."

18. Bates Gill, Chin-hao Huang, and J. Stephen Morrison, "China's Expanding Role in Africa. Implications for the United States," A Report of the CSIS Delegation to China on China-Africa-U.S. Relations (November 28–December 1, 2006): 5, 7.

19. For example, since Chad broke off ties with Taiwan in August 2006, China has signed loans, debt relief, and economic cooperation agreements with Chad worth $80 million.

20. "We wish to warn the Chinese government and its oil companies to steer well clear of the Niger delta. Chinese citizens found in oil installations will be treated as thieves. The Chinese government, by investing in stolen crude, places its citizens in our line of fire." Julie Ziegler, "Nigerian Militants Claim Bomb Attack, Warn Chinese Companies," *Bloomberg*, April 29, 2006.

21. Harry G. Broadman, *Africa's Silk Road: China and India's New Economic Frontier*, (Washington, D.C.: The World Bank: 2007), 274–275. (The World Bank notes that it is hard to compare China's assistance to Africa with that of traditional aid agencies because it is impossible to know what loans were concessional and what loans were nonconcessional.)

22. "Toward an Angola Strategy: Prioritizing U.S.-Angola Relations. An Independent Commission Report," (New York: The Council on Foreign Relations, 2007).

23. "China's Trade in Africa Carries a Price Tag," *New York Times*, August 21, 2007.

24. Western oil companies went into Nigeria with little regard for these underlying issues and only made the problem worse. Shell, the largest producer of Nigerian crude, produces more than half of the country's crude and has been extracting oil from Nigeria since 1956, and admitted in a company-commissioned, independent report in 2003 that it had "inadvertently fed corruption, poverty, and conflict through its oil activities in Nigeria." James J. F. Forest and Matthew V. Sousa, *Oil and Terrorism in the New Gulf. Framing U.S. Energy and Security Policies for the Gulf of Guinea* (Lanham, MD: Lexington Books, 2006), 9.

25. McPherson, *Governance, Transparency,* 461–464; Terry Lynn Karl, *The Paradox of Plenty: Oil Booms and Petro-States* (Berkeley: University of California Press, 1997).

26. "China's Trade in Africa Carries a Price Tag," *New York Times*, August 21, 2007.

27. Elizabeth C. Economy, "The Great Leap Backward? The Costs of China's Environmental Crisis," *Foreign Affairs* (September/October 2007): 45.

28. The Africa-China-U.S. Trilateral Dialogues are sponsored by the Brenthurst Foundation, the Chinese Academy of Social Sciences, the Council on Foreign Relations, and the Leon Sullivan Foundation. Within the framework of the dialogues, delegates from Africa, China, and the United States have met three times in South Africa, Beijing, and Washington to discuss ways to cooperate in the drive for African economic development.

CHAPTER 16

Turkey: A Case of a Transit State

Necdet Pamir

Turkey is not a major energy producer. On the contrary, though it has significant lignite reserves (roughly 10 billion tons) and significant hydroelectric potential (180 billion kilowatt-hours), when it comes to oil and gas it is heavily dependent; imports meet 92 percent of its oil demand and 98 percent of its gas demand. Yet, Turkey's strategic location, which makes it a natural energy bridge between major energy producing areas in the Middle East and Caspian Sea regions in the East and big consumer markets in Europe and further West, assigns it a place among the countries most important to global energy security. Today, 86 mbd of oil are consumed globally while almost half of this volume (roughly 43 mbd) is inter-regionally traded. A growing amount of this oil passes through Turkish territory. Three mbd pass through the dangerous waterways of the Turkish Straits (Bosporus and Dardanelles). The Baku-Tbilisi-Ceyhan (BTC) oil pipeline delivers 1 mbd to global markets and additional amounts of oil and gas are increasingly directed from Russia, Kazakhstan and Azerbaijan to the Black Sea. The volume of oil tanker transportation through the region is expected to be around 4 mbd in 2010. Turkey's role in energy security becomes increasingly salient as an integrated system of oil and gas pipelines known as the "East West Corridor" is gradually developing to transit additional energy resources from Russia and Central Asia through Turkey to Western markets. This includes the already operational Blue Stream Gas Pipeline from Russia (peak capacity: 16 bcm a year), the BTC pipeline, the Iraq–Turkey (crude oil) pipeline, a gas pipeline transporting Iranian gas (10 bcm a year), another one carrying Azerbaijani gas (up to 6.6 bcm a year), a "North-South" Corridor concept as well as several "Straits Bypass" pipeline projects which are under consideration. Currently, Turkey's Mediterranean port of Ceyhan is already one of the world's most important energy hubs and a vital outlet both for current Iraqi oil exports and for current as well as potential future Caspian oil exports. On the positive side for Turkey, these pipelines increase the country's geopolitical importance, generate revenues for Turkish entrepreneurs and transit revenues for the government, create employment opportunities and reduce congestion and danger on the Turkish Straits. Potential drawbacks include competition from other countries, particularly Russia, and increasing risks for terrorist attacks.

Turkey's major oil and gas pipelines (in operation, under construction and proposed) are listed and summarized below:

Oil Pipelines

Baku-Tbilisi-Ceyhan (BTC): Operational since June 4, 2006, the 1 mbd pipeline is the first major step after the Baku-Supsa "early oil pipeline" (with a limited capacity of 140,000 barrels per day) to break down the Russian monopoly on outlets for Caspian hydrocarbon sources. The pipeline carries Azerbaijani oil, crosses Georgian territory and ends up in Ceyhan. In the mid- and long-run the project aims to add Kazakh and Russian oil. There are plans to increase its capacity to 1.6 mbd. BTC provides significant economic benefit to all the countries it traverses and is expected to contribute to the stability of the region. In May 2008, Turkey's Energy and Natural Resources Minister Hilmi Guler stated that Turkey had earned $2 billion in BTC transit revenues on 378 million barrels of transported Azeri oil.[1] BTC is the first non-Russian main pipeline exit to the international markets built after the collapse of the Soviet Union.[2] During Soviet times, outlet capacity was designed in such a way that all export routes (pipelines, Volga-Don Water Channel, railways) from the Commonwealth of Independent States (CIS) countries had to cross the Russian Federation (RF). After the dissolution of the Soviet Union, in order to achieve absolute independence, the newly independent states sought alternative routes for oil and gas exports that did not cross Russian territory. For this purpose, the "East-West Energy Corridor" strategy was developed and the United States, Turkey and Georgia closely collaborated with suppliers like Azerbaijan, Kazakhstan and Turkmenistan to bring it to fruition. BTC formed the first and most valuable step of this corridor. It is complemented by a new and parallel gas pipeline (South Caucasus Gas Pipeline) transporting Azerbaijani gas first to Turkey and then to Greece as the first connection to a European country.

Iraq–Turkey (Kirkuk–Yumurtalık) Pipeline (ITP): This twin pipeline has a design capacity of 1.4 mbd. The initial line (615 miles) became operational in 1976 and the first tanker was loaded in May 1977. The second and parallel line (550 miles) became operational in 1987. It terminates near Ceyhan. It was closed in August 1990 in accordance with the U.N. resolutions to apply sanctions against the then Iraqi regime. It was reopened for limited flows again in accordance with the related U.N. resolutions. The pipeline was operational but transported almost half of its full capacity during the post-1991 Gulf War. For Turkey, this caused an estimated loss of $40 billion in transit revenues. Following the invasion of Iraq in 2003, flows were halted and since then, the line has suffered scores of sabotage attacks and is operating with severe interruptions and almost negligible capacity. Under stable regional geopolitical conditions and together with BTC, Ceyhan is expected to become a very important oil terminal and regional market (a "New Rotterdam") to provide and diversify energy supply to Europe. With several new pipeline proposals in the works the significance of this port will further increase. New refineries are also expected to be built near Ceyhan, making this region an energy hub. The government is also considering a new LNG terminal (initially to target the Israeli market) and examining the potential of constructing a new petro-chemical plant near Ceyhan.

Proposed Turkish Straits' Bypass Projects: The Bosporus and Dardanelles are major shipping choke points between the Black Sea and the Aegean Sea, opening to energy-thirsty Western markets through the Mediterranean (see Figure 16.1). Current oil tanker transportation volumes are as high as 3 mbd and projected to reach to 4 mbd by 2010. Even with the BTC, the tanker traffic load is unacceptably high and it threatens the Turkish Straits and the city of Istanbul. The Turkish Straits are considered to be among the most dangerous waterways of the world.[3] Only half a mile wide at their narrowest, with strong currents in opposite directions at a certain point, these are among the busiest and hardest to navigate waterways. As reported by the U.S. Department of Energy, "Past collisions in the Straits have resulted in large oil spills, and additional oil shipping from the Caspian Sea region via the Black Sea and the Bosporus could put the Istanbul metropolitan area at further environmental risk."[4] In addition, new regulations imposed by Turkish authorities due to security and environmental concerns cause frequent delays for tankers carrying Russian oil. To avoid supply disruptions and tension with Moscow there are several Straits' bypass pipeline projects under consideration. One of those bypass projects is the Trans-Thrace pipeline which could carry oil from the Black Sea to the Adriatic Sea. While initially the Russians made a compromise to join this project, Turkey, given environmental and security concerns, favors the Samsun-Ceyhan option which connects the Black Sea with the Mediterranean and which may be further extended to Israel.[5] Russia, for its part, announced its support for the Burgas-Alexandroupolis pipeline that bypasses not only the Straits but also Turkish territory, transporting oil from the Black Sea to the Mediterranean through Romania, Serbia and Croatia all the way to the Adriatic Sea. An agreement to construct the pipeline was signed by Bulgaria, Greece and Russia in March 2007. The Russian-Turkish debate on the best conduit for Caspian and Russian energy remains unresolved, which means that the environmental and security threats to the Turkish Straits will only grow.

Natural Gas Pipelines

Russia-Turkey Western Pipeline: Operational since 1987, this 14 bcm line crosses Ukraine, Moldova, Romania and Bulgaria. The Russians complain about illegal siphoning of their gas on the way to Turkey. They therefore proposed and successfully constructed a sub-sea pipeline crossing the Black Sea to directly sell their gas to Turkey. This ambitious line is called Blue Stream.

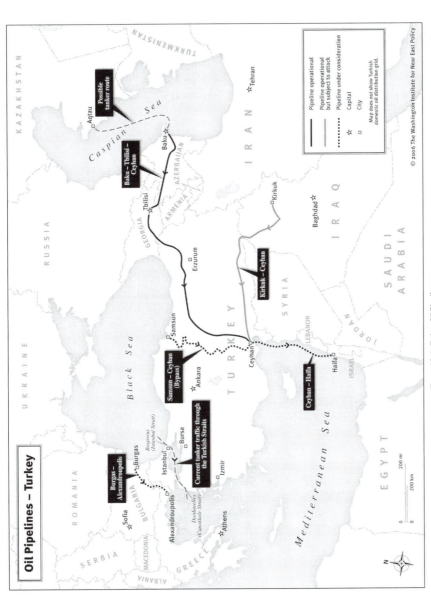

Figure 16.1 Turkey Oil Pipelines

Used by permission of Alicia Glanz, Washington Institute for Near East Policy, Director of communications.

The Blue Stream: This 2,150 meter sub-sea line started to deliver Russian gas in 2002 and its peak yearly volume will be 16 bcm. Turkey received 7.65 bcm of gas in 2006 through the Blue Stream pipeline, which transports gas from Samsun port to Ankara. Currently, 65 percent of Turkey's gas imports are from Russia (including the Russia-West pipeline deliveries), which is both economically and strategically an unacceptable rate. The Russians are proposing to extend this pipeline from Ankara to Ceyhan. There are plans to transport additional volumes of gas to Israel either by a sub-sea pipeline or by LNG tankers from Ceyhan. The former option (sub-sea pipeline) seems to be the preferred option.

Iran-Turkey: This 10 bcm capacity pipeline started to deliver gas in December 2001 and supplied 5.7 bcm of gas to Turkey in 2006. The line is operating with interruptions due to its quality problems and poor metering standards. Problems relating to Iranian gas were brought to the International Court of Justice for arbitration. Iranian gas is the next candidate, following Azerbaijani gas, to be transited to Europe. But the nuclear ambitions of the Iranian leadership are not only weakening this option but also threatening the stability of the region.

South Caucasus Gas Pipeline (SCGPL) from Azerbaijan to Turkey: The SCGPL, also known as Baku-Erzurum-Ceyhan Pipeline, was initially projected to bring Azerbaijani gas from Shakh Deniz gas and condensate field via Georgia to Turkey and then to transit additional volumes to Greece and Italy. As far as the existing gas deal is concerned, peak volumes to Turkey are limited to 6.6 bcm a year and 3 to 4 bcm will be transited to Greece. If the feasibility proves positive, 8 bcm will be transited to Italy. With almost a year of delay, BOTAŞ (Turkish Petroleum Pipeline Corporation) reported that the line became operational in July 2007. As of October 2007, the pipeline transported a cumulative volume of 755 million cubic meters to Turkey. This pipeline is important in several ways. First, it forms the second step of the "East-West Energy Corridor" and helps to decrease the reliance of Azerbaijan, Georgia and Turkey on Russian sources. The agreed price of gas is much cheaper (although there still seem to be some conflicts on the commercial terms) compared to the existing price structures of Russian and Iranian deliveries. It helps the diversification efforts of Turkey and contributes in a positive manner to the country's security concerns, mainly from the east, since there are significant supply problems with Iran, particularly in the winter season. In addition to generating transit fees from the line, Turkey aspires to alleviate its energy security concerns by keeping 15 percent of the supplied amount.

Nabucco Gas Pipeline Project to Europe: This ambitious project aims to decrease Europe's growing dependency on Russian gas by supplying the European natural gas market with gas from countries other than Russia, candidates being Azerbaijan, Turkmenistan, Iran, Iraq and Egypt. The countries initially involved on the demand side are Turkey, Bulgaria, Romania, Hungary and Austria. Their related pipeline companies (BOTAŞ, Bulgargaz, Transgaz SA, MOL Nyrt. and OMV respectively) formed a joint venture company, with each of the partners having a 20 percent stake. They were later joined by Germany's RWE AG. A French company, Gaz de France SA, was blocked from joining the consortium by Turkey's BOTAŞ after the French parliament made it a crime to deny that the mass killing of Armenians by Ottoman Turks during World War I was genocide.[6] If constructed, the 25–31 bcm pipeline is expected to help in supplying the ever growing demand of the EU while increasing the strategic and economic importance of Turkey and therefore positively affecting its relations with the EU leadership. Despite strong EU support, the project faces significant problems both on the supply and demand sides. The history and the ongoing debate of the project's evolution is a typical and significant example of the struggle over energy geopolitics among powers like the EU, the United States and Russia.

Turkey-Greece-Italy: The Turkey-Greece Gas Pipeline is planned to transport 3 bcm a year of Azerbaijani gas via Turkey to Greece and it is expected to further transport an additional 8 bcm a year gas to Italy. With almost a year of delay, the initial volumes were transited to Greece starting in November 2007. BOTAŞ has the right to resell 750 million cubic meters of the Azerbaijani gas while the rest is planned to be directly marketed by the Consortium developing the Shakh Deniz field in Azerbaijan. The already operational Turkey-Greece pipeline is a modest but important step for Turkey's ambitions of being an energy bridge, since it is the first step connecting Turkey to the European markets.

Other Projects: There are other proposed gas pipeline projects waiting for the approval of the Energy Market Regulatory Authority (EMRA) of Turkey (see Figure 16.2). Since the Turkish gas market is overburdened their realization will require time, concrete proposals and enthusiasm from the European markets. Those proposals include a 10 bcm pipeline from Iraq and a 16 and 14 bcm pipeline from Turkmenistan to Europe. Each alternative faces significant problems rising from the geopolitical power struggle in the energy arena.

Turkey's Role in the Big Power Struggle on Energy Security

While the Middle East, North Africa and the Caspian regions are the richest energy domains, developing Asia, Japan, the United States and EU will continue to be the biggest energy markets with increasing dependency on energy imports from these regions. EU officials are trying to decrease their dependency on Russia and Turkey offers one of the best options for an alternative energy corridor for Middle Eastern, Central Asian and even North African hydrocarbon resources. As stated in a recent official document, the European Commission recommends the Council "help Turkey to make full use of its potential to become a major energy transit hub and in particular promote its rapid integration into the Energy Community Treaty."[7] While the Commission intends to increase the potential of Turkey as an

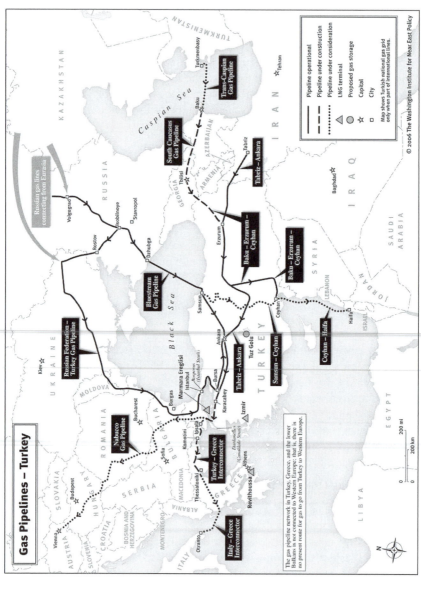

Figure 16.2 Turkey Gas Pipelines

Used by permission of Alicia Glanz, Washington Institute for Near East Policy, Director of communications.

important energy corridor for European countries, there are significant problems to be resolved (especially those created by the end results of competing and conflicting Russian and American policies in the region) in order to turn this rhetoric into concrete projects. Russia is a powerful player in the energy security game. While for importing countries diversification means diversifying sources of supply, Russia sees diversification as finding new export routes to maintain its economic and political posture. Turkey had long been favoring the East-West Energy Corridor strategy and to that end BTC and South Caucasus Gas Pipelines are significant and successful steps. Both pipelines experienced significant delays, and the former some serious cost overruns. The main reason for the delay of the latter is that Azerbaijan and Georgia, both highly dependent on Russian gas supplies, were coerced by Moscow to halt the projects. There were other reasons such as cementing problems in the production wells and allegations of corruption, but Russian policies were dominant. Both countries are unable to pay the inflated prices for Russian gas so they requested a postponement from Turkey. The SCGPL connected to the Turkish gas network in Eskişehir and recently this network was further extended and connected to an export pipeline which recently started to transport Azerbaijani gas to Greece. The North-South Corridor—Blue Stream Pipeline—is accepted as a complementary policy by the current Turkish government but it serves as an additional opportunity for increasing Turkey's dependency on Russian gas. The Nabucco Gas Pipeline Project demonstrates how the great power struggle for energy security impedes the efforts to achieve diversification. The initial efforts for this 4.8 billion euro and 2,000-mile long project started in the early 2000s and the Cooperation Agreement was signed in October 2002 in Vienna, creating a company called Nabucco Gas Pipeline Company.[8] Following a feasibility study, construction was expected to start in 2008 and the pipeline was planned to be operational in 2011. This is clearly not going to happen. There are significant barriers to this project. First, there are problems on the supply side. The alternative sources to Russian gas are Azerbaijan, Turkmenistan, Iran, Iraq, and Egypt. Azerbaijan is currently under pressure and intimidation by Russia. So is Georgia, through which the pipeline is planned to cross. The reserves in Azerbaijan's Shakh Deniz gas and condensate field that are feeding the SCGPL stand at 3.6 tcm, while the agreed volumes to be sold to Turkey will be peaking at a 6.6 bcm/year level. Azerbaijani gas will first be consumed in Turkey and a 3 bcm/year amount is dedicated to Greece. If the Italy extension is constructed, then an extra amount of 8 bcm/year will be needed, which seems to be a very hard target to reach. It also means that there will be no Shakh Deniz gas available for Nabucco. Despite an announcement that the reserves of Shakh Deniz can be almost doubled, Azerbaijani gas has volumetric constraints which decrease its reliability as a potential alternative to support the viability of the Nabucco.

An alternative to Azerbaijan as a source of natural gas to the European theater, Turkmenistan, has 2.86 tcm of recoverable reserves.[9] It produced 62.2 bcm in 2006 and consumes 18.8 bcm a year which leaves 43.4 bcm a year for exports. Except for the 8 bcm a year exported to Iran, the rest goes to Russia, where it is transported to European markets. Russian Gazprom and Turkmenneftegaz have already signed a 25 year long gas purchase agreement for Turkmen gas volumes gradually reaching to 80 bcm a year to be delivered to Russia. Some significant volumes are also dedicated to the TransAfghan Pipeline (to transport future Turkmen gas production to Pakistan and India via Afghanistan) and to China. Therefore, Turkmenistan's gas does not seem to be a reliable source of supply to the Nabucco pipeline, and the project would need billions of dollars worth of upstream investment and 8–10 years of development. Furthermore, the status of the Caspian is another important problem to be resolved since even if Turkmen gas was available in adequate volumes, its transportation via a sub-sea pipeline crossing the Caspian depends on the goodwill of Russia and Iran. Without their acquiescence one can expect those countries' open or covert attempts to stop gas transportation via the Caspian.

The third alternative is Iran. Iran's reserves (27.8 tcm, 15.5% of the world total) are second only to Russia. It produces 111.9 bcm a year (in 2008).[10] The volumes that Turkey receives from Iran (5.7 bcm a year in 2006) are in a way swapped volumes from Turkmenistan. U.S. policies against Iran are a direct obstacle to the realization of this alternative. A Memorandum of Understanding (MOU) signed between Iran and Turkey in July 2007 stated that the Turkish Petroleum Corporation (TPAO) will develop a portion of Iran's rich South Pars field, and together with Turkey's State Pipeline Transportation Corporation transport the Iranian gas first to Turkey and then to Europe. This proposal seems to be facing problems as well. The Bush administration flexed its muscles against Iran and high level U.S. officials announced their opposition and advised Turkey that this was not a suitable time to invest in the oil and gas sector of Iran. Since the Turkish government still seems aligned with the U.S. it does not seem very likely that the Turkish oil and transportation companies will be successful in taking further steps to turn this MOU into a solid agreement and then start implementation. With positive relations between France, Germany and the United States, the chance of Iran's receipt of foreign investment to develop its gas reserves does not seem high, at least for the short term. Russia and China may have a different approach, but then the flow of the possible gas production will be in a different direction and not towards the European market. The Iranian gas may either flow towards Asia in the form of LNG or towards Russia (via Armenia). The flow via Russia will only increase the already problematic Russian hegemony.

The fourth alternative, Iraq, also poses a challenge since to date there is neither sufficient stability nor a reliable government with which to negotiate. While as of this writing the security situation in the country shows improvement, a deterioration is still not out of the realm of possibility. TPAO has for almost 12 years been trying to sign oil and gas deals with the Iraqi government. Gharraf oil field and Mansuriye gas fields have been the focus. But neither during Saddam's period nor after the invasion were the efforts successful. Several MOUs were signed but none turned into a concrete agreement. TPAO and BOTAŞ (with a Turkish private company) are trying to construct a 10 bcm a year capacity pipeline to transport Iraqi gas first to Turkey and then to Europe. In May 2009 BOTAŞ announced that supply from Iraq's Kurdish region would allow the Nabucco pipeline to move gas to Europe by as early as 2014.[11]

But the instability of Iraq is a serious matter of concern and Iraqi gas also has its limits (for the aforementioned reasons) as a viable alternative for Nabucco.

The fifth option for Nabucco is Egypt. Turkey, together with its neighbors, is developing the Arab Natural Gas Pipeline Project aiming to transport Egyptian gas via Jordan and Syria to Turkey and then eventually to European markets. The initial phase of the project is complete and the pipeline reaches Syrian territory. The parties are working on an Inter Governmental Agreement. Initial volumes available for transport will be modest and as low as 1.5 to 2 bcm a year. Egyptian authorities are trying to restrict available volumes for export and preserve their reserves partially for their future generations.

There are problems on the demand side as well. All of the countries that are stakeholders of the Nabucco pipeline are highly dependent on Russian imports, making them vulnerable to Russian coercion and intimidation.

The situation is also complex in the debate on oil pipelines to bypass the Turkish Straits. As previously mentioned, there are several bypass pipeline projects proposed by different countries and companies. While there is finally a kind of consensus between Russia and Turkey that the Turkish Straits are already overloaded by dangerous oil tanker traffic, there is no consensus on a single project to reduce the traffic in the Straits. Russia favors a pipeline crossing the Turkish territory (Kıyıköy-Saros: Trans-Thrace) while the Turkish government insists on Samsun-Ceyhan (Black Sea to the Mediterranean). For a while Russia tried to convince Turkey that it had the oil volumes required to make any pipeline feasible but finally decided to promote a pipeline which also bypasses Turkey, namely the Burgas-Alexandroupolis oil pipeline. An intergovernmental agreement was signed in March 2007 in Athens by the relevant ministers of the three countries, in the presence of their leaders, Russia's President Vladimir Putin, Bulgaria's Prime-Minister Sergey Stanishev and the Greek Prime Minister Kostas Karamanlis.[12] This is another case where Russian and Turkish benefits diverged and the first round seems to have been won by the Russians. Signing an agreement does not necessarily mean that the pipeline will eventually be built. Yet, if Moscow gets its way, Turkey's role as the main bridge between the Middle East, the Caspian and Central Asia would be significantly diminished. Despite that, Turkey still plays hardball with the EU when it comes to Nabucco. Turkey wants more control over the energy projects that traverse it and demands to collect gas from the east, buy some domestically at below-market prices and charge transit fees which exceed those requested by other EU members through which pipelines pass like Bulgaria, Romania, Hungary, and Austria. Such an approach puts Turkey at odds with the EU at a time when Turkey needs to bolster its candidacy for EU membership.

Conclusion

Although Turkey's geography offers a very advantageous and unique potential to make it an energy bridge, energy policy errors over the last decades have limited this potential to a certain extent. Turkey's energy policy has suffered from the lack of a comprehensive strategic plan, and with limited integration of energy considerations into Ankara's overall foreign and economic policies. Turkey's strong dependence on Russian hydrocarbons has also limited its ability to become an effective countermeasure to Russia as a provider of energy security to Europe. In the future, continuous reliance on Russian energy coupled with European failure to embrace Turkey could lead Turkey to seek stronger bilateral relations with Moscow to balance the costs of playing a key role in EU's energy diversification efforts. Thanks to Turkey's rich indigenous resources like hydro, lignite, wind, geothermal and solar, the country can redesign its energy policy and decrease its overdependence on imported sources in the mid- and long-term. Once Turkey reshapes its own energy policies in a positive direction it will then have a greater potential to address the security concerns of Europe and the world. To this end, EU and U.S. officials should work with Turkey to remove some of the obstacles which prevent Turkey from fulfilling its potential of being a linchpin of Europe's energy security.

Notes

1. John C.K. Daly, "Turkey Seeks to Become Energy Transit Hub," *UPI*, May 28, 2008.

2. There are also limited non-Russian export outlets like Baku–Supsa (Black Sea port of Georgia, 7 million tons a year) and minor swap exports through Iran.

3. Turkey Country Analysis Brief, Energy Information Administration/Department of Energy, U.S., October 2006, http://www.eia.doe.gov/cabs/Turkey/Background.html.

4. Ibid.

5. "Israel and Russia Close to Deal on Mediterranean Pipeline," *Haaretz*, July 17, 2008.

6. "Turkey Shuns Gas Project in Genocide Row," *Times Online*, April 6, 2007.

7. "An External Policy To Serve Europe's Energy Interests," Paper from Commission/Sg/Hr For The European Council.

8. "Investment Opportunities in the Countries From Adriatic to the Black Sea," paper presented by Mehmet T. Bilgiç, General Manager of BOTAŞ, Turkey, November 8, 2004, Vienna.

9. BP Statistical Review of World Energy, June 2008, http://www.bp.com/liveassets/bp_internet/globalbp/globalbp_uk_english/reports_and_publications/statistical_energy_review_2008/STAGING/local_assets/downloads/pdf/statistical_review_of_world_energy_full_review_2008.pdf.

10. Ibid.

11. Orhan Coskun, "Iraqi Gas to Launch Nabucco by 2014: Botas Source," *Reuters*, May 17, 2009.

12. Bulgaria, Greece, Russia Finalize Details on Long-Awaited Pipeline Deal," *Associated Press*, February 7, 2007.

CHAPTER 17

NATO's Grapple with Energy Security

Robert G. Bell

On July 30, 2007, a NATO flotilla comprised of ships from six member states set sail on a historic 12,500 mile voyage circumnavigating Africa. "Maritime security, ensuring the safe passage of shipping and supporting a coordinated international approach to protect energy supplies are high priorities for NATO," said the Alliance's Secretary General, Jaap de Hoop Scheffer, in explaining the naval force's mission.[1] Among the important energy security-related seas visited by the flotilla during this cruise were the Niger Delta, where criminal gangs have been attacking oil installations and kidnapping oil workers, the Cape of Good Hope, where, beginning in August 2007, the NATO maritime group conducted joint exercises with the South African Navy for the first time in NATO's history, and, in September, the dangerous waters off the coast of Somalia, where attacks by pirates have become frequent. The intent of this two-month mission was to demonstrate NATO's ability to employ its military assets to uphold security and international law on the high seas, including protecting the right of passage for vital energy supplies. A year before this voyage, it would have been difficult to predict that it would or could take place. In the fall of 2006, as NATO made final preparations for its late November Heads of State and Government Summit in Riga, the allies were quite divided as to whether energy security was an appropriate role for the Alliance. Some member states viewed a NATO role in this area as an unacceptable encroachment on the jurisdiction of the European Union (EU). Others argued that there was no agreed military analysis available from NATO's Military Authorities (NMAs) to underpin any policy review. Others, though, were confident that NATO could demarcate where it could "add value" in this field; that is, by limiting its focus to the transshipment security and critical infrastructure protection dimensions, and leaving the security of supply challenge to the EU. For his part, Secretary General de Hoop Scheffer had been pressing member states for almost a year to agree to put energy security on the Alliance's agenda. For example, the secretary general had succeeded in late 2005 in getting this topic on to the agenda of an *informal* dinner discussion between NATO and EU Foreign Ministers. Then, at the February 2006 Munich Conference on Security Policy, he reiterated his appeal for a broadening and deepening of *formal* political-security discussions within NATO, so as to include more crucial issues, adding that "one that leaps to mind is energy security."[2]

To begin laying a foundation for such discussions, the Headquarters had scheduled a "NATO Forum on Energy Security" in Prague for later in February and announced that "a number of prime ministers, energy ministers, high-ranking NATO representatives, and senior representatives from the global energy community are expected to attend."[3] Regrettably, following strenuous objections from some allied governments, including most notably France, the secretary general had to climb back off this limb. Days before the conference, members of the NATO International Staff were told that they could not make presentations at the conference. Finally, NATO "press guidance" was prepared stating that: "NATO does not have a formal role or policy in the area of energy security or pipeline security" and that "NATO is not contemplating any type of military involvement to protect oil and gas infrastructure in [the Caucuses] or any other region."[4] Similarly, a March 17, 2006, "Reinforced North Atlantic Council" (R-NAC) on energy security called by the secretary general was characterized more by disagreements as to whether the topic was appropriate for the NAC than any significant forward movement. By Riga, however, countervailing pressures, including strong representations from the United States, together with recurring episodes in Europe of heavy-handed Russian employment of gas and oil supply disruptions as an instrument of political influence, had made it clear that the summit could not ignore this topic.[5] As the EU's High Representative for Foreign Policy (himself a former NATO secretary general) noted in an op-ed that fall, "Energy security has shot to the top of the European and wider international agenda."[6] The result was an artful compromise; one that, depending on one's perspective, either set NATO on course toward an eventual formal endorsement of an Alliance role in this area or, in the words of one unnamed NATO official, "opened the Pandora's Box on energy security."[7]

In an important policy document also approved at the summit, the Comprehensive Political Guidance (CPG), NATO leaders agreed that "the disruption of the flow of vital resources" was one of the three or four developments "likely to be the principal threats to the Alliance over the next 10 to 15 years."[8] Nonetheless, in terms of addressing how, *exactly,* NATO would address this "likely threat," the secretary general was able only to secure a consensus from them on a *tasking* to *try* to agree on a role for the Alliance in this field. In Paragraph 45 of the Riga Summit Communiqué, NATO Heads of State and Government recorded this consensus:

> As underscored in NATO's Strategic Concept, Alliance security interests can also be affected by the disruption of the flow of vital resources. We support a coordinated, international effort to assess risks to energy infrastructures and to promote energy infrastructure security. With this in mind, we direct the

Council in Permanent Session to consult on the most immediate risks in the field of energy security, in order to define those areas where NATO may add value to safeguard the security interests of the Allies and, upon request, assist national and international efforts.[9]

Since Riga, serious policy disagreements over NATO's role in energy security among allies have remained evident. While the dispatch of the naval flotilla was, to be sure, a laudatory milestone, it testifies mainly to the relative ability of the Alliance to maintain freedom of action within its Integrated Military Command, in which France does not participate. Within the various political-military bodies at the Headquarters that took up the Riga tasking, questions, rather than answers, have remained more the order of the day. For example, in late February 2007, a NATO Task Force on Energy Security met for the first time since the summit. Its task was to define the questions the allies must answer before framing any policy on energy security, including:

- Defining the role of NATO forces in energy infrastructure protection;
- Identifying the sensitivities associated with any NATO role in keeping the Strait of Hormuz and other vulnerable oil and gas transshipment choke points open, or in providing a low-visibility, stabilizing, and non-provocative presence at sensitive oil production or refining locations on land;
- Integrating security of supply policies among allies.[10]

The question of a adopting a hard military role in these areas, however, reportedly made some governments nervous: "Nations are very anxious to steer around any suggestion that there will be a militarization of this issue," said one source, adding: "even for protection of maritime shipping, there are many who question whether NATO could ever have a role, given the ambiguity of the laws of the high seas."[11] In the summer of 2007, the secretary general succeeded in securing consensus within the NAC for a tasking to the NATO strategic military commands to identify the minimum military requirements (MMR) for the Alliance associated with protecting critical energy security infrastructure (CESIP). Those reports have since been submitted, and discussions are continuing in the appropriate political venues, including the NATO Senior Political Committee (SPC), as well as in a Military Committee Working Group. However, a kind of chicken and egg standoff appears to persist, with the military complaining that it is extremely difficult to identify a MMR absent clear political guidance about the Alliance's level of ambition in taking on such roles, and the political side saying that it cannot begin a focused discussion until the military has laid out the costs and other implications of the various alternatives.

NATO's Fundamental Purposes

If NATO is to achieve a consensus on these issues, it must begin by reminding itself of the Alliance's fundamental purposes. NATO's *role* in energy security is clear. What is not clear is its *policy*. This is true both in terms of security of supply and the protection of its critical energy systems infrastructures. At the 2006 Munich conference, Secretary General de Hoop Scheffer noted that "NATO's Strategic Concept includes the protection of vital supply lines as one area critical to the security of allies." Except for the 1949 North Atlantic Treaty, the 1999 Strategic Concept, as previously noted, provides the highest and most definitive guideline for the Alliance's political-military decision-making. Paragraph 24 of the Strategic Concept was one of the most important and prescient adaptations in NATO's post-Cold War strategy agreed by the then-19 heads of state and government at NATO's Fiftieth Anniversary Summit in Washington. In its entirety, this paragraph reads as follows:

> Any armed attack on the territory of the Allies, from whatever direction, would be covered by Article 5 and 6 of the Washington Treaty. However, Alliance security must also take account of the global context. Alliance security interests can be affected by other risks of a wider nature, including *acts of terrorism*, sabotage and organized crime, *and by the disruption of the flow of vital resources*. The uncontrolled movement of large numbers of people, particularly as a consequence of armed conflicts, can also pose problems for security and stability affecting the Alliance. Arrangements exist within the Alliance for consultation among the Allies under Article 4 of the Washington Treaty, and, where appropriate, co-ordination of their efforts including their responses to risks of these kinds.[12]

As stated in the first part of the key sentence in this paragraph, NATO heads of state and government agreed, by consensus, that foreign-based or directed terrorist attacks could provide grounds for invoking the collective security guarantee contained in Article 5 of the NATO Treaty. By 1999, the Clinton Administration had been dealing with bombings of U.S. embassies and military forces by al-Qaeda for some time, and it welcomed the willingness of the allies to agree to this broadening of the traditional conception of what could constitute an Article 5 attack. Two years later, on September 11, 2001, when NATO permanent representatives met with Lord Robertson and his key staff midst the shock and horror of the video images from America, it was this set of words from Paragraph 24 of the Strategic Concept that provided the precedent and the relevant policy guidance that informed the consultations that, within hours the next day, allowed NATO for the first time in its 52-year existence to invoke Article 5. The authority provided by Paragraph 24 was specifically referenced in the Statement released by the North Atlantic Council that next day:

> The Council agreed that if it is determined that this attack was directed from abroad against the United States, it shall be regarded as an action covered by Article 5 of the Washington Treaty, which states that an armed attack against one of the Allies in Europe or North America shall be considered an attack

against them all. The commitment to collective self-defense embodied in the Washington Treaty was first entered into in circumstances very different from those that exist now, but it remains no less valid and no less essential today. When the Heads of State and Government of NATO met in Washington in 1999, they paid tribute to the success of the Alliance in ensuring the freedom of its members during the Cold War and in making possible a Europe that was free and whole. But they also recognized the existence of a wide variety of risks to security, some of them quite unlike those that had called NATO into existence. More specifically, they condemned terrorism as a serious threat to peace and stability and reaffirmed their determination to combat it in accordance with their commitments to one another, their international commitments and national legislation.[13]

The point worth emphasizing here is that the key sentence in Paragraph 24 of the Strategic Concept does not stop with the words "acts of terrorism." Rather, it goes on to specifically identify "disruption of the flow of vital resources" as an additional basis for *possible* consultations under Article 4, and, if deemed appropriate, a coordinated collective security response under Article 5. To be clear: there is no automatic response here. The existence of Paragraph 24 does not mean that any oil crisis will lead NATO to invoke Article 5. Whether such a crisis ever led to the invoking of Article 4, let alone an Article 5 response, would of course depend on the nature of the event, the success or failure of what presumably would be intense diplomatic efforts to resolve the problem, and, if that diplomacy failed, the decisions that NATO allies would reach, which require consensus.

Potential NATO Energy Security Crises

That said, those who would argue that NATO has no role in energy security must explain why the clause that NATO heads of state and government formally agreed in one part of Paragraph 24 of the 1999 Strategic Concept (i.e., that an act of terrorism can trigger an Article 5 response) does not necessarily apply to another part of that same paragraph (i.e., a cut-off of oil or gas supplies). This is not an academic argument. One does not have to look very far to identify scenarios—hypothetical, to be sure, but not unimaginable—under which NATO might be asked by a member state for consultations under Article 4 as a result of a security of energy supply crisis. To cite one example, in January 2006, Bulgaria, a NATO member state since 2002, rejected a demand from Gazprom that it agree to review the prices it will pay between now and 2010 for natural gas. Had Bulgaria's gas been shut off—as occurred with Ukraine, Moldova, and Georgia—would Bulgaria have requested NATO consultations under Article 4? Would NATO have been prepared if it had? To ask those questions is to answer them. Bulgaria is also far from the only continental European NATO ally with a very high dependency on foreign oil, as illustrated below:

NATO Ally	Dependence on Foreign Oil
Slovakia	100%
Baltics (3 nations)	100%
Poland	99%
Bulgaria	94%
Czech Republic	82%
Hungary	81%

Ukraine is, of course, not a NATO ally, at least not yet. That said, some allies, including Poland and the United States, hope that Ukraine might be ready to merit an accession invitation by the time of NATO's 2009 60th Anniversary summit. Whatever timeline one favors for Ukrainian membership in NATO, it is hard to imagine how NATO allies can proceed too far down this road until they have agreed among themselves, "at 26," on how the Strategic Concept would apply if after Ukraine joins the Alliance its gas supplies were again turned off by Russia. Similar concerns involve Georgia, another country awaiting membership. The recent military clash between Georgia and Russia in August 2008 highlights the risk associated with bringing into the Alliance former Russian allies that are playing a key role in global energy security. Had Georgia been a NATO member in the summer of 2008 the Alliance would have been under pressure to meet its military responsibilities. Finally, consider Iran and the ongoing nuclear crisis there. Both the EU and the United States have made it perfectly clear that it is "unacceptable" to permit Iran to acquire a nuclear weapons capability. While speculation intensifies with regard to the possibility of a preemptive strike against Iranian nuclear facilities (an option that President Bush has repeatedly emphasized "remains on the table"), this option is seen as a "last resort," and efforts have continued, both within the UN Security Council, by the United States bilaterally, and within the EU, to ratchet up the severity of economic sanctions, together with pledging possible incentives if Iran complies with the UN Security Council mandates. Nevertheless, Iran's president has defiantly continued to reject the Council's demands and belittle the effect of the sanctions already agreed upon. The Iranian government has also made clear that more draconian sanctions, if approved by the UN Security Council, could lead to a cut-off of its oil exports to the West. And others have warned that it would not be inconceivable in such a crisis that Iran would attempt to close the Strait of Hormuz, through which half the world's traded oil is shipped. If this crisis were, in the worst case, to escalate to include these kinds of oil denial actions by Iran, and if any NATO ally whose economy was seriously destabilized were to cite Paragraph 24 of the Strategic Concept and invoke Article 4, would NATO be prepared for that debate, especially if it had still not even agreed that it had a role to play with regard to energy security? Again, to ask that question is to answer it.

It is worth recalling that when NATO almost tore itself apart during the 2003 war against Iraq, it was not about invoking Article 5—rather, the Alliance was split by a sharp disagreement as to whether Turkey was in fact threatened by Iraq, in the context of Article 4, and whether the Alliance as a whole therefore needed to offer mutual assistance. The best way to ensure that situations do *not* get out of control and become crises is to try to anticipate them and plan accordingly. With this in mind, NATO should, as a matter of priority, expedite and intensify its decision-making on implementation of the Riga energy security tasking.

An additional illustration of the need to move now to begin conducting prudent, preparatory planning at NATO for possible energy security crises in the years ahead is the growing international interest in the Arctic region, which is believed to contain 25 percent of the world's undiscovered oil and gas reserves. The potential for the Arctic Ocean to become accessible to maritime shipping for extended periods of the year due to a warming climate offers the prospect of a renewed naval interest in the Barents Sea and, with it, the potential for a confrontation over the exploitation of the vast energy resources in the Arctic Sea comes ever closer. Four NATO allies—the United States, Norway, Denmark and Canada, as well as their partner in the 27-member NATO-Russia Council (NRC), Russia, are direct participants, and competitors, in the scramble to stake claims to this potential windfall.

Coordinating NATO and the EU

Some would say, indeed, some *are* saying: no, this is the domain of the European Union, and NATO should keep out. To be sure, the EU has a crucial role that it can and must play. It is exercising this responsibility through its diplomacy with Russia, including its efforts to persuade Russia to ratify the Energy Charter Treaty and its transit protocol. It is also intensifying its internal energy security efforts within the EU zone as well, with new initiatives focused on creating a European energy market, addressing anticompetitive market distortions, encouraging diversification and new technologies, and initiating its own critical infrastructure protection programs. The EU can and should also expand its dialogue and cooperation with the United States on energy security, as EU Commission President Jose Manuel Barroso and other EU leaders have proposed. But the EU does not include Norway (except in the context of the European Economic Area) or Turkey (at least for many years to come). That means, for example, that when EU Ministers meet, no one is formally representing a major part of the North Sea oil supply dimension, or the opportunities for reducing European dependency on Russian oil and gas represented by the Baku-Tbilisi-Ceyhan pipeline. And the United States, of course, does not include Canada. Thus an EU-US dialogue venue also leaves this major energy producing nation out. However, Norway, Turkey and Canada are all members of long-standing within NATO.

Fortunately, this does not have to be an "either/or" choice: each organization brings strengths and core competencies to bear. Coordinating NATO's and the EU's efforts in this respect can be a win-win outcome for both organizations. If nothing else, NATO and the EU should at least meet to begin this dialogue, particularly on critical infrastructure protection issues, if not formally under the auspices of the regular NAC-EU Political Security Committee (PSC) meetings, then informally. In fact, a multiplicity of venues can play a positive role, including the OSCE and the G-8 (which Russia chaired in 2007 and for which then President Putin made energy security a key theme).

The NATO-Russia Council (NRC) also seems to be tailor-made for this kind of political dialogue. Indeed, it was discussed by NATO defense ministers and Russian Defense Minister Sergei Ivanov in 2006 when the NRC convened during the Informal NATO Defense ministerial meetings in Sicily. The NRC is not meant as a forum only for issues on which NATO and Russia agree. It was intended to allow hard-nosed discussions on issues where disagreements are deep. As Winston Churchill once said, "jaw, jaw is better than war, war." If NATO and Russia can meet in the NRC to argue strong disagreements over missile defense initiatives—and they are—then they should be able to engage in a frank and open dialogue within the NRC in which allied concerns about Russia's using energy supplies as a blunt instrument of foreign and security policy can be made clear.

Critical Energy Infrastructure Protection

The Riga Summit Communiqué agreement places particular emphasis on the protection of energy infrastructure dimension of energy security. In this regard, it is important to appreciate that NATO itself owns and operates significant strategic downstream assets. Indeed, NATO owns and operates 10 different jet fuel pipeline systems covering some 7,000 miles across 12 NATO nations, linking storage depots, air bases, civil airports, pumping stations, refineries and port entry points, including the largest of NATO's pipeline systems, the Central Europe Pipeline System (CEPS). NATO has operated CEPS for over four decades and under its current commercial business model, the system is leased to industry for provision of jet fuel to major commercial airports in Europe. Indeed, CEPS is utilized to provide 100 percent of the jet fuel used by airlines at Brussels Airport, and the majority of fuel supplied at Frankfurt and Schiphol.

Designed with World War III very much in mind, CEPS was designed to extremely daunting war-survival specifications, with great redundancy of pipeline pumping stations, hardening of critical facilities, buried pipelines, and quick-reaction emergency repair teams all emphasized. Indeed, CEPS even came under direct attack by European-based anti-NATO terrorists during this era. In this context, then, NATO has much to offer in terms of hands-on experience and capability as Europe and the West engage in a broader dialogue about security of its energy transmission systems in the face of a long war against Islamic terrorism.

Conclusion

Four years ago, NATO's heads of state and government, meeting President Bush in Brussels during his rapprochement tour of Europe after the Iraq invasion, underscored their commitment "to strengthening NATO's role as a forum for strategic and political consultation and coordination among allies, while reaffirming its place as the essential forum for security consultation between Europe and North America."[14] They also pledged "to develop further our strategic partnership with the EU." There would seem to be few issues that more necessarily are appropriate for "political and security consultation and coordination" at the highest levels of the Alliance, and between NATO and the EU, than energy security. As German Chancellor Merkel has observed, it is clear that the issue of security of energy supply has now become "deeply political."[15] Moreover, as European Commission President Barroso reminded us in a major speech at Georgetown University in 2006, at which he proposed a new "Strategic Energy Dialogue" between the EU and the United States, it is not just the supply and demand—or upstream—dimensions of the energy business that has now become what he termed "major strategic policy issues," it is also the downstream dimension, including protection of pipelines, storage depots and transportation routes.[16] President Barroso's recommendation for creating "a permanent network of EU-US energy experts who could identify common policies and responses to energy crises," however, overlooked the many contributions that could be brought to bear by including NATO in this dialogue—an organization with its headquarters in the same city as the EU. Unfortunately, this EU -NATO disconnect is all too common in the interrelationship—or too often lack thereof—between these two proud organizations. Four years after NATO began wrestling with these challenges, the outcome of its efforts to clearly define a more proactive role in energy security matters, or to gain internal consent to engage the EU formally in this field, remain very much uncertain. Yet, as Senator Richard Lugar, then Chairman of the U.S. Senate's Foreign Relations Committee, said on the eve of the Riga Summit, "the most likely source of armed conflict in the European theatre and the surrounding regions will be energy scarcity and manipulation."[17] It is therefore safe to assume that NATO members will find themselves increasingly engaged in missions that are either directly or indirectly associated with energy security. If the Alliance is to continue to re-tool itself to remain both viable and relevant to the evolving global security environment of the 21st century, it must clarify its position and focus on identifying action items that produce added value and that can deliver tangible security gains while coordinating directly with other nongovernmental organizations toward the formulation of a common and comprehensive transatlantic energy security policy. In other words, NATO should use both its status as an intergovernmental organization as well as its comparative advantage over other international organizations–its military capabilities.

Notes

1. NATO News: NATO Naval Force Sets Sail for Africa," July 30, 2007, www.nato. int/docu/update/2007/07-july/e0730a.html. The six contributing nations were Canada, Denmark, Germany, the Netherlands, Portugal and the United States. The ships com-

prised NATO's Standing Naval Maritime Group 1 (SDNMG 1), one of four of NATO's standing naval forces that operate under the auspices of the Alliance's Integrated Military Command.

2. Munich Security Conference Web site, http://www.securityconference.de/konferenzen/2007/index.php?sprache=en&.

3. "NATO Forum on Energy Security," NATO Security Through Science, updated October 12, 2005, www.nato.int/science/news/2005.

4. "Press Points for the NATO Forum on Energy Security Technology," NATO Press Office, February 13, 2006.

5. Among those in the United States who skillfully pressed for a more assertive NATO role was Senator Richard Lugar, Chairman of the Senate Committee on Foreign Relations. In an important speech on the eve of the Summit, Senator Lugar called on NATO to formally define defending against oil and gas cut-offs as an Article V commitment, thereby requiring a collective security response by all Alliance member states. Senator Lugar also called on NATO to establish regular high-level consultation on energy issues with Russia and other energy rich nations. ["Lugar Speech in Advance of NATO Summit," Press Release, Office of Senator Lugar, November 22, 2006, http://lugar.senate.gov/press/record.cfm?id=266087.

6. Javier Solana, "Europeans Must Act Collectively on Energy Security," *Financial Times*, September 3, 2006.

7. "Allies Struggle to Define Energy Security," *Defense News*, March 5, 2007, 38.

8. Comprehensive Political Guidance, Paragraph 2. NATO Basic Texts (2006), www.nato.int/docu/basictxt. The CPG is intended to provide a framework and political direction for NATO's continuing transformation over the next 10–15 years and hence complements, and amplifies upon, the highest doctrinal guidance source within the Alliance, the NATO Strategic Concept, adopted by Heads of State and Government at the Washington Summit in 1999, which the CPG notes "remains valid."

9. "Riga Summit Communiqué," NATO Press Release, November 29, 2006.

10. "Allies Struggle to Define Energy Security," *Defense News*, March 5, 2007, p. 38.

11. Ibid.

12. ANNEX to C-M(99)21. (emphasis added)

13. "Statement by the North Atlantic Council," Press Release, September 12, 2001.

14. Statement Issued by the Heads of State and Government Participating in a Meeting of the North Atlantic Council in Brussels on 22 February," NATO Press Release.

15. "Merkel: Guantanamo Mustn't Exist in the Long Term," Spiegel Interview, *Spiegel Online international,* January 9, 2006, http://www.spiegel.de/international/0,1518,394180,00.html.

16. "Speaking with a Common Voice: Energy Security in the 21st Century," Remarks at Georgetown University Honorary Degree Ceremony, Jose Manuel Durao Barroso, February 9, 2006, http://ec.europa.eu/commission_barroso/president/pdf/speech_20060209_en.pdf.

17. "NATO Should 'Revive Cold War Exercise' to Counter Energy Threat: US," *Deutsche Press Agentur,* November 27, 2006.

CHAPTER 18

Liquefied Natural Gas: The Next Prize?

Cindy Hurst

The liquefied natural gas (LNG) industry is one of the fastest growing sectors in the energy market. When referring to LNG, it is important to point out that it is not a new source of energy, but rather a method for delivering an already existing form of energy—natural gas. For decades, natural gas has been transported regionally via an extensive network of pipelines. While this has long been a reliable method for delivering the gas, it has reduced the marketability of the product, forcing suppliers and consumers to be tied together through the fixed infrastructure of pipelines and long-term contracts. LNG, on the other hand, is natural gas in a liquid state. It is produced when the natural gas is cooled at high pressure to minus 256°F, which turns it into a liquid, reducing its volume to 1/600th that of its gaseous state. This makes it economically feasible and technically possible to transport in specially designed tankers rather than relying on a fixed pipeline infrastructure. Once a tanker reaches its destination, it offloads its cargo either in its liquid state into special facilities, where it is stored until it is regasified, or in its gaseous state after being regasified onboard the tanker before being fed directly into a domestic pipeline. LNG offers an alternative method to deliver much needed natural gas around the world, transforming the industry from a regional market into a global market. In 2006, LNG accounted for approximately 7 percent of the global consumption of natural gas. That market share is expected to increase to12 percent by 2030.[1]

The concept of liquefying gas is not a new one. In the early 19th century, British chemist and physicist Michael Faraday experimented with converting various gases into liquids. In 1873, the German engineer, Karl Von Linde, built the first practical compressor refrigeration machine in Munich. In 1912, the first LNG plant was built in West Virginia. The plant began operating in 1917. In 1941, the first commercial liquefaction plant was built in Cleveland, Ohio. The Cleveland plant suffered the first LNG disaster three years later, when an explosion killed nearly 130 people and destroyed 79 homes—a disaster that brought to light some of the potential dangers of LNG. In 1959, the first LNG tanker transported 2,000 tons of natural gas from Louisiana to a terminal at Canvey Island on the Thames estuary in the United Kingdom. It was not until the 1960s, however, that LNG would become a commercially viable energy option. Algeria became the first country to export LNG during the 1960s after the discovery of major gas reserves. Other countries—the United States, Libya, Brunei, and Indonesia— quickly followed suit. In the 1990s Qatar emerged as a leading LNG producer, and in 2006, as LNG production in Indonesia decreased, it bumped Indonesia out of its number one seat.

On the consumption side, Japan, Europe and South Korea have been lead- ing the way since the early 1990s. Due to geographic constraints and restricted domestic reserves Japan, which uses natural gas mostly in the electric power and gas utility industries, is the number one importing country of LNG. Having no pipelines running to the island nation and with limited domestic gas reserves, Japan is forced to rely almost wholly on LNG to meet its natural gas needs.[2] The United States introduced Japan to LNG in 1969. Then, after realizing the value of natural gas, Japan began importing LNG from Brunei in 1972. The list of import countries to Japan quickly grew over the next three decades to include the United Arab Emirates, Malaysia, Australia, Qatar, Oman, and Trinidad and Tobago. Japan's imports grew from approximately 1,939 billion cubic feet (bcf) in 1993 to over 2,858 bcf in 2005.[3] Natural gas consumption in Japan is expected to grow at an average rate of 0.7 percent per year to 3.7 tcf in 2030.[4] In order to keep up with its growing natural gas demand, by 2006 Japan had constructed 26 LNG im- port terminals with another six in the planning or proposal stages. South Korea, like Japan, suffers from geographic constraints. The best option for a pipeline to South Korea would be one that traverses North Korea; however, the North's severe political instability and the strained relations between the two countries would likely reduce South Korea's energy security. This forces South Korea to rely almost wholly on LNG for all of its natural gas needs.

Europe, with a steady pipeline flow coming from Russia, Algeria, and Norway, has been turning increasingly to LNG to supplement current piped-in natural gas supplies and, more importantly, to break free from some of the reliance on pipeline supplies from Russia. In 2005, 11 percent of Europe's gas imports came in the form of LNG, mostly from Algeria and Nigeria.[5] In Italy alone 14 LNG ter- minals are currently under construction or in different stages of planning.

Due to flattening production in both Canada and the United States, coupled with continually rising natural gas demand, the United States too is forced to increase its LNG imports. In 2006, LNG comprised only about 3 percent of all natural gas consumed in the U.S. The Energy Information Administration pre- dicted that by 2030, LNG would make up 13 percent.[6] As of August 2008 there are currently eight operating LNG terminals in the U.S. and another 17 have been approved for construction by the Federal Energy Regulatory Committee (FERC), most of them along the Gulf of Mexico and the northeast coast.[7]

Finally, emerging economies will see the biggest increases of natural gas consumption. China and India, the two fastest growing economies, desperately need fuel to support their growth. Both of these countries have been turning to LNG to help supplement planned future natural gas consumption. Prior to 2004, natural gas in China was used mostly in the production of chemical fertilizers, something that was desperately needed to feed a population of 1.3 billion people. In India, approximately one-third of the natural gas consumed was used for fertilizers. Neither of these countries relied much on natural gas, turning to coal instead for heating and cooking. All this is changing, however, and interest in LNG is increasingly growing. China's first LNG import terminal came online in 2006 in Guangdong province. Up to 10 more import terminals could be built within the following decade. While China had previously pushed to bring these terminals online sooner, its efforts have been met with a number of difficulties, including securing long term contracts at an "acceptable" rate. India's first LNG terminal began operations in 2004. A second terminal came online one year later. Two more terminals are under construction and an additional one is in the planning phases.[8]

Since 1993, the LNG trade has been growing dramatically as more and more countries, looking to natural gas as a source of energy come online with regasification terminals (see Figure 18.1). The growth of LNG will likely continue in an upward trend, increasing competition for global supplies. However, it is not an easy transition. While there are definite advantages to LNG, there are also disadvantages and challenges facing the industry.

Advantages of LNG

LNG adds to energy security in two major ways:

Eliminating the Middleman: LNG eliminates the middleman, or those countries through which a pipeline must traverse to reach its ultimate consumer. For example, natural gas consumption is expected to increase significantly in both India and Pakistan. With neighboring Iran having ample natural gas reserves, an ideal solution to ensure future natural gas supplies to both India and Pakistan is the proposed Iran-Pakistan-India (IPI) pipeline, which would connect the three countries. This pipeline, if ever constructed, will traverse part of Pakistan and continue on to India, allowing Iran to deliver natural gas to both countries. While this option could potentially contribute to improved relations between India and Pakistan, it will make India heavily dependent on Iran and Pakistan, both of which are facing significant domestic and international challenges. Traversing the restive province of Baluchistan in southern Pakistan, a pipeline could face frequent attacks by Baluchi separatists. To cut out the middleman, India could choose to import natural gas as LNG. Despite being more costly, this option would likely provide India more energy security than would a pipeline.

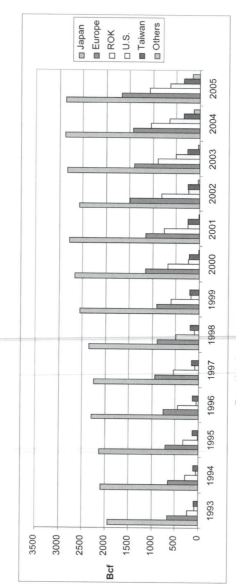

Figure 18.1 Growth of LNG Markets in Key Consuming Regions
Source: International Energy Agency

Increased Diversification: Adding LNG imports to supplement natural gas consumption provides countries with increased flexibility through alternative delivery methods. Through diversification, countries become less susceptible to political or economic coercion or even blackmail. Roughly a quarter of Europe's natural gas imports comes from Russia, mostly via pipelines traversing Ukraine and Belarus. The experience of the past few years clearly demonstrates that Russia is willing to use energy as a tool of coercion and intimidation against her former allies. Therefore, increasing dependency on Russian natural gas puts European countries at risk, especially during winter months when demand is heavy. LNG can also contribute to U.S. energy security by diversifying supply sources. Right now the United States is mostly dependent on domestic and Canadian gas. This renders it highly vulnerable to disruptions on its home continent. If terrorists or a massive storm took out a key pipeline, it would be hard to bring in alternative supplies from outside North America. By developing an LNG infrastructure the United States would be able to quickly absorb LNG from a diverse range of foreigner suppliers and hence mitigate the impact of a catastrophic supply disruption.

Disadvantages of LNG

While LNG clearly contributes to energy security through diversification and flexibility, consumers and producers are also faced with a number of complex variables that can compromise energy security and global security in general. The largest consumers of LNG are predominantly those who belong to the Organization for Economic Cooperation and Development (OECD), countries considered democratized and by and large committed to free trade and open markets. On the other hand, the majority of LNG exporting countries are not democracies and they do not uphold the values and best practices OECD countries are accustomed to. While this may not seem to be a problem in a world where money is the driving factor in business relations, the risk is in political partiality. In other words, a country may choose to deny exports to another country simply because it does not agree with the potential recipient's political point of view. The 1973 Arab oil embargo is a perfect example. Furthermore, LNG could ease the formation of a gas cartel. During the past decades in which natural gas was traded strictly via pipelines, the possibility of forming an OPEC-like natural gas cartel was low. The growth of the LNG industry is changing that. The Gas Exporting Countries Forum (GECF), which first met in May 2001 in Iran, is a loosely structured organization of gas producers. The purpose of the forum was to give member countries an informal setting in which they could exchange views and experiences. Russia, Qatar, Indonesia, Algeria, Brunei, Malaysia, Nigeria, Norway, Oman and Turkmenistan were the first members of the GECF. Since 2001, the organization has grown, although membership fluctuates. Despite previous attempts from member countries to try to deny any intention of organizing a cartel, skeptics question the organization's possible underlying intentions. In January 2007, Ayatollah Ali Khamenei, Iran's supreme leader, suggested that Iran and Russia team up to form a gas cartel. In a statement that caused an international stir Vladimir Putin, then president of Russia, called it an "interesting idea."[9] An international cartel would almost certainly be led by Russia, which possesses approximately 27 percent of global reserves, and Iran, which possesses 16 percent. A cartel that comprised these two countries would control nearly half of the world's reserves and be able to restrict production and manipulate prices. An OPEC-style gas cartel is unlikely as long as the vast majority of natural gas is traded via pipeline and through long term contracts. However, a growth of the LNG industry would turn what was once a regional market into a global market, creating new possibilities for such a cartel.

Another problem associated with LNG is the potential threat of terrorism. The potentially lethal nature of LNG was first realized in Cleveland, Ohio, in 1944 after a new cylindrical tank failed and released all of its contents into the nearby streets and sewers. The spill caused a vapor cloud to form and ultimately ignite, triggering a sequence of events that left, as mentioned before, nearly 130 people dead and destroyed 79 homes, two factories, 217 cars, and 7 trailers. The second incident occurred at the Skikda LNG plant in Algeria on January 19, 2004. This time, 27 people were killed and 72 wounded. The blast also destroyed three of the plant's liquefaction units and cut production levels in half. In both cases, these disasters were ruled accidents and not sabotage. Despite these disasters, the LNG industry touts an impeccable safety record with dangers that have been minimized through improved safety and security measures. For example, in the Cleveland accident, after the plant had already been running without incident, a large tank was added. Due to the scarcity of steel alloys during World War II, the new tank was built with a low nickel content. According to an investigation by the Bureau of Mines, the inner shell of the cylindrical tank became brittle from the low temperature of the LNG. Excessive ground vibrations are believed to have caused crack propagation in the inner shell of the tank, which ultimately led to the leak and subsequent explosions.[10] The safety of LNG has been widely debated, especially since the 9/11 attacks, after which Richard Clarke, former White House counterterrorism chief reportedly prompted the U.S. Coast Guard to close Boston Harbor to all LNG tankers, fearing terrorists could strike again. The harbor remained closed for several weeks before reopening under much tighter security. Almost weekly, LNG tankers have to pass within several hundred yards of the crowded Boston waterfront, past the end of the Logan International Airport runway and under a busy bridge before reaching the Suez Energy North America LNG terminal in Everett, Massachusetts. Safety measures in place today make it unlikely that an unintentional event could spark a major disaster. For example, an accidental collision with a small vessel would not likely reach the LNG tanks to cause any damage that would result in an LNG spill. These massive holding tanks are separated from the hull of the ship by 6–10 feet of water when the tanks are full. The true concern is in the possibility of a well orchestrated terrorist attack against an LNG tanker. While there are other potentially attractive targets, such as vessels carrying ammonium nitrate or liquid propane gas, there are four reasons

LNG could be deemed a better target. First, it is a highly visible and recognizable target. The Moss spherical LNG tanker cannot be mistaken with its giant domes sitting atop the vessel. Second, an attack would impact natural gas deliveries into the United States and probably locations abroad that could seriously impact the economy. Even if an attack were not successful in creating mass casualties, the psychological factor would send natural gas prices up and even likely put a halt to LNG imports. This would, in turn, seriously impact locations such as Massachusetts, which have become heavily dependent on LNG deliveries. It would also jeopardize plans to expand the LNG industry worldwide and slow down the approval process for new terminals. Third, widespread concerns have greatly increased LNG security measures, which could make LNG tankers and terminals, at least within the United States, extremely hard targets to attack. Therefore, although groups like al-Qaeda tend to attack soft targets, a strike against LNG would boost a group's credentials "as a meaningful force." This would tend to "build morale among existing members and attract new recruits."[11] Fourth, there is no empirical data available on the effects of an attack against an LNG tanker or terminal. Therefore it is impossible to determine the physical impact of such an incident with all the safety and security procedures in place. A perfectly executed attack against an LNG tanker could potentially create mass casualties. While LNG in itself is neither flammable nor explosive, once a spill occurs, it quickly vaporizes into 90 percent methane, which, at the appropriate levels of air to gas, is highly flammable and can explode when trapped within a confined area.[12] According to a study released by the Sandia National Laboratories in December 2004, the most significant impacts to public safety exist within half a mile of an accident site for a minor incident and up to one mile for a very large spill. In some cases, it would be possible for a vapor cloud to extend to 1.5 miles, creating a potentially high thermal hazard within the area.[13] Some experts feel that the most probable danger associated with an LNG spill is the potential for a pool fire, which could occur if LNG is spilled near an ignition source, causing the evaporating gas to combust and burn above the LNG pool. Pool fires burn at greater heat and speed than oil or gas fires. Additionally, they cannot be extinguished and must therefore burn themselves out. The heat of the pool fire could cause thermal radiation to injure people and damage property "a considerable distance from the fire itself."[14] Despite the target desirability, risks can be and are being minimized through appropriate government action. Immediately following the 9/11 attacks, the Coast Guard increased LNG tanker and port security measures. Additionally, the Coast Guard works with state, environmental and police marine units to patrol the Boston harbor on a 24-hour basis. Government-imposed regulations on both the transport and storage of LNG have become more stringent, and proposed LNG terminals must undergo a much more rigid approval processes. The siting of an LNG terminal is critical to mitigate any possible attacks. Placing an LNG terminal at least five miles out to sea mitigates the possibility or potential effect of an attack. In February 2007, the United States Government Accountability Office (GAO) released its study titled *Public Safety Consequences of a Terrorist*

Attack on a Tanker Carrying Liquefied National Gas Need Clarification.[15] The GAO reviewed six studies conducted since the 9/11 attacks and summarized the findings. It then polled a group of 19 experts from academia, the industry, government consultants and people with experience with explosives. These experts did not completely agree on the findings. However, they did generally agree that in the event of a terrorist attack on LNG the most likely danger to the public is the heat hazard of a fire and that explosions are not likely to occur unless the LNG vapors are in confined spaces. They also agreed that the previous claimed hazards of freeze burns and asphyxiation do not pose a hazard to the public. Although the experts generally agreed on the public safety impacts of an LNG spill, they disagreed on what would be the dimensions of the heat/hazard zone. Half of the experts believed that it was between one and 1.25 miles. The other half thought the estimate was either too conservative or not conservative enough. Also, the experts did not agree on the government's conclusions that only three of the five tanks on a tanker would be involved in a cascading failure. The best conclusion to draw from the GAO study is that further studies are required to clarify uncertainties that spark debate and fear surrounding LNG. According to Jim Wells, GAO Director, Natural Resources and Environment, "If the existing research underestimates, the public is exposed to inappropriate risk. If the research overestimates, we incur costly mitigation measures and we potentially lose the availability to a critical, valuable energy resource going forward."[16]

A third problem associated with LNG is the difficulty in siting regasification plants. In the United States this has been a source of heated debate in recent years as many Americans have adopted a not in my backyard mentality. Due to fears of a potential terrorist attack against an LNG tanker or terminal, the industry has been forced to come up with innovative siting alternatives; namely offshore facilities. A second challenge to siting a regasification plant, especially where the industry is privatized, is the possibility that the industry would not be able to supply qualified personnel to run these operations. It took approximately 40 years to build the first 200 LNG tankers. In 2006, 30 newly built LNG tankers were constructed. This marked a 16 percent increase in the LNG fleet and a 19 percent increase in the total shipping capacity.[17] A major challenge facing the industry is keeping up with crewing demand. Compounding the problem is the fact that many senior LNG officers are retiring and need to be replaced with new, highly skilled mariners. LNG tankers are among the most complex merchant vessels and therefore require the highest level of training for a mariner. Each vessel requires 22 seafarers, which consist of five deck officers and 17 crew members. The total number reaches upward to 70 when vacations, illness and turnover are taken into account.[18] Placing underqualified and unvetted mariners on board these tankers increases risks to safety and security.

Impact on Global Energy Security

LNG's most important attribute is the creation of trade relations and political alliances that so far geography has not allowed. Countries that previously had no energy relations are now growing increasingly dependent on each other thanks to their ability to trade in LNG. In most cases such relations are not only mutually beneficial but they also create positive economic interdependencies that contribute to global stability, prosperity, and security. However, in some cases, LNG enables relations that are not conducive to global security. One good example of this is the strengthening ties between China and Iran at a time when the international community seeks to pressure Iran to halt its pursuit of nuclear weapons technology and stop its support of terrorist groups. Despite Iran's massive reserves it has limited access to the growing Asian market. Without LNG there would be no way for Iran to sell its gas to an emerging energy-consuming giant like China. Iran's desire to strengthen its ties with China (and for that matter India) goes beyond economics. Iran needs China's diplomatic protection in the UN Security Council, where China is a permanent member with veto power. LNG is therefore Iran's geopolitical wildcard. Recognizing the benefit of LNG, Iran increased its efforts to build the necessary infrastructure. In 2004, it signed two major long-term agreements with China to ensure a steady flow of LNG for over 25 years.[19] While the agreement is a positive step toward energy security for China, the move seriously undermines Western-imposed sanctions against Iran for supporting terrorism and pursuing nuclear technology. In fact, China has outwardly opposed sanctions against Iran while paving a path for other countries to do business with Iran. Additionally, having diversity of markets can be used for political and economic leverage by some of the major producers. Russian state-owned energy giant Gazprom, the world's largest natural gas company, for example, has a growing monopoly on natural gas. Yet, Gazprom can only exert pressure on clients with whom it is connected via pipelines. As a major player in the LNG market the company will be able to expand its circle of clients and, hence, use similar tactics against countries with which Russia is at odds.

By increasing LNG imports the United States is faced with a double edge sword. While LNG can increase energy security through diversification and flexibility, so too it can actually impede energy security in that it increases dependency on foreign imports. The EIA projects that by 2030 up to 90 percent of natural gas imported into the United States will be in the form of LNG.[20] This growing dependence increases U.S. vulnerability to possible political and economic pressure as well as increasing the likelihood of placing the entire economy at risk through possible energy disruptions.

LNG is important to America's energy mix. However, for true energy security other alternative energy sources are required. For example, within the 48 contiguous states of the United States, natural gas production has leveled off. Gas fields are becoming costlier and riskier to develop because producers are required to dig deeper and add more rigs to these production sites. Meanwhile, the Outer Continental Shelf (OCS) is estimated to contain a substantial amount of oil and natural gas reserves. Some of these natural gas fields are off limits to development due to environmental concerns, prompting government-imposed drilling restrictions. Many LNG critics claim that by opening up these locations to exploration and production, the United States would become less dependent on natural gas imports. However, once the moratorium on access to these sites is lifted, access to the OCS will not have a significant impact on natural gas production much before 2030, because production would take 5–10 years to commence.[21] Therefore, even by lifting restrictions sooner, it would still be over 15 years before these resources were to make a significant impact on U.S. natural gas production.

There is no easy solution to energy security. Over time, energy efficiency, renewable energy sources and clean coal technologies will help to offset the reliance on natural gas and hence on LNG, reducing dependence on imported energy. However, until these become sufficiently available, many countries will be forced to increase future LNG intake and the sector's ability to grow will largely depend on how both consumers and producers manage the many political, economic and security risks associated with LNG.

Notes

1. *International Energy Outlook 2008,* Energy Information Administration, September 2008, http://www.eia.doe.gov/oiaf/ieo/pdf/0484(2008).pdf; James M. Kendell, *Global Gas Outlook,* Energy Information Administration, A Power Point presentation given at The Aspen Institute, 28 June 2008, http://www.eia.doe.gov/pub/oil_gas/natural_gas/presenta tions/2008/globalgas/globalgas_files/frame.html.

2. There had been discussions in the early 2000s to try to run a natural gas pipeline from the Sakhalin project to Japan. As of 2007, nothing has transpired from these discussions.

3. "International Liquefied Natural Gas (LNG) Imports by Country of Origin, All Countries, 1993–2005," Energy Information Administration, http://www.eia.doe.gov/emeu/international/gastrade.html.

4. *International Energy Outlook 2008,* Energy Information Administration.

5. "World Imports by Origin, 2005," Energy Information Administration, October 10, 2006, http://www.eia.doe.gov/emeu/international/LNGimp2005.xls.

6. *Annual Energy Outlook 2008,* 180.

7. Federal Energy Regulatory Commission, North American LNG Terminals http://www.ferc.gov/industries/lng/indus-act/terminals/lng-approved.pdf.

8. Natural Gas Market Review 2007: Security in a Globalizing Market to 2015, International Energy Agency, 2007, table 42.

9. While Putin did call the idea an interesting one, he did add that he had no plans to create a cartel. M.K. Bhadrakumar, "Gas: Iran Turns up the Heat," *Asia Times,* February 10, 2007.

10. "A Brief History of U.S. LNG Incidents," CH IV International Website, http://www.ch-iv.com/links/history.html.

11. Martin C. Libicki, Peter Chalk, and Melanie Sisson, *Exploring Terrorist Targeting Preferences* (Santa Monica: Rand Corporation, 2007), 63.

12. As the LNG is warmed and returns to its gaseous state, either at a regasification terminal or from simple exposure to the air, it begins to mix with the surrounding air while forming a vapor cloud. This vapor cloud can be ignited and burned if it is within a minimum and maximum concentration of air and vapor. However, it must first vaporize to a range of 5 to 15 percent gas to air before it is capable of burning. This is because with too little oxygen or fuel concentrations below the lower flammability limit, the cloud cannot burn.

13. Mike Hightower et al, "Guidance on Risk Analysis and Safety Implications of a Large Liquefied Natural Gas (LNG) Spill Over Water," *Sandia Report,* SAND2004-6258, December 2004.

14. Paul W. Parfomak, *Liquefied Natural Gas (LNG) Infrastructure Security: Background and Issues for Congress,* CRS Report for Congress, updated May 13, 2008. http://www.ncseonline.org/NLE/CRSreports/08Jun/RL32073.pdf.

15. "Public Safety Consequences of a Liquefied Natural Gas Spill Need Clarification," Testimony of Jim Wells, GAO Director, Natural Resources and Environment before the Committee on Homeland Security, March 20, 2007, http://www.gao.gov/new.items/d07633t.pdf.

16. Ibid.

17. *Natural Gas Market Review 2007: Security in a Globalizing Market to 2015,* International Energy Agency, 2007, table 42.

18. Ibid., 108.

19. Jephraim P. Gundzik, "The Ties that Bind China, Russia, and Iran," *Asia Times,* August 19, 2007.

20. It is difficult to determine the future direction of the global LNG market. Many new international players are entering the market and competition for available sources is growing. Amounts of LNG available to the U.S. markets will likely vary from year to year. *Annual Energy Outlook 2008,* Energy Information Administration, March 2008, http://www.eia.doe.gov/oiaf/aeo/production.html.

21. *Annual Energy Outlook 2007,* Energy Information Administration, February 2007, 51.

CHAPTER 19

Technological Solutions for Energy Security

Paul J. Werbos

The United States and other energy-consuming nations face three major energy security challenges. The first is transportation fuel security: how can we make our transportation sector robust enough to be able to survive the possibility of a major price shock—with crude oil rising to $200 per barrel or $400 or even more—in the soonest possible time? The second is daytime electricity: how can we eliminate the need for us and our allies to import natural gas in growing quantities in order to generate daytime electricity, as soon as possible? The third is baseload electricity: how can we help the world avoid the grave long-term costs of expanding any of the three well-established options for providing the majority of the world's base load electricity—coal, nuclear fission with enrichment, or solar farms—as oil and natural gas become too expensive for that application?

Some may ask: "Why should we worry, even if gasoline should go to $50 per gallon, and the cars available come from the same menu we see today? Why not just change our lifestyle? Why not take bicycles to work, or use public transportation?" Bicycles have a lot to offer our health, but they do not really help us solve the larger problems in the United States. (In some parts of the world, continued use of bicycles and motor scooters does buy us time, but the United States is in no position to tell the Chinese and Indians to keep using bicycles forever.) The reality is that nearly 90 percent of American workers get to work by car, and 84 percent of American workers take more than 10 minutes to get there. If a price shock or supply interruption kept half of these workers from getting to work, the domino effects on the U.S. economy would be devastating. It would be devastating even if we initially relied on the free market to distribute the pain as efficiently as possible. Conversely, if we all end up driving electric cars powered by renewable energy sources, individuals who choose to drive large or fast cars would be hurting no one but themselves by doing so. If Americans all moved out of houses into apartments close to their jobs, and never changed their jobs, then the need for cars would be reduced dramatically—but so would their standard of living.

In any case, this is not really feasible for a very long time to come and would certainly not be feasible politically before a major price shock. On the other hand, once we deploy the technologies that we need for true energy security, we can continue to build houses as big as we choose, without any need for constraints beyond the discipline of the free market.

Some people may ask, "Why not rely on the market to do everything here?" There are two answers. First, even the market requires that *someone* works out the technological details—from the big picture down to the essential specifics. This chapter does not ask: "What can *governments* do to achieve energy security?" It asks: "What can *we* do, all of us together, including especially industry leaders and university researchers?" Government has an essential role in encouraging and facilitating the major changes required here, but only industry can supply the new cars and new energy production systems that we need.

Second, purely economic market-based approaches to these problems tend to be a meat-axe. For example, if we imagine that we live in a world of truly perfect, precognitive markets, then the perfect way to prevent excess CO_2 emissions would be a massive tax on those emissions. The negative impact of such policy on the economy would probably be much greater than the positive impact in improving efficiency. This chapter proposes market-based strategies informed by the technical realities. If we understand the condition of the patient better, we can get away with using a scalpel instead of meat-axe.

The strategies proposed here will not be the usual bureaucratic kinds of 10-year-plan strategies, attached to 6-digit specifications of exactly how much fuel we will use of each kind in every year. Plans like that do not do justice to the uncertainties, the hazards and the opportunities that are the essence of the challenges in front of us. For example, our first goal here is not to reduce the actual use of gasoline; it is to reduce the damage that the U.S. economy would encounter in case of a major oil price rise. The larger goal is to maximize the probability that the human species as a whole attains a secure, sustainable energy system. Tiny incremental improvements that do not help make this transition are mostly worse than useless, because they distract from what we need to do. What is the optimal strategy of action, when our goal is not to make incremental improvements but to get to true energy security, as soon as possible and with maximum probability?

Transportation Fuel Security: How Can We Zero Out Dependence on Oil in the Shortest Possible Time?

The growing need to import oil from unstable parts of the world is a central challenge to U.S national security. If world dependency on those regions continues to grow at the present rate, in 20–30 years the costs and the dangers could grow even larger than they are now. New cars stay on the road in the United States for an average of 15–17 years after they are purchased. Trucks last even longer. Thus, in order to achieve 50 percent or more petroleum fuel-independence in 20–25 years, we have to change half the new cars and trucks being sold in a mere 5–10 years. By 2015 or so, this would require that roughly half the new cars and trucks must be able to operate without any use of gasoline at all, if necessary. There are four proven ways to carry the energy needed to power a car, other than liquid hydrocarbons:

1. Alternative liquid fuels, which could be alcohols like ethanol and methanol or liquids like P-series biofuels, Fischer-Tropsch liquids, mixed alcohols, hydrazine hydrate, or dimethyl hydrazine;
2. Electricity stored in batteries;
3. Gaseous fuels like natural gas (methane), dimethyl ether or hydrogen;
4. Compressed air.

In addition, there are three further serious possibilities today:

5. Electricity stored in new types of ultracapacitors with high energy density;
6. Wind up cars, similar to wind-up toy cars with large rubber bands;
7. Heat batteries, or "thermal storage units."

Any of these technologies could be used in principle to give us a transportation system able to run without hydrocarbons. However, it is not realistic to imagine that half the people buying new cars in the United States in 2015 would be willing to buy cars that cannot be filled up from an existing nationwide infrastructure—gas stations, the electric power grid or (arguably) the natural gas grid. Automobile company research has concluded that the fuel for a car must be available in at least 10 percent of the local gas stations before a normal consumer would be willing to buy the car.[1] In general, liquid fuels allow twice the driving range or more under today's technology with cars that a consumer could afford, compared to electricity or gaseous fuels. Electricity offers at least twice the overall energy efficiency and an easier fit with renewable power sources. Even in the long term, assuming motorists continue to demand a driving range of 300 miles, if liquid fuel prices continue to rise but battery prices do not fall beyond today's best market price, the optimal long-term sustainable solution may actually be similar to the near-term approach proposed below. However, that near-term approach has the advantage of opening the door to more rapid development both of alternative liquid fuels and of electricity storage; it would be a very important stepping-stone to any one of the possible long-term sustainable futures.

GEM Flexibility—The Nearest-Term Option

GEM (Gasoline-Ethanol-Methanol) fuel flexibility formally means that a car can use gasoline, ethanol (an alcohol fuel currently made from crops such as sugar cane and corn) or methanol (an inexpensive merchant fuel that can be made from a wide variety of feedstocks including coal, natural gas, biomass and urban waste) in any mixture, from one day to the next, without voiding its warranty. In practice, GEM flexibility requires two key inexpensive upgrades of a car most economically done at the factory: (a) use of corrosion-resistant gaskets, hoses, engine materials, etc.; and (b) use of adaptive engine control, so as to optimize performance for any mix of fuels. These upgrades also allow the use of more exotic liquid fuels. GEM flexibility was a well-established technology for conventional cars by 1990, and it is much less expensive than hybrid cars or gaseous fuel capability, let alone pure electric or fuel cell cars today. A quick, rough calculation suggests that U.S. consumers might have saved hundreds of billions of dollars per year if we had adopted GEM flexibility already in the 1990s. The calculation actually shows a doubling of U.S. revenue to downstream fuel distribution companies, but a deep reduction in oil import bills. Conversion to GEM flexibility in all new cars could be accomplished in 2–4 years. GEM flexibility also offers greater efficiency in the use of coal and natural gas-based liquid fuels, and something like a doubling in the sustainable potential contribution of biofuels.

In the 1980s, Ford deployed thousands of GEM-flexible Taurus cars in California, at no additional cost compared to conventional cars. Roberta Nichols, representing Ford, estimated that it would cost $300 per car to add this capability to all new cars, in mass production.[2] A major part of that estimate was the cost of better control, and the cost of a more corrosion-resistant gas tank. Because of environmental regulations, stronger gas tanks are now already in use. Advances in computer chips have lowered the cost of control. Auto industry sources estimate that the cost would be about $100–200 per car now and that it would take only about two years to convert auto production to GEM flexibility outside the United States. In the United States, it could take a little longer due to legal delays unless, of course, the law was changed to speed up the process. These facts may seem surprising; therefore, some empirical data may be in order. From January 2003 to May 2008—about five years—the share of GE (gasoline-ethanol) flexible cars sold in Brazil rose from zero to over 80 percent. The technology for GE flexibility is essentially the same as GEM flexibility (though a bit weaker). Furthermore, the companies selling these cars in Brazil are the same as the companies selling cars in the United States; they already have the experience of GE flexibility well-assimilated, as a starting point.

GEM flexibility offers significant benefits to coal-to-liquids technology and biofuels. The most promising coal-to-liquids technology is still based on oxygenated gasification. In 1981, the DOE commissioned the Rand Corporation to analyze cost escalation in the construction of synfuels plants, which were very popular at the time.[3] The report showed relatively promising numbers for the "Texaco" or "Cool Water" technology of oxygenated gasification. In recent years, General Electric purchased this technology from Texaco, and is promoting it as the best "Clean Coal" technology. In China, Shell has agreed to build major new methanol plants (to produce transportation fuel) based on oxygenated gasification. These kinds of plants can also be used to produce hydrocarbons—but at a cost. Higher efficiency and lower cost (and lower waste of resources and less emissions) can be obtained by going to methanol instead of hydrocarbons. Even lower costs can probably be obtained by doing even less processing of the liquids stream coming out of the Fischer-Tropsch process at the heart of these plants. A GEM flexible car could also use these more general Fischer-Tropsch fuels. Likewise, GEM flexible cars would allow the producers of biofuels to produce more fuel from the same biomass, while wasting less energy in the process. At the present time, there is great excitement about developing new technologies for *cellulosic ethanol*—converting sources of cellulose like switchgrass or wood or the husks of sugarcane plants into high quality ethanol, as required by GE-flexible cars not warranted to use methanol. But moonshiners have been making mixed alcohols out of wood and cellulosic plants for many decades. There are well-established processes here, far less expensive than some of the new high purity distillation schemes required for conversion of cellulosic biomass into ethanol. The alcohols are not so pure, but GEM-flexibility does not require as high of a purity level as GE flexibility. Waiting for purity—and paying for it—simply makes no economic sense. If the pure ethanol producers really can do better than expected, GEM cars would certainly open the door to their product too; however, those who doubt whether they could really compete in an open market may be worried about the competition that GEM flexibility would bring.

Electrification of Transportation through Plug-in Hybrid Electric Vehicles (PHEV)

Today's most established hybrid car, the Toyota Prius, recently showed a reduction in gasoline per mile by 47 percent compared to the conventional version of the same car. As other companies catch up with Toyota in hybrid technology, similar gains should be expected. Hybrid technology is still improving even at Toyota. For example Danil Prokhorov has reported a new software controller that can improve the mpg of the Prius hybrid by more than 15 percent with no change in the hardware of the car.[4] Toyota has announced that most of the new cars it produces will be hybrids within ten years—in part because of very strong market pressure and high gasoline prices in most of the developed world. A plug-in hybrid electric vehicle (PHEV) is essentially just a hybrid car or truck with two things added: (a) a larger battery, so that the car has a significant all-electric driving range; and (b) a plug, so that the battery can be recharged by plugging the car into an electric outlet at your home or at a parking lot. A typical consumer, driving a PHEV with 20 mile all-electric driving range, would use electricity to replace about half of the gasoline that would have been used with the usual hybrid. For several years, Toyota has succeeded in doubling its production of hybrids every year. Scaling up to produce PHEVs does not add much additional difficulty here, since a PHEV is basically the same as a hybrid except for the battery. Battery manufacturers are generally optimistic about their ability to scale up quickly— given enough demand and financing, and good enough battery designs.

A widespread use of PHEVs would be a net benefit to the grid, not a net cost. DOE's Pacific Northwest National Laboratory has estimated that 84 percent of U.S. cars, pickup trucks and SUVs could be PHEVs powered by the existing electric power system, without any increase in generation or transmission capacity.[5] A major reason for this conclusion is that the electric transmission grid is now used at less than 50 percent capacity during the night, when most people would be recharging their PHEVs. The National Renewable Energy Laboratory per-formed a similar study, concluding that "there is no need for additional generation capacity, even at 50 percent PHEV penetration."[6] How could so much gasoline be replaced by so little electricity? Part of the reason is unused nighttime trans-mission capacity. But the biggest reason is efficiency. The small gasoline engine at the heart of the Prius hybrid is only 30 percent efficient.[7] The car as a whole, however, outperforms conventional cars, mainly because conventional cars spend most of their time operating far away from the point of maximum efficiency and because they lose energy during braking (unlike hybrids.) But when natural gas (a fuel similar to gasoline in cost and scarcity) is burned to make electricity in large electric power plants, efficiencies as high as 60 percent can be achieved. Thus a PHEV running on that electricity is basically twice as efficient as a regular hybrid and four times as efficient as a conventional car. (Old car batteries also had a 30 percent loss in the charge/discharge cycle, but the new batteries for PHEVs are much better.) Of course, the electricity can also be supplied from less expen-sive or renewable sources, which makes the situation still better for the driver. This high efficiency explains the recent finding by the Electric Power Research Institute and the Natural Resources Defense Council that use of PHEVs could reduce total greenhouse gas emissions substantially, across all nine scenarios they considered, using different assumptions about where the electricity comes from. PHEVs can improve other dimensions of air quality, in addition to the CO_2 ben-efits, so long as the cars are properly controlled. With adaptive engine control, this should be straightforward.[8]

What about the bottom-line costs and benefits to the ordinary consumer? The conventional hybrid car is a borderline investment for the average consumer. With the Toyota Prius today, at $3 or $4 per gallon, the additional cost of the hybrid car is slightly more than the benefit of the fuel savings. For the Prius, the additional cost of the hybrid is about $3,000, of which $1,800 is said to be for the battery and $1,200 the ancillary equipment. Only the increased security or insurance benefit—and tax incentives that reflect that benefit—really justify the purchase. The PHEVs available today are retrofitted hybrid cars, using upgrade kits that cost well over $5,000.[9] Using batteries from the historic large and powerful U.S. battery manufacturers, it is difficult to do much better. But there have been major breakthroughs in bat-teries in the last decade. As an example, Thunder Sky of Shenzhen, China, is now able to supply the 10kwh batteries needed for a PHEV for a cost of $2,000 each in quantity—only $200 more than the usual estimate of the battery cost for a conven-tional hybrid. The manufacturing plant itself is nonpolluting, and the recycling is-sues are easier to deal with than the recycling issues for ordinary lead-acid batteries. The cost per kwh is less for larger batteries. The Massachusetts-based A123 Systems also has a modern lithium-ion battery used in Black and Decker tools, and a new relationship with GM. If batteries suitable for PHEVs can be made at a cost similar to the battery cost for conventional hybrids, then PHEVs will become a value proposi-tion for the consumer better than conventional hybrids. Strong incentives could be important in getting to that point. (For purposes of this strategy, new ultracapacitors with high energy density are just another important new battery option.)

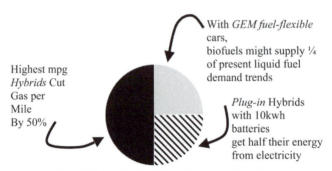

With *GEM fuel-flexible* cars, biofuels might supply ¼ of present liquid fuel demand trends

Highest mpg *Hybrids* Cut Gas per Mile By 50%

Plug-in Hybrids with 10kwh batteries get half their energy from electricity

Figure 19.1 Best Near-Term Option to Zero out Need for Gasoline

Gaseous Fuels

Several nations have experimented with cars carrying special fuel tanks capable of holding gaseous fuels such as natural gas or hydrogen. This chapter does not focus on such solutions for several reasons. First, natural gas—especially *pipeline* natural gas—is a scarce and valuable fuel, no more plentiful than oil itself. Since the lion share of the world's natural gas reserves is essentially owned by Russia and OPEC members, there is no national security benefit in shifting from oil to natural gas. Second, the upgrades cost on the order of $1,000-$3,000 and take a lot of space in the trunk of the car. PHEVs cost more, but they offer larger long-term reductions in fuel cost, and a stronger pathway to using renewables as the ultimate source of energy. Hydrogen makes even less sense. Contrary to popular belief, hydrogen is not an energy source but an energy carrier, just like electricity. In this context it should be compared with electricity. There are two ways to make hydrogen: the first is by re-forming natural gas either at the fuel station or on board the vehicle. But, again, shifting from oil to natural gas to fuel our cars would do nothing to improve energy security. The other way to make hydrogen is using electricity to split water into hydrogen and oxygen, in which case we need to store the hydrogen on board the car and use an expensive fuel cell to convert it back into electricity. This is an expensive and highly inefficient process. We could instead simply plug the car in and use electricity directly, with no new infrastructure required other than perhaps an extension cord (see Figure 19.1).

Transportation Fuel Strategy Summary

The core strategy here is simply to accelerate the arrival of GEM-flexible PHEVs as much as possible, for the sake of national security. More precisely, the four measures of progress that should be maximized are:

1. The market penetration of GEM-flexible highway vehicles, fuel-efficient hybrids, PHEVs, and—best of all—GEM-flexible PHEVs;

2. The development of technology that improves the quality and reduces the cost of GEM-flexible cars and PHEVs, such as better batteries, better battery management systems, adaptive engine control and the development of supply chain systems that accelerate the use of the best available technology;

3. Likewise, the technology (and its penetration) for supplying alternate liquid fuels, both from biological and nonbiological sources, to be selected by market forces with proper incentives for sustainability in biofuel production and proper correction for net production of greenhouse gasses; this includes GEM-flexible gas stations;

4. The penetration and technology for connecting PHEVs to the electric power grid, both at home and in parking lots, so as to provide maximum value to the electric power grid across different times of day.

These values are not designed to minimize the actual use of gasoline. The goal here is to move us away from an insecure monopoly situation, where the consumer has no choice but gasoline (or diesel fuel) to use in his/her car, to a new market competition between different forms of energy, so that a user can decide on a day-to-day basis which fuel to use, and how to make the tradeoff between driving range (always best with gasoline or advanced liquid fuels) versus cost (best with electricity). If we believe in the power of market competition and consumer choice, then this approach is far better than today's policy of enshrining gasoline as the one and only government-backed winner. More precisely, this strategy aims to serve four longer-term goals: first, to create a resilient system for transportation energy, able to adapt quickly and efficiently to changing conditions of price and availability of fuels and electricity—continuing to use gasoline so long as gasoline is affordable enough as judged by the consumer; second, to improve efficiency in the production and use of fuels and electricity; third, to improve the efficiency of the electric power grid itself, by providing additional storage available to the grid and making better use of night-time transmission capability; and fourth, as a byproduct of competition, to create a transportation system that can respond quickly and efficiently to incentives or taxes based on environmental conditions.

Transportation Fuel beyond Cars and Trucks

Oil-based fuels are used in more than just cars and trucks in the transportation sector. They are also used in buses, off-highway vehicles, trains and airplanes. Because the bulk of our dependency comes from cars and trucks, we need to focus our energy on them until and unless we are truly moving as fast as we can in that sector. Nevertheless, buses and off-highway vehicles can sometimes provide a good market-worthy test bed for GEM flexibility and battery-based technologies. Trains present a different situation. Most modern trains use highly efficient diesel-electric hybrid engines, and use massive amounts of energy per vehicle. New technologies like advanced Stirling may allow fuel flexibility in trains, but they are not yet ready for use in that sector, and trains are not the best test bed to start with. Electrification for trains is a known, expensive, technology. An academic proposal for a new form of magnetic levitation technology, which might allow electricity-based trains to move faster and more cheaply and compete more effectively with passenger jets dependent on liquid fuels, is an exciting possibility for nations like China, which already make heavy use of passenger rail and have not yet built up their jet fleets; however, it should not be allowed to distract from more urgent work on passenger vehicles.

Aviation is also quite different from cars and trucks as it is basically stuck with liquid fuels with very high energy per kilogram. Fuels with high energy density are usually more difficult to work with than low density fuels like ethanol or methanol, because high energy density implies more possibility of explosions and fires, when all else is equal. On the other hand, low density fuels require airplanes to carry more fuel. This makes little sense at a time when air carriers are looking for ways to reduce their load. Higher carbon fuels like synthetic jet fuel from coal or methane are becoming increasingly popular among airlines and air forces. But if we are to focus on low carbon fuels, fuel flexibility can only be achieved by using high-energy low-carbon fuels like hydrazine hydrate or the rocket fuel dimethyl hydrazine. These two fuels are just examples—both are easier to handle than hydrazine proper—but their penetration of the aviation fuel market still faces many technological and regulatory barriers.

New Technologies for Electricity Generation

For practical purposes, there are two very different markets for electricity—the daytime market, peaking a few hours after noon, and the 24/7 market for steady base-load power, day and night. In the United States, daytime electricity is supplied more and more by consuming natural gas. Natural gas is more expensive than coal or nuclear fuel, but the low capital cost of natural gas generators makes them attractive as a source of electricity that only gets turned on a few hours every day.

A rational energy strategy for the power sector should include efforts to bring renewable power technologies to compete with natural gas for the daytime electricity market worldwide. It should also support early research on breakthrough energy concepts that show some hope of being able to produce as much energy, sustainably and affordably, as coal or nuclear fission.

From basic physics, it is easy to calculate that solar energy has the potential to generate something like 100 times the world's total use of electricity, even if solar farms are deployed only on desert land, which is enough to meet demand, but only if the technologies become more affordable. As this book goes to press, evidence is becoming more convincing that the United States, China and several other nations also have enough raw wind resources to meet all their needs, but this would be practicable only if the storage and intelligence in the power grid could be sufficiently improved.

A combination of better batteries, thermal storage and a true, adaptive time-shifting brain-like intelligent power grid would allow us to use daytime solar energy to supply the baseload market, or wind energy to supply a larger fraction of the base load market.[10] But there is still a major cost premium involved. The rational strategy is thus to develop in parallel novel solar power technologies and the intelligent grid. These core technologies offer large unmet opportunities to make progress many times faster than is happening as yet anywhere in the world today.

Rooftop silicon based photo-voltaic solar power (like wind) can be an excellent test bed for inserting new intelligent control technology into the power grid. Well-established traditional control methods simply have not allowed us to pay solar power providers the full value of what their electricity would be worth, in an optimal power grid. Yet, rooftop solar—useful as it is—is not likely to produce enough electricity to replace the need for natural gas in electric utilities.

Challenges and Opportunities in Cutting the Cost of Earth-Based Solar Farms as Soon as Possible

There are two different technologies available to electric utilities in building solar farms to provide daytime electricity: photovoltaics (PV) or solar cells and solar thermal systems, which concentrate sunlight to provide heat, which is then converted into electricity. The key strategic goal here is to build solar farms cheaply enough that they can compete with natural gas in generating daytime electricity nationwide, as soon as possible. California utilities are the leaders in developing solar farms in the United States, in part because they pay a high price for daytime electricity from natural gas, and in part because the Mojave desert gives them a source of steady sunlight large enough to meet all the electricity needs of the country (day and night) if we could afford to use it. In 2005 Southern California Edison agreed to buy up to 500 megawatts from Stirling Energy Systems (SES) at a price "well under" the 11.3 cents per kilowatt-hour (kwh), the price Southern California Edison paid for daytime electricity from natural gas. The SES technology is a form of solar thermal power, pioneered by the Sandia laboratories of DOE, using moveable "dishes" made up of mirrors to track the sun. Because photovoltaics are more expensive than mirrors, and because they require a large investment in "balance of system" technology and installation, they are not likely to get under 11.3 cents per kwh total cost in the foreseeable future. Our best hope of displacing natural gas nationwide at the shortest possible time lies with solar thermal power. Beyond the United States, the World Bank has led the world's efforts to develop cost-effective solar farms, publishing a number of comprehensive assessments of solar thermal technology.[11] Historically, the Bank has focused on older more proven technologies, like the large-scale solar "trough" technologies or heliostats, which focus light on to a liquid like water. These technologies collect hot water from a large area, so that they can use large efficient systems to convert the heat to electricity. SCE has also funded projects to try that kind of technology in California, but the full costs in the United States have been in the neighborhood of 20 cents per kwh. The World Bank has reported costs as low as 12–13 cents in other parts of the world. Since labor costs and installation are the main cost for any of these solar systems, it is not surprising that the cost is higher in the United States than in Africa. Because the trough technology is a large-scale technology and relatively mature, it is our best hope for beating 11.3 cents in California, let alone competing across the entire country. Most of the United States pays less than California for daytime electricity—utilities in the East coast pay as little as 8 cents per kwh, on average, for electric power between noon and 8 PM, the peak time—and most of the United States has far less reliable sunlight than the Mojave desert. If one were to install gigawatt-sized solar farms in the dry and sunny parts of Texas, it would cost about 2 cents per kwh to carry that power all the way from Texas to the East Coast. Solar farms could compete with natural gas nationwide, if the total cost of generation and power conditioning could be brought down to 6 cents per kwh. But is that really possible? In order to maximize the probability of success in getting to 6 cents per kwh, consider the following strategy:

- Maximum continued support for the existing efforts led by SES and SCE (albeit with some fine tuning and augmented funding to exploit new technology opportunities) to deploy moveable dishes that maximize solar exposure.
- Substantial new efforts to try to develop two promising approaches to double the efficiency in going from heat to electricity. (This could double the electricity output from a given dish, and thereby cut the cost per kwh in half).
- Efforts to retune the design of the reflectors so that they can be mass-produced in existing underutilized factories making body parts for the automobile industry.
- High-risk background efforts to develop construction automation technology to reduce the cost of physically setting up the dishes.

The two promising approaches to doubling efficiency are: fourth generation Stirling engines, as proposed by Sobey and Johansson,[12] and a higher-risk higher-potential new technology, the Johnson Thermo-Electric Converter (JTEC).[13] JTEC is a new general-purpose technology for converting heat differences to electricity. If it works out as expected, and turns out to be inexpensive enough, it could also be used to replace the 30 percent-efficient gasoline engines in hybrid cars. This would reduce the requirements for liquid fuel by another factor of two. Cost is less of an issue in the solar power application, where the bulk of the costs are for building the dish itself. Fourth generation Stirling is less risky, technically, but presents other challenges.

Because of their modular nature, solar dishes might well be a suitable target for modern construction automation technology. Probably this would require a new partnership between the world's experts in construction robotics in Japan, a U.S. company like Caterpillar capable of building the large robot/vehicles in the United States, and leaders in brain-like computational intelligence. It is too early to know whether this is a realistic option, but the potential benefits are large enough to warrant a serious effort to find out what can be done. Construction automation may also be the greatest hope for lowering the cost of trough style solar farms to compete with natural gas. Nevertheless, dish systems may be a better test bed for construction automation, because they may be easier to assemble. All of these activities require a highly adaptive approach, of course, as we buy new information about what we can do.

Conclusion

Technologies are now within reach that could totally eliminate our need to import oil and eliminate our need to burn fossil fuel to generate electricity, at little or no cost to the consumer. To reach this goal, we need more focused and innovative near-term research, but simple regulatory fixes can get us a large part of the way.

What would it cost to require that all new cars should be GEM flexible—and to pay a $200 incentive payment back to manufacturers to compensate them for this? If 15 million new cars are sold each year in the U.S., this would work out to a cost of $3 billion per year—much less than the potential savings of oil at over $100 per barrel even when long-term national security benefits are not accounted for. Some lobbyists have labeled this idea a government mandate. But really, this is closer in spirit to the Open Standards for Digital Television that the U.S. Congress has ordered starting in 2009. The goal is not to mandate a choice of fuel, but to establish open fuel standards: open standards for competition in the fuel market. The new standards for the television industry are estimated to cost much more than the $3 billion, but it has been agreed that the value of open competition in the television industry is large enough to justify the cost and the standards. Is digital television really more important to national security and the U.S. economy than our dependence on oil from OPEC?

Notes

The author is an employee of the U.S. government. The views presented in this chapter do not represent the official views of any part of the government and should not be construed to represent any agency, determination, or policy.

1. Roberta Nichols, *The Methanol Story: A Sustainable Fuel for the Future, Journal of Scientific & Industrial Research,* 62 (January-February 2003): 97–105, www.werbos.com/energy.htm (with permission).

2. Ibid.

3. R. E. Horvath, S. J. Bodilly, R. W. Hess, E. W. Merrow and K. E. Phillips (Rand Corporation), *Analysis of Selected Energy Technology Cost Estimates,* WD-1098-2-ORNL (planned as R-2571-ORNL), March 1982. For related work see www.rand.org/pubs/notes/N1720 and www.rand.org/pubs/notes/2009/N2063.pdf.

4. Danil Prokhorov, "Toyota Prius HEV Neurocontrol and Diagnostics," *Neural Networks,* 21, no. 2–3 (March-April 2008).

5. Michael Kintner-Meyer, Kevin Schneider and Robert Pratt, *Impacts Assessment of Plug-In Hybrid Vehicles On Electric Utilities and Regional U.S. Power Grids,* Pacific Northeast National Laboratory, PNNL-SA 53700 and PNNL-SA-53523, www.pnl.gov/energy/eed/etd/publications.stm.

6. P. Denholm and W. Short, *An Evaluation of Utility System Impacts and Benefits of Optimally Dispatched Plug-In Hybrid Electric Vehicles.* National Renewable Energy Laboratory NREL Technical Report NREL/TP-620-40293, revised October 2006, 15.

7. *IEEEUSA Position Statement: Plug-In Electric Hybrid Vehicles,* June 2007, www.ieeeusa. org/policy/positions/PHEV0607.pdf.

8. M. Duvall and E. Knipping, *Environmental Assessment of Plug-In Hybrid Electric Vehicles,* Report by the Electric Power Research Institute and the Natural Resources Defense Council, July 2007, http://www.epri-reports.org/Volume1R2.pdf.

9. W. D. Jones, "Take this Car and PLUG IT," *IEEE SPECTRUM,* July 2005, http://www. spectrum.ieee.org/jul05/1572.

10. Paul Werbos, "ADP: Goals, Opportunities and Principles," in Jennie Si, Andrew G. Barto, Warren Buckler Powell and Don Wunsch, eds. *Handbook of Learning and Approximate Dynamic Programming* (IEEE Press Series on Computational Intelligence, Wiley-IEEE Press, 2004).

11. World Bank Global Environment Facility, Assessment of the World Bank/GEF Strategy for the Market Development of Concentrating Solar Thermal Power. World Bank 2006, http://siteresources.worldbank.org/GLOBALENVIRONMENTFACILITYGEFOPER ATIONS/Resources/Publications-Presentations/Solar-Thermal.pdf.

12. Sobey and Johansson (2006) The Status of Double Acting Swash Plate Drive Stirling Engines (DA/SH). www.werbos.com/energy.htm (with permission).

13. Logan Ward, "Super Soaker Inventor Aims to Cut Solar Costs in Half," *Popular Mechanics,* January 8, 2008, http://www.popularmechanics.com/science/earth/4243793.html.

CHAPTER 20

A Nuclear Renaissance?

Charles D. Ferguson

Within the confines of the current electricity production and distribution system, for the next few decades and even longer term, nuclear energy offers the capability to generate a tremendous amount of electricity. Unlike most of the readily available oil reserves, uranium ore, which is needed to fuel nuclear power plants, is largely present in non-Middle Eastern countries. Many of the major uranium mining countries, such as Australia and Canada, are friendly to the United States. Also positively for energy security, uranium is much more plentiful as a long-term energy source than oil. In addition, plutonium produced from uranium could extend the supplies of nuclear energy almost 100-fold. Moreover, thorium deposits offer another route for hundreds of years of nuclear energy.[1] Although uranium, plutonium, and thorium would make nuclear energy from fission, nuclear fusion energy could, in principle, provide thousands of years or perhaps even longer supplies of electricity. Because commercializing fusion energy and industrializing the thorium nuclear fuel cycle appear decades away, the focus here is on the prospects for uranium and plutonium to contribute to energy security in the near and intermediate terms. While expanded use of nuclear energy can enhance energy security, it can increase security risks from nuclear weapons programs and nuclear terrorism, and can pose safety hazards from highly radioactive waste and potential nuclear accidents. Thus, greater governmental and industrial attention and resources are needed to address these safety and security risks if nuclear energy is to have a longer term future.

Basics of the Nuclear Fuel Cycle: Atoms for Peace and War

The immense benefits and risks of nuclear energy stem from the vast latent power inside the tiny volume of the atomic nucleus. Fissioning only one nucleus of uranium, for example, releases several hundred times more energy than the amount of chemical energy typically needed to free an electron from an atom.

In comparison to fossil fuels, one nuclear fuel pellet has an equivalent energy of three barrels of oil or one ton of coal.[2] To illustrate that only a few nuclear weapons can cause far more damage than an armada of conventional weapons, President Dwight D. Eisenhower in his "Atoms for Peace" speech said, "A single [nuclear] air group, whether afloat or land-based, can now deliver to any reachable target a destructive cargo exceeding in power all the bombs that fell on Britain in all of World War II."[3] But it is not easy to release nuclear energy either in reactors or bombs. Both nuclear reactors and bombs need fissile material. "Fissile" refers to the ability of a nucleus to easily fission, or split in two, if it absorbs a neutron. Neutrons can move slowly or rapidly, but slow, or thermal energy, neutrons increase the odds for fission to occur in fissile material. An absorbed neutron triggers a fissile nucleus to split apart. Fission thus causes a heavy nucleus to become two medium-sized nuclei, which are radioactive. These radioactive fission products add to the burden of nuclear waste disposal. The benefit of fission comes from the released energy.

The stability of a substance's nucleus determines whether that substance is fissile. Most nuclei are not fissile because the neutrons and protons they contain are tightly bound together. Imagine a tug-of-war between two competing forces inside a nucleus. The force of electromagnetism wants to push apart the "like" positively charged protons but has no effect on the uncharged neutrons. Thus, if there were no attractive force, nuclei would fly apart. The strong nuclear force, however, provides the glue that keeps protons and neutrons stuck together. But the catch is that this force is short ranged—most effective over the width of a proton or neutron—whereas electromagnetism has an infinite range but decreases in strength as one over the distance squared. Picturing the very strong but short attractive pulls and the less strong but farther range negative pushes, one can see that small nuclei with relatively few neutrons and protons are, in general, more tightly bound than heavier nuclei with many neutrons and protons. The less tightly bound a nucleus is, the more susceptible it is to fission.

Due to the way in which protons and neutrons are arranged and thus bound inside heavy nuclei, those materials with an odd number of protons and neutrons are typically fissile in contrast to those with an even number. The number of protons and neutrons is called the atomic mass of a material, and the number of protons is called the atomic number. The atomic number determines the chemical properties of an element because chemistry depends on electromagnetic forces, resulting from the number of protons in an element's nucleus. Each element has its own unique atomic number. For example, the element uranium always has 92 protons. But the number of neutrons inside a uranium nucleus can vary and thus result in different isotopes of this element. Uranium-235, for example, has 92 protons and 143 neutrons, and uranium-238 has 92 protons but has 146 neutrons. The differing numbers of neutrons gives these two isotopes different nuclear properties. From the standpoint of reactors and bombs, uranium-235 is more desirable because it is fissile whereas uranium-238 is not.

Because uranium-235 is far less abundant than uranium-238, reactor builders and bomb makers have to work harder to fulfill their ambitions. In nature, only 0.711 percent of uranium is uranium-235 while 99.283 percent is uranium-238; the remainder of 0.0054 percent is uranium-234. The concentration of uranium-235 is much too low to power nuclear bombs, which ideally require 90 percent or greater concentrations. The concentration process is typically termed "enrichment." Highly enriched uranium (HEU), which can fuel bombs, ranges from 20 percent to more than 90 percent concentration of uranium-235. Low enriched uranium (LEU) ranges from slightly enriched 1 or 2 percent to just under 20 percent concentration of uranium-235.

Most commercial power reactors typically use LEU with 3 to 5 percent uranium-235. Some reactors such as the Canadian-designed CANDU can be fueled with natural uranium, but to compensate for the very low concentration of uranium-235 they need to use a special type of water, heavy water, to make the nuclear reactions happen. Heavy water consists of deuterium, an isotope of hydrogen with a heavier mass, bound to oxygen. By contrast, ordinary or light water consists of two atoms of hydrogen bound to one atom of oxygen. Heavy water is better than light water in providing more slow neutrons available for fission and thus less uranium-235 is needed for fueling heavy water reactors. To acquire heavy water, a CANDU reactor operator would need to invest in a heavy water distillation plant while saving money in not having to buy enriched uranium.

Light water reactor operators would need to invest in uranium enrichment services. While there are various ways to enrich uranium, only two are now used commercially. The gaseous diffusion method feeds uranium hexafluoride gas through porous barriers. These barriers are made of semi-permeable membranes that preferentially allow passage of the slightly less massive uranium-235 hexafluoride gas molecules while the slightly heavier uranium-238 hexafluoride molecules lag behind. Developed during the Manhattan Project, gaseous diffusion is still used by the United States. France also has a commercial-scale diffusion plant. But both countries are moving away from this method because it uses more energy than gaseous centrifugation, the more prevalent commercial method.

Gaseous centrifugation uses the physical principle of centrifugal force to separate uranium-235 from uranium-238. Visualize a rapidly spinning merry-go-round in which the riders feel a force directed away from the axis of rotation. Because this centrifugal force is proportional to mass, heavier riders would feel a stronger push. Similarly, heavier uranium-238 hexafluoride molecules tend to congregate near the outer wall of the centrifuge's rotor whereas lighter uranium-235 hexafluoride molecules are more concentrated near the axis of rotation. A centrifuge's enrichment ability depends on the length of the rotor and the spinning frequency. The longer the rotor and the greater the frequency, the greater enrichment capability a centrifuge has. For example, Iran would need 3,000 one-meter long P-1 centrifuges—the type procured from the A. Q. Khan nuclear black market—to make enough highly enriched uranium for one bomb in about a year.

For comparison, only a few hundred of the 10-meter tall U.S.-built centrifuges would be enough for making an equivalent amount of weapons-usable uranium. Thus, the same enrichment technology can make both LEU for commercial reactors and HEU for bombs.

Like enrichment, reprocessing of spent nuclear fuel poses proliferation dangers. Reprocessing is a chemical technique used to separate plutonium from spent fuel. This spent fuel comes from a reactor, which has consumed uranium in fresh fuel. The fissile isotope uranium-235 provides almost all of the nuclear energy during the time period shortly following fueling of a reactor. Additional nuclear energy is eventually produced by the fissioning of plutonium. While fresh uranium fuel does not contain plutonium, reactors produce fissile plutonium from non-fissile uranium-238. A uranium-238 nucleus absorbs a neutron to become uranium-239. After two radioactive decays typically occurring within a few days, uranium-239 becomes plutonium-239, a fissile material useful for powering reactors or bombs.

Because any enrichment or reprocessing plant is a latent factory for making weapons-usable nuclear materials, strict controls are needed to prevent misuse of these facilities. These controls are called nuclear safeguards. Safeguards comprise a set of inspections on a country's nuclear facilities and nuclear materials.[4] Inspectors try to determine if the operators of these facilities have diverted nuclear materials into bomb programs. Safeguards are not perfect. That is, a country that wants to make nuclear bombs could do so if it has enrichment or reprocessing technologies.

But safeguards, if diligently applied, raise the costs of nuclear proliferation. If subject to safeguards, a proliferator would have to invest in covert facilities. If inspectors have adequate access to investigate nuclear facilities and interview technicians, a proliferator would run a relatively high risk of getting caught. Nonetheless, there is always the risk that a country with nuclear facilities could abrogate its safeguards obligations, kicking out inspectors and launching an overt nuclear weapons program. But by doing so, that country has announced its intention, and then the international community, committed to stopping the spread of nuclear bombs, would have the responsibility to act. Even if a country has not abrogated safeguards but still has violated some of its safeguards commitments, the international community should act if the violation constitutes a threat to international peace and security.[5]

Whether the international community has a strong enough will to act is being tested by Iran. Iran has built a pilot-scale enrichment plant at Natanz and plans to build an even larger commercial-scale enrichment plant. In early 2008, Iran had assembled about 3,000 centrifuges into the pilot plant—thus giving the Iranians a starter-kit for making a bomb's worth of weapons-grade uranium within a year once they have mastered the operation of the plant. While this plant has been subject to safeguards inspections from the International Atomic Energy Agency, the fear is that Iran could have a covert facility or could break out of its safeguards commitments in the future. Because Iran did not declare this facility in a timely manner and had acquired enrichment technology through the nuclear black market, the United States, France, Germany, and the United Kingdom have suspected that Iran intends to make nuclear weapons. Iranian leaders, however, have always described its nuclear program as peaceful, with the intention of providing greater energy security for Iran. The purported purpose of Iran's nuclear program is to diversify electricity production, thereby freeing up more natural gas that Iran could sell. Natural gas and oil are Iran's chief export commodities.

In response to Iran's increasing latent capability to make nuclear weapons, the United States, its European partners, Russia, and China have imposed sanctions through United Nations Security Council resolutions. These sanctions, as of early 2008, are relatively weak and have yet to persuade Tehran to suspend its enrichment program. Also, apparently in response to Shia Iran's nuclear activities, neighboring Sunni Arab countries have expressed interest in nuclear power programs. While Persian Gulf states such as Kuwait, Qatar, Saudi Arabia, and the United Arab Emirates have described this interest in terms of energy diversification and power for water desalination, a peaceful nuclear power program could provide the political cover for nuclear weapons programs. As long as these countries do not acquire enrichment or reprocessing facilities, however, the proliferation likelihood would be low. In particular, these countries could be persuaded to forgo developing these facilities and only acquire nuclear fuel from existing suppliers, as many fuel service proposals in recent years have offered.[6]

Even if the nuclear proliferation danger can be minimized, new nuclear power countries pose another risk. Because they have no experience in operating commercial reactors, they have a higher likelihood of causing nuclear accidents. The nuclear industry fears that a major accident anywhere could harm the prospects for greater use of nuclear power everywhere. The widespread consequences of the 1986 Chernobyl nuclear accident caused the industry to do more to make nuclear power safer. It formed the World Association of Nuclear Operators (WANO), which performs peer reviews of commercial nuclear power plants.[7] While self-policing organizations such as WANO play an important role, regulatory agencies independent of undue industry or government influence are even more essential. Nuclear regulatory agencies in countries established in producing nuclear power and the International Atomic Energy Agency's Department of Nuclear Safety face the immense challenge of helping some two dozen countries that need regulatory assistance.

Nuclear Energy's Present Contribution to Energy Security

As of early 2008, 31 countries use nuclear power to produce electricity. For these countries, nuclear energy has provided greater energy security by reducing reliance on fossil fuels from unstable regions. It is important to realize that currently nuclear energy is used only to make electricity. Most of this electricity powers lighting and electronic appliances in homes and businesses. Some countries, such as Finland, France, and Sweden, make use of nuclear-generated electricity to supply a significant portion of home and business heating. While nuclear-generated electricity does provide some energy for public transportation in many subway systems, nuclear has yet to make a significant contribution to the transportation sector. Because almost all cars and trucks use petroleum, nuclear-generated electricity so far has a very limited role in powering vehicles. That situation could change if there is a switch to more electricity-powered vehicles and to fuel cell vehicles, as discussed in the next section.

Many nuclear power plants have more than one nuclear reactor. The total global commercial reactors have a combined electrical power rating of about 380 Gigawatts (GW). (One GW equals 1,000 Megawatts (MW).) Typically, a large commercial reactor is rated at 1,000 MW of electrical power, although some of the newer reactors under construction are larger than 1,000 MW with electrical power ratings upwards of 1,600 MW. To imagine what a 1,000 MW reactor can do, picture a city in the developed world of about a half-million people, which is comparable to Washington, DC. This reactor could provide the electricity needs of such a city.

In the United States, nuclear energy currently generates about 19 percent of the nation's electricity from 104 commercial reactors. Nuclear energy provides about 8 percent of the total U.S. energy consumption because electricity comprises about 40 percent of total U.S. energy use. To be sure, nuclear energy has reduced U.S. reliance on oil over the past thirty years. In 1975, only two years after the 1973 oil embargo, petroleum powered 15 percent of U.S. electricity. In contrast, by 2005, oil had dropped to only 3 percent of U.S. electricity needs and that was mainly for peak electrical power demands. For comparison, nuclear power, which is optimally operated at base-load electricity generation, that is, constant power output rather than cycling up and down to meet changes in demand, went from 9 percent in 1975 to almost 21 percent in 2004. From 2004 to late 2007, the share of nuclear power in the U.S. electricity production mix actually decreased. In recent years, utilities have been building and operating more power plants fired by natural gas. By contrast, no utility has ordered a new nuclear power plant in more than 30 years.

Despite this stagnation in nuclear power plant orders, at least three factors explain why nuclear power rose from 9 percent proportional use in the mid-1970s to about 20 percent in the 2004 to 2007 period. Although no new nuclear power plants have been ordered since 1978 and then built, several plants ordered prior to that date were completed during the 1980s and even into the 1990s, and several plants have received license renewals. Second, after the 1979 Three Mile Island accident, the U.S. nuclear industry devoted substantial attention to safety and power plant performance. As a result, power plants stayed at peak power for longer periods—in the industry this is called increasing the plant load factor. Concurrently, the industry shortened the shut-down time for maintenance and refueling, further allowing longer periods of operation at high power levels. Third, many U.S. nuclear power operators applied to the Nuclear Regulatory Commission to grant power up-ratings. That is, plants that were nominally rated at say 1,000 MW were allowed to bump up their power ratings a few percent more and for some reactors, more than 10 percent, thus allowing more electricity generation without building more plants.

Globally, nuclear power production has slightly declined in recent years after reaching a peak of 444 commercial reactors in 2002. As of the end of 2007, nuclear energy generated about 16 percent of the world's electricity from 439 commercial power reactors.[8] Different regions of the world vary significantly in the amount of nuclear power produced from only two commercial reactors in all of Africa to more than 120 in Europe. In Africa, only South Africa has one nuclear power plant at Koeberg. But because of severe electricity shortages resulting from poor planning in recent decades, South Africa urgently needs more electricity. The South African government has been considering building a half dozen or more nuclear plants in the coming decade and has discussed such construction with Areva, the French nuclear plant manufacturer.[9] Additionally, South Africa could try to move forward with building Pebble Bed Modular Reactors, small to medium power rating reactors that were partially developed by South African engineers. But technical and financial uncertainties have cast doubt on whether South Africa will build these reactors.[10]

In Asia, a few countries produce significant portions of their electricity from nuclear energy while most Asian countries generate little or no electricity from this source. Japan with 55 reactors, providing about 30 percent of its electricity, stands out as the Asian leader. But the July 16, 2007, Japanese earthquake, which forced the shut down of the Kashiwasaki-Kariwa nuclear power plant, the world's largest nuclear power plant, raises concerns about the further expansion of nuclear energy in Japan. Japanese officials would prefer to increase nuclear use to no more than 40 percent of the total electricity mix.[11]

Japan also stands out as one of the few countries, including France, India, Russia, and the United Kingdom, with a reprocessing plant. Energy security fears have convinced the Japanese government that it should reduce its reliance on external supplies of nuclear fuel. With scarce natural resources, Japan has mostly imported nuclear fuel from the United States. But in the 1970s, Tokyo requested U.S. permission to reprocess spent fuel to extract plutonium to fuel power plants. Although the United States at that time had changed its domestic policy to stop reprocessing and had decided to encourage other countries to also stop this practice, Japan was allowed to proceed with building a reprocessing plant. One of the conditions on the construction was to subject the Rokkasho reprocessing plant to continuous on-site inspections from safeguards inspectors. A facility that has cost more than four times its initial projected cost of $2 billion, Rokkasho is almost ready for full operations, as of early 2008. According to Japanese officials, reprocessing has raised the cost of electricity by about 10 percent. Because of energy security concerns, Japan has been willing to pay this extra price. Nonetheless, Japan has yet to fuel any reactors with fuel made from plutonium because of public concerns and delays in certification of the reactors to consume plutonium.

Like Japan, South Korea relies significantly on nuclear energy for about 38 percent of its electricity. Energy security concerns have also influenced the South

Korean government's decision to support nuclear power. But unlike Japan, South Korea had not received U.S. permission to reprocess U.S.-origin fuel. The United States has discouraged such activity because it feared a nuclear arms race on the Korean Peninsula. North Korea had exploited its medium sized research reactor at Yongbyon to make plutonium for weapons. Despite these concerns, the George W. Bush administration has brought South Korea into research on pyroprocessing, which is a reprocessing technology that may offer proliferation-resistant nuclear fuel. While pyroprocessing would not completely separate plutonium from other radioactive elements, it would not meet the strict "spent fuel standard" of proliferation resistance defined by the U.S. National Academy of Sciences.[12]

Although China and India are far behind Japan and South Korea in harnessing nuclear power, they have ambitious plans to build many nuclear power plants in the coming years. Currently, China and India produce about 2 to 3 percent of their electricity from nuclear energy. By 2020, both countries are striving to double this proportional use. But considering the projected 6 to 8 percent annual growth in electricity demand, these countries would have to almost quintuple the power production from nuclear plants. This presents a daunting challenge. Most likely, China and India will continue to rely mainly on coal to generate electricity for the foreseeable future.

Turning to Europe, the nuclear industry confronts conflicting political forces. On the one hand, public opposition has forced the phase out of nuclear power plants in Belgium, Germany, Italy, Spain, and Sweden. All but Italy still operate nuclear power plants but plan to shut down these plants when they reach or near their end of life within the next ten to twenty years. While current or future governments in these countries may change this decision, nuclear power faces a highly uncertain future there. In contrast, Finland, France, Russia, and several countries in Eastern Europe favor expanded use of nuclear power. Energy security concerns have played a major role in these countries' outlooks on nuclear energy. France presents a unique case of perhaps too much reliance on nuclear power. It has an overcapacity in electricity production and now generates about 78 percent of its electricity from nuclear power. Because of the overcapacity, France has often sold electricity to neighboring countries. But it has been at times unable to sell this energy and has been forced to shut down nuclear plants on certain weekends.[13]

Potential Future Contribution to Energy Security

As France's electricity overcapacity suggests, a country could find itself having too much nuclear energy. But if France and other countries were able to use electricity to power cars and trucks, there would be greater demand for electricity from all sources. Opening up the transportation sector to electrical power could help liberate many countries from dependence on foreign sources of oil as long as more oil was not used to generate electricity. Nuclear energy could fuel cars and trucks via two methods: electricity generation for plug-in hybrid or pure electric-powered vehicles and production of hydrogen for fuel cell powered vehicles.

To produce hydrogen from nuclear power plants, the most efficient method is to employ very high temperatures to free hydrogen either through electrolysis of steam or thermochemical processes.[14] But the current fleet of reactors does not produce temperatures high enough for these methods. Engineers are designing the next generation of reactors, so-called Generation IV, which could generate very high temperatures.[15] The steep financial cost of building such reactors has held back construction. Nonetheless, even the current generation of nuclear plants offers the potential to provide hydrogen for fuel cells by electrolysis of water using off-peak power capacity and providing heat to assist steam reforming of natural gas.

The real hold up for hydrogen use in transportation, however, is not the lack of having the most appropriate nuclear power plants. Two factors would argue against near or even longer term deployment of hydrogen fuel cell vehicles. First, although some prototype fuel cell vehicles are on roads, gasoline hybrids have already proven their efficacy with hundreds of thousands of these vehicles reliably transporting people without the need for a new infrastructure such as hydrogen fueling stations. In an oil-constrained world, gasoline hybrids could serve as a bridging technology to already technologically proven plug-in hybrids, which use a combination of plug-in electrical power and a liquid fuel powered internal combustion engine. This technology could then serve as a bridge to pure electric powered vehicles, which some auto manufacturers have already made. Longer life and longer charge batteries on future electric cars would offer more reliability for consumers and a viable alternative to hybrid cars that use an internal combustion engine.

The second and most powerful argument working against hydrogen-powered vehicles is that on a total energy consumption basis, they use far more energy than even standard gasoline powered vehicles. In particular, a hydrogen-powered vehicle uses about three times more energy than a pure electric vehicle and about one-and-a-half times more energy than a gasoline-powered vehicle.[16] According to the World Nuclear Association, "The energy demand for hydrogen production could exceed that for electricity production today."[17] Looking at transportation from a total energy consumption standpoint, nuclear power or any form of non-oil electricity generation would make a bigger contribution to energy security through generation of electricity to power vehicles than through production of hydrogen for fuel cells in vehicles. While using hydrogen to fuel cars and trucks may never reach widespread deployment, the production of hydrogen is today a major industry for many other commercial applications, including food, aerospace, cosmetics, and electronics. Current techniques to produce hydrogen commonly employ fossil fuels, thus increasing demand for these scarce resources. Thus, nuclear and solar energies to produce hydrogen offer ways to help break dependence on fossil fuels. To determine how to deploy these alternative hydrogen production sources effectively, the U.S. National Academy of Sciences recommended in a 2007 report that the federal government help form an industry consortium including the petroleum industry and other applications that need hydrogen.[18] As part of this effort, the Department of Energy is researching the Next Generation

Nuclear Plant, which would create very high temperatures for efficient hydrogen production. But the projected timescale for deployment is around 2030.

From a U.S. energy security perspective, the tar sands of Alberta, Canada represent a source of oil free from the geopolitical encumbrances of the Middle East. Presently, industry uses natural gas to generate steam pumped into the bitumen of the tar sands in order to free oil deposits. Utilizing nuclear power to generate steam for the process would free natural gas for export, should the proper pipeline infrastructure be built. Methane, the principal component of natural gas, is a potent greenhouse gas. Proponents of the nuclear power idea argue that their method would reduce this greenhouse gas emission because nuclear power is a near zero emission energy source. Up to 20 CANDU reactors may be needed for this project.[19] Nevertheless, the energy made by these reactors might be more wisely consumed on powering plug-in hybrid or pure electric vehicles instead of perpetuating use of oil.

Impediments to Further Growth of Nuclear Power

Near term financial, material, and personnel barriers are blocking greatly increased use of nuclear power plants. Nuclear power plants have had high capital costs compared to coal and natural gas power plants. In addition, a nuclear power plant's long licensing and construction time—seven to ten years typically—has also increased financing costs. According to financial analysis by Moody's, Merrill Lynch, and other major investment firms, the cost to pay for nuclear plant construction, as of early 2008, has soared to more than $4,000 per kilowatt. Thus, a 1,000 MW plant would cost a minimum of $4 billion. This amount represents 10 percent or more of a typical U.S.-based utility's capital valuation. Thus, a utility would run a substantial financial risk if it defaulted on such a capital-intensive project.

To stimulate growth of nuclear power in the United States, Congress passed the Energy Policy Act of 2005, which offers incentives for nuclear power as well as other near-zero or low-carbon emission sources of energy, including wind and solar. This Act provides the direct incentive of a tax credit of 1.8 cents per kilowatt-hour for up to 6,000 megawatts of new nuclear capacity for the first eight years of operation. This credit equates to $125 million annually per 1,000 MW or a total eight-year credit of up to $6 billion. To be eligible for this tax credit, a utility would have to apply for a combined construction and operating license by December 31, 2008, begin reactor construction prior to January 1, 2014, and acquire Department of Energy certification. If more than 6,000 MW of eligible reactor applications are received by December 31, 2008, the tax credit would be distributed on a proportional basis among the eligible reactors. This 2008 deadline has spurred about two dozen applications, but few of these reactors are likely to be built because of near and intermediate term shortages in critical components such as reactor pressure vessels and steam generators and in qualified personnel to build and operate these plants.[20]

For those plants that start construction, the 2005 Energy Policy Act also offers regulatory risk insurance, which is an incentive specifically for nuclear power. This insurance would cover the principal and interest on debt and other costs incurred in buying replacement power as a result of licensing delays. The intention is to reduce the uncertainty about the combined construction and licensing process. The Act also makes new nuclear plants eligible for federal loan guarantees. Because the federal government (i.e., U.S. taxpayers) would bear the financial risk, these loan guarantees could make investment in the first handful of reactors more enticing for Wall Street. While these incentives will likely stimulate a half dozen reactors built in the United States by 2020, the projected growth in electricity demand and the aging fleet of reactors will more likely result in a proportional decline of nuclear energy in the U.S. electricity mix. Most reactors have received twenty year license renewals, but by 2030, without further life extensions, which might increase the risk of accidents, the U.S. fleet will face a retirement cliff without further construction.

In other regions, nuclear power could experience proportional growth in those countries with state-owned nuclear enterprises in contrast to the private U.S.-based utilities. China, France, India, and Russia, for instance, have provided significant government support and ownership of nuclear power plants. But even demand from national governments cannot accelerate nuclear growth faster than material and personnel limits. To put these daunting challenges in perspective, the Keystone Center's report on nuclear energy states that building 700 GW of nuclear power capacity (an amount needed to keep pace with projected mid-century demands for electricity) "would require the industry to return immediately to the most rapid period of growth experienced in the past (1981–1990) and sustain this rate of growth for 50 years."[21] Nonetheless, a sustained level of demand would stimulate increased supplies of parts and people needed to build and operate nuclear plants. But faced with higher capital costs and relatively long construction times, nuclear power appears uncompetitive compared to coal and natural gas plants despite the relatively high costs of natural gas. Longer-term substantial growth of nuclear power as well as other near-zero and low-carbon emission sources will likely depend on whether governments set a price on carbon dioxide emissions through taxes or cap-and-trade schemes.

Paving the way for the long term viability of nuclear power, government action is also required to address permanent waste disposal and to invest in research and development for technologies that provide for new proliferation-resistant fuel and might reduce the waste burden. No country has yet opened a permanent repository for waste from commercial nuclear power. As the country with the largest amount of such waste, the United States serves as special test case of leadership on this issue. As of early 2008, the U.S. nuclear industry produced more than 55,000 metric tons of spent fuel; it makes an additional 2,000 tons per year. By U.S. law, Yucca Mountain in Nevada was selected as the repository. But political opposition from Nevada politicians has threatened to block use of this facility. Even if the Department of Energy grants a license by 2009 to store waste there, Yucca Mountain will likely not start receiving waste until 2020 at the earliest. Moreover, potential expanded use of nuclear energy would generate more spent fuel.

To try to alleviate the waste disposal problem, provide for substantially more fuel, and limit the proliferation of nuclear weapons, the Bush administration in 2006 launched the Global Nuclear Energy Partnership (GNEP). If successful, this initiative would offer complete fuel services in which a handful of supplier states would provide fuel to many client states and agree to take back spent fuel for safe and secure keeping. Thus, by reducing the need for most countries to make their own fuel and store fissile materials such as plutonium, GNEP hopes to lessen the likelihood of proliferation. Supplier countries like the United States would reprocess the spent fuel but in a proliferation-resistant way, that is, by keeping other radioactive elements around the plutonium mixture, thus rendering it less useful for nuclear weapons. But because this mélange of plutonium and other radioactive materials would not be as radioactive as spent fuel, terrorists or thieves could, in principle, handle this reprocessed material without running the risk of immediate lethal radiation exposure. To try to counter that potential threat, GNEP envisions basing reprocessing facilities next to special reactors designed to burn the new fuel. These reactors would use fast, or high energy, neutrons, to cause fission, thus producing electricity while consuming some plutonium and other radioactive materials that would pose long term hazards in repositories. The caveat is that the fissionable mixture would have to be recycled multiple times in fast reactors to burn up most of the original plutonium and other fissionable elements.

Nonetheless, even if this method does not significantly reduce the storage burden on waste repositories, proponents of GNEP argue that eventually the world will need to use plutonium if it wants to greatly expand use of nuclear power. Based on the current demand for uranium at 68,000 metric tons annually and the known recoverable resources at 4,743,000 metric tons, the world would have sufficient uranium at current prices for the next 70 years.[22] But as the demand for uranium increases and as the price rises, the incentives for more uranium mining and prospecting would grow, resulting in more supplies. Even at the recent high historical price of $130 per kilogram of uranium, a uranium fuel cycle is cheaper than a plutonium fuel cycle. But there may come a point in the coming decades in which greater plutonium use looks relatively cost competitive. Perhaps more importantly, following the examples of France, India, and Japan, more countries may turn toward using plutonium because of energy security concerns.

Notes

1. Mujid S. Kazimi, "Thorium Fuel for Nuclear Energy," *American Scientist*, September-October 2003.

2. Neil M. Cabreza, "Nuclear Power VS. Other Sources of Power," Department of Nuclear Engineering, University of California, Berkeley, CA, http://www.nuc.berkeley.edu/thyd/ne161/ncabreza/sources.html.

3. President Dwight D. Eisenhower "Atoms for Peace," speech, December 8, 1953.

4. IAEA Safeguards Department, *IAEA Safeguards: Staying Ahead of the Game,* International Atomic Energy Agency, 2007.

5. For a recent book length study on safeguards, see Henry Sokolski, ed., *Falling Behind: International Scrutiny of the Peaceful Atom* (Carlisle, PA: Strategic Studies Institute, 2008), http://www.npec-web.org.

6. For several papers and presentations on the various fuel service proposals, see International Atomic Energy Agency, "New Framework for the Utilization of Nuclear Energy in the 21st Century: Assurances of Supply and Non-Proliferation," Conference Proceedings, September 2006, http://www-pub.iaea.org/mtcd/meetings/Announcements.asp?ConfID=147.

7. For more information about the World Association of Nuclear Operators, see http://www.wano.org.uk/.

8. Mycle Schneider and Antony Froggatt, "The World Nuclear Industry Status Report 2007," Commissioned by the Greens-EFA Group in the European Parliament, January 2008.

9. "France and South Africa Sign Nuclear Skills Agreements," *World Nuclear News,* March 3, 2008.

10. Jim Harding, "Pebble Bed Modular Reactors—Status and Prospects," February 2004, https://www.rmi.org/images/PDFs/Energy/E05-10_PebbleBedReactors.pdf.

11. Author interview with Japanese officials, Rokkasho-mura, Japan, August 2007.

12. Panel to Review the Spent Fuel Standard for Disposition of Excess Weapon Plutonium, Committee on International Security and Arms Control, *The Spent Fuel Standard for Disposition of Excess Weapon Plutonium: Application to Current DOE Options* (Washington, D.C.: National Academy of Sciences Press, 2000).

13. Schneider and Froggatt, "The World Nuclear Industry States."

14. Leon Walters, David Wade, and David Lewis, "Transition to a Nuclear/Hydrogen Energy System," World Nuclear Association Annual Symposium, London, September 4–6, 2002.

15. L. Sandell, EPRI Project Manager, "High Temperature Gas-Cooled Reactors for the Production of Hydrogen," Technical Report, Electric Power Research Institute, October 2004.

16. AllianceBernstein, "The Emergence of Hybrid Vehicles: Ending Oil's Stranglehold on Transportation and the Economy," Research on Strategic Change Report, June 2006, 37.

17. World Nuclear Association, "Transport and the Hydrogen Economy," Information Paper no. 70, January 2008.

18. National Research Council of the National Academies, *Review of DOE's Nuclear Energy Research and Development Program* (Washington, D.C.: The National Academies Press, 2007).

19. John K. Donnelly and Duane R. Pendergast, "Nuclear Energy in Industry: Application to Oil Production," Proceedings of the 20th Annual Conference of the Canadian Nuclear Society, May 30–June 2, 1999.

20. Charles D. Ferguson, *Nuclear Energy: Balancing Benefits and Risks,* Council on Foreign Relations, Council Special Report no. 28, April 2007.

21. The Keystone Center, *Nuclear Power Joint Fact-Finding,* June 2007.

22. Nuclear Energy Agency, *Uranium 2005: Resources, Production, and Demand,* Organization of Economic Cooperation and Development, 2005. The estimate in the chapter is based on a price of $130 per kilogram of uranium.

CHAPTER 21

The Decentralized Energy Paradigm

David M. Sweet

In the context of violent conflict the asymmetric nature of today's clashes demand a new response that conventional defense strategies cannot offer. As conflicts shift from easily identified enemies to the new style of stealthy guerilla tactics, traditional defenses aimed at protecting large power plants and other energy infrastructure become moot. Resilience in the grid can only be maintained by adapting the energy system to new realities, such as creating a distributed network of intelligent and interconnected yet autonomous generators.

Decentralized energy (DE) is neither a new nor an unfamiliar concept. The very first commercial electricity plant in the world, installed in 1882 in New York City at Pearl Street Station, was a combined heat and power plant. In different parts of the world and in different circles DE is known by names as diverse as distributed generation, on-site power, embedded generation, captive power, backup generation, uninterruptible power, cogeneration, and district energy. Although some may debate the commonalities among the various terms what they all share is the notion of generating electricity where it is needed. On average, a phenomenal two thirds of each unit of fuel burned to make electricity is wasted. The majority of each unit of fuel is vented up smoke stacks as waste heat. Once the power has been generated an additional 5–10 percent of the energy is lost as it is delivered to end users. So the potential for reducing the need for new supplies via improved energy conservation and efficiency is great. DE is one important part of the demand-side equation. It is defined as: "electricity production at or near the point of use, irrespective of size, technology or fuel used—both off-grid and on-grid." It can include on-site renewable energy, high efficiency cogeneration or combined heat and power (CHP), industrial energy recycling, and on-site power. Because DE installations are more numerous than conventional generators and, by definition, are located close to where the energy is required, energy infrastructure is also much less vulnerable to natural threats and sabotage. DE increases efficiency, relieves supply shortages and creates a more robust grid, thereby reducing infrastructure vulnerability.

DE Technologies

DE consists of a diverse portfolio of technology options that in most cases complement each other as well as conventional centralized grid technologies.

Reciprocating Engines: The most common DE technology is the internal combustion engine, just like the ones found in our cars and trucks. Engines for power generation can employ spark or compression combustion technology and can use a variety of fuels from regular gas and diesel to natural gas or biofuels—many engines can even use a variety of fuels. They are a proven technology and in many applications are the cheapest option. The main drawback of engines as a DE technology is that waste heat tends to be of a temperature too low for many industrial processes; however, there are still a wide range of applications where low grade heat can be employed, including heating and cooling buildings but also for many industrial processes.

Steam Turbines: A turbine is analogous to a household fan; steam passing over special blades forces the blades to turn. Steam turbines are most often used in central generating plants be they coal, oil or nuclear. They can also be employed in DE applications; however, they are usually found in larger industrial applications where high temperatures are required for some industrial process. With steam turbines water is heated in a boiler and the resulting steam turns a turbine which in turn powers a generator. Any fuel can be used. What differentiates centralized steam turbine plants from DE steam plants is that DE plants are sited close to heat load in order to optimize fuel use. In such DE applications waste heat from some industrial application can be used to heat the boiler water rather than venting waste heat to the environment (thus doubling fuel efficiency); or waste heat from the steam generator can be used for some industrial process. In other words steam turbines can either be used in top or bottom cycle cogeneration applications.

Gas Turbines: In the case of gas turbines, hot gases rather than steam pass across the turbine blades, causing them to spin. Gas turbines lend themselves very well to DE applications, partly because every year smaller and smaller models become available on the market. Gas turbines can be fueled by fossil-based natural gas or by renewable methane derived from agricultural waste, waste water or urban organic wastes such as food scraps. Like steam turbines or reciprocating engines, gas turbines are optimal when waste heat is put to use.

Microturbines: A microturbine, as the name suggests, is a miniaturized version of a gas turbine. It consists of a single shaft connecting a turbine, compressor and generator. Air is drawn in through a compressor into a recuperation unit that has been heated by the exhaust gases. The air flows into a combustion chamber where it is mixed with the fuel and burned. The hot gas is expanded through the turbine, creating mechanical energy. The exhaust gases pass out through the recuperation unit to capture some of the remaining heat. Microturbines are predominantly fuelled by natural gas, but other liquid and gaseous fuels can also be used. They typically range in capacity from about 25kWe to 500kWe and, like all DE technologies, are ideal for modular applications; if more than 500kW are required multiple units can be added and operated in tandem. Their small size makes them an ideal choice for providing power and heat/cooling for buildings.

Fuel Cells: Fuel cells generate electricity via a chemical reaction rather than a combustion process. Most commonly, a hydrogen rich fuel, such as coal or natural gas, is converted into hydrogen by a reformation process. Another way to make hydrogen is to use electricity to split water though a process called electrolysis. The fuel cell then uses the hydrogen as a fuel to produce electricity. The main advantage of fuel cells is that they can provide heat for a wide range of applications and show high electrical efficiencies under varying load. In addition, because they have no moving parts, they are very quiet and, of course, they create no emissions (apart from the fuel reformation process or the generation of electricity used for electrolysis). They remain one of the more expensive DE technologies.

Stirling Engines: Stirling engines are also known as external combustion engines. A source of heat (for example from the combustion of natural gas) is supplied to the engine that causes the working fluid to expand, moving a piston. A displacer then transfers the fluid into the cold zone of the engine where it is recompressed by the working piston. The fluid is then transferred back to the hot region of the engine and the cycle continues. In theory any source of heat is practical and some designs are powered by solar energy. Stirling engines hold great promise and are being used widely in Europe in residential cogeneration applications. The major challenge facing developers of Stirling engines is overcoming the barriers to mass production and thus cost reduction. As a result the market for Stirling engines is not as mature as some of the other DE technologies.

Photovoltaics: Solar electric photovoltaic panels generate electricity directly from the sun's rays. Usually fabricated from silicon with traces of other elements, PV cells are solid state semiconductors. PV cells work by absorbing particles of light (photons), which liberate electrons (negative) from the semiconductor layer, leaving behind a positive "hole." Electricity is thus generated. Generally arranged into modules, PV cells can be designed to match a wide range of electrical needs. Efficiencies for commercial PV cells range from 7–17 percent. Perhaps the most elegant of all DE technologies, they are silent, and because they can be integrated directly into the fabric of a building or mounted on a roof they require no extra space. They have a low environmental impact; and their modular nature allows for flexibility of application. Their main drawback is high cost.

Wind Turbines: A wind turbine creates electricity directly when the wind turns a turbine attached to a generator. Wind turbines generate power silently and are a good investment, however, wind is an intermittent resource, so some backup technology is typically required, whether the grid or a store of batteries. Wind energy is commonly used in both onsite and offsite applications. An example of 'decentralized' wind would be a rooftop turbine or a turbine supplying electricity to a single farm house. A group of larger turbines feeding power to a village or industrial park could also be considered decentralized wind. Larger wind farms feeding into the high voltage grid, although desirable, would not fall into the decentralized energy category.

DE Benefits

The benefits of decentralized energy are numerous and are attracting more and more adherents every day. If venture capitalists are any indication, we are in the process of witnessing a flood of interest in the clean tech sector, which includes clean DE.[1] Research by the World Alliance for Decentralized Energy (WADE) indicates that approximately 36 percent of electricity generation capacity added in 2006 can be attributed to DE capacity. Why the popularity? DE offers substantial economic savings via reduced capital requirements, increased fuel efficiency, reduced green house gas emissions, reduced emissions of health-debilitating air contaminants, a smaller land use footprint, heightened power reliability, free grid services such as voltage support and operating reserves, and is often the most affordable option for bringing power to communities without a modern grid. Of most relevance to this discussion, however, is that DE can increase the energy security outlook of the regions in which it is employed both in terms of reduced infrastructure vulnerability and reduced dependence on imported fuels.

Reduced Vulnerability to Supply Disruptions

The case of Azerbaijan illustrates how a more decentralized approach can make a grid infrastructure more resilient to both natural and human threats while simultaneously reducing dependency on fuel imports. Bordering Russia to the north and Iran to the south, Azerbaijan lies in a relatively politically volatile region of the world. Compare it to Georgia, which has a smaller population and relies more heavily on hydro for its power needs. Whereas Georgia has chosen to invest in upgrading its existing centralized thermal power plants, build new Combined Cycle Gas Turbine (CCGT) plants and new high voltage transmission lines, Azerbaijan has chosen instead a more decentralized development model. To meet its thermal generation capacity Georgia must rely on gas imports, but because its main plant, the Gardabani plant, does not recover heat, 40–60 percent of each unit of imported gas is lost in the form of waste heat, and an additional 16 percent of the electrical energy is lost in the form of line losses.[2] Because the plant is some distance from the capital Tbilisi, recovering heat is impractical and increased losses are unavoidable. In the event of a plant shut down (as a result of scheduled or unscheduled maintenance or sabotage), Georgia is fortunate enough to have hydro backup, but the difference in generation must either be met entirely from expensive imports or the nation is forced to rely on rolling blackouts. In January 2006, a series of terrorist attacks on Georgian energy infrastructure, including gas pipelines and electrical grid infrastructure, incapacitated the Georgian economy and left almost the entire population of 4.5 million without heat during the coldest winter in 20 years. The path that Azerbaijan has chosen is not only more amenable to waste heat recovery (which nearly doubles fuel use efficiency and reduces import dependency) but is also much less vulnerable to attack. In 2005, due to increasing need for power as a result of continued economic growth in Azerbaijan, it was necessary to find a way to ease tight supplies. Upon examining the various options available to meet the anticipated demand, the Azerbaijani administration decided that a decentralized energy infrastructure was better able to meet requirements than the conventional approach of building a large centralized power plant. It was therefore decided that five smaller plants would be built in strategic locations of high energy demand.[3] Each plant was to be composed of 10 identical 9MW gas engines making for a total addition of 450MW. Because the plants were sited where the power was needed no additional transmission capacity was required, and because power did not have to be moved large distances across the grid 16 percent less generation capacity could be built in order to meet the same demand (i.e., additional power did not have to be generated to make up for grid losses). In February 2006, just 10 months after the original order was placed, the first of the five plants was up and running. Now all five of the plants are in operation, producing reliable electricity where it is needed.[4] Furthermore, in three of the locations waste heat is being captured in the wintertime in order to heat greenhouses and produce value-added crops for export (a technique pioneered in the Netherlands). Using the power plants in such cogeneration applications greatly improves the fuel efficiency, reducing the need for additional fuel imports. Currently, Azerbaijani engineers are looking at further ways to use waste heat at the remaining plants. The project has been so successful that a sixth and seventh plant have been commissioned which will make further use of waste heat, using absorption chillers for cooling in the summer time and heating of greenhouses in the winter.[5]

The decentralized model being employed in Azerbaijan has a multiplicity of security benefits, particularly at a time of great geopolitical uncertainty in light of Russia's 2008 invasion of Georgia. Data is not yet available on total fuel savings resultant from the approach, but using the conservative estimate that fuel efficiency has been improved by 25 percent would translate into 25 percent less gas that would have to be imported for power generation, decreasing significantly the bargaining power of Russia, on which Azerbaijan relies for gas. Reduced imports also translated into significant economic savings and allowed scarce budgetary resources to be allocated elsewhere. Capital cost savings were also realized through the elimination of both the need to build extra capacity to meet peak demand and additional new grid capacity to move power to end users.

In addition, the vulnerability of Azerbaijan's power system to deliberate attack or natural disaster has been reduced considerably. In order for Azerbaijan to lose even 50MW, six engines at one of the plants would have to fail at once. In order for a larger act of sabotage to be effective terrorists would have to coordinate five simultaneous attacks and each attack would have to be successful—perhaps not impossible but considerably more challenging than targeting a single large plant. Robustness of the system is similarly improved from a perspective of natural disasters, water shortages (which make cooling difficult), and so forth.

A Modular Approach

One of the main drawbacks of centralized power plants is the fact that there is such a lag between the time when the perceived need for a plant is identified and when the plant is finally up and running and delivering actual power. In many cases the planning, design, construction and commissioning of a large coal, nuclear or hydro plant can span decades. In the case of decentralized energy, a small plant can be up and running in months or even days. For example, when the construction of the Comanche Peaks nuclear plant in Texas was delayed Texas Utilities contracted with several CHP facilities to provide firm capacity in the meantime.[6] Because of the greater flexibility and ease of siting and constructing DE plants they can more easily match incremental load growth and are therefore a much more secure financial investment. A misplaced bolt found inside the generator at Koeberg nuclear power plant in South Africa in December 2005 required the replacement of much of the generator.[7] Long lead times for repairing the 900MW unit, including difficulty finding spare parts, resulted in rolling blackouts for much of 2006 until it was repaired in May. As the case of Azerbaijan illustrates, a nation can get more power faster by investing in DE rather than conventional centralized plants. When contrasted with the groundswell of public opposition to new nuclear build in the UK, DE is also a much more politically palatable option.

Reduced Critical Infrastructure Vulnerability

The benefit of the decentralized model in terms of resilience to natural disasters can be illustrated by a multitude of case studies. Most of New York City's 58 hospitals experienced backup power failures during the Northeast blackout of 2003.[8] At the South Oaks Hospital, however, the staff was not even aware of the blackout plaguing their neighbors until they received a phone call from the local police.[9] The smooth transition to the CHP system allowed the hospital to be fully operational throughout the outage. Similar stories are common wherever disaster strikes. Shortly after the Northeast blackout, Italy witnessed a blackout that plunged almost the entire nation, more than 56 million people, into darkness. However, the lights of at least one hospital, equipped with a CHP plant, provided a glowing example of how decentralized energy ensures reliability. The Padua City Hospital, equipped with a modern onsite power system, handled the blackout without difficulties, exhibiting a seamless transition from grid power to fully autonomous operation.

Hurricane Katrina, in August 2005, knocked out power to millions of people in and around the Gulf of Mexico. Jackson, Mississippi, was one of the many cities affected. Again, a hospital with a cogeneration plant was the sole clear spot radiating in the surrounding gloom. The Mississippi Baptist Medical Center in Jackson managed to stay operational for the duration of the emergency thanks to its onsite system.

Of course, hospitals are not the only structures affected by blackouts, nor are they the only ones that benefit from decentralized energy during times of emergency. Over 9.7GW of CHP capacity was operational in the region affected by the August 2003 Northeast blackout.

The Swedish city of Malmö, a major commercial centre in southern Sweden, has attained a high level of self-sufficiency through heavy investment in a diverse portfolio of energy generation sited in the heart of the city. Energy technologies applied include solar/PV, wind, geothermal, and biomass cogeneration. The energy sources are largely connected and integrated in the buildings, which are in turn connected to the district heating network and therefore benefit the surrounding community, ensuring constant supply of heat and electricity. The end result is that the community is largely energy self-sufficient and few imports are required to meet local demands. The city has in effect created a cocoon for itself that protects it from energy price volatility and other whims of the international energy markets.

Improved Resilience to Emerging Strategic Threats

In addition to conventional threats of terrorism against energy infrastructure, a growing range of weapons are designed specifically to immobilize electricity infrastructure on a large scale. The graphite bomb for example, also known as a blackout bomb, showers an area in fine carbon filaments that interfere with electrical components. A version of the graphite bomb was used by NATO forces against Serbia in May 1999, disabling 70 percent of that country's power grid. E-bombs, a related weapon, are similarly designed to target electrical infrastructure. High power microwaves bombs, flux compression generator bombs (FCGs), and nuclear E-bombs are some of the weapons in the arsenal aimed at incapacitating electrical infrastructure and electronics. The weapons are attractive partly because they can seriously damage someone's ability to fight without any direct harm to living things. However, a serious e-bomb attack could very dangerous indeed, imperiling critical services such as medical services, communications, and water and sanitation. Another emerging threat is cyber attack. In April 2007,

Russian hackers shut down overnight the economy of neighboring Estonia.[10] Using a technique known as a distributed denial of service attack (DDoS), the perpetrators overwhelmed Estonian servers en masse, using armies of zombie computers from countries around the world, including those as diverse as Egypt, Vietnam, and Peru. The attacks rocked the nation, shutting down the major newspaper, electronic banking and automatic tellers, as well as the Internet. Although the power system was not targeted in this attack, it shows how a coordinated attack, in this case allegedly the work of volunteer pranksters, can have very real effect. Most centralized power systems are extremely vulnerable to cyber attacks. In a recent experiment designed to test the vulnerability of power systems to attack in the United States, the U.S. Department of Energy's Idaho National Laboratory showed it was possible to hack successfully into the control system of a major power plant and shut down operations.[11] In 2006, a U.S. security expert successfully hacked into a nuclear power plant control room, which controlled cooling of the reactor core.[12] The implications are obvious. According to a 2002 U.S. Government Accountability Office report, 70 percent of energy and power companies had experienced some kind of severe cyber attack and the frequency and sophistication of attacks is growing.[13]

Because graphite bombs and E-bombs tend to have limited ranges, a decentralized energy model is far more resilient to such weapons. A single blast from one of the above could shut down a major power plant, in effect cutting power on the order of hundreds or thousands of megawatts capacity—enough to power a small city. In order to wreak similar havoc on a largely decentralized system, a coordinated attack on hundreds or thousands of individual plants would be required. A successful attack on only a fraction of the plants would have limited local effects, as neighboring plants, using smart meters and communications, could seamlessly make up for the difference. Cyber attacks too would prove comparatively ineffective on a decentralized network. As explained above, shutting down a single multi-GW capacity coal, nuclear or hydro plant would affect millions of people. With a system of hundreds of smaller plants supplying the same people, hundreds of security systems of varying sophistication would have to be breached in tandem—a far more unlikely and labor-intensive possibility. This is to say nothing of the possible disastrous consequences of a successful attack on a nuclear power plant.

Reduced Costs

WADE research shows that in addition to direct security benefits considerable cost savings arise from a shift to a more decentralized model. WADE demonstrated in a report commissioned in the UK that Britain could save about £1.4 billion of avoided capital costs (roughly 27 percent lower than the central alternative) and reduced delivered energy cost of 0.38 pence/kWh by using DE to meet demand rather than central plant, largely as a result of reduced need for expensive high voltage transmission.[14] Savings of a similar magnitude were projected in fuel use, along with a reduction in pollution. Carbon dioxide emissions would be reduced by 17 percent. A synthesis of similar WADE research from around the world shows that a shift from investment in centralized power generation to decentralized generation typically saves anywhere between 15 percent and 40 percent of total delivered energy costs by displacing the need for generation capacity to meet peak electricity demand as well as grid capacity to transport the displaced power.[15] Independent research reinforces these findings. Work by IEA, for example, estimates savings in excess of $125 billion as a result of increased global DE investment between now and 2030.[16]

Of course cost savings are a different issue from security, but the evidence suggests that decentralized energy could create security benefits surpassing that offered by military hardware for a price tag comparable to a fraction of the military budget of many nations. Even compared to the costs of securing existing central infrastructure—not including new build—the costs to build new secure DE plants can seem modest. For example the International Atomic Energy Agency has estimated that "hundreds of millions of dollars would have to be spent around the world to improve construction and operating standards and enhance emergency response procedures" of existing nuclear plants.

A Shift Is Possible

In the mid-1980s Denmark realized the enormous benefits of DE and mandated a large scale and rapid shift to more decentralized energy, including combined heat and power plants connected to community energy grids. Now Denmark enjoys the benefits of an energy system with more than 50 percent decentralized energy. The United States almost doubled its CHP capacity between 1989 and 1999 without the kind of explicit policy support witnessed in Denmark. Unfortunately the proportion has since dwindled, but given sufficient political will it is possible to quickly shift to a more decentralized energy paradigm.

Some commentators have argued that infrastructure rebuilding efforts in conflict ridden areas such as Iraq or Lebanon should focus on decentralized energy rather than the typical centralized approach. As one of Iraq's leading power sector experts put it, in reference to efforts to rebuild Iraq's power sector after the U.S. offensive: "Had the bulk of the funds allocated for electricity works been devoted to installing smaller plants dispersed nearer load centers, full load demand could well have been met. The increasingly common power cuts could well have been substantially reduced, if not eliminated, country wide. Furthermore, the effects of sabotage or looting of transmission assets in the wake of the 2003 war would have been considerably lessened."

As conventional energy sources dwindle and demand for energy is increasing around the world, the need for increased energy security is becoming more apparent. Decentralized energy technologies offer enormous security benefits. By reducing a region's vulnerability to energy supply interruptions and threats to critical electricity infrastructure, both natural and human, DE can offer great comfort at a low comparative cost. DE is a practical way of mitigating risks associated with energy insecurity while simultaneously allowing communities to adapt to energy interruptions from disrupted supply chains and damaged infrastructure alike.

Notes

1. Richard Schlesinger, "Venture Capital Flood," Energy Central, *EnergyBiz Insider,* October 15, 2007, http://www.energycentral.com/site/newsletters/ebi.cfm?id=397.

2. IEA Electricity Information 2004, (Paris: International Energy Agency, 2003).

3. "Power in Numbers: Why Multiple, Decentralized Power Plants are Better," *Cogeneration and Onsite Power Magazine,* September October 2006, http://www.cospp.com/articles/article_display.cfm?Section=ARCHI&C=Featu&ARTICLE_ID=273406&KEYWORDS=%7Bklimstra%7D.

4. Personal communication with Jacob Klimstra, Wartsila.

5. Wartsila CHP Plant for Guba Azerbaijan. Wartsila Press release, October 29, 2007, http://www.wartsila.com.

6. "CHP in Texas," *Cogeneration and Onsite Power Production Magazine,* November-December 2007.

7. Melanie Gosling, "Sabotage Probed at Koeberg Nuclear Station," *Cape Times,* January 20, 2006, http://www.int.iol.co.za/index.php?set_id=1&click_id=14&art_id=vn20060120071013263C336169.

8. C. Levy and K. Zernike, "The Blackout: Hospitals: Lessons Learned on 9/11 Help Hospitals Respond," *New York Times,* August 16, 2003.

9. Bruce A. Hedman, "Energy and Environmental Analysis, Inc., Combined Heat and Power: Enhancing Power Reliability While Reducing Operating Costs," Presentation at the Energy 2006 Conference, August 8, 2006.

10. "Hackers Take Down the Most Wired Country in Europe," *Wired Magazine,* August 21, 2007, http://www.wired.com/politics/security/magazine/15-09/ff_estonia.

11. "Staged Cyber Attack Reveals Vulnerability in Power Grid," *CNN,* September 26, 2007, http://www.cnn.com/2007/US/09/26/power.at.risk/index.html.

12. "U.S. Takes New Tack To Defend Power Grid," *CBS News,* October 30, 2007, http://www.cbsnews.com/stories/2007/10/30/tech/main3431478.shtml.

13. "Critical Infrastructure Protection. Significant Challenges Need to Be Addressed," Testimony of Robert F. Dacey, Director, Information Security Issues, U.S. Government Accountability Office, before the Subcommittee on Government Efficiency, Financial Management and Intergovernmental Relations, Committee on Government Reform, House of Representatives, July 24, 2002, http://www.gao.gov/new.items/d02961t.pdf.

14. "Decentralizing UK Energy: Cleaner, Cheaper, More Secure Energy for the 21st Century Application Of The WADE Economic Model to the UK," Greenpeace UK, March 2006, http://www.localpower.org/documents/reporto_greenpeace_modelrun.pdf.

15. Sytze Dijkstra, "The WADE Economic Model, Previous Results and Future Application," WADE, February, 2006, http://www.puc.nh.gov/EPAB/Symbiotic%202006-02-20%20WADE%20DE%20Economic%20Model%20-%20Article.pdf.

16. *World Energy Investment Outlook 2003,* (Paris: International Energy Agency, 2003) http://www.iea.org/Textbase/nppdf/free/2003/weio.pdf.

CHAPTER 22

Balancing Energy Security and the Environment

Deron Lovaas

> The question remains: how quickly and painlessly can we negotiate that shift
> [from oil to another energy source] now? Alan Greenspan assures us that we
> have always managed to move on to the next great fuel before the resources
> available to us have been fully exploited. But he neglects to mention how
> close we have cut it, and how desperate we have become before the shift was
> accomplished.
>
> —Peter Tertzakian, *A Thousand Barrels A Second*

As a society we face an energy transition. The book that includes Tertzakian's
passage above described a transition we made in the 1800s, from whale oil to
petroleum-derived kerosene. The analogy is apt, at least in terms of environmental implications. Humanity hunted these mammalian creatures to the point where
their dwindling numbers made a transition inevitable if difficult. Hence, there is
often a tension between energy production and environmental protection, ne-
cessitating difficult tradeoffs. Energy demand during the 20th century and early
21st century has climbed steadily upwards, with jumps as countries scale the
industrialization curve. This has been led by OECD countries. However, there is
already a shift, as non-OECD countries, particularly highly populous China and
India, take the lead as the world's largest energy users. Due to global reliance on
fossil fuels, this ever-climbing demand has left its mark on landscapes around
the globe, from the scarred and polluted landscapes of Shanxi Province in China,
where coal is king, to the felling of hundreds of thousands of acres of rainforest
in Ecuador for the sake of oil drilling, to the denuded, contaminated and rapidly
growing swath of the boreal forest in the Canada's Alberta Province where high
oil prices are driving a boom in tar-sands production.[1] Is it a "hard truth," as the
National Petroleum Council recently announced, that humanity must adopt a
no-holds-barred approach to wrestling with the global energy challenge?[2] Is the
way forward a combination of everything conceivable, tapping what some refer

to as a bottomless well of sources, including coal, unconventional oil, and even methane hydrates, to low-carbon alternatives such as biomass? The way forward requires more discernment and care, so that both of the epic challenges before us, energy security and climate change, can be addressed. Thankfully, as this chapter will detail, there are synergies between energy security and the environment: through conservation, efficiency and substitution humanity can reduce harmful environmental effects while meeting energy needs.

Conventional Energy Sources and the Tradeoffs They Present

The 20th century was dominated by oil. Oil's share of the energy picture grew to eclipse coal, which was king in the 19th century. This makes sense given the greater energy content and the easy transportability of this liquid fuel. Non-fossil energy sources have on the other hand played a tiny role, with regional variations depending on resource availability or government commitments–for example, the northwestern United States relies in part on hydropower, and nuclear power plays a large role in France. The environmental effects of these sources vary. Currently, one concern looms above all others: The effects of greenhouse gas emissions, especially the most voluminous by far, carbon dioxide (CO_2). Figure 22.1 shows the relative contribution of different fossil energy sources to increases in carbon dioxide levels in the atmosphere.[3]

Coal

This fossil fuel is arguably the most environmentally damaging of our energy sources, and certainly the most carbon-intensive. It was first used in large scale in the 1600s in England, due to widespread deforestation. The price of wood had

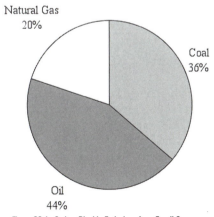

Figure 22.1 Carbon Dioxide Emissions from Fossil Sources

skyrocketed due to the clash between this supply constraint and unrelenting demand for wood as a source of construction material and fuel. Plentiful coal was the substitute of choice. Coal really came into its own in the 18th century, when the world—led by the industrializing U.S., entered the age of coal, lasting until the mid-20th century. Use of coal accelerated in the wake of Thomas Edison's invention of the first coal-fired electric power plant in New York City in 1882. Electrification of nations of the world followed, and continues in the developing world. Air pollution from processing and combustion of coal has been a concern ever since its first widespread use in England. By the mid-20th century, sulfur dioxide (SO_2) from coal combustion was identified as a contributor to acid rain, and the U.S. Congress adopted a program to address this threat in amendments to the Clean Air Act of 1990. The program issued emission permits that were tradable among sources, allowing a market system to identify and implement the most cost-effective means to cut SO_2. As a result, costs were 20 times less than some industry estimates and even lower than optimistic estimates from environmentalists, saving as much as one billion dollars per year while cutting 10 million tons of pollution. SO_2, however, remains a concern with 300,000 people living in areas with unhealthy levels of this pollution and 18 states experiencing rises in this pollutant from power-plant smokestacks in recent years.[4] Other harmful pollutants from coal combustion include mercury, particulate matter (commonly referred to as soot), oxides of nitrogen (NOx), a contributor to smog, and mercury.

While burning coal contributes a great deal more to increased morbidity and mortality rates worldwide, upstream effects are noteworthy too. In the United States, black lung disease kills about 1,000 miners a year, which is down from 2,500 in the early 1980s after regulations promulgated pursuant to new laws required the reduction of mineworker exposure to coal dust.[5] However, last year, a government study found that rates of black lung among experienced miners unexpectedly doubled in the last decade.[6] Coal mining itself kills 40 miners in a bad year (and the U.S. has had several bad years of late). Strip mining and mountaintop removal, standard practices in the United States, contribute mightily to habitat and waterway degradation.

These figures, however, pale in comparison to mortality due to coal use in rapidly industrializing China. The state mine safety agency notes that the death rate for every 100 tons of coal mined is 100 times that of the United States, and that 70,000 additional miners contract black lung disease every year.[7] Downstream figures are even more eye-popping, with SO_2 from coal combustion "contributing to about 400,000 premature deaths a year" and causing widespread acid rain damage.[8] Pollution from coal combustion has even been transported by wind to other countries, including the United States[9]

New power generation technologies would reduce the environmental harms caused by combustion of coal for that purpose. Specifically, a plant using integrated gasification combined cycle (IGCC) in lieu of the norm (pulverized coal or PC) would cut emissions of various air pollutants (NO_x, SO_2, CO, PM, VOCs) and substantially reduce solid waste and water use by coal plants.[10] Building them is a challenge, since IGCC plants are more costly than PC ($1,567/kW compared to $1,442/kW according to one recent study); however, this differential flips if one assumes carbon capture and sequestration ($2,076/kW for IGCC vs. $2,345/kW for PC).[11] This is an important technology for addressing the problem of CO_2 emissions. In fact, capturing and sequestering the carbon generated during production safely in appropriate geologic formations could slash emissions. Perfecting and commercializing this technology (which resembles the longtime oil production practice of injecting CO_2 into formations in order to enhance oil recovery) is the sine qua non for continued coal uses in a carbon-constrained world. As NRDC summed up in a recent report on coal in the United States and China: "Marginal improvements in coal plant efficiency will not deliver reductions on the scale needed to stabilize concentrations at reasonable levels."[12]

Besides electricity generation, there is another possible route for the carbon locked in coal to be released into the atmosphere: liquefying coal for use in the transportation sector. Using technology developed in Germany in the 1920s, South Africa relies on this source of liquid fuel for 30 percent of its gasoline and diesel fuel. High oil prices and concerns about energy security have boosted commercial interest in the liquefaction of coal (hereinafter referred to as liquid coal) by the Fischer-Tropsch process, named after the two German chemists who invented it in the early 20th century, so much so that the EIA projects under its high price scenario ($100/bbl) that by 2030 more than two mbd of coal-to-liquids will be produced globally.[13] The EIA projects that liquid coal will make up 2 percent

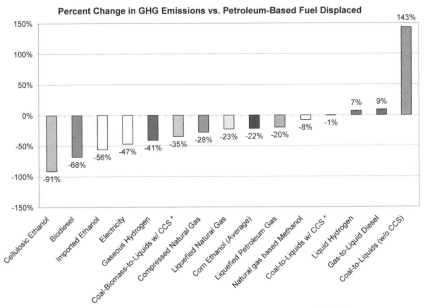

Figure 22.2 Percent Change in GHG Emissions vs. Petroleum-based Fuel Displaced

of all liquid fuel production in the United States alone by 2030 (400,000 barrels per day).[14] According to its 2007 outlook, China (second only to the United States in coal reserves) could produce more than three times that amount in 2030.[15] In 2006, China announced a plan to invest $128 billion in the development of liquid coal, and about 30 projects are currently being planned or built.[16] This increased activity presents a huge environmental challenge. The carbon dioxide emissions from the entire life cycle of U.S. liquid coal production are more than twice that of conventional gasoline, as shown in Figure 22.2.[17]

Use of liquid coal to power transportation is also highly inefficient compared to an alternative that is growing in popularity, with major automakers including GM and Toyota committing to commercialization in just a few years: plug-in hybrids. Even using optimistic assumptions about conversion efficiency in liquid coal plants, plug-in hybrids displace more than twice as much oil per ton of coal used. And the difference in carbon dioxide emissions is even greater; assuming the same vehicles, carbon capture, and sequestration for both liquid coal and coal-fired power plants, the former yields 10 times as much carbon dioxide as the latter. And even assuming the commercial viability of new emissions control technology, dramatic increases in production of liquid coal would require dramatic increases in coal mining, which as described above entails a host of environmental harms. The coal industry itself estimates that displacing just 10 percent of total U.S. oil demand would increase U.S. mining by 42 percent, or an additional 475 million tons of coal per year.[18]

Some experts have pointed to another possibility for making fuel, one that entails use of CO_2 as a raw material rather than a waste product. While a long-shot vis-à-vis commercial viability, this process is attracting attention as the need to develop carbon-neutral to carbon-negative means to fuel transportation sinks in, and is described by Nobel-Prize-winning chemist Dr. George Olah and his colleagues, with a specific focus on CO_2 based methanol:

> The recycling of CO_2 via its chemical reduction with hydrogen to produce methanol . . . is . . . an attractive alternative. As fossil fuels become more scarce, the capture and recycling of atmospheric CO_2 would become and remain feasible for the production of methanol, together with synthetic hydrocarbons and associated products. The hydrogen required would be obtained by the electrolysis of seawater (an unlimited resource), while also releasing oxygen. The electrical power required would be provided by atomic energy, and/ or by any suitable alternate energy source [for example, solar power]. Upon their combustion, methanol and the synthetic hydrocarbons produced would be transformed back to CO_2 and water, thereby closing the methanol cycle.[19]

Oil and Natural Gas

Petroleum is the second biggest fossil source of carbon dioxide, mirroring its role as the largest supplier of global energy. Furthermore, global demand for oil is projected to rise by 29–82 percent by 2030, depending on the projection in question, from the EIA high economic growth scenario to the IEA alternative policy scenario.[20] Natural gas is also projected to rise substantially by 2030, by 47–139 percent depending on the scenario.[21] This energy source was often discovered when exploring for oil, and was routinely flared off (and still is in too many places) until its value as an energy source was realized and capturing and marketing it became common practice. A similar cradle-to-cradle logic may apply to the use of CO_2 as a feedstock for producing methanol, as described above.[22] The technology is not environmentally benign, with substantial environmental damage caused by drilling for oil as well as natural gas. As described in a 2005 NRDC analysis:

> Offshore development is associated with onshore infrastructure, including pipelines, which has caused significant harm to salt marshes and other coastal resources . . . development also brings with it the risk of toxic oil spills, which in turn threaten a wide variety of marine species. Extraction of oil or gas from beneath the ocean floor creates massive amounts of drilling waste containing toxic metals and other contaminants, most of which is dumped untreated into surrounding waters. [Although the U.S. EPA forbids discharges within three miles of the U.S. coastline] . . . operations generate large amounts of "polluted water," which is brought up from wells . . . [it] also contains a variety of toxic pollutants and typically is discharged into the ocean with minimal treatment. Offshore seismic exploration means noise pollution harmful to whales and other marine mammals . . . drilling generates tons of air pollutants as well.
> Onshore development . . . results in heavy industrialization of affected areas. Exploration activities degrade wildlife habitats and roadless areas, harm fragile soils and archaeological resources, and encourage damaging off-road vehicle use.[23]

However, the physical infrastructure footprint is only a small portion of the overall environmental effects of oil and natural gas. Viewed on a life-cycle basis, the greatest effect is in end-uses. And this is where natural gas has an advantage, since it burns much more cleanly than oil and coal. In fact, due to dramatically lower carbon intensity, displacement of oil and coal with natural gas reduces CO_2 emissions. For example, a new combined cycle gas-fired power plant emits about 40 percent less CO_2 than a traditional pulverized coal plant.[24] But in spite of the clean burn, substantial CO_2 emissions still result, compounding the damage to the environment due to resource extraction as described above.

Unconventional Oil and Gas

High oil prices, concerns about security and peaking of conventional oil production have also spurred an interest in substitutes for conventional oil, with production of unconventional oil on the rise. These substances "have a high viscosity, flow very slowly (if at all) and require processing or dilution to be produced through a well bore."[25] The global endowment of this resource is huge, numbering in the trillions of barrels. However, producing it is very expensive and environmentally damaging compared to conventional oil, as a specific case in North America showcases: Canada's tar sands. There is a huge deposit in the province of Alberta. It comes in the form of bitumen, a heavy substance that clings to sand grains. In fact, only 10 percent of the sands is actually oil. This resource is very diffusely deposited and very low quality. It is exceedingly costly to extract and refine, requiring the tearing up of the boreal forest as well as huge amounts of energy and water for extraction and processing. Production of Canadian tar sands has nonetheless doubled over the last 10 years to more than one million barrels a day and is slated to continue increasing.[26] Production is also the source of spiraling carbon dioxide emissions, with projections that emissions from sands-related activities will quadruple by 2015, derailing chances that Canada would attain its agreed-upon goal of lowering emissions from 1990 levels by 2008–2012.[27] The sands have been largely exploited by surface mining, a practice that strips the boreal forest bare, with the world's largest trucks ferrying tons of bitumen out of the pits. The environmental legacy is a denuded moonscape and huge ponds of toxic tailings as a byproduct. A different process is used to access the 80 percent of the sands that are more deeply deposited throughout Alberta: in situ extraction, more akin to oil drilling than surface mining, can take various forms (two are currently used commercially in sands production—Cyclic Steam Simulation and Steam-Assisted Gravity Drainage).[28] In situ techniques still entail a damaging footprint in a forested region. One assessment finds that if all the deep deposits are developed, 11,454 square kilometers of boreal forest will be cleared and a network of 441,600 kilometers of roads, pipelines and power lines will be spread across more than one-fifth of Alberta.[29] Jeopardizing the boreal forest is a global problem—it is host to many migratory waterfowl and is the world's largest terrestrial reservoir of carbon—as well as a local one, due to the massive amounts of water needed to extract oil from the sands with existing production techniques.[30]

High energy prices and improving technology have spurred interest in another unconventional fossil fuel: gas shale, a sedimentary rock that is less porous than sandstone where traditional natural gas is found. With horizontal drilling, producers can move laterally beneath cities and neighborhoods to extract the product, and promising U.S. fields include the Barnett Shale in Texas, the Haynesville Shale in Louisiana and the Marcellus Shale in Pennsylvania and New York. But like other unconventional hydrocarbons, gas shale presents environmental challenges. Millions of gallons of water as well as chemicals to reduce drilling friction must be pumped deep down into the wells, straining water resources and potentially contaminating groundwater.

Biomass

Globally, the role of biomass in meeting humanity's energy needs has been eclipsed by the economic boom fueled by fossil fuels. In the 19th century wood was the energy source choice for home heating, cooking and industrial activities. But, as one expert notes, "In terms of millions of barrels of oil equivalent consumption per day, biomass energy usage had increased from about 5 out of a total consumption of 7 in 1860, to about 20 out of a total consumption of 200 in 2000."[31] As the world contemplates another big energy shift, renewed interest in biomass is sparking a boom, most notably through the production of biofuels such as ethanol, methanol and biodiesel. Ethanol production doubled and biodiesel production expanded sixfold from 2001 to 2006 alone.[32] In the United States, this has meant an explosion in corn cultivation. Sugar ethanol in Brazil has also experienced phenomenal growth, making up 52 percent of the world's ethanol market in 2006. While the growth rates are impressive, fossil fuels still dominate after more than a century of development: biofuels account for about 1 percent of global liquid fuel consumption.[33]

As the biofuels boom continues, concerns about unintended consequences grow. The environmental effects of biofuels are variable depending on the feedstock, the process used to transform that feedstock to fuel, and the distance to market and mode of transport.

Feedstock cultivation is more land-intensive than fossil resource exploitation—although as described above the latter is far from benign—yielding a host of harmful effects such as polluted runoff into water bodies. Arguably, these effects can be mitigated more easily than those of fossil exploitation, for example by adopting low-till techniques and relying on feedstocks such as switchgrass or miscanthus that require little or no fertilizer or pesticide input and can even serve as wildlife

Table 22.1 Fossil Energy Balance for Select Biomass Feedstocks

Fuel	Fossil Energy Balance
Gasoline (from conventional crude)	0.8
Ethanol (sweet sorghum)	1
Ethanol (corn)	1.5
Ethanol (wheat)	2
Ethanol (sugar beets)	2
Ethanol (sugar cane)	8
Cellulosic ethanol and methanol	2–36
Diesel (from conventional crude)	0.8–0.9
Biodiesel (rapeseed, EU)	2.5
Biodiesel (castor)	2.5
Biodiesel (sunflower)	3
Biodiesel (waste veg. oil)	5–6
Biodiesel (palm oil)	9

habitat. A big question about the use of biofuels, if greenhouse gas emissions are a primary concern, is how much energy is generated compared with how much fossil energy is put into the process.[34] Table 22.1 shows some of the most recent attempts to answer this question, in some cases a range of values is listed, and feedstocks are in parentheses.[35]

While the data shows that ethanol from sugarcane or cellulose and biodiesel from waste vegetable oil or palm oil displace the most fossil fuels, the overall environmental benefit is contingent on the previous use of the land. The ultimate cautionary tale involves palm oil. An EU mandate requires increasing substitution of biodiesel for diesel, driving up demand for this feedstock. Indonesia and Malaysia account for more than 80 percent of global palm oil production, having ramped up steeply since the 1970s.[36] In a mere dozen years (1985–1997), Indonesia cleared 60 percent of the lowland rainforest of Kalimantan, on the island of Borneo, and Sumatra—deforestation primarily undertaken to facilitate the planting of oil palm.[37] Palm oil plantations are profoundly inhospitable to the rare wildlife found in Malaysian and Indonesian rainforests, a veritable "biological desert." The World Bank concluded that Indonesia is "almost certainly undergoing a species extinction spasm of planetary proportions."[38]

In Brazil, where "plantations for sugar and ethanol production have expanded predominantly into areas once used for cattle grazing, as cattle move on to new pastureland (often cleared rainforests)."[39] Soybean production is having a similarly devastating effect on the Brazilian rainforest, and is considered "one of the main causes of tropical deforestation in the Brazilian Amazon."[40] Algae holds substantial promise, and offers double environmental dividends. As demonstrated in a project at the Massachusetts Institute of Technology, micro algae colonies process pollutants emitted from smokestacks, reducing levels of oxides of nitrogen pollution by 80 percent and CO_2 by 30–40 percent.[41] These organisms also yield 40–50 percent of their weight in oil, producing more than 50 percent more gallons per acre per year of fuel as palm oil.[42] This technology remains a long shot, costing more than $200 per barrel to produce, but costs will come down and the huge yield coupled with the fact that it can grow in marginal (i.e., nonbiodiverse) lands make it a compelling possibility.[43]

Next generation options include biofuels derived from the cellulose of plants and municipal solid waste. Viability of these options is expected in 8–15 years, although sustained high oil prices should bring that horizon closer.[44] While the feedstocks are widely and cheaply available, the challenge is the effort and expense needed to break cellulose down into parts that can be processed, something that it resists naturally.

There are two candidate processes for cellulosic biofuels: biochemical and thermochemical. The latter relies on the Fischer-Tropsch process described above. The technology has been commercially viable for production of electricity and liquid fuels from fossil fuel feedstocks; as of 2004 there were 117 such facilities worldwide that could theoretically be adapted to use biomass feedstocks too.[45] The biochemical process, while dependent on reduced costs of breaking down cellulose with the use of enzymes, requires "less capital-intensive facilities and can be economical on a smaller scale" assuming the technological hurdles are cleared.[46] If and when commercial viability is achieved, scaling up is likely to happen quickly due to new policy and sustained high oil prices. One study, which assumes commercialization by 2012, finds that U.S. production alone would increase approximately 10-fold from its current annual level to 60 billion gallons.[47]

Other Renewables

Other renewables (i.e., wind, solar, geothermal) are promising low-carbon alternatives and are growing rapidly, and projected to keep doing so. World Energy Outlook shows this energy category growing 6.7 percent annually from 2005–2030, a blistering pace. However, given the relative small base it only increases from less than 1 percent to about 2 percent of world energy production by 2030.[48] Alternative policies can have an effect, but they must be quite aggressive. In its most recent Alternative Policy Scenario, IEA finds that growth is 44 percent higher than in the reference case, with its share of the whole increasing to a mere 3 percent.[49]

Fast-growing wind power capacity reached about 60,000 megawatts (MW) in 2005, a 12-fold increase from the 1995 level.[50] Germany is by far the leader with more than 18,000 MW of this total, thanks to a policy context that is prodding development of this technology forward. However, the wind boom is spreading to places including China, which is building the world's largest wind energy facility, and Texas, which has joined a majority of U.S. states in establishing a "Renewable Portfolio Standard" (RPS), specifying a percentage of electricity that must come from renewable sources by a certain date.[51] In fact, production tax credits (PTCs), RPS policies and concerns about climate are among the drivers the Department of Energy lists in a recent scenario showing that a healthy 20 percent share for wind power is feasible by 2030, a projection that would avoid 7.6 million metric tons of CO_2 emissions and save four trillion gallons of water normally consumed by electricity generation.[52]

While under the IEA's Reference Scenario, wind power's share of total electricity would be merely 5 percent; one analysis suggests that with the spread of aggressive policies such as RPS and economic incentives its share could be 29.1 percent.[53] Siting the new facilities may be a challenge given concerns among some environmentalists that large windmills may be little more than "bird Cuisinarts." However, while windmills can pose a threat to bats, right now other factors such as buildings and cats are responsible for far more avian deaths than wind turbines.[54] If sited intelligently (i.e., not in migration or heavy travel paths), major conflicts with wildlife can be avoided. Aesthetic concerns can also be minimized, although Americans must learn to see the beauty in the wind made visible as environmentalist Bill McKibben poignantly puts it.[55]

In the solar realm, as one author notes, "Japan's sunshine program and Germany's 100,000 solar roofs program, which have used various types of subsidies to stimulate robust domestic solar-energy industries, now account for 69 percent of the world market for PV [photovoltaics]."[56] PV cells and arrays and thermal methods—such as the large mirror arrays in the western United States that concentrate and collect power—are the two active solar-energy technologies; they can be deployed in centralized or distributed ways. Thanks largely to the leadership of these two OECD countries, the global PV market leaped more than 10-fold between 1995 and 2005, an eye-popping 29 percent per annum growth rate.[57] While challenges remain, including most notably storage of energy between sunny days and the comparatively high cost per kilowatt-hour of solar energy, as it scales up—with China and India among others setting aggressive growth targets—technological breakthroughs are likely.[58]

As these industries achieve takeoff, negative effects must be monitored and mitigated. In economic terms, there will be positive externalities, such as the spread of best practices and technological knowhow, and negative externalities, such as pollution. A cautionary tale is unfolding in China, where polysilicon plants manufacturing components for photovoltaic cells are dumping highly toxic waste into the surrounding environment.[59] Cross-border upstream consequences of shifts in the energy economy deserve scrutiny since the control of some air and water pollutants may be subject to the environmental Kuznets curve hypothesis whereby emissions increase along with per capita income until a certain point, after which countries slide down the opposite slope of a U-shaped curve with pollution controls increasing along with increases in income.[60]

Nuclear Energy

Some point to energy released by radioactive decay through nuclear reaction, fission, or fusion of atomic nuclei as a potentially promising, low-carbon source of power. This is certainly the conclusion of the IEA's outlook, which found under its alternative policy scenario that nuclear power capacity would increase twice as fast as the reference scenario, reaching a point 27 percent higher than reference by 2030.[61] By IEA's lights, the largest increases, assuming new policies, would be in the EU, China and the United States in that order. Notably, in the past few years, some high-profile environmentalists claim nuclear power is a low-carbon alternative that should not be dismissed, among them Stewart Brand (founder of the Whole Earth Catalog), James Lovelock (author of the Gaia hypothesis), Patrick Moore (Greenpeace founder) and Christine Todd Whitman (former EPA head). However, it is telling that in IEA's reference case nuclear's share by 2030 plummets six points from the 2005 level, to a mere 9 percent. In spite of concerns about energy security and prices as well as climate change, nuclear power therefore appears, at least according to the IEA projections, to have a relatively dim future.[62] Why is that the case?

First, public concerns about safety and radioactive waste have not abated despite improvements in technology. Also of concern is expansion of nuclear power in countries with "significant weaknesses in legal structure (rule of law);

construction practice; operating, safety, and security cultures; and regulatory oversight."[63] Insufficient safeguards are a danger in a world where states such as Iran are pursuing nuclear technology.[64] The issue of cost—of capital, operations, maintenance and fuel—is also a huge hurdle for expansion, leading one expert to conclude recently that "the most likely case is that the U.S. net nuclear capacity will rise very slightly over the next 15 years. EU nuclear capacity will in all likelihood fall. Growth in China and India will be significant, but may also fall short of either EIA or IEA expectations, primarily because both use extremely optimistic cost estimates."[65]

Hydrogen

Especially in transportation, the bloom is off the rose with this supposed energy alternative, which, as an energy carrier rather than an energy source, loses in the comparison to electricity. Joe Romm lists some of the reasons hydrogen is unlikely to compete with other emission-reducing technologies:

- The competition—more fuel-efficient internal combustion engine vehicles—is getting tougher, so the incremental benefits of using fuel cell vehicles will be smaller.
- In the near term, hydrogen is likely to be made from fossil fuel sources.
- Annual operating costs of a fuel cell vehicle are likely to be much higher than those of the competition for the foreseeable future.
- Fuels used to make hydrogen for transportation could achieve larger greenhouse gas savings at lower cost if used instead to displace the dirtiest stationary electric power plants.[66]

The infrastructure dilemma seems insurmountable. Onboard storage of hydrogen, in either gaseous or liquid form, makes for incredibly expensive vehicles,[67] and a large-scale shift to hydrogen entails supplementing or supplanting the existing liquid fuel delivery infrastructure. This is a tough proposition, to put it mildly.

Carbon Dioxide and Climate Change

Despite great strides in pollution control, the environmental outlook remains cloudy because of the growing problem of greenhouse gas emissions, by far the most voluminous of which is carbon dioxide. Due to what scientists refer to as their forcing power, concentrations of other gases produced anthropogenically—such as methane and nitrous oxide—must also be reduced.

Managing the risks of climate change is a huge challenge. How can humanity manage it? Reducing deforestation helps, as does efficiency. But de-carbonizing our energy system over time is an indispensable component in a strategy to lower atmospheric carbon concentrations. Concentrations of CO_2 continue to increase in part due to the loss of carbon sinks such as forests that retain the carbon in their biomass and fix it in the soil, as well as oceans. However, carbon dioxide is also released during combustion of fossil fuels for energy production, most notably coal and oil. The IPCC finds that it is 90 percent likely that most of the warming over the past fifty years is due to anthropogenic emissions of heat-trapping gasses including CO_2, and holds that slowing this growth such that concentrations stabilize at 450 ppm is essential to avoiding climatic forcing that would yield more than 1–2 degrees of additional warming.

The Way Forward

If energy demand trends continue, the big question is whether or not there is a path forward to address the energy security concerns described so vividly by other contributors to this book without undermining efforts to reduce greenhouse gas emissions. Fortunately, trends are not destiny and there is ample evidence that energy demand can be moderated substantially in the near-term via an efficiency surge. Improvements in efficient use of energy have historically paid large dividends in the United States, helping to drive down the energy intensity of the economy (a phenomenon that has also been helped by structural changes in the U.S. economy as it moves from manufacturing to services). Two recent estimates underscore the potential to increase energy efficiency, sometimes called the First Fuel, globally, thereby moderating demand. The first, by the McKinsey Global Institute, finds that 20–24 percent of projected demand could be cut by 2020, achieving up to half of the carbon dioxide reductions needed to stabilize the climate tolerably. The other, the IEA's Alternative Policy Scenario in its 2007 outlook, finds a possible reduction of 11 percent by 2030. Under this scenario the biggest gains can be achieved in China and India. Coal consumption would be substantially lower due to greater efficiency of power plants and use of nonfossil alternatives: 23 percent less in China and 37 percent less in India. And oil savings of 19 percent for China and 17 percent for India would be achieved by a more fuel-efficient vehicle fleet and greater use of biofuels.[68]

More broadly, new policy can help bring down costs rapidly and Professors Robert Socolow and Stephen Pacala of Princeton University have devised a useful analytical guide for policymakers considering the large-scale carbon emission reductions required to achieve the monumental task of stabilizing carbon dioxide concentrations that we need to avert the costly consequences that scientists warn about of warming of more than 2 degrees centigrade. (Some warming is already built into the climate system given anthropogenic carbon emissions and the fact that a carbon dioxide molecule can remain in the atmosphere for as much as a century.) An element of urgency is added when we consider that the climate system has been likened to a canoe in that it may simply lean in response to increasing concentrations of carbon, but it may also reach a tipping point, yielding much more abrupt change.[69] Socolow and Pacala propose a global commitment to seven technological-improvement wedges that would halve emission from 14 gigatons by mid-century. Possibilities include a doubling of fuel economy of cars from 30 to 60 miles per gallon, cutting electricity use in buildings by 25 percent, increasing windpower 40-fold (displacing coal), or adding twice today's nuclear output (displacing coal).[70]

Fleshing out the practical nature of each wedge, as well as the possible tradeoffs and synergies with energy security goals, is crucial. The challenge is daunting but, as Socolow and Pacala have pointed out, it is not insurmountable if one sees the tremendous infrastructure investments envisioned in the IEA scenarios as opportunities. Most structures, vehicles and their contents are yet to be designed and built. As Socolow and Pacala put it, "dramatic changes are plausible over the next 50 years because so much of the energy canvas is still blank."

Notes

1. Keith Bradsher, "Pollution from Chinese Coal Casts a Global Shadow," *New York Times,* June 11, 2006; W. Corbett Dabbs, "Oil Production and Environmental Damage," Research Paper 15, Trade and Environment Database, (Washington, D.C.: American University, 1996), http://www1.american.edu/TED/projects/tedcross/xoilpr15.htm; Ann Bordetsky, et al., *Driving It Home: Choosing the Right Path for Fueling North America's Transportation Future,* NRDC, Western Resource Advocates, Pembina Institute, New York, NY, June 2007, http://www.nrdc.org/energy/drivingithome/contents.asp.

2. *Facing the Hard Truths about Energy,* National Petroleum Council, 2007, http://www.npchardtruthsreport.org.

3. Energy Information Administration, Department of Energy, Annual Energy Review 2006, 344, http://tonto.eia.doe.gov/FTPROOT/multifuel/038406.pdf. "Other" includes the use of municipal solid waste, coal coke net imports and geothermal sources for energy.

4. Office of Air Quality Planning and Standards, Environmental Protection Agency, *Latest Findings on National Air Quality—Status and Trends through 2006,* Research Triangle Park, North Carolina, EPA-454/R-07-007, January 2008, http://www.epa.gov/air/airtrends/2007/report/trends_report_full.pdf; Zachary Corrigan, et al. *Pollution on the Rise: Local Trends in Power Plant Pollution* (Washington, D.C.: U.S PIRG Education Fund, January 2005), http://static.uspirg.org/reports/pollutionontherise.pdf.

5. National Institute for Occupational Safety and Health, Centers for Disease Control, Occupational Respiratory Disease Surveillance, "Coal Workers' Health Surveillance Program," Fall 2008 Update, http://www.cdc.gov/niosh/topics/surveillance/ords/CWHSP-News-Fall2008.html.

6. Ken Ward, Jr., "Black Lung Rates Double in 10 Years," *The Charleston Gazette,* September 19, 2007.

7. Xiaohui Zhao and Jiang Xueli, "Coal Mining: Most Deadly Job in China," *China Daily,* November 13, 2004.

8. Keith Bradsher and David Barboza, "Pollution From Chinese Coal Casts a Global Shadow," *New York Times,* June 11, 2006.

9. Ibid.

10. Office of Air and Radiation, Environmental Protection Agency, *Final Report: Environmental Footprints and Costs of Coal-Based Integrated Gasification Combined Cycle and Pulverized Coal Technologies,* EPA-430/R-06/006, Washington, D.C., July 2006.

11. Edward S. Rubin, Chao Chen and Anand B. Rao, "Cost and Performance of Fossil Fuel Power Plants with SO_2 Capture and Storage," Energy Policy, 35, no. 9 (2007): 4444–4454, September 2007, Elsevier Ltd.

12. Daniel A. Lashof, et al., *Coal in a Changing Climate,* NRDC Issue Paper, Natural Resources Defense Council, New York, February 2007, http://www.nrdc.org/global-Warming/coal/coalclimate.pdf.

13. Energy Information Administration, Department of Energy, *Annual Energy Outlook 2006,* DOE/EIA-0383(2006), http://www.eia.doe.gov/oiaf/archive/aeo06/index.html.

14. Energy Information Administration, Department of Energy, *Annual Energy Outlook 2007,* DOE/EIA-0383(2007), http://www.eia.doe.gov/oiaf/archive/aeo07/index.html.

15. Ibid.

16. Ibid.

17. U.S. EPA, Office of Transportation and Air Quality, EPA420-F-07-035, April 2007 (the source for the methanol bar is natural gas); Bordetsky, *Driving It Home.*

18. Thomas G. Kraemer, et al., *Coal: America's Energy Future,* National Coal Council, Washington, D.C., 2006, http://nationalcoalcouncil.org/Documents/NCC_Report_Vol1.pdf.

19. George A. Olah, Alain Goeppert, G.K. Surya Prakash, *Beyond Oil and Gas: The Methanol Economy* (Weinheim: Wiley-VCH, 2006).

20. *Facing the Hard Truths about Energy,* National Petroleum Council, 2007, http://www.npchardtruthsreport.org.

21. Ibid.

22. For more on cradle-to-cradle thinking see William McDonough and Michael Braungart's *Cradle-to-Cradle: Rethinking the Way We Make Things* (New York: North Point Press, 2002).

23. *Managing America's Latest Natural Gas Crisis*, NRDC analysis, November 2005.

24. R.E.H. Sims, et al., Energy supply. In Climate Change 2007: Mitigation, Contribution of Working Group III to the Fourth Assessment Report of the Intergovernmental Panel on Climate Change (Cambridge and New York: Cambridge University Press, 2007).

25. Ibid.

26. Bordetsky, *Driving It Home.*

27. Ibid.; Deron Lovaas, "Taking the High Road to Energy Security," *In Business,* 28, no. 3 (May/June 2006), http://www.jgpress.com/inbusiness/archives/_free/000987.html.

28. "Fact Sheet: In Situ Technology," Oil Sands Discovery Center, Fort McMurray, Alberta, http://www.oilsandsdiscovery.com/.

29. Rick Schneider and Simon Dyer, *Death by a Thousand Cuts: The Impacts of In Situ Oil Sands Development on Alberta's Boreal Forest,* Canadian Parks and Wilderness Society and the Pembina Institute, Calgary, Alberta, August 2006, http://www.oilsandswatch.org/pub/1262.

30. National Commission on Energy Policy, Bipartisan Policy Center, *Unconventional Fossil-Based Fuels Issue Brief,* Issue Brief #1, Washington, D.C., October 8, 2008, http://www.energycommission.org/ht/display/ReleaseDetails/i/8700/pid/500.

31. Donald L. Klass, "Biomass Energy," in *Dictionary of Energy*, eds., Cutler J. Cleveland and Christopher Morris (Amsterdam: Elsevier Press, 2006).

32. Suzanne Hunt et al., *Biofuels for Transport: Global Potential and Implications for Sustainable Energy and Agriculture,* prepared by Worldwatch Institute for the German Ministry of Food, Agriculture and Consumer Protection in coordination with the German Agency for Technical Cooperation and the German Agency of Renewable Resources (London: Earthscan, 2007).

33. Ibid.

34. Ibid.

35. Ibid.

36. Ellie Brown, *Cruel Oil: How Palm Oil Harms Health, Rainforest & Wildlife,* Center for Science in the Public Interest, May 2005, http://www.cspinet.org/new/pdf/palm_oil_final_5-27-05.pdf.

37. Ibid.

38. Jean Aden et al., World Bank. *Indonesia: Environment and Natural Resource Management in a Time of Transition* (Washington, D.C., February 2001), http://www-wds.worldbank.org/servlet/main?menuPK=64187510&pagePK=64193027&piPK=64187937&theSitePK=523679&entityID=000094946_01110804163281.

39. Hunt, *Biofuels for Transport.*

40. R. Schneider, et al. (2000) as quoted in *Biofuels for Transport.*

41. Hunt, *Biofuels for Transport.*

42. Ibid., and John Sheehan, presentation at the Commercial Aviation Alternative Fuels Initiative 2007 conference, Washington, D.C., November 7–8, 2007.

43. John Sheehan presentation.

44. Ibid.

45. Ibid.

46. Ibid.

47. Daniel De La Torre Ugarte, et al. "Conditions that Influence the Economic Viability of Ethanol from Corn Stover in the Midwest of the USA," *International Sugar Journal* 108, no. 1287, 2006.

48. International Energy Agency, *World Energy Outlook 2007,* OECD/IEA, Paris, France, 2007

49. Ibid.

50. Greenpeace, Global Wind Energy Council, *Global Wind Energy Outlook,* Brussels, Belgium, September, 2006, http://www.gwec.net/.

51. Gingrich book, Pew Center on Global Climate Change, http://www.pewclimate.org/what_s_being_done/in_the_states/rps.cfm.

52. Energy Efficiency and Renewable Energy Administration, Department of Energy, *20% Wind Energy by 2030: Increasing Wind Energy's Contribution to U.S. Electricity Supply,* DOE/GO-102008-2567, Oak Ridge, TN, July 2008, http://www1.eere.energy.gov/windandhydro/pdfs/41869.pdf.

53. Greenpeace, *Global Wind Energy Outlook.*

54. Jason W Horn, Edward B. Arnett and Thomas H. Kunz, "Behavioral Responses of Bats to Operating Wind Turbines," *Journal of Wildlife Management* 72 no. 1, 2008, http://www.bu.edu/cecb/wind/video/Horn_et_al_2008.pdf; Wallace Erickson, et al., Western EcoSystems Technology, *Avian Collisions with Wind Turbines: A Summary of Existing Studies and Comparisons with Other Sources of Avian Collision Mortality in the U.S.,* National Wind Coordinating Committee, Washington, D.C., August 2001, http://www.nationalwind.org/publications/wildlife/avian_collisions.pdf.

55. Bill McKibben, "Serious Wind: Environmentalists Should be Careful What They Wish for," *Orion Magazine,* 187 (July-August), http://www.adirondackwind.com/SERIOUS_WIND.htm.

56. Travis Bradford, *Solar Revolution: The Economic Transformation of the Global Energy Industry* (London: MIT Press, 2006).

57. Ibid.

58. Ibid.

59. Ariana Eunjung Cha, "Solar Energy Firms Leave Waste Behind in China," *Washington Post,* March 9, 2008.

60. Environmental Kuznets curve as defined in the *Encyclopedia of Energy* from Elsevier Press.

61. IEA, *World Energy Outlook 2007*.

62. To be clear, its role is likely to be much larger if climate policies are widely adopted; the IEA for example finds that its share by 2030 would be 27 percent higher in its alternative policy vs. reference case.

63. Catherine Morris et al., *Nuclear Power Joint Fact-Finding,* The Keystone Center, Keystone, Colorado, June 2007, http://www.nuclear.gov/pdfFiles/rpt_KeystoneReportNuclear PowerJointFactFinding_2007.pdf.

64. See Douglas Frantz and Catherine Collins, "Those Nuclear Flashpoints are Made in Pakistan," *Washington Post,* November 11, 2007.

65. Jim Harding, "Economics of Nuclear Power and Proliferation Risks in a Carbon-Constrained World," *Electricity Journal,* Elsevier, Inc., November, 2007.

66. Joseph Romm, *The Hype About Hydrogen,* (Washington D.C.: Island Press 2004).

67. Tim Moran, "Tanks are key to hydrogen economy's growth," *Automotive News,* November 19, 2007.

68. Ibid.

69. Richard A. Posner, *Catastrophe: Risk and Response* (New York: Oxford University Press 2004).

70. Robert Socolow and Stephen Pacala, "A Plan to Keep Carbon in Check," *Scientific American,* September 2006.

CHAPTER 23

Realism and Idealism in the Energy Security Debate

Gal Luft and Anne Korin

In this book we sought to inquire how different actors in the global energy system view energy security, to assess some of the growing energy security challenges that the 21st century holds in store for humanity and, with the help of leading experts, reflect on how the world is likely to address them. This inquiry stemmed from a sense that there is a strong disconnect between the publicly stated policies, coming from officials and experts in net energy producing and consuming countries alike, in praise of international cooperation, collective security, free markets, fair distribution of resources and commitment to sustainable growth and the welfare of future generations, and the reality on the ground, characterized by volatile energy prices, rising geopolitical instability, suppliers using strong-arm tactics against consumers while consumers beat their chests about energy self-sufficiency and boost their military capabilities to ensure their access to energy. If everybody agrees on the bedrock principles of an effective global economic system why do we face today the gravest risks to our energy supply? And why is the maximal degree of energy security we can hope for, according to James R. Schlesinger, a keen observer of the energy and security world, "various degrees of insecurity"?[1]

The short answer, as described throughout the book, is that per capita energy use is growing by leaps and bounds and this makes nations more prone than ever to compete over access to cheap and depleting energy sources. "The diagnosis of the energy crisis is quite simple," reiterated President George W. Bush, "Demand for energy is increasing while supplies of oil and natural gas are diminishing."[2] In the process of securing energy supplies, energy-hungry nations are often forced to compromise other important security, economic and environmental concerns. At the same time, exporters are nationalizing their energy industries, leaving less and less room for the private sector and foreign investors while increasingly using energy as tool to advance their foreign policy agenda.

Under such conditions, agreeing on a unified energy security agenda will be increasingly difficult and each country is likely to pursue its own interests based on what it perceives as energy security. As the first half of this book showed, one complicating factor in the effort to create a common energy security agenda is that there is no uniform view of what energy security really is. Countries' understanding of energy security depends on their geographical location, resource endowment, level of economic development, system of governance and many other factors. For some countries energy security means producing more energy at home and relying less on foreigners. For others, it is about creating economic and political interdependencies with their suppliers even if those suppliers are unsavory. Some countries are more concerned about natural gas and electricity; others about oil and transportation. Many are dependent on external sources for both. Some place high hopes in the use of military force to secure energy supply; others put their faith in collective security arrangements, loose alliances and even looser international treaties and organizations. For China, energy security means securing supply through government-to-government deals and buying stakes in foreign oil fields—in Sudan, Nigeria, Angola and so on. Others, like India and Japan, prefer to buy oil on the global market, seeing little sense in China's overseas investments. For Russia, OPEC and others who generate the overwhelming share of their governments' revenues from energy exports, energy security is all about security of demand that they hope to achieve by creating a vertical monopoly over the supply of energy, discouraging and undermining consumers' diversification efforts and imposing restrictions on foreign investment in domestic oil and gas fields. A few like Bahrain, Indonesia and even Norway and the UK, whose hydrocarbon sectors have either leveled off or are already in decline, are making the transition from an exporter mindset to that of an importer.

Variety but Not Variety Alone

Despite variations in the perceptions about energy security, there are few universal principles that dominate almost every country's energy security strategy. The first is the doctrine articulated by Winston Churchill before the British Parliament in 1913, stating that "safety and certainty in oil lie in *variety* and *variety* alone."[3] Different countries have different interpretations of the term "variety." Consumers seek variety of suppliers and supply lanes so that if one or more suppliers go offline the impact can be minimized. Producers are uncomfortable with their dependence on a single market and seek to expand their portfolio of clients. Hugo Chavez' attempts to break Venezuela's dependence on the U.S. market by diverting an increasing part of his country's oil to China is one example. Like consumers, producers to want to diversify their supply lanes and avoid blockades or terrorist acts that could devastate their economies. Efforts by both producers and consumers to diversify supply lines have given rise to a new breed of countries in the energy security picture: transit countries. Turkey, Cameroon and Georgia and in the future perhaps Bangladesh, Afghanistan, Israel, Pakistan, Niger, and Colombia are some of the countries that are currently in the process of gaining increasing international status and national wealth by being conduits for oil and gas.

The temptation to be a transit state is great: revenue earning from granting right of way, an influx of foreign investment and increased energy security as some of the oil or gas can be diverted to the transit state's market. But as Necdet Pamir described in the case of Turkey, with the benefits come some diplomatic and security challenges. By enabling Caspian energy to bypass Russia and flow to European markets, Azerbaijan, Georgia and Turkey find themselves at odds with Moscow. The Trans-Saharan gas pipeline that could, if built, connect Nigeria's gas reserves to Europe via Algeria's Mediterranean coast will make Niger, through which 470 miles of the pipeline is planned to traverse, a key contributor to European energy security. EU officials say the pipeline could supply 20 bcm a year of gas to Europe by 2016. But, as in the case of the BTC pipeline, such a project could threaten Russia's security of demand and Nigeria, Niger, and Algeria are likely to come under pressure from Moscow to abandon this effort. Allowing Iranian gas to pass to India through Pakistan's territory would no doubt incur Washington's wrath. The United States would also be equally unhappy if Colombia went ahead and lent its territory to become a land bridge for Venezuelan oil to reach the Pacific coast, from where it can be easily shipped to China instead of the United States. And if Afghanistan somehow succeeded in becoming a conduit for Turkmen gas en route to India that would be a challenge to Iran, which competes over access to the Indian market. Indeed, for every winner there is a loser.

As oil and gas become increasingly difficult to obtain, the definition of variety broadens from *geographical* variety to variety of *energy* sources. In other words, countries seek to diversify their energy basket to include as many sources of energy as can contribute to the grid and the transportation sector. Broadening a country's energy portfolio through increased use of alternative fuels, nuclear energy and renewable energy sources reduces the impact of a disruption in hydrocarbon supply. Even within the oil and gas sector there are calls for increased variety. The definition of oil is expanding to include a variety of nonconventional forms of petroleum made from tar sands, heavy oil, oil shale, coal-to-liquids and gas-to-liquids. Conventional natural gas is now being increasingly augmented by coal-bed methane, shale gas, tight sandstone gas, and, in the future, possibly methane hydrates.

Redundancy and Liquidity

Redundancy and liquidity are also universal principles of energy security. As described by several contributors, both the power and oil sectors have too little wiggle room to deal with supply disruptions, whether man-made or due to natural reasons. For years, disruptions in the oil sector could be offset by OPEC's spare capacity—the ability of some producers, chiefly Saudi Arabia, to inject extra oil into the market when other suppliers falter. This spare capacity was the oil market's main source of liquidity. In 2002, spare capacity amounted to nearly 10 percent of the 76 mbd global oil market. A year later, with demand climbing to 78 million barrels, spare capacity dropped to about 5 percent. This cushion was sufficient to prevent an oil crisis when a labor strike in Venezuela, ethnic riots in

Nigeria and a war in Iraq took major producers out of the market for extended periods. With global daily demand at 86 mbd spare capacity is barely 2 mbd, which is at the dangerous level of 2 percent. Despite Saudi Arabia's reassurance that it is accelerating plans to bring new oil fields into production, this is all too little, too late. The IEA estimates that spare capacity will rise to 4 mbd in 2010 as new projects come on stream but will fall again toward 2013 as demand continues to grow.[4] As a result, the oil market in the decades to come will resemble a car without shock absorbers: the tiniest bump on the road can send a passenger to the ceiling. Without liquidity, only one mechanism is left to bring the market to equilibrium: rapid and uncontrolled price increases.

To compensate for the erosion in OPEC's spare capacity, major oil consuming countries would have to take steps to insulate their economies from supply disruptions by creating liquidity mechanisms of their own in the form of strategic reserves. More than 4 billion barrels are held in strategic reserves, roughly a third of which is government-controlled (the rest is held by private industry). The United States alone holds an emergency stockpile of some 700 million barrels, a number it intends to increase in the coming years. Japan owns 580 million barrels; South Korea has 150 million; and the EU mandates that each member country keep the equivalent of 90 days of imports. Meanwhile, China is in the process of building a 310 million-barrel reserve, and India, 37 million. The IEA has made clear that the emergency stockpiles of its member countries are for strategic purposes only. But were the United States and Europe to increase their reserves significantly and major Asian nations encouraged to break that constraint and establish larger oil banks, within a few years a new global Strategic Petroleum Reserve could begin to serve as a liquidity mechanism, replacing the failings of OPEC. But it is important to remember that strategic stocks can only strengthen energy security when they are handled properly and when they are activated in a concerted manner as part of an effective international framework. Unfortunately, despite the global nature of the oil market, there is insufficient international coordination of strategic reserves, and most countries have opaque procedures on when and how to fill the stocks and on when oil can be released. Furthermore, the big emerging economies of China and India are not part of the IEA, which coordinates the reserves held by the rich countries. Barring their inclusion in the international emergency management system China and India will be tempted to build massive stockpiles, adding extra demand to an already stretched market. David Victor and Sarah Eskreis-Winkler correctly point out that "a better-run and better-coordinated international system of oil caches could help convince China and India that treating oil as a true commodity and trusting the markets more are better ways to improve their energy security than pursuing oil mercantilism."[5]

Redundancy is also an imperative for producers. In order to bring their product to market energy exporters depend on vast pipeline networks, export terminals and LNG liquefaction facilities. A failure of one of those components in the supply chain would hurt not only the economic well being of the producer but also its image as a reliable supplier. In this, Saudi Arabia is perhaps the most vulnerable producer. As Ali Koknar described in Chapter 2, the Kingdom's oil system is target rich and extremely vulnerable to terrorist acts. This is not only due to al-Qaeda's strong presence there and its ability to carry out coordinated attacks but also to the structure of the Kingdom's oil infrastructure. Over half of Saudi Arabia's oil reserves are contained in just eight fields, among them the world's largest onshore oil field—Ghawar, which alone accounts for about half of the country's total oil production capacity—and Safaniya, the world's largest off-shore oilfield. About two-thirds of Saudi Arabia's crude oil is processed in a single enormous facility called Abqaiq, 25 miles inland from the Gulf of Bahrain. On the Persian Gulf, Saudi Arabia has just two primary oil export terminals: Ras Tanura—the world's largest offshore oil loading facility, through which a 10 percent of global oil supply flows daily—and Ras al-Ju'aymah. A successful terrorist attack on each one of these hubs could take up to half of Saudi oil off the market for an extended period of time and with it most of the world's spare capacity, causing a major economic shock. In addition to this, Saudi Arabia now faces the threat of Iranian blockage of the Strait of Hormuz. Iran possesses a stockpile of mines that could be used to disrupt the flow of transportation and provoke the United States to engage in extended military conflict. Such emerging threats to Saudi access to global markets have revived interest in the Trans-Arabia oil pipeline project that would circumvent the Strait of Hormuz by carrying Saudi oil from Ras Tanura to export terminals in Oman, UAE and Yemen. As Ariel Cohen described, Russia too is increasingly interested in diversification of its supply routes to both the European and Asian markets. Unlike Saudi Arabia, whose primary concerns are terrorism and war in the Persian Gulf, for Moscow supply route diversification is aimed at Russia's dominating access to its markets and preventing competing conduits of Caspian energy from capturing a significant share of the European market.

Redundancy is no less important in the power sector. As David Sweet pointed out, the vulnerabilities of power grids throughout the world to intrusions and terrorist attacks are at all-time highs with potential for major and economically devastating disruptions. Not withstanding advances in both cyber and physical security as well as attempts to decentralize power sources through DE, the short-term or long-term disruption of electricity to banks, refineries, hospitals, airports, water systems and military installations still presents a terrifying scenario. Power companies, policymakers and regulators throughout the world are waking up to this reality, developing tactics and technologies to defend high impact targets like transformers and supervisory control and data acquisition, or SCADA, systems.[6] In increasingly integrated markets like Europe a main strategy to add redundancy is to interconnect national transmission grids that were initially constructed to be independent and stand-alone.

Realists vs. Idealists

In most cases the universal principles discussed above are not enough to fulfill countries' energy security needs, and this brings us to the biggest question facing the energy security community: will humanity manage to peacefully balance the interests of all of the players in the energy security system or will the world descend into a series of diplomatic skirmishes, fierce economic contest and energy wars. Michael Klare's and Chris Fettweis' chapters shed some light on one of the most interesting debates in the field of international relations today between energy security realists and what can be called energy security idealists.

Energy security realists see the world grappling with a cluster of challenges that will only get worse as time goes by. They assume that countries are predisposed to pursue their self-interest using every aspect of their national power. They therefore tend to view energy as a subset of global power politics and a legitimate tool of foreign policy, and they are skeptical of the current energy market's ability to guarantee long term supply. Realists point out that throughout history, certain commodities, and in particular energy commodities, minerals, water and food, have had a strategic value beyond their market price and as such they have been repeatedly used as tools of foreign policy by exporters and have been among the prime catalysts for armed conflict. As the world is evolving into what Michael Klare calls a system of "rising powers/shrinking planet," the risk of energy wars is in the minds of many. Klare's predictions are bleak, seeing the earth transforming into "a barely habitable scene of desolation" due to a series of energy conflicts and environmental degradation, and this view is not uncommon among energy security realists.[7] While realists accept the role of collaboration and interdependencies as a way to enhance collective energy security, they do insist on weighing this against other material forces, together with an understanding of the history, culture and economics of the societies comprising the international system. In a world of jihad, terrorism, proliferation of weapons of mass destruction and deepening divide between Islam and the West, realists cannot ignore the fact that more than three quarters of the world's proven conventional oil reserves and nearly half of its natural gas reserves are concentrated in Muslim countries. Realists recognize the power and threat of the oil cartel, and they sharply distinguish between nationalized resources used as tools of the state and resources owned and commercially handled by international companies that adhere to free market rules. In light of all this, realists see a role for the state in a concerted effort to reduce the strategic value of oil and gas, in effect putting energy policy in the service of foreign policy as opposed to the current situation in which foreign policy is increasingly subjugated to energy policy concerns.

Idealists on the other hand view a slightly rosier future, believing that war to control territories that contain fossil fuels will continue to be a very rare phenomenon as the new century unfolds. Fettweis explains that fighting over energy is futile since it will always be cheaper to buy oil than to seize it. He argues that "the interests of consumers and producers do not conflict—all parties involved in oil production have serious interests in stability, without which no one can benefit," and this reflects the bedrock principle of energy security idealism: strong faith in the power of markets and the concept of "interdependence" as the key to ensure energy security. Idealists point out that because oil and gas are traded globally, a supply disruption anywhere will affect prices everywhere. They have a fundamental belief that energy market players are rational and motivated by profit maximization. Markets should be left to work and higher prices are not an energy security problem but a solution as they depress demand and increase efficiency. Idealists tend to downplay ideological, cultural and geopolitical drivers, and they view efforts by consumers to insulate their economies through greater self-reliance as futile and undesirable. International competitive and integrated markets, on the other hand, are viewed as tension reducers that increase market certainty and create a healthy equilibrium between the economic interests of consumers and producers. Popular among idealists is the idea of a "grand bargain" among producers and consumers, one that, in the words of World Bank President Robert Zoellick, involves "sharing plans for expanding supplies, including options other than oil and gas; improving efficiency and lessening demand; assisting with energy for the poor; and considering how these policies relate to carbon production and climate change policies."[8] Such calls for improved multilateralism on energy security are not new. The problem is that they do not seem to work. In June 2008, when global oil prices hit a record near $140 a barrel, the world's major oil producers and consumers, as well as leaders from big oil firms and international organizations convened in Jeddah, Saudi Arabia, to seek ways to bring stability to the international oil market for the benefit of all. At the conference British Prime Minister Gordon Brown called for a long-term deal whereby the oil-consuming nations would diversify energy supplies, moving into nuclear and renewables, and the oil-producing countries would increase production, as well as recycle some of their huge profits into western renewable technologies.[9] But despite these calls for adoption of win-win solutions, tensions between producers and consumers worsened further in the month that followed and the prospects for such a grand bargain, and even, more, the prospects of actors fulfilling their promises, seem highly unlikely.

The belief in the rationality of markets causes idealists to play down the notion that producers would use their energy as a weapon. The Arab oil embargo of 1973, which demonstrated the danger of a conflict between suppliers and consumers, is viewed as a solitary incident that acted as a boomerang, hurting the exporters more than the consumers. The threats of using the energy weapon by Hugo Chavez and Mahmoud Ahmadinejad are viewed as empty rhetoric, and Russia's repeated use of the natural gas weapon can be avoided through stronger integration of European markets and enhanced dialogue with Moscow.

The acolytes of energy security idealism also sweep away views calling for increased energy independence. As Daniel Yergin wrote in *Foreign Affairs,* real energy security requires setting aside the pipe dream of energy independence and embracing interdependence.[10] Pierre Noël alleges that calls for energy independence "reinforce prejudices in China and India about the need for aggressive foreign energy policies—a process that looks like a vicious circle."[11] And Frank Verrastro and Sarah Ladislaw called for "a much more sophisticated approach to energy policymaking, one that more fully appreciates the interdependencies of global markets, the complex nature of energy security, and the need to manage the trade-offs inherent in energy policy decision making."[12]

If realists are less "sophisticated" in their thinking it is primarily because they assume that most countries—consumers and producers alike—are still motivated by nationalistic sentiments and that market forces and economic interdependence do not guarantee peace and stability. The notion that interdependence reduces the risk of conflict does not pass the test of historical scrutiny. World War I broke among the most economically interdependent countries. Despite high trade levels in 1913–14 German leaders decided to attack, to ensure long-term access to markets and raw materials. In the 1930s, the two most aggressive states, Germany and Imperial Japan, were also the most highly interdependent despite their efforts towards autarky relying on other states for critical raw materials. In fact, Japan had a much higher level of economic interdependence with other countries than it did in the 1920s, but nonetheless embarked on aggressive imperialism.

Energy security realists' skepticism of the ability of energy markets to deliver energy security also stems from their view of energy markets as anything but free. Nearly 80 percent of the world's oil reserves are controlled by governments through their national oil companies. These governments set prices by their investment and production decisions, and they have wide latitude to shut off the spigot for political reasons, just as Libya did as we were writing these lines in October 2008 when it decided to stop oil supply to Switzerland in response to the arrest in Geneva of the son of Libyan leader Muammar Gaddafi.[13]

OPEC countries that rely heavily on energy revenues are inclined to keep prices high. In Winter 2008, as the price of oil plunged from its historical high of $147 a barrel to under $40, the IMF assessed that Saudi Arabia must earn at least $49 a barrel to avoid going into deficit, Iran and Venezuela need $90 and Iraq $110 to balance their books.[14] This is the main reason why those countries are likely to continue to constrict supply and restrict access to foreign investment. To this end, Saudi Arabia's King Abdullah ordered some new oil discoveries left untapped to preserve oil wealth in the world's top exporter for future generations.[15] Russia also showed that it aims to restrict production. "The idea of mothballing oilfields seems very interesting to me," Russian Energy Minister Sergei Shmatko said.[16] These are not necessarily displays of greed and focus on short term economic considerations but also a reflection of a different perception of time in some of the producers' cultures. Unlike well-diversified industrialized economies where there is strong belief in the power of technology and innovation to ensure economic progress, countries heavily reliant on energy revenues for their economic well being see their reserves as an insurance policy that guarantees their future economic security. This may also explain exporters' lack of transparency, denying energy markets the information that is so vital to their healthy functioning. Recent nationalization efforts of energy assets in places like Venezuela, Russia, and Bolivia promise more government control and less hospitable investment climates for IOCs in the decades to come. Furthermore, in many countries energy prices are controlled by governments and petroleum products are either sold for way below market prices or are heavily taxed. Finally, trade barriers on alternative fuels are still prevalent in the United States and EU and are blocking the road to international free and open trade among consumers and producers.

Make no mistake, despite intensive efforts by Western oil companies in recent decades to develop non-OPEC sources of supply in West Africa, the Caspian, Latin America and the tar sands of Canada, the Middle East remains and will continue to remain the world's primary supplier of crude oil. The IEA projects that the share of Middle Eastern members of OPEC of world oil production will grow from 28 percent today to 43 percent in 2030. This will no doubt allow OPEC members to wield tremendous geopolitical power and an ability to manipulate the oil prices to the detriment of the global economy. Russia's recent international behavior is a source of great concern in the West. Just one month after its attack on Georgia, Russia's President Dmitry Medvedev delivered a hard blow to the prospect of multilateralism in energy security when he told the UN Security Council that Russia would unilaterally claim part of the energy-rich Arctic, sidestepping efforts to reach multinational agreement on the future of this region. "This is our responsibility, and simply our direct duty, to our descendents," he said. "We must surely, and for the long-term future, secure Russia's interests in the Arctic."[17]

As we move deeper into the 21st century many of the challenges of the oil market will be duplicated in the natural gas market. Due to high oil prices natural gas will continue to replace oil wherever possible. In addition, because natural gas emits less CO_2 when it is burned than either coal or petroleum, governments implementing national or regional plans to reduce greenhouse gas emissions may encourage its use. As a result, according to the EIA, total natural gas consumption is projected to increase from 104 tcf in 2005 to 158 tcf in 2030.[18] On the supply side, almost three-quarters of the world's natural gas reserves and half of the world's undiscovered reserves are located in the Middle East and Eurasia. Russia, Iran, and Qatar together account for about 57 percent of the world's natural gas reserves. With such growing control over reserves the temptation to create an OPEC-like natural gas cartel will be strong. In January 2007, Iran's supreme leader Ayatollah Ali Khamenei proposed that Iran and Russia create a cartel. Later that year then Russian President Vladimir Putin and Qatari Emir Sheik Hamad bin Khalifa Al Thani agreed to explore the idea. President Abdelaziz Bouteflika of Algeria and President Hugo Chávez of Venezuela are also known to support creation of such a cartel. And in October 2008, Iran, Russia and Qatar announced that they would form a "big gas troika."[19] But many energy security idealists still play down this possibility, pointing to the complexity of natural gas markets compared to oil. Natural gas is less fungible than oil and unlike oil, which is traded on an exchange that constantly updates the market price based on supply and demand, it is sold under tight contracts that allow buyers to lock in prices for up to 25 years. This makes a gas cartel difficult to achieve, according to the skeptics. But as more natural gas is traded in the form of LNG and as fewer countries control its reserves the feasibility of such a cartel and likelihood of its effectiveness increase. Whether or not the 16-member Gas

Producing Countries Forum will evolve into a cartel is hard to tell at this point but many of this group's members are clearly interested in the option. It is worth remembering that OPEC was first formed in 1960, but it did not function as a true cartel until 1999, when Saudi Arabia began to assert its will to push prices higher.

Finally, the financial crisis that began in 2008 and is unfolding as these lines are being written is likely to leave energy-producing countries in a more advantageous position to solidify control over the world's energy system as alternatives to hydrocarbons become less competitive. The collapse of the global credit system has reduced the volume of investment in renewable energy from $7 billion in 2007 to $5 billion in 2008 and a forecasted $4 billion in 2009.

There is no doubt that in the era of globalization countries become increasingly interdependent in a variety of fields. There is also little dispute that in a perfect world interdependence is a wonderful idea. But the world is far from perfect and the world's top energy exporters are the most imperfect of all. Regretfully, to date, the idealist approach to energy security has proven ineffective in checking the emboldened posture of energy exporters and the overt challenges they pose to global energy security and to international security writ large. This is particularly true for Europe, where the approach of soft security is applied to energy security as well and where energy security idealism is therefore pervasive. European action in face of Russia's coercion has been weak, disunited and unfocused. This has given the Kremlin greater political influence, to the detriment of Europe's economic security. The EU's purported policy of promoting greater competition in energy supplies and diversification of the continent's natural gas sources has been largely unsuccessful, and projects like Nabucco, which could help diversify European energy supply, seem to have gained little traction. High level European officials who publicly lament the EU's inability to diversify its sources are often the same ones who give endorsements to Russian projects that are going to make things worse. As Robert Bell noted in Chapter 17, energy security idealism is one of the main reasons behind some EU governments' reluctance to enable an expanded role for NATO in energy security, believing that the discussion on energy security in the framework of NATO would send the wrong signal to Russia. Pierre Noël's assertion that "NATO for energy is a dangerous nonsense" is reflective of this mindset.[20]

When it comes to Washington, the idealists' approach to energy security also leaves much to be desired. The years of the Bush administration were dedicated to promotion of anti-terrorism best practices abroad and collaboration on critical energy infrastructure protection as well as an effort to promote political reforms in energy-producing regions and democratize Arab regimes in the hope that such policy could put U.S. relations with such regimes on a sound political footing and hence ensure security of supply.[21] But the Middle East is slow to embrace democracy, and while as of this writing it is premature to determine whether or not the Iraqi experiment is a success, in other parts of the region, as well as in other key energy producing countries like Russia, Kazakhstan, and Venezuela, freedom and democracy are in retreat. In fact, the Middle East is becoming increasingly volatile as most of the region's players have declared their intentions to follow Iran's path and develop nuclear capabilities, albeit for "peaceful purposes."

Environment and Security

In recent years, climate change concerns have been injected into the discussion on energy security, exposing another divergence of opinion in the energy security community. Some security experts hold that climate change poses a serious threat to international security. According to this view projected climate change acts as a threat multiplier in already fragile regions, exacerbating conditions that lead to failed states—the breeding grounds for extremism and terrorism—and adding to tensions even in stable regions of the world.[22] Those who view climate change as a global security threat of equal urgency to the current energy security challenge demand that the potential national security consequences of climate change be fully integrated into national security and national defense strategies, and that energy security solutions should only be applied if they also address climate change concerns. In Chapter 22, Deron Lovaas shows how difficult the tradeoffs are between energy security and environmental challenges. Energy security concerns can breed policies that environmentalists consider devastating. One example is coal-to-liquids. During the apartheid years, South Africa faced economic sanctions, which threatened its oil imports. The country addressed its energy security challenge by building coal-liquefaction facilities. Today, coal-rich countries like China and the United States, eager to cut petroleum dependence, are increasingly interested in similar coal-to-liquids technology, which is profitable as long as crude oil remains above $60 a barrel. But, for environmentalists, using coal to displace oil is a nightmare scenario, as coal-derived fuel produces twice as much CO_2 as petroleum-based fuel. Coal is not the only source of energy that improves energy security while increasing CO_2 emissions. Canadian tar-sands and oil shale have tremendous potential for additional liquid fuels, but the environmental impact of extracting them far exceeds that of conventional oil. Indonesia's attempt to supply the world with biodiesel made from palm oil led it to burn its rainforests, releasing such vast amounts of CO_2 that the country turned into the world's third biggest emitter after China and the United States.

While some put greater emphasis on energy security at the expense of the environment, others are willing to sacrifice energy security in order to address environmental concerns. The prime exhibit here is Germany, whose chancellor Angela Merkel named confronting climate change as her country's top priority. The German government announced that it will seek to totally phase out the country's coal-mining industrial sector by 2018. It also intends to phase out its nuclear-power industry by 2020 (this despite the fact that nuclear power plants do not emit CO_2). Considering the fact that 80 percent of Germany's electricity comes from coal and nuclear power, these are astonishing decisions. Replacing these sources of base load power with Russian natural gas and a slew of renewable-energy technologies, many of which are not yet competitive, could put the German economy at the mercy of the Kremlin, which has shown no compunction in using energy as a geopolitical weapon.[23] India also highlights the challenge in squaring security and climate-change considerations. India's growing demand for electricity puts it on the horns of dilemma: As Jeremy Carl showed, as owner of 10 percent of the world's coal reserves it could provide for most of its own power needs. Coal power for one billion Indians means a lot of CO_2. Yet, security-minded people are even more concerned about India shifting to the cleaner alternative to coal, natural gas. Should India decide to power its turbines with natural gas it is likely to become increasingly dependent on neighboring Iran, the world's second largest natural gas reserve. Pressuring India to reduce its emissions may slow down the melting of the ice-caps, but such a policy will send India right into the welcoming arms of Iran, undermining Western efforts to isolate Iran economically.

If there is an inconvenient truth relating to our energy system it is that we may not be able to address both issues in one strike, and too much emphasis on one could worsen the other. This is not to say that there are no policies that could successfully address both. Investment in efficiency, conservation, and clean technology is desirable and should be promoted. Renewable sources of energy like solar, wind and geothermal are critical. So are technologies to recycle CO_2 into usable liquid fuels like methanol and biodiesel from algae. But if one is to look at the big picture, such agreeable-to-all-sides remedies in and off themselves cannot solve problems of this magnitude. In times of peace and prosperity, security and the environment tend to compete for resources and public support on an equal footing, and the challenge policymakers face is to find an optimal balance between the two. But history shows that as geopolitical and economic concerns loom larger, environmental concerns tend to be put on the back burner, sometimes with painful long term consequences.

The Choice to Have Choice Is Ours

Nice as it would be to have a global energy system in which consumers, producers and transit states work harmoniously to the benefit of all, the current realities leave little room for optimism. Turning a blind eye to the destabilizing elements, indulging in wishful thinking or kowtowing to unsavory regimes all on the altar of interdependence is exactly what brought to some of the worst calamities of the last century. To reach true and lasting energy security we must understand the strategic value of energy resources and most specifically the implications of maintaining oil's monopoly in the transportation sector. As both Gal Luft and Paul Werbos pointed out in their chapters, the unique strategic importance of oil to the modern economy stems from the fact that the global economy's very enabler, the transportation sector, is utterly dependent on it. More than 95 percent of transportation energy is petroleum based. And yet, throughout the world, the energy debate is focused, from a foreign policy perspective—as articulated by the Carter Doctrine—on ensuring uninterrupted access to oil including by military force if necessary, and from a domestic policy perspective, on policies that increase either the availability of petroleum or the efficiency of its use. The reality is that efforts to expand petroleum supply or to crimp petroleum demand do not address the roots of the energy vulnerability: oil's monopoly in the transportation sector (the reason oil is a strategic commodity), and the stranglehold of OPEC over the consuming nations' economies. To enhance energy security there should be a focus on transformational policies that aim to reduce oil's strategic value through choice and competition in the transportation fuel market—in effect expanding Churchill's variety doctrine to include variety of fuels. Since oil's strategic status derives from its domination of ground transportation, this requires, first and foremost, vehicles that can run on a variety of fuels—not just petroleum-based fuel. Such vehicles reduce the importance of any one feedstock or fuel to the transportation sector. Cars that can run only on gasoline prevent significant market penetration of alternative fuels and thus maintain the monopoly of oil in the transportation sector and with it the excessive power of the oil cartel. As Paul Werbos described, for a cost of roughly $100 extra compared to a gasoline-only vehicle, automakers can make virtually any car a flex-fuel vehicle, capable of running on any combination of gasoline and a variety of alcohols such as ethanol and methanol, made from a variety of feedstocks, including agricultural material, waste, coal, and natural gas. (Alcohol does not just mean ethanol, and ethanol does not just mean corn.) Flex-fuel vehicles provide a platform on which fuels can compete and let consumers and the market choose the winning fuels and feedstocks based on economics. Electric cars and plug-in hybrid electric vehicles (PHEVs) also provide access into the transportation sector to non-petroleum energy sources, placing electricity—which in net consuming countries is for the most part not generated from oil—in competition with liquid fuel. Flex-fuel PHEVs enable electricity and alcohols from a variety of energy sources to compete against petroleum based fuel, thereby breaking oil's monopoly in the transportation sector and with it OPEC's growing control over the world's economy. Policies that accelerate the shift to competition-enabling cars are key to stripping oil of its strategic status. When cars and trucks throughout the world become platforms on which fuels can compete, oil will be forced to compete at the pump (or the socket) against other sources of energy like coal, biomass, natural gas and the broad spectrum of electricity sources. Such competition will not only drive down the price of oil but it will also alter the geopolitical balance of power in favor of oil importers and developing countries with resources to become alternative fuels producers.

The rise in oil prices constitutes a regressive tax on the world's poorest nations—many of which are located in Africa, South Asia and Latin America—with an adverse impact on global security. At the same time, these nations have a significant potential for energy production through their agricultural sectors, particularly considering the large swaths of degraded land suitable for cultivation of energy crops. Instead of importing their oil from OPEC, poor developing countries could export alternative fuels (not to mention supply fuel to their own markets), driving world development and facilitating healthy economic interdependencies. An international focus on breaking oil's transportation fuel monopoly would therefore be an engine for world development and poverty alleviation. According to author Robert Zubrin, "We could take something like a trillion dollars a year now going to the oil cartel, and redirect it to the world agricultural sector instead—about half going to advanced sector farmers and the other half going to the third world. This would create a huge financial engine for world development, and allow hundreds of millions of people to be lifted out of poverty."[24] Unfortunately, progress in this direction is thwarted by trade barriers put in place by developed nations, one example being the 54 cent per gallon tariff the United States imposes on ethanol imports.

A fuel choice strategy would enable the two fastest growing oil consumers, China and India, to avoid tying their transportation sectors exclusively to oil, a course that could become a complicating factor in their future relations with the West and with other regional powers. Maintaining oil's monopoly in the transportation fuel market bears the risk of putting the United States and China on a collision course over access to oil as demand increases. It is therefore in the interest of both countries to strive for fuel choice by utilizing their coal and biomass endowments as well as a broad spectrum of electricity sources, all of which can displace oil in the transportation sector.

But none of this will happen without committed leadership and government action to remove barriers to competition, through policies affecting technology (e.g., by enacting an open fuel standard, as discussed by Luft and Werbos) and trade (e.g., by repealing import tariffs on alternative fuels). Consuming countries will have to strike the right balance between security and environmental concerns and work in concert against anti-market forces and coercion by non-democratic energy exporters. And yes, there will be times that aircraft carriers will be put to use in the service of energy security.

Sheikh Zaki Yamani, a Saudi who served as his country's oil minister three decades ago is known for his reflection that "The Stone Age did not end for lack of stone, and the Oil Age will end long before the world runs out of oil." But whether or not the world is running out of oil 150 years after the discovery of oil in Titusville, Pennsylvania, the age of oil and gas is showing the first signs of slowing down and the curtain is being raised on a new energy era. What this era will look like, who will be its power brokers and how smooth will be the transition to it is premature to determine. What is clear is that it will be up to consumers to raise the curtain and do so pulling all their weight, as defenders of the old order are guaranteed to try to drag the curtain down to prolong the economic system on which they thrive. The ultimate question is who will pull harder.

Notes

1. Statement of James Schlesinger before the Committee on Foreign Relations, U.S. Senate, November 16, 2005, http://www.planetforlife.com/oilcrisis/oilschlesinger.html.

2. "Still Holding Customers Over a Barrel," *The Economist,* October 25, 2003.

3. Winston Churchill, *Parliamentary Debates* (Commons, July 17, 1913), 1474–1477.

4. "IEA's Tanaka: Spare Oil Capacity will Tighten Again," *Reuters,* August 27, 2008.

5. David G. Victor and Sarah Eskreis-Winkler, "In the Tank: Making the Most of Strategic Oil Reserves," *Foreign Affairs,* July/August 2008.

6. *Making the Nation Safer: The Role of Science and Technology in Countering Terrorism,* National Academy of Committee on Science and Technology for Countering Terrorism and National Research Council, 2002, http://www.nap.edu/openbook.php?isbn=0309084814.

7. Michael Klare, *Rising Powers, Shrinking Planet* (New York: Metropolitan Books 2008), 261.

8. "Modernizing Multilateralism and Markets," speech by Robert B. Zoellick, President, The World Bank Group, The Peterson Institute for International Economics, Washington, DC, October 6, 2008, http://siteresources.worldbank.org/BRAZILEXTN/Resources/Zoellickspeech6October2008.pdf.

9. "Demand, not Speculation, at Heart of Oil Shock, Says Brown," *The Guardian,* June 23, 2008.

10. Daniel Yergin, "Ensuring Energy Security," *Foreign Affairs,* March/April 2006.

11. Pierre Noël, "Challenging the Myths of Energy Security," *Financial Times,* January 10, 2008.

12. "Frank Verrastro and Sarah Ladislaw, "Providing Energy Security in an Interdependent World," The Washington Quarterly, Autumn 2007, http://www.twq.com/07autumn/docs/07autumn_verrastro.pdf.

13. "Libya Cuts Swiss Oil and Economic Ties in Protest," *Reuters,* October 11, 2008.

14. "Saudi Needs Oil Above $49 to Avoid Deficit," *Gulf Times,* September 21, 2008.

15. "Saudi King Says Keeping Some Oil Finds for Future," *Reuters,* April 13, 2008.

16. "Russia Wants to Influence Global Oil Price," *Reuters,* September 25, 2008.

17. Miriam Elder, "Russia Threatens to Seize Swathe of Arctic," *The Daily Telegraph,* September 18, 2008.

18. EIA, International Energy Outlook 2008, http://www.eia.doe.gov/oiaf/ieo/nat_gas.html.

19. "OPEC Style Gas Cartel Established," *RTE Business,* October 22, 2008, http://www.rte.ie/business/2008/1022/gas.html.

20. Pierre Noël, "Challenging the Myths."

21. Patrick Clawson and Simon Henderson, *Reducing Vulnerability to Middle East Energy Shocks, A Key Element in Strengthening U.S. Energy Security,* Washington Institute for Near East Policy, Policy Focus #49, November 2005, http://www.washingtoninstitute.org/pubPDFs/PolicyFocus49.pdf.

22. Center for Naval Analysis (CNA), *National Security and the Threat of Climate Change,* http://securityandclimate.cna.org.

23. Frank Umbach, "Germany's Energy Insecurity," *Journal of Energy Security,* October 2008, http://www.ensec.org/index.php?option=com_content&view=article&id=153:germanysenergyinsecurity&catid=81:europe&Itemid=324.

24. Robert Zubrin, *Energy Victory: Winning the War on Terror by Breaking Free of Oil* (Amherst, NY: Prometheus, 2007).

Index

About the Contributors

Robert G. Bell is a Senior Vice President with SAIC. In 1999–2003 he was NATO's Assistant Secretary General for Defense Investment. Prior to that he worked at the White House National Security Council (NSC) as a Special Assistant to President Clinton for National Security Affairs and as the NSC Senior Director for Defense Policy and Arms Control. In 1981–1993, Mr. Bell served on the Senate Committees on Foreign Relations and Armed Services, working for Senators Percy and Nunn, respectively. His career also includes six years at the Congressional Research Service (CRS), including a one year assignment in Brussels, where he served as staff director of the Military Committee of the NATO Parliamentary Assembly. From 1969 until 1975, he served as an air force officer in the air traffic control and communications field. Robert Bell holds a Master of Arts degree in International Security Studies from Tufts University's Fletcher School of Law and Diplomacy and a Bachelor of Science degree in International Affairs from the United States Air Force Academy.

Jeremy Carl is a Research Fellow in the Program on Energy and Sustainable Development at Stanford University and research fellow at the Institute for the Analysis of Global Security. He came to Stanford by way of New Delhi, India where he worked on energy and resource economics issues at The Energy and Resources Institute (TERI), India's leading energy think tank. His research interests are in energy security and the political economy and environmental effects of energy development, with a particular focus on India and China. His current research focuses on the political economy and environmental effects of the global coal sector. He received his B.A. with distinction in history from Yale University, and an MPA from the John F. Kennedy School of Government, Harvard University.

Dr. Ariel Cohen is Senior Research Fellow in Russian and Eurasian Studies and International Energy Security at The Heritage Foundation. Dr. Cohen is author of *Russian Imperialism: Development and Crisis* (1998); *Eurasia in Balance* (2005), *Kazakhstan: Energy Cooperation with Russia—Oil, Gas and Beyond; Kazakhstan:*

The Road to Independence (2008) and over 25 book chapters and 400 articles in academic and popular media. Olena Krychevska, a 2007 intern at The Heritage Foundation, has greatly contributed to research and production of the Russia chapter. Carla Bock, a 2007 Heritage intern, has greatly contributed to research and production of chapter on Central Asia.

Dr. Charles D. Ferguson is a Fellow for Science and Technology at the Council on Foreign Relations, an Adjunct Assistant Professor in the Security Studies Program at the School of Foreign Service at Georgetown University, and an Adjunct Lecturer in the National Security Program at the Johns Hopkins University. At the Council, he focuses his research and writing on nuclear energy and nuclear security. He wrote the Council Special Report *Nuclear Energy: Balancing Benefits and Risks.* He has worked on nuclear safety issues as a physical scientist in the U.S. State Department. After graduating with distinction from the United States Naval Academy, he served as a nuclear engineering officer on a ballistic-missile submarine. He holds a Ph.D. in physics from Boston University.

Dr. Christopher J. Fettweis returned to Tulane University in the fall of 2008, after having spent three years teaching national security studies at the U.S. Naval War College. He is the author of *Losing Hurts Twice as Bad: The Four Stages to Moving Beyond Iraq* and *Angell Triumphant: The International Politics of Great Power Peace,* as well as a number of articles in policy and scholarly journals. He is a research fellow at the Institute for the Analysis of Global Security. He holds a Ph.D. from the University of Maryland.

David L. Goldwyn is President of Goldwyn International Strategies LLC, an international energy consulting firm. He is a Senior Fellow in the Energy Program at the Center for Strategic and International Studies (CSIS) and serves on the Council of Foreign Relations (CFR) Task Force on Energy Security and CFR Center for Preventive Action Task Forces on Angola, Venezuela and Bolivia. Goldwyn served as Assistant Secretary of Energy for International Affairs, Counselor to the Secretary of Energy, and national security deputy to U.S. Ambassador to the UN Bill Richardson. Mr. Goldwyn received a Bachelors of Arts degree from Georgetown University, a Masters in Public Affairs degree from the Woodrow Wilson School of Public and International Affairs at Princeton University and a law degree from New York University School of Law.

Sabrina Howell is a China expert at the Institute for the Analysis of Global Security, focusing on energy economics and energy security. She has conducted research in Central Asia, China and the Caucasus. She holds a degree in Economics and East Asian Studies from Yale University.

Cindy Hurst is a political-military research analyst with the U.S. Army's Foreign Military Studies Office. Her research is centered on various energy issues. She is a lieutenant commander in the U.S. Navy Reserve and currently is writing a book on the potential global implications of LNG.

Amy Myers Jaffe is the Wallace S. Wilson Fellow in Energy Studies at the Baker Institute of Rice University. Jaffe's research focuses on oil geopolitics, strategic energy policy including energy science policy, and energy economics. Jaffe is widely published and served as co-editor of *Energy in the Caspian Region: Present and Future* (2002) and *Natural Gas and Geopolitics: From 1970 to 2040* (2006). Jaffe served as a member of the reconstruction and economy working group of the Baker/Hamilton Iraq Study Group, as project director for the Baker Institute/ Council on Foreign Relations Task Force on Strategic Energy Policy, and as a principal advisor to USAID's project on Options for Developing a Long Term Sustainable Iraqi Oil Industry. She is currently serving as a strategic advisor to the American Automobile Association (AAA) of the United States. Prior to joining the Baker Institute, Jaffe was the senior editor and Middle East analyst for *Petroleum Intelligence Weekly*.

Michael T. Klare is a Five College Professor of Peace and World Security Studies, a joint appointment of Amherst, Hampshire, Mount Holyoke, and Smith Colleges and the University of Massachusetts at Amherst. He is the author of several books on world security affairs including *Resource Wars* (2001), *Blood and Oil* (2004) and *Rising Powers, Shrinking Planet: The New Geopolitics of Energy* (2008)

Ali M. Koknar is an Associate Fellow of the Institute for the Analysis of Global Security. He is a private security consultant in Washington, DC, specializing in counterterrorism and international organized crime. A native of Turkey, he studied law and business management in Turkey and in South Africa.

Anne Korin is co-director of the Institute for the Analysis of Global Security (IAGS). She chairs the Set America Free Coalition, an alliance of national security, environmental, labor and religious groups promoting ways to reduce America's dependence on foreign oil. Ms. Korin appears frequently on Capitol Hill and her advice is sought by members of Congress. Her education includes engineering degree in computer science from Johns Hopkins University and work towards a doctorate at Stanford University.

Deron Lovaas is vehicles campaign director at Natural Resources Defense Council (NRDC) in Washington, DC. He directs the "Break the Chain" oil security campaign and served earlier as the chief lobbyist on the federal Transportation Equity Act for the 21st Century (TEA-21) reauthorization bill. A graduate of the University of Virginia, Deron has worked in environmental policy and advocacy for more than a decade, including as director of the Sierra Club's "Challenge to Sprawl" campaign and a specialist in transportation and air-quality planning at Maryland's Department of the Environment.

Dr. Gal Luft is executive director of the Institute for the Analysis of Global Security (IAGS). He specializes in strategy, geopolitics, energy security and economic warfare. Dr. Luft has published numerous studies and articles on security and energy issues in various newspapers and publications and testified before committees of the U.S. Congress. He holds degrees in international relations, international economics, Middle East studies and strategic studies and a doctorate in strategic studies from the Paul H. Nitze School of Advanced International Studies (SAIS) Johns Hopkins University.

Dr. Johanna Mendelson Forman is Senior Associate in the Americas Program at the Center for Strategic and International Studies (CSIS) in Washington, D.C. Her work focuses on the Caribbean, Brazil and Central America. She also serves the executive director of the Jatropha Foundation, an organization dedicated to the development of renewable energy alternatives in the Caribbean and Latin America, and on the board of the Latin American Council on Renewable Energy. A former co director of the Post-Conflict Reconstruction Project and co-author of *Play to Win: a Framework for U.S. Post-Conflict Reconstruction*, framework for rebuilding war-torn societies. Her research includes studies on security-sector reform in conflict states, economic development in postwar societies, and the role of the United Nations in peace operations. She has written extensively about reconstruction programs from Iraq, Guatemala, and Haiti. Recently, she served in Haiti as a senior advisor to the UN Mission (MINUSTAH), where she worked on development of renewable energy programs to sustain rural communities. She holds a J.D. from Washington College of Law at American University, a Ph.D. in Latin American history from Washington University, St. Louis, and a Master's of International Affairs, with a certificate of Latin America studies, from Columbia University in New York.

Susana Moreira is a Ph.D. candidate at the School of Advanced International Studies (SAIS), Johns Hopkins University and Summer Intern Scholar, Center of Strategic International Studies (CSIS).

Dr. Donna J. Nincic is Associate Professor and Chair of the Department of Global and Maritime Studies at the California Maritime Academy, California State University. She received her doctorate in Political Science/International Relations from New York University, and has held previous positions at the University of California, Davis; the Hoover Institution; and the US Department of Defense. Her research focuses on maritime security, particularly piracy and terrorism. Recent publications include "Sea Lane Security and US Maritime Trade" in Sam J. Tangredi, ed., *Globalization and Maritime Power*, Washington D.C.: National Defense University Press (2002), and "The Challenge of Maritime Terrorism: Threat Identification, WMD, and Regime Response," *Journal of Strategic Studies* (August 2005). Her current research focuses on maritime piracy in Africa, and U.S.-Canadian conflict over the Northwest Passage.

Necdet Pamir is an expert in Turkey's energy policy. He is member of the Executive Board of the Turkish National Committee of the World Energy Council, an advisor to the Chairman of the Attila Dogan Construction & Installation Company and General Manager of the Attila Dogan Petroleum Corporation. He writes frequently for various Turkish and international publications including a monthly "Energy Edition" of *Cumhuriyet* daily newspaper. He holds a B.Sc. in Petroleum Engineering Department from the Middle East Technical University.

Dr. Kevin Rosner is Senior Fellow at the Institute for the Analysis of Global Security (IAGS) specializing in Russian and European energy security, security of critical energy infrastructure, and international energy-security policy. He is managing editor of IAGS' *Journal of Energy Security*. In 2006 he served as the Co-Director for the NATO Forum on Energy Security. Dr. Rosner is the editor of a series of reports published (2005–2007) by Global Markets Briefings on Russian Foreign Energy Policy covering Russian downstream investment in Central European and FSU energy systems. Past positions held include Senior Oil and Gas Advisor, Thales Information Systems, Senior Security Advisor to the Baku-Tbilisi-Ceyhan pipeline company, Project Director with the Program on Cooperation with the Russian Federation at the OECD, and Project Manager with the UNESCO Science Division in Paris.

Devin Stewart is program director at the Carnegie Council for Ethics in International Affairs. Previously, he was Assistant Director of Studies and Japan Studies Fellow at the Center for Strategic and International Studies (CSIS) in Washington, D.C. He remains affiliated with CSIS as an Adjunct Fellow. From 2000 to 2003, Devin was a researcher at the Research Institute of Economy, Trade, and Industry and in 2004 a staff writer for *The Daily Yomiuri* in Tokyo. He also chaired the Korea-Japan Study Group in Tokyo and in Washington. He was also a researcher at the Japan External Trade Organization New York and has served on the staffs of the U.S. Senate Committee on Foreign Relations and Senator Barbara Mikulski. Devin's articles have appeared in more than 10 languages in numerous publications. He received a B.A., cum laude, from the University of Delaware, where he won a scholarship to study Arab immigration in France. He holds an M.A. from the Paul H. Nitze School of Advanced International Studies (SAIS) at Johns Hopkins University in Washington, D.C., and Bologna, Italy. He would like to thank Chris Janiec and Warren Wilczewski for their invaluable contributions to this chapter.

David M. Sweet is the Executive Director of the World Alliance for Decentralized Energy (WADE). Prior to joining WADE, Mr. Sweet served as Director of the United States Energy Association, the U.S. arm of the World Energy Council, as Executive Director of the International LNG Alliance, Vice President of the Independent Petroleum Association of America, an attorney in private practice, and as an expert witness on financial, rate and permitting issues at the Federal Energy

Regulatory Commission. Mr. Sweet serves as president of the Natural Gas Round-table, a member of the North American Energy Standards Board, a vice chairman of the ABA Section of Public Utility, Communications and Transportation Law and its gas committee, a member of the World Energy Council Committee on Cleaner Fossil Fuel Systems, and on the Board of Advisors of the Institute for the Analysis of Global Security. He received his law degree with honors from George Washington University, an M.B.A. from the University of Maryland, and a B.S. degree magna cum laude also from the University of Maryland.

Dr. Paul J. Werbos is program director at the National Science Foundation. Prior to arriving full-time at NSF in 1989, he worked at the Energy Information Administration (EIA) of the Department of Energy where he was lead analyst for long-term energy futures and developed the econometric models used in EIA's Annual Energy Outlook for industrial and transportation energy demand and for oil and gas production. He has given a number of major talks to Congress on energy policy, and is a member of IEEE-USA. He holds four degrees from Harvard and the London School of Economics in economics, international political systems, emphasizing European economic institutions, applied mathematics, with a major in quantum physics and a minor in decision and control and applied mathematics.